# Evolution's Empress

*Darwinian Perspectives on the*
*Nature of Women*

EDITED BY
MARYANNE L. FISHER
JUSTIN R. GARCIA
ROSEMARIE SOKOL CHANG

OXFORD
UNIVERSITY PRESS

# OXFORD
UNIVERSITY PRESS

Oxford University Press is a department of the University of Oxford.
It furthers the University's objective of excellence in research, scholarship,
and education by publishing worldwide.

Oxford   New York
Auckland   Cape Town   Dar es Salaam   Hong Kong   Karachi
Kuala Lumpur   Madrid   Melbourne   Mexico City   Nairobi
New Delhi   Shanghai   Taipei   Toronto

With offices in
Argentina   Austria   Brazil   Chile   Czech Republic   France   Greece
Guatemala   Hungary   Italy   Japan   Poland   Portugal   Singapore
South Korea   Switzerland   Thailand   Turkey   Ukraine   Vietnam

Oxford is a registered trade mark of Oxford University Press in the UK
and certain other countries.

Published in the United States of America by
Oxford University Press
198 Madison Avenue, New York, NY 10016

Library of Congress Cataloging-in-Publication Data

Evolution's empress : Darwinian perspectives on the nature of women / edited by
Maryanne L. Fisher, Justin R. Garcia, Rosemarie Sokol Chang.
pages cm
ISBN 978-0-19-989274-7
1. Women—Psychology.   2. Sex differences (Psychology)   3. Evolutionary psychology.
4. Human evolution.   I. Fisher, Maryanne.   II. Garcia, Justin R., 1985–
III. Chang, Rosemarie Sokol.
HQ1206.E956 2013
155.3′33—dc23
2012044983

3  5  7  9  8  6  4  2
Printed in the United States of America
on acid-free paper

# ACKNOWLEDGMENTS

We have been extremely fortunate to collaborate and interact with many fabulous scholars during our work on this volume. We thank the following people who provided support and helpful advice and in many cases reviewed chapters or shared additional insights: Alice Andrews, Carola Borries, Leslie Heywood, Sarah Blaffer Hrdy, Glenn Geher, Hanna Kokko, Tami Meredith, Joan Silk, Sarah Strout, and Griet Vandermassen. We also thank the support of the Feminist Evolutionary Psychology Society and the NorthEastern Evolutionary Psychology Society. Our editorial team at Oxford University Press, Abby Gross, Joanna Ng, and Suzanne Walker have been delightful and shown consistent support through the duration of this project. Last, we thank our contributors, who have written thought-provoking chapters that span a formidable range of topics and viewpoints on how women are active agents in evolution.

# CONTENTS

# CONTRIBUTORS

**Laura Betzig**
The Adaptationist Program
Ann Arbor, MI

**Nicole M. Cameron**
Departments of Psychology and
  Biology
Center for Development and
  Behavioral Neuroscience
Binghamton University, State
  University of New York
Binghamton, NY

**Lorne Campbell**
Department of Psychology
The University of Western Ontario
London, Ontario, Canada

**Rosemarie Sokol Chang**
Department of Psychology
State University of New York at New
  Paltz
New Paltz, NY

**Kathryn Coe**
Indiana University Richard M.
  Fairbanks School of Public Health
  at IUPUI
Indianapolis, IN

**Nancy Easterlin**
English Department
Women's and Gender Studies
  Program
University of New Orleans
New Orleans, LA

**Michelle J. Escasa-Dorne**
Department of Anthropology
University of Nevada, Las Vegas
Las Vegas, NV

**Linda Marie Fedigan**
Department of Anthropology
University of Calgary
Calgary, Alberta, Canada

**Maryanne L. Fisher**
Department of Psychology
Program in Women and Gender
  Studies
St. Mary's University
Halifax, Nova Scotia, Canada

**David A. Frederick**
Crean School of Health and Life
  Sciences
Chapman University
Orange, CA

**Justin R. Garcia**
The Kinsey Institute for Research in
  Sex, Gender, and Reproduction
Indiana University, Bloomington
Bloomington, IN

**Patricia Adair Gowaty**
Department of Ecology and
  Evolutionary Biology
University of California, Los Angeles
Los Angeles, CA

**Peter B. Gray**
Department of Anthropology
University of Nevada, Las Vegas
Las Vegas, NV

**Leslie Heywood**
Department of English
Institute for Evolutionary Studies
Binghamton University
Binghamton, NY

**Sarah Blaffer Hrdy**
Department of Anthropology
University of California, Davis
Davis, CA

**Katharine M. Jack**
Department of Anthropology
Tulane University
New Orleans, LA

**Johannes Johow**
Center of Philosophy
University of Giessen
Giessen, Germany

**Laurette Liesen**
Department of Political Science
Lewis University
Romeoville, IL

**Bobbi S. Low**
School of Natural Resources and
  Environment
University of Michigan
Ann Arbor, MI

**Tami Meredith**
Department of Mathematics and
  Computing Science
St. Mary's University
Halifax, Nova Scotia, Canada

**Liza R. Moscovice**
Department of Primatology
Max Planck Institute for Evolutionary
  Anthropology
Leipzig, Germany

**Lesley Newson**
College of Life and Environmental
  Sciences
University of Exeter
Exeter, UK
Department of Environmental Science
  & Policy
University of California, Davis
Davis, CA

**Elisabeth Oberzaucher**
Department of Anthropology
University of Vienna
Vienna, Austria

**Craig T. Palmer**
Department of Anthropology
University of Missouri-Columbia
Columbia, MO

**Michele Pridmore-Brown**
Office for History of Science and
  Technology
University of California, Berkeley
Berkeley, CA

**Chris Reiber**
Program in Biomedical Anthropology
Department of Anthropology
Institute for Evolutionary Studies
Binghamton University, State
  University of New York
Binghamton, NY

**Tania A. Reynolds**
Department of Psychology
Florida State University
Tallahassee, FL

**Peter J. Richerson**
Department of Environmental Science
  and Policy
University of California, Davis
Davis, CA

**Julie Seaman**
Emory University School of Law
Atlanta, GA

**Eckart Voland**
Center of Philosophy
University of Giessen
Giessen, Germany
Alfried-Krupp Institute for Advanced
  Studies (Wissenschaftskolleg)
Greifswald, Germany

**Christopher J. Wilbur**
Department of Psychology
University of Wisconsin Colleges
UW-Marathon County Campus
Wausau, WI

**Kai P. Willführ**
Lifecourse Dynamics and Demographic
  Change
Max Planck Institute for Demographic
  Research
Rostock, Germany

**Sharon M. Young**
Department of Anthropology
University of Nevada, Las Vegas
Las Vegas, NV

# OVERDUE DIALOGUES: FOREWORD TO
## *EVOLUTION'S EMPRESS*

SARAH BLAFFER HRDY

Essays in this book promote long-overdue conversations between Darwinians and feminists. The delay is understandable, if short-sighted on both sides. For all its originality and power, Darwin's view of human nature was distorted by overly narrow, often misleading stereotypes about females. In writing his classic account of *The Descent of Man and Selection in Relation to Sex*, Darwin assumed that "the most able men will have succeeded best in defending and providing for themselves, their wives and offspring" (1871/1981, Part II: 383) and that off-spring sired by hunters with "greater intellectual vigor and power of invention" would be most likely to survive. Invoking his theory of sexual selection, which combines male-male competition followed by female choice of the winning male (easily the most original of Darwin's many brilliant ideas), Darwin assumed that women would preferentially select as mates the best and the brightest of pro-vider/defenders and thereafter single-mindedly devote themselves to rearing that male's young. With selection acting more strongly on this vigorous and active sex than on what Darwin regarded as the more "passive" female sex, it followed that men would attain "a higher eminence, in whatever he takes up, than woman can attain— whether requiring deep thought, reason, or imagination" (1871/1981, Part II: 327). Altogether, it was a very neat, internally consistent—if entirely androcentric— package, leaving out crucial female contributions to subsistence as well as all the strategizing females engage in to ensure their local clout and the survival of any young at all.

Over time, this bias grew more pronounced among some of Darwin's disciples, persisting to the present day. No wonder many of those in the humanities and social sciences subscribed to Virginia Woolf's assessment: "Science it would seem, is not sexless; she is a man, a father, and infected too" (1938). Feminists were understandably put off by more than a century of male-centered constructs, including constructs whereby our ancestors evolved big brains so that males could outwit competitors or collaborate with one another the better to kill game or prevail over neighboring groups, or evolved to walk upright so males could carry meat back to females and offspring who waited back at camp (e.g., Lovejoy, 1981, among many other distinguished evolutionists). Feminists wrote off biology as a field unhelpful to women seeking either to improve their lot or to better understand themselves. But these same feminists may be surprised by the very different scenarios and highly variable female organisms that emerge from the pages of this book.

Over the last four decades a growing assortment of sociobiologists and evolutionary-minded anthropologists and psychologists have started to employ a wider angled evolutionary lens to study a range of creatures including humans. The result is a more accurate picture encompassing the evolutionary interests and perspectives of females as well as males, along with selection pressures across the life course beginning in utero and continuing long after women cease to be fertile.

And what of generations of Darwinians whose confidence in their own objectivity led them to ignore feminist critiques as too ideologically motivated to merit attention? A growing number of them as well are beginning to recognize that no amount of hypothesis-testing and extra data-collection matter if hypotheses being tested are built on flawed or seriously incomplete starting assumptions. A few of these committed evolutionists are even wondering out loud how it was possible that sex differences apparent in some species could have been projected onto nature at large without taking into account just how flexible sex roles between and within species often are (especially Gowaty, this volume). How could widely accepted assumptions about *universal* sex differences have persisted and shaped evolutionary theorizing for so long after abundant evidence contradicting such presumptions had been reported? How could mainstream scientists ever have taken it as granted that females were too preoccupied with nurturing to compete in wider spheres, as in this statement: "primate females seem biologically unprogrammed to dominate political systems, and the whole weight of the relevant primates' breeding history militates against female participation in what we can call 'primate public life'" (Tiger, 1977, p. 28)? How could the finest textbook in the field back in the 1970s have so casually pronounced that "most adult females . . . are likely to be breeding at or close to the theoretical limit" while "among males by contrast there is the probability of doing better" (Daly & Wilson, 1978, p. 59), with the obvious implication that somehow what matters most is competition between males for mates? (Hint: sometimes it does, except when it doesn't!). Given just how much evidence there was before our eyes, why did so many years elapse before stereotypes about sexually "ardent" males and universally discriminating "coy" females started to be challenged (e.g., Hrdy, 1986/2006) and before long-standing stereotypes about evolved female nature were revised (Angier, 1999; Eckholm, 1984; Gowaty, 1987)?

Right along with Darwin's immense curiosity, powers of observation, imagination, and diligence, one of his great strengths was humility. Darwin fretted constantly that he might be wrong. Were he alive today, I imagine he would be at the fascinated forefront studying the new and highly variable female life-forms taking shape from behind the shadows of biased presumptions. I would even go so far as to speculate that Darwin himself might entertain a novel twist to his own theory of sexual selection. Quite possibly it was in the interests of well-born men in social contexts where males are considered superior, control resources, and dominate females, *not* to notice certain things about their daughters and wives. Even the most well intentioned and upright of gentlemen could go right on believing that a woman was naturally inclined and even eager to give birth to one closely spaced child after another, devoting herself single-mindedly to their care while lovingly and charitably also devoting her (naturally empathetic) Emma-like nature to improving her husband's quality of life. In patriarchal worlds where inheritance and property rights overwhelmingly favored sons, where paternity mattered a great deal, women's autonomy was highly constrained. In societies where any challenge to a woman's chastity would be disastrous, no wonder a woman might prefer to preserve herself for the one "best"— which of course was too often taken to mean the most propertied— male. And well might the discretion of such a woman lead to the impression (as the famous medical authority of Darwin's day William Acton put it) that "the majority of women (happily for them) are not much troubled with sexual feelings of any kind" (Acton, 1865, pp. 112–113). How convenient to assume that if women behaved passively, opted out of "primate public life," or remained monandrous, it was because they were naturally inclined to do so! Such blinders would have eased the existence of a kindly Victorian gentleman, while also enhancing his professional as well as reproductive success.

Whatever their sources, Darwin's blind spots constituted a highly adaptive obliviousness shared by a succession of brilliant researchers in the evolutionary sciences. I still vividly recall a conversation with an eminent British zoologist about the many newly recognized sources of variance in female reproductive success and the question of why their recognition had been so long in coming. "Females were just harder to study," he told me, with a perfectly straight face. Note that this was in the 1980s, before fieldworkers had ready access to noninvasive methods for determining genetic paternity. Variation between the lifetime reproductive success of females should have been, if anything, easier to measure than that of males.

So what changed? A great deal! The transformations can be detected in the way psychologists and anthropologists interpret an increasingly broad range of human behaviors (e.g., see chapters by Moscovice; Newson & Richerson; Escasa-Dorne, Young, & Gray; Fedigan & Jack) as well as those by scholars with backgrounds in political science, law, comparative literature, and gender studies (e.g., chapters by Liesen; Easterlin or Pridmore-Brown). In my own case, the process began as I increasingly began to identify with the female monkeys that I studied in the arid zone forests of Rajasthan. Observing them day after day, I could not help but empathize with langur mothers, who every 27 months on average had to cope with the appearance in their midst of a new male bent on killing infants sired by his predecessor. By this point in the 1970s, feminist critiques of science were also (however awkwardly and belatedly) percolating into my consciousness. I was increasingly aware of the disconnect between evolutionary generalizations by mentors (all male in those days) and the sexual, maternal, and competitive emotions I routinely noticed and experienced firsthand.

Thus when the behavior of females I was watching failed to conform to theoretical expectations, instead of dismissing seemingly idiosyncratic antics I grew curious. Rather than write off as insignificant the behavior of females who temporarily left their groups to sexually solicit strange males (even females who were already pregnant so hardly after the "best" genes), I tried to imagine why a female would ever do so. A field study originally focused on a particularly striking male reproductive strategy (eliminating the offspring of rival males so as to compress female fertility into his tenure of access) expanded to include an array of previously undreamed of female counterstrategies, such as females engaging in not-possibly-conceptive matings with extragroup males so as to manipulate information about paternity (Hrdy, 1977, 1981). Over time, I began to rethink why women like myself would ever feel conflicted or ambivalent about motherhood and recognize how impossible it would have been for the apes in the line leading to the genus *Homo* to evolve had mothers *not* been able to rely on help from a wider range of others (allomothers of both sexes) than previously supposed (Hrdy, 1999).

It is by now clear from many sources that throughout the evolution of our species, the majority of conceptions and births ended in untimely demise. And if so, female status-striving and quests for autonomy, and quite a bit else that mothers, older sisters, grandmothers, and others do to ensure at least some infants remain safe from predators and conspecifics and well-enough fed and positioned so as to prosper long enough to breed themselves, would have rendered the female sex wide open to Darwinian selection in realms far broader than simply choosing the "right" mate and then committing to every fetus conceived, selflessly rearing every baby born.

Can the f-word "feminist" so dreaded by empirically minded scientists introduce sources of bias? Yes, of course it can, and sometimes does. But keep in mind just how often the same rigorously scientific intellects that once were bent on rejecting any taint of feminist thought failed to notice how "masculinist" were the models they themselves had so long endorsed. It is important to acknowledge and recall this history lest old biases creep back in.

As I employ the term "feminist" it simply refers to anyone, male or female, who advocates equal rights and opportunities for both sexes. In an evolutionary context, this means paying equivalent attention to selection pressures on females as well as those acting on males. "Feminism" becomes political only when countervailing biases deny females equal consideration, which of course in the case of much early Darwinian and especially social-Darwinian (Spencerian) theorizing, they did. Rather than introducing new sources of bias, or seducing researchers into politically correct positions unsupported by evidence, feminist critiques led many of us to revise incorrect starting assumptions. Eyes newly opened to old sources of bias started to see females who were competitive and sometimes violent (see especially the chapters by Liesen and Fisher) as well as affiliative and cooperative, females who could be nurturing in one context and quite destructive in another and also, as in almost all primates, often characterized by decidedly polyandrous tendencies. Such females were every bit as strategic as males. Indeed in some species (Cercopithecine monkeys come to mind) a daughter's rank— and with it her reproductive success—is determined by her mother's, while in other species the mother's rank influences the reproductive success of sons. This is the case among bonobos, muriqui monkeys, and under some circumstances among humans as well (see the "empresses" in Laura Betzig's chapter of this volume!). The female status-seekers and perpetuators in these instances are anything but uninvolved in "primate public life," often playing for more enduring stakes than males do. Read on and see for yourselves.

# References

Acton, W. (1865). *The functions and disorders of the reproductive system* (4th ed.). London: Churchill.

Angier, N. (1999). *Woman: An intimate geography*. Boston: Houghton Mifflin.

Daly, M., & Wilson, M. (1988). *Sex, evolution and behavior.* North Scituate, MA: Duxbury Press, p. 59.

Darwin, C. (1871/1981). *Descent of man and selection in relation to sex* (Facsimile of 1871 edition published by J. Murray, London). Princeton, NJ: Princeton University Press.

Eckholm, E. (1984). New view of female primates assails stereotypes. *New York Times*, Sept. 18, 1984.

Gowaty, P. A., (Ed.). (1997). *Feminism and evolutionary biology: Boundaries, intersections and frontiers.* New York: Chapman and Hall.

Hrdy, S. (1977). *The langurs of Abu: Female and male strategies of reproduction.* Cambridge, MA: Harvard University Press.

Hrdy, S. (1981). *The woman that never evolved.* Cambridge: Harvard University Press.

Hrdy, S. (1986/ 2006). Empathy, polyandry and the myth of the coy female. In E. Sober (Ed.), *Conceptual issues in evolutionary biology* (3rd ed., pp. 254–256). Cambridge, MA: MIT Press.

Hrdy, S. (1999). *Mother Nature: A history of mothers, infants and natural selection.* New York: Pantheon.

Knight, J. (2002). Sexual stereotypes. *Nature, 415,* 254–256.

Lovejoy, O. (1981). The origin of man. *Science, 211,* 341–350.

Tiger , L. (1977). The possible biological origins of sexual discrimination. In D. Brothwell (Ed.), *Biosocial man.* London: Eugenics Society.

Woolf, V. (1938). *The Three Guineas.* New York: Harcourt, Brace and World.

# Introduction to *Evolution's Empress*

MARYANNE L. FISHER, ROSEMARIE SOKOL CHANG, AND
JUSTIN R. GARCIA

## Introduction

We are at a thrilling point in academia; at long last, we are on the verge of seeing two distinct areas of scholarship, previously at odds, come together. We are
witnessing the beginnings of reconciliation between evolutionary theory and
feminism—two fields with vastly different intellectual approaches, and both with
a contentious past and a mysterious future. These two broad areas are rooted in
entirely distinct histories. They often lead to conclusions that are so juxtaposed,
there seems to be little or no middle ground. Each carries a set of assumptions on
the forces and mechanisms shaping the human condition. Evolutionary behavioral scientists immerse themselves in the scientific method, asking questions
they believe arise from past, objective research. Feminist theorists raise questions
about that very objectivity, pointing to the ways that bias in research and action
can have real-world social and political effects. With these disparate views, how is
it possible to have any common ground?

One must first realize that although feminism can be defined in many ways,
it is largely a "social movement and political program aimed at ameliorating
the position of women in society" (Campbell, 2006, p. 63). As Anne Campbell
discusses, "This is a goal endorsed by women and men from a variety of backgrounds—including a very large number of evolutionary psychologists" (ibid.).
She points out that many within the field of evolutionary psychology (including
human behavioral ecology, sociobiology, ethology, etc.) have written about feminist issues, and reviews the ways in which feminism can help inform evolutionary
psychology. Campbell's writings represent only a beginning, rather than an endpoint, and have sadly received far too little attention. Moreover, the piece quoted
above was aimed at an evolutionary psychology audience, rather than a broader,

interdisciplinary audience that contains feminist scholars, including those in women's and gender studies, which we try to rectify in this volume. In addition, there have been significant strides in recent years to show how feminism and evolutionary perspectives can work together, and this volume is an attempt to highlight some of that new work.

Both evolutionary psychology and academic feminism are grounded in frameworks that can be used to investigate a variety of phenomena, which perhaps represents one of the most important areas of similarity. These two disciplines are based in perspectives that are used to inform topics of inquiry, and although this pattern represents a similarity, it also means that there exists a chasm between them. Bridging this gap has clear obstacles, but we, along with others (e.g., Fedigan, 1986; Gowaty, 1997; Hrdy, 1981; Vandermassen, 2005), do not believe them to be insurmountable. The integration of evolutionary and feminist perspectives to the study of human behavior, culture, and biology has provided, and continues to provide, novel and holistic insights for scholars in a variety of disciplines. Rather than list examples here, we ask you, the reader, to turn to this book as evidence of these insights.

It is extremely challenging to write an introduction to a volume that attempts to move toward bringing together two fields that have been at odds for so long. Our goal in editing this book was not to provide a comprehensive, authoritative view; instead, we hope it will provide sufficient background to initiate a discussion among scholars in both fields. Here is an attempt, from a wide variety of perspectives, to bridge some of the gaps between feminism and evolutionary psychology.

Over the last decade there has been increasing debate as to whether feminism and evolutionary psychology are compatible. Such debates often conclude with a resounding "no," possibly because of the way each has been defined by the other. While these debates have been taking place, there has been growing dissatisfaction within the field of evolutionary psychology for the way the discipline has repeatedly shown women to be in passive roles when it comes to survival and reproduction (see Milam, 2010, for a review of how females were seen as passive versus active from an evolutionary perspective). Evolutionary behavioral research has been misled due to assumptions of women as docile in mating, and has too often neglected topics such as mothering, female alliances, female aggression, female physiology, female intrasexual competition, and women's role in human evolution at large. When these topics are examined, they are often viewed in terms of how they affect women, rather than human evolution overall.

Our goal, and that of our contributors, is not to diminish the role of men in evolution, but rather to augment this perspective by showing that women have been active players on the evolutionary landscape.[1] We were inspired to edit a volume regarding the active role of women in human evolution in 2009, in part as a reaction to the book by Sarah Blaffer Hrdy, *Mothers and Others: The Evolutionary Origins of Mutual Understanding*, which casts women in a leading role in human evolution. Surely this book reinvigorated many scholars to consider women as equally, if at times differently, influential as men in human evolution (e.g., Heywood, 2010).

We begin this introduction with a short summary of the evolution-feminism debate and the topics in evolutionary psychology that have been applied to women. We next consider two main obstacles that need to be overcome: addressing the mixing of science with policy, and the value of studying sex differences from an evolutionary perspective. Finally, we end with a discussion of academic areas in which the active role of women has been neglected, and how these problematic disciplinary shortcomings are addressed in the volume you now hold in your hands.

## We've Come a Long Way: A Short Summary of the Contention Between Evolutionists and Feminists

An early indication of the gendered bias in evolutionary theory comes from Charles Darwin himself. In *The Descent of Man, and Selection in Relation to Sex* (1872), he wrote:

> The chief distinction in the intellectual powers of the two sexes is shown by man's attaining to a higher eminence, in whatever he takes up, than can woman—whether requiring deep thought, reason, or imagination, or merely the use of the senses and hands…if men are capable of a decided pre-eminence over women in many subjects, the average of mental power in man must be above that of women…(men have had) to defend their females, as well as their young, from enemies of all kinds, and to hunt for their joint subsistence. But to avoid enemies or to attack them with success, to capture wild animals and to fashion weapons requires the aid of the higher mental faculties, namely, observation, reason, invention, or imagination. These variance faculties will thus have been continually put to the test and selected during manhood. (p. 311)

Feminists who were Darwin's contemporaries, such as Antoinette Brown Blackwell, responded to this sexist view, but had little effect on the scientific community. Brown Blackwell wrote in *The Sexes Throughout Nature* (1875):

> [Charles Darwin and Herbert Spencer are] both thinkers who have more profoundly influenced the opinions of the civilized world than perhaps any other two living men—when these two, endorsed by other world-wide authorities, are joined in assigning the mete and boundary of womanly capacities…it is time to recognize the fact that the "irrepressible woman question" has already taken a new scientific departure.

Woman herself must speak hereafter....She must consent to put in evidence the results of her own experience, and to develope [sp] the scientific basis of her differing conclusions. (pp. 234–235)

Disappointingly, Brown Blackwell's criticisms and call for action appear to have gone largely ignored. Part of the reason for such a lack of reaction is likely because she did not have data, which is the scientific gold standard to support a claim. Instead, her work reads as a politically focused passage, aligned with an early women's rights movement. It is hard to argue with Darwin's theses regarding sexual selection, which appeal to logic and evidence-based reason, albeit at times relying on circular and association-based reasoning.

Darwin was not at all alone in his position that accorded men higher cognitive abilities than women, and it remained a subject that echoed into the early 20th century. During this time, physicians and scientists placed the stake of a woman's psychology and health on her ovaries, which culminated in the belief that a woman's fecundity was inversely related to her education (see Ehrenreich & English, 2005). These voices of authority (including the noteworthy G. Stanley Hall, a reputable member of psychology's history) recommended that women not attend college, as the development of their brains would interfere with the development of their ovaries. As women were granted access to college, research was dedicated to the sterilizing effects of higher education among women (e.g., Goodsell, 1936; Hodson, 1929; Moore, 1930). Women's colleges were even accused of "breeding unintelligence by sterilizing intelligence" (Carey, 1929, abstract).

While the view of females as passive in the evolutionary process has been altered in the subdisciplines more akin to anthropology (e.g., behavioral ecology), there seems to be a general reluctance to change the traditional evolutionary psychology paradigm (see Liesen, 2007, 2012). The former has moved forward from the Man the Hunter model (Lee & DeVore, 1968), which sees the importance of hunting as a male trait that is responsible for the major human milestones such as bipedalism and encephalization. Anthropologists have since examined the data from comparative models, foraging societies, and fossil and material evidence, and found little support for this model. For example, Fedigan (1986, p. 24) writes, "the ethnographic evidence on contemporary hunter-gatherers in tropical and subtropical zones supports the economic independence claimed in the Woman the Gatherer model, and...no ethnographic examples exist of sedentary women in foraging societies being provisioned by their husbands with plant foods." Yet, the provisioning hypothesis of pair-bonding (see Lovejoy, 1981) is still advocated in evolutionary psychology (e.g. Buss, 1999). The provisioning hypothesis is related to the Man the Hunter model, as it is proposed that females are attracted to men who give provisions (usually in terms of food and protection) because to do so increases the probability that the pair's children will survive to an age of reproductive maturity.

This hypothesis has been used as the basis of much research and has gained some support (e.g., Stirrat, Gumert, & Perrett, 2011), however, there exists significant counter-evidence; data show men provide more meat to the children of other men than their own children via food sharing, and often use meat to acquire additional wives rather than invest more in existing children (Blurton Jones, Marlowe, Hawkes, & O'Connell, 2000). Furthermore, the physical record shows an increase in female but not male body size since the origin of the *Homo* line (McHenry, 1992), rather than the increasing sexual dimorphism in size, as might be expected by the male provisioning hypothesis. Despite these findings, current textbooks in evolutionary psychology still tout male provisioning as the most likely hypothesis to explain human mating systems and strategies (e.g., Workman & Reader, 2008).

Models in evolutionary psychology that are based on the mechanism of sexual selection likewise still imply that men are the forerunners of creativity and intelligence; take for example the idea that art and literature have been sexually selected much like a peacock's train feathers. Fedigan (1986) refers to this approach as the "coat-tails" theory of human evolution. Traits have been selected for in males, and characterize females (in part) only after the selection in males takes place. While not as boldly stated as by Darwin himself, contemporary approaches (e.g., Miller, 2000) seem reminiscent of this approach, explaining major cognitive developments in human evolution by the process of female choice for the traits in males. Clearly, psychological traits lack the distinction of sexually selected physical, morphological, traits in species such as peafowl. While the difference in appearance of a peacock and peahen are stark, the cognitive differences between men and women are not. In the case of the arts, many of the sex differences can be interpreted as a lack of exposure rather than a lack of aptitude (an example being female painters; see Nochlin, 1971/2003).

Among many evolutionary psychologists, the axiomatic position of male-male competition serving as the primary driver of human (behavioral) evolution is taken as a given and readily accepted at face value as "fact." Moreover, much of evolutionary psychological research on sex differences in mating, for example, rests on the reasoning that male mate choice shaped the development of female's physical attractiveness, while female choice shaped male's development of physical traits linked to dominance (e.g., Puts, 2010). These findings are framed using evolutionary theory, and at the surface level represent informative, logical results. However, as Dawkins (1976) originally pointed out, the human situation is highly unusual given that in many other species males are the attractive sex, due to the fact that females are the commodity being competed over and are the limited reproductive resource. In such species, females do not have to do very much to find a high-quality mate; they can simply wait for the winner of the male-male competition, or use their own mate preferences to help decide which mate is suitable. Why is it, then, that in humans, females are the more subjectively attractive sex, the ones who undergo efforts to make themselves abide with standards of beauty? Why do they emphasize their youth, and its associated fecundity? The answer might reside in competition; women compete with other women to obtain the most high quality mate possible (see Fisher, this volume). Despite the obviousness of this possibility, Darwin himself proposed that the evolution of female traits are not subject to the same intense pressures as male traits that result from competition (for review see Hrdy, 1999). Indeed, as Brown Blackwell (1875, p. 16) points out, four years after the publication of Darwin's *The Descent of Man and Selection in Relation to Sex* (1871); "Mr. Darwin...has illustrated how his theory of how the male has probably acquired additional masculine characters, but he seems never to have thought of looking to see whether or not the females had developed equivalent feminine characters."

This is, largely, the state of contemporary thinking and scholarship regarding the evolutionary origins of human behavior in evolutionary psychology: males competed with each other, which was the driving force of human evolution, and the ramifications of female mate choice remain(ed) debated (e.g., for a review see Milam, 2010). Meanwhile, this perspective leads to the presumption that females are passive, acting coy, and waiting to be in the position of being able to select the winner of the competition as their mate (for a well-researched alternate perspective to the "coy female" see Small, 1995). Of course, this type of thinking and reasoning certainly does not represent the logic of all human evolutionary behavioral scientists, as we hope the current volume reflects. However, given this view, is it any surprise that those working in feminist programs of study would be offended by evolutionary psychology?

Finally, the starting point in much of evolutionary psychology research begins with an approach that resonates more clearly with male scholarship: the idea of linear relations. Certainly it was evolutionary theory, as Darwin conceived it, that led to an overhaul in this idea. The *scalae naturae* idea of progression up a ladder toward modern humans espoused by Plato and other philosophers has been rewritten due to knowledge of descent with modification, and a hominid fossil record that shows more of a branching than linear evolution. Despite these efforts, the image of the "march of progress" depicted in popular versions of human evolution (Howell, 1965) is hard to erase from our culture. Similarly, human group living has been constructed as based in linear dominance hierarchies similar to gorillas, an idea that has received feminist criticism (see Dagg, 2004). Reflection on a female perspective offers a more branching or web-like approach to social groups (see for example, Liesen, this volume). Shifting the view to the interrelations among humans, rather than a hierarchical view of social interactions, leads to different testable predictions regarding evolved psychologies. For one, it shifts the focus to the unique level of cooperativeness among humans contrasted with even our closest relatives, rather than focusing on our tendencies toward conflict (see Hrdy, 2009; or for an example of social tolerance among bonobos, Hare, Melis, Woods, Hastings, & Wrangham, 2007).

Much of the scholarship pertaining to women and evolution has been directed toward what happens *to* women rather than how women actively influence and are fully part of human evolution. For example, female orgasm was initially proposed as a functionless by-product of male orgasm (Symons, 1979). This hypothesis resonated with many scholars as an unpleasant and short-sighted explanation. Since Symons's proposal, nearly 20 arguments have been put forth to explain the adaptive utility of female orgasm (see Lloyd, 2005). It is important to note (as does Lloyd, a philosopher of evolutionary science) that these conclusions are drawn based on the available scientific evidence, and are not, and should not, be used to make a value statement about either men or women. Incidentally, and begrudgingly to many, following more careful examination in recent years it appears the science still currently points to the by-product view as the most likely explanation (see Lloyd, 2005; Zietsch et al., 2011). Meanwhile, as a different example, early work on motherhood focussed on pregnancy and gestation as women's main role in evolutionary history. More nuanced work has cast motherhood as center stage in human evolution (Hrdy 1999), and even proposed that the infant-mother (and other) relationship has led to cooperation (Hrdy, 2009) and language (Falk, 2009).

Over the last few decades, major strides have been taken in overturning male-bias to the study of human evolution. Some notable examples include the topic of mothering and female sexuality, as mentioned. Yet, there is still a tendency to portray *any* research that involves women as feminist, such as research that examines sex differences. We fully admit that this volume contains work that could be critiqued on these grounds; some of the chapters are included simply because they focus on women, rather than encompassing feminist perspectives per se. Such work understandably leaves outsiders to the field of evolutionary psychology wondering if women will benefit from the union of evolution and feminism, and whether evolutionary scientists "get" feminist scholarship (and vice versa). Or, perhaps, to borrow the term from the late evolutionist Stephen Jay Gould, if the theories and ideologies of evolutionary science and academic feminism are "non-overlapping magisteria." In the current volume we attempt to bridge *some* aspects of the divide between evolutionary studies and women's studies, in what we hope is a positive step in the right direction: to examine and question those ways in which women are active agents in the evolutionary process. We also, though, include work that might not be considered as truly feminist. We do so partly to show the range of work that is ongoing, and fully expect that readers will find themselves nodding with some chapters and adamantly disagreeing with other chapters. If this is the case, we have reached our mission: to generate discussion and initiate what we hope will be a turning point for both evolutionary-minded scholars and those working within a feminist paradigm. This volume is a starting point, not an endpoint, and the various perspectives used by the contributors will hopefully lead to further theorizing and bridging by future theorists.

## Two Main Obstacles to the Integration of Feminism and Evolutionary Theory

The first obstacle to the integration of a feminist perspective and evolutionary psychology pertains to the somewhat artificial distinction between what *is* and what *ought* to be. Evolutionary psychology's goal is to explain human psychology as it *is*, and explain how it has been shaped over vast spans of time. This goal sometimes leads to easily digestible findings (e.g., humans may have evolved a craving for sweets; Birch, 1999) and sometimes it leads to more politically loaded findings (e.g., men may have an evolved tendency to rape under certain conditions; Thornhill & Palmer, 2000). The door for criticizing such findings is opened by people who claim that by researching explanations for a behavior as violent as rape, the researchers are in fact justifying the act (also known as the *naturalistic fallacy* in evolutionary circles; but see the *Stanford Encyclopedia of Philosophy*, 2008, for a critique of how this fallacy has been misconceptualized, and instead, it is actually what philosophers refer to as the fallacy of *Argumentum ad Naturam* or the *Appeal to Nature*; David Livingston Smith, personal communication). Furthermore, feminists, including feminist biologists such as Anne Fausto-Sterling (1985), have pointed out that the types of questions asked by evolutionary psychologists, the way language is used, the conclusions that are reached, and so on, represent bias, and that any claims of objectivity are ludicrous. Fausto-Sterling argues that, "by using the word rape, [evolutionary psychologists] have transformed its meaning. First to describe certain animal behaviors they use a word originally applied to a human interaction . . . that includes . . . conscious will. Then they employ the animal behavior in theories about rape in human society. In the process they confuse the meanings of two different behaviors and offer a natural justification for a human behavior that Webster's [dictionary] calls criminal" (1981, p. 161).

The successful future of evolutionary approaches to human behavior depends partially on the ability of scholars to carefully interpret and present their findings in a way that is conscious of the naturalistic fallacy and the way in which research may be (mis)interpreted (Garcia et al., 2011). In the case of human rape, which has perhaps become a hallmark example for the contentious divide between evolutionists and feminists, it is especially important to consider the scientific and social obligation to distinguish between what "is" and what "ought" to be. As Melissa Emery Thompson states in her careful review of the multiple evolutionary arguments thus far put forward to explain the etiology of such socially unacceptable behavior, "the role of biology in understanding human rape has been the subject of heated and not always scientific debate" (2009, p. 346). This is no doubt due to missteps on *both* sides of the debate. For instance, in Thornhill and Palmer's cage rattling book on the topic, there are multiple instantiations of the naturalistic fallacy being committed (Wilson, Dietrich & Clark, 2003). Thus, continued scientific discourse refutes claims based on evidence—that is, based on more data about what actually *is*, and not simply on our desires for what *ought* to be. As scholars rooted in evolutionary studies, we have an obligation to be aware of the potential to polarize entire disciplines with certain work, and in such cases, take the utmost caution in clearly, carefully, and consciously presenting our work, which includes policing the field from within, by other scholars operating in the same paradigm.

There are some recent integrations of the *is* of evolutionary theory with the *ought* of policy, notably in the area of improving public policy. The Evolution Institute presided by David Sloan Wilson is a think tank that assists public policy makers in applying evolutionary research to improve policy issues such as childhood education and risky adolescent behavior (Evolution Institute, 2011). At the time of writing, we are aware of no public outcry surrounding this integration. This example of successful integration of the "is" and "ought" deserves attention, as it might represent one promising way for evolutionary psychology and feminist thinking to meet: in the land of applied public policy (see Seamen, this volume).

The need for positive examples of integration is critical, in light of the fact that past attempts have been met with ambiguity or failure. A good case in point is the admirable attempt to explain how evolutionary psychology and feminist theory can work together, made by Griet Vandermassen (2005). She proposed that evolutionary psychology could provide insights, especially on the "ultimate" causes of behavior, whereas feminist thinking could aim to construct social reform and betterment on these findings, while simultaneously ensuring that male bias was removed. As Campbell (2006) discusses, probably the most notable problem to overcome is the source of sex differences, as evolutionary scholars propose they are grounded in processes stemming from natural and sexual selection, while many feminist scholars rely on explanations based in social construction and role theory. In many ways, Vandermassen's view could be used to show how both social construction and evolutionary processes can lead to behavior we see today, thus beginning to rectify the debate. To date, however, it seems that no one is directly working within the solution that Vandermassen offered. Evolutionary psychologists are continuing to pursue questions similar to those prior to Vandermassen's book, and feminists still are resistant to acknowledge any benefits of the evolutionary perspective. The greater contention for combining evolution with feminism than evolution with public policy seems rooted in the second obstacle to closing the evolution-feminism gap: sex differences in human behavior.

This second main obstacle to an integration of feminism and evolutionary theory pertains to the politicization of research on sex differences. Disciplines in which feminists often find themselves, such as sociology and gender studies, have a history of looking toward the ways in which people are socialized to explain human behavior (i.e., "nurture"). Evolutionary psychologists eschew this approach and look instead toward the ways in which our minds and behavior have been shaped over time (i.e., "nature"), although they do so with an awareness of the environmental pressures that caused these developments. While recent approaches in evolutionary psychology have tempered their approach with a more integrative and complete perspective toward human nature (e.g., behavioral ecology or evolutionary-developmental psychology; see Heywood, this volume), sociocultural constructivist scholars have been slower to temper their socialization approach. It is also worth noting that most sophisticated researchers no longer rely on the "nature versus nurture" divide, as it has become an intellectually bankrupt distinction; human behavior must, by all intelligent accounts, be the combined result of interacting biological and sociocultural pressures. The challenging questions that remain are about how, when, and why these forces interact.

A recent study provides an extreme example of how scholars in particular disciplines view the causes of sex differences. Compared to scholars in psychology or biology, those in sociology and women's studies believed that psychological sex differences in human adults and children are due to nurture, as are sex differences in chickens (Geher & Gambacorta, 2010). More scholars working in sociology and women's studies ascribed any sex difference in mating, such as roosters' preference to mate with multiple hens but hens' preference to mate with one rooster, as a socialization process among chickens. However, where the story becomes interesting is that these same academics believed that nature does play a large role in some human universals, such as a disgust response. Certainly, developmental and ecological conditions will alter any biological proclivity, but it is precisely an appreciation for this nuanced relationship that is necessary for complex and promising scholarship; outright rejection of one school of thought by the other does little to improve our understanding of the human condition.

Clearly, when sex differences enter the equation there is a line drawn in the sand between traditional evolutionary psychologists and traditional feminist scholars (not that either necessarily have archetypal "traditional" viewpoints in current academia). Despite this line, in recent years there has emerged a small but growing movement to unite the two fields in scientific circles. Scholars who address the female side of evolution (e.g., Fisher, 1999; Gowaty, 1997; Hrdy, 1999; Low, 2005; Rosvall, 2011; Smuts, 1995; Vandermassen, 2005; Vitzthum, 2008; Zuk, 2002; for a review see also Campbell, 2006), sometimes called Darwinian Feminists (see Low, 2005), have examined how a potentially male biased view of evolution has misshaped the predictions and interpretations we make about (human) evolutionary processes. Most recently, Hrdy (2009) takes issue with the lopsided attention that has been given to human competition versus cooperation. She argues that humans alone among the great apes will both tolerate and help nonrelated individuals on a consistent basis. Using a multitude of scientific sources, she then builds a strong argument that our propensity to cooperate is deeply entwined with the need for multiple caregivers to invest in human offspring: cooperative breeding leads to cooperation across groups. Such a shift in thought is only possible when scholars examine and correct historical bias in evolutionary science, and this bias, when present, has deep and knotted roots.

## Topical Areas in Which Women Have Been Left Out of Evolutionary Studies

We are not the first, by far, to talk about how evolutionary psychology often overlooks areas of relevance to women. However, here we briefly review a few examples to provide more of a background to this volume. In modern evolutionary psychology there exists a small literature on motherhood, mating, and sexuality that is relevant to the evolution of women. The conclusions drawn from the more extensive literature specific to the evolution of men are far grander. Men are argued to take risks, to compete with each other for mates, and to hunt for food to sustain families—all tasks that have been linked to major human milestones, such as language, cooperation, and tool use. These large claims cannot be made with the same equanimity for women. The claims about women are much tighter, smaller, and fewer. One area in which women are granted an active role is that of mate choice, as they are thought to be the selective, choosier, sex. For example, they are shown to select characteristics that lead to specific outcomes in male psychology (e.g., Miller, 2000) and engage in extra-pair copulations at opportune times to sequester optimal genes for children (e.g., Thornhill & Gangestad, 2003), both of which show that women have a role in shaping, if nothing else, the type of men whose genes are being furthered in subsequent generations. Yet, we do not see many arguments for women's role in the "bigger" human evolutionary milestones in evolutionary psychology that mirror those of men's roles (contrary to developments in anthropology discussed earlier, such as the Woman the Gatherer model, see Tanner, 1983; or women's role in cooperation, see Hrdy, 2009). Given that both sexes have endured natural and sexual selection, this lopsided attention seems strange, theoretically incomplete, and intellectually unsophisticated.

Essentially, then, what we are not seeing is a focus on issues that show women in a central role of human evolution. However, there are a few prominent scholars who have broached this gap to incorporate women into the larger picture. For example, Falk (2009) has proposed that human language evolved following the intimate tones used by mothers to infants (termed motherese, parentese, or infant-directed speech). In addition, Hrdy (2009) has used the caregiver-infant bond—which includes women and men—to explain the evolution of cooperation. But as a whole, issues that are central to women's evolutionary story are not being talked about at academic conferences or published with regularity in the academic literature within the field of evolutionary psychology.

The topic of mothering represents a big fish in a small pond; it is one of the most prevalent topics of evolutionary studies on women, but it is still disheartening to see that it is not more discussed. Human survival depends on the strategies that women employ for mothering; they are faced with a multitude of decisions, such as whether or not to invest in a child, whom they should have a child with, whom they should align themselves with for support systems, whom they must compete against in order to acquire a good mate, what their gametes might be doing to ensure fertilization, and so on. Some scholars, such as Sarah Blaffer Hrdy, author of *Mother Nature: Natural Selection and the Female of the Species* (1999), have made inroads into this area, but given the importance of these issues, one would expect hordes of researchers would be focused on these topics. There was great promise in the 1990s, given that one of the first compendiums on evolutionary psychology, *The Adapted Mind: Evolutionary Psychology and the Generation of Culture* (1992), contained a section dealing with maternal vocalizations, pregnancy sickness, and maternal nurturance versus neglect. Yet, something has changed: the academic landscape no longer contains this focus, which reflects the startling lack of scientific progress on this front.

*Evolution's Empress* is one way to address this problem. We do not take the perspective that only women know about women, which is often (although becoming less so) a firm belief of those in women's studies or those who work within a feminist framework (for a review see Hebert, 2007). Instead, we sought to bring together some of those who have examined women's active role in evolution into a single volume. We also endeavored to create a "sampler" such that there would be a noticeable range of topics to inspire future researchers. We contend that ignoring a female viewpoint in an age of gender-equality has merely led to the default assumption that what is true for men is true for women, except in the cases where researchers examine sex differences. In this volume, the collection of diverse contributors show how shifting the role of women from passive to active agents in evolution changes the way we envision human evolution and modern psychology.

This volume will not please everyone, but our hope is that it will initiate a discussion. In the future, it would be rewarding to see a volume, edited by scholars in feminist studies, on how to apply an evolutionary framework to some of *their* questions. Until then, we are pleased that there has recently (2011; Feminist Reappraisals of Evolutionary Psychology, edited by Smith and Konik) been a special issue of the journal *Sex Roles* where scholars talk about these two distinct approaches, and there has also been the formation of the Feminist Evolutionary Psychology Society. This is an exciting time indeed.

# Evolution's Empress

This volume is divided into five sections in order to encompass a range of ways in which evolutionary and feminist perspectives can work together to provide novel insights into behavior.

In Section One, "Sex Roles, Aggression, Competition, and Cooperation," we begin with female social relationships. This section starts with Fisher's overview of the advances in our understanding of women's intrasexual competition for mates then moves into an analysis by Liesen of female aggression, alliance development, and how females view status. Moscovice examines female alliances in a close genetic relative to humans, the bonobo. Section One ends with an examination of a bigger context, whereby Gowaty discusses the development of theoretical (and mathematical) predictions pertaining to sex differentiated behavior and the study of individual differences.

In Section Two, "Mothering and Parenting," Coe and Palmer discuss the role of women in transmitting traditions regarding cooking and storytelling. Cameron and Garcia then review the unique biological contributions that maternal effects have on adaptive offspring development. Newson and Richerson analyze the reasons and consequence for the development of female cooperation in the raising of children, while Chang presents vocalizations used in attachment relationships as evidence to show how the course of women's evolution has led them to solicit help in child rearing. Betzig then ends this section with historical evidence on conflict between fathers and sons, and makes the case that sons win when they have strong mothers.

For Section Three, "Health and Reproduction," Reiber first presents an overview of how scientific knowledge on women's reproductive physiology is lacking, and how an evolutionary feminist perspective can help inform this important topic. Then, Low reviews women's fertility as it relates to many social, cultural, and ecological factors. The issue of trade-offs between present and future reproduction is investigated by Johow, Voland, and Willführ in their discussion of women's postreproductive life. Escasa-Dorne, Young, and Gray then examine woman's life history decisions regarding how much care to provide to children, and how to view her romantic relationships, as influenced by life course development.

In Section Four, "Mating and Communication," Fedigan and Jack present a view of women's reproduction by examining various ways in which female capuchins (as an example species) are not passive recipients to male mating strategies, but rather are active throughout the entire reproductive process. Returning to humans, Frederick, Reynolds, and Fisher discuss female mate choice across various circumstances to display how women use variable mating strategies. Wilbur and Campbell show how one trait, humor, has been a topic of female mate choice, and how this preference has actively led to the shaping of men's evolved psychology. This section concludes with a chapter by Oberzaucher, who presents an approach to understanding the importance of sex differences in communication style.

And, finally, in Section Five, "New Disciplinary Frontiers," our contributors present a very diverse range of ideas to show how evolutionary and feminist perspectives can work together to arrive at novel insights into a range of topics. For example, Meredith reviews how women's priorities and motivations are distinct from those of men, and how this view might allow a reinterpretation of existing evolutionary psychology research. Easterlin performs a biocultural reading of Charlotte Brontë's classic novel *Jane Eyre*, stressing Jane's need to resist male control in her pursuit of both reproductive fitness and personal autonomy within the pair-bond. Seaman then enters the legal arena, and calls for a constructive engagement between feminist legal scholars and evolutionary psychologists, which would ideally enable insights of the latter group to be incorporated and thereby enable a deeper understanding of the human behavior that the law seeks to shape and regulate. Pridmore-Brown merges queer theory and recent work on the evolutionary consequences of cooperative breeding to discuss the ongoing "queering" of nature and the biologization of culture. Our final chapter, by Heywood, reviews the status of evolutionary psychology and feminist theory, and applies the *extended synthesis* as a model that leads to a common ground for both. As editors, we feel that this volume will serve as the starting point for many interesting discussions, and that these sections represent a wide array of varying perspectives on the ways that feminism and evolutionary psychology can interact.

# Note

1. Readers are referred to Farrell and Sterba (2008) to read more about the costs that may or may not be associated with focusing on women exclusively. In particular, Farrell's arguments show (and we agree) that it is not simply a case that most of evolutionary psychology is "male psychology."

# References

Birch, L. L. (1999). Development of food preferences. *Annual Review of Nutrition, 19,* 41–62.

Blurton Jones, N. G., Marlowe, F. W., Hawkes, K., & O'Connell, J. F. (2000). Paternal investment and hunter-gatherer divorce rates. In L. Cronk, N. Chagnon, & W. Irons (Eds.), *Adaptation and human behavior: An anthropological perspective* (pp. 69–90). New York: Aldine de Gruyter.

Brown Blackwell, A. (1875). *The sexes throughout nature.* New York: G. P. Putnam's Sons.

Buss, D. M. (1999). *Evolutionary psychology: The new science of the mind.* Boston: Allyn and Bacon.

Campbell, A. (2006). Feminism and evolutionary psychology. In J. H. Barkow (Ed.), *Missing the revolution: Darwinism for social scientists* (pp. 63–99). New York: Oxford University Press.

Carey, H. R. (1929). Sterilizing the fittest. *North American Review, 228,* 519–524.

Dagg, A. I. (2004). *"Love of Shopping" is not a gene: Problems with Darwinian psychology.* Montreal: Black Rose Books.

Darwin, C. (1872). *The descent of man, and selection in relation to sex* (Vol. 2). New York: D. Appleton and Company.

Dawkins, R. (1976). *The selfish gene.* Oxford, UK: Oxford University Press.

Ehrenreich, B., & English, D. (2005). *For her own good: Two centuries of the experts' advice to women* (Rev. ed.). New York: Anchor Books.

The Evolution Institute (2011). *The Evolution Institute: Understanding and Improving the Human Condition.* http://evolution-institute.org/

Falk, D. (2009). *Finding our tongues: Mothers, infants, and the origins of language.* New York: Basic Books.

Farrell, W., & Sterba, J. P. (2008). *Does feminism discriminate against men? A debate.* New York: Oxford University Press.

Fausto-Sterling, A. (1985). *Myths of gender: Biological theories about women and men.* New York: Basic Books.

Fedigan, L. M. (1986). The changing role of women in models of human evolution. *Annual Review of Anthropology, 15*, 25–66.

Fisher, H. E. (1999). *The first sex: The natural talents of women and how they are changing the world.* New York: Random House.

Garcia, J. R., Geher, G., Crosier, B., Saad, G., Gambacorta, D., Johnsen, L., & Pranckitas, E. (2011). The interdisciplinary context of evolutionary approaches to human behavior: A key to survival in the ivory archipelago. *Futures, 43*, 749–761.

Geher, G., & Gambacorta, D. (2010). Evolution is not relevant to sex differences in humans because I want it that way! Evidence for the politicization of human evolutionary psychology. *EvoS Journal: The Journal of the Evolutionary Studies Consortium, 2*(1), 32–47.

Goodsell, W. (1936). The size of families of college and non-college women. *American Journal of Sociology, 41*, 585–591.

Gowaty, P. A. (1997a). Darwinian feminists and feminist evolutionists. In P. A. Gowaty (Ed.), *Feminism and evolutionary biology* (pp. 1–7). New York: Chapman.

Gowaty, P. A. (Ed.). (1997b). *Feminism and evolutionary biology.* New York: Chapman.

Hare, B., Melis, A. P., Woods, V., Hastings, S., & Wrangham, R. (2007). Tolerance allows bonobos to outperform chimpanzees on a cooperative task. *Current Biology, 17*(7), 619–623.

Hebert, L. A. (2007). Taking "difference" seriously: Feminisms and the "man question." *Journal of Gender Studies, 16*, 31–45.

Heywood, L. (2010). *The quick and the dead: Gendered agency in the history of Western science and evolutionary theory.* Paper presented at the Fourth Annual Meeting of the NorthEastern Evolutionary Psychology Society, New Paltz, New York.

Hodson, C. B. S. (1929). Feminism and the race. *Eugenics, 2*, 3–5.

Howell, F. C. (1965). *Early man.* New York: TIME-LIFE Books.

Hrdy, S. B. (1981). *The woman that never evolved.* Cambridge, MA: Harvard University Press.

Hrdy, S. B. (1999). *Mother nature: Natural selection and the female of the species.* Phoenix, AZ: Firebird Distributing.

Hrdy, S. B. (2009). *Mothers and others: The evolutionary origins of mutual understanding.* Cambridge, MA: Harvard University Press.

Lloyd, E. A. (2005). *The case of the female orgasm: Bias in the science of evolution.* Cambridge, MA: Harvard University Press.

Lee, R. B., & DeVore, I. (Eds.) (1968). *Man the hunter.* New York: Aldine.

Liesen, L. T. (2007). Women, behavior, and evolution: Understanding the debate between feminist evolutionists and evolutionary psychologists. *Politics and the Life Sciences, 26*(1), 51–70.

Liesen, L. T. (2012). Feminists need to look beyond evolutionary psychology for insights into human reproductive strategies: A commentary. *Sex Roles.* doi: 10.1007/s11199-012-0153-3

Lovejoy, C. O. (1981). The origin of man. *Science, 211*, 341–350.

Low, B. S. (2005). Women's lives there, here, then, now: A review of women's ecological and demographic constraints cross-culturally. *Evolution and Human Behavior, 26*, 64–87.

McHenry, H. M. (1992). Body size and proportions in early hominids. *American Journal of Physical Anthropology, 87*, 407–431.

Milam, E. L. (2010). *Looking for a few good males: Female choice in evolutionary biology.* Baltimore, MD: Johns Hopkins University Press.

Miller, G. (2000). *The mating mind: How sexual choice shaped the evolution of human nature.* New York: Anchor Books.

Moore, H. T. (1930). Women's colleges and race extinction. *Scribner's, 87*, 280–284.

Nochlin, L. (1971/2003). Why have there been no great women artists? In A. Jones (Ed.), *The feminism and visual culture reader* (pp. 229–233). London: Routledge.

Puts, D. A. (2010). Beauty and the beast: Mechanisms of sexual selection in humans. *Evolution and Human Behavior, 31*, 157–175.

Rosvall, K. A. (2011). Intrasexual competition among females: Evidence for sexual selection? *Behavioral Ecology, 22*, 1131–1140.

Small, M. F. (1995). *Female choices: Sexual behavior of female primates.* Ithaca, NY: Cornell University Press.

Smith, C. A., & Konik, J. (2011). Feminism and evolutionary psychology: Allies, adversaries, or both? An introduction to a special issue. *Sex Roles, 64*, 595–602.

Smuts, B. (1995). The evolutionary origins of patriarchy. *Human Nature, 6*, 1–32.

*Stanford Encyclopedia of Philosophy*. (2008). http://plato.stanford.edu/entries/moral-non-naturalism/

Symons, D. (1979). *The evolution of human sexuality*. New York: Oxford University Press.

Stirrat, M., Gumert, M., & Perrett, D. (2011). The effect of attractiveness on food sharing preferences in human mating markets. *Evolutionary Psychology, 9*, 79–91.

Tanner, N. M. (1983). Hunters, gatherers, and sex roles in space and time. *American Anthropologist, 85*(2), 335–341.

Thornhill, R. & Gangestad, S. W. (2003). Do women have evolved adaptation for extra-pair copulation? In E. Voland & K. Grammar (Eds.), *Evolutionary aesthetics* (pp. 341–369). New York: Springer-Verlag.

Thornhill, R., & Palmer, C. (2000). *A natural history of rape: Biological bases of sexual coercion*. Cambridge, MA: MIT Press.

Vandermassen, G. (2005). *Who's afraid of Charles Darwin? Debating feminism and evolutionary theory*. Lanham, MD: Rowman & Littlefield.

Vitzthum, V. J. (2008). Evolutionary models of women's reproductive functioning. *Annual Review of Anthropology, 37*, 53–73.

Wilson, D. S., Dietrich, E., & Clark, A. (2003). On the inappropriate use of the naturalistic fallacy in evolutionary psychology. *Biology and Philosophy, 18*(5), 669–681.

Workman, L., & Reader, W. (2008). *Evolutionary psychology: An introduction* (2nd ed.). New York: Cambridge University Press.

Zietsch, B. P., Miller, G. F., Bailey, J. M., & Martin, N. G. (2011). Female orgasm rates are largely independent of other traits: Implications for "Female Orgasmic Disorder" and evolutionary theories of orgasm. *Journal of Sexual Medicine, 8*(8), 2305–2316.

Zuk, M. (2002). *Sexual selections: What we can and can't learn about sex from animals*. Berkeley: University of California Press.

# SEX ROLES, COMPETITION, AND COOPERATION

# 1

# Women's Intrasexual Competition for Mates

MARYANNE L. FISHER

## Introduction

Here then is the puzzle. Competition between females is documented in every well-studied species of primate save one: our own....Women are no less competitive than other primates, and the evidence will be forthcoming when we begin to devise methodologies sufficiently ingenious to measure it. Efforts to date have sought to find "lines of authority" and hierarchies comparable to those males form in corporations. No scientist has yet trained a systematic eye on women competing with one another in the spheres that really matter to them. The difficulty is not simply narrowness of vision and the mistaken assumption that female competition will take the same form as competition between males, but also the subtlety of interaction between females....How do you attach a number to a calumny? How do you measure the sweetly worded put-down? Until we are able to solve such problems, evidence for this hypothesized competitive component in the nature of women remains anecdotal, intuitively sensed but not confirmed by science.

—Hrdy, 1981/1999, pp. 129–130

This chapter is a reply to Hrdy's (1981/1999) call for researchers to examine women's competition in a sphere that matters to them. I will outline various types of evidence that clearly indicate that women's intrasexual competition can be measured. The above quotation from Hrdy sums up the problems involved in researching one of the most neglected aspects of evolved human mating psychology: how women compete intrasexually to acquire and retain mates. The quotation also applies equally well to women's intrasexual competition in other domains, such as relational status, social dominance, and obtaining resources for the support of one's children; in other words, areas that matter to women. Indeed, in polygynous societies, co-wives intrasexually compete for food and money, paternal care for their children, and for their children's inheritance (Burbank, 1987), and yet these behaviors have remained understudied. Unlike many of the overt, physical ways that men compete, women's competition is subtler, hidden, and disguised. In this chapter I will review why women's intrasexual competition takes this form and what we know at this point about women's competitive behavior. Although women indubitably compete in many ways, I will focus exclusively on the acquisition and retention of mates, as the majority of recent evolutionary-informed research is in this area.

There has been an increase in the number of papers published on this topic since Hrdy made her call, but still, there is much that needs to be studied. Theorists are drawing attention to the fact that we must dispel the negativity surrounding, or placement of values on, women's competition and instead focus on the evolutionary basis of this activity (Ingo, Mize, & Pratarelli, 2007). Many recent studies have illuminated the various strategies that women use, and how factors such as women's fertility impact on their behavior. However, empirical evidence is particularly lacking, possibly because of the difficulty involved in measuring its occurrence. This lack of attention is highly noticeable when compared to the level of research that is conducted on the topic of female mate choice. Although researchers have devoted substantial time and energy into exploring women's mate preferences, including personality, humor, voice, and height preferences, they have not yet spent a comparable level of effort addressing how women actually obtain the men whom they prefer. This chapter will provide an overview of this neglected topic, and show that studying female mate choice, although important, is only part of women's mating effort.

# Why Do Women Compete?

## Theoretical Review of Definitions

Darwin's (1871) theory of sexual selection is composed of two similar but distinct processes: intersexual selection and intrasexual selection. *Intersexual selection* is the preferential choice exerted by members of one sex for members of the opposite sex possessing particular traits. *Intrasexual selection* is the selection of characteristics that benefit individuals in the competition between members of the same sex for mating access to members of the opposite sex. In the former, individuals express preferences and actively choose mates, and in the latter, individuals compete for access to mates. Thus, according to Darwin's view of sexual selection, characteristics evolve that enable individuals to gain advantage over same-sex competitors and consequently obtain successful matings. Moreover, both elements have evolved in unison, such that characteristics most preferred by the opposite sex are those that are of most benefit in intrasexual competition.

Intrasexual competition has evolved as an important behavioral adaptation for attracting mates and for gathering resources necessary for reproduction (Darwin, 1871). Strategies used for intrasexual competition may be overt, such as physically fighting with a known rival, or they may be subtler, such as applying cosmetics to enhance attractiveness, where the rival may or may not be known. At first glance, one might think that cosmetic use is akin to the peacock's train, in that the individual is displaying her attractiveness to woo potential mates, and to signal to rivals whether competition would be potentially productive or not. Like the peacock flaunting its train, women are advertising their attractiveness when they use cosmetics. However, women can consciously apply cosmetics to make themselves look younger, with smoother, glowing skin, large eyes, red lips, and thereby deceive potential mates and rivals into thinking that they are more attractive than they might otherwise be.

But let us step back for a moment and think about competition more broadly, because there are many different ways to conceptualize competition. I propose that competition must be seen as rivalry; when two or more individuals are in pursuit of the same resource and that resource is perceived to be insufficient in quantity, the individuals can be considered as being engaged in a competition. The individuals do not have to be conscious of the rivalry, or be even aware of their competitors, but they must be partaking in an activity that draws them closer to attaining the desired resource (Hrdy, 1999). In terms of our topic, I propose that the scarce resource is "good men," as defined below, and the behaviors include a wide range of activities, including dressing up for a night out on the town, telling a rival that the male is a homosexual when he is not, casually making a negative comment about another woman, and calling the male frequently to ensure he is not with another woman.

Returning to sex differences, the literature clearly shows that women compete, but in a different way than men (for a review and application to workplaces, see Buunk, Goor, & Solano, 2010; Buunk, Pollet, Dijkstra, & Masser, 2011). This conclusion mirrors the findings on sex differences in aggression; both sexes are aggressive but express and demonstrate it differently (e.g., Bettencourt & Kernahan, 1997; Björkqvist, Lagerspetz, & Kaukiainen, 1992; Björkqvist, Österman, & Lagerspetz, 1994; Frodi, Macaulay, & Thome, 1977; Liesen, this volume). In tandem to the issue of how competition is defined is the quandary of measurement. Women's competition is often subtle and, thus, difficult to quantify (e.g., Cashdan, 1999; Hrdy, 1999). Therefore, the techniques used often have to be similarly indirect and innovative, often relying on observations or changes in perception.

## The Link Between Competition and Aggression

There exists a link between competition and aggression that underscores much of the research, so in an effort to be transparent in my logic, I present that link here. I consider *aggression* as any form of behavior or action directed at the goal of harming or irritating another person (Barron, 1977; Eron, 1987). One type, *indirect aggression* is when a perpetrator tries to cause harm while simultaneously attempting to make it appear as though there was no harmful intention (Björkqvist, Lagerspetz, & Kaukiainen, 1992). In this way, indirect aggression is akin to *relational aggression* (Crick & Grotpeter, 1995; Henington, Hughes, Cavell, & Thompson, 1998), which is the manipulation of peers via their relations and reputation, and interference with friendships and group inclusion. Often indirect aggression is used within the context of relationships, directed at someone's reputation, or for the purposes of group exclusion, for example. While indirect aggression means that there is an unknown aggressor or that the aggressor can claim that s/he was not performing an act for aggressive purposes, relational aggression can involve direct or indirect tactics with the only criterion being that it happens within the context of a relationship.

For example, indirect aggression among girls and women includes behaviors such as breaking confidences; criticizing others' clothing, appearance, or personality; trying to win others to one's side; shunning; excluding from the group; writing nasty notes; and spreading false stories and gossip (Björkqvist, 1994; Owens, Shute, & Slee, 2000; Simmons, 2002). It often involves the use of social networks, third parties, or other means to inflict harm on another individual (Fry, 1998). This social manipulation is usually performed to obscure any intention to cause harm, thus reducing the possibility of retaliation and counter-aggression (Björkqvist, et al., 1992). Thus, the victim is attacked circuitously so that the attacker can inflict harm without being correctly identified (Björkqvist, 1994; Björkqvist et al., 1992). Furthermore, girls and women tend to perform their aggressive acts from within a tightly woven group of allies, thereby intensifying the damage to the victim (Simmons, 2002), as more aggressors are involved.

Researchers have proposed a link between aggression and competition, such that aggression is necessary for competition to occur (e.g., Schuster, 1983). This theory has wide support in the literature (e.g., Burbank, 1987). Moreover, it seems that indirect aggression is linked to sexual readiness, as earlier onset in sexual behavior has been documented in aggressive girls (White, Gallup, & Gallup, 2010).

Historically, researchers have focused on men's aggression and their competitive nature, often arguing that the two are interlinked (e.g., Daly & Wilson, 1990; Geary, Byrd, Hoard, Vigil, & Numtee, 2003; Marlowe, 2000; Mazur & Booth, 1998; Symons, 1979; Trivers, 1985; Van de Vliert & Janssen, 2002; Wilson & Daly, 1985). Many researchers have noted that men are more physically aggressive than women (e.g., Cashdan, 1998; Fry, 1998; Maccoby & Jacklin, 1974), which has been used to show that men are competitive and women are not (e.g., Symons, 1979). This conclusion is simply inaccurate. For example, in a cross-cultural examination, Burbank (1987) found that in 61% of the 137 cultures she analyzed, women engaged in physical aggression, typically fighting other women over men, thereby showing that women can be directly aggressive and competitive. Other researchers have argued that the sexes do not differ significantly with respect to the frequency of aggressive behavior in general (e.g., Bettencourt & Miller, 1996; Frodi, Macaulay, & Thome, 1977; Ramirez, Andreu, & Fujihara, 2001). Overall, it seems that researchers have only begun to explore forms of female aggression and have largely neglected female intrasexual competition, especially as it applies to acquiring mates. Indeed, it remains "a vast area of ignorance" (Berglund, Magnhagen, Bisazza, König, & Huntingford, 1993, p.186). So, why is it that women's intrasexual competition has been overlooked?

Perhaps the answer lies in the fact that women rarely compete in physical ways, as overtly as men. Women, more than men, often compete in ways that do not involve direct physical contact, instead using verbal attacks or indirect social aggression (e.g., Barash, 2006; Campbell, 1999; Valen, 2010). It may be the case that, because women possess less physical strength than men, they develop alternative methods of competing, and thereby have developed unique strategies (Björkqvist, 1994). Campbell (1999; but see Liesen, this volume) suggests that this lack of physical competitiveness reflects not merely an absence of male-type risk-taking, but rather a successful female adaptation that results in reproductive benefit. She argued that when women become mothers, they become the primary caregivers and protectors of their children. Thus, it is more important for the mother to remain alive than the father, leading to the use of indirect, low-risk, strategies to resolve disputes. Taylor et al. (2000) similarly posits that in stressful situations, women do not have a "fight or flight" response. A fight response might cause them to "put themselves and their offspring in jeopardy, and the flight response...may be compromised by pregnancy or the need to care for immature offspring" (p. 412; see also Moscovice, this volume). Instead, they propose that women have evolved a "tend or befriend" response to stress, with tending being the quieting and caring for children and blending into the environment, and befriending being the creation of networks of associations containing individuals who will provide resources and protection for the woman and any children.

## The Scarcity of Good Men

The advantages, in terms of individual fitness, of finding and then retaining a mate of sufficient quality cannot be overstated. Consequently, most of the theory surrounding female competition for mates is framed with respect to seeking a mate for a long-term relationship (with the duration of the long-term being undefined). The standard argument, then, is that intrasexual competition may be beneficial for gathering resources that are needed for reproduction and childcare. Men who are good providers and possess the physical ability to serve as protectors (i.e., protect against "infanticide, sexual harassment, theft of valued resources, and general coercion;" Rodseth & Novak, 2006, p. 196) are a resource for which women may intrasexually compete. Women have faced sex-specific reproductive circumstances during evolutionary history; in contrast to men, women have energetically costly gametes that are comparatively few in number. Once fertilization occurs, it involves a substantial investment in terms of energy and time. Due to this differential in required reproductive effort, men's optimal reproductive strategy may be to seek as many matings as possible and invest little in any resulting children, while women's optimal strategy may be to carefully seek a mate and invest heavily in any children (as based on mammalian parental investment strategies as elaborated by Trivers, 1985). It is probable that these differences in reproductive strategy have influenced methods of competition. For example, men may compete for access to fertile women, while women may compete for access to men with resources and who are willing to provide paternal care (Buss, 1989; Cashdan, 1998).

What is missing from this standard argument is the acknowledgment that women sometimes seek short-term, primarily sexual relationships (Buss & Schmitt, 1993). When seeking a brief interaction, women are thought to prefer a mate with high "gene quality" given that the man will presumably not invest any resources or parental care in any resulting children (see for example, Gangestad & Simpson, 2000). I propose that women's competition follows the type of relation- ship they are seeking; if seeking a brief interaction, women will compete in ways to advertise their physicality, sexuality, and lack of commitment, while if they are seeking a long-term partner, women will compete in ways that advertise their parenting abilities and fidelity. Indeed, this appears to be the case, as Schmitt and Buss (1996) found that women pursuing a short-term relationship emphasized their sexuality and attractiveness, whereas women pursuing a long-term relation- ship promoted their faithfulness and sexual restrictiveness. Similarly, they found women pursuing a short-term relationship described other women, whom they perceived as potential competitors, as "ugly," "frigid," and "unhygienic," whereas in a long-term scenario they emphasized a competitor's promiscuity. Although these findings are promising, they are based on self-reported behavioral surveys, and it would be beneficial to have data from other methods for additional sup- port. I should note that another possibility exists; women seeking a short-term relationship simply might not need to compete as much as women seeking a lon- ger relationship. This prediction is based on the findings of Kenrick, Groth, Trost, and Sadalla (1993), who reported that, when considering women for relationships of various durations, men place more importance on female attractiveness as the expected duration increases. In other words, men have lower standards for a woman's attractiveness (which is an important element of male mate preference) when seeking a mate for a one-night stand, as opposed to steady dating or mar- riage. Subsequently, perhaps not the *form* but instead the *quantity* of competition changes in parallel to the length of the relationship.

Furthermore, it must be emphasized that competition does not end at mate acquisition; once a good mate has been selected, he must be retained, and the strategies used in the former situation will presumably be distinct from those in the latter. The strategies used may therefore vary depending on relationship status. To acquire a mate, one might advertise her positive qualities, make herself maximally attractive, and try to appear kind, friendly, and helpful. To keep a mate, though, one might claim that a potential rival is cruel, has a sexually transmitted infection, or a poor reputation, all features that are invisible and not readily confirmed (Fisher & Cox, 2011). Moreover, one might actually alter her own views; for example, Johnson and Rusbult (1989) demonstrated that individuals who were highly committed to their relationships actively, and perhaps even consciously, derogated available, attractive opposite-sex individuals on interpersonal dimensions such as intelligence and faithfulness (see also Simpson, Gangestad, & Lerma, 1990; Lydon, Meana, Sepinwall, Richards, & Mayman, 1999; Maner, Rouby, & Gonzaga, 2008; but also Fisher, Tran, & Voracek, 2008). This issue of how one's relationship status (i.e., whether or not one is attached, one's level of commitment) relates to the use of competitive strategy is far from resolved.

# What We Know About Women's Intrasexual Competition

## Results From Social Psychological Investigations

To begin, it is important to recognize that there are various behavioral strategies individuals use in intrasexual competition for mates. Two that have been documented are self-promotion and competitor derogation. *Self-promotion* is the enhancement of one's positive qualities, relative to those possessed by members of the same sex. In one of the first studies on the topic, Buss (1988) assessed via surveys people's use of self-promotion for the purpose of mate attraction and found women self-promoted by manipulating their appearance and men by displaying and bragging about their resources. Whereas the intention of Buss (1988) was to examine self-promotion for the sole purpose of mate attraction, Walters and Crawford (1994) examined self-promotion for the purpose of intrasexual competition and largely replicated his results. The second strategy, *competitor derogation* is any act used to decrease a rivals' mate value relative to oneself. Using a similar method to Buss (1988), Buss and Dedden (1990) found women tended to derogate rivals' appearance, while men typically derogated rivals' physical abilities and resources.

In a two-part study, Fisher, Cox, and Gordon (2009) examined sex and relationship status differences in selecting self-promotion versus competitor derogation in specific situations. For example, participants chose between "Sometimes when you see the man you're involved with, you say something to him about your own attractiveness, how fit and healthy you are looking" versus "Sometimes when you see the man you're involved with, you say something to him about your rival's unattractiveness, how unfit and unhealthy she is looking." In the first part, a convenience sample of undergraduate students was provided with forced choice items, which revealed self-promotion was selected significantly more often, regardless of context, sex, or relationship status. In the second part, the researchers asked a sample from the community to complete continuous measures (with the same contextual information as part one). For example, participants were asked, "How often have you tried to improve your appearance (e.g., dieted, dressed well, whitened teeth)?" with a scale ranging from never or very rarely to more than once a day. They found that women, more than men, reported using self-promotion, while men reported higher levels of competitor derogation. Those who were dating and those who were romantically uninvolved used both strategies more than those in common-law or married relationships.

More recently, Fisher and Cox (2011) performed a qualitative study in which participants listed all the ways in which they compete for mating attention, which revealed two additional strategies. One is *mate manipulation*, where one removes the target or goal of the competition so that no competition is necessary, such as by sequestering the mate or displacing his attention from a potential rival. The other was *competitor manipulation*, which is where one attempts to convince a rival that the potential mate is not worth the costs of competition. The methods of persuasion need not be honest, but because the price of deception is frequently high in terms of ostracism or retaliation, individuals utilizing deception must do so with caution (Hess, 2009). The results showed that the majority of listed tactics were those related to self-promotion, followed by mate manipulation, competitor derogation, and competitor manipulation. Women were significantly more likely than men to list self-promoting tactics concerning their general physical appearance and concerning their body and athleticism. Men were significantly more likely to list direct actions, including bullying or intimidating a rival or putting down a rival's material possessions, when derogating a competitor.

Fisher and Cox (2011) then used the qualitative data to create a survey to assess how frequently people performed these behaviors. They found self-promotion to be the most-used strategy, followed by mate manipulation, while competitor manipulation and competitor derogation were used an equivalent amount. In light of this finding and the data from Fisher, Cox, and Gordon (2009), in which social desirability influenced the use of competitor derogation, they proposed that self-promotion improves one's presentation to a mate, while other strategies may lead to negative evaluations (Fisher & Cox, 2009, for a review). Self-promotion can be disguised as self-improvement, which is socially desirable. Moreover, it does not necessitate knowing the identity of one's rivals, and it can be used to attract a large number of mates rather than to identify a specific mate. Interestingly, Fisher and Cox (2011) did not find any sex difference in strategy use, but did confirm that those in romantic relationships competitor derogate more than those who are romantically uninvolved. Regarding the lack of a sex difference in comparison to previous work by others, perhaps by keeping the survey items intentionally broad, they captured more behaviors. Walters and Crawford (1994) reported that several tactics had to be omitted from their analysis because judges were required to agree that the tactic was competitive and also agree on the tactic's purpose. That is, "if one sex makes more use of subtle competitive tactics, the method used in this study may not detect ... such tactics" (p. 12). This exclusion is important in light of the large body of research that reveals women's use of indirect, subtle forms of competition (Björkqvist, Österman, & Lagerspetz, 1994).

Fisher, Shaw, Worth, Smith, and Reeve (2010) then sought to explore the possibility that those who use competitor derogation would be negatively evaluated by potential mates, which would partly explain the greater reliance on self-promotion. To do so, they conducted a study with a pre-post design. In the first part, men rated photographs of women in terms of how friendly, kind, physically attractive, promiscuous, and trustworthy they thought the woman was, her overall desirability as a mate, her potential to make a fit parent, and how much they would consider her for a long-term relationship or for a brief sexual relationship. In the second part of the study, the stimuli were constructed so that it appeared that one woman had made a negative statement (i.e., derogation) about another woman; both women's photographs were included, and fake names were assigned. A new group of participants then rated the derogator on the dimensions, allowing for a comparison. Overall, men significantly decreased their evaluations of the derogator's friendliness, kindness, trustworthiness, and overall desirability as a mate. A comparison group of female participants were also included; instead of rating how much they would consider the model for a relationship, they indicated whether they believed they could improve the model's appearance by giving her a makeover, which may indirectly suggest whether women believed the model was "trying her hardest" to look attractive. Women's results mirrored those of men, but women also significantly decreased their views of the derogator's fitness as a parent and her physical attractiveness. The study design incorporated the idea that the type of derogation might matter, and thus included derogations that were based on either sexuality, appearance, or personality. These more in-depth results of how derogators are viewed by men are presented in Table 1.1, while Table 1.2 shows the results for the comparison group of women. Surprisingly, derogators are not rated negatively with regard to how likely men are to consider them for a long-term relationship or sexual relationship, nor in terms of their promiscuity or physical appearance. Concerning this last characteristic, previously we found men's views of women's physical attractiveness remains quite stable, regardless of gaining information about a woman's sexual history or expected duration of any future romantic relationships, while women's views are influenced by this type of information in potential mates (Williams, Fisher, & Cox, 2008).

Using a different approach, DeBacker, Nelissen and Fisher (2007) studied the role of gossip in rivalry for mates. One form of gossip, "sexual rivals reputation gossip," is information about the mating skills of competitors, which helps

*Table 1.1* **Negative changes in men's views of various dimensions of female derogators according to the type of derogation; "X" indicates significant decrease, see Fisher et al. (2010)**

|  | *Appearance Derogation* | *Sexuality Derogation* | *Personality Derogation* |
|---|---|---|---|
| Friendliness | X |  | X |
| Kind | X | X | X |
| Physically attractive |  |  |  |
| Parenting ability |  |  | X |
| Promiscuity |  |  |  |
| Trustworthiness | X | X |  |
| Consider for long-term relationship |  |  |  |
| Consider for sexual relationship |  |  |  |
| Overall desirability | X | X | X |

*Table 1.2* **Negative changes in women's views of various dimensions of female derogators according to the type of derogation; "X" indicates significant decrease, see Fisher et al. (2010)**

|  | *Appearance Derogation* | *Sexuality Derogation* | *Personality Derogation* |
|---|---|---|---|
| Friendliness | X | X | X |
| Kind | X | X | X |
| Physically attractive | X | X | X |
| Parenting ability | X | X | X |
| Promiscuity | X |  |  |
| Trustworthiness | X | X | X |
| Could be improved with a makeover |  |  |  |
| Overall desirability | X | X | X |

to identify rivals and allow individuals to more readily select a winning strategy. Individuals could also manipulate the information to alter rivals' reputations, such as by exaggerating or supplying additional details. Hess (2009) viewed this as "informational warfare" and proposed that gossip is a strategy for within-group competition and for attacking and defending reputations; it may be more useful in women's intrasexual competition than in men's intrasexual competition, which would increase selection for psychological adaptations for informational aggression in women (Hess, 2009). Using a recall study of vignettes manipulated for content, DeBacker et al. (2007) found sex differences in the ability to remember information about rivals. They predicted women would recall more same-sex information than men, because gossip may be a useful tool in future derogation of rivals (Buss & Dedden 1990; Schmitt & Buss 1996), particularly for women who rely on indirect aggression (Hess, 2009). As predicted, Debacker et al. found women recalled more information about the mating skills of female characters than men recalled about the mating skills of male characters. Moreover, female characters' physical attractiveness was recalled more by both sexes than that of male characters, and male characters' wealth was recalled more by both sexes than that of female characters. These findings suggest that both men and women attend to the attractiveness of women, either to determine their potential mate value (in the case of men) or to assess them as threats for intrasexual competition (in the case of women). Similarly, both men and women attend to the wealth of men for the same reasons.

Attending to the features of rivals is a critical facet of intrasexual competition. It is logical that knowing about the local mating market, particularly about one's rivals, can influence one's own behavior. Hill and Durante (2011) found that priming women with images of attractive local women representing potential competitors caused them to self-report a stronger desire to engage in attractiveness-enhancing but also risky behaviors such as tanning and using diet pills. Interestingly, women in romantic relationships seemed particularly interested in taking diet pills, which indicates that competitive behavior remains when mated. The proposition is reasonable, given one's mate could be poached or commit infidelity.

Although it would presumably be advantageous to be able to accurately assess the mate quality of one's rival in the immediate environment, Hill (2007) proposed that people have a tendency to overestimate how much members of the opposite sex find those of the same sex attractive as potential mates, which she termed, "the mate competition overestimation bias." She argues that while it would be ideal to be able to perfectly estimate the mate value of rivals, the temporal shifts of mate preferences as well as individual differences, and people's tendency to hide or deceive their true preferences, makes it unlikely that the related evaluation of rivals can be accurate. She further posits that the harm of underestimating the value of a rival is worse than overestimation, and showed that indeed, both women and men are prone to the latter.

## Cross-Cultural and Developmental Findings

Intrasexual competition among girls and women is prevalent across cultures. The most convincing evidence is from Burbank's (1987) cross-cultural investigation of 317 societies that revealed women are the most common target of female aggression. She discovered that cross-culturally, women are physically aggressive, destroy property, refuse to perform duties, and insult others nonverbally (e.g., through gestures, locking someone out of a domicile). These findings must be considered with some caution, though, because it is very likely that women spend the majority of their time in the presence of other women, and because Burbank excluded measures of indirect aggression.

Other studies provide further cross-cultural evidence for intrasexual competition for mates, albeit through documenting indirect aggression. In most of these studies, the authors note that sexual jealousy was a strong motivation for aggressive acts. In Argentina, Hines and Fry (1994) found women use more indirect aggression (e.g., gossiping, lying, ridiculing, invidious comparisons of clothing and attractiveness) than men, and that men use more physical aggression. Olson (1994) obtained similar results in her examination of Tongan women. An account of a holiday in Greece by Kostash (1987) demonstrated indirect aggression via exclusion and "cold stares." Even the small island society of Vanatinai, New Guinea, provided support for the idea that women frequently use indirect aggression (Lepowsky, 1994). In addition to these studies, to date, female indirect aggression has also been documented in Australia (Owens, Shute, & Slee, 2000); Finland, Israel, Italy, and Poland (Österman, et al., 1998); and the United Kingdom (Campbell, 1995).

One investigation clearly showed women's aggression is linked to reproduction via mate attainment. In her 1983 study of Zambian society, Schuster documented that women were faced with a scarcity of desirable (e.g., reliable and resourceful) men due to pronounced social and economic stratification based on an economy of surplus rather than subsistence. Over time, women grew increasingly dependent on men for resources, and men became increasingly unreliable as providers, resulting in a scarcity of highly desirable men. Promiscuity became more prevalent, and thus marital relationships were considered to be unstable, such that a man was often a potential target of sexual advances from other women. Women, especially co-wives, competed by gossiping, quarrelling, and often by physical fighting.

Some of these studies found gossip to play an important role in women's competition (e.g., Schuster, 1983). One use of gossip is to alter reputations. Although not framed as such, Rucas and colleagues' (2006) study of the Tsimane women in Bolivia specifically focused on the manipulation of other women's reputation. Evaluations of women's attractiveness were found to be altered according to reputational information concerning trustworthiness, social intelligence, wealth, status, mothering ability, and housekeeping ability, but there was no effect based on manipulations of promiscuity. Thus, they showed that gossip may be effectively used to alter evaluations of mating rivals.

In a study framed as an inquiry into the adaptive function of menopause, evidence of competition in Gambia has also been documented. Mace and Alvergne (2011) recently presented preliminary findings that in rural Gambian households competition exists among women living in the same compound of a reproductive age. They found several instances of mothers who became grandmothers before reaching menopause, and that for these individuals, having a grandchild significantly reduced their reproductive rate. They argue that menopause thus evolved as a way to reduce intrasexual competition for mates. As an aside, there is likely more evidence of women's intrasexual competition from anthropological studies than has been documented; researchers probably notice women's intrasexual competition for mates but do not focus on it, as it is not the central topic of their study. Hopefully at some point, someone will collect these observations into a coherent document to show the universality of this behavior, and how it can be influenced by context, such as the presence of young children, number and age of co-wives, and resource scarcity.

As for developmental evidence, it seems that for girls, increases in indirect aggression align with reproductive onset. Björkqvist et al. (1992) found dramatic increases in indirect aggression among girls who were approximately 11 years of age, followed by still higher rates among 15-year-olds; meanwhile, boys' rates remain stable. Indeed, Österman and colleagues (1998) reported that girls, aged 8, 11, and 15, in Finland, Israel, Italy, and Poland, primarily rely on indirect aggression (and boys on physical or verbal aggression). In terms of adult populations, this sex difference remains, such that women often use indirect aggression, especially in social relationships, whereas men have a decreased use of physical aggression and increased use of verbal aggression.

Studies on relational aggression also support the prediction that intrasexual competition increases at reproductive onset. With a sample of approximately 900 second and third grade children, Henington and associates (1998) found boys received higher peer ratings of relational aggression than girls. However, among children in grades three through six, Crick and Grotpeter (1995) reported that girls scored higher on relational aggression than boys. Together, these results suggest female aggression changes in response to reproductive development. This possibility remains to be tested, though, because the difference might stem from contrasting definitions and measures.

## Results From Biological Investigations

For brevity, I have excluded comparative investigations into female intrasexual competition, although there have been important strides made, especially in the nonhuman primate literature. Similarly, I omit anthropological discussions about the influence of hunting and gathering on the development of female peer relationships, and how these activities may have affected the evolution of female intrasexual competition, as compared to other apes (see Rodeth & Novak, 2006, for a review).

One of my first investigations into women's intrasexual competition involved ratings of female (and for comparison, male) facial attractiveness, according to ovulatory cycle phase (Fisher, 2004). I argued that decreases in attractiveness ratings were akin to competitor derogation, whereby one is devaluing a rival, and later proposed that the purpose of this behavior might be to inadvertently persuade a potential mate that a rival is not attractive (see Fisher & Cox, 2009).

The results showed that ovulating women had significantly lower evaluations of female faces as compared to non-ovulating women. Interestingly, there was no difference for male faces. I posited that these findings indicated women derogated competitors at a time most critical for conception. In a follow-up study, Lucas, Koff, and Skeath (2007) documented women in the highly fertile part of their cycle were less likely to share monetary rewards in a game, and more likely to reject a chance to share in a monetary stake when it was a low offer. They propose that their finding shows that women in the most fertile part of their cycle may be prone to competing for resources.

Further, evidence of endocrinological influence on women's intrasexual competition was indirectly obtained by Welling et al. (2011), who found that mate retention tactics are higher among women using hormonal contraceptives (especially for synthetic estradiol) than nonusers, especially tactics related toward their mates. Men whose mates were users also reported an have increased rates of mate retention tactics, but directed them toward rivals and mates. Both forms of mate retention are likely competitive behaviors, in that one is manipulating a mate by ensuring that he does not attend to potential rivals (see Fisher & Cox, 2011).

There is a sizable body of literature addressing how women behave according to their ovulatory cycle hormones. In general, it seems that some women modify their behaviors during times of high fertility to appear maximally enticing to potential mates. For example, women may dress more fashionably and select more revealing clothing when in a phase of high fertility (Haselton et al., 2007; see also Durante, Li, & Haselton, 2008, for a review of cues to ovulation). Durante et al. (2008) propose that women might be dressing sexier as a way of outcompeting other women on the mating market during a time when it matters most in terms of probability of conception. Moreover, they found that for those involved in a romantic relationship, satisfaction mattered; women who were satisfied with their mate shifted their preferences toward revealing clothes when maximally fertile. Durante et al. (2011) then went one step further and showed, using shopping behavior at a retail clothing website, that ovulating women chose sexier and more revealing attire (including shoes and accessories). This effect was particularly salient when women were first primed to notice attractive local women (i.e., mating rivals), as opposed to unattractive women, and attractive or unattractive men.

Recently, Markey and Markey (2011) suggested that although men attend to women's physical attractiveness, it is not the only characteristic that is evaluated, and hence, not the only one that might be susceptible to hormonal shifts. They found that men are most attracted to women with a warm interpersonal manner; that is, men like women who act kind, accommodating, sympathetic, and gentle. Interestingly, they demonstrated that women who are in the highly fertile part of their cycle exhibited more of these warm characteristics and less dominance, as compared to other parts of their cycle.

# What We Still Need to Investigate

## Friend or Rival?

There are many options for future research, based on the findings reviewed in this chapter.

I have investigated the topic of women's intrasexual competition for mates for over a decade, and one question in particular has constantly troubled me: How do women know when someone is an ally, someone that they should befriend (à la Taylor et al. 2000) versus someone who is a rival? Women's alliances are extremely important, especially given that they serve the adaptive purpose of providing all-omothering (Hrdy, 2009). At the same time, women absolutely must compete for mates and to retain mates. How is this path between friend and rival navigated? Is there an empirical design that can explore the decision-making process that would capture the nuances of such a delicate balance between friend and foe? I hope so, but it remains to be performed. Likewise, I propose that group dynamics, composition, and demographics influence the use of competitive strategies. For example, women may only compete with other women who are not in their immediate social group, and the derogation of rivals may be an effective way of maintaining social bonds. This possibility is supported by research on the use of gossip as an important mechanism for the maintenance of women's friendships (e.g., Dunbar, 1996).

The nonhuman primate literature clearly indicates that human females are distinct. Rodseth and Novak (2006) discuss this uniqueness as follows. Although there is noteworthy variation among populations, female chimpanzees have a relatively solitary existence with few social alliances, partly due to natal dispersion to reduce feeding competition. This aversion to competition prevents them from forming bonds with female kin. However, women, even when they move into a group of unrelated individuals in a highly patriarchal society form close and lasting friendships. They propose that these friendships represent alliances "for the purposes of competition against others" (p. 203). Does this model fit when talking about mate acquisition and retention? That is, do models of social bonds such as this one capture the nuances of women's intrasexual competition for mates? If so, how women select their alliances needs to be explored, considering these friends also represent rivals for mates.

Akin to deciding whether someone is a friend or rival is the decision of strategy use. Many factors likely impact on this decision-making process, including the quality of the mate, identity of the rival, or past experience with a particular tactic. An obvious example concerns attractiveness; women's attractiveness is an important component of men's mate preference (Buss, 1989) and consequently a vehicle of women's competition (e.g., Fisher, 2004). Therefore, perhaps women evaluate their own attractiveness with respect to other women to determine the type of strategy they should use. Research has shown that a woman who is unattractive is relatively ineffective in derogating the appearance of a rival, as compared to an attractive woman (Fisher & Cox, 2009). As a result, she should rely on alternative tactics. Although this decision seems straightforward, it is confounded by the fact that evaluations of the physical attractiveness of one's rivals are rarely accurate, as people tend to overestimate rivals' attractiveness (Hill, 2007). Therefore, if a woman's decisions regarding strategy are based only on physical attractiveness, there is a reasonable chance for failure. Instead, her decision should include multiple sources of information, such as the relationship one has with rivals, the number of rivals, their personality features, whether the rivals are romantically involved, and the riskiness of the tactic.

## The Influence of Mate Value

Another issue that needs to be more adequately explored is how to measure the frequency and effectiveness of self-promotion tactics in daily life. Ways to capture competitor derogation are relatively easier; one can note decreases in attractiveness ratings (e.g., Fisher, 2004), or listen to what is overheard in women's washrooms (Blennerhassett & Fisher, 2011). Documenting and measuring self-promotion is much trickier, though, as these behaviors can be disguised as self-improvement mediated by social norms, or simply as dimensions of one's personality (e.g., "I'm not *acting* nice, I *am* nice"). Casual observation leads me to predict one could examine primping behavior at a dance club, or how women interact with each other when in the presence of desirable men, but extending these findings to study typical daily life seems problematic given that self-promotion can be so readily disguised as self-improvement, for example.

In a similar vein, researchers still have not discovered the role of self-perceived and other-perceived mate value in women's intrasexual competition. We know that people who engage in social comparison tend to adjust their competitive strategy. For example, Buunk and Fisher (2009) found that women who engaged in social comparison self-reported that they engaged in intrasexual competition. Likewise, Buss et al. (2000) found women experienced distress when they believed potential rivals had more attractive faces and bodies, and proposed that jealousy might be a way to examine this phenomenon. That is, jealousy might be an emotional reaction to the self-comparison against rivals. Maner et al. (2009) found that once primed about concerns of infidelity, those with high chronic jealousy attend vigilantly to the attractiveness of potential rivals, remember those individuals, and think of them negatively, as compared to those with lower jealousy.

Recently, Arnocky and colleagues (2011) documented that women in romantic relationships who made frequent social comparisons in terms of attractiveness also were most likely to engage in indirect aggression. They argue that these are women who might perceive themselves to have low mate value in terms of physical attractiveness, and thus, will perceive more threats to existing relationships. This perception leads them to try to control their partner and also ensure that rivals are kept at arms' length. As Arnocky et al. (2011) review, behaving indirectly aggressively toward rivals may be useful in that it can reduce the social standing of the target, such as by spreading a false rumor, and "because of the negative symptoms associated with indirect victimization, such as depression or social anxiety" (p. 11), and increase one's own standing via popularity.

Indeed, it seems that having an awareness of one's attractiveness (and hence, at least a partial assessment of self mate-value) influences competitive behaviors. Durante et al. (2008) showed that women with lower self-perceived attractiveness showed larger shifts toward preferring revealing clothes when most fertile, while Bleske-Rechek and Lighthall (2010) found that within pairs of female friends, the woman who was lower in physical attractiveness perceived higher mating rivalry than the friend who was more attractive. These results build on Bleske and Shackelford (2001), who investigated intrasexual competition among same-sex friends in terms of mating rivalry. They hypothesized that people are very selective about their friends because friends are often in close proximity to one's mate. Moreover, they predicted that people take into consideration features such as a friend's promiscuity and physical attractiveness, as these may increase the chances that the friend will successfully poach their mate. Bleske and Shackelford's findings supported this claim; women, more than men, became distressed when female friends enhanced their attractiveness and were sexually available.

Perceptions of potential rivals' attractiveness has also been investigated via uncontrolled muscle contractions. Hazlett and Hoehn-Saric (2000) investigated women's physiological responses to potential rivals using facial electromyographic techniques, and found highly attractive rivals elicited a greater corrugator (brow lowering) muscle reaction and greater self-reported arousal than less attractive women. The authors concluded that attractiveness is particularly salient for women's assessments of other women, and this muscle reaction is due to a defensive display in response to a perceived threat. However, Hazlett and Hoehn-Saric were only able to measure facial muscle movements in response to two categories (attractive or unattractive) of facial stimuli, and thus, it remains for future researchers to continue with this potentially fruitful line of investigation.

Fisher et al. (2008) have also made initial inroads into this area, beginning with the development of a comprehensive self-perceived mate value inventory, and the next step is to investigate how it relates to competitive strategy use. A potentially more interesting question, though, is how one's mate value relates to the mate value of potential competitors; presumably, people compete only with those they perceive as having a similar value. Competing with someone possessing a much higher mate value would be a waste of energy, time, and resources, whereas one would likely win with little effort against someone with a much lower mate value. Competition should therefore maximally exist among those of similar mate values. Although much of the past research reviewed in this chapter logically leads to this prediction, until we can accurately determine the composition of women's mate value and measure the various parts, it remains an unaddressed issue.

## Other Avenues for Future Research

There are numerous other lines of investigation to be pursued. Although I have focused on competition solely for the purposes of mating, it remains to be experimentally shown that intrasexual competition, as conceptualized in this chapter, is performed in reference to mating behavior and not other factors. For example, women may derogate other women as a way of maintaining friendships, and the competition might be used for the purposes of sharing information, deepening trust, and excluding others. A longitudinal or cross-sectional life history study could directly test whether female intrasexual competition is solely performed for mating purposes. Young, adolescent women could be observed during prepuberty and postpuberty intervals, and if competition for mates significantly increases in conjunction with reproductive onset, the conclusion would be that competition is performed, at least partly, for reproductive reasons. Similarly, participants could be older women, tested prior to and after menopause. If competition noticeably decreases with the cessation of reproductive capacity, then it would be possible to conclude, to some extent, that competitive behavior is performed for the purposes of mating. Studies of relational and indirect aggression suggest this result will be obtained, but it remains to be tested for competition.

A different potential line of research to explore is the influence of economic independence on women's competition for mates. As reviewed, the literature suggests that women who are seeking a long-term relationship benefit from selecting a mate with resources. What happens, though, if the woman has her own resources; does her wealth influence her mate preferences, and in turn, her strategies or frequency of competition? Likewise, does the number of potential mates influence competition? Presumably in situations of scarcity, competition would increase. However, Cantu and colleagues (2011) reported the results of a preliminary study in which they found women who were primed (via a story or arrays of photographs) to believe that there was a shortage of available men expressed a desire for a high-paying career and to delay starting a family. This finding suggests that at least some women remove themselves from the mating market temporarily, and thus do not engage in competition.

Furthermore, future research is necessary to determine the characteristics in potential mates that elicit female intrasexual competition. Do women compete more strongly for men with resources in comparison to attractive men? What are the traits or characteristics of potential mates that are most preferred, and hence, the features for which women compete? Evolutionary psychologists (e.g., Buss, 1989) have suggested that women most prefer men who demonstrate resources, and value the personality characteristics that result in financial security such as ambition. In contrast, social psychologists (e.g., Hatfield, Aronson, Abrahams, & Rottman, 1966) have suggested that the sexes do not significantly differ in the importance they place on attractiveness in potential mates. The characteristics of potential mates that elicit women's competition need to be identified.

Another line of future inquiry may address how people intrasexually compete in relation to same-sex family members. Kin selection theory suggests that individuals with overlapping genes may assist each other in realizing their reproductive potentials (Hamilton, 1964). Therefore, future research could examine how genetically related sisters versus genetically unrelated sisters respond to potential threats via intrasexual competition. For example, do genetically related sisters discuss each other's attractiveness in a positive way more often than genetically unrelated sisters? Do genetically related sisters attempt to deflect gossip about each other, and defend each other's reputations more so than genetically unrelated sisters? By extension, do genetically related sisters assist each other in acquiring a desirable mate more than genetically unrelated sisters, and if so, how do they use intrasexual competition? Recently, Nitsch and Lummaa (2011) reported preliminary findings based on a preindustrial Finnish dataset of 20,000 individuals. They found that women's (and men's) reproductive success was encumbered by having elder siblings of the same sex, and concluded that once individuals reach sexual maturity, they compete with same-sex siblings for mating opportunities, among other resources. There remains much to be explored in this area.

Female intrasexual competition may also be evident among various professions. For example, due to the intense selection criteria based on attractiveness, professional fashion models would be a potentially viable population to study. Fashion models depend, at least mostly, on their appearance to retain their jobs. For example, Wilson and Edwards (2000) document that female fashion models must be a minimum of 5'8" in height, have clear and flawless skin, healthy hair, long legs, wide-set eyes, high facial symmetry, and typically must be under 22 years of age. Moreover, employers have specific requirements on hip, bust, waist, and thigh measurements, and employers weigh and measure the models weekly (Wilson & Edwards, 2000). Due to this intense pressure to retain a particular appearance, it is possible that models may exhibit higher than usual levels of intrasexual competition specifically in terms of attractiveness. Beauty-show contestants would also be a potential sample of interest for the same reasons. I must note this approach conflates career success with mating success, given that one must be maximally attractive to be well employed, and thus broadens intrasexual competition to include rivalry that is not strictly limited to the mating arena.

One final area that I will mention concerns the interpersonal dynamics underlying strategy use. Cox and Fisher (2008) proposed a rudimentary framework for intrasexual competition that outlined the fact that these behaviors involve an actor (person performing the behavior), the target (e.g., the mate), and the rival. They presented how nine different relationships occur, and how they relate to strategy use. The key is to identify for whom a competitive act is intended, and the consequence of that act. Little attention has been paid to the dynamics of those involved, particularly with respect to whom the behavior is intended to influence.

# Conclusion

Women's intrasexual competition for the acquisition and retention of mates exists. The literature on indirect aggression and relational aggression was used to show that intrasexual competition is documented cross-culturally, and seems to be related to the age of reproductive onset, suggesting deep evolutionary roots that underpin women's mating strategies. I then reviewed some of the ways women's intrasexual competition has been explored to date. Women engage in competition using a variety of strategies; they may derogate the attractiveness of a competitor, choose to self-promote, or attempt to manipulate the availability or value of the male who is the target of the competition. I also reviewed the influence of women's fertility on some of their behaviors, such as competitor derogation. Finally, I reviewed several promising lines of research that remain to be pursued. Many exciting, unanswered questions remain, and the research described here is hopefully just the beginning of a long journey of exploration.

# References

Arnocky, S., Sunderani, S., Miller, J., & Vaillancourt, T. (2011). Jealousy mediates the relationship between attractiveness comparisons and females' indirect aggression. *Personal Relationships, 19*, 290–303.

Barash, S. S. (2006). *Tripping the prom queen: The truth about women and rivalry.* New York: St. Martin's Griffin.

Barron, R. A. (1977). *Human aggression.* New York: Plenum.

Berglund, A., Magnhagen, C., Bisazza, A., König, B., & Huntingford, F. (1993). Female-female competition over reproduction. *Behavioural Ecology, 4*, 184–187.

Bettencourt, B. A., & Kernahan, C. (1997). A meta-analysis of aggression in the presence of violent cues: Effects of gender differences and aversive provocation. *Aggressive Behavior, 23*, 447–456.

Bettencourt, B. A., & Miller, N. (1996). Gender differences in aggression as a function of provocation: A meta-analysis. *Psychological Bulletin, 119*, 422–447.

Björkqvist, K. (1994). Sex differences in physical, verbal, and indirect aggression: A review of recent research. *Sex Roles, 30*, 177–188.

Björkqvist, K., Lagerspetz, K. M., & Kaukiainen, A. (1992). Do girls manipulate and boys fight? Developmental trends in regard to direct and indirect aggression. *Aggressive Behavior, 18*, 117–127.

Björkqvist, K., Österman, K., & Lagerspetz, K. M. (1994). Sex differences in covert aggression among adults. *Aggressive Behaviour, 20*, 27–33.

Blennerhassett, C., & Fisher, M. (2011, March). *Intrasexual competition for mates in the woman's bathroom.* Paper presented at the annual meeting of the Association for Women in Psychology, Philadelphia, PA.

Bleske, A. L., & Shackelford, T. K. (2001). Poaching, promiscuity, and deceit: Combating mating rivalry in same-sex friendships. *Personal Relationships, 8*, 407–424.

Bleske-Rechek, A., & Lighthall, M. (2010). Attractiveness and rivalry in women's friendships with women. *Human Nature, 21*, 82–97.

Burbank, V. K. (1987). Female aggression in cross-cultural perspective. *Behavior Science Research, 21*, 70–100.

Buss, D. M. (1988). The evolution of human intrasexual competition: Tactics of mate attraction. *Journal of Personality and Social Psychology, 54*, 616–628.

Buss, D. M. (1989). Sex differences in human mate preferences: Evolutionary hypotheses tested in 37 cultures. *Behavioral and Brain Sciences, 12*, 1–49.

Buss, D. M., & Dedden, L. A. (1990). Derogation of competitors. *Journal of Social and Personal Relationships, 7*, 395–422.

Buss, D. M., & Schmitt, D. P. (1993). Sexual strategies theory: An evolutionary perspective on human mating. *Psychological Review, 100*, 204–232.

Buss, D. M., Shackelford, T. K., Choe, J., Buunk, B. P., & Dijkstra, P. (2000). Distress about mating rivals. *Personal Relationships, 7*, 235–243.

Buunk, A., & Fisher, M. (2009). Individual differences in intrasexual competition. *Journal of Evolutionary Psychology, 7*, 37–48.

Buunk, A., Goor, J., & Solano, A. (2010). Intrasexual competition at work: Sex differences in the jealousy-evoking effect of rival characteristics. *Journal of Social and Personal Relationships, 27*, 671–684.

Buunk, A. P., Pollet, T. V., Dijkstra, P. & Massar, K. (2011). Intrasexual competition within organizations. In G. Saad (Ed.), *Evolutionary psychology in the business sciences* (pp. 41–70). New York: Springer.

Cantu, S., Durante, K, Griskevicius, V., & Simpson, J. (2011, June). *Briefcase over baby: The influence of sex ratio on career aspirations.* Paper presented at the annual meeting of the Human Behavior and Evolution Society, Montpellier, France.

Campbell, A. (1995). A few good men: Evolutionary psychology and female adolescent aggression. *Ethology and Sociobiology, 16*, 99–123.

Campbell, A. (1999). Staying alive: Evolution, culture and women's intra-sexual aggression. *Behavioural and Brain Sciences, 22*, 203–252.

Cashdan, E. (1998). Are men more competitive than women? *British Journal of Social Psychology, 37*, 213–229.

Cashdan, E. (1999). How women compete. *Behavioral and Brain Sciences, 22*, 221.

Cox, A., & Fisher, M. (2008). A framework for exploring intrasexual competition. *Journal of Social, Evolutionary, and Cultural Psychology, 2*, 144–155.

Crick, N. R., & Grotpeter, J. K. (1995). Relational aggression, gender, and social-psychological adjustment. *Child Development, 66*, 710–722.

Daly, M., & Wilson, M. I. (1990). Killing the competition. *Human Nature, 1*, 83–109.

Darwin, C. (1871). *The descent of man and selection in relation to sex.* London: John Murray.

DeBacker, C., Nelissen, M., & Fisher, M. (2007). Let's talk about sex: A study on the recall of gossip about potential mates and sexual rivals. *Sex Roles, 56*, 781–791.

Dunbar, R. (1996). *Grooming, gossip and the evolution of language.* Cambridge, MA: Harvard University Press.

Durante, K., Li, N., & Haselton, M. (2008). Changes in women's choice of dress across the ovulatory cycle: Naturalistic and laboratory task-based evidence. *Personality and Social Psychology Bulletin, 34*, 1451–1460.

Durante, K., Griskevicius, V., Hill, S., Perilloux, C., & Li, N. (2011). Ovulation, female competition, and product choice: Hormonal influences on consumer behavior. *Journal of Consumer Research, 37*, 921–934.

Eron, C. D. (1987). The development of aggressive behaviour from the perspective of a developing behaviorism. *American Psychologist, 42*, 435–442.

Fisher, M. (2004). Female intrasexual competition decreases female facial attractiveness. *Proceedings of the Royal Society of London, Series B (Supplemental), 271*, S283–285.

Fisher, M., & Cox, A. (2009). The influence of female attractiveness on the effectiveness of competitor derogation. *Journal of Evolutionary Psychology, 7*, 141–155.

Fisher, M., & Cox, A. (2011). Four strategies used during intrasexual competition for mates. *Personal Relationships, 18*, 20–38.

Fisher, M., Cox, A., Bennett, S., & Gavric, D. (2008). Components of self-perceived mate value. *Journal of Social, Evolutionary, and Cultural Psychology, 2*, 156–168.

Fisher, M., Cox, A., & Gordon, F. (2009). Deciding between competition derogation and self-promotion. *Journal of Evolutionary Psychology, 7*, 287–308.

Fisher, M., Shaw, S., Worth, K., Smith, L., & Reeve, C. (2010). How we view those who derogate: Perceptions of female competitor derogators. *Journal of Social, Evolutionary, and Cultural Psychology, 4*, 265–276.

Fisher, M., Tran, U., & Voracek, M. (2008). The influence of relationship status, mate seeking and sex on intrasexual competition. *Journal of Social Psychology, 148*, 493–508.

Frodi, A., Macaulay, J., & Thome, P. (1977). Are women always less aggressive than men? A review of the experimental literature. *Psychological Bulletin, 84*, 634–660.

Fry, D. P. (1998). Anthropological perspectives on aggression: Sex differences and cultural variation. *Aggressive Behavior, 24*, 81–95.

Gangestad, S. W., & Simpson, J. A. (2000). The evolution of human mating: Trade-offs and strategic pluralism. *Behavioral and Brain Sciences, 23*, 573–644.

Geary, D. C., Byrd, C. J., Hoard, M. K., Vigil, J., & Numtee, C. (2003). Evolution and development of boys' social behavior. *Developmental Review, 23*, 444–470.

Hamilton, W. D. (1964). The genetical evolution of social behavior. *Journal of Theoretical Biology, 7*, 1–16.

Haselton, M., Mortezaie, M., Pillsworth, E., Bleske-Rechek, A., & Frederick, D. (2007). Ovulatory shifts in human female ornamentation: Near ovulation, women dress to impress. *Hormones and Behavior, 51*, 40–45.

Hatfield, E., Aronson, V., Abrahams, D., & Rottman, L. (1966). The importance of physical attractiveness in dating behavior. *Journal of Personality and Social Psychology, 4*, 508–516.

Hazlett, R. L., & Hoehn-Saric, R. (2000). Effects of perceived physical attractiveness on females' facial displays and affect. *Evolution and Human Behavior, 21*, 49–57.

Henington, C., Hughes, J. N., Cavell, T., & Thompson, B. (1998). The role of relational aggression in identifying aggressive boys and girls. *Journal of School Psychology, 36*, 457–477.

Hess, N. (2009). *Informational warfare: The evolution of female coalitions and gossip.* Doctoral dissertation. Retrieved from http://anthro.vancouver. wsu.edu/media/PDF/on March 28, 2010.

Hill, S. (2007). Overestimation bias in mate competition. *Evolution and Human Behavior, 28*, 118–123.

Hill, S., & Durante, K. (2011). Courtship, competition, and the pursuit of attractiveness: Mating goals facilitate health-related risk taking and strategic risk suppression in women. *Personality and Social Psychology Bulletin, 37*, 383–394.

Hines, N. J., & Fry, D. P. (1994). Indirect modes of aggression among women of Buenos Aires, Argentina. *Sex Roles, 30*, 213–236.

Hrdy, S. (1999). *The women that never evolved.* Cambridge, MA: Harvard University Press. Republished from 1981.

Hrdy, S. (2009). *Mothers and others: The evolutionary origins of mutual understanding.* Cambridge, MA: Harvard University Press.

Ingo, K., Mize, K., & Pratarelli, M. (2007). Female intrasexual competition: Toward an evolutionary feminist theory. *Theory and Science, 9.* http://theoryandscience.icaap.org/content/vol9.1/ingo.html

Johnson, D. J., & Rusbult, C. E. (1989). Resisting temptation: Devaluation of alternative partners as means of maintaining commitment in close relationships. *Journal of Personality and Social Psychology, 57*, 967–980.

Kenrick, D. T., Groth, G. E., Trost, M. R., & Sadalla, E. K. (1993). Integrating evolutionary and social exchange perspectives on relationships: Effects of gender, self-appraisal, and involvement level on mate selection criteria. *Journal of Personality and Social Psychology, 64*, 951–969.

Kostash, M. (1987). Feminism and nationalism. In V. Miner & H. E. Longino (Eds.), *Competition: A feminist taboo* (pp. 40–56). New York: The Feminist Press.

Lepowsky, M. (1994). Women, men, and aggression in an egalitarian society. *Sex Roles, 30*, 199–211.

Lucas, M., Koff, E., & Skeath, S. (2007). A pilot study of relationship between fertility and bargaining. *Psychological Reports, 101,* 302–310.

Lydon, J. E., Meana, M., Sepinwall, D., Richards, N., & Mayman, S. (1999). The commitment calibration hypothesis: When do people devalue attractive alternatives? *Personality and Social Psychology Bulletin, 25,* 152–161.

Maccoby, E. E., & Jacklin, C. N. (1974). *The psychology of sex differences.* Stanford, CA: Stanford University Press.

Mace, R., & Alvergne, A. (2011, June). *Female female competition in rural Gambian households.* Paper presented at the annual meeting of the Human Behavior and Evolution Society, Montpellier, France.

Maner, J. K., Miller, S. L., Rouby, D. A., & Gailliot, M. T. (2009). Intrasexual vigilance: The implicit cognition of romantic rivalry. *Journal of Personality and Social Psychology, 97,* 74–87.

Maner, J. K., Rouby, D. A., & Gonzaga, G. (2008). Automatic inattention to attractive alternatives: The evolved psychology of relationship maintenance. *Evolution and Human Behavior, 29,* 343–349.

Markey, P., & Markey, C. (2011). Changes in women's interpersonal styles across the menstrual cycle. *Journal of Research in Psychology, 45,* 493–499.

Marlowe, F. (2000). Paternal investment and the human mating system. *Behavioural Processes, 51,* 45–61.

Mazur, A., & Booth, A. (1998). Testosterone and dominance in men. *Behavioral and Brain Sciences, 21,* 353–397.

Nitsch, A., & Lummaa, V. (2011, June). *Are elder siblings helpers or competitors.* Paper presented at the annual meeting of the Human Behavior and Evolution Society, Montpellier, France.

Olson, E. (1994). Female voices of aggression in Tonga. *Sex Roles, 30,* 237–248.

Österman, K., Björkqvist, K., Lagerspetz, K. M., Kaukiainen, A., Landau, S. F., Fraczek, A., & Caprara, G. V. (1998). Cross-cultural evidence of female indirect aggression. *Aggressive Behavior, 24,* 1–8.

Owens, L., Shute, R., & Slee, P. (2000). "Guess what I just heard!": Indirect aggression among teenage girls in Australia. *Aggressive Behaviour, 26,* 67–83.

Ramirez, J. M., Andreu, J. M., & Fujihara, T. (2001). Cultural and sex differences in aggression: A comparison between Japanese and Spanish students using two different inventories. *Aggressive Behaviour, 27,* 313–322.

Rodseth, L., & Novak, S. (2006). The impact of primatology on the study of human society. In J. Barkow (Ed.), *Missing the revolution: Darwinism for social scientists* (pp. 187–220). New York: Oxford University Press.

Rucas, S., Gurven, M., Kaplan, H., Winking, J., Gangestad, S., & Crespo, M. (2006). Female intrasexual competition and reputational effects on attractiveness among the Tsimane of Bolivia. *Evolution and Human Behavior, 27,* 40–52.

Schmitt, D., & Buss, D. (1996). Strategic self-promotion and competitor derogation: Sex and content effects on the perceived effectiveness of mate attraction tactics. *Journal of Personality and Social Psychology, 70,* 1185–1204.

Schuster, I. (1983). Women's aggression: An African case study. *Aggressive Behaviour, 9,* 319–331.

Simmons, R. (2002). *Odd girl out: The hidden culture of aggression in girls.* New York: Harcourt.

Simpson, J., Gangestad, S., & Lerma, M. (1990). Perception of physical attractiveness: Mechanisms involved in the maintenance of romantic relationships. *Journal of Personality and Social Psychology, 59,* 1192–1201.

Symons, D. (1979). *The evolution of human sexuality.* New York: Oxford University Press.

Taylor, S., Klein, L., Lewis, B., Gruenewald, T., Gurung, R., & Updegraff, J. (2000). Biobehavioral responses to stress in females: Tend-and-befriend, not fight-or-flight. *Psychological Review, 107,* 411–429.

Trivers, R. L. (1985). *Social evolution.* Menlo Park, CA: Benjamin/Cummings Press.

Valen, K. (2010). *The twisted sisterhood: Unraveling the dark legacy of female friendships.* New York: Ballantine Books.

Van de Vliert, E., & Janssen, O. (2002). Competitive societies are happy if the women are less competitive than the men. *Cross-Cultural Research, 36*, 321–337.

Walters, S., & Crawford, C. B. (1994). The importance of mate attraction for intrasexual competition in men and women. *Ethology and Sociobiology, 15*, 5–30.

Welling L., Puts, D., Roberts, S., Little, A. & Burriss, R. (2011, June). *Hormonal contraceptive use and mate retention behavior in women and their male partners.* Paper presented at the annual meeting of the Human Behavior and Evolution Society, Montpellier, France.

White, D. D., Gallup, A. C., & Gallup, G. G. (2010). Indirect peer aggression in adolescence and reproductive behavior. *Journal of Evolutionary Psychology, 8*, 49–65.

Williams, L., Fisher, M., & Cox, A. (2008). The impact of sexual history and desired relationship duration on evaluations of attractiveness and recall. *Journal of Evolutionary Psychology, 6*, 1–23.

Wilson, M. I., & Daly, M. (1985). Competitiveness, risk taking, and violence: The young male syndrome. *Ethology and Sociobiology, 6*, 59–73.

Wilson, M. J., & Edwards, A. (2000). *A model's primer* (2nd ed.). Riverview, FL: Advanced Multimedia Designs.

# 2

# The Tangled Web She Weaves

## *The Evolution of Female-Female Aggression and Status-Seeking*

LAURETTE LIESEN

## Introduction

Women of all ages have stories to tell of their battles with other women over recognition, acceptance, and inclusion. They want to be recognized as being attractive, talented, and sociable; they also want to be accepted by other women and men. Groups of girls and women define who is acceptable and who is to be excluded, especially if they are high-status groups. Not being socially included in some group, especially at a young age, may have profound social, psychological, and reproductive consequences for those girls or women who are deemed unacceptable, isolated, and excluded by their peers. For those who are targeted and excluded, the consequences can be reproductively difficult at best and physically devastating at worst.

In recognition of the harm women can inflict, there have been many popular books that describe girls and women's various aggressive tactics and the injuries caused by these machinations (for example Simmons, 2002; Wiseman, 2002). Interestingly, among these various popular books, only a few make any reference to biological or evolutionary perspectives and these are tangential at best (for example Chesler, 2001; Garbarino, 2006; Tanenbaum, 2002). While all of these accounts are interesting reading, they do not explain why women use aggression against each other and strive for status.

Prior to the 1980s, both female aggression and female dominance relationships were nearly invisible to scholars, particularly those in the evolutionary sciences. It was assumed that females did not pursue dominance, rank, or status because there were few physical conflicts involving females, and their relationships lacked the more observable hierarchical structures that characterized male social structures. The most compelling explanations for female-female aggression are rooted in the research by feminist evolutionists and primatologists. Their groundbreaking work was informed by feminism and looked beyond sexual stereotypes. For example, Sarah Hrdy (1981/1999), Linda Fedigan (1982), and Barbara Smuts (1987a) all have provided insights into female aggression, dominance, and status-seeking behaviors and their long-term reproductive benefits. Years later, this research eventually led to new examinations of human female aggression (for example Bjorkqvist, Osterman, & Kaukiainen, 1992; Campbell, 1999, 2002) and dominance structures among female adolescents (for example Benenson, 1999, 2009; Hawley, 1999, 2003, 2007).

In this chapter, I will present an overview of feminist evolutionists' contributions, especially in primatology, to the contemporary understanding of female aggression, dominance, and status-seeking. Not only does this literature clearly demonstrate that girls and women are aggressive, using both physical and indirect tactics, it also demonstrates that they pursue dominance and status. Similar to their nonhuman primate relatives, the status girls and women pursue has reproductive benefits in terms of material and social resources that over time will benefit them and their children. These resources include regular access to the physical resources for survival and reproduction (food, space, and males), higher rank that frees them from harassment from other females, and the establishment of alliances. Finally, I will suggest that the way girls and women pursue status leads to dominance structures that are like a web or matrix. Rather than wanting to be at "the top" like males, girls and women (like other nonhuman female primates) want to be the "center of attention," for that is where the most social, material, and reproductive benefits are located. They can do this either by dominating their own social groups or by being associated with the dominant group itself. When the resources necessary for survival and reproduction are scarce, the pursuit of these personal needs can lead to daily political struggles and conflicts of interest among girls and women that may have a long-term impact on their reproductive success.

## Female Primates and Aggression

Beginning in the late 1970s, various feminist evolutionists, especially primatologists, closely examined nonhuman primate female reproductive behavior, including female aggression and dominance structures. While feminism did influence these primatologists (Hrdy 1981/1999), they were first scientists using the theories and methodologies of sociobiology, evolutionary biology, and behavioral ecology who consciously decided to pay more attention to female behavior. They challenged earlier assumptions that male aggression was an innate trait and the determinant of dominance hierarchies within human groups (Barash, 1982; Wilson, 1978). They found that their data on nonhuman primate females did not fit the assumptions that females passively pursued their own reproductive interests, and that males were innately aggressive and the only sex that competed for dominance. From their work with primates, various feminist evolutionists, such as Hrdy (1977, 1981/1999), Lancaster (1985, 1991), Fedigan (1982, 1983), and Smuts (1985, 1987a, 1987b, 1992), brought new insights into female reproductive behavior in general and aggressive behavior in particular.

Within primatology, aggression refers to several types of behaviors. It is defined as intentional behavior that may cause physical injury to another individual, as well as nonphysical or self-assertive behaviors—such as displays, supplantations, harassment, and territorial vocalizations (Fedigan, 1982). While these aggressive behaviors may not cause injury, they may cause an individual to physically withdraw, possibly away from resources that are important for that individual's rank, survival, or reproductive success. For example, Strier (2011) cites several instances among different primate groups in which high-ranking females have forced lower ranked females out of their territories when there is a scarcity of food and water. Feminist primatologists certainly broke new ground by observing the various manifestations of female primate aggression. For example, Smuts (1987a) found no consistent sex differences between primate males and females in the frequency of agonistic interactions, specifically supplantations, threats, chases, and fights. However, there are qualitative differences among various primates in the way males fight in comparison to how females do. Male baboons, vervet monkeys, and macaques use ritualized threats—yawns, teeth grinding, or charging— more often to intimidate their rivals. Beyond these visual threats and displays, male primates may also hit, bite, slap, or grapple, usually resulting in injury, but rarely death. In rare instances, female primates have also used ritualized threats and physical aggression against rivals (Smuts, 1987a; see also Walters & Seyfarth, 1987). Just because female primates have low rates of physical aggression does not mean they are uncompetitive.

In an attempt to explain why primate females do not use physical aggression as often as males, Smuts (1987a) draws on parental investment theory (Trivers, 1972) and suggests that nonhuman primate males who use aggression may make greater gains in terms of immediate mating opportunities. Indeed nonhuman primate females who use physical aggression may not experience great immediate increases in their own reproductive success in terms of mating. In fact, Smuts (1987a) suggests that when females use physical aggression, they may be undertaking a higher risk than males in these attacks since they may not only injure themselves, but also harm their own fetuses or infants. However, this explains only one specific context in which primate females would probably shy away from physical aggression. It does not explain why some primate females do use physical aggression to harm and injure their rivals and their rivals' offspring, and why they use harassment, supplantations, and vocalization toward rivals.

While the behavior is rare compared to males, primate females have been observed inflicting physical harm, including death, on rivals. Rather than looking for short-term reproductive success to explain sex differences in aggression, Fedigan (1982) argues that it may be more useful to examine the social interactions and contexts within which they take place and determine if there are longer term benefits for females and their offspring to engage in aggressive behaviors. Physical aggression has been observed among primate females in these contexts:

- *During daily interactions between dominant and subordinate individuals over higher rank* (Fedigan, 1982). This was observed among troops of wild baboons in which the females exhibited types of behavior that had been considered primarily male—ritualized threats, face lacerations, and mounting of potential allies (Smuts, 1987a).
- *For the protection of infants.* Females have attacked males and higher ranking females to protect their infants (Fedigan, 1982; Hrdy, 1981/1999; Smuts, 1987a, 1987b).
- *Over scarce resources, such as food, water, territory, or mates* (Fedigan, 1982; Hrdy, 1981/1999; Smuts, 1987a; see also Thompson, Stumpf, & Pusey, 2008).
- *During encounters with unfamiliar animals or predators* (Fedigan, 1982; Smuts, 1987a).
- *Committing infanticide.* Researchers have also observed high-ranking chimpanzee females committing infanticide against the infants of low-ranking females (Hrdy, 1981; Pusey, Williams, & Goodall, 1997; Pusey et al., 2008), thus removing future competitors for food for their own offspring.

Both physical and indirect aggression are tools that primate females use to enhance their own and their offspring's long-term reproductive success. Part of the competitive pursuit of reproductive success is acquiring high rank within the group. Hrdy (1981/1999) maintains that nonhuman primate females are highly competitive with each other, especially for dominance and higher status, and will use various aggressive tactics that are usually nonphysical and subtle. In the context of female primates' social organization, aggression can be a means to obtain as well as maintain dominance.

## Female Primates and Dominance

When examining status among humans, it useful to look at social structures in other primate species since dominance and rank are closely related concepts. Among ethologists, dominance is defined in terms of preferential access to valuable resources, such as food, water, space, or mates (Barkow, 1975). Dominance also refers to an individual who can take resources from another individual (Lee & Johnson, 1992). This does not mean that a dominant individual is always physically aggressive; she can use self-assertion and threats (Fedigan, 1982, 1983). In determining where individuals fall in a dominance structure, observers identify the rank of an individual in a social group. Rank is defined in terms of basic rank and dependent rank. Basic rank is a dominance relationship that occurs when an identified individual is alone with no allies present. Dependent rank is a dominance relationship that occurs when an individual has a dominant relative or ally present (de Waal & Harcourt, 1992). Among primates, including humans, an individual's rank within a group is contextual as well as fluid. In one social situation, an individual may achieve his or her goals very easily, while in other situations that individual may be thwarted by more dominant individuals with higher ranks (Bernstein & Gordon, 1980). These relationships are distinguished by the presence of ritualized submission, and they are distinct from just winning fights (Martin, 2009).

Researchers measure dominance and deference behaviors in several ways: through direct observations of conflict resolution, physical fights, threats, submissive behaviors, and patterns of conflict avoidance among individuals. Therefore, dominance is determined by how an individual responds to a threat. When Hrdy (1981/1999) describes a primate as dominant, she means that she won a one-on-one encounter by approaching, displacing, or threatening another primate. If the individual is submissive or retreats from approaches or interactions, she is considered subordinate (Fedigan, 1982).

Prior to the work by feminist evolutionists, researchers interested in dominance and rank only observed male behavior because it is more physical and overt. This led the evolutionary theorists of the 1960s and 1970s to define dominance only as a relationship among individuals (males) in which one demonstrates the ability to achieve a goal against the strivings of others through conflict, self-assertion, or physical aggression (Fedigan, 1982). Another factor contributing to the lack of research on female dominance structures was that researchers widely assumed that competitiveness, status-seeking, and ambition are not compatible with being a good mother (Hrdy, 1999). Rather than considering dominance to be just an inherent male trait, feminist evolutionists have demonstrated that female primates have dominance structures. These structures are not determined by physical aggression alone, but also by other types of aggressive tactics and demographic and ecological variables. Shifts in dominance and rank can occur because of deaths, group fission and fusion, and migrations, which may or may not involve aggressive behavior (Fedigan, 1983). For both studies of primate and human females, feminist evolutionists (Fedigan, 1982; Hrdy, 1981/1999; Smuts, 1985) redefined dominance structures and rank to include females, leading the way for other scholars to take female aggressive and dominance behavior seriously.

Female primates who face increased competition over resources use physical and nonphysical aggression to gain and maintain dominance rank, attaining a better quality of life in terms of greater access to resources, more offspring, and less harassment and injury from others. Recent research in primatology has further supported their groundbreaking work. During times of scarcity, higher ranked primate females have better access to food and water. When these resources are scarce, higher ranked females will have greater reproductive success

(Lancaster, 1985; Lee & Johnson, 1992). Access to better food and water is also related to having access to better space. In a recent study conducted by Murray, Mane, and Pusey (2007), higher ranked female chimpanzees occupied more resource rich habitats, while subordinates were forced to the peripheral territories that contain fewer resources and a greater risk of predation.

As high-ranked females have better access to resources, their rank will affect their and other females' reproductive physiology (Fedigan, 1983; Hrdy, 1981; Pusey et al., 2008). Among rhesus macaques, baboons, and chimpanzees, the daughters of high-ranked females reach sexual maturity and give birth earlier than lower ranked females (Masetripieri, 2007; Pusey et al., 1997; Silk, 1987). In addition, among bonobos, high-ranking females have their choice of mates without restrictions (Low, 2000). In a study of mountain gorillas, Robbins, Robbins, Stekles, and Stekles (2007) found that females with higher rank and who were in groups with more than one male silverback had greater reproductive success. The higher rank was associated with greater survival rates, shorter birth intervals, and greater success in raising offspring. Typically, in several primate species not only is the mother's rank passed on to her daughters, it also benefits her sons during their juvenile years. Among baboons, the sons of high-ranking mothers experience several positive maternal effects—faster growth, earlier reproductive maturity, and lower levels of glucocorticoid (Onyango, Gesquiere, Wango, Alberts, & Altmann, 2008). Finally, a higher ranked female in a group, through her mere presence, can affect the menstrual cycles of subordinates, either by delaying maturation, inhibiting ovulation, or causing spontaneous abortions (Hrdy, 1981/1999). Lower ranked females who experience psychosocial pressures and resulting elevated glucocorticoid levels will see the impact on their offspring in terms of lower birth weight, growth rate, immunity, and survival (Onyango et al., 2008).

Along with these reproductive benefits, high-ranked primate females get away with a variety of aggressive behaviors against subordinates. Ongoing harassment of subordinate females causes such stress that over time it reduces lower ranked females' fertility and thus their long-term reproductive success. In addition, high-ranked females will target lower ranked females and their offspring for harassment, and sometimes murder. Among macaques and baboons, a high-ranking female may take an infant from the subordinate female. If she refuses to return it, the infant will starve to death (Hrdy, 1981/1999). During her work with the Gombe chimpanzees, Jane Goodall observed high-ranking females murdering the infants of lower ranked females (cited in Hrdy, 1981/1999; Pusey et al., 2008). Among nonhuman primates, higher rank provides females and their offspring with protection from harassment, injury, and even death.

Another factor that influences female dominance structures are coalitions with related and unrelated females. Coalitions involve three or more individuals who cooperate and assist each other within an aggressive or competitive context (de Waal & Harcourt, 1992). For primate females, the development of coalitions is contingent on the female's age, size, and kinship structure within the group

(Datta, 1992), and has important survival and reproductive consequences. In a recent study, Silk et al. (2009) found that offspring of female baboons who formed strong social bonds with other females lived significantly longer than those offspring who formed weaker bonds. According to Cords, Sheehan, and Ekernas (2010), juvenile female monkeys can actively establish networks with higher ranked adult females for future allies (see also Moscovice, this volume). Even as adults, primate females may be dependent on their kin allies to maintain their rank above lower ranked females (Chapais, 1992), and it is stressful if a female loses her preferred partners in her coalition (Silk, Altmann, & Albers, 2006). The contexts in which coalitions are formed include repulsing strange males who have entered the group (Smuts, 1992), protecting another adult female from an attack by a male (Smuts, 1987a), protecting infants (Hrdy, 1981/1999; Smuts, 1985, 1987a), harassing and attacking lower ranked females and their offspring (Hrdy, 1981/1999; Pusey et al., 2008), and excluding other females from their groups to reduce competition for food (Benenson, Hodgson, Heath, & Welch, 2008).

In sum, primate females will use various types of aggression and strive for dominance within their social groups for the resources, protection, and coalitions necessary for their long-term reproductive success. Indeed, Hrdy maintains that among nonhuman primates, competition among females is:

> The central organizing principle of primate social life....Whereas males compete for transitory status and transient access to females, it is females who tend to play for more enduring stakes. For many species, female rank is long-lived and can be translated into longstanding benefits for descendents of both sexes. Females should be, if anything, *more* competitive than males, not less, although the manner in which females compete may be less direct, less boisterous, and hence more difficult to measure. (1981/1999, pp. 128–129)

Consequently, these contributions and insights by feminist evolutionists and primatologists have enabled us to see and understand why girls and women are aggressive and strive for status.

## Women and Aggression

Among many of the recent scholarly and popular publications on female aggression, only a few look to the evolutionary sciences for insight. This may be related to the fact that early evolutionary scientists typically focused on human male aggression because its physical manifestations are easily observed. Even when the object of research was female aggression, the operationalization of aggression favored "male" forms, that is, physical aggression. Feminist evolutionists' reliance on primate studies and evolutionary theory help us to better see aggression among girls and women. As the studies on nonhuman female primate aggression expanded, eventually the conceptualization of human female aggression changed and available data grew. By the 1980s and 1990s, researchers were looking at the various forms of aggression—indirect, verbal, and relational—and how it is used differently by males and females (Bjorkqvist et al., 1992; Burbank, 1987; Crick & Grotpeter, 1995). While aggression is one reproductive strategy available to males, early accounts did not recognize that aggression can also be a strategy used by females.

By examining the behavior of humans' closest genetic relatives, researchers not only learned how to observe the more subtle examples of female aggression but also they began to ask why some girls and women intentionally use aggressive tactics for physical, social, and reproductive gain. Even though they tend to be smaller and lack the physical strength of males, these characteristics do not prevent girls and women from being hostile or make them less prone to conflicts (see Archer, 2000, 2009; Campbell, 2002). Human female aggression is reported in all regions of the world. Women display a wide range of aggressive behaviors—ranging from insulting, excluding, or silently snubbing a person, to physically fighting, destroying property, and killing.

In response to their anger and frustration, women use both direct and indirect aggressive tactics. Direct aggression includes physical assaults, threats, and verbal insults, while indirect aggression includes exclusion, gossip, and social manipulation. Bjorkqvist et al. (1992) make further distinctions between direct verbal aggression and indirect aggression in their study of Finnish schoolchildren. Direct verbal aggression consists of yelling, directing insults, and teasing, which are overt forms of aggression that are easily observed. Indirect aggression, also called relational aggression, enables the aggressor to avoid direct physical contact with her target. It can consist of gossiping, ignoring, and various social manipulations, such as withdrawing friendship or exclusion, that purposefully damage relationships (Crick & Grotpeter, 1995; Little, Jones, Henrich, & Hawley, 2003; Underwood, 2003). The popular literature, which examines the lives of American adolescents (Chesler, 2001; Simmons, 2002; Tanenbaum, 2002; Wiseman, 2002), has many accounts of what these writers call relational aggression along with the pain and isolation girls and women have experienced at the hands of their peers. For example, relational aggression can include "ignoring someone to punish them or get one's own way,...using negative body language or facial expressions, sabotaging someone else's relationships, or threatening to end a relationship unless the friend agrees to a request" (Simmons, 2002, p. 21). Overall, girls and women are aggressive and are more likely to use direct verbal and indirect aggression than direct physical aggression (Bjorkqvist & Niemele, 1992; Campbell, 2002; Crick & Grotpeter, 1995).

Who then are the targets of women's aggression? In her cross-cultural review of 137 societies, Burbank (1987) states that women were the targets of female aggression in 91% of those societies, while men were targets in 54% of them. Yet, she found that men were the primary reason for women's aggression. In order to protect their relationships and resources for their children, women very often will lash out at other women when their husbands commit adultery. Even in polygynous societies, aggression between women can erupt because of jealousy, potential loss of resources, and competition from a new wife. When female aggression is verbal or physical and property is destroyed, women are more often the targets. In her research on Zambian women, Schuster (1983) found that physical violence is more common among women outside the household. In her cross-cultural study, Burbank (1987) also found that women rarely attacked their sisters, mothers, daughters, and related males. In a study of British schoolgirls, Campbell (1986) found that 73% of their physical fights were with another girl, consisting of punching, kicking, or slapping. Finally, Campbell (2004) found that female physical aggression occurs more often among lower socioeconomic classes, presumably because the competition for resources is more intense.

In societies where a few men control scarce resources, their distribution, and formal political power, there is an increase in the competition not only among men but also among women who are trying to attract and keep the men capable of providing those resources. They will very often compete with each other indirectly in order to cater to male preferences in women (Cashdan, 1998). For example, Western women spend significant amounts of time and resources to enhance/create a youthful appearance using cosmetics and dieting (see also Seaman, this volume) since these are cues of health and fertility for men. When men are looking for long-term mates, they prefer women who exhibit signs of fidelity. For those girls and women who want to attract a long-term mate who will invest in a relationship and future children, a reputation for fidelity is vital and worth fighting to protect (Campbell, 2002, 2004; Cashdan, 1998). From an evolutionary perspective, female-female aggression is one type of female competition over males, resources, and status, all of which are vital for long-term female survival and reproduction (Burbank, 1987; Glazer, 1992; Hawley, 1999, 2008; Hrdy, 1981/1999, 1999; Paul & Baenninger, 1991).

## Women and Status-Seeking

In addition to using various types of aggression to secure the benefits of long-term mates and resources, women will use it to gain status. In studies on dominance structures, "status" is a term used that is related to "rank." Psychologists recognize that striving for status in one's social group is vitally important for individuals, having consequences for an individual's self-esteem, personal well-being, and social experiences (Anderson, John, Keltner, & Krieg, 2001; Barkow, 1975). Here "status" refers to the standing an individual has within face-to-face groups, not just high levels of socioeconomic success. Higher status results in prominence (being visible and known), respect (peers holding an individual in high regard), and influence over the group (controlling decisions within the group) (Anderson et al., 2001). Another term used in dominance research, especially among children, is "popular." In studies of American school-aged children, higher ranked children are considered "popular" by their peers, who consider them to be more visible and well known (Adler & Adler, 1998; Eder, 1995).

Before examining the link between aggression and status, it is necessary to address those who argue that women are not interested in status. One evolutionist who argues that women do not compete for status is Anne Campbell (2002, 2004, 2006). She maintains that women compete for resources, but not status, by using indirect aggression to avoid injuries. Drawing on evolutionary psychology and parental investment theory (Trivers, 1972), she states that women have an evolved psychological response to avoid physical aggression in order to maintain their survival and their offspring's since they invest more than males in gestation, lactation, and care. Those females in human evolutionary history who avoided physical aggression and resulting injury were able to increase their inclusive fitness. Therefore, Campbell argues that women then have little to gain, if not more to lose, by engaging in risky, physical aggression for status. In fact, she maintains that the achievement of dominance for females is not worth fighting for (see also Pinker, 2002). She states that the competition for access to resources is low risk and indirect in form. Therefore, women have a fear of physical injury because of the possibly huge reproductive costs, which she states is the factor that diminishes physical aggressive behavior among women and their striving for status.

There are several problems with Campbell's argument. First, she too believes that males have greater variations in their reproductive success, which has led to intense male-male competition for copulations. Yet, according to Hrdy (1999), there is variation in female reproductive success, but it is not measured in terms of copulations as it is for males. There are selection pressures on females, especially when they are mothers. Among primates, if a mother does not secure the resources, space, and dominance rank to enhance her own survival, the survival of her offspring could be compromised in the future. These "maternal effects" are passed on to future generations, but not as genes. As Hrdy states, "a female's quest for status—her ambition, if you will—has become inseparable from her ability to keep her offspring and grand-offspring alive. Far from conflicting with maternity, such a female's 'ambitious' tendencies are part and parcel of maternal success" (1999, p. 52). In addition, Benenson (2009) points out that females are engaged in breeding competition for food, territory, helpers, protection, and status. Women rely heavily on men for protection and provisioning their children, and therefore compete to maintain their men's loyalty and to fend off competitors. While it is true that some human females may avoid direct physical aggression out of fear of harm, there is significant evidence that human females will use verbal, indirect, and relational aggression to achieve and to maintain their status.

Second, Campbell's argument that women are indifferent to status is based on males' experiences of competing for status. When one disconnects status from the socioeconomic measures, it helps us to see that girls and women seek status too (Benenson, 1999). In Anderson et al.'s (2001) study, college women did consider status important (the authors defined status as having an asymmetrical amount of attention, respect, and esteem as well as having more influence and control within a group), and those with high status were highly extroverted. In a study by Jokela and Keltikangas-Jarvinen (2009), they found that the personality characteristic of leadership, which is associated with status-striving and social dominance, did lead to reproductive success for women in terms of having more children after 30 years of age compared to those with low leadership.

Finally, Campbell does not root her analysis in feminist evolutionists' primate studies. Not only do these studies show that females will use physical aggression (Hrdy, 1981/1999; Pusey et al., 2008) but also there are additional studies that demonstrate that females will use other tactics in pursuit of dominance rank that will bring them reproductive benefits. Just because female dominance structures are harder to observe and the criteria for female reproductive success is more stringent does not therefore mean that dominance and status are unimportant for girls and women. Overall, Campbell's (2002, 2004, 2006) reliance on parental investment theory leads her and many other scholars to assume that women do not care about their own status in association with their own reproductive success.

Based on feminist evolutionists' work, there has been fascinating research on the dominance structures and status among girls, which has contributed to our understanding how and why women seek status. For example, Hawley (1999) examined the adaptiveness of social dominance, which she defines as "the differential ability to control resources" (p. 97). Hawley's (2007a) "resource control theory" focuses on the function of behavior as individuals attempt to control scarce material, social, and informational resources. The material resources humans want to control are those things related to growth, survival, and cognitive and behavioral development. While children are not directly competing for food and water, they are competing for cognitive stimulation from toys, interaction with others, and new exciting situations (Hawley, 1999). The social resources individuals compete for include alliances, mates, and models for social learning (friends whom they like, admire, and respect). Younger children want friends with whom to play and want to be around those they like and admire, and teens' lives are centered around their friends and pursuing dating opportunities. Finally, the informational resources humans compete for include those things that help us ascertain both material and social resources. As Taylor et al. (2000) discuss in their work, female groups are vital sources of information and an important means of dealing with stress. Children want to know what is going on with their peers, and are acutely aware of what is acceptable or "cool" in terms of material goods, behaviors, and friends.

It is also evident that women in non-Western cultures are concerned about their own status, and will use various aggressive tactics to ensure that they are respected, prominent within their groups, and influential in order to enhance their future reproductive success. Burbank (1987) examined 137 cultures using Human Relations Area Files survey data, and among the various reasons that women use aggression was status. She states that in 13% of the societies she examined women reported behaving aggressively because of sorcery, gossip, or some other injury directed against them. In 20% of societies, women behaved aggressively when others treated them in a negative manner. Finally, women used aggression as a means of coercion and domination (Burbank 1987).

In another study of Zambian women, Schuster (1983) states that women used various means of aggression to protect their status as wives or girlfriends of the males they desired. She also reported that women competed for socially desirable men by using aggression to protect their reputations as good wives and mothers. For example, political elite women identified themselves as mothers who are concerned with the general welfare, and criticized female subelites for creating moral chaos in their society. As Schuster describes the situation,

> Sub-elites are the out-group in these interstrata relations. Unlike elites...their concerns are personal. Unlike the urban poor...they consider themselves liberated from many patterns of behavior that define traditional women's roles....They look and act differently from other strata and are therefore highly visible in society...[and] men could not resist them. (1983, p. 327)

Besides aggression there are different strategies for securing these resources that children and adults use that develop over the course of an individual's life history. Some individuals use prosocial strategies (cooperation, assistance, persuasion). They are socially competent individuals with good social skills, who are agreeable and conscientious, and who are well liked by their peers (Hawley, 2003). Cillessen and Rose (2005) define these individuals as "sociometrically popular"; they are usually cooperative and prosocial, and rarely use aggressive behavior. In contrast, there are some individuals who rely primarily on coercive strategies (aggression, threats, and insults). They are not well liked and not considered popular by their peers, who usually try to avoid them (Hawley, 2003).

Finally, there are individuals that use both prosocial and coercive strategies, and Hawley (1999, 2003, 2007a, 2007b) calls these individuals "bi-strategic controllers," who use aggression to maintain popularity in the eyes of outsiders and manage competitors within their groups. This research definitely shows the link between aggression and status for girls. There are several studies analyzing Western school-aged girls who are bi-strategic controllers who use both overt and relational aggression strategically to achieve or to maintain their perceived popularity (Benenson et al., 2006; Cillessen & Mayeux, 2004; Cillessen & Rose, 2005; Salmivalli, Kaukiainen, & Lagerspetz, 2000). As Hawley, Little, and Card (2008) found, these girls had many friends, attracted social attention, and had peers who wanted to be like them. In the popular literature, Wiseman (2009) offers a description of Hawley's bi-strategic controller as the center of many girls' cliques. This "queen bee"..."feels power and control over her environment. She's the center of attention, and people pay homage to her" (Wiseman, 2009, p. 89).

In addition to creating and maintaining a social network, another benefit of using aggression is that it can be used against competitors. If one member of the group acts too confidently or as if she were better than the other members, she risks criticism if not rejection by her group (Campbell, 2002). This type of aggression has a leveling effect, ensuring that the group maintains stability and that its members do not become competitors with the leader. Girls and women may use relational aggression more often against their friends with whom they have shared personal information (Benenson et al., 2006). Social exclusion works well for girls and women as they compete for the resources they need for reproductive success (Benenson, 2009).

According to Schuster and Hartz-Karp (1986), women certainly use indirect aggression to maintain the status quo within in their social groups. In their study of an Israeli kibbutz, they found that among women there were significant levels of "verbal violence"—bickering, quarreling, gossiping, criticism, and ostracism. Most women in this community were relegated to service work in kitchens, laundries, or childcare while having primary responsibility for their own housework and caring for their own children. If any woman tried to go beyond the prescribed sex roles, such as taking a professional job, they were considered to be uncooperative and irresponsible, gossiped about, and even ostracized. This behavior reinforced both the overall social structure and reinforced subordination. According to Schuster and Hartz-Karp, "the expression of aggression is socially legitimated. Even its strongest expression, aggression is intended to 'help' victims by assisting conformity" (1986, p. 198).

While individuals who are socially competent gain social benefits from aggression, they also can impose costs to their rivals (Hawley, 2003, 2007a). As with other female primates, higher status can reduce the amount of harassment one receives, and puts one in the better position of being the harasser. In turn, those who are victimized can indeed bear substantial costs. Children and adolescents who are victimized find themselves marginalized from their peer groups (Martin, 2009; Nansel, Craig, Overpeck, Gitanjali, & Ruan, 2004), and this isolation can have a profound impact on a girl's health, social learning, and academic performance. The popular literature (Simmons, 2002; Wiseman, 2002) provides numerous accounts of how girls can suffer at the hands of other girls as these victims are shunned, struggle at school, and in some cases deal with depression and eating disorders (see also Mealey, 1999).

Building on primate studies and evolutionary perspectives, it is clear that women use a variety of aggressive tactics to gain status, and these tactics can be considered types of reproductive strategies that lead to the resources necessary for reproductive success. As Hawley et al. (2008) argue, biologists and psychologists have been underestimating the overt competitiveness among adolescent females. Just because girls and women opt for verbal and indirect types of aggression does not mean that the stakes are not as important as mating opportunities are for men. In certain situations, they will diminish or denigrate any possible female competitors for the resources that are vital to the long-term survival and reproductive success of their offspring (Hrdy, 1999). For many women, their reproductive success depends on their reputation and status as good long-term mates and on their ability to attract males who will invest resources over a long period of time. Like nonhuman primate females, girls and women form their own groups and cliques as part of the competition for men, resources, and status that contribute to their long-term reproductive success.

## The Tangled Web of Social Dominance and Women

The research by feminist evolutionists has contributed greatly to our understanding of female aggression, dominance, and status-seeking. Not only did these pioneering researchers (Fedigan 1982, 1983; Hrdy, 1981/1999; Smuts, 1987a,b) take the time to watch and study nonhuman primate female behavior, they also formed new hypotheses informed by feminist perspectives that challenged and eventually replaced sexist assumptions about passive female reproductive behavior. Therefore, this research leads to new insights into female social structures and how status-seeking impacts them. When researchers look at our closest genetic relatives, they find that they have a female dominance structure, but it is not as obvious or linear as males' (Pusey et al., 1997). With the high-ranked female at the center of the group's territory and the focus of other members' attention, it could be argued that female dominance structures are organized like a matrix or web. In fact, the dominant females in chimpanzee social groups have control and priority access to the resource-rich space at the center and away from the edge of the territory. This not only gives the dominant female and her offspring access to the best food and water, they expend less energy acquiring these resources and are safer from outside predators (Murray et al., 2007). As described above, female nonhuman primates do not hesitate to use aggressive tactics to gain and preserve their dominance and the long-term benefits that comes with it for themselves and their offspring.

Based on the research on female aggression and status-seeking, it is now a good time to reexamine female dominance structures. Historically, male hierarchies have been more readily observed. However, Martin (2009) states that pure linear hierarchies are exceptions and not the rule among animals, and reminds us that earlier studies examined these hierarchies in small captive populations that could not disperse (see Figure 2.1). In addition, much of the literature on social dominance has focused on male behavior and has assumed that based on parental investment theory females do not pursue status (Campbell, 2002, 2004, 2006).

It can be argued that girls and women—like many of their nonhuman primate relatives—tend to organize themselves in webs of peer groups in which there are high status individuals in the center and lower status members in the periphery. Fisher (1999) describes female groups as "networks of vital human connections"

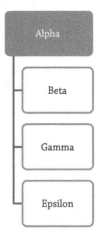

*Figure 2.1* Linear male dominance hierarchy. Adapted from Martin (2009).

based on cooperation, harmony, and connections that are lateral rather than hierarchical, and egalitarian rather than competitive (pp. 29–30). However, Hawley (1999, 2007) states that there is competition and even aggression between and within girls' groups. As Burbank (1987) and Schuster (1983) suggested, women can use aggression against women who threaten their reputations and attempt to diminish their social status. Like primates, dominant individuals have central and very visible roles within their groups and are well known by those outside their cliques. In Anderson et al.'s (2001) study of college women, they found that extraverted women, those who were sociable, assertive, and charismatic, had higher status in terms of respect, esteem, and influence in their groups.

In addition, the research and popular literature consistently states that those females who are perceived as popular are the center of attention of their groups. Wiseman's (2009) *Queen Bees and Wannabes* suggests that adolescent girls have different roles in their groups. The girl in the center she labels the "Queen Bee": "through a combination of charisma, force, money, looks, will, and social intelligence, this girl reigns supreme over the other girls and weakens their friendships with others, thereby strengthening her own power and influence" (Wiseman 2009, p. 87). The next influential person in the girl group Wiseman (2009) calls the sidekick, who is the closest ally to the Queen Bee. Another powerful person in the clique is the "banker," who controls and distributes information about the group's members. A more benign trafficker of information is the "messenger," who uses information in attempts at peace-making within the group. There are also pleasers/wannabes who want desperately to be in the group and be close to the Queen Bee. Those girls who do not challenge the Queen Bee are called "torn bystanders." Another role player in these cliques is the floater or champion, who is not controlled by others and has friends in different groups. Finally, there are the "targets" that are excluded from the groups and are humiliated and ridiculed. Sometimes they are within a clique, and sometimes they are on the periphery hoping to be accepted (Wiseman, 2009; see Figure 2.2).

As difficult as it is to navigate these female groups, even those who are followers of the "queen bee" or "bi-strategic controller" have many social benefits from this network—the support of friends, protection from harassment by outsiders, and status as a group member. As Hawley maintains, "social dominance attracts social attention and is gained by individuals who possess highly attractive social skills and less pleasant aggressive attributes" (2007b, p. 170). At the same time, those on the peripheries of these social groups can be targeted for various types of aggression, which can have profound psychological and physical effects for victims. Future investigation is needed to determine if these excluded individuals have comparative difficulty in acquiring the material, social, and informational resources needed for their development, health, and future reproductive success.

At this point, much of the research on social dominance examines the social lives and strategies of children and adolescents. They are easier to study since they are "captive" populations in schools (Martin, 2009). Nonetheless, researchers are now starting to look at adult populations. For example, Hawley, Shorey, and Alderman (2009) examined the relationship between attachment orientations and social dominance among college students. Until recently, much of the literature on female aggression, status-seeking, and social dominance presents anecdotal accounts of women's experiences. Hopefully scholars will attempt to do more quantitative work examining this behavior in the future.

In conclusion, when politics is defined as the management of conflicts of interests, it is easy to see how women are engaged in political struggles every day, starting at a very young age. As feminists have adeptly observed, the

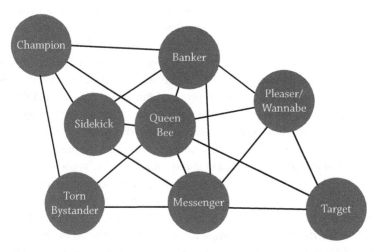

*Figure 2.2* Proposed female dominance structure. Based on Wiseman (2009).

personal is very political, especially in the pursuit of long-term resource security for themselves and their children. Yet, the competition women engage in is not just against men, but with other women who are also pursuing mates, resources, and status. Girls and women will use various aggressive tactics (verbal, indirect, relational, and at times physical) against each other for men, resources, and status that benefit them and their children. We see this recounted in the popular literature about aggression and girls and even among the modern mothers of 21st-century America as they aggressively strive for the best resources for their children in terms of home, schools, social opportunities, extracurricular activities, and material goods. In traditional societies outside the West, if mothers do not have access to enough resources, it can have significant physical, developmental, and social impacts on their children. Therefore, women must be aggressive *because* the stakes are significant for their long-term reproductive success. Feminist evolutionists' insights, rooted in primate studies, has helped us see the aggressive and status-seeking behaviors of girls and women, and "untangle" the volatility, instability, and complexity of their web-like dominance structures that many have not seen.

# References

Adler, P. A., & Adler, P. (1998). *Peer power: Preadolescent culture and identity*. New Brunswick, NJ: Rutgers University Press.

Anderson, C., John, O., Keltner, D., & Krieg, A. (2001). Who attains social status? Effects of personality and physical attractiveness in social groups. *Journal of Personality and Social Psychology, 81*(1), 116–132.

Archer, J. (2000). Sex differences in aggression between heterosexual partners: A meta-analytical review. *Psychological Bulletin, 126*(5), 651–680.

Archer, J. (2009). The nature of human aggression. *International Journal of Law and Psychiatry, 32*, 202–208.

Barash, D. (1982). *Sociobiology and behavior* (2nd ed.). New York: Elsevier Science.

Barkow, J. (1975). Prestige and culture: A biosocial interpretation. *Current Anthropology, 16*, 553–752.

Benenson, J. (1999). Females' desire for status cannot be measured using male definitions. *Behavioral and Brain Sciences, 22*, 216–217.

Benenson, J. (2009). Dominating versus eliminating the competition: Sex differences in human intrasexual aggression. *Behavioral and Brain Sciences, 32*(3), 268–269.

Benenson, J., Hodgson, L., Heath, S., & Welch, P. (2008). Human sexual differences in the use of social ostracism as a competitive tactic. *International Journal of Primatology, 29*, 1019–1035.

Benenson, J., Sinclair, N., & Dolenszky, E. (2006). Children's and adolescents' expectation of aggressive responses to provocation: Females predict more hostile reactions in compatible dyadic relationships. *Social Development, 15*(11), 65–81.

Bernstein, I., & Gordon T. (1980). The social component of dominance relationships in rhesus monkeys (macaca mulatte). *Animal Behavior, 28*(4), 1033–1039.

Bjorkqvist, K., & Niemela, P. (1992). New trends in the study of female aggression. In K. Bjorkqvist & P. Niemela (Eds.), *Of mice and women: Aspects of female aggression* (pp. 3–16). San Diego, CA: Academic Press.

Bjorkqvist, K., Osterman, K., & Kaukiainen, A. (1992). The development of direct and indirect aggression in males and females. In K. Bjorkqvist & P. Niemela (Eds.), *Of mice and women: Aspects of female aggression* (pp. 51–66). San Diego, CA: Academic Press.

Burbank, V. (1987). Female aggression in cross-cultural perspective. *Behavioral Science Research, 21*, 71–100.

Campbell, A. (1986). Self-reporting of fighting by females. *British Journal of Criminology, 26*, 28–46.

Campbell, A. (1999). Staying alive: Evolution, culture, and women's intrasexual aggression. *Behavioral and Brain Sciences, 22*, 203–252.

Campbell, A. (2002). *A mind of her own: The evolutionary psychology of women.* Oxford, UK: Oxford University Press.

Campbell, A. (2004). Female competition: Causes, constraints, content, and contexts. *Journal of Sex Research, 41*(1), 16–26.

Campbell, A. (2006). Sex differences and indirect aggression: What are the psychological mediators? *Aggression and Violent Behavior, 11*, 237–264.

Cashdan, E. (1998). Women's mating strategies. *Evolutionary Anthropology, 5*(4), 134–143.

Chapais, B. (1992). The role of alliances in social inheritance of rank among female primates. In A. H. Harcourt & F. B. de Waal (Eds.), *Coalitions and alliances in humans and other animals* (pp. 29–60). Oxford, UK: Oxford University Press.

Chesler, P. (2001). *Woman's inhumanity to woman.* New York: Thunder's Month Press/Nation Books.

Cillessen, A. H. N., & Mayeux, L. (2004). From censure to reinforcement: Developmental change in the association between aggression and social status. *Child Development, 75*(1), 147–163.

Cillessen, A. H. N., & Rose, A. J. (2005). Understanding popularity in the peer system. *Current Directions in Psychological Science, 14*(2), 102–105.

Cords, M., Sheehan, M., & Ekernas, L. (2010). Sex and age differences in juvenile social priorities in female philopatric nondespotic blue monkeys. *American Journal of Primatology, 72*, 193–205.

Crick, N. R., & Grotpeter, J. K. (1995). Relational aggression, gender, and social-psychological adjustment. *Child Development, 66*, 710–722.

Datta, S. B. (1992). Effects of availability of allies on female dominance structures. In A. H. Harcourt & F. B. de Waal (Eds.), *Coalitions and alliances in humans and other animals* (pp. 61–82). Oxford, UK: Oxford University Press.

De Waal, F. B., & Harcourt, A. H. (1992). Coalitions and alliances: A history of ethological research. In A. H. Harcourt & F. B. de Waal (Eds.), *Coalitions and alliances in humans and other animals* (pp. 1–22). Oxford, UK: Oxford University Press.

Eder, D., Evans, C., & Parker, S. (1995). *School talk: Gender and adolescent culture.* New Brunswick, NJ: Rutgers University Press.

Fedigan, L. (1982). *Primate paradigms: Sex roles and social bonds.* Montreal, Canada: Eden Press.

Fedigan, L. (1983). Dominance and reproductive success in primates. *Yearbook of Physical Anthropology, 26*, 91–129.

Fisher, H. (1999). *The first sex: The natural talents of women and how they are changing the world.* New York: Ballatine Books.

Garbarino, J. (2006). *See Jane hit: Why girls are growing more violent and what can be done about it.* New York: Penguin Press.

Glazer, I. M. (1992). Interfemale aggression and resource scarcity in a cross-cultural perspective. In K. Bjorkqvist & P. Niemela (Eds.), *Of mice and women: Aspects of female aggression* (pp. 163–172). New York: Academic Press.

Hawley, P. (1999). The ontogenesis of social dominance: A strategy-based evolutionary perspective. *Developmental Review, 19*, 97–132.

Hawley, P. (2003). Prosocial and coercive configuration of resource control in early adolescence: A case for the well-adapted Machiavellian. *Merrill-Palmer Quarterly, 49*(3), 279–309.

Hawley, P. (2007a). Social dominance in childhood and adolescence: Why social competence and aggression may go hand in hand. In P. H. Hawley, T. D. Little, & P. C. Rodkin (Eds.), *Aggression and adaptation: The bright side to bad behavior* (pp. 1–30). Mahwah, NJ: Erlbaum.

Hawley, P. (2007b). The allure of a mean friend: Relationship quality and processes of aggressive adolescents with prosocial skills. *International Journal of Behavioral Development, 31*(2), 170–180.

Hawley, P., Little, T. D., & Card, N. (2008). The myth of the alpha male: A new look at dominance-related beliefs and behaviors among adolescent males and females. *International Journal of Behavioral Development, 32*(1), 76–88.

Hawley, P., Shorey, H., & Alderman, P. (2009). Attachment correlates of resource control strategies: Possible origins of social dominance and interpersonal power differentials. *Journal of Social and Personal Relationships, 26*(8), 1097–1118.

Hrdy, S. B. (1977). *Langurs of abu: Female and male strategies of reproduction.* Cambridge, MA: Harvard University Press.

Hrdy, S. B. (1999). *Mother nature: A history of mothers, infants, and natural selection.* New York: Pantheon Books.

Hrdy, S. B. (1981/1999). *The woman that never evolved.* Cambridge, MA: Harvard University Press.

Jokela, M., & Keltikanga-Jarvinen, L. (2009). Adolescent leadership and adulthood fertility: Revisiting the "central theoretical problem of human sociobiology." *Journal of Personality, 77*(1), 213–229.

Lancaster, J. (1985). Evolutionary perspectives on sex differences in higher primates. In A. S. Rossi (Ed.), *Gender and the life course* (pp. 3–28). New York: Aldine Press.

Lancaster, J. (1991). A feminist and evolutionary biology looks at women. *Yearbook of Physical Anthropology, 34,* 1–11.

Lee, P. C., & Johnson, J. A. (1992). Sex difference in alliances and the acquisition and maintenance of dominance status among immature primates. In A. H. Harcourt & F. B. de Waal (Eds.), *Coalitions and alliances in humans and other animals* (pp. 391–414). Oxford, UK: Oxford University Press.

Little, T. D., Jones, S., Henrich, C., & Hawley, P. (2003). Disentangling the "whys" from the "whats" of aggressive behavior. *International Journal of Behavioral Development, 27*(2), 122–133.

Low, B. (2000). *Why sex matters: A Darwinian looks at human behavior.* Princeton, NJ: Princeton University Press.

Martin, J. L. (2009). Formation and stabilization of vertical hierarchies among adolescents: Towards a quantitative ethology of dominance among humans. *Social Psychology Quarterly, 72*(3), 241–264.

Masetripieri, D. (2007). *Macachiavellian intelligence: How rhesus macaques and humans have conquered the world.* Chicago: University of Chicago Press.

Mealey, L. (1999). Evolutionary models of female intrasexual competition. *Behavioral and Brain Sciences, 22,* 234.

Murray, C., Mane, S. V., & Pusey, A. (2007). Dominance rank influences female space use in wild chimpanzees, *pan troglodytes*: Towards an ideal despotic distribution. *Animal Behavior, 74,* 1795–1804.

Nansel, T. R., Craig, W., Overpeck, M. D., Gitanjali, S., & Ruan, J. (2004). Cross-national consistency in the relationship between bullying behaviors and psychosocial adjustment. *Archives of Pediatric and Adolescent Medicine, 158,* 730–736.

Onyango, P., Gesquiere, L., Wango, S., Alberts, S., & Altmann, J. (2008). Persistence of maternal effects in baboons: Mother's dominance rank at son's conception predicts stress hormone levels in subadult males. *Hormones and Behavior, 54,* 319–324.

Paul, L., & Baenninger, M. A. (1991). Aggression by women: Mores, myths, and methods. In R. Baenninger (Ed.), *Targets of violence and aggression* (pp. 401–442). Amsterdam: Elsevier Science.

Pinker, S. (2002). *The blank slate: The modern denial of human nature.* New York: Viking.

Pusey, A., Williams, J., & Goodall, J. (1997). The influence of dominance rank on the reproductive success of female chimpanzees. *Science, 277,* 828–831.

Pusey, A., Murray, C., Wallauer, W., Wilson, M., Wrobelewski, E., & Goodall, J. (2008, July 29). Severe aggression among female *pan troglodytes schweinfurthii* at Gombe National Park, Tanzania. *International Journal of Primatology, 29.* Published online.

Robbins, M., Robbins, A., Stekles, N., & Stekles, H. (2007). Socioecological influences on the reproductive success of female mountain gorillas (gorilla beringei beringei). *Behavioral Ecology and Sociobiology, 61*, 919–931.

Salmivalli, C., Kaukiainen, A., & Lagerspetz, K. (2000). Aggression and sociometric peers: Do gender and type of aggression matter? *Scandinavian Journal of Psychology, 41*, 17–24.

Schuster, I. M. (1983). Women's aggression: An African case study. *Aggressive Behavior, 9*, 319–331.

Schuster, I., & Hartz-Karp, J. (1986). Kinder, kueche, kibbutz: Women's aggression and status quo maintenance in a small scale community. *Anthropology Quarterly, 59*, 191–199.

Silk, J. (1987). Social behavior in evolutionary perspective. In B. Smuts, D. Cheney, R. Seyfarth, R. Wrangham, & T. Strusaker (Eds.), *Primate societies* (pp. 318–329). Chicago: University of Chicago Press.

Silk, J., Altmann, J., & Albers, S. (2006). Social relationships among adult female baboons (papio cynocephalus) I. Variation in the strength of social bonds. *Behavioral Ecology and Sociobiology, 61*, 183–195.

Silk, J., Beehner, J., Bergman, T., Crockford, C., Engh, A., Moscovice, L., ... Cheney, D. (2009). The benefits of social capital: Close social bonds among female baboons enhance offspring survival. *Proceedings of the Royal Society of Biology, 276*, 3099–3104.

Simmons, R. (2002). *Odd girl out: The hidden culture of aggression in girls*. New York: Harcourt.

Smuts, B. (1985). *Sex and friendship in baboons*. New York: Aldine.

Smuts, B. (1987a). Gender, aggression, and influence. In B. Smuts, D. Cheney, R. Seyfarth, R. Wrangham, & T. Strusaker (Eds.), *Primate societies* (pp. 400–412). Chicago: University of Chicago Press.

Smuts, B. (1987b). Sexual competition and mate choice. In B. Smuts, D. Cheney, R. Seyfarth, R. Wrangham, & T. Strusaker (Eds.), *Primate societies* (pp. 385–399). Chicago: University of Chicago Press.

Smuts, B. (1992). Male aggression against women: An evolutionary perspective. *Human Nature, 3*, 1–44.

Strier, K. (2011). *Primate behavioral ecology* (4th ed.). Boston: Prentice Hall.

Tanenbaum, L. (2002). *Catfight: Women and competition*. New York: Seven Stories Press.

Taylor, Shelley E., Klein, L.C., Lewis, B.P., Gurung, R.A.R., & Updegraff, J.A. (2000). Biobehavioral responses to stress in females: Tend-and-befriend, not fight-or-flight. *Psychological Review, 107*(3), 411–429.

Thompson, M., Stumpf, R., & Pusey, A. (2008). Female reproductive strategies and competition in apes: An introduction. *International Journal of Primatology, 29*, 815–821.

Trivers, R. (1972). Parental investment and sexual selection. In B. Campbell (Ed.), *Sexual selection and the descent of man* (pp. 136–207). Chicago: Aldine.

Underwood, M. K. (2003). *Social aggression among girls*. New York: Guilford Press.

Walters, J. R., & Seyfarth, R. M. (1987). Conflict and cooperation. In B. Smuts, D. Cheney, R. Seyfarth, R. Wrangham, & T. Strusaker (Eds.), *Primate societies* (pp. 306–317). Chicago: University of Chicago Press.

Wilson, E. O. (1978). *On human nature*. New York: Bantam Books.

Wiseman, R. (2002). *Queen bees and wannabees: Helping your daughter survive cliques, gossip, boyfriends, and other realities of adolescence* (1st ed.). New York: Crown.

Wiseman, R. (2009). *Queen bees and wannabees: Helping your daughter survive cliques, gossip, boyfriends, and the new realities of girl world* (2nd ed.). New York: Crown.

# 3

# Getting by With a Little Help From Friends

## The Importance of Social Bonds for Female Primates

LIZA R. MOSCOVICE

## Introduction

Among the distinguishing features of humans are their high levels of sociality. Humans maintain stable, affiliative relationships with a larger and more diverse range of social partners than typical of other species, including relatives and also unrelated individuals (Dunbar, 2009). In addition, humans show concern for the welfare of complete strangers, facilitating forms of large-scale cooperation that are fundamental to modern societies (Fehr & Fischbacher, 2003). The outcomes of such high levels of sociality are striking. From the unconditional physical aid and emotional support that occurs within the context of close friendships, to out-pourings of humanitarian aid in response to global crises, humans exhibit more altruism, or providing of costly aid to others, than any other species.

Adaptations related to maintaining affiliative social relationships with a broad range of partners undoubtedly played a critical role during human evolution, by facilitating increased social cohesion and forms of cooperation as social group size expanded (van Schaik & Kappeler, 2006). In modern societies as well, social relationships continue to have major impacts on human fitness. In longitudinal, cross-cultural studies, people who maintain stronger social relationships, often measured in terms of perceived social support, have greater longevity (Moen, Dempstermcclain, & Williams, 1989) and reduced risks for a range of physical and mental health problems (Seeman, 1996), compared with people who are more socially isolated. The association between strong social relationships and health outcomes remains after controlling for other potential confounds, such as age, socioeconomic status and preexisting health conditions (House, Landis, &

Umberson, 1988). Similarly, greater levels of interpersonal conflict in relationships are associated with decreased emotional well-being, increased risks of depression and greater susceptibility to infectious disease (Abbey, Abramis, & Caplan, 1985; Cohen, Gottlieb, & Underwood, 2000). A recent meta-analysis reviewing results of 148 studies concluded that people with stronger social relationships have a 50% reduced chance of mortality compared to people with weaker social relationships (Holt-Lunstad, Smith, & Layton, 2010).

While it is clear that social relationships have major fitness implications for humans, little is currently known about the cognitive and emotional adaptations that allow humans to form and maintain flexible social relationships and about *how* social relationships impact health outcomes. Among the models that have been proposed to explain how social relationships impact health, the main effects model emphasizes ways that social relationships directly influence cognitive, emotional, and behavioral processes that support health, for example by reinforcing self-esteem, providing a sense of self-worth and encouraging healthy behaviors (Cohen et al., 2000). The social buffering model emphasizes the ways that social relationships may improve health outcomes by providing physical resources and emotional support to cope with stressful situations (DeVries, Glasper, & Detillion, 2003). Humans and all other mammals respond to a perceived physical or psychological stressor with activation of the hypothalamic-pituitary-adrenal (HPA) axis, resulting in the release of the steroid hormone cortisol from the adrenal gland (reviewed in Sapolsky, 2002). This so-called stress hormone is typically released within minutes following the onset of a stressor, and in the short-term facilitates a range of adaptive physiological responses, including mobilization of energy and suppression of costly anabolic processes such as digestion and reproduction. However, long-term or chronic cortisol release can have detrimental effects on health and fitness, including hypertension, immune and/or reproductive suppression, and even death (Sapolsky, 2002). Circulating levels of cortisol can be measured in blood, saliva, or feces, providing a sensitive index of an individual's stress levels. Support for the social buffering model comes from a range of experimental studies in which humans exposed to minor stressors such as public speaking while in the presence of a supportive social partner exhibited significant reductions in cortisol release, blood pressure, and heart rate, compared to subjects who underwent the same stressor but without any social support (reviewed in Thorsteinsson & James, 1999). It is likely that social relationships work through both main effects and stress buffering pathways to reinforce positive behaviors and self-image and reduce stress responses to negative events.

## Social Relationships and Gender

There is a substantial literature indicating gender differences in patterns of social relationships in humans (Taylor, Klein, Lewis, Gruenewald, Gurung, & Updegraff, 2000; Umberson, Chen, House, Hopkins, & Slaten, 1996). Several studies report that relative to men, women maintain a larger and more diverse range of social bonds, are more active in providing and receiving support from their social networks, and report more benefits from contact with same-sex friends (Shye, Mullooly, Freeborn, & Pope, 1995; Smith & Christakis, 2008). These gender differences are observed across the life cycle. Among adolescent children and college students, females report consistent differences in the size of their social networks and in their extent of reliance on social partners relative to their male counterparts (reviewed in Taylor et al., 2000).

There is also evidence for gender differences in which aspects of social relationships have the greatest impact on health outcomes. For females, the size of their social groups is closely linked to health outcomes (Kendler, Myers, & Prescott, 2005; Shye et al., 1995), while for males the presence of specific social partners, such as spouses, appears to have a greater impact on health (Shye et al., 1995). Women also exhibit a two-fold stronger relationship between assessments of social support and self-perceived health compared with men (Denton & Walters, 1999). Females exhibit a stronger desire than males to affiliate in response to stress (Belle, 1987), and while social support from opposite-sex partners can be effective in reducing physiological and behavioral signs of stress in males (Kirschbaum, Klauer, Filipp, & Hellhammer, 1995), support from same-sex partners appears to be more effective in reducing stress in females (reviewed in Taylor et al., 2000).

In reviewing this evidence, it is important to consider two related issues: How robust are these reported gender differences in social relationships, and to the extent that there are robust gender differences, what is their cause? The first issue can be addressed through the use of meta-analysis, a statistical tool that analyzes results from many studies to calculate the extent to which a specific variable of interest impacts patterns of results. In the context of gender studies, the effect size measures the extent of differences in the distribution of scores for specific behaviors between males and females. Hyde (2005) undertook an extensive meta-analysis of reported gender differences in cognition, communication, social variables, and psychological well-being. She found that the vast majority of reported gender differences, including several differences in social relationships, had small effect sizes, indicating that gender explained very little of the overall variability in the traits. However, there was one robust effect of gender on social behavior; in multiple studies assessing personality, females scored higher on measures of nurturance, empathetic behavior, and altruism compared with males ($d = -0.91$, reviewed in Hyde, 2005). It is also important to note that meta-analyses are not yet available for many of the gender differences reviewed here, especially related to the role of social relationships in stress buffering and mediating health outcomes.

The second issue is to explain the sources of any robust gender differences in patterns of social relationships. One dominant theory in the psychological literature is the social role theory, which interprets gender differences in social behavior as flexible, context-dependent outcomes of socialization (reviewed in Archer, 1996). From this perspective, historical inequalities in status and differences in social roles and division of labor between the sexes result in different opportunities for developing friendships. These differences are perpetuated through social learning and through direct impacts of inequalities on behavior.

A different perspective supported by evolutionary psychology suggests that gender differences in social relationships and other aspects of human behavior are the result of sex-specific strategies to optimize individual fitness during human evolutionary history. This framework was first proposed by Darwin (1871), who introduced sexual selection as a subset of natural selection focusing on individual strategies to maximize reproductive success. Through sexual selection theory, parental investment is viewed as a costly and limited resource, so whichever sex invests more toward the rearing of young will be competed over by the sex that contributes less. Among mammals, females typically contribute more toward the rearing of young than do males, in part due to obligate internal gestation and lactation. As a result, males are expected to compete among each other for access to mating opportunities with fertile females, in order to maximize their reproductive success. Females on the other hand are expected to be more discriminating about their mates, in order to select males who will contribute to offspring fitness, either directly by providing some paternal care, or indirectly by contributing good genes. As a result of this conflict of interest, the sexes are hypothesized to differ in a range of behaviors including courtship, mate choice, and intrasexual aggression. Sexual selection theory remains the primary framework for understanding sex differences in behavior among nonhuman species, although the theory continues to be modified and expanded by a growing body of research indicating that intrasexual competition and mate choice can operate in both sexes to varying degrees (Clutton-Brock, 2007).

Applying sexual selection theory to human behavior, gender differences in social behavior and patterns of affiliation may also represent the outcome of conflicting strategies related to optimizing reproductive success during human evolutionary history. For example, within the context of high levels of male-male competition for access to mates during human evolution, emotional vulnerability within friendships could be exploited by potential competitors (Archer, 1996), possibly resulting in smaller social networks and more limited reliance on social relationships for males. This framework may also account for the prominent role of opposite-sex partners in providing social buffering and health benefits for males, reviewed earlier in this section. Through sexual selection theory, male coercion and harassment of females is viewed as one potential strategy for increasing mating opportunities during human evolutionary history. From this perspective, females' high levels of empathy within same-sex relationships and greater reliance on same-sex social partners for social buffering from stress may reflect adaptive counterstrategies to gain protection and respite from male harassment (Taylor et al. 2000).

The relative extent to which perceived human gender differences in social relationships and other behaviors represent deep-rooted socialization or evolved biological differences remains an open question, and it is important to note that these two theories are not mutually exclusive. Where cross-cultural consistencies in gender stereotypes are found, this may reflect ways that cultural learning interacts with biological dispositions to reinforce and enhance gender differences in traits with different underlying fitness implications for males and females (Archer, 1996).

We are still at the initial stages of evaluating the extent of cross-cultural consistency in gendered patterns of social relationships and health impacts. This is because the majority of studies of social relationships and health have occurred within Westernized countries, and sampled populations share similarities in ethnic and cultural backgrounds, racial identities, sexual orientation, and socialized gender norms. Research in more diverse geographical and cultural environments, reflecting differences in the patterns and extent of gender roles, is critical to further characterize the relative influence of socialization on gender differences in social relationships. In addition, a comparative approach to examining patterns of social relationships in nonhuman species can help to evaluate a possible biological basis for gender differences in social relationships. A comparative approach is also important for elucidating the various mechanisms related to forming and maintaining social relationships, which remain largely unknown in humans.

## Social Relationships in Comparative Perspective

### Methods for Measuring Social Relationships Across Primates

Researchers characterize human social relationships in several ways. One common measurement is the extent of social integration, referring to the number and diversity of different social roles that individuals maintain, with close partners and within the broader community (Seeman, 1996; Brissette, Cohen, & Seeman, 2000). Another strategy is to assess an individual's perception of social support, which is also predictive of health outcomes (Lakey & Cohen, 2000). Social network theory provides a more quantitative approach to characterizing an individual's social world and relating social relationships to health outcomes (Smith & Christakis, 2008). In social network theory, the structure of an individual's social world is represented graphically as sociograms, with nodes representing individuals within a network and lines between nodes representing social connections. Several studies have examined how network size, referring to the number of nodes in an individual's social network, and network density, referring to the extent to which network members maintain ties with each other, impact health outcomes (House, Landis, & Umberson, 1988). More recent research has found that health measures of the social contacts within an individual's broad social network are predictive of an individual's own health outcomes, including the likelihood of obesity, smoking, and other risk factors for health problems (Christakis & Fowler, 2009).

Importantly, all of these approaches rely to some degree on subjective assessments of social relationships. For example, when measuring social integration or constructing social networks, researchers must determine which subset of a subject's social relationships to include in the analysis. These decisions are often based on the respondents' subjective assessments of the relative importance of their various social relationships. In contrast, ethologists studying the behavior of non-human species have no means of determining their subjects' perceptions of social relationships and social support and rather must rely entirely on quantitative assessments of social relationships. Social relationships among nonhuman primates are often defined at the dyadic level using some version of a dyadic association index (DAI; Boesch & Boesch-Achermann, 2000), which measures the proportion of time that two animals spend in close spatial proximity to each other. Typically this is index is calculated as:

$$\frac{(\text{Social time }_{A+B \text{ together}})}{(\text{Social time }_{A \text{ without } B} + \text{social time }_{B \text{ without } A} + \text{social time }_{A+B \text{ together}})}$$

A higher DAI value indicates higher levels of social tolerance and affinity. The strength of dyadic relationships is also characterized by the frequency of species-specific social interactions such as grooming, which is a common form of affiliation across primate species (Silk, 2002; see Figure 3.1). In addition, the quality of social relationships has been assessed by the extent of symmetry in exchange of affiliative behaviors between partners and the stability of relationships has been indexed by determining whether an individual's preferences for social partners remain constant over time (Silk, Alberts, & Altmann, 2006).

Ethologists are typically able to characterize the social relationships among all possible partners within a social group, something that is often prohibitively difficult to achieve in humans. Measures of association and affiliation among specific dyads can be divided by the average scores across all dyads, to determine whether two individuals associate more often than on average (Gilby & Wrangham, 2008). Or dyadic association levels can be divided by expected values based on the null hypothesis that social behaviors are randomly distributed among group members (Langergraber, Mitani, & Vigilant, 2007). Dyads with measures that exceed average or chance levels are then identified as preferential associates. The threshold criteria for identifying dyadic relationships that are significantly stronger than average or chance levels vary across studies, but often include DAIs at least half a standard deviation above the mean, or in the 90th percentile of all dyads (Hohmann & Fruth, 2002; Langergraber et al., 2007; Gilby & Wrangham, 2008). If these preferential associations are also relatively stable and enduring over time, they are described as social bonds (Parish, 1996). Recent studies have also begun to incorporate social network analysis into examinations of animal social behavior (e.g., Lehmann & Boesch, 2009), suggesting an important tool for moving beyond

*Figure 3.1* Female baboons grooming at the Moremi Game Reserve, Botswana. Photograph by Liza R. Moscovice. Reprinted with permission from Liza R. Moscovice.

dyadic analyses to quantify differences among individuals in their extent of social integration within larger groups.

## Patterns of Primate Social Bonding and Implications for Fitness

The majority of mammalian species live in permanent social groups, and sociality confers a range of benefits, including protection from predation, enhanced success in locating and defending resources, enhanced mating opportunities, and reduced vulnerability to infanticide (Silk, 2007). Not just the presence of group members, but also the nature of relationships with specific partners has fitness implications for individuals. This is especially true for primates, given their long life spans and high levels of social cognition (Cheney & Seyfarth, 1990). Within social groups, social interactions can range from agonistic to affiliative, and social behaviors can be indiscriminate, directed at any members of a group or selective, directed at specific individuals. Across a range of primate species, individuals maintain selective, affiliative social bonds with a subset of other group members who are often also close relatives. In the majority of Old World monkeys such as baboons (*Papio hamadryas* sp.), females are the philopatric sex, remaining in their natal groups for their entire lives, while males disperse into new groups at sexual maturity. Female baboons form long-term, differentiated social bonds primarily with close female relatives or age-matched female peers who have grown up together (Silk, Alberts, et al., 2006; Silk, Altmann, & Alberts, 2006). Close social partners exchange high levels of affiliative behaviors, such as grooming, and female relatives provide each other with greater levels of coalitionary support in conflicts with other group members than do unrelated females (Silk, Alberts, & Altmann, 2004; Wittig, Crockford, Seyfarth, & Cheney, 2007). In contrast, relationships among adult male baboons tend to be largely competitive, and for many males their most affiliative social relationships involve short-term associations with lactating females and their dependent young (Palombit et al., 2000).

Selective social bonds impact individual fitness in part by facilitating rank acquisition in species with dominance hierarchies. Baboon females inherit ranks immediately below their mothers. Alliances among relatives play an important role in establishing these ranks, and can be critical in reinforcing dominance status during rare cases of female hierarchy instability (Engh et al., 2006b). Higher rank in turn can provide fitness advantages, through priority of access to important resources, such as mating opportunities and preferred foraging sites. These fitness advantages can translate into differences in long-term reproductive success (Silk, 2007; Wroblewski et al., 2009).

In addition to the ways that social relationships impact fitness by influencing rank, selective social bonds also provide social buffering against stress for primates, similar to evidence in humans. In laboratory settings, primates exposed to novel, potentially stressful stimuli in the presence of a familiar and highly affiliative social partner, such as a close relative or a pair-bonded mate in monogamous species, have reduced stress responses than when exposed to the same stressor alone or with unfamiliar individuals (reviewed in Kikusui, Winslow, & Mori, 2006). In natural settings as well, there is evidence that social relationships can mediate stress responsivity. Among wild female chacma baboons (*P. h. ursinus*), females who maintained strong and stable social bonds with a subset of close female partners had lower average cortisol levels and exhibited smaller increases in cortisol in response to stressful situations, compared with females who had weaker and more diffuse social relationships (Crockford, Wittig, Whitten, Seyfarth, & Cheney, 2008). When a female's social bonds were disrupted by the loss of close female relatives to predation, the affected females exhibited increases in cortisol in the month following their relatives' death (Engh et al., 2006a). These females also actively recruited new social partners, and subsequently had reductions in cortisol to baseline levels.

Thus, there is ample evidence that selective social relationships provide a range of fitness benefits to nonhuman primates, suggesting that selection pressures for forming differentiated social bonds likely occurred among evolutionary ancestors of humans. Humans however gain enhanced fitness benefits as a result of their ability to maintain cooperative social bonds with nonrelatives and in situations where individuals have little prior history of social interactions. High levels of sociality and cooperation in humans are supported by cultural innovations, including the use of language to establish intentions, and the use of reputation to cooperate preferentially with those who behave more altruistically toward others (Fehr, Fischbacher, & Gachter, 2002). In addition, humans have neurocognitive adaptations that selectively reinforce the rewarding aspects of cooperation (Rilling et al., 2002). The extent to which nonhuman species may exhibit some of the same cognitive and emotional adaptations related to maintaining flexible social bonds outside of kinship remains an open question.

The patterns of social bonding found in baboons and many other primate species are largely consistent with socioecological models predicting high levels of sociality and affiliation among the philopatric sex, due to lifetime residency with individuals who are often close relatives (Kappeler, 2008). According to kin selection theory, by cooperating with relatives and competing with non-kin for rank and access to resources, individuals propagate a proportion of their genes shared in common with their relatives (Hamilton, 1964). However, some patterns of primate social bonding defy basic predictions from kin selection theory and suggest the potential for more flexible social bonding in nonhuman primates as well. For example Assamese macaques share with baboons a female philopatric social system, but a recent study suggests that unlike the largely agonistic relationships among male baboons, dispersing male macaques form strong and stable social bonds with a subset of other unrelated males, characterized by higher than average measures of association, grooming, and coalitionary support (Schulke, Bhagavatula, Vigilant, & Ostner, 2010). There is also increasing evidence that bonds with non-kin as well as with kin can have important fitness implications for primates. Among female baboons, variation in the strength, quality, and stability of social bonds with nonrelatives as well as with relatives has direct impacts on female longevity and reproductive success (Silk et al., 2009, 2010). Among unrelated Assamese macaque males, those with stronger social bonds attain higher dominance rank and have greater paternity success (Schulke et al., 2010).

Some of the most interesting exceptions to general predictions of kin selection theory occur among unrelated female great apes. In contrast with the majority of other primate species, great apes live in nonmatrilineal social systems, each characterized by some degree of female dispersal, typically into social groups without close female relatives present (Meder, 2007). As a result, female great apes experience more variable and diverse social environments than typical of most primate species. For dispersing female great apes, forming social bonds may be an important means of integrating into a new social group, but these bonds must be formed in the absence of kinship or a shared history of social interactions.

Due to their close phylogenetic relationship to humans, the apes are an especially relevant taxonomic group for exploring the origins of human social bonding. Moreover, female social bonding in great apes shares some important parallels with humans. Cross-culturally modern human societies are characterized by bisexual philopatry, indicating that both sexes may live near close relatives or disperse from their natal groups. However, across modern hunter-gatherer groups, males are significantly more likely than females to coreside with close kin (Hill et al., 2011). In addition, in a recent analysis of the strontium isotope composition of fossil teeth from two species of ancestral humans, the composition of male teeth matched the local geography where the fossils were found while the composition of female teeth did not, indicating that the females may have emigrated from other areas (Copeland et al., 2011). This combined evidence suggests that ancestral human social groups were likely characterized by greater levels of male philopatry and female dispersal, similar to patterns for extant great apes. This also suggests that any behavioral or physiological adaptations that enhance social bonding with non-kin may have been especially important for female fitness in ancestral humans and may continue to be important for female great apes.

A better understanding of patterns of social bonding among unrelated female great apes is thus directly relevant to exploring possible mechanisms underlying the evolution of more flexible social bonding and cooperation in humans. Moreover, by exploring exceptions to more typical patterns of affiliation based on kinship in primates, we can begin to examine the external factors and internal mechanisms that promote flexible social bonding among non-kin in a range of species, including humans.

# Patterns of Sociality Among Female Great Apes: The *Pan* Species

Among the great apes, the two *Pan* species, the bonobo (*Pan paniscus*) and chimpanzee (*Pan troglodytes* sp.) are the closest phylogenetic relatives to humans, having shared a common ancestor with humans as recently as six million years ago, and diverging from a shared ancestor only two million years ago (Bradley & Vigilant, 2002). In both species, the core social structure consists of large mixed-sex social groups, or communities, ranging from 30 to over 100 individuals. Both species also exhibit a flexible fission-fusion social system, in which members of a larger community form temporary associations in parties of fluctuating size and composition (Wrangham, 2000). Such extreme flexibility in social grouping is rare in other primate species, and may result from a relaxation of predation risks, due to the relatively large body size of *Pan* species. Fission-fusion grouping patterns help to reduce food competition, by facilitating foraging in smaller parties during periods of food scarcity (Wrangham, 2000). Both species are characterized by male philopatry and female dispersal, and genetic analyses have confirmed that females typically immigrate into groups without close female relatives present (Hohmann, Gerloff, Tautz, & Fruth, 1999; Langergraber et al., 2009). However, there is also a great deal of variability in aspects of *Pan* social behavior, primarily involving patterns of female affiliation and social bonding within groups.

## Social Bonding Among Female Chimpanzees

The earliest studies of chimpanzee social behavior occurred at a handful of field sites in East Africa, containing the *P.t. schweinfurthii* subspecies. These studies presented a picture of relatively asocial females in comparison with the more gregarious males (Goodall, 1986). At several East African sites, male chimpanzees spend most of their time in same-sex or mixed-sex parties, and males maintain stable, affiliative social bonds with maternal brothers and with a subset of unrelated males (Langergraber et al., 2007; Mitani, 2009). Males exchange more frequent forms of aid with their close male associates than with other group members, including food sharing and providing coalitionary support in social conflicts (Langergraber et al., 2007). In contrast female chimpanzees at many East African sites spend the majority of their time alone or with their dependent offspring (Williams, Liu, & Pusey, 2002; Wrangham, Clark, & Isabirye-Basuta, 1992). As a result, average dyadic association indices (DAIs) among females are much weaker than DAIs among males, and between males and females (Gilby & Wrangham, 2008).

However, as data have become available from an increasing number of study sites and subspecies, including the West African subspecies, *P. t. verus*, it has become clear that female chimpanzees exhibit considerable variation in patterns and extent of social bonding, both within and between sites (Gilby & Wrangham, 2008; Lehmann & Boesch, 2009). Females at the Tai Forest study site in Cote d'Ivoire, West Africa, are much more gregarious than their counterparts at some East African sites, spending up to 82% of their time in either same-sex or mixed-sex parties, and 84% of females had at least one long-term preferred female associate (Lehmann & Boesch, 2009). At the Kanyawara, Uganda, field site in East Africa, more female than male same-sex dyads were classified among the strongest DAIs in the community (Langergraber et al., 2009). Thus, while female chimpanzee social relationships tend to be weaker than those of males on average, across sites a subset of unrelated females maintain stable, long-term preferences for association that are among the strongest in the community (Gilby & Wrangham, 2008; Langergraber et al., 2009; Lehmann & Boesch, 2009).

Interestingly, in contrast with patterns among male chimpanzees, exchanges of affiliation such as grooming, coalitionary support, and food sharing tend to be relatively rare in female chimpanzees, even among preferred spatial associates (Gilby & Wrangham, 2008; Langergraber et al., 2009). At some sites, female dyadic associations are positively correlated with grooming (Langergraber et al., 2009), suggesting that these associations may reflect genuine social affinities. But at Tai Forest, preferential grooming relationships were more rare and less stable than preferential spatial associations, and did not correlate with association preferences (Lehmann & Boesch, 2009). The lack of high rates of affiliation among female spatial associates has led some to propose that associations may reflect similar preferences for core ranging areas, rather than social preferences (Emery Thompson, Kahlenberg, Gilby, & Wrangham, 2007) It is also possible that different types of social interactions may serve different purposes for female chimpanzees. For example, grooming patterns may reflect short-term goals to receive social support or reduce conflict among less preferred social partners (Lehmann & Boesch, 2009), while more stable spatial associations may reflect long-term social bonds.

One of the first studies to apply social network analysis to great apes suggests that fluctuations in demographic factors impact patterns of social bonding in female chimpanzees. The social networks of female chimpanzees at Tai Forest were analyzed during two time periods reflecting changes in the number of female community members due to poaching and disease (Lehmann & Boesch, 2009). At larger community sizes, the social network had low density since only a subset of all possible female dyads were characterized by strong social bonds, and the social network was clustered, due to subgroupings of several females with high levels of association. When group size decreased, network density increased, due to an increased proportion of dyads with strong social bonds, and clustering was eliminated.

Available evidence points to extensive variation in patterns of social bonding in female chimpanzees, across sites and even within sites, possibly in response to changes in demographic or ecological factors. In addition, direct forms of affiliation and cooperation are relatively rare among females in comparison with the philopatric males, even when considering preferred female partners for spatial association. Related to this, the benefits that female chimpanzees receive from same-sex social relationships remain unclear.

## Social Bonding Among Female Bonobos

Despite their similar relevance for exploring the evolution of human social relationships, bonobos have received less attention than their more thoroughly studied congeners, the chimpanzees. This is due in part to the longer history of research on chimpanzees, and to the relatively few long-term study sites with habituated bonobo communities. However, available evidence from field sites consistently depicts high levels of gregariousness and affiliation, and low levels of aggression among female bonobos (Hohmann et al., 1999; Kano, 1980; White, 1989). Females are disproportionately represented in both mixed-sex and same-sex parties and associate in parties more often than males at some sites (Furuichi, 2009; Hohmann & Fruth, 2002). Across sites, the strongest dyadic associations consistently involve females, either with other unrelated females, or with males, including their adult sons, and very few females exhibit active avoidance (Hohmann et al., 1999). In contrast with patterns in chimpanzees, in bonobos, the weakest associations and highest levels of aggression occur among males.

While close spatial associations among female chimpanzees are not necessarily characterized by high frequencies of other forms of affiliation, among bonobo females, close spatial associates groom each other more often than do random associates (Hohmann et al., 1999). More generally, high levels of sociality among female bonobos are associated with high levels of cooperation in a range of contexts, including cofeeding within close proximity in food patches (Kano, 1980; White & Wood, 2007), sharing preferred, monopolizable foods (Fruth & Hohmann, 2002, see Figure 3.2), and providing coalitionary aid, often against males (Parish, 1996). In contrast, these forms of cooperation occur less frequently between the sexes (with the exception of mother-son bonds) and among males. High levels of female sociality are hypothesized to provide a range of fitness benefits for females, including priority of access to food (White et al., 2007), ability to dominate males in aggressive contexts (Furuichi, 1989), and improved reproductive success (Parish, 1996).

The ability of female bonobos to outcompete males for access to resources and in aggressive contexts contrasts so markedly with more typical patterns of male dominance over females in chimpanzees and the majority of other primate species, that researchers initially interpreted these patterns

*Figure 3.2* Bonobos at the Lui Kotale field site in the Democratic Republic of Congo co-feed on a fresh duiker carcass. Photograph by Robin Loveridge. Reprinted with permission from Robin Loveridge.

anthropomorphically as arising from male chivalry (reviewed in Parish & De Waal, 2000), rather than considering how unique social strategies among female bonobos may allow them to outcompete males. We still have much to learn about how female bonobos maintain high levels of cooperation, not only with preferred female associates, but with a wide range of other unrelated females as well.

One unique feature of female bonobo social behavior that may provide some insights into their sex-specific patterns of cooperation involves their high frequency of sociosexual behaviors. While sociosexual behaviors occur among all group members, adult females exhibit higher frequencies of same-sex sexual behavior than any other age or sex class (Fruth & Hohmann, 2006). The most common sociosexual behavior among females is genital contacts, which consists of ventro-ventral embrace between two females and lateral rubbing of genitals against each other (Hohmann & Fruth, 2000). This behavior is largely absent in chimpanzees. Interestingly, genital contacts occur more frequently during periods of potential social conflict, such as while feeding on preferred and potentially monopolizable foods (Hohmann & Fruth, 2000). Also, genital contacts occur more frequently among females who associate at chance levels, rather than among preferred associates (Hohmann & Fruth, 2000). This suggests that genital contacts may serve a specific function, possibly in reducing social tension and promoting cooperation among females with weaker social bonds. This might be analogous to the proposed role of grooming for female chimpanzees at Tai Forest, in facilitating social interactions among females with weaker social bonds (Lehmann & Boesch, 2009).

Affiliative interactions such as grooming may facilitate social bonding by triggering the release of neurotransmitters that interact with the brain's reward pathways to reinforce preferences for association with specific partners (Dunbar, 2010). The neuropeptide hormone oxytocin is one of the main molecules believed to be responsible for the changes in brain chemistry that mediate social bonding. Oxytocin is regulated by the female gonadal hormone estrogen, and is involved in a range of female reproductive and sociosexual behaviors including orgasm, parturition, and lactation (reviewed in Turner, Altemus, Enos, Cooper, & McGuinness, 1999). In addition, oxytocin has been implicated in aspects of social bonding in a range of mammalian species. For example, in the monogamous prairie vole (*Microtus ochrogaster*), mating triggers the release of oxytocin in the brain, and oxytocin binding in reward regions of the brain such as the nucleus accumbens is necessary for the formation of female preferences for male partners (reviewed in Ross & Young, 2009). Similarly, in a monogamous New World monkey, the cotton-top tamarin (*Saguinus oedipus*), the frequency and duration of sexual and affiliative behavior among mates were positively correlated with peripheral oxytocin levels measured in urine (Snowdon et al., 2010). While the neurobiology of same-sex preferential associations has not been thoroughly explored, it is likely that female social bonds are also mediated by oxytocin. If so, it is possible that sociosexual interactions among female bonobos function as a potent releaser of oxytocin, possibly providing a shortcut to attain high levels of affiliation with specific female partners that would otherwise take longer periods of association and affiliation to establish.

Available evidence also suggests that preferential associations among female bonobos may fluctuate more often than typical of female chimpanzees, or of mixed-sex or male associations in bonobos. At the Lomako field site in the Democratic Republic of Congo, preferred partners for spatial associations fluctuated every 5–7 months among females, while mixed-sex and male-male close associations remained stable over several years (Hohmann et al., 1999). In contrast with this evidence from female bonobos, at several chimpanzee sites females' preferences for specific social partners remained stable over multiple years (Langergraber et al., 2009; Lehmann & Boesch, 2009). By flexibly switching among preferred female associates over shorter time periods, female bonobos may be able to maintain more egalitarian social bonds with a greater number of female group members than is possible for female chimpanzees.

Current evidence from across chimpanzee and bonobo study sites confirms that female social bonding is common in both species, even though adult females typically live apart from other female relatives. However, there are also important differences in patterns of female social bonding between the two *Pan* species. Wild female bonobos exhibit more widespread social tolerance, likely mediated by unique behavioral and physiological mechanisms mediating female social bonding. High levels of social tolerance in turn may facilitate high levels of female cooperation and the ability to dominate males in many contexts. In captive settings, unrelated bonobos of both sexes exhibit higher levels of success on cooperative tasks than chimpanzees (Hare, Melis, Woods, Hastings, & Wrangham, 2007) and even provide costly aid to individuals from other social groups (Hare & Kwetuenda, 2010), suggesting that bonobos may exhibit high levels of altruism toward unrelated group members and even strangers. Based on this combined evidence, bonobos may provide one of the best living models to explore the evolution of flexible social bonding in humans. Further research examining behavioral and non-invasive endocrine correlates of social bonds among female bonobos, as well as determining the benefits that females receive from same-sex social bonds, will help to identify factors that may have been critical in the evolution of social bonds among ancestral humans.

## Conclusions and Broader Implications

An extensive and cross-disciplinary body of research indicates an important role of social relationships in influencing measures of health and fitness in humans. In several nonhuman species as well, the maintenance of a strong and diverse network of social relationships has major fitness implications, especially for female mammals (Cameron, Setsaas, & Linklater, 2009; Silk et al., 2009). Further investigation of the causes and consequences of individual and gender differences in patterns of social bonding in humans and other species is greatly needed. This research should occur on several fronts.

From a sociological perspective, human research would benefit from integration of greater cross-cultural perspectives on the patterns and function of social relationships for males and females. As one important step in this direction, Hruschka (2010) demonstrates cross-cultural similarities in dynamics of friendships, including tolerance for long-term imbalances in exchanges of aid within the context of close friendships, but not with strangers or casual acquaintances. Hruschka (2010) also suggests that many reported gender differences may not be consistent across cultures. More cross-cultural gender comparisons of social relationships are needed, especially concerning how friendships are formed and how they impact health outcomes for males and females.

From a psychobiological perspective, experimental studies of humans in laboratory settings indicate some interesting potential gender differences in how individuals perceive their role in social relationships and their extent of reliance on social relationships to diffuse stressful situations (e.g., Kirschbaum, Klauer, Filipp, & Hellhammer, 1995). In addition, novel methodologies for noninvasive measurement of brain activation and hormone release are providing new insights into the physiology and neurobiology of social bonding and emotional identification with others, in humans and other species (Baumgartner, Heinrichs, Vonlanthen, Fischbacher, & Fehr, 2008). In particular, the neuropeptide hormone oxytocin has been implicated in mediating the rewarding aspects of social bonding in a range of mammalian species (reviewed in Donaldson & Young, 2008) and has been shown to increase trust and generosity in humans when administered intranasally in experimental settings (Kosfeld, Heinrichs, Zak, Fischbacher, & Fehr, 2005; Zak, Stanton, & Ahmadi, 2007).

While the experimental work provides fascinating insights, more emphasis should be given to applying experimental approaches to understand complex social interactions in natural settings. The majority of studies to experimentally manipulate and measure oxytocin levels in humans have occurred in males and have involved simulated interactions with strangers in laboratory settings that may have limited relevance for understanding natural social interactions. Despite the prominent role of oxytocin in mediating female maternal care and monogamous pair bonding, we still know very little about the role of oxytocin in mediating other types of affiliative social bonds for females, such as those with same-sex partners. Further research in humans and other species should apply non-invasive methodologies to characterize how the identity of social partners and different types of social interactions in natural settings may influence peripheral release of oxytocin and other neuropeptide hormones, and what role these hormones may play in reinforcing selective social bonds, especially for females.

From a comparative biological perspective, long-term field studies of wild chimpanzees and bonobos are continuing to provide important insights into the social lives of our closest evolutionary relatives. Social network analysis has been used at some chimpanzee study sites to better understand social dynamics within larger groups. It would be interesting to characterize female social networks across a greater number of chimpanzee study sites and during periods with differences in demographic factors such as group size or ecological factors such as food availability. This analysis would help to understand whether observed differences in female sociality among sites may reflect adaptive adjustments to differences in resource competition, stemming from ecological or demographic factors. It would also be interesting to determine whether individual variation in the strength and quality of social bonds with non-kin has consequences for female fitness in chimpanzees, as has been found for other female primates with matrilocal social systems, such as baboons (Silk et al., 2009, 2010).

Our knowledge of the social behavior of wild bonobos arises from only a handful of study sites and remains limited in comparison with the larger number of long-term field studies of chimpanzees. We do not yet understand the function of diverse social interactions such as genital contacts in mediating social bonds and cooperation among female bonobos. We also do not know whether evidence for greater fluctuations in preferred social partners among female bonobos indicates less stability in social bonds compared with female chimpanzees, or a unique strategy to maintain high levels of affiliation across a broad range of social partners. In addition, more rigorous methods are needed to identify and compare the range of fitness benefits that female bonobos gain through same-sex social bonds, similar to recent research on fitness implications of mother-offspring bonds for male bonobos (Surbeck, Mundry, & Hohmann, 2011). It would be particularly interesting to determine whether greater gregariousness and cooperation among female bonobos facilitates the rearing and social development of infants by increasing alloparental care by unrelated females. Ancestral humans may have received similar benefits as a result of increased mechanisms for social bonding (Hrdy, 2009). By protecting wild populations of chimpanzees and bonobos from ongoing anthropogenic threats, and by establishing new bonobo study sites within protected areas, primatologists will continue to gain insights into flexible patterns of social bonding among our closest phylogenetic relatives.

Humans exhibit high levels of sociality and cooperation with a diverse range of social partners, including relatives, close associates, casual acquaintances and even strangers. Human sociality is facilitated by a combination of cultural and neurocognitive adaptations that increase motivation to cooperate with others toward shared goals. Female bonobos regularly exchange diverse affiliative behaviors with a broader range of unrelated social partners than typical of many other species, and there is evidence that this widespread affiliation facilitates a range of fitness benefits for females. A better understanding of the causes and consequences of female social bonding in bonobos will provide a clearer picture of the social environment in which ancestral humans may have evolved.

# References

Abbey, A., Abramis, D. J., & Caplan, R. D. (1985). Effects of different sources of social support and social conflict on emotional well-being. *Basic and Applied Social Psychology, 6*(2), 111–129.

Archer, J. (1996). Sex differences in social behavior: Are the social role and evolutionary explanations compatible? *American Psychologist, 51*(9), 909–917.

Baumgartner, T., Heinrichs, M., Vonlanthen, A., Fischbacher, U., & Fehr, E. (2008). Oxytocin shapes the neural circuitry of trust and trust adaptation in humans. *Neuron, 58*(4), 639–650.

Belle, D. (1987). Gender differences in social moderators of stress. In R. C. Barnett, L. Biener, & G. K. Baruch (Eds.), *Gender and stress* (pp. 257–277). New York: Free Press.

Boesch, C., & Boesch-Achermann, H. (2000). *The chimpanzees of the Tai forest: Behavioural ecology and evolution*. New York: Oxford University Press.

Bradley, B. J., & Vigilant, L. (2002). The evolutionary genetics and molecular ecology of chimpanzees and bonobos. In C. Boesch, G. Hohmann, & L. F. Marchant (Eds.), *Behavioural diversity in chimpanzees and bonobos* (pp. 259–276). New York: Cambridge University Press.

Brissette, I., Cohen, S., & Seeman, T. E. (2000). Measuring social integration and social networks. In C. Sheldon, L. G. Underwood, & B. H. Gottlieb (Eds.), *Social support measurement and intervention* (pp. 53–85). New York: Oxford University Press.

Cameron, E. Z., Setsaas, T. H., & Linklater, W. L. (2009). Social bonds between unrelated females increase reproductive success in feral horses. *Proceedings of the National Academy of Sciences of the USA, 106*(33), 13850–13853.

Cheney, D. L., & Seyfarth, R. M. (1990). *How monkeys see the world: Inside the mind of another species*. Chicago: University of Chicago Press.

Christakis, N. A., & Fowler, J. H. (2009). *Connected: The surprising power of our social networks and how they shape our lives*. New York: Little & Brown.

Clutton-Brock, T. (2007). Sexual selection in males and females. *Science, 318*(5858), 1882–1885.

Cohen, S., Gottlieb, B., & Underwood, L. (2000). Social relationships and health. In S. Cohen, L. Underwood, & B. Gottlieb (Eds.), *Measuring and intervening in social support* (pp. 3–25). New York: Oxford University Press.

Copeland, S. R., Sponheimer, M., de Ruiter, D. J., Lee-Thorp, J. A., Codron, D., le Roux, P. J., et al. (2011). Strontium isotope evidence for landscape use by early hominins. *Nature, 474*(7349), 76–78.

Crockford, C., Wittig, R. M., Whitten, P. L., Seyfarth, R. M., & Cheney, D. L. (2008). Social stressors and coping mechanisms in wild female baboons (*Papio hamadryas ursinus*). *Hormones and Behavior, 53*(1), 254–265.

Darwin, C. (1871). *The descent of man and selection in relation to sex*. New York: Appleton.

Denton, M., & Walters, V. (1999). Gender differences in structural and behavioral determinants of health: An analysis of the social production of health. *Social Science and Medicine, 48*(9), 1221–1235.

DeVries, A. C., Glasper, E. R., & Detillion, C. E. (2003). Social modulation of stress responses. *Physiology and Behavior, 79*(3), 399–407.

de Waal, F. (1998). *Chimpanzee politics: Power and sex among apes* (Rev. ed.). Baltimore: Johns Hopkins University Press.

Donaldson, Z. R., & Young, L. J. (2008). Oxytocin, vasopressin, and the neurogenetics of sociality. *Science, 322*(5903), 900–904.

Dunbar, R. I. M. (2009). Mind the bonding gap: Constraints on the evolution of hominin societies. In S. Shennan (Ed.), *Pattern and process in cultural evolution* (pp. 223–234). Berkeley: University of California Press.

Dunbar, R. I. M. (2010). The social role of touch in humans and primates: Behavioural function and neurobiological mechanisms. *Neuroscience and Biobehavioral Reviews, 34*(2), 260–268.

Emery Thompson, M., Kahlenberg, S. M., Gilby, I. C., & Wrangham, R. W. (2007). Core area quality is associated with variance in reproductive success among female chimpanzees at Kibale National Park. *Animal Behaviour, 73*, 501–512.

Engh, A. L., Beehner, J. C., Bergman, T. J., Whitten, P. L., Hoffmeier, R. R., Seyfarth, R. M., et al. (2006a). Behavioural and hormonal responses to predation in female chacma baboons (*Papio hamadryas ursinus*). *Proceedings of the Royal Society of London, Series B, 273*(1587), 707–712.

Engh, A. L., Beehner, J. C., Bergman, T. J., Whitten, P. L., Hoffmeier, R. R., Seyfarth, R. M., et al. (2006b). Female hierarchy instability, male immigration, and infanticide increase glucocorticoid levels in female chacma baboons. *Animal Behaviour, 71*(5), 1227–1237.

Fehr, E., & Fischbacher, U. (2003). The nature of human altruism. *Nature, 425*(6960), 785–791.

Fehr, E., Fischbacher, U., & Gachter, S. (2002). Strong reciprocity, human cooperation, and the enforcement of social norms. *Human Nature, 13*(1), 1–25.

Fruth, B., & Hohmann, G. (2002). How bonobos handle hunts and harvests: Why share food? In C. Boesch, G. Hohmann, & L. F. Marchant (Eds.), *Behavioural diversity in chimpanzees and bonobos* (pp. 231–243). New York: Cambridge University Press.

Fruth, B., & Hohmann, G. (2006). Social grease for females? Same-sex genital contacts in wild bonobos. In V. Sommer & P. L. Vasey (Eds.), *Homosexual behaviour in animals: An evolutionary perspective* (pp. 294–315). New York: Cambridge University Press.

Furuichi, T. (1989). Social interactions and the life history of female *Pan paniscus* in Wamba, Zaire. *International Journal of Primatology, 10*(3), 173–197.

Furuichi, T. (2009). Factors underlying party size differences between chimpanzees and bonobos: A review and hypotheses for future study. *Primates, 50*(3), 197–209.

Gilby, I. C., & Wrangham, R. W. (2008). Association patterns among wild chimpanzees (*Pan troglodytes schweinfurthii*) reflect sex differences in cooperation. *Behavioral Ecology and Sociobiology, 62*(11), 1831–1842.

Goodall, J. (1986). *The chimpanzees of Gombe: Patterns of behavior*. Cambridge, MA: Harvard University Press.

Hamilton, W. D. (1964). The genetical evolution of social behavior: I and II. *Journal of Theoretical Biology, 7*, 17–52.

Hare, B., & Kwetuenda, S. (2010). Bonobos voluntarily share their own food with others. *Current Biology, 20*(5), R230–R231.

Hare, B., Melis, A. P., Woods, V., Hastings, S., & Wrangham, R. (2007). Tolerance allows bonobos to outperform chimpanzees on a cooperative task. *Current Biology, 17*(7), 619–623.

Hill, K. R., Walker, R. S., Bozicevic, M., Eder, J., Headland, T., Hewlett, B., et al. (2011). Co-residence patterns in hunter-gatherer societies show unique human social structure. *Science, 331*(6022), 1286–1289.

Hohmann, G., & Fruth, B. (2000). Use and function of genital contacts among female bonobos. *Animal Behaviour, 60*(1), 107–120.

Hohmann, G., & Fruth, B. (2002). Dynamics in social organization of bonobos (*Pan paniscus*). In C. Boesch, G. Hohmann, & L. F. Marchant (Eds.), *Behavioural diversity in chimpanzees and bonobos* (pp. 138–150). New York: Cambridge University Press.

Hohmann, G., Gerloff, U., Tautz, D., & Fruth, B. (1999). Social bonds and genetic ties: Kinship, association, and affiliation in a community of bonobos (*Pan paniscus*). *Behaviour, 136*(9), 1219–1235.

Holt-Lunstad, J., Smith, T. B., & Layton, J. B. (2010). Social relationships and mortality risk: A meta-analytic review. *PLoS Medicine, 7*(7), e1000316.

House, J. S., Landis, K. R., & Umberson, D. (1988). Social relationships and health. *Science, 241*(4865), 540–545.

Hrdy, S. B. (2009). *Mothers and others: The evolutionary origins of mutual understanding.* Cambridge, MA: Harvard University Press.

Hruschka, D. J. (2010). Friendship: Development, ecology, and evolution of a relationship. Berkeley: University of California Press.

Hyde, J. S. (2005). The gender similarities hypothesis. *American Psychologist, 60*(6), 581–592.

Kano, T. (1980). Social behavior of wild pygmy chimpanzees (*Pan paniscus*) of Wamba: A preliminary report. *Journal of Human Evolution, 9,* 243–260.

Kappeler, P. M. (2008). Genetic and ecological determinants of primate social systems. In J. Korb & J. Heinze (Eds.), *Ecology of social evolution* (pp. 225–243). London: Springer.

Kendler, K. S., Myers, J., & Prescott, C. A. (2005). Sex differences in the relationship between social support and risk for major depression: A longitudinal study of opposite-sex twin pairs. *American Journal of Psychiatry, 162*(2), 250–256.

Kikusui, T., Winslow, J. T., & Mori, Y. (2006). Social buffering: Relief from stress and anxiety. *Philosophical Transactions of the Royal Society of London B, Biological Sciences, 361*(1476), 2215–2228.

Kirschbaum, C., Klauer, T., Filipp, S. H., & Hellhammer, D. H. (1995). Sex-specific effects of social support on cortisol and subjective responses to acute psychological stress. *Psychosomatic Medicine, 57*(1), 23–31.

Kosfeld, M., Heinrichs, M., Zak, P. J., Fischbacher, U., & Fehr, E. (2005). Oxytocin increases trust in humans. *Nature, 435*(7042), 673–676.

Lakey, B., & Cohen, S. (2000). Social support theory and measurement. In S. Cohen, L. G. Underwood, & B. H. Gottlieb (Eds.), *Social support measurement and intervention: A guide for health and social scientists* (pp. 29–52). New York: Oxford University Press.

Langergraber, K. E., Mitani, J. C., & Vigilant, L. (2007). The limited impact of kinship on cooperation in wild chimpanzees. *Proceedings of the National Academy of Sciences of the USA, 104*(19), 7786–7790.

Langergraber, K. E., Mitani, J., & Vigilant, L. (2009). Kinship and social bonds in female chimpanzees (*Pan troglodytes*). *American Journal of Primatology, 71*(10), 840–851.

Lehmann, J., & Boesch, C. (2009). Sociality of the dispersing sex: The nature of social bonds in West African female chimpanzees, *Pan troglodytes. Animal Behaviour, 77*(2), 377–387.

Meder, A. (2007). Great ape social systems. In W. Henke & I. Tattersall (Eds.), *Handbook of paleoanthropology* (pp. 1235–1271). Berlin, Germany: Springer.

Mitani, J. C. (2006). Reciprocal exchange in chimpanzees and other primates. In P. M. Kappeler & C. van Schaik (Eds.), *Cooperation in primates and humans: Mechanisms and evolution* (pp. 107–119). New York: Springer.

Mitani, J. C. (2009). Male chimpanzees form enduring and equitable social bonds. *Animal Behaviour, 77*(3), 633–640.

Moen, P., Dempstermcclain, D., & Williams, R. M. (1989). Social integration and longevity: An event history analysis of women's roles and resilience. *American Sociological Review, 54*(4), 635–647.

Palombit, R. A., Cheney, D. L., Fischer, J., Johnson, S., Rendall, D., Seyfarth, R. M., et al. (2000). Male infanticide and defense of infants in chacma baboons. In C. van Schaik & C. H. Janson (Eds.), *Infanticide by males and its implications* (pp. 123–152). New York: Cambridge University Press.

Parish, A. R. (1996). Female relationships in bonobos (*Pan paniscus*): Evidence for bonding, cooperation, and female dominance in a male-philopatric species. *Human Nature, 7*(1), 61–96.

Parish, A. R., & De Waal, F. B. M. (2000). The other "closest living relative": How bonobos (*Pan paniscus*) challenge traditional assumptions about females, dominance, intra- and intersexual interactions, and hominid evolution. *Annals of the New York Academy of Sciences, 907,* 97–113.

Rilling, J. K., Gutman, D. A., Zeh, T. R., Pagnoni, G., Berns, G. S., & Kilts, C. D. (2002). A neural basis for social cooperation. *Neuron, 35*(2), 395–405.

Ross, H. E., & Young, L. J. (2009). Oxytocin and the neural mechanisms regulating social cognition and affiliative behavior. *Frontiers in Neuroendocrinology, 30*(4), 534–547.

Sapolsky, R. M. (2002). Endocrinology of the stress-response. In J. Becker, S. Breedlove, D. Crews, & M. McCarthy (Eds.), *Behavioral endocrinology* (2nd ed., pp. 409–450). Cambridge, MA: MIT Press.

Schulke, O., Bhagavatula, J., Vigilant, L., & Ostner, J. (2010). Social bonds enhance reproductive success in male macaques. *Current Biology, 20*(24), 2207–2210.

Seeman, T. E. (1996). Social ties and health: The benefits of social integration. *Annals of Epidemiology, 6*(5), 442–451.

Shye, D., Mullooly, J. P., Freeborn, D. K., & Pope, C. R. (1995). Gender differences in the relationship between social network support and mortality: A longitudinal study of an elderly cohort. *Social Science and Medicine, 41*(7), 935–947.

Silk, J. B. (2002). Using the "F"-word in primatology. *Behaviour, 139*(2–3), 421–446.

Silk, J. B. (2007). The adaptive value of sociality in mammalian groups. *Philosophical Transactions of the Royal Society of London B Biological Sciences, 362*(1480), 539–559.

Silk, J. B., Alberts, S. C., & Altmann, J. (2004). Patterns of coalition formation by adult female baboons in Amboseli, Kenya. *Animal Behaviour, 67*(3), 573–582.

Silk, J. B., Alberts, S. C., & Altmann, J. (2006). Social relationships among adult female baboons (*Papio cynocephalus*): II. Variation in the quality and stability of social bonds. *Behavioral Ecology and Sociobiology, 61*(2), 197–204.

Silk, J. B., Altmann, J., & Alberts, S. C. (2006). Social relationships among adult female baboons (*Papio cynocephalus*): I. Variation in the strength of social bonds. *Behavioral Ecology and Sociobiology, 61*(2), 183–195.

Silk, J. B., Beehner, J. C., Bergman, T. J., Crockford, C., Engh, A. L., Moscovice, L. R., et al. (2009). The benefits of social capital: Close social bonds among female baboons enhance offspring survival. *Proceedings of the Royal Society B, Biological Sciences, 276*(1670), 3099–3104.

Silk, J. B., Beehner, J. C., Bergman, T. J., Crockford, C., Engh, A. L., Moscovice, L. R., et al. (2010). Strong and consistent social bonds enhance the longevity of female baboons. *Current Biology, 20*(15), 1359–1361.

Smith, K. P., & Christakis, N. A. (2008). Social networks and health. *Annual Review of Sociology, 34*, 405–429.

Snowdon, C. T., Pieper, B. A., Boe, C. Y., Cronin, K. A., Kurian, A. V., & Ziegler, T. E. (2010). Variation in oxytocin is related to variation in affiliative behavior in monogamous, pairbonded tamarins. *Hormones and Behavior, 58*(4), 614–618.

Surbeck, M., Mundry, R., & Hohmann, G. (2011). Mothers matter! Maternal support, dominance status, and mating success in male bonobos (*Pan paniscus*). *Proceedings of the Royal Society B, Biological Sciences, 278*(1705), 590–598.

Taylor, S. E., Klein, L. C., Lewis, B. P., Gruenewald, T. L., Gurung, R. A., & Updegraff, J. A. (2000). Biobehavioral responses to stress in females: Tend-and-befriend, not fight-or-flight. *Psychological Review, 107*(3), 411–429.

Thorsteinsson, E. B., & James, J. E. (1999). A meta-analysis of the effects of experimental manipulations of social support during laboratory stress. *Psychology and Health, 14*, 869–886.

Turner, R. A., Altemus, M., Enos, T., Cooper, B., & McGuinness, T. (1999). Preliminary research on plasma oxytocin in normal cycling women: Investigating emotion and interpersonal distress. *Psychiatry, 62*(2), 97–113.

Umberson, D., Chen, M. D., House, J. S., Hopkins, K., & Slaten, E. (1996). The effect of social relationships on psychological well-being: Are men and women really so different? *American Sociological Review, 61*(5), 837–857.

van Schaik, C. P., & Kappeler, P. M. (2006). Cooperation in primates and humans: Closing the gap. In P. M. Kappeler & C. van Schaik (Eds.), *Cooperation in primates and humans: Mechanisms and evolution* (pp. 3–21). New York: Springer.

White, F. J. (1989). Social organization of pygmy chimpanzees. In P. G. Heltne & L. A. Marquardt (Eds.), *Understanding chimpanzees* (pp. 194–207). Cambridge, MA: Harvard University Press.

White, F. J., & Wood, K. D. (2007). Female feeding priority in bonobos, *Pan paniscus*, and the question of female dominance. *American Journal of Primatology, 69*(8), 837–850.

Williams, J. M., Liu, H. Y., & Pusey, A. E. (2002). Costs and benefits of grouping for female chimpanzees at Gombe. In C. Boesch, G. Hohmann, & L. F. Marchant (Eds.), *Behavioural diversity in chimpanzees and bonobos* (pp. 192–203). New York: Cambridge University Press.

Wittig, R. M., Crockford, C., Seyfarth, R. M., & Cheney, D. L. (2007). Vocal alliances in chacma baboons (*Papio hamadryas ursinus*). *Behavioral Ecology and Sociobiology, 61*(6), 899–909.

Wrangham, R. W. (2000). Why are male chimpanzees more gregarious than mothers? A scramble competition hypothesis. In P. M. Kappeler (Ed.), *Primate males: Causes and consequences of variation in group composition* (pp. 248–258). New York: Cambridge University Press.

Wrangham, R. W., Clark, A. P., & Isabirye-Basuta, G. (1992). Female social relationships and social organization of Kibale Forest chimpanzees. In T. Nishida et al. (Eds.), *Topics in primatology. Vol. 1: Human origins* (pp. 81–98). Tokyo, Japan: University of Tokyo Press.

Wroblewski, E. E., Murray, C. M., Keele, B. F., Schumacher-Stankey, J. C., Hahn, B. H., & Pusey, A. E. (2009). Male dominance rank and reproductive success in chimpanzees, *Pan troglodytes schweinfurthii*. *Animal Behaviour, 77*(4), 873–885.

Zak, P. J., Stanton, A. A., & Ahmadi, S. (2007). *Oxytocin increases generosity in humans. PLoS One, 2*(11), e1128.

# 4

# A Sex-Neutral Theoretical Framework for Making Strong Inferences About the Origins of Sex Roles

PATRICIA ADAIR GOWATY

## Introduction

To understand better women's role in evolution, as this volume seeks to do, it is critical that we understand and test alternative hypotheses for the origins of sex roles. As I use the term, "sex roles" refers to aspects of sex-differentiated behavior and physiology associated with "reproductive decisions." Reproductive decisions are probably not often conscious, but are behavioral or physiological alternatives that individuals take during a lifetime of options about reproduction. Early reproductive decisions may strongly affect or even determine later reproductive decisions; thus sex roles can be thought of a cascade of reproductive decisions or options, as a syndrome of connected (sometimes loosely) behavioral (physiological) alternatives.

Has anyone ever used a strong-inference (Platt, 1964) approach to testing alternative hypotheses about the *origins* of sex roles? Perhaps it is time to do so, as sex-neutral models for choosy and indiscriminate behavior of individuals exist. Without the foil of rigorous sex-neutral models, we are left with consistency through correlation. Is that good enough in the face of logically and mathematically robust alternatives? If reigning explanations of the origins of sex-differentiated behavior are correct, empirical tests of the predictions from a strong-inference perspective will clearly reject the sex-neutral forces of social and ecological contingency. Without empirical tests of the alternatives, we will never know.

For me theory is a tool, neither an end in itself nor the truth. For me theory is a guide to the design of tests that would eliminate, that is, rule out alternative possibilities. Forty years ago, my professors taught me to look for crucial experiments, those capable of testing two or more alternative ideas at once, so that if the experiments are well carried out, their results could simultaneously soundly reject one strongly inferential hypothesis and support another. This well-known method of "strong inference" tests crucial predictions (Platt, 1964). I began my empirical work on bluebirds in the 1970s under Platt's sway and I remain committed to his practice because it is an efficient way to get to the truth of nature. And, as Platt emphasized, using strong inference can help protect us against one of science's greatest perils, self-deception.

I start with (1) a clarification of what I think, what I seek to know, and the source of my commitments to theoretical guides. Then I describe (2) what have seemed to me the most contentious arguments about sex roles, and (3) a theoretical path to parsing alternative hypotheses. I end with (4) a series of potential tests that will efficiently tell us if an alternative sex-neutral model of mating behavior can explain more of the nature of women/females (and men/males) than the—often circular—ideas that begin with sex differences to predict more sex differences.

## Why Quantitative Theory Is Essential

That I like sex-neutral models emphatically does not mean I think intrinsic sex differences do not exist. Female mammals give birth; males never do. Female mammals lactate; male mammals very rarely do. Sex differences exist. My interests here lie in sex-differentiated behavior, and since behavior is usually contingent on external circumstances rather than intrinsic sex-determined circumstances, I am asking simple questions about the contingencies of behavior that we call "reproductive decision-making" and their real time fitness effects. My intellectual romance with sex-neutral, null models is because I am concerned that we will never know the truth of nature unless we have guiding null models (those without assumptions about preexisting adaptation or selection) with sex-neutral assumptions (meaning assumptions about individuals not sexes) that can tell us theoretically what a null and sex-neutral world might look like. To be excessively clear, please keep in mind that sex-neutral, null models can and do predict adaptive (fitness enhancing) behavior of individuals. To some readers null and sex neutral may seem on the face of it useless. But, that is wrong, particularly when the sexes differ, as they so often do, because when the sexes do differ we must partition what we see into adaptation and stochastic processes. Are sex differences in reproductive decision-making due to adaptive processes or to statistical mechanical probabilistic processes? A fundamental example from basic genetics is Hardy-Weinberg's equilibrium theory of gene frequency variation between generations. The Hardy-Weinberg equilibrium theory proved mathematically that gene frequencies do not change unless the simple assumptions of the theory are violated: that is, if drift or selection or both occur. The Hardy-Weinberg theory became and remains in genetics a powerful, ubiquitous tool that allows insights into the many ways adaptive and stochastic processes modify gene frequencies. My point here is that null, sex-neutral models hold similar promise for understanding important between- and within-sex variation in behavior and fitness.

Null and sex neutral models of sex roles guide new observations and experiments that might tell us some very surprising things, things that the dominant modern views of narrow sense sexual selection obscure, hamstringing our imaginations and our experiments. Null models might tell us an enormous amount about women as they do about female flies, fish, ducks, and mice and perhaps about chimpanzees. For example, we now do have sex neutral theoretical solutions that allow us to characterize the generalities of demography associated with human and nonhuman female multiple mating and failures to mate (Gowaty & Hubbell, 2012), and these are currently providing guides to strong inference empirical tests of fitness variations of different options, such as mating once, mating more than once, and even not at all. And, the payout of these models is that combined with tractable experimental systems, we can examine in a strongly inferential frame, alternative hypotheses about the fitness costs and benefits to females of polyandry and to males of polygyny (Gowaty, 2012).

## The Intuitive Hypothesis of Origins of Sex Differences and Sex Roles

The "Bateman-Trivers paradigm" (Dewsbury, 2005) organizes most modern studies of sexual selection. It says variation in gamete sizes or parental investment patterns determine sex roles, a set of ideas I call collectively the cost of reproduction (COR) hypotheses (Gowaty, 2012). The arguments go like this: in species with female-biased gamete sizes (Parker, Baker, & Smith, 1972) or postgamete parental investment (Trivers, 1972) (1) genes in males for ardent, profligate mating and aggression are fixed, whereas genes in females for "coy," reticent, choosy passivity are fixed. In species with larger male than female gametes (never observed so far) or greater male parental investment, the choosy genes are in males and the profligate competitive genes are in females. Typical sex differences associated with typical bigger female gametes or greater female parental investment were then said to result in typical fitness differences between males and females (Bateman, 1948), namely (2) lower reproductive success variance in females than males, (3) because sexual selection acts on males through female choice and male-male competitive interactions. Bateman said all of this followed from (4) male multiple mating having a greater effect on achieved fitness than female multiple mating. Bateman argued that this was why "in females there would be selection in favour of females obtaining only one mate after which they would become relatively indifferent" (p. 365). The hypotheses of the Bateman-Trivers paradigm are now called "Bateman's principles" (Arnold, 1994) instead of "Bateman's conclusions" or "Bateman's hypotheses." Bateman's conclusions continue to hold sway (Jones, 2009) as an up-to-date citation analysis of Bateman (1948) would demonstrate.

But some are surprised of the hold of Bateman's hypotheses on sex differences research. More than 25 years ago, Sutherland (1985) showed that chance could explain Bateman's results. And, two years after that, Hubbell and Johnson (1987) published another quantitative alternative hypothesis to the COR hypotheses. Their stochastic mating model proved theoretically that real-time environmental variation—ecological and social contingency—produced fitness variances that Bateman and the COR theorists said sex differences in choosy and indiscriminate behavior produced. Their work proved that under stochastic demography fixed sex differences such as universally indiscriminate males and universally choosy females *would be selected against*, independent of their gamete sizes or their patterns of parental investment (discussed in Gowaty & Hubbell, 2005) and independent of any sexual selection. The Hubbell and Johnson mating model showed that choosy and indiscriminate behavior need not have been originally dependent on either or both the evolution of anisogamy or sex differences in parental investment. No compulsory linkage exists between anisogamy/parental investment and variation in choosy/indiscriminate behavior.

But, what about the empirical linkage Bateman made between behavior and fitness variances? In the last decade reanalyses of Bateman's paper suggested his conclusions were wrong (Snyder & Gowaty, 2007), his data were selectively presented (Dewsbury, 2005; Tang-Martinez & Ryder, 2005), and his method for observing number of mates was fatally flawed. Bateman's method overestimated the number of individuals with zero mates and underestimated the individuals with one or more mates (Gowaty, Kim, & Anderson, 2012), so that he (Snyder & Gowaty, 2007) and others using his method mismeasured the key variable—variance in number of mates. Bateman's "principles" are in fact only Bateman's hypotheses.

Empirical failures of the Bateman-Trivers paradigm came even earlier than Sutherland's (1985) theoretical challenge and the more recent methodological challenges: I thought the data Sarah Hrdy (1981) discussed in 1981 in *The Woman That Never Evolved* soundly rejected COR. Others must not have agreed with me, as many still posit and conclude Bateman's "principles," even when their data remain inconsistent with COR's assumptions. For example, more than a hundred studies (reviewed in Ah-King & Gowaty, draft May 5, 2012), most published since 2000, show that individuals switch from choosy to random mating when their environmental and social circumstances change, *putting the lie to the force of parental investment to shape choosy and indiscriminate mating—at least in the "choosy sex."* Instead of saying, "Observations failed to match the predictions of anisogamy or parental investment," investigators erect ad hoc, usually correlational hypotheses to tack onto COR hypotheses to explain observations; most of these posit some kind of unique, species-specific, sometimes peculiar-to-that species, believable trade-off between mate choice and something odd about the tested species. In the studies Ah-King and Gowaty (MS draft May 5, 2012) found, subjects changed from random to choosy mating when their encounters with potential mates changed (Chapman & Partridge, 1996); under predation risk (Forsgren, 1992); when their condition (Poulin, 1994), experience (Kodric-Brown & Nicoletto, 2001; Marler et al., 1997), or disease risk changed; as their own access to resources changed (Itzkowitz & Haley, 1999); when the density of potential mates changed (McLain, 1992); and under variation in the operational sex ratio (Berglund, 1994; Jirotkul, 1999) and other factors. This within-sex phenotypic plasticity means that COR did not fix choosy behavior. In this body of studies COR's predictions failed to capture the truth of nature.

Even in the face of contrary data rejecting the COR assumptions, it seems impossible for some to imagine that sex differences in parental investment did not shape sex differences in choosy and indiscriminate behavior. The power of this paradigm (Dewsbury, 2005; Tang-Martinez & Ryder, 2005) is so strong that most of the authors exploring empirically the environmental circumstances associated with changes from choosy to random mating in *the* choosy sex almost never simultaneously asked if the low-investing sex changes from random to choosy mating. Would empiricists be more willing to say that their data reject the parental investment idea if there were other compelling models, perhaps about individuals rather than sexes? Would we then be more willing to ask: Do males in species with no male parental investment switch from random to choosy? I wish more investigators would ask that question. We have needed for a long time a theory of individuals that could refocus our gaze on *individuals, not sexes*, and to release the vice-grip on our imaginations.

Despite the extraordinary power of the Bateman-Trivers paradigm, it is crumbling under the weight of its own success: without the intuitive and inspiring ideas of Geoff Parker and Robert Trivers, investigators in our field, including this author, would have been unlikely to pursue an understanding of the sexual behavior of nonhuman animals nor would they have been funded to do it.

I have been seeking a strongly inferential approach for parsing between the alternative explanations for the origin of sex roles since my first read of Trivers (1972). I stumbled in October 2001 on an alternative while reading Hubbell and Johnson (1987), a widely overlooked and sometimes misrepresented paper that set me on a new path to the switch point theorem (SPT) (Gowaty & Hubbell, 2009). If the ideas Hubbell and I have on offer are wrong, it will be easy to find out. The tools for the rejection of our ideas are built into them, and I have tried very hard to be explicit about this. So, to be further emphatic about my goals and motives: I am not claiming the only path to the truth, just a unique idea that may make our search for the origins of sex differences more efficient. For me, we reach the stopping rule in the search for truth when no simpler explanation for this or that explains what we see.

## Three Hypotheses of the Origins of Sex Roles

A familiar argument, which evolutionary psychologists and some behavioral ecologists habitually use, assumes that sex roles (Box 4.1) are essential and binary,

BOX 4.1  **Some Meanings of the Word "Sex"**

*"Sex" is combining and mixing of genetic material.* Biologists define sex as occurring when chromosomes undergo meiosis so that genetic material of two individuals mixes together—recombines—to produce a unique gamete. The "sex" in recombination—that is, the genetic mixing, however, is not dissimilar to the genetic mixing that occurs with transposable elements, so "sex" is not unique to genetic mixing. During the sex of meiosis and genetic mixing, individuals need not be differentiated into different embodied sexes; the individuals need only be different individuals.

*"Sex" indicates whether an individual has large or small gametes.* The sex of an individual is usually defined in terms of the size of gametes that an individual produces: individuals with big, often sedentary gametes—eggs, are defined female, while individuals with small, mobile gametes—sperm, are defined male. There are ambiguities even with this gamete-size definition of sex because in some species sperm might be bigger than eggs. For example, see the remarkable series of papers documenting sperm size variation in *Drosophila* sp. from the lab of Therese Markow (Knowles & Markow, 2001; Markow, 2002; Pitnick & Markow, 1994a, 1994b; Pitnick, Markow, & Spicer, 1995; Pitnick, Spicer, & Markow, 1995; Snook et al. 1994; Snook & Markow 1996, 2001). Defining sex in terms of gamete sizes of individuals is a convenient starting point for a general challenge to how we study the evolution of sex roles. Obviously differences in the size of combining gametes are not essential prerequisites for sex, because in many organisms isogamous (same-sized) gametes from two different individuals come together to produce offspring. If we focus on the idea that two *individuals* rather than individuals of *two sexes* come together and share genetic and somatic resources to produce offspring, it becomes clear that differences in male and female parents are not necessary prerequisites to recombination.

*"Sex" indicates the type of genitalia an individual has.* The presence or absence of a penis can indicate an individual's gametic sex; however, in humans at least considerable variation in internal and external genitalia exists, some-times making it hard to bin or categorize an individual to sex (Dreger, 2008; Fausto-Sterling, 2000; Gowaty, 2008) something that is also true in species besides humans. For example, brown hyena *Crocuta crocuta* females have a "pseudo-penis," an enlarged clitoris (Hamilton, Tilson, & Frank, 1986), through which they give birth (Frank & Glickman, 1994) and which females erect to signal submission (East, Hofer, & Wickler, 1993). In most bird spe-cies males lack intromittant organs altogether (Gowaty & Buschhaus, 1998), so lacking a penis does not indicate "male" or "female." (Some birds like ducks do have remarkable intromittant organs; passerines do not as a rule. Rather

BOX 4.1 *(Continued)*

for sperm to pass to the female's cloaca both sexes evert a compartment of the cloacae and touch them together in a "cloacal kiss" which transfers sperm from male cloaca to female cloaca). Sex similarity, monomorphism, and ambiguity put the lie to the universal utility of genitalia as a marker of one's sex.

*"Sex" is what we call the behavioral acts that precede gamete sharing.* For some investigators the first inklings of sex role differences are obvious in behavior that precedes copulation. For example, in many species most familiar to us, it is common for males to court with displays of showy plumage, outrageous "dances," and so forth, which females (or others?) may respond to or not. So, investigators often call a species "sex role reversed" if females in a given species are more colorful or have more-developed plumage than the males (Darwin 1871), or even if females court males. Or consider this: the male "role" of being on top during copulation has such salience in the minds of researchers that they often infer the sex of an individual if it is the one on top or not during copulation. The strength of the "male-on-top" assumption hid—sometimes for a very long time—the fact that in some species, homosexual pairs are common (MacFarlane et al., 2007): individuals express gendered behavior. Take the case of same-sex parenting in albatross (Young et al., 2008), overlooked until DNA inference of chromosomal sex of adults. To other investigators, the fact that some individuals readily can take on the behavior, reified as a "role" of opposite sexes, suggests that some "sex role behavior" is in fact contingent, optional, and developmentally plastic, clearly not sex-specific.

genetically determined traits, whose adaptive significance lies in past selection of "environments of evolutionary adaptation, EEA" (see the dissenting arguments in Irons, 1998), namely the environments Parker et al. (1972) and Trivers (1972) hypothesized to select for genes for choosy females and ardent males. Less familiar, but similarly strong arguments, which academic feminists and some social psychologists promote, assume that sex and sex roles are plastic, nonadaptive traits that arise under the influence of nurture. A third perspective is more interesting than the essentialist gene-centric, EEA argument or the prediction-free arbitrary trait argument. The third argument is that sex-differentiated behavior is individually flexible (an extreme form of developmental plasticity) arising under the influence of nurture and nature, but hardly arbitrary. Sutherland (1985) and Hubbell and Johnson (Hubbell & Johnson, 1987) originated null (selection-free) and sex-neutral (starting with individuals) models of variation in fitness and reproductive decision-making. These two models inspired the third argument that says that developmentally plastic sex roles are made up of *adaptively flexible behavior and physiology* serving the fitness interests of *individuals* in real time, that is, as they live their lives in ecological time, rather than in evolutionary time (Gowaty & Hubbell, 2005, 2009). According to the third argument, genes and environments are "inextricably intertwined during development" (West-Eberhard, 2003) and jointly determine sex roles. This third perspective provides strong justification for the idea that sex and sex roles are developmental reaction norms (Ah-King & Nylin, 2010; Gorelick & Heng, 2010), which I discuss a bit below to introduce evolutionary scenarios for the evolution of contingent behavior of individuals under different ecological constraints.

## Changing Worldviews: Reaction Norms and Phenotypic Plasticity

The set of phenotypic responses of the same genotype in different environments defines a reaction norm. However, a more integrated perspective includes West-Eberhard's (2003) important viewpoints on developmental plasticity and the developmental reaction norm perspective (Pigliucci, 2005; Schlichting & Pigliucci, 1998). The developmental reaction norm perspective starts with the ideas that (1) individuals are integrated units—phenotypes—not disconnected parts (the whole is greater than the sum of the parts and genes are part of bigger integrated units); (2) ecological constraints—and their effects on epigenetics, culture, learning, and other ontogenetic processes including chance (see Jablonka & Lamb, 2005)—are keys to determination of adult forms; and (3) environmental heterogeneity affects trait expression throughout ontogeny. "Phenotypic plasticity" and "developmental reaction norm" refer to integrated phenotypes and stimulate new ways to think about the origins of phenotypes (Ah-King & Nylin, 2010) that forego the tensions of essentialist gene centric ideas about sex roles. As Anne Fausto-Sterling (2000) so eloquently put it: "organisms—human and otherwise—are active processes, moving targets, from fertilization to death" (p. 235). The developmental reaction norm perspective facilitates study of adaptive effects of within-individual, within-lifetime changes in phenotypes.

An extreme form of developmental plasticity, a part of the developmental reaction norm perspective, is *individual adaptive flexibility* (IAF). Many investigators recognize this extreme form of developmental plasticity as behavior (Dukas, 1998). As I see it, the tenets of individual adaptive flexibility are that individuals are more than their genes. Individuals are integrated phenotypes that deterministic (adaptive) and stochastic (chance) environmental and social constraints shape and reshape throughout individuals' lives. Epigenetic and other ontogenetic processes (like culture and learning) proximately mediate changes in what individuals do (induce individual behavior) in ways that enhance individual Darwinian fitness (reproductive success and survival). This generalized view of IAF assumes that ancient selection occurred leaving all individuals in all species—including humans—able to sense and respond in adaptive ways (to increase fitness or decrease fitness losses) to indicators of their prospects for reproduction and survival, which may change moment-to-moment. According to the IAF hypothesis, selection occurred resulting in individuals who can sense variation in their reproductive and survival prospects. According to IAF, individuals "predict" their fitness rewards and costs from alternative decisions open to them, most often correctly, based on current circumstances. Darwinians observe such sensitivity and responsiveness all the time (Dukas, 1998). Thus, it is possible and likely that sex does not fix sex-differentiated choosy and indiscriminate behavior, but that the social and ecological environments in which individuals find themselves induce choosy and indiscriminate behavior (Gowaty & Hubbell, 2005).

How can we find out? We need to ask the same questions of individuals of both sexes under similar ecological and social circumstances. To help design such tests we need a theory of environmentally and socially induced behavior predicting the behavior of individuals, *not sexes*, who experience similar or different ecological and social environments, and who then, depending on social and ecological constraints (Gowaty, 1997), behave as "choosy" or "indiscriminate." Hubbell and Johnson's (1987) mating model gave us exactly that. Gowaty and Hubbell's (2009) SPT relaxed one of the assumptions of Hubbell and Johnson's (1987) mating model to provide a theoretical "analytical solution" allowing predictions of what adaptively flexible individuals do when mate quality comes in as many varieties as the number of mates. Do individuals in this or that demographic and social circumstance mate at random or wait for a better option (be choosy). Thus, the SPT predicts the fraction of potential mates acceptable to a given individual given a specified set of circumstances. Experimentalists can compete the SPT's predictions *about flexible individuals* against the predictions of parental investment and anisogamy theory (Parker, Baker, & Smith, 1972) *about fixed sexes*.

## The Hypothesis of Individually Adaptive Flexibility

Schematics describing a scenario for the evolution of individuals making individually adaptively flexible (IAF) reproductive decisions are in Gowaty and Hubbell (2005, 2009). In contrast to the COR arguments, the scenario for individually adaptive flexibility (IAF) as in Sutherland (1985) and in Hubbell and Johnson's (1987) mating model and in the SPT starts with stochastic demography, meaning that chance variation in individual survival and mate encounter were the first determinants of lifetime variance in fitness. The IAF scenario assumes that selection acted so that all individuals sense and respond to the changing environmental and social circumstances that affect their options for reproduction and survival.

So, in the IAF the force of selection was on sense organs, cognitive processes, and motor patterns that constitute integrated proximate mechanisms of behavior of individuals fitting them to their circumstances, as those circumstances may change moment-to-moment.

The IAF scenario "turned the arrow of causation from behavior to fitness around" (Gowaty & Hubbell, 2005). COR says behavior causes variances in fitness, but the mating model of stochastic demography shows that lifetime variances in fitness must come also or even primarily from the probabilities of chance demography, which in turn provides the information to individuals that induce their real-time variation in behavior. COR scenarios instantiated evolved, fixed sex differences in behavioral alternatives to accept or reject potential mates, leaving individuals with fixed choosy or indiscriminate behavior. The IAF scenario (Gowaty & Hubbell, 2005) instantiated the idea that in all individuals have the mechanisms for adjusting—when individuals' circumstances changed in ecological time—their reproductive decisions in such a way to enhance fitness benefits and decrease fitness costs. IAF makes clear that the usually assumed one-way ticket—behavior to fitness—is in fact a round-trip ticket with the arrows of causation going in both directions.

Strong alternative, testable hypotheses could end the long-standing debates that opened this chapter. Whether you are more comfortable with the assumptions of COR or IAF, whether or not your political views fit you to prefer ideas about evolved and fixed sex differences or evolved individual flexibility is beside the point of discerning which among the three ideas above are nearer the truth of nature.

The series of models below (Gowaty & Hubbell, 2005, 2009, 2010; Hubbell & Johnson, 1987) predict the moving targets of individual fitness gains and losses of the "active processes"—individual reproductive decisions—resulting in trajectories of adaptive individual reproductive careers from an individual's first period of receptivity to mating to death. These mathematical theorems proved that individuals able to make adaptive reproductive decisions evolve, whenever the theorem's assumptions are met in nature. The models prove that individuals can change their behavior and physiology moment-to-moment as their ecological and social circumstances change in ways that enhance their lifetime fitness. If one proves a theorem mathematically, it remains only for the empiricist to test its assumptions. *Do the theorem's assumptions match real-world observations?*

A caution: A reviewer asked me to remark on the many models exploring the circumstances for the "the direction of sexual selection" (Kokko & Monaghan, 2001; Kokko, Jennions, & Brooks, 2006). I have not, as they mostly predict the behavior of sexes, not individuals. When they predict fitness outcomes, they predict for sexes not individuals. Assuming things about sexes to predict things about sexes seemed not on topic for my goal to understand whether or not the origins of choosy and indiscriminate behavior or the origins of fitness variances are about sexes or about individuals. The phrase "direction of sexual selection" seems to imply some assumptions of compulsory sex differences of some sort at the outset in most of these models, even if one is looking at ecological contingencies. In addition sexual selection is a within-sex process (Darwin, 1871), so I have always found it hard to understand how greater sexual selection in one sex actually lessens sexual selection in another (I think the usual justification for the "direction" argument requires narrowest sense sexual selection, meaning that the mechanisms of sexual selection only work through variance in number of mates). Bateman's and Arnold's (1994) claims notwithstanding, the operation of sexual selection in one sex does not depend on the operation of sexual selection in the other (Altmann, 1997). It may be possible to set up the "direction of sexual selection" models in a strong-inference framework, but I didn't see these hypotheses as alternatives to COR about *origins*, but rather as modifications of COR that allowed newer observations that were inconsistent with the paradigmatic worldview to again fit with COR. Ad hoc approaches to theory and theory modification is, of course, time honored and honorable. And, has no doubt been useful in nudging our enterprise of discovering the truth of nature forward. Perhaps others will pick up the challenge to show how the models that I am not discussing actually do allow for strongly inferential tests of the classic debates that interest me here and that impelled me to write this chapter. That is a discussion that I suspect would be useful and that many would welcome.

## Conceptual Similarities of the Mating Model and the Switch Point Theorem

Hubbell and Johnson's (1987) mating model, and the switch point theorem (SPT) (Gowaty & Hubbell, 2009) both capture mathematically IAF. The difference between the mating model and the SPT is that the SPT has some "improvements" in the form of some modified assumptions, that is, the SPT is an ad hoc quantitative hypothesis, designed to overcome the limitations of one of Hubbell and Johnson's original assumptions. Hubbell and Johnson (1987) were among the first, if not the first, to formally model the lifetime fitness effects (including lifetime variance in mating success) of individually adaptive flexibility in expression of choosy and indiscriminate mating behavior under the assumptions that time and chance are universal constraints on what individuals do and the fitness gained or lost as a result of what they do or do not do. Both are silent overall about the exact mechanisms of information transfer between generations (Maynard Smith & Szathmáry, 1997). Both are about individuals, not sexes. Both assume that within (and between) individual variation in acceptances/rejections (random/choosy) of potential mates occurs under stochastic demography, in which individuals vary in their likelihood of survival, $s$, their encounters with potential mates $e$, and the availability of potential mates, and the "quality" of those mates. Both predict under what environmental and social circumstances stereotypical sex role behavior might emerge from induced behavior of individuals who are in different ecological and social circumstances, rather than from fixed sex-specific traits. In addition, both models predict the fitness associated

with individual behavior: the fitness costs and benefits for an individual of a particular mating and within-sex variances in mating success. The models differ in their
assumptions about fitness variation among potential mates. In the original mating
model, an individual mating with any potential mate would result in high ($W_H$) or
low ($W_L$) fitness. One of the points of the original mating model was to find the
magnitude of difference in fitness—the fitness ratio $W_L/W_H$—at which choosy and
indiscriminate mating yielded equal fitness (Figure 4.1). The space above and below
the isocline of equal fitness showed the conditions that would select against fixed
choosy or fixed individual behavior.

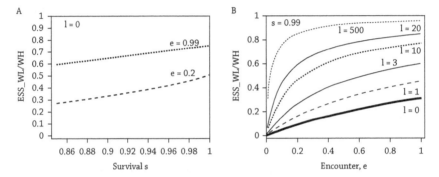

*Figure 4.1* Graphs of the lines of equal fitness for choosy versus random mating of
an individual calculated from the analytical results in Hubbell and Johnson (1987).
Each line on each graph represents an individual, independent of its sex. The line of
equal fitness in A is a function of $s$, and in B a function of $e$. The y-axis in both graphs
is the ratio of fitness conferred when mating with a low or high "quality" mate. The
area below each line on each graph shows conditions when choosy mating will yield
greater fitness; the area above each line shows when indiscriminate mating will yield
higher fitness. In A all individuals are virgins, meaning they have never experienced a
postmating latency, so their $l = 0$. There are two lines: for $e = 0.99$ and $e = 0.2$. Choosy
behavior yields higher fitness at higher $e$ than lower $e$, and increases at both $e$ values
as $s$ increases. A shows that all else equal when individuals have a higher $s$, they
are more likely to be "choosy": that is, the area under the curve is greater than the
area over the curve. In comparison if $s$ is lower, more space over the curve indicates
indiscriminate behavior yields higher fitness. It says, for example, that if males are
more vulnerable to predation than females, it may be that predators reduce the
time they have for mating, favoring indiscriminate mating over choosy mating. In B
when $s$ is always high (0.99) the $W_L/W_H$ of equal fitness conferred for choosy versus
indiscriminate mating varies with $e$, with choosy always more frequent as $e$ increases,
and as $l$ increases from 0 to 500. Note that the effect of $l$ divides the fitness space
more dramatically at smaller values of $l$ than larger. Note also that the position of
the line of equal fitness is determined jointly by $e$, $s$, and $l$. B says that virgins ($l = 0$),
independent of their sexes, are more indiscriminate than nonmated individuals, and
that even individuals with small $l$ or large $l$ will be both choosy and indiscriminate
under some conditions. The fact that $l = 0$ for virgins provides an empirical path
forward in the goal of testing for the origins of sex differences.

In contrast to Hubbell and Johnson's mating model, in the SPT the fitness that would be conferred was not limited to two mate "qualities," but could occur in up to n "qualities," where n equals the number of potential mates. The problem the SPT solves is the fraction of all potential mates (n) a given individual would find acceptable to mate. The fraction of potential mates ranked acceptable defines the switch point for an individual. The SPT (Gowaty & Hubbell, 2009) is an analytical solution to the problem of the proportion of potential mates that a focal individual, *independent of their sex*, will accept or reject as a mate, under the assumption that there are n mate "qualities" (n = the number of potential mates). It predicts differences in what individuals do when they experience different constraints (Figure 4.2). Figure 4.3

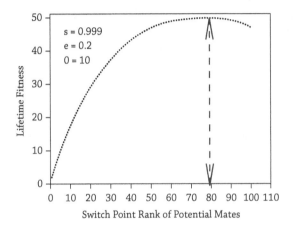

*Figure 4.2* Switch point for accepting or rejecting potential mates for an individual. Read the x-axis as a series of switch point rules: Accept up to rank x and reject all from x + 1 to n. On the x-axis of a switch point graph for a particular focal individual is all potential mates arranged according to the rank the focal individual assigns to each. Each rank then represents a particular rule, so that at rank *x*, for instance, the rule is "accept potential mates as encountered from rank 1 up to rank *x* and reject all potential mates up to rank *x* + 1 to *n*," where n is the number of potential mates in the population. No focal individual in a population needs to rank a given potential mate the same way. This means no requirement exists for a best male or a best female that all opposite sex individuals prefer over any others; that is, the x-axis for each focal individual may hold different potential mates in each rank; females need not rank a given male the same way, and males need not rank a given female the same way. The highest point on the y-axis of lifetime fitness is *f*\*, the average lifetime fitness of individuals with a given *e*, *s*, *n*, *l*, and *w-distribution*, when they use the accept/reject rule associated with *f*\*. To figure out the switch point, find the highest point on the curve of lifetime fitness and note the corresponding rank of potential mates on the x-axis: the switch point rule between accept and reject is the one that maximizes lifetime fitness for given values of *e*, *s*, *n*, *l*, and *w-distribution*. The SPT proved that an individual maximizes its lifetime fitness if it encounters and accepts any potential mate up to and on the left of the switch point and encounters and rejects any individual on the right hand side of the switch point rule.

is an example of a comparison graph of two individuals under high and low survival regimes. Its results say that if there are systematic differences in the ecology of the sexes (say greater environmental vulnerability, rather than intrinsic vulnerability, of one sex than the other to predation, or competitive control due to social constraints unrelated to individuals' intrinsic constraints, of their encounters with potential mates), then sex differences in choosy and indiscriminate mating may be due entirely to ecological circumstances, not intrinsically embedded in their sex, but embedded in their ecological and social circumstances. If there are no differences in the ecological and social constraints for individuals, it predicts similar behavior of individuals whether their sexes differ or not. It also predicts the circumstances under which sex-associated differences exist in constraints, but which do not result in differences in behavior. The SPT, like Hubbell and Johnson's mating model, does this without appeal to or dependence on knowledge of fancy traits that may or may not mediate an individual's acceptance/rejection behavior. The theorem relies on the universal certainty of demographic stochasticity but it can also facilitate a deeper understanding of the deterministic forces that also may act on individuals to affect sex roles. It provides a quantitative approach to a new area of study: the ecological and social contingencies of sex roles.

Now, I describe how one might use the SPT to test alternative scenarios for the origins of choosy and indiscriminate behavior. Does an individual's sex determine its behavior? Is individual behavior contingent, dependent on the ecological circumstances and developmental histories of individuals? That is, do inextricably intertwined nature and nurture induce individual adaptive behavior?

## The Assumptions of the Switch Point Theorem: What to Test

Individuals are an important unit of selection (Lewontin, 1970) through which the heritable mechanisms of evolution—genetic, cultural, developmental, and ecologically induced epigenetics—operate. Our focus on individuals allows us to study between- and within-individual variation and to critically challenge and test alternative hypotheses about individuals of different and same sexes. Empiricists who draw individuals at random, irrespective of their sex, for future tests of behavior (random vs. choosy mating) and fitness will be in a position to prove whether this assumption matches their system. If empiricists control the variables associated with the SPT, for example, with tests of virgin individuals (all of which regardless of their sex have identical latencies or timeouts of zero), a single failure to observe predicted changes in individuals of either sex would indicate that the SPT does not apply in that system.

We assumed that individual lifetimes were finite and the tempo of reproductive opportunities has profound effects on reproductive decisions. We assumed that selection has acted so that individuals can sense and respond to cues of time constraints. We assumed that individuals do often sense when they are or are not under predation risk; know when they are ill; when they have greater or fewer attractive resources. We assumed individuals do sense variation in encounters with potential mates, and do predict their future encounters. We assumed that individuals do sense the duration of the latency to remating that they experience relative to their time for mating and reproduction. And, we assumed individuals do respond to this variation in themselves and in others. These assumptions seemed self-evident. If individuals have no sense organs, the SPT would not apply. If individuals cannot change their behavior in response to their particular ecological circumstances during receptive periods, the SPT would not apply. The fact that individuals do respond to predators, disease, and so forth, provides an opportunity to explore how finely they modulate their behavior in response to the effects of stochastic demography on an individual's time for mating and reproduction.

When encounter rates are low, so that individuals must spend more time searching for or advertising for, or waiting to encounter potential mates, individuals have less time available for mating and reproduction. This assumption is self-evident. The following statements would be straightforward to test: high encounters increase opportunities to mate, and under most, but not all configurations of the SPT, high $e$ increases the fitness payout for choosy behavior for an individual regardless of its sex. An individual likely will change her behavior whether mated or virgin when her risk of being eaten or killed changes.

Stochastic effects on demography arise because individuals sometimes leave or enter populations by chance; by chance some individuals enter or leave receptivity to mating; by chance individuals may have variable durations of time-outs after mating. Thus, in keeping with Hubbell and Johnson's mating model, this assumption of the SPT allows us to study how chance variation in encounters, survival, and the durations of time-out affect means and variances in fitness, including number of mates. Empiricists could put the assumption of stochastic demography to powerful uses. It is self-evident that chance effects on demography happen; and it is likely that deterministic forces also work on $e$, $s$, and $l$. Thus, an important question, very seldom addressed is what part of fitness variances are due to stochastic demography versus selection (Hubbell & Johnson, 1987; Gowaty, 2003). A way for empiricists to study this crucial question is to put the analytical solutions from Hubbell and Johnson's mating theory to work to calculate what the null model predicts fitness variances to be under variation in $s$ and $e$ and to compare the predicted null variances to observed variances. Readers interested in a worked example using a simple model of null variance should study Bill Sutherland's (1985) model showing that chance effects on encounters coupled with fixed (not available for selection to act on) durations of latency can account entirely for Bateman's (1948) data.

We assumed that during development, prior to first receptivity to mating, individuals acquire information about who they are relative to others in the population so that on encounter, all individuals—irrespective of their sex—can assess, more or less instantaneously, the likely fitness outcomes of mating with this or that potential mate. Does individual ability to assess alternative potential mates vary with developmental exposures to conspecifics? It does in *Drosophila paulastorum* (Kim & Ehrman, 1998; Kim, Ehrman, & Koepfer, 1992, 1996; Kim, Koepfer, & Ehrman, 1996; Kim, Phillips, Chao, & Ehrman, 2004). Clever empiricists have tested for Westermarck effects in many species, so I suspect that additional studies on the effects of variation in exposure to conspecifics during development will have effects on what individuals know about themselves when they reach first receptivity to mating: how quickly can virgins in different species make decisions about whom they prefer? We need controlled experiments to find out. Because we assume that mate assessment is self-referential, if empiricists show that mate assessment is not self-referential, one of our informal assumptions (not critical to the structure of the model but to our interpretations of the model) will be refuted.

Individuals assess fitness cognitively—not necessarily consciously, and assessment need not be a behavioral motor act. Assessment according to the IAF scenario is separate from the behavioral motor act of accepting/rejecting a potential mating (and therefore potentially confusing to investigators who conflate cognitive assessment processes with the behavioral acts of mating or not mating). Investigators sometimes confound this dichotomy between a cognitive process and a behavioral act probably because most of our information comes from what individuals do (including, if they are human, what they say, which might be lies or self-deceptive statements), so that the two concepts of *assessment* and *accepting/rejecting* a potential mate are often inappropriately conflated in empirical practice. As the mating model and the SPT prove theoretically, assessment is not the same as accepting or rejecting a potential mate. Evaluating appetitive behavior or intention movements in a series of three linked experiments can verify this assertion of assessment as a cognitive process different from the behavioral act of accepting/rejecting:

1. Put subjects (an individual whose assessments we wish to infer) and "discriminatees" (individuals the subject is to assess) into choice arenas that do not allow touching, but do allow seeing, hearing, smelling, and so forth. (Discriminatees may be placed in arenas at random with respect to their phenotypes or not.) Using a priori criteria, such as fraction of time spent in front of one discriminatee or the other in a fixed time trial, determine which discriminatee the subject "likes," in this case, using duration of time with or near.

2. If subjects reach criterion time with one discriminatee, randomly assign the subject to breed with the one they liked or the one they did not like, and evaluate the fitness outcomes of the enforced experimental matings. (Steps 1 and 2 have been completed in a number of species as reviewed in Gowaty et al., 2007).

3. Redo step 1 with new virgins and then place the subject and the two discriminatees together in an "open field" so that all three individuals can

interact, so that mate preferences and within sex competitive interactions like aggression or interference may occur, and note with whom the subject mates first. It is highly likely that these matings will appear to occur at random with respect to the previously evaluated assessment behavior in step 1.

This series of experiments demonstrate that the cognitive process of assessment is different from accepting or rejecting an encounter with a potential mate. Such results indicate how important it is to evaluate the *w-distribution*, the background fitness variation under which individuals make their decision to mate or not.

Fitness is a relative expression of some component of fitness; relativized fitness always varies between 0 and 1. Therefore in the Hubbell and Johnson mating model and the SPT it remains an empirical question what exactly is the component of fitness that individuals "predict" when they assess each other. Because we assumed that individuals know about themselves relative to others in the population, it became clear that the shape of the distribution of fitness that would be conferred that comes from the matrix of all virgin males mated to all virgin females simultaneously (i.e., random mating)—the *w-distribution*— could have an important effect on individuals' decisions. We prefer to imagine that assessment of "mate" quality is self-referential and about the likely survival of offspring to adulthood. This SPT assumption is consistent with the many studies suggesting that complementarity at immune coding loci fuels mate preferences. How often this assumption is true is "in the air"; many recent studies show consistency with the assumption of mate choice for immune-gene complementarity. I look forward to those that do not, for surely some counterexamples do or will exist. If they do not, these observations of mate preferences for complementarity strongly support the SPT's formal and informal assumptions about fitness.

We assume that mate assessment is "self-referential," so that not only do individuals assess the fitness outcomes of mating with this or that potential mate but that they can rank them, from best (1) to worst (n). The switch point is the rank among all potential mates at which an individual switches. It is important that in the SPT the way one individual, say a male, ranks potential mates is unique to that male, and that no other individual need rank potential mates the same way. We also assume that individuals encounter potential mates at random with respect to the way an individual ranks them. Therefore, the distribution of fitnesses of potential mates *for a given individual can be unique to them*, as seems reasonable in a flat distribution of fitness with nearly equal probability that a given potential mate yields any fitness between 0 and 1. To test this idea one would need an experimental device, perhaps a round "Amsterdam" arena in which one would place a single subject, who could see, smell, and hear, but not touch or copulate with the discriminatees. The investigator could then use the subject's appetitive behavior to evaluate whom they do and do not like. Hold the set of discriminatees constant, but vary the subjects. If all subjects preferred the same individual or ranked individuals the same way, under the stringent case of a flat w distribution, the SPT would be at risk, that is, inconsistent with the nature of the test system.

We assumed a particular mathematical approach. Because we wanted to count up what individuals do, we made a model of what happens in discreet time. We assumed that individuals enter and exit a series of states until they enter the state of death, a state they cannot exit. We assumed that individuals move through these states with some probabilities, and with some probabilities have a chance of moving from one state to the state of death. We imagined individuals starting their reproductive careers in a state of receptivity to mating, in which they "search" for mates actively (which could be searching) or passively (which could be staying in place, being attractive or calling, etc.). If they are lucky and do not die in the state of receptivity and if they are lucky and encounter a potential mate, they may enter the state of encountering and mating or encountering and not mating. If they encounter and do not mate or die, they will reenter receptivity to mating. If they encounter and mate, they reenter a state of latency to receptivity, the duration of which can vary between individuals. Because individuals move into and out of states, we can count up the number of times they pass through a given state. Because we can count up what individuals do, we can compute means and variances in important components of fitness like mean number of mates for individuals who experience certain values of $s$, $e$, and $l$, and thereby also the variance in number of mates. This approach allows us to ask questions like this: Is the variance in number of mates for individuals with an encounter probability of 0.2 potential mates per unit of time greater or lesser than individuals with an encounter probability of 0.99 potential mates per unit of time? A question empiricists should ask is whether the particular sequence of states and their assumptions match their system. The current model might fail to predict common chimpanzee behavior because we assume that after each mating that individuals enter a compulsory time-out and we count fitness at the end of the latency. But, chimpanzee females often mate with several different males within minutes of each other. To predict chimpanzee behavior what's needed is modification of the assumptions of the SPT so that individuals can mate multiply before entering any time-out (Gowaty & Hubbell, forthcoming).

The SPT suggests that some questions are more important than others: What is the likely fitness that would be conferred via random mating? We need to know to interpret why we might collectively fail to find predicted differences in the fitness outcomes. For example, could it be that some or even many (presumed) unpublished studies that sought the predicted relationship between fancy male traits and enhanced offspring health (Hamilton & Zuk, 1982) failed to find the expected answer because the *w-distribution*—was skewed so that most potential mates conferred similar fitness on females. If our tests of key predictions do not take the *w-distribution* into account, we may prematurely conclude that a given trait provides no information on offspring health. We risk finding that nature is inconsistent with the hypothesis, even if the hypothesis is true.

How often in social behavior and mating systems do we know the number of potential mates in study populations? How often do we operationally define *e* to estimate the mean and variance of individual encounters? We need more estimates of variation among individuals in predation risk and disease risk and mortality risk from other factors. What is an individual's likelihood of survival from one unit of time to the next, in one stage to the next? For example, many investigators assume that mated females survive more poorly than unmated or that multiply mated females die sooner than singly mated females. However, recent field data and laboratory experiments challenge these common assumptions: Wild mated females in *Drosophila* survive longer after capture than wild virgin females (Markow, 2011). In a laboratory study, polyandrous (multimated) *D. pseudoobscura* died no faster than females with a single copulation or females that mated many times with the same male (Gowaty, Kim, Rawlings, & Anderson, 2010). We need many more empirical observations from wild-living and captive individuals of their likelihood of survival under different conditions.

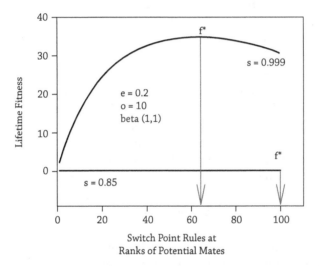

*Figure 4.3* Two switch points given instantaneous changes in survival probability, *s*, when *e*, *o*, and *w-distribution* are held constant. When *s* = 0.85, lifetime fitness accrual from mating is very low (expected future life is 6.67 time-units) and the switch point so high that every potential mate is acceptable as a mate; when *s* = 0.999 (expected future life is 1,000 time units) lifetime fitness accrual is much higher, and individuals can afford to wait, and so the SPT predicts they reject many encountered potential mates. Notice that with declining *s*, *f\**—the fitness among all switch points yielding the highest fitness—moves to lower fitness with declining *s*, so that the switch point moves to the right: individuals with lower *s*, accept more potential mates than individuals with higher *s*. Because survival probability can change rapidly, the SPT says the most adaptive reproductive decision for an individual is to change acceptance and rejection rules rapidly too.

Figure 4.3 makes the point that the time constraints on individuals may change moment-to-moment so that an individual may have different switch points moment-to-moment too. The switch-point that maximizes an individual's lifetime fitness may change instantaneously as ecological and social conditions change. Many readers are familiar with behavioral data consistent with this idea (cited earlier).

For future tests of the origins of sex roles, the duration of latency before remating, what we called $l$ before, we now call a time-out period after mating, $o$, and $o$'s effect on the switch point is one the most important results of the SPT: at least for empiricists, because the result is nonintuitive. Sensitivity analyses of the rate of change in $f^*$, the fitness that defines the best switch point rule, given variation in each of the parameters of the SPT indicate that variation in time-out is the least important of the parameters affecting $f^*$ (Gowaty & Hubbell, 2009, online supplemental material and forthcoming). Nonetheless, the fact that $o = 0$ for virgins is a crucial point useful in constructing strongly inferential experimental tests of different hypotheses for origins of sex roles, because virgins—no matter what their sex—have the same value of time-out ($o = 0$ for female and male virgins). Consideration of Figure 4.4 also emphasizes the crucial difference between the SPT and the assumptions of COR. COR, being about the effects of past selection, like potential reproductive rate theory (Clutton-Brock & Parker, 1992), predicts fixed different outcomes for females and males even when $e$, $s$, $o$, $n$, and $w$-distribution are the same—in dramatic contrast to the SPT.

Figure 4.5 shows that individuals making reproductive decisions under identical time constraints (the same $s$, $e$, $l$, and $n$) but experiencing different $w$-distributions have different, fitness-enhancing switch points. When $w$-distributions are right-skewed, fitnesses are clumped toward high fitness; when $w$-distributions are left-skewed, potential mates are clumped toward low fitness. In the examples of Figure 4.5, $f^*$ and the switch points for individuals in populations with right-skewed $w$-distributions are further to the right, so that individuals accept more potential mates. In populations with left-skewed $w$-distributions, it pays individuals to reject more potential mates.

The SPT model is synthetic: it unifies what might have been thought of as different explanations, such as one about acceptances and rejections of potential mates under different encounters, one for predator risk, one for pathogen risk, one for population size, and so forth. With information on $s$, $e$, $o$, $n$, and $w$-distribution, the SPT predicts behavior and fitness conferred. We no longer need a special ad hoc trade-off hypothesis to explain why individuals change from choosy to random mating (1) in the presence of a predator, (2) under pathogen risk, or (3) under resource variation. Importantly one does not need to know what trait or traits in potential mates mediate preferences; rather one need only ask about constraints on the chooser's time and their fitness benefits or costs of a particular decision to accept or reject. The trade-off between time and fitness can explain the already-observed behavioral switches of individuals in the lab and in the field without appeal to the fancy traits in the chosen mediating preferences or sex differences in parental investment.

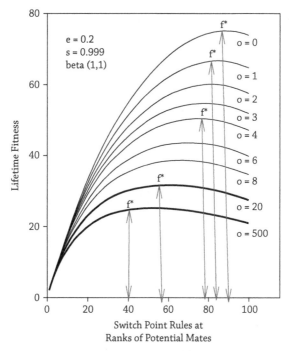

*Figure 4.4* When all else is equal, virgins (*o* = 0) accept more potential mates than individuals who are rmating (who may have *o* = 0 to infinity). Given that *e*, *s*, *n*, and *w-distribution* are constant, virgins adaptively accept more potential mates than nonvirgins. Two things happen with increases in 0: the curse of lifetime fitness is lower at successively higher values of latency; while the switch point moves closer to the origin of the x-axis, meaning that already-mated individuals having experienced longer time-outs after previously mating reject more potential mates than individuals with shorter previous time-outs. The maximum lifetime fitness, *f\**, that determines the switch point rank for a given set of parameter values, moves closer to the origin of the x-axis, where the accept-reject rule becomes increasingly stringent and fewer potential mates are in the acceptable range. As time-out takes up a greater proportion of a nonvirgin's life, the *f\** fitness associated with each accept-reject rule is less and the switch point rule maximizing fitness converges: The differences between *f\** of *o* = 20, *o* = 50, and *o* = 100 are much less than the difference in *f\** at *o* = 0 and *o* = 1 or between *o* = 1 and *o* = 2.

# Testing the Assumptions and Predictions of the Switch Point Theorem

The veracity of a quantitative theory is of two types: Is the math correct? Do the theory's assumptions capture the truth of nature? Some readers will doubt that individual animals can predict (can assess) the fitness that may be gained or lost from mating with this or that mate. Readers' doubts are welcome, because most

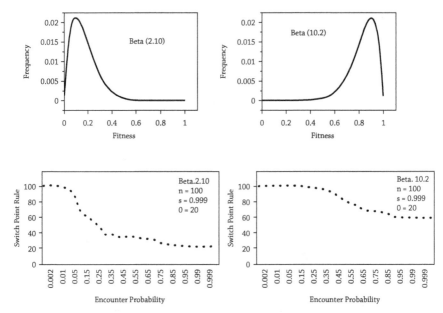

*Figure 4.5* Top panel shows two *w-distributions* indicated by their beta 2.10, a left-skewed distribution with mostly low fitnesses and beta 10.2, a right-skewed curve with mostly high fitnesses. The bottom panel shows how the switch point rules change with encounter probability, holding *s, n, o* constant under two different *w-distributions*. Given the values of *o, s, e,* and *n*, the switch points are on average at lower ranks when the *w-distribution* has a high frequency of lower fitness conferred than when the *w-distribution* has a high frequency of high fitness conferred. At similar values of *e*, say *e* = 0.55, individuals in a population with this left skewed *w-distribution* will accept mates up to about rank 39 and reject those potential mates ranked 40 to 100, while those experiencing the right-skewed *w-distribution* will accept up to about rank 80 and reject potential mates from 81 to 100. The *w-distribution* can have a profound effect on the behavior of individuals.

of the existing empirical work on mate preferences does not inform this question. Our field needs more empirical studies of the fitness variation of different reproductive decisions. Most studies of mate choice designed to explain traits in potential mates assume that choosers gain higher fitness from liking this one or that one, but very, very few studies, relative to the bulk of mate choice studies have evaluated the fitness accrual of a focal's preference(s) (Bluhm & Gowaty, 2004; Drickamer, Gowaty, & Holmes, 2000; Drickamer, Gowaty, & Wagner, 2003; Gowaty, Drickamer, & Holmes, 2003; Gowaty et al., 2007; Nicoletto, 1995; Reynolds & Gross, 1992). Yet, many experimental data do inform the question of whether or not individuals are able to assess potential mates for the likely fitness that would be conferred if the focal mated with them.

For example, Gowaty et al. (2007) reviewed experimental studies showing that in male and female flies, in male and female mice, in male and female fish, and in female ducks individuals behaved as though they preferred some potential mates and disliked others. Most of the experiments were silent about the traits in potential mates that may mediate preferences, because the experimentalists included potential mates in the trials at random with respect to their phenotypes. However, the tests were not silent about the fitness rewards and costs of mating with partners that focal choosers behaviorally preferred or did not prefer. After preference testing, we placed subjects randomly in enforced monogamous pairs with the ones they liked or did not like. In experimental enforced pairs, subjects in enforced pairs with potential mates they did prefer laid fewer eggs or gave birth to fewer young, but produced significantly more adult offspring than subjects assigned to potential mates they did not prefer. These results empirically proved that focal individual assessment behavior predicts fitness rewards of mating with this or that potential mate. In the species in which the investigators were able to use "choosers" (the SPT's equivalent of a focal individual) of both sexes, the behavior of focal males indicated fitness enhancing preferences of potential mates, just as happened in females. We can take at least two important messages from these results: (1) A major assumption of the SPT was verified: behavioral assessments "predict" fitness outcomes. (2) Germane to the question at hand about the origins of sex role behavior, the experimental data rejected the hypothesis that individual premating assessment behavior is arbitrary.

But, does sex fix and determine individual behavior or do contingencies affecting dynamic trade-offs between time and fitness determine individual behavior? A strongly inferential test would proceed in two parts. (1) Investigators will evaluate the *w-distribution* of the source population and at the same time (2) perform experimental tests of focals' accept-reject behavior. As far as I know, this set of tests has not yet been completed.

- To estimate the shape of the *w-distribution*, randomly pair 30–50 virgins and allow them to breed; evaluate egg-to-adult (birth-to-adult) survival and productivity (number of offspring who reach reproductive age). Fit a beta distribution to the frequency distribution of fitness, which estimates the background shape of the fitness distribution that behaving individuals confront.
- Control the developmental exposure of all subject individuals (those whose reproductive decisions you will observe and categorize), so that individuals of both sexes have equal access to information about conspecifics; that is, so that individuals' opportunities to learn who they are relative to others in the population are identical or at least similar. Holding individuals in identically sized same-sex populations in nearby containers so that they can smell, hear, and see opposite-sex individuals, but not touch them and certainly not copulate with them would control development exposures.
- Until the start of experimental trials for assessment, hold—under identical conditions—virgins with same-sex conspecifics, so that all individuals—regardless of their sex—are treated the same, and unable to mate. At the same time, hold them so that they are able to gain visual, olfactory, and auditory

information about the number of potential mates. Note the numbers of males in the male colony; note the number of females in the female colony (your estimate of $n$ for females and $n$ for males).

- Draw subjects at random from groups of same-sex virgins to serve as focal individuals and potential mates.
- Test individuals for operationally defined assessment behavior under similar conditions controlling for the number of potential mates focals get to see during assessment testing. Assessment testing should be in an arena of some sort. For example, one might construct a behavioral arena, like an "Amsterdam arena," in which the focal can move along a corridor allowing investigators to observe the behavior of subjects, when focals can see, smell, and hear, but not touch potential mates who are in separate cells so that they cannot interact. Run from 30 to 100 tests for individuals of each sex.
- Develop criteria for determining in controlled trials that an individual assesses one of the potential mates as "more likable" than another. Make sure any result for an individual is repeatable, (e.g., on different days). Sum the number of trials with an unambiguous result (meets criteria for demonstrating a preference) of one potential mate for males and the number of unambiguous assessments for females; calculate the proportion of assessments meeting operational criteria.
- If $e$, $s$, $n$, and the $w$-distribution were indeed identical and if all subjects of both sexes were indeed virgins and receptive to mating at the start of the trials, and if males fail to meet criteria for demonstrating a preference more often than females or vice versa, the result would be inconsistent with the SPT, but only under the assumption that those being discriminated were placed in trials at random with respect to phenotype. This experiment thus constitutes a strong-inference test (Platt, 1964) with a crucial prediction, meaning that the experimental outcome of a carefully carried-out experiment will simultaneously support one hypothesis and reject the other.

## Switching the Status Quo

Obviously a sex-neutral science of sex-differentiated behavior and psychology is possible. The assumptions and predictions of the theorems I discussed are testable, so further proof is in the pudding clever experimentalists concoct.

It is also my hope that the SPT will inspire a new round of testing of nonintuitive notions. For example, are males choosy in species with no parental investment? The answer is "yes" in the few species that have put males to the test (e.g., Anderson, Kim, & Gowaty, 2007). I look forward to the time when investigators will be able to describe how males in their species say "no."

Judy Stamps (personal communication) once said, "If it's intuitive, test it." I think she predicated her advice on the general ease with which most of us believe in what is comfortable. Going with beliefs that make us comfortable makes us vulnerable to accepting uncritically assumptions that fail in nature. Assumptions in our comfort zones of intuition are the ones *we are least likely to test*, but perhaps the ones we should most rigorously test. Intuitive but false assumptions fall into Rumsfeld's category of unknown unknowns. How many unknown unknowns remain about sex differences in behavior and mating, where intuition and politics have colluded to keep us ignorant?

# Acknowledgments

Steve Hubbell and I have been collaborating on these ideas since 2001. I thank him for his patience, generosity, kindness, and remarkable originality (full disclosure: we're married and I'm biased, but what I say about Hubbell is nonetheless true). I thank Sarah Hrdy for her sage advice. I thank the editors of the volume for inviting me to contribute. I gratefully acknowledge NSF Grants IBN-9631801, IBN-0911606, IOS-1121797 each of which supported empirical work testing ideas related to the models I discuss herein.

# References

Ah-King, M., & Gowaty, P. A. (draft May 5, 2012)). Random and choosy mating: Within-sex developmental plasticity or individual flexibility? *Ecology and Evolution*.

Ah-King, M., & Nylin, S. (2010). Sex in an evolutionary perspective: Just another reaction norm. *Evolutionary Biology*, *37*, 234–246.

Altmann, J. (1997). Mate choice and intrasexual reproductive competition: Contributions that go beyond acquiring more mates. In P. A. Gowaty (Ed.), *Feminism and evolutionary biology: Boundaries intersections and frontiers* (pp. 320–333). New York: Chapman and Hall.

Anderson, W. W., Kim, Y. K., & Gowaty, P. A. (2007). Experimental constraints on mate preferences in *Drosophila pseudoobscura* decrease offspring viability and fitness of mated pairs. *Proceedings of the National Academy of Sciences of the United States of America*, *104*, 4484–4488.

Arnold, S. J. (1994). Bateman principles and the measurement of sexual selection in plants and animals. *American Naturalist*, *144*, S126–S149.

Bateman, A. J. (1948). Intra-sexual selection in *Drosophila*. *Heredity*, *2*, 349–368.

Berglund, A. (1994). The operational sex ratio influences choosiness in a pipefish. *Behavioral Ecology*, *5*, 254–258.

Bluhm, C. K., & Gowaty, P. A. (2004). Social constraints on female mate preferences in mallards, Anas platyrhynchos, decrease offspring viability, and mother productivity. *Animal Behaviour*, *68*, 977–983.

Chapman, T., & Partridge, L. (1996). Female fitness in *Drosophila melanogaster*: An interaction between the effect of nutrition and of encounter rate with males. *Proceedings of the Royal Society of London Series B, Biological Sciences*, *263*, 755–759.

Clutton-Brock, T. H., & Parker, G. A. (1992). Potential reproductive rates and the operation of sexual selection. *Quarterly Review of Biology*, *67*, 437–456.

Darwin, C. (1871). *The descent of man and selection in relation to sex*. London: John Murray.

Dewsbury, D. (2005). The Darwin-Bateman paradigm in historical context. *Integrative and Comparative Biology, 45*, 831–837.

Dreger, A. (2008). Sex beyond the karyotype. In D. L. Kleinman, K. A. Cloud-Hansen, C. Matta, & J. Handelsman (Eds.), *Controversies in science and technology: From climate to chromosomes* (pp. 481–492). Madison: University of Wisconsin Press.

Drickamer, L. C., Gowaty, P. A., & Holmes, C. M. (2000). Free female mate choice in house mice affects reproductive success and offspring viability and performance. *Animal Behaviour, 59*, 371–378.

Drickamer, L. C., Gowaty, P. A., & Wagner, D. M. (2003). Free mutual mate preferences in house mice affect reproductive success and offspring performance. *Animal Behaviour, 65*, 105–114.

Dukas, R. (1998). *Cognitive ecology: The evolutionary ecology of information processing and decision making.* Chicago: University of Chicago Press.

East, M. L., Hofer, H., & Wickler, W. (1993). The erect "penis" is a flag of submission in a female-dominated society: Greetings in serengeti spotted hyenas. *Behavioral Ecology and Sociobiology, 33*, 355–370.

Fausto-Sterling, A. (2000). *Sexing the body: Gender politics and the construction of sexuality.* New York: Basic Books.

Forsgren, E. (1992). Predation risk affects mate choice in a gobid fish. *American Naturalist, 140*, 1041–1049.

Frank, L. G., & Glickman, S. E. (1994). Giving birth through a penile clitoris: Parturition and dystocia in the spotted hyaena (*Crocuta crocuta*). *Journal of Zoology, 234*, 659–690.

Gorelick, R., & Heng, H. H. Q. (2010). Sex reduces genetic variation: A multidisciplinary review. *Evolution, 65*, 1088–1098.

Gowaty, P. A. (1997). Sexual dialectics, sexual selection, and variation in mating behavior. In P. A. Gowaty (Ed.), *Feminism and evolutionary biology: Boundaries, intersections, and frontiers* (pp. 351–384). New York: Chapman Hall.

Gowaty, P. A. (2003). Sex roles, contests for the control of reproduction, and sexual selection. In P. M. Kappeler & C. P. van Schaik (Eds.), *Sexual selection in primates: New and comparative perspectives.* Cambridge, UK: Cambridge University Press.

Gowaty, P. A. (2008). Perception bias, social inclusion, and sexual selection: Power dynamics in science and nature. In D. L. Kleinman, K. A. Cloud-Hansen, C. Matta, & J. Handelsman (Eds.), *Controversies in science and technology: From climate to chromosomes* (pp. 401–420). Madison: University of Wisconsin Press.

Gowaty, P. A. (2012). The evolution of multiple mating: Costs and benefits of polyandry to females and of polygyny to males. *Fly, 6*, 1–9.

Gowaty, P. A., Anderson, W. W., Bluhm, C. K., Drickamer, L. C., Kim, Y. K., & Moore, A. J. (2007). The hypothesis of reproductive compensation and its assumptions about mate preferences and offspring viability. *Proceedings of the National Academy of Sciences of the United States of America, 104*, 15023–15027.

Gowaty, P. A., & Buschhaus, N. (1998). Ultimate causation of aggressive and forced copulation in birds: Female resistance, the CODE hypothesis, and social monogamy. *American Zoologist, 38*, 207–225.

Gowaty, P. A., Drickamer, L. C., & Holmes, S. S. (2003). Male house mice produce fewer offspring with lower viability and poorer performance when mated with females they do not prefer. *Animal Behaviour, 65*, 95–103.

Gowaty, P. A., & Hubbell, S. P. (2005). Chance, time allocation, and the evolution of adaptively flexible sex role behavior. *Integrative and Comparative Biology, 45*, 931–944.

Gowaty, P. A., & Hubbell, S. P. (2009). Reproductive decisions under ecological constraints: It's about time. *Proceedings of the National Academy of Sciences of the United States of America, 106*, 10017–10024.

Gowaty, P. A., & Hubbell, S. P. (2010). Killing time: A mechanism of sexual selection and sexual conflict. In J. Leonard & A. Cordoba-Aguilar (Eds.), *The evolution of primary sexual characters in animals* (pp. 79–96). Oxford, UK: Oxford University Press.

Gowaty, P. A., & Hubbell, S. P. (2012, in press). The evolutionary origins of mating failures and multiple mating. *Entomologia Experimentalis et Applicata.*

Gowaty, P. A., Kim, Y. K., & Anderson, W. W. (2012). No evidence of sexual selection in a repetition of Bateman's classic study of *Drosophila melanogaster. Proceedings of the National Academy of Sciences of the United States of America. 109* (29), 11740–11745.

Gowaty, P. A., Kim, Y. K., Rawlings, J., & Anderson, W. W. (2010). Polyandry increases offspring viability and mother productivity but does not decrease mother survival in *Drosophila pseudoobscura. Proceedings of the National Academy of Sciences of the United States of America, 107,* 13771–13776.

Hamilton, W. D., & Zuk, M. (1982). Heritable true fitness and bright birds: A role for parasites. *Science, 218,* 384–387.

Hamilton, W. J., Tilson, R. L., & Frank, L. G. (1986). Sexual monomorphism in spotted hyaenas, *Crocuta crocuta. Ethology, 71,* 63–73.

Hrdy, S. B. (1981). *The woman that never evolved.* Cambridge, MA: Harvard University Press.

Hubbell, S. P., & Johnson, L. K. (1987). Environmental variance in lifetime mating success, mate choice, and sexual selection. *American Naturalist, 130,* 91–112.

Irons, W. (1998). Adaptively relevant environments versus the environment of evolutionary adaptedness. *Evolutionary Anthropology, 6,* 194–204.

Itzkowitz, M., & Haley, M. (1999). Are males with more attractive resources more selective in their mate preferences? A test in a polygynous species. *Behavioral Ecology, 10,* 366–371.

Jablonka, E., & Lamb, M. (2005). *Evolution in four dimensions: Genetic, epigenetic, behavioral, and symbolic variation in the history of life.* Cambridge, MA: MIT Press.

Jirotkul, M. (1999). Operational sex ratio influences female preference and male-male competition in guppies. *Animal Behaviour, 58,* 287–294.

Jones, A. G. (2009). Mate choice and sexual selection: What have we learned since Darwin? *Proceedings of the National Academy of Sciences of the United States of America, 106*(Suppl. 1), 10001–10008.

Kim, Y. K., & Ehrman, L. (1998). Developmental isolation and subsequent adult behavior of Drosophila paulistorum: IV. Courtship. *Behavioral Genetics, 28,* 57–65.

Kim, Y. K., Ehrman, L., & Koepfer, H. R. (1992). Developmental isolation and subsequent adult behavior of Drosophila paulistorum: I. Survey of the six semispecies. *Behavioral Genetics, 22,* 545–556.

Kim, Y. K., Ehrman, L., & Koepfer, H. R. (1996). Developmental isolation and subsequent adult behavior of Drosophila paulistorum: II. Prior experience. *Behavioral Genetics, 26,* 15–25.

Kim, Y. K., Koepfer, H. R., & Ehrman, L. (1996). Developmental isolation and subsequent adult behavior of Drosophila paulistorum: III. Alternative rearing. *Behavioral Genetics, 26,* 27–37.

Kim, Y. K., Phillips, D., Chao, T., & Ehrman, L. (2004). Developmental isolation and subsequent adult behavior of *Drosophila paulistorum*: VI. Quantitative variation of cuticular hydrocarbons. *Behavioral Genetics, 34,* 385–394.

Knowles, L. L., & Markow, T. A. (2001). Sexually antagonistic coevolution of a postmating-prezygotic reproductive character in desert Drosophila. *Proceedings of the National Academy of Sciences of the United States of America, 98,* 8692–8696.

Kodric-Brown, A., & Nicoletto, P. F. (2001). Age and experience affect female choice in the guppy (*Poecilia reticulata*). *American Naturalist, 157,* 316–323.

Kokko, H., Jennions, M. D., & Brooks, R. (2006). Unifying and testing models of sexual selection. *Annual Review of Ecology, Evolution, and Systematics, 37,* 43–66.

Kokko, H., & Monaghan, P. (2001). Predicting the direction of sexual selection. *Ecology Letters, 4,* 159–165.

Lewontin, R. C. (1970). The units of selection. *Annual Review of Ecology and Systematics, 1,* 1–18.

MacFarlane, G. R., Blomberg, S. P., Kaplan, G., & Rogers, L. J. (2007). Same-sex sexual behavior in birds: Expression is related to social mating system and state of development at hatching. *Behavioral Ecology, 18,* 21–33.

Markow, T. A. (2002). Perspective: Female remating, operational sex ratio, and the arena of sexual selection in Drosophila species. *Evolution, 56,* 1725–1734.

Markow, T. A. (2011). "Cost" of virginity in wild Drosophila melanogaster females. *Ecology and Evolution, 1*, 596–600.

Marler, C. A., Foran, C., & Ryan, M. J. (1997). The influence of experience on mating preferences of the gynogenetic Amazon molly. *Animal Behaviour, 53*, 1035–1041.

Maynard Smith, J., & Szathmáry, E. (1997). *The major transitions in evolution*. New York: Oxford University Press.

McLain, D. K. (1992). Population density and the intensity of sexual selection on body length in spatially or temporally restricted natural populations of a seed bug. *Behavioral Ecology and Sociobiology, 30*, 347–356.

Nicoletto, P. F. (1995). Offspring quality and female choice in the guppy, *Poecilia-Reticulata. Animal Behaviour, 49*, 377–387.

Parker, G. A., Baker, R. R., & Smith, V. G. F. (1972). The origin and evolution of gamete dimorphism and the male-female phenomenon. *Journal of Theoretical Biology, 36*, 529–553.

Pigliucci, M. (2005). Evolution of phenotypic plasticity: Where are we going now? *Trends in Ecology and Evolution, 20*, 481–486.

Pitnick, S., & Markow, T. A. (1994a). Large-male advantages associated with costs of sperm production in *Drosophila hydei*, a species with giant sperm. *Proceedings of the National Academy of Sciences of the United States of America, 91*, 9277–9281.

Pitnick, S., & Markow, T. A. (1994b). Male gametic strategies: Sperm size, testes size, and the allocation of ejaculate among successive mates by the sperm-limied fly *Drosophila pachea* and its relatives. *American Naturalist, 143*, 785–819.

Pitnick, S., Markow, T. A., & Spicer, G. S. (1995). Delayed male maturity is a cost of producing large sperm in *Drosophila. Proceedings of the National Academy of Sciences of the United States of America, 92*, 10614–10618.

Pitnick, S., Spicer, G. S., & Markow, T. A. (1995). How long is a giant sperm? *Nature, 375*, 109–109.

Platt, J. (1964). Strong inference. *Science, 146*, 347–353.

Poulin, R. (1994). Mate choice decisions by parasitized female upland bullies, *Gobiomorphus breviceps. Proceedings of the Royal Society of London. Series B, Biological Sciences, 256*, 183–187.

Reynolds, J. D., & Gross, M. R. (1992). Female mate preference enhances offspring growth and reproduction in a fish, *Poecilia-Reticulata. Proceedings of the Royal Society of London. Series B, Biological Sciences, 250*, 57–62.

Schlichting, C., & Pigliucci, M. (1998). *Phenotypic evolution: A reaction norm perspective*. Sunderland, MA: Sinauer Associates.

Snook, R. R., & Markow, T. A. (1996). Possible role of nonfertilizing sperm as a nutrient source for female *Drosophila pseudoobscura Frolova* (*Diptera: Drosophilidae*). *Pan-Pacific Entomologist, 72*, 121–129.

Snook, R. R., & Markow, T. A. (2001). Mating system evolution in sperm-heteromorphic *Drosophila. Journal of Insect Physiology, 47*, 957–964.

Snook, R. R., Markow, T. A., & Karr, T. L. (1994). Functional-nonequivalence of sperm in *Drosphophia pseduoobscura. Proceedings of the National Academy of Sciences of the United States of America, 91*, 11222–11226.

Snyder, B. F., & Gowaty, P. A. (2007). A reappraisal of Bateman's classic study of intrasexual selection. *Evolution, 61*, 2457–2468.

Sutherland, W. J. (1985). Chance can produce a sex difference in variance in mating success and account for Bateman's data. *Animal Behaviour, 33*, 1349–1352.

Tang-Martinez, Z., & Ryder, B. T. (2005). The problem with paradigms: Bateman's worldview as a case study. *Integrative and Comparative Biology, 45*, 821–830.

Trivers, R. L. (1972). Parental investment and sexual selection. In B. Campbell (Ed.), *Sexual selection and the descent of man* (pp. 136–179). Chicago: Aldine.

West-Eberhard, M. J. (2003). *Developmental plasticity and evolution*. Oxford, UK: Oxford University Press.

Young, L. C., Zaun, B. J., & VanderWerf, E. A. (2008). Successful same-sex pairing in Laysan albatross. *Biology Letters, 4*, 323–325.

# SECTION TWO

## MOTHERS AND PARENTING

# 5

# Mothers, Traditions, and the Human Strategy to Leave Descendants

KATHRYN COE AND CRAIG T. PALMER

> There are no incentives to individualistic invention or creativity in
> Ojibwa culture. [Myths] ... are "repeated, not invented."
> —Hallowell, 2002, pp. 80–81

## Introduction

Jane Lancaster (1991), in her paper "A Feminist and Evolutionary Biologist Looks at Women," argues that the human female reproductive strategy is characterized by a phenotypic and behavioral plasticity that was a result of having to adjust to shifts in available social and physical resources. Individual females, by adjusting their reproductive investments in unique ways to those environmental shifts, could optimize access to resources. This view of the role of female reproductive behavior is consistent with, and can be seen as a subset of, the widely accepted view that human behavior is highly plastic and that human culture is "built for speed" (Richerson & Boyd 2000, p. 1). In other words, natural selection favored an increasing reliance on socially learned and individually unique behaviors because they allowed for creativity—that is, they allowed for greater changes in human behavior from one generation to the next.

While we agree with Lancaster that female reproductive patterns have been crucial in the recent evolution of our species and that they are context driven because there was fluctuation in the various environments in which our ancestors lived, we carefully examine the meaning of the term" behavioral plasticity." If behavioral plasticity is defined as the development of alternative phenotypes that improve fitness in response to environmental changes (see Relyea, 2001), or as implying creativity, change, and individualism, then the evidence regarding maternal behavior that is found in the ethnographic record is perplexing (see quote at the beginning of this chapter). Instead of seeing significant variation in maternal behavior from one year to another or one generation to another over time, in response to environmental contingencies, we find that human mothers apparently developed a strategy that worked—that is, it was successful in leaving descendants across environments and generations. Indeed, a great deal of ethnographic evidence indicates that while many aspects of maternal behavior involve social learning, the basic strategies used are consistent across cultures. These strategies involve building and sustaining, over the lifetime, social relationships that are crucial to the transmission of information from one generation to the next, important in protecting and providing for fragile offspring, and, as we argue in this chapter, appear to be aimed at reducing and constraining the potential ways that the behavior of offspring could potentially vary from the behavior of their mothers.

If we define traditions as "the continuation of behavioral practices across generations through social learning" (Fragaszy & Perry, 2003, p. 1), rather than by formalized codes of conduct or belief systems, then other species, particularly those with extended parental care (birds, cetaceans, rodents, and primates—Japanese macaques, orangutans, chimpanzees, and capuchin monkeys), can be said to have traditions. In some cases, chimpanzee and orangutans, traditions can be quite complex (van Schaik, 2002). Unfortunately, identifying the precise factors involved in the transmission of traditions (e.g., how does social learning work?) has been shown to be difficult (King, 1994); however, it is probably safe to assume that many traditions are learned from one's caretakers and that the traditional skills demonstrated by older females are copied, or replicated by, younger females when they encounter the same situation that requires use of those skills. To the extent a female learns to be an alloparent, to provide one example, she presumably learned the skills by observing older conspecific females caring for immature offspring. Similarly, males would often learn their skills through close contact with older conspecific males (see Agostini & Visalbergh, 2005). These traditions, while having adaptive value, also can be quite fragile and can go extinct if something, such as death and/or habitat loss, disrupts the transmission process (van Schaik, 2002).

Before we begin, we now need to clarify the meaning of words like social learning, change, creativity, and persistence and tradition. In its broadest sense, social learning refers to behavior acquired by one individual observing or paying attention to another individual who behaves differently (Box, 1994). While there is a great deal of controversy, social learning generally is not seen as merely a passive process involving copying because, for one reason, the development of a level of skill requires repeated practice and the effect of the behavior—the consequences it can evoke—will influence whether or not the act is replicated (Galef, 1992). The word "creativity" is regularly used in a number of senses. One usage is related to the idea of change; creativity, for these scholars, is thought or behavior that leads to changes in culture, in the sense of invention and development of novel ideas and artifacts (Craft, 2003). Other scholars, however, use the word creativity to refer to thoughtfulness or the ability to direct one's own actions (Masini, 1994). This use of the term in this case does not imply change. We are arguing that mothers have used the second kind of "creativity" to limit the kind of change implied by the first kind of "creativity," and thus allow for cultural persistence and tradition. Further, although persistence and tradition are sometimes used to refer to behaviors that may last for a only few years or generations, we are emphasizing that some practices last thousands and even tens of thousands of years, transmitted from one generation of kin to the next.

We use the cross-cultural record to build our argument that, "the notion of creativity [in the sense of change] may be value laden and culture-specific" (Craft, 2003, p. 113) "with a strong emphasis on individuality and the value it places on being able to think independently of social norms" (p. 120) and that human behaviors, including traditional female reproductive behaviors, have resisted the change that this kind of creativity often implies. A mother has, as Masini (1994) writes, "the creative capacity to keep her culture alive despite an environment that seems bent on crushing it" (p. 52). This means that any tendencies that humans, at least human mothers, had to monitor the environment and change their behavior in response, was largely restrained by culture. Thus we argue that although human mothers were indeed monitoring the environment and were indeed active agents in the human evolutionary process, this process, rather than instigating cultural change, apparently involved making a large investment in building and sustaining social relationships that are necessary for the transmission of information from one generation to the next, and actively restraining creativity and cultural change.

This focus on traditions—on placing restraints on change—is counter to normal approaches to the evolution of culture, and indeed counter to what many people living in modern societies tend to view as worth studying. People living in modern societies tend to value innovation highly, while viewing the continuity with past forms of behavior as somehow inferior, and often undesirable. This can be seen in Diamond's (2001, p. 24) reference to the new forms of culture originating about 35,000 years ago, as "the Great Leap Forward." Given this prejudice, it seems clear that in this case, as in all of science, it is crucial to separate the question of the role played by mothers in evolution—whether this role involved increasing or decreasing culture change—from any assumptions we bring to the table regarding what behaviors are desirable.

Current evolutionary explanations of culture also tend to see cultural change as an *active process* involving such activities as "the hard work of invention" (Schiffer, 2005, p. 485), or as due to the operation of various cultural transmission biases (Henrich, 2001, p. 992), or even random copying errors (Lipo & Eerkins, 2005, p. 316). Cultural persistence, or the lack of cultural change from one generation to the next, is seen as merely a *passive state* that occurs when the active processes of change are not taking place. Our view reverses this common view that cultural continuity is merely evidence of failure in the difficult process of innovation, and replaces it with the view that at least some forms of cultural change are the consequence of failure of the difficult process of cultural preservation. That is, the modification in thinking that we are suggesting involves viewing the *absence of cultural change as also being the result of an active process*, instead of merely a *passive state* that exists when the active processes of change are not taking place. This view is compatible with Campbell's (1975, p. 1105) observation that in cultural evolution, deviation from tradition "seems unproblematic" because "there has no doubt always been a sufficient raw dross of both haphazard and 'intelligent' variations on the social tradition to provide the 'mutations' or 'trials' the process requires, imperfect transmissions of tradition being only one source," while it is "retention and duplication" that is "more problematic." Although the exact timing of changes in the amount and role of traditions in human behavior remains an intriguing question for future study, as it extends far beyond the scope of this paper, we suggest the following very rough time line. Copying, and thus replicating, the behavior of parents (especially mothers) has played a large role in many species of mammals for millions of years (see Avital & Jablonka, 2001). However, the technology and ability to survive in varying climates clearly indicate far greater social learning is taking place between parents and offspring in anatomically modern humans by 100,000 years ago than has ever occurred in any other mammalian species. We suggest that a key benefit to traditions sometime between 100,000 years ago and 40,000 years ago was the identification of kin, through such things as ancestral names (e.g., clan and tribal names) and other identifiers of common ancestry, such as tribal dress and or other body decoration. This identification, when combined with traditional behavior that encourages cooperation among those identified as kin, had the crucial advantage of producing cooperation between second and perhaps even third cousins, and thus larger cooperating sets of allies.

While identification of close kin is perhaps possible through such things as phenotype matching, one also would learn who one's close kin are through interactions centered, initially, around a shared mother. When traditions that allow for kin identification (e.g., descent names, body decoration, or stories that trace kinship links back to a distant ancestor) are passed down through many generations they can come to identify many distant cousins as kin. Indeed, such traditional practices typically come to identify individuals as kin even when they live far away. People living in modern, nontraditional societies tend to think of kin as a small subset of a much larger gathering of non-kin who cooperate because they belong to the same "society." Therefore it takes some effort to conceptualize that during this period of human evolution the only people cooperating together were kin, and they were doing so because they identified each other as kin and had been influenced by other traditions to be kind to kin. As these traditions were transmitted to each generation of descendants, the number of individuals a person could cooperate with increased because their number of kin increased.

Traditions identified kin, and the cooperation among those kin created "society." That is, traditions created a social environment for offspring which consisted of numerous cooperating kin who acted as the teachers, protectors, and providers of those costly human offspring. These larger networks of kin would also be advantageous in hunting, protection from predators, and conflict with both other anatomically modern humans and closely related species. As we argue in a paper on the transition between tribal law and law of the emerging city-states, traditions about how to cooperate with people not identified as kin appear much later (Coe & Palmer, 2008).

The benefits to passing on these traditions, and the resulting increase in population, may have ironically led to what is commonly seen in the new forms of cultural behavior, which started to occur around 35,000 years ago, and which Diamond refers to as "the Great Leap Forward." The items perhaps most often used to mark this cultural "takeoff" are art and burials, both of which are hypothesized to indicate the presence of religion. Although the initial appearance of any cultural behavior is, by definition, a form of cultural change and a deviation from previous cultural traditions, what is not appreciated is that art and religion were profoundly traditional activities for tens of thousands of years after this initial appearance. Thus, we propose that both art and religious behavior, initially, were indeed new aspects of behavior, but the primary consequence of these behaviors was to dramatically increase the ability of ancestors to pass on traditions much more effectively *through these new traditions*. In other words, these new traditions facilitated the transmission of other traditional behaviors, particularly proper kinship behavior.

Not only were ancestors able to influence their offspring more effectively through traditional art and traditional religious rituals, but they were able to influence their offspring to pass on these same traditional behaviors to their own offspring more effectively, and so on and so forth through many more generations than was previously possible (for a discussion of traditional art see Coe, 2003, and for the consequence of traditional religious behavior see Palmer, 2010; Steadman & Palmer, 2008).

This enabled the members of subsequent generations to identify far more distant relatives as kin, and thus greatly increased the size of cooperating allies. An irony here is that the origin of the new behaviors of art and religion may have been the success that previous traditions had in increasing the number of surviving descendants. However, eventually, as the population of humans increased, humans became more likely to encounter other humans who, due to the lack of recent common ancestry, had developed somewhat different traditions. This exposure to different traditions, as anthropologists have long noted (see discussion in Cameron, 1990), may have further stimulated the new ideas of such aspects of culture as art and religion and subsequent cultural change.

Regardless of what caused the origin of art and religion or when that origin occurred and/or was evident in the archaeological record, it is clear that religion and art were highly traditional for tens of thousands of years from the time of their origin to the time of the first city-states (Coe, 2003; Coe & Palmer, 2006). It is also clear that these city-states brought together sets of codescendants, once called tribes, now often referred to as ethnic groups, thus introducing new ideas and practices and resulting in changes in behavior. The changes seen in classical Greece and Rome are clear evidence of such a process. The "dark ages" then represent a relative return to tradition resulting from the power of a relatively homogeneous religion in much of Europe (Coe, 2003), which brought with it traditions encouraging cooperation among non-kin at least partially though the use of metaphorical kinship terms (e.g., we are brothers and sisters, all children of God the father). The "Renaissance" may be seen as another end, or "death," of many traditions in Europe, as much as it is a rebirth of cultural innovation and change (Coe, 2003). The various "revolutions" (e.g., political, industrial, informational) since that time are typically further accelerations of tradition abandonment.

If our view is correct, an examination of the mechanisms that preserve cultural traditions, and the incorporation of these mechanisms into scenarios of human evolution, is warranted. We suggest that such mechanisms do exist, and that mothers have played an integral role in their development and implementation. Indeed, we will argue that mothers were maintaining traditions long before males became engaged in doing so, and that mothers have continued to play at least as large a role as men in maintaining traditions in the vast majority, if not all, traditional cultures.

The goal of this reconsideration of the role of innovation in human evolution is not to replace current theories of technological innovation and culture change, but to supplement them by proposing testable answers to two questions about cultural preservation:

1. How can patterns of cultural behavior remain essentially unchanged over many generations? That is, what are the proximate mechanisms preserving cultural traditions?
2. What was the evolutionary advantage, or advantages, of preserving cultural traditions over many generations?

We will argue that mothers played the major role in preserving cultural traditions, and will provide ethnographic examples of some of the most important ways this was accomplished. In regard to question number two, we will argue that traditions had two distinct evolutionary benefits. First, traditions implied the replication of behaviors that were evolutionarily successful in past generations. This minimized the occurrence of the infinite potential deviations from those traditional behaviors that could prove to be evolutionarily unsuccessful, and promoted the preservations of traits necessary for the gradual accumulation of innovations in succeeding generations. That is, traditions provided cultural evolution with the "descent" part of the concept "descent with modification." Second, the preservation of certain cultural behaviors was necessary for the formation of the *extended networks of cooperating kin* that were crucial to the recent evolutionary success of our species. The failure to find such networks of kin, and the mechanisms we propose to account for their creation, in the ethnographic material would falsify this part of our hypothesis.

# Mothers and the Transmission of Traditions: The "Empress" of the Kitchen, and Beyond

We hope to support our proximate and ultimate explanations by making four specific arguments: (1) mothers, and grandmothers, were the primary transmitters of traditions during most of the vast majority of time humans have existed; (2) the transmission of traditions was important to human existence and evolution; (3) the faithful transmitting of traditions is far from something that just happens when no effort is being expended to change them, but instead requires considerable effort; and (4) the ubiquity and importance of the transmission of traditions during most of human existence is difficult to comprehend because it—along with the honoring of elders and ancestors who created and preserved the traditions— has become so rare in "modern" societies.

## Cooking

Given that our approach deviates from many standard theories about human evolution, we ease into our theory with an example that is both familiar to standard conceptions of motherly behavior and of a time depth where the lack of cultural change may be noteworthy, but not incomprehensible. The setting for our discovery of just such an example could not have been more ironic because it occurred in what must be one of the most novel of human environments, traveling at 600 miles per hour, 35,000 feet over the Atlantic ocean, amid fellow passengers absorbed with technological devices that did not exist the year before. Yet there it was in the in-flight magazine, in an article showing an elderly woman next to the title "Guess Who's Cooking Dinner?" (Raub, 2008). Not only did the word "tradition" appear again and again in the article, the article focused on the behavior of mothers and grandmothers, referred to respectfully as "Empresses":

> Sensing a culinary collapse in her own country, 71-year-old Italian sociology professor Egeria Di Nallo, a Bologna native, teamed with the University of Bologna and the Association for the Guardianship and Exploitation of the *Traditional* Culinary-Gastronomic Heritage of Italy in 2004 and dreamed up a little something called Home Food. Like the name suggests, Home Food is a network of home cooks—mainly Italian

women, known as Cesarine ("*empresses*"), named such as a nod to the mothers, aunts, and grandmothers who have *passed* on the *traditional* recipes of the country through the ages—who are fervently preserving the culinary *traditions* of one of the most gastronomically blessed places on earth. (Raub, 2008; emphasis added)

Then came the perfect intermediary time frame necessary to make these maternally transmitted traditions of sufficient length to be very impressive to modern readers, but not so long as to be unfathomable: "So the next time you are in Bologna, you can forgo the exhaustive search through the university town's lovely medieval streets that ends up with you on the losing end of bad Bolognese, and instead feast on salsiccia passita (traditional pork sausage) and Bolognese-style veal cutlet, a recipe that first appeared in local cookbooks in *800 AD*" (Raub, 2008; emphasis added).

The fact that the transmission of these important recipes is performed by "empresses" is consistent with our first premise, that women were the primary transmitters of traditions, or as the article phrased it: "the people who are *repositories of the ancient knowledge* of our cookery" (Raub, 2008; emphasis added). The very existence of the "Home Food" program supports our second premise that the transmission of traditions, at least to those wanting to eat high quality but home-like (note: important that it is home-cooked food—prepared by mothers during childhood!) Italian food, is important. Our third point, that great effort is needed to transmit traditions faithfully, is then given as the reason there is an open niche for the Home Food program: "First of all, it is possible to taste foods prepared *completely traditionally*. Restaurants, since they run businesses and have to optimize resources and time, cannot be as *precise and devoted to tradition* as a *traditional* 'lady of the house' can be" (Raub, 2008; emphasis added). Not only is the replication and transmission of traditions an active process, it is one that requires "devotion."

Finally the article emphasizes the rarity of experiencing something truly traditional:

Each time you step into a Cesarina's home, you are embarking on a *rare* journey of taste that harks back to the region's *traditional* cuisine before it was pierced and prodded by the modern world. In the words of Home Food, you will be "avoiding flights of imagination, fusion, or contamination that have taken the foods away from their *traditional* form. (Raub, 2008; emphasis added)

Traditions in general have been "pierced and probed by the modern world" to the extent that a "rare journey" is required to experience actual traditions of any kind, not just those related to food preparation. Further, traditions have become so scarce and unappreciated that it is a challenge to convince people of their importance: "But perhaps most unbelievable of all is that in the beginning, getting people into the idea of authentic Italian meals in authentic Italian homes took some persuasion. "We must admit that sometimes we were considered a little bit crazy," says Di Nallo. "So the first difficulty was to convince people of the validity of our project. But then, as you can now taste, we did it!" (Raub, 2008). Unfortunately, we cannot provide you with a taste of delicious traditional Bolognese sauce to convince you that our argument that mothers and grandmothers were repositories of ancient knowledge about essentially all aspects of human existence is not crazy, we can only link you to memories of such meals or build a solid argument by using logic and evidence.

Before the transmission of traditional culinary skills is cast off as only a sexist example reinforcing the triviality of male created stereotypes of the role of women, remember that eating is a fairly important aspect of human existence. As primatologist Richard Wrangham (2009) argues in *Catching Fire: How Cooking Made Us Human*, cooking gave early humans an advantage over other primates as it increased the quality of the diet, thus leading to larger brains and more leisure time. Thus, traditional ways of cooking may have represented one of the very ancient and crucial traditions in human evolution. Further, keep in mind that many other aspects of human culture (e.g., moral rules, history of their people, role of elders) are transmitted during the hours of interaction devoted to transmitting such seemingly mundane activities as food preparation (Coe, 2003). Foremost among these aspects of culture that accompanied the transmission of behaviors like cooking were stories about proper social behavior (Coe, 2003).

However, lest the reader still assume that we are being biased in describing women as doing the cooking, a review of all the African cultures included in the Human Relations Area Files (HRAF) search (N = 39), indicates that women are mentioned as the cooks in all the ethnographies that addressed cooking. Typical of the descriptions is this: "The preparation of food is a woman's task" (Tallensi; Fortes & Fortes, 1936, p. 261), or "women's work" (Mendi; Leach, 1994, p. 77), "Nkundo's wife is to him the person who will attend to the satisfaction of his daily needs with respect to nourishment" (Mongo; Hulstaert & Vizedom, 1938, p. 20), and "cooking belongs to the women's sphere of life" (Bena; Culwick, Culwick, & Kiwanga, 1935, p. 380), and, finally, "the preparation of food by churning, pounding, grinding, cooking are brewing are the exclusive privilege of women" (Evans-Pritchard, 1951, p. 129). Cooking stopped being a woman's responsibility only when she grew very old, and her hands became unsteady while cooking (Cox & Mberia, 2004).

The ethnographic record makes it clear, however, that cooking was not a passive role for women. For example, Zande males report "We don't have any usual meal times, we eat when our wives decide to cook" (Culwick, 1950, pp. 50–51). Women among the Bunyoro were actively involved in teaching cooking skills to their daughters (Nyakatura & Kwamya, 1970, pp. 41, 204) and, while doing so, "whisper tales to one another about men" and teach their daughters what they must know about marriage and sexual relations (Calame-Griaule, 1986, p. 114). So important was the accuracy of the replication that mothers spent a considerable amount of time teaching their daughters. Ames (n.d., p. 73) reports that Wolof girls "learn adult patterns of work at an early age. The girls learn from their mothers by observation and imitation, except for instruction in cooking certain dishes which are quite difficult to prepare." Yet another indication that women were actively not passively involved in cooking is the fact that women did not have to "put up" with a husband who eats so much of what she cooks that there is nothing left for her or who "does not eat what she cooks" (Barundi; Palume, 1963, p. 200).

Any exceptions, which might lead to a male doing the cooking, such as times when his wife was bedridden, were likely to be met with disapproval (Libyan Bedouin; Abu-Lughod, 1989, p. 47). Many ethnographers mention the sexual division of labor and how ignoring that division has consequences. In Bagisu society, for example, "there is a distinct division of labor between men and women" and generally the women are responsible for preparing meals; if a man tried to cook, he could be ridiculed (Beierle, 2004, p. 6). Heald (1989, p. 150) reported that among the Bagisu, "age mates acted as guardians of the male division of labor and would beat or fine one of their number who was caught doing 'women's work', such as cooking." Among the Mendi, such a man would be called a *nyahagbahama*, or woman-like man (Bledsoe, 1990, p. 286). Only among the Tallensi were men clearly said to cook and then "only on ritual and special occasions and, as a rule, out of doors" (Fortes & Fortes, 1936, p. 261).

## Traditional Stories

Hand wrote that "I have always thought the oldest profession was that of professional story teller" (1996, p. 17). However, before there was any division of labor and specialization sufficient for anyone to qualify as a professional anything, mothers telling stories to their descendants, and telling those descendants to repeat the stories to their own descendants, was crucial to human existence. Perhaps the best insight into these stories comes from the mythology of Australian Aboriginal people.

These stories are "simple and brief accounts of the lives of the totemic ancestors" (Strehlow, 1947, p. 1). That is, the ancestors were made more interesting by their association with certain species of plants or animals (Palmer et al., 2008). The traditional stories about totemic ancestors were passed for so many generations that they are often claimed to have originated in a time so ancient that it is known as the "Dreaming." As Clarke explained, "Whenever I have asked Aboriginal people to explain the Dreaming they have mostly responded in the same manner; it is the story of their old ways, how the land was formed, what they used to do and what they learned from their grandparents generation about their Ancestors" (Clarke, 2003, p. 16). Although there are many different types of

Aboriginal myths, not only were many myths clearly "charters" for moral behavior (Hiatt, 1975, pp. 5–7) but also they emphasized that moral behavior included the faithful copying of traditions. Thus, as was true in the case of the recipes prepared by the Italian culinary empresses and by the African cooks, great effort was taken to "preserve the original myth in its traditional form through the passing centuries" (Strehlow, 1947, p. 1).

The hard work involved in a child's efforts to copy a parent (Castro & Toro, 2004) is significant. Just as it can take considerable time and effort to learn how to cook, copying traditional stories and the associated rituals from one generation to the next also requires considerable time and effort. Nganyintja Ilyatjari, "a prominent Pitjantjatjara woman who lived her early years in a largely traditional setting" (Edwards, 1998, p. viii), describes a specific ritualized type of traditional storytelling method, used by *Pitjantjatjara* women, and known as *milpatjunanyi*. It involves drawing symbols and placing objects like leaves and stones in the sand to represent people and places of the story with one hand, while rhythmically beating the ground with a stick held in her other hand. Ilyatjari describes both how, and what, she learned from such stories told to her by her mother and father, especially from the stories about how they were related to the water holes and camps created by their Ancestral Totems during the "Dreaming":

> Father and Mother taught us the names of all the places as the whole family together looked after them, brothers, aunts and sisters. We who were related to those places [by virtue of descent from the same Totemic Ancestor that created the places] lived here together...As they taught and taught us we learned about all of the places and their stories...And we learned the stories of the country. They kept telling them again, again and again. Father told me many stories and I learned....as they told story after story I listened and listened and learned. (1998, p. 2)

The most significant identifiable effect of the telling and retelling of these stories was the promotion of kinship cooperation among the participants. Ilyatjari provides specific examples of parents telling their offspring traditional stories that "taught them to share" (1998, p. 4):

> They told these kinds of stories, about a man, or a good child, or a bad child who was hit. A child who was bad was punished. These are the things they taught us using the leaves: living good lives, about a man getting plenty of meat and about sharing everything. They placed leaves also to represent our relationships and moieties. These are people of our moiety, and those are from the other moiety. This is a daughter and this is an uncle. Mother would teach us and we watched. (1998, p. 3)

Edwards concisely summarized the function of these traditional stories by stating, "Through these stories children learned about relationships and behaviours" (Edwards, 1998, p. 5).

Although the concept of the "Dreaming" might seem exotic to most members of modern societies, when viewed from a cross-cultural perspective it is having "no dreaming"—that is, no ancestors—that is the exception to the way humans have lived for many thousands of years. When you have no ancestors, you have no blueprint for how to succeed. According to Stanner, an elderly aboriginal man told him, "White man got no dreaming, Him go 'nother way. White man, him go different, Him got road belong himself" (1956, p. 51). The traditionalness of "traditional" cultures, as illustrated by the Aboriginal peoples of Australia, was obvious to many earlier anthropologists. Kroeber (1948, pp. 256–257) observed that "cultures are...inclined to be persistent ....Even in times of the most radical change and innovation there are probably several times as many items of culture being transmitted from the past as there are being newly devised." The statement by Boas that culture acted as a "restriction of inventiveness" (1955, p. 156) also suggests an active role for metatraditions as a cause of this cultural persistence. It is Frazer, however, who makes the most forceful conclusion about traditional cultures: "No human being is so hidebound by custom and tradition as your democratic savage;... [In such a traditional society] the individual's lot is cast from the cradle to the grave in the iron mold of hereditary custom" (Frazer, 1979, p. 352).

It is unfortunate that Frazer combined his description of the pervasiveness of traditional behavior in some cultures with such a negative judgment of those cultures. Frazer's disparaging view of traditional cultures has led to the perception that the word "traditional" is derogatory because it implies "backward" (Douglas, 2003, p. 6). This is why the much-used category of "traditional" culture or society has become "problematic" (Keen, 2004, p.1). The current stigma associated with tradition, combined with the tendency to exaggerate cultural differences (Bloch, 1977), has obscured the apparently universal existence of traditions. Thus, it has prevented an appreciation of the likely importance of traditions in human culture and evolution.

# We Are All Descended From Mothers Who Transmitted Traditions

We suggest that the passing of traditions by mothers had two distinct evolutionary benefits. First, transmitting traditions facilitated the replication of behaviors that were evolutionarily successful in past generations. This minimized the occurrence of the infinite potential deviations from those traditional behaviors that would have been evolutionarily unsuccessful and promoted the preservation of traits necessary for the slow and gradual accumulation of innovations in succeeding generations. That is, mothers transmitting traditions provided cultural evolution with the "descent" part of the concept "descent with modification." Second, the preservation of certain cultural behaviors was necessary for the formation of the *extended networks of cooperating kin* that were crucial to the recent evolutionary success of our species.

Language, including the development of descent names, may have been necessary for the creation of the social environment experienced by humans at least the last 30,000 or 40,000 years. This social environment consisted of webs of cooperative social relationships among individuals identified as kin. These webs cannot be explained by kin selection because they universally far exceeded the small set of very closely related individuals where kin selection would play a major role. While a great deal has been written by anthropologists about the nuances and variations of these large webs of kinship (lineages, clans, moieties, etc.), only one mechanism for their *creation* has been seriously put forth (Palmer & Steadman, 1997) and this mechanism *requires* traditional behavior.[1]

Starting at least several tens of thousands of years ago the creation of the social environments of our ancestors required two types of traditions. The *identification* of large numbers of kin requires giving offspring some symbol that they are your descendant, such as a descent name or body decoration including tribal outfits, and influencing your offspring to copy your behavior (see Coe, 2003; Palmer & Steadman, 1997). When, *and only when*, this type of tradition exists and is copied relatively perfectly over many generations do "large lineages or clans...grow up over time as the descendants of the original ancestor/ancestress" accumulate (Fox, 1967, p. 122). Influencing these large numbers of identified descendants to *cooperate* with each other required a second tradition that consisted of influencing your offspring to cooperate with individuals identified as kin and to copy that behavior. The existence of such traditions is succinctly demonstrated by a saying among the Lugbara of Africa: "the rules of social behaviour are the 'words of our ancestors'" (Middleton, 1960, p. 27).

The predictable consequences of these two types of traditions being copied over a great many generations is illustrated by the axiom of kinship amity that "applies to all of the Tiv" (Fortes, 1969, p. 237) where "the whole population of some 800,000 traces descent by traditional genealogical links from a single founding ancestor" (Keesing, 1975, pp. 32–33). The benefit of even much smaller extended networks of kin would exist even in situations where environmental fluctuations were so rapid, or children migrated to environmental patches so different, that "parental generation behavior is a useless guide" (Richerson & Boyd, 2000, p. 7), if indeed such conditions ever existed.

Multiple lines of evidence, biological, archaeological, and historical, indicate that humans have long been wanderers. While this may seem to suggest that over the course of human evolutionary history humans were repeatedly forced to adjust to new ecosystems and that families often have been split by migration, there is strong evidence supporting that until fairly recently—perhaps when cities and trade routes first emerged—groups of kin migrated together. Even today, there is evidence that patterns of migration are highly influenced by kin networks; kin migrate to areas where kin already have settled (Winters, de Janvry, & Sadoulet, 2001) and when highly traditional people migrate, they may migrate en masse, as in the case of the Triquis, who fairly recently migrated from Oaxaca into Northern Mexico to work in agriculture. In these cases, much of the traditional lifestyle is replicated, including traditions guiding kinship and leadership behavior, health practices, and even village layout. In these cases, traditions can be strengthened (Field, 2009).

However, when migrants start modifying their behaviors, and losing their traditions through the process of acculturation, we find something called the Hispanic paradox. While these studies lack both breadth and methodological rigor, there is strong support for claims that acculturation has negative effects and is associated with worse health outcomes; those migrants who have acculturated have a lower health status than do those who are recent migrants (Lara, Gamboa, Kahramanian, Morales, & Bautista, 2005). To account for this phenomenon, Balcazar, Peterson, and Cobas (1996) argue that the breakdown of kinship, or the lack of locally based kinship relationships, may play a role through such things as maternal encouragement of safe health practices and discouragement of high risk behaviors. Highly acculturated Mexican American adolescents, they found, were more likely to have engaged in risk behaviors, including taking illegal substances, and, when pregnant, more likely to experience a fetal or postnatal death. Traditions, particularly those of kinship centered around an involved mother, they and others have argued, provide "protective mechanisms" that shelter pregnant women from adverse health conditions, including the most serious risk factors of pregnancy (Balcazar, Peterson, & Krull, 1997, p. 16; see also Scribner & Dwyer, 1989).

# Conclusion

It should be clear that the fact that women have been the primary transmitters of the traditions discussed in this chapter should not be taken to imply the nonexistence of other traditions that may have been transmitted through both sexes, or primarily through males. Indeed, the obvious existence of such traditions does not change our argument in any way. Further, our argument does not imply anything about what behaviors should or should not be considered "womanly" or "manly" in the future. Information about the role of women in transmitting traditions regarding cooking and storytelling during the past can increase our understanding of human evolution, but it cannot tell us what future patterns of behavior may, at any point in time, seem to be desirable.

We want to emphasize that our focus on the primacy of mothers as opposed to fathers as transmitters of traditions is not done in an attempt to establish that mothers are in any sense better than women without children or better than fathers. To read such a position would be to commit the naturalistic fallacy. Human fathers, as well as mothers, have obviously been transmitting important traditions to their offspring for many centuries of recent human evolution. Aunts and uncles often reinforced this teaching. Our argument for the primacy of mothers is simply based on the fact that human mothers on average probably spent more time with offspring in the past and continue to do so in most cultures today. Further, for much of our earlier evolutionary history, motherly behavior was the only form of parental behavior in our species, although the exact onset of fatherly behavior in our species continues to be a source of great debate (Gibbons, 2009). As Edel and Edel (1957, p. 34) conclude from their cross-cultural study: "Mother take care of your child" is a "universal imperative." While anthropologists have reported variation in mothering behaviors, mothering behaviors are held to be so important that they are seen cross-culturally to generate moral sentiments and to have an "absolute structuring effect on morality, serving as the foundation for restrictions and positive ideas and values" (Edel & Edel, 1957, p. 34).

Feminism is typically seen as a call for change, and a breaking away from traditions and stereotyped sex roles deemed as patriarchal and oppressive to women. Thus, when assertions that women performed activities previously thought to be the domain of men (e.g., hunting, warfare) are made, there appears to be an easy connection between the role women are claimed to have played in human evolutionary history and the sought-after change in contemporary sex roles. In contrast, there is a certain irony in the hypothesis that the underappreciated role of women in recent human evolution is related to an underappreciation of the role of traditions in recent human evolution. This irony is illustrated by the "empress of the kitchen" example, where the "stereotyped domestic role" of women is argued to have been of great importance in human evolution. This irony, however, should not be any cause for concern to those who strive for a future without such gender stereotypes. This is because there is no need to fear that the patterns of behavior favored by natural selection in the past dictate what we should desire or what is possible to achieve in the future. To think otherwise, is to commit the naturalistic fallacy. Indeed, all the accurate knowledge of our evolutionary past can provide us with is knowledge that we can reject or that we can use to create whatever future is deemed desirable.

## Note

1.  For a humorous alternative mechanism see Vonnegut's novel *Slapstick; or, Lonesome no More* (1976), where a character named Dr. Wilbur Daffodil-11 Swain promises to reduce the sterile isolation of modern society by using the computers of the federal government to assign everyone a new middle name and number, thus recreating large webs of kinship like those of our ancestors where everyone is obligated to help fellow clan members.

# References

Abu-Lughod, L. (1989). *Veiled sentiments: Honor and poetry in a Bedouin society.* Berkeley: University of California Press.

Agostini, I., & Visalbergh, E. (2005). Social influences on the acquisition of sex-typical foraging patterns by juveniles in a group of wild tufted capuchin monkeys (*Cebus nigritus*). *American Journal of Primatology, 65,* 335–351.

Ames, D. (n.d.). *Plural marriage among the Wolof in the Gambia: With a consideration of problems of marital adjustment and patterned ways of resolving tensions.* Microfiche HRAF MS30 116 8.

Avital, E., & Jablonka, E. (2001). *Animal traditions: Behavioural inheritance in evolution.* New York: Cambridge University Press.

Balcazar, H., Pererson, G., & Krull, J. (1997). Acculturation and family cohesiveness in Mexican American pregnant women: Social and health implications. *Family and Community Health, 20*(3), 16–31.

Balcazar, H., Peterson, G., & Cobas, J. (1996). Acculturation and health-related risk behaviors among Mexican-American pregnant youth. *American Journal of Health Behavior, 20*(6), 425–433.

Beierle, J. (2004). *Culture summary: Bagisu.* New Haven, CT: HRAF.

Bledsoe, C. (1990). School fees and the marriage process for Mende girls in Sierra Leone. In P. Reeves Sanday & R. Gallagher Goodenough (Eds.), *Beyond the second sex: New directions in the anthropology of gender* (pp. 283–309). Philadelphia: University of Pennsylvania Press.

Bloch, M. (1977). The past and present in the present. *Man* (N.S.), *12,* 278–292.

Boas, F. (1955/1927). *Primitive art.* New York: W. W. Norton.

Box, H. O. (1994). Comparative perspectives in primate social learning: New lessons for old traditions. In J. Roeder, B. Thierry, J. Anderson, & N. Herrenschmidt (Eds.), *Current primatology* (pp. 321–327). Strausbourg, Germany: Université Louis Pasteur.

Calame-Griaule, G. (1986). *Words and the Dogon world* (D. LaPin, Trans.). Philadelphia, PA: Institute for the Study of Human Issues.

Cameron, C. (1990). Avant-gardism as a mode of cultural change. *Cultural Anthropologist, 5*(2), 217–230.

Campbell, D. T. (1975). On the conflicts between biological and social evolution and between psychology and moral tradition. *American Psychologist, 30,* 1103–1126.

Castro, L., & Toro, M. A. (2004). The evolution of culture: From primate social learning to human culture. *Proceedings of the National Academy of Sciences, 101*(27), 10235–10240.

Clarke, P. A. (2003). *Where the ancestors walked: Australia as an Aboriginal landscape.* Crow's Nest, N.S.W., Australia: Allen and Unwin.

Coe, K. (2003). *The ancestress hypothesis.* New Brunswick, NJ: Rutgers University Press.

Coe, K., & Palmer, C. T. (2006). The words of our ancestors: Kinship, tradition, and moral codes. *World Cultures, 16*(1), 2–27.

Coe, K., & Palmer, C. T. (2008). The words of our ancestors: kinship, tradition, and moral codes. *World Cultures* ejournal, University of California at Irvine, 16(1). http://repositories.cdlib.org/wc/worldcultures/vol16/iss1/art1/

Cox, F. M., & Mberia, N. (2004). Aging and elderhood. In C. P. Edwards & B. B. Whiting (Eds.), *Ngecha: A Kenyan village in a time of rapid social change* (pp. 179–214). Lincoln: University of Nebraska Press.

Craft, A. (2003). The limits to creativity in education: Dilemmas for the educator. *British Journal of Educational Studies, 51*(2), 113–127.

Culwick, G. (1950). *A dietary survey among the Zande of the south-western Dudan Khartoum.* Khartoum, Sudan: Agricultural Publications Committee, Ministry of Agriculture, Sudan Government.

Culwick, A., Culwick G., & Kiwanga, T. (1935). *Ubena of the rivers.* London: G. Allen and Unwin.

Diamond, J. (2001). The great leap forward. In P. Whitten (Ed.), *Anthropology: Contemporary perspectives* (8th ed., pp. 24–33). Boston: Allyn and Bacon. (Original work published 1989).

Douglas, B. (2003). Christianity, tradition, and everyday modernity: Towards an anatomy of women's groupings in Melanesia. *Oceania, 74*(1/2), 6–23.

Edel, M., & Edel, A. (1957). *Anthropology and ethics*. Springfield, IL: Charles C. Thomas.

Edwards, W. H. (1998). Leadership in aboriginal society. In W. Edwards (Ed.), *Traditional aboriginal society* (2nd ed., pp. 161–181). South Yarra, Australia: Macmillan Education Australia.

Evans-Pritchard, E. E. (1951). *Kinship and marriage among the Nuer*. Oxford, UK: Clarendon Press.

Field, L. W. (2009). Global indigenous movements. In K. Fine-Dare & S. Rubenstein (Eds.), *Border crossings: Transnational Americanist anthropology* (pp. 230–246). Lincoln: University of Nebraska Press.

Fortes, M. (1969). *Kinship and social order*. Chicago: Aldine.

Fortes, M., & Fortes, S. (1936). *Food in the domestic economy of the Tallensi*. London: Oxford University Press.

Fox, R. (1967). *Kinship and marriage*. Middlesex, UK: Penguin.

Fragaszy, D., & Perry, S. (2003). Towards a biology of traditions. In D. Fragaszy & S. Perry (Eds.), *The biology of traditions: Models and evidence* (pp. 1–32). New York: Cambridge University Press.

Frazer, J. (1979). Sympathetic magic. In W. Lessa & E. Vogt (Eds.), *Reader in comparative religion* (4th ed., pp. 337–352). New York: Harper Collins. (Original work published 1911).

Galef, B. (1992). The question of animal culture. *Human Nature, 3*, 157–158.

Gibbons, A. (2009). Breakthrough of the year: *Ardipithecus ramidus*. *Science, 326*, 1598–1599.

Hallowell, A. I. (2002). *The Ojibwa of Berens River, Manitoba*. Belmont, CA: Wadsworth.

Hand, E. (1996). Writing the supernatural novel. *The Writer, 109*(5), 17–20.

Heald, S. (1989). *Controlling anger: The sociology of Gisu violence*. Manchester, UK: Manchester University Press for the International African Institute.

Henrich, J. (2001). Cultural transmission and the diffusion of innovations: Adoption dynamics indicate that biased cultural transmission is the predominate force in behavioral change. *American Anthropologist, 103*, 992–1013.

Hiatt, L. R. (1975). Introduction. In L. Hiatt (Ed.), *Australian aboriginal mythology* (pp. 1–23). Carlton, N.S.W., Australia: Excelsis Press.

Hulstaert, G., & Vizedom, M. (1938). *Marriage among the Nkundu*. Brussels, Belgium: Librarie falk Fils.

Keen, I. (2004). *Aboriginal economy and society*. South Melbourne, Australia: Oxford University Press.

Keesing, R. (1975). *Kin groups and social structure*. New York: Holt, Rinehart, and Winston.

King, B. (1994). *The information continuum: Evolution of social information transfer in monkeys, apes and hominoids*. Santa Fe, NM: SAR Press.

Kroeber, A. (1948). *Anthropology*. New York: Harcourt, Brace, and Company. (Original work published 1923).

Lancaster, J. B. (1991), A feminist and evolutionary biologist looks at women. *Yearbook of Physical Anthropology, 34*, 1–11.

Lara, M., Gamboa, C., Kahramanian, M. I., Morales, L., & Bautista, D. E. (2005). Acculturation and Latino health in the United States: A review of the literature and its sociopolitical context. *Annual Reviews of Public Health, 26*, 367–397.

Leach, M. (1994). *Rainforest relations: Gender and resource use among the Mende of Gola, Sierra Leone*. Edinburgh, UK: Edinburgh University Press for the International African Institute.

Lipo, C. P., & Eerkens, J. W. (2005). Cultural transmission, copying errors, and the generation of variation in material culture and the archaeological record. *Journal of Anthropological Archaeology, 24*, 316–334.

Masini, E. B. (1994). The creative role of women in a changing world: The case of women in developing countries. *Leonardo, 27*(1), 51–56.

Middleton, J. (1960). *Lugbara religion*. London: Oxford University Press.

Nyakatura, J., & Kwamya Rigby, Z. (1970). *Aspects of Bunyoro custom and tradition*. Nairobi, Kenya: East African Literature Bureau.

Palmer, C. T. (2010). Cultural traditions and the evolutionary advantages of non-innovation. In M. O'Brien & S. Shennan (Eds.), *Innovation in cultural systems: Contributions from evolutionary anthropology* (pp. 161–174). Cambridge, MA: MIT Press.

Palmer, C. T., & Steadman, L. B. (1997). Human kinship as a descendant-leaving strategy: A solution to an evolutionary puzzle. *Journal of Social and Evolutionary Systems, 20*, 39–51.

Palmer, C. T., Steadman, L. B., Cassidy, C., & Coe, K. (2008). Totemism, metaphor, and tradition: Incorporating cultural traditions into evolutionary psychology explanations of religion. *Zygon: Journal of Religion and Science, 43*(3), 713–729.

Palume, D. (1963). Women of Burundi: A study of social values. In D. Palume (Ed.), *Women of tropical Africa* (pp. 179–215). London: Routledge & Kegan Paul.

Raub, K. (2008, July 1). Guess who's cooking dinner? Retrieved March 6, 2010, from http://www.americanwaymag.com/food-egeria-di-nallo-italy-association-for-the-guardianship-and-exploitation-of-the-traditional-culinary

Relyea, R. (2001). The lasting effects of behavioral plasticity. *Ecology, 83*, 1947–1955.

Richerson, P. J., & Boyd, R. (2000). Built for speed: Pleistocene climate variation and the origin of human culture. *Perspectives in Ethology, 13*, 1–45.

Schiffer, M. B. (2005). The devil is in the details: The cascade model of invention processes. *American Antiquity, 70*, 485–502.

Scribner, R., & Dwyer, J. (1989). Acculturation and low birthweight among Latinos in the Hispanic HANES. *American Journal of Public Health, 79*(9), 1263–1267.

Stanner, W. E. H. (1956). The dreaming. In T. Hungerford (Ed.), *Australian signpost* (pp. 51–65). Melbourne, Australia: F. W. Cheshire.

Strehlow, T. G. H. (1947). *Aranda traditions*. Melbourne, Australia: Melbourne University Press.

van Schaik, C. (2002). Fragility of traditions. *International Journal of Primatology, 23*(3), 527–538.

Vonnegut, K. (1976). *Slapstick; or, Lonesome no more*. New York: Delacorte Press.

Winters, P., de Janvry, A., & Sadoulet, E. (2001). Family and community networks in Mexico-U.S. migration. *Journal of Human Resources, 36*(1), 159–184.

Wrangham, R. (2009). *Catching fire: How cooking made us human*. New York: Basic Books.

## 6

# Maternal Effect and Offspring Development

NICOLE M. CAMERON AND JUSTIN R. GARCIA

## Introduction

Motherhood is an important investment for most mammals, particularly for humans. Contrary to males, for which physiological minimal parental investment is simplified to spermatozoids, minimal maternal contribution often involves a long pregnancy (gestation). Of course, for humans, time and energy spent on courtship, copulation to conception patterns, maintenance of long-term socio-sexual pair-bonds, and family expectations all require significant sex-specific efforts as well (Gray & Garcia, 2013). Moreover, as cooperative breeders, human offspring benefit from maternal, paternal, and others' investments (Hrdy, 2009). Yet, there are still many aspects of reproduction specific to maternal investments. For most mammals, reproductive costs to females are far greater than the costs to males. In particular, consider the fetal environment (in utero), birthing, long periods of caring for and in some cases transporting their infant, physical nurturing through lactation, and extended (lactational) amenorrhea, as some of the unique contributions mothers make for their offspring. Humans are no exception, with gestation being approximately 40 weeks and women generally being primary caregivers of children until at least early adolescence. Consequently, it is important to consider the role of motherhood in child development and ultimately in human evolution. In this chapter we use a comparative approach to consider the important role of mothers on the development of their offspring, with the hope of gaining a better understanding of the evolutionary biology of maternal effect.

# A Forecast of Environmental Conditions

From psychologists to geneticists, researchers have long recognized the importance of maternal effects on offspring. Across species, maternal effect is defined as
the influence of the maternal environment (genotype or phenotype) on any component of the phenotype of the offspring apart from the nuclear genes (Bifulco
et al., 2002; Legates, 1972). Such maternal effects have been described across a
variety of species ranging from plants to mammals. Indeed, even in plants, phenotypic response to environmental changes is thought to include nongenomic,
transgenerational, processes that integrate epigenetic and maternal factors such
as organellar processes (Galloway, 2005).

In animals, there are a variety of mechanisms by which maternal effect can
take place: through preloading of messenger RNAs (ribonucleic acid) into unfertil-
ized eggs, through maternal provisioning of a fertilized egg, or through maternal
behaviors such as oviposition, feeding, licking, grooming, and generally caring
for the offspring. Maternal effects are usually mediated via the ecological context (i.e., one's environment). The quality of the prevailing environment, defined
primarily as the abundance of nutrients and the risk for mortality, directly influences mother-offspring interactions. The quality of this interaction will then
influence the life history strategies (e.g., defensive, foraging, reproductive) of the
offspring. Hinde (1986) suggests that such effects are likely due to natural selection having shaped offspring to respond to subtle variations in parental behaviors. Thus, maternal effects are adaptations that forecast the likely environmental
conditions in which offspring shall emerge, develop, and compete for survival
and reproduction themselves. Likewise, Vitzthum (2009) has demonstrated that
women's reproductive biology varies considerably in response to local ecological conditions—adaptively adjusting to environmental pressures throughout a
woman's reproductive life. Taken together, it reasons that offspring outcomes are
a response—often adaptive, but occasionally a byproduct—to variation in maternal physiology and behavior.

## Maternal Investment: Costs and Benefits

In roughly 90% of mammalian species, parental care is provided by the mother
(Hrdy, 1999). Humans are actually quite unique in the amount of paternal care
fathers provide (Gray & Anderson, 2010). Female mammals entering motherhood
must make a series of cost-benefit calculations to evaluate the trade-offs needed
to do what is best for herself versus what is best for her offspring. This represents
the delicate evolutionary balance between survival and reproduction. Pregnancy
and raising offspring may be tremendously costly, and may often affect a female's
health and ability to avoid depredation. For a mother, the price of pregnancy
(utilization of her energy and nutrients to grow offspring), lactation (milk production), and the consequences of changes in her behaviors (e.g., spending more

time feeding, building a nest) have to be worth the ultimate gain: transmitting one's genes to future generations. The risks associated with parturition and raising offspring (e.g., more time foraging, protecting the offspring) need to also be balanced. These behaviors have an impact on the mother's own safety and health. In other words, motherhood affects survival and future reproduction, and thus a female's long-term fitness.

In mammals, maternal investments differ greatly between species. The pregnancy length varies, from a short period of less than 2 weeks in the opossum (12 days) to almost 2 years in the Indian elephant (624 days). The postbirth time spent with offspring can also vary greatly; some species produce fairly mature young (precocial) while others produce helpless young (altricial) that require lots of care. For a species like the rat (with which much laboratory research has been conducted), an almost constant contact with the mother is needed. This is in part because rat offspring cannot regulate their own body temperature or defecate/urinate without the physical stimulation/licking from the mother. In contrast, rabbits only spend approximately 3 minutes per day nursing their young. Human mothers give birth to semiprecocial offspring that can thermoregulate, but still need lots of care and nursing, including (particularly in preindustrial societies) several years of nursing (Dettwyler, 1995; Hrdy, 1999). In rodents, offspring are independent less than a month after birth. In comparison, the investment required of a human mother is enormous; human children take a relatively long time to mature to independence (late childhood). Whatever the magnitude of maternal investment for the female, the effect on offspring often precedes birth and continues long after.

## Effects on Offspring Development

Maternal gauge of the environment can influence reproduction in a variety of ways, with some arguing environmental assessment can even partially determine biological sex of offspring. Trivers and Willard (1973) proposed that breeding success among males is more variable than among females, thus reasoning that maternal condition should skew offspring sex ratios based on local ecology. This adaptive offspring sex ratio adjustment has been documented in several species. As an example, higher maternal rank is associated with birth of more sons than daughters in red deer (Clutton-Brock, Albon, & Guinnes, 1984). Local resource competition (among kin) in the galago "bush babies" also results in male-biased sex ratio, possibly to promote a greater proportion of offspring that are the dispersing sex for this species', which will leave the low local resource area (Clark, 1978). More recent evidence among humans even suggests that in harsh environmental conditions with low resources (i.e., famine), maternal physiology will skew offspring sex ratio to produce more boys than girls (Song, 2012). Similarly, as a possible adaptive shift in secondary sex ratio, between the years 1940 and 1980 in North America, relatively more boys were born than girls during times of war (Ellis & Bonin, 2004).

Early in the development of the embryo, maternal effects begin influencing growth. The fetal programming hypothesis suggests that the prenatal environment can drastically modify the proclivities of the offspring (Cameron, del Corpo, et al., 2008; Phillips, 2002). Maternal food consumption and a mother's overall health and endocrine profile can all affect the development of her offspring. In mammals, maternal nutrition during pregnancy and lactation has a direct impact on the physiology of the offspring. In humans, undernourished mothers yield low birth weight babies, with substantial influence on the short-term morbidity susceptibility of the newborn (Belkacemi, Nelson, Desai, & Ross, 2010). These offspring are also at increased risk of developing cardiovascular disease and diabetes in later adult life (Jansson & Powell, 2007).

In addition to maternal diet, the maternal endocrine milieu also has a major impact on offspring. Maternal stress and sex hormones can cross the feto-placental barrier, an adaptive barrier to prevent teratogens from reaching the fetus. There, hormones can influence fetal development and birth outcomes. Although the feto-placental barrier may be efficient to protect the fetus against low levels of maternal stress hormones (corticosteroids), it has limited effects when the mother is chronically stressed (Welberg, Thrivikraman, & Plotsky, 2005). In turn, exposure to stress during gestation results in alterations of cognitive, endocrine, and neurochemical responses in adult offspring (Bowman et al., 2004). Sex steroids such as estrogens and androgens can affect the development of the embryo in a variety of ways as well. Fetal testosterone may impact gender specific behavior in human children (Hines et al., 2002), with levels of prenatal testosterone associated with gender-typical play behavior (Auyeung et al., 2009). Some have even linked male sexual orientation with fraternal birth order, suggesting that maternal histocompatibility antigens act on the developing fetal brain (Blanchard, 2001). Fetal testosterone's organizational effects on subsequent behavior and morphology persist into adulthood, with examples such as fetal testosterone's effect on 2D:4D, the relative lengths of the index and ring finger (Manning, 2002). High maternal plasma androstenedione levels (a precursor of testosterone and estrogen) are associated with an increased risk for male children to later develop testicular cancer (Holl et al., 2009). Maternal exposure to endocrine disrupting compounds, such as pesticides and chemicals used in the plastics industry, may also have important consequences, including disturbances to a fetus's developing reproductive system (Patisaul & Adewale, 2009). Thus, during fetal development the quality of the maternal compartment has direct short-term and long-term effects on the behavior and health of offspring.

## Nursing

One of the hallmark features of a mammal is production of milk for young, and thus the presence of functional mammary glands in females. Lactation is energetically costly for females. It has been argued that among mammals the costs of lactation to a mother's subsequent survival are greater than the relative fitness costs of the previous gestation (Clutton-Brock et al., 1989). In humans, lactation occurs as a reflex following infant suckling at the nipple. Suckling stimulates activation in the hypothalamus to direct release of oxytocin; oxytocin in turn acts at the mammary gland to produce milk letdown/ejection (Borrow & Cameron, 2012; Nishimori et al., 1996). Nursing young requires substantial time investments, increases potential for depredation, can limit movement, and can potentially occur at a cost to a mother's health, survival, and social interactions. Human nursing, as in several other primates, includes a sizable learning curve for new mothers, suggesting that breastfeeding in humans is not an entirely automatic event (the reasons for which remain unclear; see Volk, 2009). Moreover, lactating/nursing mothers often experience lactational amenhorrhea, or postnatal subfecundity. In humans, like many other mammals, continuous breastfeeding of offspring will typically result in lactational amenorrhea to prevent women from renewing their menstrual cycle after childbirth. Lactational amenorrhea is an adaptation to space pregnancies and allow mothers time to care for initially dependent offspring. Breastfeeding as a natural form of birth control can be rather effective, and is practiced by women cross-culturally (Stuart-Macadam & Dettwyler, 1995). However, the time duration and total number of nursing episodes per day vary considerably among different populations (see Woodbridge, 1995). For instance, iKung mothers have a high average feed frequency of 4.1 episodes of feeding per hour, with each feeding episode lasting 1.9 minutes (Konner & Worthman, 1980); Inuit mothers nurse offspring for an overage of 5 minutes on each breast every 2–3 hours (Berman, Hanson, & Hellman, 1972). Despite maternal costs in time and energy, evidence suggests that breastfeeding is remarkably positive for the growth and development of human offspring (Dettwyler, 1995).

While nursing can be costly to females, it can also help promote the survival of offspring. Some have argued that lactation itself also contributes to maternal effect, by way of "lactational programming"—in other words, providing offspring with a forecast of the environment in which their mother lives (Hinde & Capitanio, 2010; Hinde & Milligan, 2011). Using primate models, Katie Hinde and colleagues have argued that mother's milk has organizational effects on offspring outcomes. In rhesus monkeys, quality of milk varies considerably with respect to ecological demands (Hinde, 2009), and predicts infant behavior and temperament (Hinde & Capitanio, 2010). Moreover, cortisol concentrations in maternal milk have even been linked to offspring behavioral syndromes (Sullivan et al., 2011). As is the case in utero, maternal assessment of the environment in which newborns are nursing can impact growth and development in young. This is possible both by adaptations in the mother to respond to offspring demands, and by offspring responding to honest signals forecasting the environment in which they are likely to develop.

# Laboratory (Rodent) Models of Maternal Care Effects

In mammals and in humans in particular, nervous system development continues after birth. During this sensitive developmental period, maternal care plays a crucial role in influencing brain development and consequently the systems it controls, leading to important effects on behaviors. For example, in rhesus monkeys, infants separated from their mothers at birth and raised in social deprivation become behaviorally disrupted and hyperaggressive individuals in adulthood, and females may become abusive mothers (Harlow, Rowland, & Griffin, 1964; Seay, Alexander, & Harlow, 1964).

Animal models have been extremely useful to help understand the mechanism involved in maternal "programming" of offspring neural and endocrine systems. Forty years ago, Levine, Denenberg, Ader, and others, showed that early experience has a major effect on emotional development and stress reactivity (Ader, 1969; Denenberg, 1963; Levine, 1967). They found that in rats, contrary to long periods of maternal absence, short periods of maternal separation or handling (usually 15–20 minutes daily) lowered the stress reactivity of the offspring. In 1975 Levine hypothesized that this handling paradigm elicits a change in mother-pup interaction that could be responsible for the effects on stress responses (see Cameron, del Corpo, et al., 2008). Twenty years later, a series of studies described by Liu et al. (1997) showed that handling increases maternal care when the pups are returned to their mother. They also reported that the amount of maternal care in rats is correlated with the adequacy of offspring stress responses. We now know that variation in maternal care in rats influences offspring gene expression (Francis, Champagne, Liu, & Meaney, 1999), brain activity (Liu, Diorio, Day, Francis, & Meaney, 2000), function of the endocrine system (Cameron, del Corpo, et al., 2008; Champagne, Weaver, Diorio, Sharma, & Meaney, 2003; Liu et al., 1997), and behaviors (Cameron, Fish, & Meaney, 2008; Champagne & Meaney, 2007). There is no need for a complete maternal deprivation to observe important effects in offspring, as even subtle variations in maternal behavior can produce such change.

In the rat model, there is considerable variation among lactating dams in the amount of maternal care that is given to offspring. Of all the behaviors that can be observed in lactating females, the frequency of pup licking and grooming (LG) over the first week of life is the one that varies the most between dams (Francis, Champagne, et al., 1999; Francis, Diorio, Liu, & Meaney, 1999; Weaver, Cervoni, et al., 2004). This behavior is also important because it stimulates the pup to support thermoregulation. The variations in maternal behavior among dams permit the characterization of different behavioral types: High LG mothers and Low LG mothers (Champagne, Francis, Mar, & Meaney, 2003). Lactating females for which the LG score is 1 standard deviation (SD) greater than the mean of the breeding cohort are deemed to be High LG mothers; those for which the LG scores are 1 SD below the mean are considered Low LG mothers. High LG mothers commonly engage in pup LG at about twice the frequency as Low LG mothers, with this difference only persisting for the first week of life (Champagne, Francis, et al., 2003). Interestingly, this difference in LG frequency is transmitted from mother to female offspring (Champagne, Francis, et al., 2003; Francis, Champagne, et al., 1999). As adults, offspring of High LG mothers show increased pup LG compared to those of Low LG mothers. Differences in pup LG are associated with increased estrogen receptor alpha (ERα) expression in the medial preoptic area (MPOA) (Weaver, Diorio, Seckl, Szyf, & Meaney, 2004), a brain area involved in the display of maternal behaviors. However, the differences in maternal behavior and ERα expression in the MPOA are reversed with cross-fostering (Champagne, Francis, et al., 2003; Francis, Champagne, et al., 1999). When offspring of a Low LG mother is raised by a High LG mother, the adult offspring maternal behavior is similar to the High LG mother, and the opposite is also true for female offspring raised by Low LG mothers. In contrast to the findings in the MPOA, ERα expression is significantly increased in the ventromedial hypothalamus (VMH) and the anteroventral paraventricular nucleus (AVPv) in the offspring of Low LG mothers (Cameron, del Corpo, et al., 2008). This suggests that variations in mother-pup interactions directly alter the expression of genes in the brain (particularly the ERα promoter) that regulate maternal behavior of female offspring, and serve as the basis for nongenomic transmission of individual differences in maternal behaviors (Brouette-Lahlou, Godinot, & Vernet-Maury, 1999; Champagne, Weaver, et al., 2003; Francis et al., 2002; van Hasselt et al., 2012).

The VMH and AVPv are important for the control of ovulation and sexual behavior in the rat. Some hormones (luteinizing hormone and progesterone) involved in the reproductive system show a greater level of release in female rats that receive lower levels of maternal care (Cameron, del Corpo, et al., 2008). This is also associated with a greater motivation to mate, and the display of more receptivity toward males (Cameron, Fish, et al., 2008) compared to female offspring that receive higher levels of maternal care. Female offspring of Low LG mothers also display an earlier onset of puberty (Cameron, del Corpo, et al., 2008). Not surprisingly, the Low LG females are also more capable of reproducing under laboratory conditions (Cameron, del Corpo, et al., 2008). These findings demonstrate the importance of maternal care on the development of the reproductive function and the expression of sexual behavior in the rat. See Table 6.1 for a summary of maternal effects in rat offspring and see Cameron (2011) for review.

## Transgenerational Effects

The quality of the prevailing environment regulates maternal investment, which in turn, is reflected in the mating and maternal behavior of the offspring. If this is true, then conditions that favor early sexual development in human females

*Table 6.1* **Summary of differences between high licking/grooming (High LG) and low licking/grooming (Low LG) offspring**

| Measure | Findings | Low vs. High LG |
|---|---|---|
| Stress/Fear | Startle response | > |
| Behaviors | Fear of novelty | > |
| Cognition | Learning and memory | < |
| Sexual Behavior | Receptivity | > |
| | Motivation | < |
| Development | Onset of puberty | > |
| Estrogen Receptor | Medial preoptic area | < |
| alpha Expression | Ventromedial hypothalamus | > |
| | Anteroventral paraventricular Hypothalamus | > |
| Sex Hormones | Progesterone | > |
| | Luteinizing hormone | > |
| Maternal Behavior | LG behavior with own offspring | < |

should also diminish parental care of offspring. Further, decreased parental investment in female offspring should result in a comparable pattern of parenting in daughters. As in the rat and other species, in humans there is evidence that individual differences in maternal care are transmitted across generations (Francis, Diorio, et al., 1999; Maestripieri, 1999). Conditions that characterize abusive and neglectful homes such as economic hardship, marital strife, and a lack of social and emotional support, all breed individuals who themselves are more likely to become neglectful parents. The best predictor of perpetrating child abuse or child neglect is the parents' own parent-child history. Even measures of parent-child attachment are highly correlated across generations of mothers and daughters (Miller et al., 1997). There is also strong evidence for the transmission of stable individual differences in maternal behavior in nonhuman primates (Maestripieri, 1999). Since parenting influences pubertal development, such factors may also contribute to the observed correlation between the age of menarche in the mother and that of her daughter (Chang & Chen, 2008).

# Effects on Female Reproductive Function

There is also strong evidence of parental and particularly maternal effects on reproductive development in humans, especially on the timing of puberty in females (much as in nonhuman animal models). Both poor nutrition and high rates of infection have been shown to favor a delay in the onset of puberty, likely due to valuable energetic costs (Ellison, 2003; Eveleth & Tanner, 1990; MacDonald, 1999; Worthman, 1999). In Western industrialized societies, low socioeconomic status predicts earlier onset of puberty in females independently of father's absence (Downing & Bellis, 2009). Such effects are difficult to relate to more biologically tangible factors such as nutrition and immune function. Instead, there is strong psychobiological support for parental effects on reproductive development in females.

Jay Belsky and colleagues (Belsky, 2010; Belsky, Steinberg, & Draper, 1991; Jansson & Powell, 2007) suggested that environmental adversity is associated with a decreased quality of parental care that leads to early menarche (onset of menstruation) and sexual activity in girls. Insecure attachment, child neglect, and child abuse are more prevalent in populations living under impoverished conditions (Griffin & Harlow, 1966; Harlow & Harlow, 1966), and there is strong evidence for familial influences, including mother-daughter relationship, on sexual maturation in human females (Parera & Surís, 2004). In contrast, familial cohesion and increased parental investment (e.g., time spent with children) is associated with a later onset of puberty (Ellis & Garber, 2000; Romans, Martin, Gendall, & Herbison, 2003). Importantly, early menarche predicts a younger age at first intercourse (Andersson-Ellstrom, Forssman, & Milsom, 1996; Bingham, Miller, & Adams, 1990; Phinney, Jensen, Olsen, & Cundick, 1990; Udry & Cliquet, 1982), first pregnancy, and age at birth of first child (Roosa, Tein, Reinholtz, & Angelini, 1997; Ryder & Westoff, 1971; Udry & Cliquet, 1982). Likewise, an impoverished family environment predicts an earlier onset of sexual activity (Rychtarikova, 1986). Earlier puberty onset is also associated with increased risk-taking (e.g., alcohol use, smoking, drug abuse; Downing & Bellis, 2009) and sexual risk (e.g., frequency of vaginal sex, unplanned pregnancy; Belsky, Steinberg, Houts, & Halpern-Felsher, 2010).

These findings suggest an evolutionary pathway from environmental adversity (and effects on parental well-being) to parent-child interactions, and subsequent effects on reproductive development in offspring, particularly females (see Belsky, 2012). This is also likely due to the fact that natural selection has shaped offspring to respond to subtle variations in parental care as a forecast of the environmental conditions they will ultimately face following independence from the parent (Groothuis, Muller, von Engelhardt, Carere, & Eising, 2005; Hinde, 1986). The rationale for such "phenotypic plasticity" is that under high-risk environmental conditions, when the probability of extended periods of growth and survival are low, the optimal strategy is to shift efforts to maximize the number of offspring through accelerated mating, increasing the chances that at least some offspring will survive to reproductive maturity. Moreover, since adverse environments are characterized by high, unavoidable risks, additional maternal investment in offspring quality is seen as less important (Coall & Chisholm, 2003). The trade-off, then, is that increased risk of mortality favors a shift in maternal investment toward quantity of offspring (Coall & Chisholm, 2003; Gangestad & Simpson, 2000). In contrast, more favorable environmental conditions favor greater investment in individual offspring at the cost of mating. In these environments, offspring quality predicts successful competition for available resources and is thus relevant to an individual's reproductive fitness.

# The r/K Reproductive Strategies

Variations in reproductive phenotypes as just discussed are reminiscent of r and K reproductive strategies (Pianka, 1970), which reflect conditional adaptations of a female's investment in offspring. The r strategy emphasizes mating effort to maximize the quantity of offspring. The K strategy emphasizes parental care and the quality of offspring. Studies of phenotypic variation in mating tactics reveal that both strategies are often represented within the same species depending on prevailing environmental conditions (Gross, 1996; Rhen & Crews, 2002) and are reflected in within-sex variations in reproductive function. There are considerable within-sex variations in reproductive tactics among members of the same species in insects, amphibians, fish, birds, and mammals, which suggests that evolutionary pressures produce phenotypic diversity resulting in a range of conditional reproductive strategies, rather than a single optimal strategy for males or females (Gangestad & Simpson, 2000; Gross, 1996; Rhen & Crews, 2002). This is consistent with cross-species models in evolutionary biology (Dugatkin, 2009). Reproductive fitness is determined by the ability to survive to sexual maturity, reproduce, and rear viable offspring to reproductive age. Success reflects time and energy investments in the reproductive processes, as well as in growth and survival. Almost all resources are limited; energetic allocation for survival ultimately limits investment in reproduction. The challenge every reproducing individual must thus face is to establish the most effective investment strategy. The efficacy of any such potential solution inevitably varies across environments. There is no static optimal strategy—one phenotype does not fit all ecological conditions.

## Early Socioemotional Relationship Experience and Development

Most developmental theories (e.g., attachment theory, Bowlby, 1958; psychoanalytic theory, Freud, 1940; neo-Freudian psychoanalytic theory, Horney, 1950) stress the importance of early socioemotional relationship experiences for the expression of normal social and psychological development. Parental behaviors such as emotional support, mutuality, synchrony, and appropriate reciprocal social exchange are related to child secure attachment (Bakermans-Kranenburg, van IJzendoorn, & Juffer, 2003). Maternal responsiveness and secure attachment during infancy predict better social and mental abilities later in life (Bradley, Corwyn, Burchinal, McAdoo, & García Coll, 2001). The importance of maternal-child interaction for the development of a healthy child has been well documented (Feldman, 2007), typically emphasizing social and emotional development. For instance, insecure attachment is related to increased behavioral problems later in life (Stams, Juffer, & van IJzendoorn, 2002).

The quality of the caregiver (mothers or others) can also be important for physical development. A recent study has emphasized the role of early caregiver-child social-emotional relationship experiences in the physical development of institutional children (Team, 2008). The study took place in St. Petersburg, Russian Federation, in orphanages that were acceptable with respect to medical care, nutrition, sanitation, and safety, but lacking with respect to social-emotional relationship experience between caregivers and children. Two interventions were implemented to promote positive social-emotional relationships and warm, caring, responsive caregiver-child interactions. The first concerned training of the caregiver in basic child development aimed at improving caregiver-child relationship during routine caregiving chores. The second consisted in structural changes such as reduced group size, changes in schedules and implementation of primary caregivers designed to spend most waking hours with a particular group of children. These interventions were aimed to promote caregiver-child attachment and relationship. One institution received both training and structural changes, another received only training, and a last one had no intervention. The results of this study demonstrated a general improvement in children's development during the first few years of life from the orphanage that received both interventions over the orphanage that received only one. The institution that received only one intervention showed progress over the orphanage that had received none. Child development in the intervention scenario included improvements in social skills and mental ability, as well as physical development. Physical growth such as height, weight, and chest circumference were recorded although nutrition was never modified and was equivalent in all orphanages. Furthermore, children in institutions that had received interventions displayed fewer physical limitations. The results from this study suggest that as the quality of the caregiver-child relationship improved, the social, mental, and physicaldevelopment of children also improved.

## Mother-Child Relationship and Risk-Taking Behaviors

As discussed, parental behaviors have been shown to have a direct impact on a child's health. On the extreme end, effects of child maltreatment and abuse on mental and physical health are important (for a review, see Emery & Laumann-Billings, 1998), but are outside the scope of the current chapter. However, subtle variation in mother's behavior may have important effects on children's well-being. Mothers are generally the principal caregiver for their children, and the quality of the mother-child dyad influences the organization of secure-based attachment and behavior in the infant (Coall & Chisholm, 2003). Although the strength of the effect may vary according to the child or the environment (van den Berg & Boomsma, 2007), lower levels of mother-child attachment security have been shown to affect the capacity of toddlers to cope with novel stimuli (Houtsmuller, de Jong, Rowland, & Slob, 1995). Moreover, lower levels of mother-child attachment also result in fewer coping strategies among older children (9–10 years old; Manuck, Craig, Flory, Halder, & Ferrell, 2011), and potentially impact later romantic relationships when these children reach adulthood (Fraley & Shaver, 2000). Though children vary in their susceptibility to rearing experience (Belsky & Pluess, 2009), a child's relationship with their mother is of major importance for human development.

Maternal investment during childhood often translates to the amount of time spent supervising offspring, which has a direct impact on the chances of survival of the offspring. For instance, in most developed countries accidental injury is the primary cause of death in children over 1 year of age (Belsky et al., 2010). Child supervision is a critical determinant of child injury in both preschool age children (Bredy, Humpartzoomian, Cain, & Meaney, 2003) and those 7–10 years old (Fish et al., 2004). Mothers reporting less supervision raise children who sustain more injuries.

Quality of maternal care also has a direct effect on the behavior of the child. Several studies have shown that parental monitoring of teenagers protects them against early onset of sexual activity (Meschke & Silbereisen, 1997) and sexual risk behaviors such as sexual intercourse, becoming pregnant, and having multiple sexual partners (Crosby, DiClemente, Wingood, Lang, & Harrington, 2003). Another study showed that having a good relationship with their mother has a protective effect against sexual risk behaviors in adolescent girls (14–19 years old), even when parents do not live together (Parera & Suris, 2004). In a recent study, Belsky and colleagues (Belsky et al., 2010) found that in American white, black, and Hispanic girls, greater maternal harshness (assessed when the children were 4.5 years old) correlated with more sexual risk taking by age 15 years. Less maternal support and nurturance were also associated with more alcohol misuse in boys and girls (13 to 22 years old; Barnes, Reifman, Farrell, & Dintcheff, 2000). These data reveal that the quality of maternal care and the mother-child relationship have a direct impact on the behavior, and ultimately the psychological and physical well-being of children, particularly developing girls.

## Summary

Motherhood is an important investment female mammals make in their offspring. The ultimate rewards can include increased reproductive fitness, but the costs to mothering can be substantial. For female mammals, the costs of motherhood loom in ways that conspecific males do not experience. At the same time, this costly maternal gestation and lactation provide a time during which maternal care translates into offspring survival, growth, and development. High costs for high rewards.

Maternal effects on offspring start in utero during fetal development and continuethrough adulthood. Maternal influence affects offspring physiology, psychobiology, and behavior. In humans, monkeys, and rats, we know that maternal behavior not only impacts developing offspring, but can also be transmitted across generations to future grand-offspring. Maternal effect can have heritable epigenetic consequences for one's reproductive lineage. In some cases, this occurs as unintended consequences (e.g., exposure to teratogens). In other cases, this adaptive process of fetal programming allows offspring to respond to the environment in which they will develop and potentially one day attempt to reproduce themselves.

In humans, the mother-child relationship has been shown to influence the physiology of the child, including the endocrine system, metabolism, and onset of puberty. The mother-child relationship also influences behaviors, such as coping, sexual behavior, and risk-taking. A mother's influence shapes children who grow up to become the men and women participating in their respective social groups around the world. While humans are cooperative breeders and care may come in many forms, maternal care imbues specific contributions. This is particularly the case during gestation and lactation, but continues throughout early childhood. It is likely that throughout human evolution the mother-child relationship played a unique and pivotal role in shaping human behavioral expression. The mother-child bond is the filter through which offspring assess their environment, and subsequently engage with their environment and conspecifics. A mother's contribution to human evolution is not just through producing another biological agent of the same species, but shaping the very nature of the individual that child will become.

# References

Ader, R. (1969). Early experiences accelerate maturation of the 24-hour adrenocortical rhythm. *Science, 163*, 1225–1226.

Andersson-Ellstrom, A., Forssman, L., & Milsom, I. (1996). Age of sexual debut related to life-style and reproductive health factors in a group of Swedish teenage girls. *Acta Obstetricia et Gynecologica Scandinavica, 75*, 484–489.

Auyeung, B., Baron-Cohen, S., Ashwin, E., Knickmeyer, R., Taylor, K., Hackett, G., & Hines, M. (2009). Fetal testosterone predicts sexually differentiated childhood behavior in girls and in boys. *Psychological Science, 20*, 144–148.

Bakermans-Kranenburg, M. J., van IJzendoorn, M. H., & Juffer, F. (2003). Less is more: Meta-analyses of sensitivity and attachment interventions in early childhood. *Psychological Bulletin, 129*, 195–215.

Barnes, G. M., Reifman, A. S., Farrell, M. P., & Dintcheff, B. A. (2000). The effects of parenting on the development of adolescent alcohol misuse: A six-wave latent growth model. *Journal of Marriage and Family, 62*, 175–186.

Belkacemi, L., Nelson, D. M., Desai, M., & Ross, M. G. (2010). Maternal undernutrition influences placental-fetal development. *Biology of Reproduction, 83*, 325–331.

Belsky, J. (2010). Childhood experience and the development of reproductive strategies. *Psicothema, 22*, 28–34.

Belsky, J. (2012). The development of human reproductive strategies: Progress and prospects. *Current Directions in Psychological Sciences, 21*, 310–316.

Belsky, J., & Pluess, M. (2009). Beyond diathesis stress: Differential susceptibility to environmental influences. *Psychological Bulletin, 135*, 885–908.

Belsky, J., Steinberg, L., & Draper, P. (1991). Childhood experience, interpersonal development, and reproduction strategy: An evolutionary theory of socialization. *Child Development, 62*, 647–670.

Belsky, J., Steinberg, L., Houts, R. M., & Halpern-Felsher, B. L. (2010). The development of reproductive strategy in females: Early maternal harshness → earlier menarche → increased sexual risk taking. *Developmental Psychology, 46*, 120–128.

Berman, M. L., Hanson, K., & Hellman, I. L. (1972). Effect of breast-feeding on postpartum menstruation, ovulation, and pregnancy in Alaskan Eskimos. *American Journal of Obstetrics and Gynecology, 114*, 524–534.

Bifulco, A., Moran, P. M., Ball, C., Jacobs, C., Baines, R., Bunn, A., & Cavagin, J. (2002). Childhood adversity, parental vulnerability, and disorder: Examining inter-generational transmission of risk. *Journal of Child Psychology and Psychiatry, 43*, 1075–1086.

Bingham, C. R., Miller, B. C., & Adams, G. R. (1990). Correlates of age at first sexual intercourse in a national sample of young women. *Journal of Adolescent Research, 5*, 18–33.

Blanchard, R. (2001). Fraternal birth order and the maternal immune hypothesis of male homosexuality. *Hormones and Behavior, 40*, 105–114.

Borrow, A. P., & Cameron, N. M. (2012). The role of oxytocin in mating and pregnancy. *Hormones and Behavior, 61*, 266–276.

Bowlby, J. (1958). The nature of the child's tie to his mother. *International Journal of Psychoanalysis, 39*, 350–373.

Bowman, R. E., MacLusky, N. J., Sarmiento, Y., Frankfurt, M., Gordon, M., & Luine, V. N. (2004). Sexually dimorphic effects of prenatal stress on cognition, hormonal responses, and central neurotransmitters. *Endocrinology, 145*, 3778–3787.

Bradley, R. H., Corwyn, R. F., Burchinal, M., McAdoo, H. P., & García Coll, C. (2001). The home environments of children in the United States: Part II. Relations with behavioral development through age thirteen. *Child Development, 72*, 1868–1886.

Bredy, T. W., Humpartzoomian, R. A., Cain, D. P., & Meaney, M. J. (2003). Partial reversal of the effect of maternal care on cognitive function through environmental enrichment. *Neuroscience, 118*, 571–576.

Brouette-Lahlou, I., Godinot, F., & Vernet-Maury, E. (1999). The mother rat's vomeronasal organ is involved in detection of dodecyl propionate, the pup's preputial gland pheromone. *Physiology and Behavior, 66*, 427–436.

Cameron, N. M. (2011). Maternal programming of reproductive function and behavior in the female rat. *Frontiers in Evolutionary Neuroscience, 3*, 10.

Cameron, N. M., del Corpo, A., Diorio, J., McAllister, K., Sharma, S., & Meaney, M. J. (2008). Maternal programming of sexual behavior and hypothalamic-pituitary-gonadal function in the female. *PLoS One, 3*, e2210.

Cameron, N. M., Fish, E. W., & Meaney, M. J. (2008). Maternal influences on the sexual behavior and reproductive success of the female rat. *Hormones and Behavior, 54*, 178–184.

Cameron, N. M., Soehngen, E., & Meaney, M. J. (2011). Variation in maternal care influences ventromedial hypothalamus activation in the rat. *Journal of Neuroendocrinology, 23*, 393–400.

Champagne, F. A., Francis, D. D., Mar, A., & Meaney, M. J. (2003). Variation in maternal care in the rat as a mediating influence for the effects of environment on development. *Physiology and Behavior, 79*, 359–371.

Champagne, F. A., & Meaney, M. J. (2007). Transgenerational effects of social environment on variations in maternal care and behavioral response to novelty. *Behavioral Neuroscience, 121*, 1353–1363.

Champagne, F. A., Weaver, I. C. G., Diorio, J., Sharma, S., & Meaney, M. J. (2003). Natural variations in maternal care are associated with estrogen receptor α expression and estrogen sensitivity in the medial preoptic area. *Endocrinology, 144*, 4720–4724.

Chang, S.-R., & Chen, K.-H. (2008). Age at menarche of three-generation families in Taiwan. *Annals of Human Biology, 35*, 394–405.

Clark, A. B. (1978). Sex ratio and local resource competition in a prosimian primate. *Science, 201*, 163–165.

Clutton-Brock, T. H., Albon, S. D., & Guinness, F. E. (1984). Maternal dominance, breeding success and birth sex ratios in red deer. *Nature, 308*, 358–360.

Clutton-Brock, T. H., Albon, S. D., & Guinness, F. E. (1989). Fitness costs of gestation and lactation in wild animals. *Nature, 337*, 260–262.

Coall, D. A., & Chisholm, J. S. (2003). Evolutionary perspectives on pregnancy: Maternal age at menarche and infant birth weight. *Social Science and Medicine, 57*, 1771–1781.

Crosby, R. A., DiClemente, R. J., Wingood, G. M., Lang, D. L., & Harrington, K. (2003). Infrequent parental monitoring predicts sexually transmitted infections among low-income African American female adolescents. *Archives of Pediatrics and Adolescent Medicine, 157*, 169–173.

Denenberg, V. H. (1963). Early experience and emotional development. *Scientific American, 208*, 138–146.

Dettwyler, K. A. (1995). A time to wean. In P. Stuart-Macadem & K. A. Dettwyler (Eds.), *Breastfeeding: Biocultural perspectives* (pp. 40–75). New York: Aldine.

Downing, J., & Bellis, M. A. (2009). Early pubertal onset and its relationship with sexual risk taking, substance use, and anti-social behaviour: A preliminary cross-sectional study. *BMC Public Health, 9*, 446.

Dugatkin, L. A. (2009). *Principles of animal behavior* (second edition). New York, NY: W.W. Norton & Company.

Ellis, B. J., & Garber, J. (2000). Psychosocial antecedents of variation in girls' pubertal timing: Maternal depression, stepfather presence, and marital and family stress. *Child Development, 71*, 485–501.

Ellis, L., & Bonin, S. (2004). War and the secondary sex ratio: Are they related? *Social Science Information, 43*, 115–122.

Ellison, P. T. (2003). *On fertile ground: A natural history of human reproduction.* Cambridge, MA: Harvard University Press.

Emery, R. E., & Laumann-Billings, L. (1998). An overview of the nature, causes, and consequences of abusive family relationships: Toward differentiating maltreatment and violence. *American Psychologist, 53*, 121–135.

Eveleth, P. B., & Tanner, J. M. (1990). *Worldwide variation in human growth* (2nd ed.). Cambridge, UK: Cambridge University Press.

Feldman, R. (2007). Parent–infant synchrony and the construction of shared timing: Physiological precursors, developmental outcomes, and risk conditions. *Journal of Child Psychology and Psychiatry, 48*, 329–354.

Fish, E., Shahrokh, D., Bagot, R., Caldji, C., Bredy, T., Szyf, M., & Meaney, M. (2004). Epigenetic programming of stress responses through variations in maternal care. *Annals of the New York Academy of Sciences, 1036*, 167–180.

Fraley, R. C., & Shaver, P. R. (2000). Adult romantic attachment: Theoretical developments, emerging controversies, and unanswered questions. *Review of General Psychology, 4*, 132–154.

Francis, D. D., Champagne, F. A., Liu, D., & Meaney, M. J. (1999). Maternal care, gene expression, and the development of individual differences in stress reactivity. *Annals of the New York Academy of Sciences, 896*, 66–84.

Francis, D. D., Diorio, J., Liu, D., & Meaney, M. J. (1999). Nongenomic transmission across generations of maternal behavior and stress responses in the rat. *Science, 286*, 1155–1158.

Francis, D. D., Young, L. J., Meaney, M. J., & Insel, T. R. (2002). Naturally occurring differences in maternal care are associated with the expression of oxytocin and vasopressin (V1a) receptors: Gender differences. *Journal of Neuroendocrinology, 14*, 349–353.

Freud, S. (1940). *An outline of psychoanalysis.* Wiltshire: Redwood Press Ltd.

Galloway, L. F. (2005). Maternal effects provide phenotypic adaption to local environmental conditions. *New Phytologist, 166*, 93–100.

Gangestad, S. W., & Simpson, J. A. (2000). The evolution of human mating: Trade-offs and strategic pluralism. *Behavioral and Brain Science, 23*, 573–644.

Gray, P. B., & Anderson, K. G. (2010). *Fatherhood: Evolution and human paternal behavior.* Cambridge, MA: Harvard University Press.

Gray, P. B., & Garcia, J. R. (2013). *Evolution and human sexual behavior.* Cambridge, MA: Harvard University Press.

Griffin, G. A., & Harlow, H. F. (1966). Effects of three months of total social deprivation on social adjustment and learning in the rhesus monkey. *Child Development, 37*, 533–547.

Groothuis, T. G., Muller, W., von Engelhardt, N., Carere, C., & Eising, C. (2005). Maternal hormones as a tool to adjust offspring phenotype in avian species. *Neuroscience and Biobehavioral Reviews, 29*, 329–352.

Gross, M. R. (1996). Alternative reproductive strategies and tactics: Diversity within sexes. *Trends in Ecology and Evolution, 11*, 92–98.

Harlow, H. F., & Harlow, M. (1966). Learning to love. *American Scientist, 54*, 244–272.

Harlow, H. F., Rowland, G. L., & Griffin, G. A. (1964). The effect of total social deprivation on the development of monkey behavior. *Psychiatric Research Reports (American Psychiatric Association), 19*, 116–135.

Hinde, K. (2009). Richer milk for sons but more milk for daughters: Sex-biased investment during lactation varies with maternal life history in rhesus macaques. *American Journal of Human Biology, 21*, 512–519.

Hinde, K., & Capitanio, J. P. (2010). Lactational programming? Mother's milk energy predicts infant behavior and temperament in rhesus macaques (Macaca mulatta). *American Journal of Primatology, 72*, 522–529.

Hinde, K., & Milligan, L. A. (2011). Primate milk: Proximate mechanisms and ultimate perspectives. *Evolutionary Anthropology, 20*, 9–23.

Hinde, R. A. (1986). Some implications of evolutionary theory and comparative data for the study of human prosocial and aggressive behaviour. In D. Olweus, J. Block, & M. Radke-Yarrow (Eds.), *Development of anti-social and prosocial behaviour* (pp. 13–32). Orlando, FL: Academic Press.

Hines, M., Golombok, S., Rust, J., Johnston, K. J., & Golding, J. (2002). Testosterone during pregnancy and gender role behavior of preschool children: A longitudinal, population study. *Child Development, 73*, 1678–1687.

Holl, K., Lundin, E., Surcel, H. M., Grankvist, K., Koskela, P., Dillner, J., ... Lukanova, A. (2009). Endogenous steroid hormone levels in early pregnancy and risk of testicular cancer in the offspring: A nested case–referent study. *International Journal of Cancer, 124*, 2923–2928.

Horney, K. (1950). *Neurosis and human growth.* New York, NY: W.W. Norton & Company.

Houtsmuller, E. J., de Jong, F. H., Rowland, D. L., & Slob, A. K. (1995). Plasma testosterone in fetal rats and their mothers on day 19 of gestation. *Physiology and Behavior, 57*, 495–499.

Hrdy, S. B. (1999). *Mother nature: Natural selection and the female of the species.* Phoenix, AZ: Firebird Distributing.

Hrdy, S. B. (2009). *Mothers and others: The evolutionary origins of mutual understanding.* Cambridge, MA: Harvard University Press. Jansson, T., & Powell, T. L. (2007). Role of the placenta in fetal programming: Underlying mechanisms and potential interventional approaches. *Clinical Science, 113*, 1–13.

Konner, M., & Worthman, C. (1980). Nursing frequency, gonadal function, and birth spacing among !Kung hunter-gatherers. *Science, 207*, 788–791.

Legates, J. E. (1972). The role of maternal effects in animal breeding: IV. Maternal effects in laboratory species. *Journal of Animal Science, 35*, 1294–1302.

Levine, S. (1967). Maternal and environmental influences on the adrenocortical response to stress in weanling rats. *Science, 156*, 258–260.

Liu, D., Diorio, J., Day, J. C., Francis, D. D., & Meaney, M. J. (2000). Maternal care, hippocampal synaptogenesis, and cognitive development in rats. *Nature Neuroscience, 3*, 799–806.

Liu, D., Diorio, J., Tannenbaum, B., Caldji, C., Francis, D., Freedman, A., ... Meaney, M. (1997). Maternal care, hippocampal glucocorticoid receptors, and hypothalamic-pituitary-adrenal responses to stress. *Science, 277*, 1659–1622.

MacDonald, K. (1999). An evolutionary perspective on human fertility. *Population and Environment, 21,* 223–246.

Maestripieri, D. (1999). The biology of human parenting: Insights from nonhuman primates. *Neuroscience and Biobehavioral Reviews, 23,* 411–422.

Manning, J. T. (2002). *Digit ratio: a pointer to fertility, behavior and health.* Piscataway, NJ: Rutgers University Press.

Manuck, S. B., Craig, A. E., Flory, J. D., Halder, I., & Ferrell, R. E. (2011). Reported early family environment covaries with menarcheal age as a function of polymorphic variation in estrogen receptor-α. *Development and Psychopathology, 23,* 69–83.

Meschke, L. L., & Silbereisen, R. K. (1997). The influence of puberty, family processes, and leisure activities on the timing of first sexual experience. *Journal of Adolescence, 20,* 403–418.

Miller, L., Kramer, R., Warner, V., Wickramaratne, P., & Weissman, M. (1997). Intergenerational transmission of parental bonding among women. *Journal of the American Academy of Child and Adolescent Psychiatry, 36,* 1134–1135.

Nishimori, K., Young, L. J., Guo, Q., Wang, Z., Insel, T. R., & Matzuk, M. M. (1996) Oxytocin is required for nursing but is not essential for parturition or reproductive behavior. *Proceedings of the National Academy of Sciences of the USA, 93,* 11699–11704.

Parera, N., & Surfís, J.-C. (2004). Having a good relationship with their mother: A protective factor against sexual risk behavior among adolescent females? *Journal of Pediatric and Adolescent Gynecology, 17,* 267–271.

Patisaul, H. B., & Adewale, H. B. (2009). Long-term effects of environmental endocrine disruptors on reproductive physiology and behavior. *Frontiers in Behavioral Neuroscience, 3,* 10.

Phillips, D. I. (2002). Endocrine programming and fetal origins of adult disease. *Trends in Endocrinology and Metabolism, 13,* 363.

Phinney, V. G., Jensen, L. C., Olsen, J. A., & Cundick, B. (1990). The relationship between early development and psychosexual behaviors in adolescent females. *Adolescence, 25,* 321–332.

Pianka, E. R. (1970). On r and K selection. *American Naturalist, 104,* 592–597.

Rhen, T., & Crews, D. (2002). Variation in reproductive behaviour within a sex: Neural systems and endocrine activation. *Journal of Neuroendocrinology, 14,* 517–531.

Romans, S. E., Martin, J. M., Gendall, K., & Herbison, G. P. (2003). Age of menarche: The role of some psychosocial factors. *Psychological Medicine, 33,* 933–939.

Roosa, M. W., Tein, J., Reinholtz, C., & Angelini, P. J. (1997). The relationship of childhood sexual abuse to teenage pregnancy. *Journal of Marriage and Family, 59,* 119–130.

Rychtarikova, J. (1986). Nuptiality and fertility of minors in the Czech Socialist Republic. *Demografie, 28,* 97–109.

Ryder, N. B., & Westoff, C. F. (1971). *Reproduction in the United States, 1965.* Princeton, NJ: Princeton University Press.

Seay, B., Alexander, B. K., & Harlow, H. F. (1964). Maternal behavior of socially deprived Rhesus monkeys. *Journal of Abnormal and Social Psychology, 69,* 345–354.

Song, S. (2012). Does famine influence sex ratio at birth? Evidence from the 1959–1961 Great Leap Forward Famine in China. *Proceedings of the Royal Society B, 279,* 2883–2890.

Stams, G.-J. J. M., Juffer, F., & van IJzendoorn, M. H. (2002). Maternal sensitivity, infant attachment, and temperament in early childhood predict adjustment in middle childhood: The case of adopted children and their biologically unrelated parents. *Developmental Psychology, 38,* 806–821.

Stuart-Macadem, P., & Dettwyler, K. A. (1995). *Breastfeeding: Biocultural perspectives.* New York: Aldine.

Sullivan, E. C., Hinde, K., Mendoza, S. P., & Capitanio, J. P. (2011). Cortisol concentrations in the milk of rhesus monkey mothers are associated with confident temperament in sons, but not daughters. *Developmental Psychobiology, 53,* 96–104.

Team, T.S.P.U.O.R. (2008). I. Theoretical, empirical, and practical rationale. *Monographs of the Society for Research in Child Development, 73,* 1–15.

Trivers, R. L., & Willard, D. E. (1973). Natural selection of parental ability to vary the sex ratio of offspring. *Science, 179,* 90–92.

Udry, J. R., & Cliquet, R. L. (1982). A cross-cultural examination of the relationship between ages at menarche, marriage, and first birth. *Demography, 19*, 53–63.

van den Berg, S., & Boomsma, D. I. (2007). The familial clustering of age at menarche in extended twin families. *Behavior Genetics, 37*, 661–667.

van Hasselt, F. N., Cornelisse, S., Yuan Zhang, T., Meaney, M. J., Velzing, E. H., Krugers, H. J., & Joëls, M. (2012). Adult hippocampal glucocorticoid receptor expression and dentate synaptic plasticity correlate with maternal care received by individuals early in life. *Hippocampus, 22*, 255–266.

Vitzthum, V. J. (2009). The ecology and evolutionary endocrinology of reproduction in the human female. *American Journal of Physical Anthropology, 140*(Suppl 49), 95–136.

Volk, A. A. (2009). Human breastfeeding is not automatic: Why that's so and what it means for human evolution. *Journal of Social, Evolutionary, and Cultural Psychology, 3*, 305–314.

Weaver, I. C., Diorio, J., Seckl, J. R., Szyf, M., & Meaney, M. J. (2004). Early environmental regulation of hippocampal glucocorticoid receptor gene expression: Characterization of intracellular mediators and potential genomic target sites. *Annals of the New York Academy of Sciences, 1024*, 182–212.

Weaver, I. C. G., Cervoni, N., Champagne, F. A., D'Alessio, A. C., Sharma, S., Seckl, J. R.,. . . Meaney, M. J. (2004). Epigenetic programming by maternal behavior. *Nature Neuroscience, 7*, 847–854.

Welberg, L. A. M., Thrivikraman, K. V., & Plotsky, P. M. (2005). Chronic maternal stress inhibits the capacity to up-regulate placental 11{beta}-hydroxysteroid dehydrogenase type 2 activity. *Journal of Endocrinology, 186*, R7–12.

Woodbridge, M. W. (1995). Baby-controlled breastfeeding: Biocultural implications. In P. Stuart-Macadem & K. A. Dettwyler (Eds.), *Breastfeeding: Biocultural perspectives*. New York: Aldine.

Worthman, C. M. (1999). Evolutionary perspectives on the onset of puberty. In W. Trevethan, E. O. Smith, & J. J. McKenna (Eds.), *Evolutionary medicine*. New York: Oxford University Press.

# 7

# The Evolution of Flexible Parenting

LESLEY NEWSON AND PETER J. RICHERSON

## Introduction

Women in contemporary Western societies perceive that they have a choice about when they should produce offspring, how many they should have, or if they should have any offspring at all. No innate drive or "maternal instinct" forces them to behave in ways that maximize their reproductive success. It is not just modern birth control technology or abortion that provides them with this choice. Historical and anthropological studies show that women never produced children in an uncontrolled way. Many used breastfeeding to space their pregnancies. As long as their previous child continued to suckle frequently, their risk of getting pregnant again was lower. Abstinence from sexual intercourse was common—or at least sexual intercourse that involved semen being placed in the vagina (e.g., Coale & Watkins, 1986; Low, 2000; McLaren, 1990).

There is also wide variation in how women bring up their children once they are born (e.g., Hrdy, 1999; Whiting & Whiting, 1975). The flexibility of our parenting behavior presents a challenge for scholars who attempt to explain human behavior from an evolutionary perspective. A human child must be cared for and socialized for many years if it is to develop into a successful adult and our ancestors obviously succeeded in raising offspring. But despite this, evolution does not seem to have equipped humans with a specific set of parenting behaviors. Women possess the standard mammalian equipment for gestating, delivering, and feeding offspring but they don't exhibit one "species typical" mode of parenting. The age women become mothers, how we care for our children, and how we fit them into our other relationships varies from culture to culture, from time to time, and from family to family.

This chapter will present an argument for why human parenting behavior is so diverse. We know that in spite of the flexibility, all contemporary human mothers have one characteristic in common. They receive help raising their young. Even the "single parents" in modern societies depend on others. For example, others gather food and place it in convenient supermarkets; others manufacture parenting tools, such as high chairs and slings; and institutions have been set up to help parents care for and educate their children. This is not just a modern phenomenon. For a substantial portion of human evolutionary history, those mothers who left surviving offspring received a considerable amount of help feeding and caring for their children (Hrdy, 1999). If this cooperative style of parenting evolved some time ago, if humans are "cooperative breeders," then flexible parenting and a number of other human characteristics make sense. But if those who study human behavior from an evolutionary perspective accept that humans evolved as cooperative breeders, then many of the evolutionary explanations that psychologists have offered to explain human reproductive behavior need to be reexamined.

## An Environment Favoring Flexibility

The findings of paleoclimatologists during the last two decades (e.g., Ditlevsen, Ditlevsen, & Andersen, 2002; Greenland Ice Core Project, 1993; Lehman, 1993) suggest an explanation for natural selection's favoring of behavioral flexibility in humans. For much of the last two and a half million years, during the Pleistocene epoch, the Earth's climate has been highly unstable with extreme temperature fluctuations during recurring ice ages. The number of abrupt climate change events during glacial periods seems to have been increasing over the last 4–8 major glacial cycles (Loulergue et al., 2008; Martrat et al., 2007), roughly paralleling human brain size increases and other features associated with the modernization of humans, such as increasingly sophisticated stone tools (Richerson & Boyd, in press). Animals that could adapt rapidly to changing conditions or to disperse to new habitats had an advantage over animals that were well adapted to exploit a narrow range of habitats. For long-lived creatures such as hominids, adapting to such rapid environmental changes would have required that they change dramatically in just a few generations. Genetic adaptations could not have evolved quickly enough to keep pace with such a rapid rate of change (Richerson & Boyd, 2001). The individuals who succeeded in raising offspring were not simply those whose genes provided them with innate responses to the environmental stimuli experienced by their ancestors. Successful individuals were those whose genes also provided them with the ability to make appropriate responses to environmental stimuli that their ancestors may *never* have encountered.

The oldest fossils of hominids assigned to our own "*Homo*" genus are of individuals who lived in Africa between 2 and 2.3 million years ago (Klein, 2009). The appearance of our genus coincides with a period when moist woodland and rainforest habitats were retreating and being replaced with areas of dry, heterogeneous, and unstable climate (Bobe & Leakey, 2009; Kingdon, 2007; Trauth, Maslin, Deino, & Strecker, 2005). Fossil evidence suggests that *Homo* was the only hominid who exploited these expanding habitats (Potts, 1998a; Reed, 1997). Fossils of the now extinct *Australopithecus* genus, believed to be precursors of *Homo*, have been found among fossil flora and fauna associated with moister, more wooded habitats. It is therefore likely that they occupied habitats similar to those in which some groups of chimpanzees have been observed to range (McGrew, Baldwin, & Tutin, 1988).

What was special about members of the *Homo* genus that allowed them to exploit this expanding habitat when their more ape-like relatives stayed in the shrinking wooded habitats? One plausible suggestion is that *Homo* had adaptations that allowed them to be flexible and mobile enough to survive in habitats where food and water resources were sparsely distributed and variable (Potts, 1998b). The *Homo erectus* fossils found in Asia dating back over 1.8 million years show that early *Homo* was able to survive a long migration and provides further evidence of their flexibility and mobility (Foley, 1987; Wells & Stock, 2007).

Speculation about the adaptations that would have provided this flexibility and mobility has tended to concentrate on adaptations likely to have improved the survival of hominids trying to exploit drier and more variable habitats. But survival is irrelevant to fitness unless the individuals who survive are also able to produce offspring that survive, mature, and have offspring themselves. Less consideration has been given to determining how hominids successfully raised offspring in drier more variable habitats (O'Connell, Hawkes, & Blurton Jones, 1999). How are they likely to be different from the earlier hominids that exploited moister and more stable habitats? Fossils can only hint at the parenting behavior of long-extinct hominids. But we do know about the parenting behavior of extant apes and of contemporary humans.

## Ape Life History and Parenting

In many ways the growth, development, and reproductive biology of contemporary humans is similar to that of great apes. The fossil evidence suggests that *Australopithecus* and early *Homo* were even more ape-like (Smith & Tompkins, 1995). By comparing life history variables and encephalization (brain mass in relation to body mass) in a range of primates, Barrickman and colleagues (2008) showed greater encephalization to be associated with a longer, slower life history. The speed of growth of infants is limited by the speed at which it can be provided with nourishment, and brain tissue has especially high nutritional demands (Aiello & Wheeler, 1995; Kramer & Ellison, 2010). Therefore the larger its brain, the longer it takes for each offspring to be supplied with nutrition sufficient for the brain to reach adult size. This also affects total lifespan because for the investment in brain size to be evolutionarily stable, mothers need to live long enough to raise an average of two children who go on to produce offspring themselves.

Consistent with this, large-brained apes grow very slowly, need a great deal of care for several years at the beginning of life, and have a relatively long lifespan (Charnov & Berrigan, 1993). Humans, of course have an even larger brain, longer period of dependency, and longer lifespan than our ape relatives. Another difference is the style of parenting. Compared to contemporary humans, the parenting of extant great apes is very inflexible. In the more social apes, chimpanzees, bonobos, and gorillas, membership in a group affords mothers and infants some protection but when it comes to care of infants, mother apes literally do all the heavy lifting. Primates produce milk at a slow rate compared to other mammals of a similar size, and primate milk is dilute and low in nutrients so infants have to stay near to their mother all the time and suckle frequently (Hinde & Milligan, 2011). As infants get older they begin to forage beside their mothers but continue to suckle. The ovulation of the mother is suppressed by a hormonal mechanism induced by the physical action of the infant sucking on the nipple (Freeman, Kanyicska, Lerant, & Nagy, 2000; Konner & Worthman, 1980). As the infant's own foraging becomes more competent it suckles less, the ovulatory inhibition ends and the mother becomes fertile again. If her infant dies, a female usually experiences estrus within a month or two. Chimpanzees are weaned at around the age 4.5 years. In gorillas, weaning occurs at a slightly younger age and orangutan it occurs at an older age (Sellen, 2007).

Female great apes spend virtually all their adult lives pregnant, caring for an infant, or both. The effort involved in parenting reduces the degree to which female chimps can be flexible and mobile compared to males. For example, in chimpanzee groups that regularly hunt colobus monkeys, females rarely participate in hunts (Mitani & Watts, 1999). Young infants need to be carried and even when they have developed enough to move independently they still require constant protection and help. The burdens of motherhood prevent females from moving around the canopy fast enough to hunt successfully (Mitani, personal communication). In at least some chimpanzee groups, therefore, the diet of females is different from that of males. It includes less meat and more insects (McGrew et al., 1979; McGrew, 1992). It is reasonable to conclude, therefore, that for an ape with an ape-like parenting style, females and their infants would have found it far more difficult than males to survive in drier more variable habitats where food was more widely spaced.

Apes are also limited in the extent to which they can match their rate of reproduction to changes in the abundance of resources. The slow growth and development of their babies severely limits their fecundity. In groups of chimpanzees observed in the wild, interbirth intervals tend to be in excess of 5 years (Wallis, 1997). Since the reproductive life of female chimpanzees is less than 30 years, even the most successful female is unlikely to produce more than five surviving offspring throughout her life. The interbirth interval of other great apes is similar to that of chimpanzees, or even longer (Furuichi et al., 1998; Robbins et al., 2004; Wich et al., 2004). If times are good and resources are abundant, apes cannot respond by producing offspring faster. And if times are hard, a mother may not be able to find enough nourishment to make the milk necessary to keep her infant alive. This is not such a problem in stable homogeneous habitats but it might make raising young impossible in harsher environments.

## The Evolution of Human Parenting

We know that at some point in human evolutionary history, hominids abandoned the mother-only parenting style of apes and adopted a cooperative breeding style of raising their young. In all contemporary human cultures, mothers receive considerable amounts of help raising their children, and males contribute a substantial amount of parenting effort (Gurven & Hill, 2009; Hill & Hurtado, 2009; Hrdy, 1999, 2009; Mace & Sear, 2005). As a result, the rate of human reproduction is far more flexible than that of apes. Even though we have larger brains than apes and our children grow more slowly, human females have shorter interbirth intervals. The maximum recorded fertility sustained by a human population is that of Protestant group called Hutterites, which settled as farmers in the Western Canada and the United States. Their birth records reveal the population had a total fertility rate of 12.8 from 1921 to 1930. This means that the "average" Hutterite woman gave birth to over 12 children during her lifetime, but many had even greater fecundity (Coale & Treadway, 1986). It would probably be physiologically possible for a chimpanzee female to produce over 12 offspring during her lifetime, but her infants would have to be taken away before they were weaned and raised for her.

The age human mothers wean their children varies from culture to culture, but it is common for children to begin to receive other foods to supplement breastmilk by about six months of age, food that has been foraged and processed by their mother and her helpers (Sellen, 2006). Human infants may need this extra food to support the rapid growth of their brain. As her baby starts to get less of its nourishment from her milk, a fit and well-nourished human mother will become fertile again even though she is still breastfeeding and this means she will give birth to her next child long before her previous one can forage for itself (Valeggia & Ellison, 2001). On the other hand, if resources are very scarce, a woman can delay producing her own children and help to raise her siblings or their children instead (Hill & Hurtado, 2009).

The cooperative breeding of contemporary humans relies strongly on complex culture and the psychological mechanisms that allow human groups to maintain and adjust social norms. All human populations have cultural institutions such as marriage during which a couple publicly acknowledges a sexual relationship and the female's children are acknowledged to also belong to her husband and his family (Brown, 1991). This serves to formalize an arrangement designed to ensure that the woman will receive help caring for her children. Who provides the help and what kinds of help they provide varies between cultures and families, but all cultures have strong norms about shared responsibility for the welfare of children. Mothers also rely on culturally transmitted information about things like safe weaning foods and the tools that make childcare easier, such as slings, blankets, and cradles (Hrdy, 1999; Whiting & Whiting, 1975).

Cultural institutions and technology facilitate cooperative breeding in *contemporary* human populations, but does this imply that cooperative breeding is a relatively recent adaptation that only arose after our ancestors had acquired complex culture? Three lines of argument suggest that members of the hominid line began to breed cooperatively more than two million years ago, during a time when the culture of hominid groups was unlikely to have been much more complex than that which has been observed in chimpanzee groups (Whiten et al., 1999).

The first argument that raising young cooperatively has a long history in the hominid line is based on the unique life history of contemporary humans, which limits reproduction to the middle part of our lives. Humans have an extended juvenile stage. Our children grow relatively slowly until they approach puberty and they then experience a growth spurt. During this childhood stage we are mature enough to help our parents and care for younger children but not yet sexually mature (Bogin, 2006; Kramer, 2005). One explanation for the evolution of this extended childhood is that our ancestors were able to enhance their inclusive fitness more by helping family members raise their young than by raising their own offspring without help. It appears that when a population is well nourished females begin to reach puberty earlier (Gluckman & Hanson, 2006; R. Walker et al., 2006); perhaps this is another mechanism by which females match their reproductive rate to resource availability. At the latter end of life many women, including women in hunter-gatherer societies, remain healthy and vigorous until their late sixties and seventies. They are therefore able to help their children and grandchildren long after they cease to be able to reproduce themselves (Hawkes, O'Connell, Blurton Jones, 1997; Alvarez, & Charnov, 1998; Kaplan & Robson, 2002). Again such a long nonreproductive period is unlikely to have been favored by natural selection if women had not been contributing to their fitness by helping their relatives during this period.

The second argument for the antiquity of cooperative breeding in the hominin line is based on the fossil evidence showing brain size beginning to increase with the appearance of *Homo erectus* about 1.8 million years ago. It was at this point that the encephalization of hominins increased beyond that of chimpanzees. It is unlikely that this increase would have been possible without an adaptation that increased the efficiency of parenting because the foraging of the mother alone could not have obtained sufficient resources to support the brain-growth of offspring with a brain larger than that of a chimpanzee. (Barrickman, Bastian, Isler, & Van Schaik, 2008). It is probable, therefore, that females of the genus Homo had begun to receive help provisioning their young earlier than 1.8 million years ago.

The third argument is based on the observation that developing complex culture requires prosocial motivations and skills and not just the more Machiavellian social skills observed in chimpanzees (Chapais, 2008). Hrdy (2009) argues that natural selection is more likely to favor these characteristics in the social environment of a group that is raising its young cooperatively. She points out that behaviors such as shared attention and teaching are more commonly observed in cooperatively breeding species than in apes. The evolution of complex culture is unlikely to occur if youngsters are raised only by their mothers (Henrich, 2010). In cooperatively breeding groups, the young can observe a number of more experienced individuals who use slightly different foraging techniques and have different competencies. In such conditions, individuals able to judge the best model to imitate will be the most successful, and their judgments will drive adaptive change in the culture of the group. It seems plausible, therefore, that the cooperation seen in modern humans and our capacity for complex culture evolved together. Once hominin groups began to share more and more information, they could begin to culturally evolve ways to make their cooperative care of young more effective.

It also seems unlikely that hominids could have begun to exploit the dry unstable African habitats if mothers did not receive help with caring for and provisioning their infants. In providing milk to their infants, lactating females give up water from their bodies (Bentley, 1998; Hinde & Milligan, 2011; James et al., 1995; Stumbo, Booth, Eichenberger, & Dusdieker, 1985). And because primate milk is dilute, a female ape with an unweaned child may lose a substantial amount of water each time her child feeds. The need to stay near a source of water would have constrained the foraging activities of lactating females particularly during dry seasons. Other primates who live in dry environments, such as baboons, deal with this by timing their births so that greatest lactational stress occurs during the wet season (Dunbar, Hannah-Stewart, & Dunbar, 2002) or by limiting the amount of milk produced and slowing down the growth of the infant (Altmann & Alberts, 2003). Neither of these options were likely solutions for hominids, whose infants needed to be fed all year round for at least 3 years and were already very slow growing.

If mothers needed to be near a source of water while suckling their infants and this prevented them from being mobile enough to gain sufficient food, mothers would not have been able to raise young in these habitats unless they received help. But who would have provided the help and what kind of help might a mother have received? One source of help might have been her infant's father. While the mother and infant stayed near water, the father could have foraged further away and brought back food for the mother, which she could share with her infant once it was old enough to eat solid food. Another source of help would have been other adult females. They could have taken turns babysitting each other's children with some staying near water caring for and protecting the young ones while the others foraged.

Lovejoy (2009) has suggested that *Ardipithecus ramidus*, which he argues is ancestral to Homo, were monogamous biparental carers. If he is correct, then paternal care was established in the hominid line long before the move to drier more variable habitats. It is unlikely to be that simple, however. In pair-bonded primate species, such as gibbons and titi monkeys, the pairs stay close together (Chivers, 1977; Mendoza & Mason, 1986). This increases paternity certainty by allowing the male to prevent other males mating with the female, and once the infant is born, the male is there to protect the mother and infant. Also, in these species, the paternal care does not extend to provisioning mothers and offspring. Male titi monkeys take on the energetic cost of carrying the infant, allowing the mother to forage more efficiently. But they give the infant to the mother to suckle. A mating system that involves a pair-bonded couple separating while the male forages in a habitat where food is sparsely distributed carries severe risks. The female and infant would be dependent on the successful foraging of a single male for the years that it takes for the offspring to become able to survive on its own. And a male off foraging would be unable to protect his mate and offspring. Biparental care which involves males provisioning females and their offspring has not been observed in other mammal species (Clutton-Brock, 1991).

By contrast, communal care of young by females has been observed in mammals as taxonomically diverse as lemurs (Eberle & Kappeler, 2006), sperm whales (Whitehead, 2003), and house mice (Konig, 1993), with females protecting each other's offspring and allowing them to suckle.

During times of water scarcity, hominin mothers would have had to congregate near remaining sources of water. They would have been safer if they formed groups that perhaps also included weaned but not yet mature offspring. Being able to leave her infant with this group while she foraged would have allowed a mother to forage more efficiently and search for food further away from the water source. Having some time to forage unencumbered by their infants might have allowed cooperating females to gain sufficient nutrition to survive and feed their young during dry periods and allow further exploitation of the expanding dry habitats. They may have further enhanced the cooperation by bringing food back from foraging trips to share with the baby sitters and older infants. Bringing back foraged food could have led to an increase in flexibility in the rate of offspring production. During times of relative abundance in the new highly variable habitat more food could be brought back, allowing infants to be weaned earlier and their mothers to become fertile sooner.

Cooperation between mothers may have been sufficient to allow hominids to raise young in habitats where an infant could not be raised by a mother on her own. But much larger gains in reproductive efficiency can be achieved if males also contribute to the provisioning of offspring. Pair-bonding and biparental care would have been highly risky in dry unstable habitats, but the risks would have been less for groups of cooperating males provisioning groups of cooperating females. In a number of social primates species females mate with several males and dominant males have been observed to acquiesce to subordinates matings with females (Henzi, Clarke, van Schaik, Pradhan, & Barrett, 2010). Mating with several males obscures the paternity of the offspring, and confusion over its paternity can increase the chances of an infant surviving and thus the fitness of its parents (Hrdy, 1979, 1999). If there is a possibility that a male might be the father of an infant, it is less likely to harm the infant and more likely to protect it from other males. An infant whose mother has mated with a number of males therefore has a number of male protectors. In a species in which fathers and possible fathers help to feed infants as well as protect them, the benefits of confused paternity are even greater.

A dry and variable habitat would present many opportunities for cooperation between groups of cooperative males and groups of cooperative females. Males would be attracted to water and to potentially fertile females. If the males contributed to the provisioning of the females and their offspring, infants could be weaned sooner and their mothers become fertile sooner. The more males provisioned, the more frequently females would be fertile. Thus, groups that cooperated and foraged more effectively would produce offspring more rapidly. These groups would, in fact, be reproductive units. Groups that maintained a culture of cooperation would out-compete those whose members were less cooperative. Thus through cultural evolution and gene-culture coevolution, hominin groups could evolve more complex cultures that allowed them to exploit the chaotic Pleistocene habitats more flexibly and more efficiently (Richerson & Boyd, 2005).

Having more than one male as the possible father of her children may have been helpful for part of human evolutionary history and some contemporary cultures still practice polyandry (Smith, 1998) or partible paternity (Beckerman & Valentine, 2002). However, in most contemporary cultures a child is recognized as having a single father who acknowledges that he and his family have an obligation to the child (Brown, 1991). Genetically evolved mechanisms that encourage bonding and empathy undoubtedly play a role in supporting the sexual fidelity and altruism that encourages the investment of a child's paternal kin. This support network is not, however, maintained by these mechanisms alone; culturally evolved institutions, norms, and values that a population shares also play an essential role. The wide variability in human sexual and reproductive behavior does not support the belief that humans have genes that drive them to form pair bonds with mates of the opposite sex and deliver biparental care.

Chapais (2008) and Henrich et al. (2012) argue that groups gain advantages from developing mechanisms to establish paternity of offspring and ensure that most men have wives. Members of such groups will be able to develop larger kinship networks to call on for help, and groups in which most men have access to a woman are more peaceful. It may be, therefore, that the more successful human groups were those that culturally evolved the best systems for encouraging and maintaining bonds that ensured that a child had the support of both its maternal and paternal kin. This does not always mean that support comes from the father himself. For example, the degree to which fathers provide food or direct care for their offspring varies substantially across habitats and cultural groups (Gurven & Hill, 2009; Hill & Hurtado, 2009), and studies of a number of horticultural and hunter-gatherer subsistence populations have found the death or absence of a father to have no effect on child survival or success (Sear & Mace, 2008; Winking, Gurven, & Kaplan, 2011).

Perhaps the most successful institutions for ensuring children get the support they need are those that help to arrange and maintain stable marriages in which multiple generations of the children's kin provide them with lifelong support. Marriage has become severely weakened as institution in contemporary Western cultures (Cherlin, 2004), and these cultures are unusual in the extent to which young adults are left on their own to find and choose the person with whom they will have children (Apostolou, 2007, 2010). Smaller scale societies afforded much less opportunity for observing and choosing a potential spouse, and networks of family and friends helped to match up young adults. On the basis of phylogenetic analyses using data from contemporary hunter-gatherers, R. S. Walker, Hill, Flinn, and Ellsworth (2011) determined that the arranging of marriages in human populations began before anatomically modern humans left Africa more than 50,000 years ago.

## Cooperative Breeding and the Evolution of Human Behavior

The argument we have presented here includes a great deal of speculation about what might have gone on in the past. Our purpose in presenting it is not to persuade readers of the details of this particular account. The currently available evidence only provides an outline of what might be the course of human evolution. Our purpose is to review a growing body of evidence that demands we consider new accounts of human evolution and question assumptions that have underpinned much of the research in evolutionary psychology for the last two decades.

Evolutionary psychologists have argued that psychological mechanisms that enabled our ancestors to survive and reproduce as foragers during the Pleistocene continue to influence the behavior of humans living today (e.g., Barkow, Cosmides, & Tooby, 1992). They argue that we are descended from males and females who monitored their environment and scrutinized potential mates in order to make fitness-maximizing reproductive decisions. However, most of the hypotheses developed to explain human mating are based on the assumption that these Pleistocene men and woman formed pair bonds and their offspring received biparental care. For example, according to Gangestad and Simpson (2000, p. 586):

> Given the demands of biparental care during evolutionary history, both men and women were selected to use long-term mating tactics and invest in offspring. However, they were also selected to use ecologically

contingent, conditional mating strategies, dedicating some effort to short term and extra-pair mating under specific conditions. Women may have evolved to trade off evidence of a man's genetic fitness for evidence of his ability and willingness to invest in offspring.

On the strength of such assumptions, investigations have been carried out on many undergraduates in Western universities in the hope of gaining an understanding of the evolved psychological mechanisms that are likely to have influenced the choosing of mates with whom to pair-bond or with whom to have extra-pair copulations.

However, if conditions during the Pleistocene obliged human females to raise their children as part of cooperatively breeding groups, their choices would have been constrained and rewarded very differently than if they raised their young independently or with the help of only a mate. For cooperative breeders, willing helpers in the social group are an essential resource that must be available if they are to achieve reproductive success. Individuals must therefore be sensitive to social cues when deciding whether it is a good time to mate. When developing hypotheses to explain these decisions we should consider the behavior of other cooperatively breeding mammals such as callitrichid monkeys, mongooses, and wolves. It has been demonstrated in some of these species that females receive information during social interactions that causes them to help raise the children of other females rather than give birth to children themselves (French, 1997).

Contemporary humans are undoubtedly also sensitive to social cues when making reproductive decisions. Many of these come in the form of cultural norms and values, but humans are constantly exchanging information about the sexual behavior and parenting behavior of other members of their social group (Dunbar, 1996). Although reproductive norms vary between cultures, it has been shown in a number of cultures that, by adhering to the norms of their culture, individuals tend to make reproductive decisions consistent with maximizing fitness (Borgerhoff-Mulder, 1988; e.g., Chagnon, 1988; Cronk, 1989; and reviews by Cronk, 1991; Hill & Hurtado, 1996; Irons, 1979; Low, 1993, 1999, 2000; Wang, Lee, & Campbell, 1995). Even cultural norms that cause her to delay becoming pregnant, such as a rule that a woman should not have sex until her child is weaned, can increase fitness by allowing her to have a greater lifetime fertility or to raise healthier children who go on to give her many grandchildren.

Reproductive norms are not a set of inflexible rules. They prescribe how individuals should respond to the changing circumstances they and their group-mates are experiencing. Reproductive norms have been shown to regulate the fertility of a population in response to resource availability. For example, in late medieval and early modern northern Europe, men were not "eligible bachelors" (i.e., considered as potential husbands) until they had economic means to set up an independent household (Hajnal, 1982; Watkins, 1989), and many men remained unmarried and childless. The strict enforcement of monogamy meant that men with a high income could only have legitimate offspring with one woman, and so many women also remained unmarried and childless. A study of birth and marriage rates in early modern England shows that the fertility of the population rose and fell with the price of grain (i.e., the availability of food) and that lower birthrates during the lean times were not due to married women having fewer children, but by women marrying late or remaining unmarried (Wrigley, 1978; Wrigley & Schofield, 1981; Coale, 1986).

It is interesting that when a population begins to undergo economic development the beliefs and values of its members begin to change in characteristic ways (Inglehart & Welzel, 2005; Inkeles & Smith, 1974; Newson & Richerson, 2009). For example, before economic development people tend to share certain "traditional values" such as a belief that women and men should do different work, that elders should be respected, and that families should have as many children as they can afford to raise. With economic development these begin to be replaced. One of the earliest and easiest to detect changes is the adoption of the belief that it is prudent to limit family size. For evolutionary theorists this change is puzzling because people begin to produce fewer children at a time when they are becoming more prosperous. They cease to behave as if they are competing for reproductive success.

Recognizing the cooperative nature of human reproduction suggests a reason why this change occurs—the social cues change. Economic development causes a dramatic change in the structure of social groups as people pursue new opportunities to work and gain education (Newson, Postmes, Lea, & Webley, 2005; Newson et al., 2007). People's social networks widen so that a far higher proportion of the social interaction they experience is with non-kin. As a population undergoes economic development its members increasingly identify with social groups other than their families and are influenced mostly by people who have no interest in their reproductive success. Within families, the importance of marriage and motherhood may still be discussed. But at work, in school, in the streets of towns, and in the media, other options get talked about. For example, women may learn about the benefits of getting a job and earning money to buy fashionable clothes rather than helping at home or earning money to help their family. Reproductive norms do not change immediately but they gradually diverge from that which encourages reproductive success.

With the human population now over seven billion and continuing to rise rapidly, it is good know that our reproduction is flexible. Our genes do not compel us to compete for mates and reproductive success and have as many children as we can afford. It is also a relief that human populations are capable of culturally evolving solutions to problems our species has never faced before. Not only can we produce new technology, we are capable of changing our values, beliefs, and goals. An evolutionary approach to understanding human behavior and the way we cooperate as well as compete has a great deal to offer. We also have a great deal more to learn about human evolution.

# References

Aiello, L. C., & Wheeler, P. (1995). The expensive-tissue hypothesis: The brain and the digestive system in human and primate evolution. *Current Anthropology, 36*(2), 199–221.

Altmann, J., & Alberts, S. C. (2003). Variability in reproductive success viewed from a life-history perspective in baboons. *American Journal of Human Biology, 15*, 401–409.

Apostolou, M. (2007). Sexual selection under parental choice: The role of parents in the evolution of human mating. *Evolution and Human Behavior, 28*, 403–409.

Apostolou, M. (2010). Sexual selection under parental choice in agropastoral societies. *Evolution and Human Behavior, 31*(1), 39–47.

Barkow, J. H., Cosmides, L., & Tooby, J. (Eds.). (1992). *The adapted mind: Evolutionary psychology and the generation of culture.* New York: Oxford University Press.

Barrickman, N. L., Bastian, M. L., Isler, K., & Van Schaik, C. (2008). Life history costs and benefits of encephalization: A comparative test using data from long-term studies of primates in the wild. *Evolution, 54*(5), 568–590.

Beckerman, S., & Valentine, P. (Eds.). (2002). *Cultures of multiple fathers: The theory and practice of partible paternity in lowland South America.* Gainesville: University Press of Florida.

Bentley, G. (1998). Hydration as limiting factor in lactation. *American Journal of Human Biology, 10*, 151–161.

Bobe, R., & Leakey, M. G. (2009). Ecology of plio-pleistocene mammals in the Omo-Turkana basin and the emergence of *Homo.* In F. E. Grine, J. G. Fleagle, & R. E. Leakey (Eds.), *The first humans: Origins and early evolution of the genus Homo* (pp. 173–184). Dordrecht, The Netherlands: Springer.

Bogin, B. (2006). More than human life history: The evolution of human childhood and fertility. In K. Hawkes & R. R. Paine (Eds.), *The evolution of human life history* (pp. 197–230). Santa Fe, NM: School of American Research Press.

Borgerhoff-Mulder, M. (1988). Behavioural ecology in traditional societies. *Trends in Ecology and Evolution, 3*(10), 260–264.

Brown, D. E. (1991). *Human universals.* Philadelphia: Temple University Press.

Charnov, E., & Berrigan, D. (1993). Why do female primates have such long lifespans and so few babies? Or life in the slow lane. *Evolutionary Anthropology, 1*(6), 191–194.

Chagnon, N. A. (1988). Life histories, blood revenge, and warfare in a tribal population. *Science, 239*, 985–992.

Chapais, B. (2008). *Primeval kinship: How pair-bonding gave birth to human society.* Cambridge, MA: Harvard University Press.

Cherlin, A. J. (2004). The deinstitutionalization of American marriage. *Journal of Marriage and the Family, 66*(4), 848–861.

Chivers, D. J. (1977). The lesser apes. In H. P. Ranier & G. H. Bourne (Eds.), *Primate conservation* (pp. 539–598). New York: Academic Press.

Clutton-Brock, T. H. (1991). *The evolution of parental care.* Princeton, NJ: Princeton University Press.

Coale, A. J. (1986). The decline of fertility in Europe as a chapter in demographic history. In A. J. Coale & S. C. Watkins (Eds.), *The decline of fertility in Europe.* Princeton, NJ: Princeton University Press.

Coale, A. J., & Treadway, R. (1986). A summary of the changing distribution of overall fertility, marital fertility, and the proportion married in the provinces of Europe. In A. J. Coale & S. C. Watkins (Eds.), *The decline of fertility in Europe* (pp. 31–181). Princeton, NJ: Princeton University Press.

Coale, A. J., & Watkins, S. C. (Eds.). (1986). *The decline of fertility in Europe.* Princeton, NJ: Princeton University Press.

Cronk, L. (1989). Low socio-economic status and female biased parental investment: The Mukogodo example. *American Anthropologists, 91*, 441–429.

Cronk, L. (1991). Human behavioral ecology. *Annual Review of Anthropology, 20*, 25–53.

Ditlevsen, P. D., Ditlevsen, S., & Andersen, K. (2002). The fast climate fluctuations during the stadial and interstadial climate states. *Annals of Glaciology*, *35*, 457–462.

Dunbar, R. I. M. (1996). *Grooming, gossip, and the evolution of language*. London: Faber.

Dunbar, R. I. M., Hannah-Stewart, L., & Dunbar, P. (2002). Forage quality and costs of lactation for female gelada baboons. *Animal Behaviour*, *64*(5), 801–805.

Eberle, M., & Kappeler, P. M. (2006). Family insurance: Kin selection and cooperative breeding in a solitary primate (*Microcebus murinus*). *Behavioral Ecology and Sociobiology*, *60*, 528–588.

Foley, R. (1987). *Another unique species: Patterns in human evolutionary ecology*. Harlow, UK: Longman.

Freeman, M. E., Kanyicska, B., Lerant, A., & Nagy, G. (2000). Prolactin: Structure, function, and regulation of secretion. *Physiological Reviews*, *80*, 1523–1631.

French, J. A. (1997). Proximate regulation of singular breeding in callirichid primates. In N. G. Solomon & J. A. French (Eds.), *Cooperative breeding in mammals* (pp. xx–xx). Cambridge, UK: Cambridge University Press.

Furuichi, T., Idani, G., Ihobe, H., Kuroda, S., Kitamura, K., Mori, A., et al. (1998). Population dynamics of wild bonobos (*Pan paniscus*) at Wamba. *International Journal of Primatology*, *19*(6), 1029–1043.

Gangestad, S. W., & Simpson, J. A. (2000). The evolution of human mating: Trade-offs and strategic pluralism. *Behavioral and Brain Sciences*, *23*, 573–587.

Gluckman, P. D., & Hanson, M. A. (2006). Evolution, development and timing of puberty. *Trends in Endocrinology and Metabolism*, *17*(1), 7–12.

Greenland Ice Core Project. (1993). Climate instability during the last interglacial period recorded in the GRIP core. *Nature*, *364*, 203–207.

Gurven, M., & Hill, K. (2009). Why do men hunt? A reevaluation of the "man the hunter" sexual division of labor. *Current Anthropology*, *50*(1), 51–62.

Hajnal, J. (1982). Two kinds of preindustrial household formation system. *Population and Development Review*, *8*(3), 449–494.

Hawkes, K., O'Connell, J. F., & Blurton Jones, N. G. (1997). Hadza women's time allocation, offspring provisioning, and the evolution of post-menopausal lifespan. *Current Anthropology*, *38*, 551–578.

Hawkes, K., O'Connell, J. F., Blurton Jones, N. G., Alvarez, H., & Charnov, E. (1998). Grandmothering, menopause, and the evolution of human life histories. *Proceedings of the National Academy of Sciences of the United States of America*, *95*, 1336–1339.

Henrich, J. (2010). The evolution of innovation-enhancing institutions. In M. J. O'Brien & S. Shennan (Eds.), *Innovation in cultural systems: Contributions from evolutionary anthropology* (pp. 99–120). Cambridge, MA: MIT Press.

Henrich, J., Boyd, R., & Richerson, P. J. (2012). The puzzle of monogamous marriage. *Philosophical Transactions of the Royal Society B*, *367*, 657–669.

Henzi, S. P., Clarke, P. M. R., van Schaik, C. P., Pradhan, G. R., & Barrett, L. (2010). Infanticide and reproductive restraint in a polygynous social mammal. *Proceedings of the National Academy of Sciences of the United States of America*, *107*(5), 2130–2135.

Hill, K., & Hurtado, A. M. (1996). *Ache life history: The ecology and demography of a foraging people*. New York: Aldine de Gruyter.

Hill, K., & Hurtado, A. M. (2009). Cooperative breeding in South American hunter-gatherers. *Proceedings of the Royal Society B*, *276*(1674), 3863–3870.

Hinde, K., & Milligan, L. A. (2011). Primate milk: Proximate mechanisms and ultimate perspectives. *Evolutionary Anthropology*, *20*, 9–23.

Hrdy, S. B. (1999). *Mother nature: A history of mothers, infants, and natural selection*. New York: Pantheon/Chatto & Windus.

Hrdy, S. B. (2009). *Mothers and others: The evolutionary origins of mutual understanding*. Cambridge, MA: Harvard University Press.

Inglehart, R., & Welzel, C. (2005). *Modernization, cultural change, and democracy: The human development sequence*. New York: Cambridge University Press.

Inkeles, A., & Smith, D. H. (1974). *Becoming modern: Individual change in six developing countries.* Cambridge, MA: Harvard University Press.

Irons, W. (1979). Cultural and biological success. In N. A. Chagnon & W. Irons (Eds.), *Evolutionary biology and human social behavior* (pp. 257–272). North Scituate, MA: Duxbury Press.

James, R. J. A., Irons, D. W., Holmes, C., Charlton, A. L., Drewett, R. F., & Baylis, P. H. (1995). Thirst induced by a suckling episode during breast feeding and its relation with plasma vasopressin, oxytocin, and osmoregulation. *Clinical Endocrinology, 43,* 277–282.

Kaplan, H. S., & Robson, A. J. (2002). The emergence of humans: The coevolution of intelligence and longevity with intergenerational transfers. *Proceedings of the National Academy of Sciences of the United States of America, 99,* 10221–10226.

Kingdon, J. D. (2007). Shifting adaptive landscapes: Progress and challenges in reconstructing early hominid environments. *Yearbook of Physical Anthropology, 50,* 20–58.

Klein, R. G. (2009). *The human career: Human biological and cultural origins* (3rd ed.). Chicago: Chicago University Press.

Konig, B. (1993). Maternal investment of communally nursing female house mice (*Mus musculus domesticus*). *Behavioural Processes, 30,* 61–73.

Konner, M., & Worthman, C. (1980). Nursing frequency, gonadal function, and birth spacing among !Kung hunter-gatherers. *Science, 207,* 788–791.

Kramer, K. L. (2005). Children's help and the pace of reproduction: Cooperative breeding in humans. *Evolutionary Anthropology, 14*(6), 224–237.

Kramer, K. L., & Ellison, P. T. (2010). Pooled energy budgets: Resituating human energy allocation tradeoffs. *Evolutionary Anthropology, 19,* 136–147.

Loulergue, L., Schilt, A., Spahni, R., Masson-Delmotte, V., Blunier, T., Lemieux, B., et al. (2008). Orbital and millennial-scale features of atmospheric CH4 over the past 800,000 years. *Nature, 453,* 383–386.

Lehman, S. (1993). Ice sheets, wayward winds, and sea change. *Nature, 365,* 108–109.

Lovejoy, C. O. (2009). Reexamining human origins in light of *Ardipithecus ramidus. Science, 236,* 74.

Low, B. S. (1993). Ecological demography: A synthetic focus in evolutionary anthropology. *Evolutionary Anthropology, 1,* 177–187.

Low, B. S. (1999). Sex, wealth, and fertility: Old rules in new environments. In L. Cronk, N. A. Chagnon, & W. Irons (Eds.), *Human behavior and adaptations: An anthropological perspective* (pp. 323–344). New York: Aldine de Gruyter.

Low, B. S. (2000). *Why sex matters.* Princeton, NJ: Princeton University Press.

Mace, R., & Sear, R. (2005). Are humans cooperative breeders? In E. Voland, A. Chasiotis, & W. Schiefenhoevel (Eds.), *Grandmotherhood: The evolutionary significance of the second half of female life* (pp. 143–159). Piscataway, NJ: Rutgers University Press.

Martrat, B., Grimalt, J. O., Shackleton, N. J., de Abreu, L., Hutterli, M. A., & Stocker, T. F. (2007). Four climate cycles of recurring deep and surface water destabilizations on the Iberian margin. *Science, 317,* 502–507.

McGrew, W. C. (1992). *Chimpanzee material culture: Implications for human evolution.* Cambridge, UK: Cambridge University Press.

McGrew, W. C., Baldwin, P. J., & Tutin, C. E. G. (1988). Diet of wild chimpanzees (*Pan troglodytes verus*) at Mt. Assirik, Senegal: I. Composition. *American Journal of Primatology, 16,* 213–226.

McGrew, W. C., Tutin, C. E. G., & Baldwin, P. J. (1979). Chimpanzees, tools, and termites: crosscultural comparisons of Senegal, Tanzania, and Rio Muni. Man, 185–214.

McLaren, A. (1990). *A history of contraception.* Oxford, UK: Basil Blackwell.

Mendoza, S. P., & Mason, W. A. (1986). Parental division of labour and differentiation of attachments in a monogamous primate (*Callicebus moloch*). *Animal Behaviour, 34,* 1336–1347.

Mitani, J., & Watts, D. P. (1999). Demographic influences on the hunting behavior of chimpanzees. *American Journal of Physical Anthropology, 109,* 439–454.

Newson, L., Postmes, T., Lea, S. E. G., & Webley, P. (2005). Why are modern families small? Toward an evolutionary and cultural explanation for the demographic transition. *Personality and Social Psychology Review, 9*(4), 360–375.

Newson, L., Postmes, T., Lea, S. E. G., Webley, P., Richerson, P. J., & McElreath, R. (2007). Influences on communication about reproduction: The cultural evolution of low fertility. *Evolution and Human Behavior, 28*, 199–210.

Newson, L., & Richerson, P. J. (2009). Why do people become modern: A Darwinian mechanism. *Population and Development Review, 35*(1), 117–158.

O'Connell, J. F., Hawkes, K., & Blurton Jones, N. G. (1999). Grandmothering and the evolution of Homo erectus. *Journal of Human Evolution, 36*, 461–485.

Potts, R. (1998a). Environmental hypotheses of hominin evolution. *Yearbook of Physical Anthropology, 41*, 93–136.

Potts, R. (1998b). Variability selection in hominid evolution. *Evolutionary Anthropology, 7*(3), 81–96.

Reed, K. E. (1997). Early hominid evolution and ecological change through the African Plio-Pleistocene. *Journal of Human Evolution, 32*, 289–322.

Richerson, P. J., & Boyd, R. (2001). Built for speed, not for comfort: Darwinian theory and human culture. *History and Philosophy of the Life Sciences, 23*, 423–463.

Richerson, P. J., & Boyd, R. (2005). Not by genes alone: How culture transformed human evolution. Chicago: University of Chicago Press.

Richerson, P. J., & Boyd, R. (in press). Rethinking palaeoanthropology: A world queerer than we supposed. In G. Hatfield & H. Pittman (Eds.), *Evolution of Mind*, Brain and Culture. Philadelphia: University of Pennsylvania Museum of Archaeology and Anthropology Press.

Robbins, M. M., Bermejo, M., Cipolletta, C., Magliocca, F., Parnell, R. J., & Stokes, E. (2004). Social structure and life-history patterns in Western Gorillas (*Gorilla gorilla gorilla*). *American Journal of Primatology, 64*, 145–159.

Sear, R., & Mace, R. (2008). Who keeps children alive? A review of the effects of kin on child survival. *Evolution and Human Behavior, 29*(1), 1–18.

Sellen, D. W. (2006). Lactation, complementary feeding, and human life history. In K. Hawkes & R. R. Paine (Eds.), *The evolution of human life history* (pp. 155–196). Santa Fe, NM: School of American Research Press.

Sellen, D. W. (2007). Evolution of infant and young child feeding: Implications for contemporary public health. *Annual Review of Nutrition, 27*, 123–148.

Smith, B. H., & Tompkins, R. L. (1995). Toward a life history of the Hominidae. *Annual Review of Anthropology, 24*, 257–279.

Smith, E. A. (1998). Is Tibetan polyandry adaptive? *Human Nature, 9*(3), 225–261.

Stumbo, P. J., Booth, B. M., Eichenberger, J. M., & Dusdieker, L. B. (1985). Water intakes of lactating women. *American Journal of Clinical Nutrition, 42*, 870–876.

Trauth, M. H., Maslin, M. A., Deino, A., & Strecker, M. R. (2005). Late Cenozoic moisture history of East Africa. *Science, 309*, 2051–2053.

Valeggia, C. R., & Ellison, P. T. (2001). Lactation, energetics, and postpartum fecundity. In P. T. Ellison (Ed.), *Reproductive ecology and human evolution* (pp. 85–105). New York: Aldine de Gruyter.

Walker, R. S., Hill, K. R., Flinn, M. V., & Ellsworth, R. M. (2011). Evolutionary history of hunter-gatherer marriage practices. *PLoS ONE, 6*(4), e19066.

Walker, R., Gurven, M., Hill, K., Migliano, A., Chagnon, N., Souza, R. D., et al. (2006). Growth rates and life histories in twenty-two small-scale societies. *American Journal of Human Biology, 18*, 295–311.

Wallis, J. (1997). A survey of reproductive parameters in the free-ranging chimpanzees of Gombe National Park. *Journal of Reproduction and Fertility, 109*, 297–307.

Wang, F., Lee, J., & Campbell, C. (1995). Marital fertility control among the Qing nobility: Implications for two types of preventive checks. *Population Studies, 49*, 383–400.

Watkins, S. C. (1989). The fertility transition: Europe and the third world compared. In J. M. Stycos (Ed.), *Demography as an Interdiscipline* (pp. 27–55). New Brunswick, NJ: Transaction Publishers.

Wells, J. C. K., & Stock, J. T. (2007). The biology of the colonizing ape. *Yearbook of Physical Anthropology, 50*, 191–222.

Whitehead, H. (2003). *Sperm whales: Social evolution in the ocean.* Chicago: University of Chicago Press.

Whiten, A., Goodall, J., McGrew, W. C., Nishida, T., Reynolds, V., Sugiyama, Y., et al. (1999). Cultures in chimpanzees. *Nature, 399,* 682–685.

Whiting, B., & Whiting, J. (1975). *Children of six cultures, a psycho-cultural analysis.* Cambridge, MA: Harvard University Press.

Wich, S., Utami-Atmoko, S., Mitra Setia, T., Rijksen, H., Schurmann, C., van Hooff, J., et al. (2004). Life history of wild Sumatran orangutans (*Pongo abelii*). *Journal of Human Evolution, 47,* 385–398.

Winking, J., Gurven, M., & Kaplan, H. (2011). Father death and adult success among Tsimane: Implications for marriage and divorce. *Evolution and Human Behavior, 32,* 79–89.

Wrigley, E. A. (1978). Fertility strategy for the individual and the group. In C. Tilly (Ed.), *Historical studies of changing fertility* (pp. 135–154). Princeton University Press.

Wrigley, E., & Schofield, R. S. (1981). The Population History of England (pp. 1541–1871). Cambridge: Harvard Univ. Press.

# 8

# Human Attachment Vocalizations and the Expanding Notion of Nurture

ROSEMARIE SOKOL CHANG

## Introduction

In this chapter, I review the evidence that listeners are more responsive to vocalizations used between attachment partners than they are to everyday, adult-directed speech. On average, listeners of both sexes and with varying levels of parenting experience show increased responsiveness to these vocalizations, and as such I propose that humans share an auditory sensitivity to the acoustic properties exploited by multiple *attachment vocalizations*. This sensitivity begins in infancy and continues throughout life, reflecting the expanse of potential caregivers in the evolutionary history of hominins, and the importance of child rearing to a range of individuals in addition to the mother. While in humans attachment begins between the mother and infant before birth, attachment relationships extend to multiple caregivers after birth, and these are all maintained through the use of attachment vocalizations. Such a reframing of these vocalizations to include nonmothers requires expanding the nurturing role of "mother" to include not only siblings, parents, and other relatives, but other nonrelated group members as well.

Much of the caregiving research follows from the attachment tradition laid out by Bowlby (1969/1982). Bowlby proposed that attachment is proximity seeking between a caregiver and infant (though this has been extended to adult romantic relationships among others of late; for review see Cassidy & Shaver, 2008). An attachment partnership includes those behaviors that function to decrease the proximity between primary caregiver and infant, including vocalizations, physical movement toward a partner, and infant smiles and coos. Those who have adopted Bowlby's definition have almost exclusively focused on the attachment relationship as the one involving mother and infant. Using the relationship of mother and infant is not an arbitrary starting point. In mammalian species, roughly 3–5% practice monogamous pairings (Alcock, 2001) in which infants would reliably experience interaction with fathers as well as mothers. In the remaining 95% or so, it is far more common that mammalian mothers rear infants alone. Yet humans show indications of a lengthy history of shared childcare that cannot be overlooked when examining human attachment relationships (see Hrdy, 2009, for an overview).

Early studies of infant cries likewise emphasized the mother-infant dyad by looking for the ability of mothers to discriminate between types of cries (e.g., Wasz-Höckert et al., 1964; Wolff, 1969), and later for the perceptual and physiological responses of mothers and fathers compared to nonparents in response to cries (e.g., Boukydis & Burgess, 1982; Frodi, Lamb, Leavitt, & Donovan, 1978). The prevailing view largely remains that women, regardless of parenting experience, are more uniquely responsive to infant cries than fathers, who more often show signs of orientation but not positive action when presented with cries (see Zeifman, 2001).

Early research on the vocalizations directed toward infants likewise examined the mother-infant dyad, using the terms "maternal speech" (Dale, 1974), "mothers' speech" (Murata & Ohara, 1966), or "motherese" (Newport, 1975); though later these were revised to include fathers with the terms "paternal speech" (Rondal, 1980), "parental speech" (Slobin, 1972), or "parentese" (Chafetz, Feldman, & Wareham, 1992). A shift to the terms "infant-directed speech" (Karzon, 1985) and "child-directed speech" (Warren-Leubecker & Bohannon, 1984) reflected a change in emphasis from who is speaking (i.e., a mother or parent) to whom a vocalization is being directed toward (i.e., an infant or child), rather than an updated view of who constitutes a caregiver.

There is certainly a primacy in the early attachment relationship between mother and infants as echoed in a mother's increased responsiveness to cries and their motivation to action when compared to other potential caregivers. However, as researchers examine infant responsiveness to infant-directed speech produced by multiple caregivers, and the responsiveness of many adults to whining, the picture slowly changes. Rather than an exclusive relationship between mother and infant, in humans it appears that attachment relationships become an increasingly wider circle with each year of the infant's life and with each vocalization added to the repertoire of those employed between intimate partners.

Recently, more attention has been given to the role of others in early human attachment relationships. While mothers clearly have the largest effect on child survival, the effect of fathers, though more variable, appears to have some influence on child survival, particularly after weaning (Sear & Mace, 2008; see also Gray & Anderson, 2010). Grandmothers, both maternal and paternal, have an effect on child survival (Mace & Sear, 2004), as do older siblings in the few studies in which their role has been examined (e.g., Crognier, Baali,

& Hilali, 2001). The role of these alloparents is most notable in the context of the nonindustrialized populations that made up the bulk of the Sear and Mace (2008) analysis. When looking proximately, we see evidence that gains in a child's cognitive and emotional development peaks with three attachment partners, not one—and so long at the attachment is secure, to whom one is attached makes little difference (van Ijzendoorn, Sagi, & Lambermon, 1992). Compared to the living primates to which humans are most closely related, human mothers guard their offspring from group members much less closely. Chimpanzee, gorilla, and orangutan mothers do not allow others to hold their infants for 3.5–6 months after birth; human mothers allow others to hold the infant almost immediately following birth (see Hrdy, 2009). In this way, humans are much more similar to primate species that cooperatively breed, namely marmosets and tamarins.

Even in humans, the role of the mother in child rearing cannot be ignored. In all societies, mothers spend more time on caregiving responsibilities than fathers (Gray & Anderson, 2010). When mothers work outside of the home, they spend on average one-third to one-half more time with children than do working fathers (Lamb, Pleck, Chamov, & Levine, 1987). I consider that while mothers are predominantly the primary caregiver in humans, the fact that other people consistently care for infants and children indicates that over the course of human evolution the relationship between mother and infant seems likely to have affected humans at large. For example, Hrdy (2009) considers the role of mutual gaze and theory of mind, both characteristic of humans, as most likely stemming from the social bond between mother and infant and having major implications for the evolution of cooperation. I believe the extension of attachment vocalizations from mother and child to the larger group is one vestige of the strong role of women in human evolution.

Some of the distinctive aspects of human attachment vocalizations that I will present here are better explained by the view that humans have undergone selection for alloparental care and small group living. For example, in the few primate species that have consistent maternal vocalizations, mothers vocalize when the infant is in the care of an alloparent and thus the mother needs a nonphysical form of proximity regulation (see, for example, Biben, 1992). Babbling, which is produced by infants only when not in physical contact with a caregiver, has been noted in primates only among those that cooperatively breed—humans, marmosets, and tamarins (Elowson, Snowdon, & Lazaro-Perea, 1998; Hrdy, 2009). Human infants begin babbling around 6 months, when alloparents are more engaged in caretaking (Oller & Eilers, 1988), and infant cries are past their peak (Barr, 1990). Finally, while temper tantrums have been noted in other primate species (see Butovskaya, Verbeek, Ljungberg, & Lunardini, 2000, for review), humans also whine, which is less dramatically physical, and primarily a vocal form of protest that peaks around the time of independence, and thus when more potential caregivers are engaged (Chang & Thompson, 2010).

# An Overview of Attachment Vocalizations

Human infants are noisy from the moment of birth. They make a remarkable range of noises, from whimpers to cries, and later babbles, words, and whines. People around them respond in kind with smiles, coos, and by producing an infant-directed sound known as motherese. The vocal repertoire of human infants and caregivers is unique for the range of contexts in which an infant will produce sounds, and the extensiveness of caregivers who will likely give a response. Despite the extent to which humans vocalize compared to other mammals, the basic function across mammalian species appears similar. Infants, and in some cases adults, reliably produce vocalizations in an attempt to bring an attachment partner nearer. Thus, my colleagues and I (see Sokol et al., 2005) employ the term "attachment vocalizations" to mean vocalizations that serve a proximity-seeking function between two partners involved in an intimate relationship.

Of these attachment vocalizations, infant cries, motherese, and whines are the most studied among human subjects. These vocalizations share key acoustic features; they are spoken at a slower rate, and with higher and more variable pitch than the neutral, or adult-directed speech used in every day conversation (see Sokol, Webster, Thompson, & Stevens, 2005). These vocalizations sound more melodic than adult-directed speech (Fernald, 1992a; Fernald & Kuhl, 1987; Katz, 1999).

Neurological evidence implicates the same areas in the brain in both the production of infant calls, and the maternal response to them (Newman, 2007). The rostral midline cortex is involved in the production of crying sounds (Newman, 2003), as well as being activated in human mothers when they hear infant cries (Lorberbaum et al., 2002). The amygdala and anterior cingulate gyrus show activation for both production of and response to crying sounds in human and non-human primates (Newman, 2003). Such similarities have led Newman (2003) to consider a mammalian cry circuit linking production to response as one of the earliest forms of vocal communication among mammals.

My colleagues and I have conducted research that implies a functional and perceptual similarity among these vocalizations as well. Listeners are more distracted by infant cries, whines, and motherese than other human- and nonhuman-produced sounds (Chang & Thompson, 2011). Further, listeners attend more to whines and motherese than competing adult-directed speech played simultaneously (Chang & Thompson, 2010). That humans on average, regardless of sex and parenting experience, are distracted by and drawn to listen to these vocalizations suggests a common role in attachment relationships.

These similarities in acoustic structure, neurology, and function are sufficient for us to consider them as a group rather than isolated vocalizations. There are features of these human-produced attachment vocalizations that mirror counterparts in the mammalian world; however, there are also features that clearly distinguish them from the vocal communication systems of other mammals. For example, human infant cries are produced even once reunited with a caregiver, and are directed at and responded to by a wealth of caregivers rather than only the mother. Motherese is used by caregivers other than mothers (including men), and infants show responsiveness to mother- and other-produced motherese. Whines appear to involve a deceptive element, rather than the extortion model proposed for nonhuman primate tantrums related to weaning conflict (e.g., Trivers, 1974). In the following sections I outline these comparisons and contrasts with nonhuman attachment vocalizations.

## From Isolation Calls to Infant Cries

Vocalizations are integral for restoring proximity between mother and infant upon separation across most, if not all, mammalian species (Newman, 1985, 2003). Infants of many species employ species-specific calls that function to bring the mother nearer, known as separation or isolation calls. Those species in which the infant is at the greatest risk of predation are those who most often employ isolation calls, including mammals and precocial birds that are mobile soon after birth. The costs of these signals are offset by the advantage mothers have, compared to predators, in pinpointing the location of the infant. Part of that advantage comes from having been the last individual in contact with the infant.

As the name implies, in nonhuman species, isolation calls are limited to cases in which the mother and infant are separated. For example, infant squirrel monkeys produce the isolation call more frequently the farther they are from the natal group (Masataka & Symmes, 1986). Further, isolation calls decline in frequency as the infant becomes more independent, such as in the phyllostomid bat, whose infants begin emitting echolocation pulses when they start to fly, and decrease use of pulses as their confidence in flying increases (Sterbing, 2002).

Responsiveness to isolation calls differs across species and is dependent on the identity of the typical caregivers. In many bird species that feature care from both parents, both females and males are responsive to isolation calls. This includes white-throated sparrows, the females and males of which experience a peak response to distress vocalizations when the young are still dependent, but not when made by independent young (Stefanski & Falls, 1972). For most mammals, mothers alone have a perceptual sensitivity to distress vocalizations, as typically only the mother rears the infants. In rats, mothers but not virgin females are responsive to isolation calls (Farrell & Alberts, 2002) indicating the role of experience in mothering in responding to sounds produced by infants.

Mothers from many species can identify their own infants on the basis of the isolation call alone (see Newman, 2007 for a review). Bottlenose dolphins have whistles that are specific to the mother-infant dyad; among herd living animals, mothers can recognize their infants based on vocalization alone, and squirrel monkey isolation "peeps" are individually recognizable (Symmes & Biben, 1985; Symmes, Newman, Riggs, & Lieblich, 1979). In general, mammalian mothers do not respond to isolation calls indiscriminately, but rather a mother's responsiveness depends on whether the vocalizer is her own offspring. In rats, mothers need scent cues coupled with vocalizations before approaching a distressed infant, and Japanese macaques respond to the call of their own more than another mother's infant (see Newman, 2007). While humans are sensitive to a newborn's smell, pheromones are not as integral to the bonding relationship in humans as other animals.

Human neonates produce cries that are most similar to the isolation calls used by infants of species that carry, as opposed to créche their infants (Blurton-Jones, 1972). The cries of temporarily distressed infants have a higher pitch and shorter, more frequent bursts than those of nondistressed infants (Johnston & Strada, 1986; Porter, Miller, & Marshall, 1986). Further, these stress cries are rated as more distressing, urgent, and arousing than other cries (Crowe & Zeskind, 1992; Frodi, 1981; Wood & Gustafson, 2001). A similar pattern has been established in cries in which the pitch has been manipulated; as the pitch of cries increases, so do subjective ratings of urgency, aversiveness, and distress indicated in the infant cry (Dessureau, Kurowski, & Thompson, 1998; Thompson, Olson, & Dessureau, 1996).

Like isolation calls, early infant cries function to bring an attachment figure nearer. Infants cry more when further from their mothers, and typically stop crying when contact is resumed (Bell & Ainsworth, 1972; Christensson, Cabrera, Christensson, Uvnas-Moberg, & Winberg, 1995). The closer an infant is to a caregiver, the shorter the duration of each crying bout. For example, among the !Kung San, who carry their infants continuously, infants cry as frequently as Western-reared infants, but are responded to more quickly and thus cry for less time overall (Barr, Konner, Bakeman, & Adamson, 1991).

Though infant cries share the proximity-seeking function with isolation calls, their timing and organization appear to have some distinct features in comparison to isolation calls. Infants will continue to cry even when in contact with a caregiver (Zeifman, 2001). Further, they appear to be self-perpetuating, in that once an infant begins to cry full-force, it is harder to stop. Cries are presumed to have metabolic and predatory costs to the signaler much like isolation calls (see Thompson, Dessureau, & Olson, 1998, for an alternative perspective), but given their extended length they also impose the cost of annoying and repelling a caregiver, and have been linked to abuse and infanticide (Frodi, 1981; Zeskind & Shingler, 1991)

The shifting pattern of infant cries also distinguishes them from isolation calls. Infant cries reliably begin at birth, peaking within the first 6 weeks and leveling out around 4 months, with little change during the rest of the first year (Barr, 1990). Coupled with this shift in crying is a shift in maternal responsiveness; mothers are less responsive to the cries of 4-month-old infants than of younger infants, corresponding with the increase in alloparental care (Hrdy, 2009). While early crying has been attributed to internal causes (e.g., hunger, temperature changes), later crying is attributed more to external causes such as the social environment (Zeifman, 2001). Between 7 and 9 months of age, the infant begins to cry when near the caregiver, and quiet at her/his approach; and at 9–12 months, the infant will cry in the presence of a stranger even when with a caregiver. At this age the infant has other proximity-seeking behaviors, such as crawling (Zeifman, 2001). At around 2 years old, the child shows a decrease both in stranger anxiety and crying, and an increase in "noncompliance" behaviors such as temper tantrums (Gesell & Ilg, 1943; Potegal & Davidson, 2003) and whining (Sears & Sears, 1995).

As with mammalian counterparts, human mothers show sensitivity to the cries of their infants. Mothers can recognize the cries of their own infants within days of birth (Formby, 1967; Green & Gustafson, 1983; Weisenfeld, Malatesta, & DeLoach 1981). Mothers in particular show a heightened ability to assess the amount of risk indicated in a cry voiced by their own infants compared to unknown infants (Weisenfeld et al., 1981). Mothers also show more immediate response to cries indicating pain than hunger (Wolff, 1969), though their ability to distinguish between cry types depends on the cries of their own, and not an unfamiliar infant. Mothers have physiological changes that indicate responsiveness when listening to cries, namely an immediate decrease in heart rate followed by a rapid increase, indicating preparation for action (Weisenfeld et al., 1981), an increase in breast temperature when listening to cries (Vuorenkoski, Wasz-Höckert, Koivisto, & Lind, 1969), and a milk-letdown response to cries (Mead & Newton, 1967).

Fathers also show responsiveness to infant cries. Forty-five percent of fathers (compared to 80% of mothers) can recognize their infants on the basis of cry alone (Green & Gustafson, 1983). Given the limited daily exposure Western men, on average, have with their infants (estimated around 1 hour a day during the work week, Sayer, Bianchi, & Robinson, 2004), this percentage is rather impressive. Fathers show physiological changes in response to infant cries as well, more so than in response to infant smiles (Brewster, Nelson, McCanne, Lucas, & Milner, 1998), though the changes are more indicative of general orientation or passive attention than action (Brewster et al., 1998; Weisenfeld et al., 1981). We know from hormonal studies that similar to mothers, expectant fathers experience an increase in prolactin and cortisol right before the birth of a new infant, and decreases in testosterone and estradiol following birth (Storey, Walsh, Quinton, & Wynne-Edwards, 2000). Similarly, fathers show greater increases in testosterone and prolactin in response to infant cries than nonfathers, a change particularly pronounced among those with more fathering experience (Fleming, Corter, Stallings, & Steiner, 2002).

Looking beyond the parents to potential alloparents, there is a general responsiveness to infant cries shown by all adult listeners. Perceptual ratings of cries are similar among men and women, regardless of parental status (Falcon, Stevens, &

Thompson, 2001; Gustafson & Green, 1989). Mothers and midwives (Morsbach, McCulloch, & Clark, 1986) and men and women (Chang & Thompson, 2011) show impaired cognitive functioning when presented with infant cries in comparison to aversive machine noise. Women and men show physiological changes in response to infant cries, including changes in heart rate and skin conductance when listening to infant cries compared to positive stimuli (Boukydis, 1985; Brewster et al., 1998; Crowe & Zeskind, 1992; Frodi, 1985).

While infant cries show similarities in function and maternal response to isolation calls, they clearly differ in the prolonged nature of the cry, pattern of crying over the first few years, and the response to cries by many adults rather than mother alone. The production of cries reflects the developmental immaturity of the infant in the first few months (Zeifman, 2001), as well as the relatively helpless nature of the child during the first year of life (see Montagu, 1961). The extensiveness of isolation calls in the animal world, as well the primacy of cries and the responsiveness of adult listeners to them, indicates that infant cries have an earlier phylogenetic history than other attachment vocalizations (Newman, 2007), including those produced by mothers (and others) in response to temporarily separated infants.

## Maternal Vocalizations and Motherese

While isolation vocalizations are present in most mammalian species, maternal vocalizations in response are much less common. Maternal vocalizations are used particularly by species in which there are reliable instances in which mother and infant are not in contact. There are mammalian and bird species that employ maternal vocalizations to maintain contact when physically separated. Yet in great ape species, in which infants stay within at least visual contact of the mother for the first few years, maternal vocalizations are not heard (Hrdy, 2009). Common chimpanzee infants maintain almost continual contact with the mother during the first year, and at 2 years begin to separate, maintaining a distance from her of about 5 meters (Bard, 1995); bonobo infants still remain within 10 meters of the mother by 3 years of age (Kuroda, 1989). Members of these species do not employ maternal vocalizations.

Among primates, maternal and caregiver vocalizations are emitted in species that have shared care, where the mother needs to communicate with the absent infant. Squirrel monkey infants remain on their mothers' backs during the first few weeks of life and their mothers vocalize very little to their own infants during this time (Biben, 1992). Allomothers, however, communicate with caregiver calls quite frequently starting in the first week, and up to a rate of 100 times per hour. Once the infants begin to be cared for by these allomothers, mothers vocalize to separated infants quite frequently, most often to retrieve the infant (Biben, 1992). Squirrel monkey maternal calls vary acoustically based on context, such as when emitted to begin nursing or initiate retrieval from an allomother (Biben, Symmes, & Bernhards, 1989).

Humans too display maternal vocalizations, which I refer to here as motherese. While the term "motherese" might be misleading given its use by humans of all ages and both genders, I use it to emphasize the connection to maternal vocalizations in other species, and the likely origin of this form of speech—with mothers. Motherese is spoken at a slower rate and with higher and more varied pitch than the conversational speech known as adult-directed speech (Fernald, 1992b; Fernald & Kuhl, 1987). There are slight alterations in motherese spoken in different languages, but in general men and women speak to infants in a higher pitch way distinct from they way they speak to adults in all but one culture examined (see Falk, 2009 for a review), including English, French, German, Italian, and Japanese (Fernald et al., 1989). In the one culture observed in which mothers make no prosodic alterations toward infants, a Quiché speaking group in Guatemala, children show consistent language delays (Falk, 2009). Infants show a preference for motherese soon after birth (Cooper & Aslin, 1994; Fernald, 1985) and can distinguish between context-dependent variants of motherese, such as the form used as a prohibition (Kearsley, 1973).

Motherese is a rather unique form of maternal vocalization because of the breadth of caregivers who use it. While among squirrel monkeys, allomothers produce similar calls to maternal calls, among humans motherese is used by mothers and fathers, other adults, and even children (Snow, 1977). Adults will lapse into motherese with infants that they do not know in line at the grocery store, and have been observed extending this vocalization to other caregiving situations, such as speaking in motherese to pets (Burnham, Kitamura, & Vollmer-Conna, 2002) and the elderly (Whitbourne, Culgin, & Cassidy, 1995). The best supported functions of motherese are getting the attention of infants (Fernald, 1992b), regulating the infant's affect (Trainor, Austin, & Desjardins, 2000; Werker & McLeod, 1989), and assisting in language development (Karzon, 1985). Because of the slow rate at which it is spoken, and the simplicity of the language, motherese is the most conducive type of speech for prelinguistic infants to parse.

Infants are responsive to motherese produced by mothers and fathers, and other female and male caregivers (see, for example, Werker & McLeod, 1989). In fact when compared to adult-directed speech, infants are responsive to motherese uttered by strangers, as illustrated by the majority of motherese studies that use speech samples produced by unfamiliar speakers rather than parents (e.g., Fernald, 1985). Though responsiveness generalizes to other speakers, motherese produced by one's mother still apparently takes preference over unfamiliar females (Barker & Newman, 2004); however to my knowledge a study has not been performed contrasting responsiveness to the speech of fathers with males unfamiliar to the infants.

That infants are spoken to and responsive of motherese produced by a wealth of potential caregivers indicates a human history of shared childcare. Among species in which mothers maintain physical attachment to the infant, maternal vocalizations are not observed, such as chimpanzees, bonobos, and gorillas. Maternal vocalizations are only observed in species in which there is a physical separation between infant and mother, such as ocean animals like dolphins (Newman, 2003), or species that feature shared childcare, such as squirrel monkeys (Hrdy, 2009). Yet even in these examples, maternal vocalizations are shared among the *adult females* of a group. That human males and children produce motherese distinguishes this vocalization from its close counterparts in the world of mammals.

## Tantrums and Whines

Nonhuman primates emit "whines," or "whistles," most often around the time of weaning. Stump-tailed macaques have a whistle used during a weaning tantrum, Japanese macaques have a whine uttered when the mother accepts them following a weaning tantrum, and common chimpanzees have a hoo-whimper upon separating from the mother or during a tantrum (Newman & Symmes, 1982). Adult golden lion tamarins emit a whine when they spot a predator, as this vocalization makes it harder to detect the source of the sound (Boinski, Moraes, Kleiman, Dietz, & Baker, 1994).

In the nonhuman literature, whines are not often noted in isolation from temper tantrums. Nonhuman tantrums have been described among many primate species, most often linked to weaning conflict as a form of extortion (Trivers, 1974; but see also Thompson et al., 1998). A tantrum is possibly dangerous to the juvenile, as the behavior often includes flailing oneself around and possibly into other objects, and thus serves as a way of extorting a response from the caregiver to end the tantrum. As with humans, tantrums are also a social event; rhesus monkey mothers are more likely to give in to tantrums if other monkeys are nearby (Semple, Gerald, & Suggs, 2009).

Humans certainly throw temper tantrums, and according to one study whines are a component of tantrums around 13% of the time (Potegal & Davidson, 2003). However, whines in the absence of a tantrum seem to be a more unique event in the primate world. Whines are subtler than temper tantrums and unless coupled with a tantrum, the child is not harming her/himself. Whining appears more closely linked with deception, in the sense that the child is trying to appear more helpless or in pain than s/he really is. This use of deception has also been proposed as a function of infant cries, which mimic the aspects of respiratory distress such as choking (Thompson et al., 1998). A mathematical model developed by these authors suggests that because of the extensive common interest between parents and offspring, infants are unlikely to extort benefits from their parents. However, they are likely to fake distress because the net cost to the parent of responding to such fakery is so insignificant that it pays for parents to be gullible.

Human whines share with cries and motherese salient acoustic features as well, including increased pitch and a more melodic pattern of rises and falls

(Sokol et al., 2005). Different from cries, though, whines peak at a time of linguistic competence, making them more likely to be coupled with words. This peak, between 2.5–4 years of age (Sears & Sears, 1995), also corresponds with the time of increased independence and proximity from parents, making the whiners at a prime age for receiving care from nonparent caregivers.

Adults tend to focus on the negative aspects of children's whining, and as such the vocalization is rated as more annoying than other vocalizations (Sokol et al., 2005). When shifting the focus to the child, Katz (1999) proposes that whines are a way for the child to self-sooth, just as a mother might sooth with motherese. Indeed its melodic pattern indicates a closer relation to motherese than one might infer on first listen. Despite the negative ratings of whines, they clearly "work" in that they get attention from caregivers.

The few empirical observations of human whines indicate that listeners of both sexes, with and without children, have similar responses to whining. Men and women showed the same perceptual responses to whines (Sokol et al., 2005), rating them as more annoying and whiney than other types of speech. When engaged in simple cognitive tasks, adult listeners made more errors per math problems completed when listening to whines than to a similar sounding, high-pitched machine noise (Chang & Thompson, 2011). Adult listeners showed similar physiological increases in galvanic skin response and performed worse in a recitation task when listening to whines than to adult-directed speech (Chang & Thompson, 2010). Despite this impaired performance, these same adults actually recognized more words spoken in a whine than spoken in motherese or adult-directed speech bouts of equal length. Whines might have a directive, as well as distracting ability. However, this last point needs further examination.

More research needs to be performed on whines when considering their role in attachment relationships. If my colleagues and I are correct in our presumption that these vocalizations are of the same group, and that they similarly function to bring caregivers (both parents and others) and infants or children nearer to each other (see Sokol et al., 2005), then specific predictions need to be tested. For example, whether whines are uttered and responded to more in securely attached relationships; if there is a similar amount of crying, whining, and motherese employed in an attachment-dyad; and if whines are produced to a larger number of caregivers than earlier produced infant cries.

# The Relationship Between Attachment Vocalizations and Small Group Living

Having established the patterns of usage of infant cries, motherese, and whines, I now have the onus of supporting the notion that these vocalizations indicate the importance of child rearing for multiple group members, and reflect the formation of small group living in human history. I consider, in turn, some important aspects of the human ancestral environments, maternal infanticide, and the childhood period of development.

Molecular evidence suggests that the modern human species evolved from an extremely small population of between 10,000 and 12,000 individuals, somewhere in southern Africa approximately 200,000 years ago (Dawkins, 2005; Vigilant, Stoneking, Harpending, Hawkes, & Wilson, 1991). Together with the harsh conditions of the Pleistocene in which the human species subsequently prospered and spread, this fact suggests a powerful role for selection at a small group level for individual characteristics that promoted small group coherence and continuity. Such a characteristic would promote the engagement of all group members in the care of infants and juveniles and the breakdown in the discrimination that many species make between the distress sounds of their own and others' offspring. In such a group, the care and protection of the young becomes a bonding mechanism for group members. As I have reviewed in this chapter, such a breakdown is present in the generalized human production of and response to attachment vocalizations.

Human infants and children pose a child-rearing challenge because of their extreme helplessness, the extended period of dependence, and the shortened birth-interval. While many primate species are precocial, human infants display an extreme altriciality demarcated by their relatively underdeveloped brains, and lack of locomotive ability (Rosenberg & Trevathan, 2002). The reason for this helplessness is a matter of some disagreement, however there is evidence for the role of the size and shape of the human pelvis limiting the size of the head at birth. The enlarged brain appears to have had some influence on the female pelvis in *Homo erectus*, but to some it seems most likely the pelvis underwent selection *prior* to the increase in brain size (Rosenberg & Trevathan, 2002). Specifically, the broad shoulders of human ancestors, a vestige of suspension from trees, required a pelvic change to pass the birth canal. The difficulties posed to women for such a dramatic birthing process necessitates the assistance of others during labor, and indeed midwifery (not prostitution) has as a result been proposed as the first female profession (Rosenberg & Trevathan, 2002). The need for assistance in caregiving begins immediately preceding birth for humans.

The practice of infanticide committed by mothers is also indicative of the extreme altriciality of humans. Males have been noted to commit infanticide in many primate species to induce ovulation in, and mate with the mothers (Hausfater & Hrdy, 1984, for a review); however, the only primate species in which infanticide has been documented by mothers are those that cooperatively breed, including marmosets, tamarins, and humans (Hrdy, 2009). Infanticide in these species is a way of weighing investment options such as committing infanticide due to a lack of resources, or poor infant health (Hrdy, 1979). Interestingly, the latter is also an established link between infant cries and child abuse. The cries that show the most extreme pitch fluctuations are those of infants with health problems, and are also the cries most likely to evoke an abusive response from caregivers, both male and female (Crowe & Zeskind, 1992; Frodi, 1981, 1985; Zeskind & Shingler, 1991). Since a mother who depends on assistance from others is more at the mercy of others than one who provides all of the care, mothers of those species that feature alloparents are more likely to weight the costs of childcare, and on rare occasions opt for infanticide.

Humans appear unique in another way when compared to nonhuman primates by possessing a period of childhood (Bogin, 1997). Our closest living relatives, chimpanzees, bonobos, and gorillas, have a juvenile period of dependence following weaning but preceding sexual maturity. During this time, nonhuman primate juveniles are able to procure their own food but are still under protection from group members. In addition to this juvenile period, humans have a period of childhood that likewise follows weaning and precedes sexual maturity, but during which children are still dependent solely on caregivers for food. Between the ages of 3 and 7 years, human children have immature teeth and small digestive systems, making them require softer foods and denser nutrients than adults. This extended period of dependence poses an interesting problem to human mothers, who in addition to the lengthened dependence of offspring, have a shorter birth-interval than other primates. Thus, the demands of motherhood include greater overall length of investment for each child, while juggling investment in many children at once. Being able to maintain contact by using motherese, as well as to rely on others is needed to raise such needy children.

That human infants require more cooperative care from adults (Hrdy, 2009) has influences on group living. One major shift is the blurred distinction between kin and non-kin. Human females most often leave their natal groups, in distinction from Old World monkeys, whose females stay put (Wrangham, 1980; for implications see also Moscovice, this volume). The combination of infants requiring extensive care, and women raising infants among non-kin requires a shift from kin to reciprocal altruism in childcare. Perhaps as Hrdy (2009) proposes, it is no coincidence that humans are both cooperative breeders and the most reciprocally altruistic of all documented species; something reflected as well in the use of attachment vocalizations.

# Conclusions

Humans are not unique in producing specific vocalizations for use with attachment partners. Yet, they are unique in the generalizability of these vocalizations to multiple contexts and attachment partners. Though the form of these vocalizations alters with development—from infant cries, to whines, to motherese—the general acoustic and functional pattern of these vocalizations remains constant. The breadth of caregivers is reflected in the production of and response to these calls. To raise helpless human infants and dependent children requires a reorganization of group living such that all adults provide care for many children, rather than the relationship consisting primarily of mother and child.

In the vast majority of mammalian species, attachment relationships are isolated to mother and offspring, and mostly for a brief period of time. What are we to make of the fact that humans show such a willingness to engage in attachment specific vocalizations, and across most, if not all, of the lifespan? Vocalizations are a microcosm of attachment relationships. In humans, vocalizations make up an essential part of a repertoire of attachment behaviors (Chang, 2009). As we see when looking to attachment studies in general, forming early and lasting attachments is essential for social development and later intimate relationships. Bowlby's research shows us the link between lack of early attachment and later antisocial behavior (Bowlby, 1944), which is more strongly reiterated by Harlow's and McKinney's (1971) work with rhesus monkeys raised in isolation that later exhibited signs of irreparable psychoses. Infant attachment is connected to emotional regulation and social relatedness (Sroufe, 2005), and attachment style can inform us about adult romantic relationships (Feeney & Noller, 1990). The relationship between attachment and one's ability to function within a group seems undeniable.

I propose, as have others, that the intimate relationship between infant and mother—that still takes a primacy in early infancy and later development—actually led to major human developments. I argue here that attachment was a forerunner for heightened human sociality, which is not unlike Sarah Hrdy's (2009) argument that the mother-infant relationship in humans led to complex cognitive abilities such as theory of mind, empathy, and cooperation. Alternatively, Dean Falk (2009) considers motherese a necessary predecessor to human language. These are important hypotheses to test, and offer alternatives to the earlier models of social group living that focused on dominance and aggression.

An important focus of future research will be the variation in the use of attachment vocalizations. Variation in parenting quality has been established, for example by contrasting allocation in mating and parenting within the life history theory framework (see Kaplan & Gangestad, 2005). The quality of early care has multiple influences including on infant stress response (e.g., Francis, Champagne, Liu, & Meaney, 1999) and attachment style (e.g., Belsky, 1997). Individual differences in the use of one attachment vocalization, romantic babytalk (termed *loverese*) has been documented (Bombar & Littig, 1996; Chang & Garcia, 2010). Presumably, there will be variations in the use of motherese and whining that might in part be explained by variation in attachment style.

Examining attachment vocalizations offers a good addition to allow us to consider the role of mother-infant relationships and the history of human evolution. That these vocalizations are isolated to mothers and infants in almost all other mammalian species makes the human generalizability of attachment vocalizations stand out all the more. Starting with the physical capability to birth bigger brained babies, mothers have driven change in human group arrangement. While researchers have considered the African proverb that "it takes a village to raise a child," more recently there has been a focus on the intimate (and demanding) relationship between infants and mothers in changing social relationships. In the case of humans, it might be just as likely that it takes a child—and the associated primary and other caregivers—to raise a village.

# Acknowledgment

I am greatly indebted to Nicholas Thompson for all of the feedback he has given me on this chapter, and all of the attachment vocalization work I have produced.

# References

Alcock, J. (2001). *Animal behavior: An evolutionary approach* (7th ed.). Sunderland, MA: Sinauer Associates.

Bard, K. A. (1995). Parenting in primates. In M. H. Bornstein (Ed.), *Handbook of parenting: Vol. 2. Biology and ecology of parenting* (pp. 27–58). Mahwah, NJ: Erlbaum.

Barker, B. A., & Newman, R. S. (2004). Listen to your mother: The role of talker familiarity in infant streaming. *Cognition, 94*, 45–53.

Barr, R. G. (1990). The normal crying curve: What do we really know? *Developmental Medicine and Child Neurology, 32*, 356–362.

Barr, R. G., Konner, M., Bakeman, R., & Adamson, L. (1991). Crying in !Kung San infants: A test of the cultural specificity hypothesis. *Developmental Medicine and Child Neurology, 33*, 601–610.

Bell, S. M., & Ainsworth, M. D. S. (1972). Infant crying and maternal responsiveness. *Child Development, 43*, 1171–1190.

Belsky, J. (1997). Attachment, mating, and parenting. *Human Nature, 8*(4), 361–381.

Biben, M. (1992). Allomaternal vocal behavior in squirrel monkeys. *Developmental Psychobiology, 25*(2), 79–92.

Biben, M., Symmes, D., & Bernhards, D. (1989). Contour variables in vocal communication between squirrel monkey mothers and infants. *Developmental Psychobiology, 22*, 617–631.

Blurton Jones, N. (1972). Comparative aspects of mother-child contact. In N. Blurton Jones (Ed.), *Ethological studies of child behaviour* (pp. 305–328). Cambridge, UK: Cambridge University Press.

Bogin, B. (1997). Evolutionary hypotheses for human childhood. *Yearbook of Physical Anthropology, 20*, 63–89.

Boinski, S., Moraes, E., Kleiman, D. G., Dietz, J. M., & Baker, A. J. (1994). Intra-group vocal behaviour in wild golden lion tamarins, *Leontopithecus rosalia*: Honest communication of individual activity. *Behaviour, 130*, 53–75.

Bombar, M. L., & Littig, L. W. (1996). Babytalk as a communication of intimate attachment: An initial study in adult romances and friendships. *Personal Relationships, 3*, 137–158.

Boukydis, C. F. Z. (1985). Perception of infant crying as an interpersonal event. In B. M. Lester & C. F. Z. Boukydis (Eds.), *Infant crying: Theoretical and research perspectives* (pp. 187–215). New York: Plenum Press.

Boukydis, C. F. Z., & Burgess, R. L. (1982). Adult physiological response to infant cries: Effects of temperament of infant, parental status, and gender. *Child Development, 53*, 1291–1298.

Bowlby, J. (1944). Forty-four juvenile thieves: Their characters and home-life. *International Journal of Psychoanalysis, 25*, 19–53.

Bowlby, J. (1982). *Attachment*. New York: Basic Books. (Original work published 1969).

Brewster, A., Nelson, J., McCanne, T., Lucas, D., & Milner, J. (1998). Gender differences in physiological reactivity to infant cries and smiles in military families. *Child Abuse and Neglect, 28*, 775–788.

Burnham, D., Kitamura, C., & Vollmer-Conna, U. (2002). What's new pussycat? On talking to babies and animals. *Science, 296*(5572), 1435.

Butovskaya, M., Verbeek, P., Ljungberg, T., & Lunardini, A. (2000). A multicultural view of peacemaking among young children. In F. Aureli & F. B. M. de Waal (Eds.), *Natural conflict resolution* (pp. 243–258). Berkeley: University of California Press.

Cassidy, J., & Shaver, P. R. (2008). *Handbook of attachment: Theory, research, and clinical applications* (2nd ed.). New York: Guilford Press.

Chafetz, J., Feldman, H. M., & Wareham, N. L. (1992). "There car": Ungrammatical parentese. *Journal of Child Language, 19*(2), 473–480.

Chang, R. S. (2009). From mother's mouth to baby's world and back again: Shaping one's attachments through vocalization. In R. S. Chang (Ed.), *Relating to environments: A new look at Umwelt*. Charlotte, SC: Information Age.

Chang, R. S., & Garcia, J. R. (2010). *Loverese: Bonding through intimate baby talk*. Paper presented at the 4th Annual NorthEastern Evolutionary Psychology Society, State University of New York, New Paltz.

Chang, R. S., & Thompson, N. S. (2010). The attention-getting capacity of whines and child-directed speech. *Evolutionary Psychology, 8*(2), 260–274.

Chang, R. S., & Thompson, N. S. (2011). Whines, cries, and motherese: Their relative power to distract. *Journal of Social, Evolutionary, and Cultural Psychology, 5*(2), 131–141.

Christensson, K., Cabrera, T., Christensson, E., Uvnas-Moberg, K., & Winberg, J. (1995). Separation distress call in the human neonate in the absence of maternal body contact. *Acta Paediatrica, 84*, 468–473.

Cooper, R. P., & Aslin, R. N. (1994). Developmental differences in infant attention to the spectral properties of infant-directed speech. *Child Development, 65*, 1663–1677.

Crognier, E., Baali, A., & Hilali, M. K. (2001). Do "helpers at the nest" increase their parents' reproductive success? *American Journal of Human Biology, 13*, 365–373.

Crowe, H. P., & Zeskind, P. S. (1992). Psychophysiological and perceptual responses to infant cries varying in pitch: Comparison of adults with low and high scores on the Child Abuse Potential Inventory. *Child Abuse and Neglect, 16*, 16–29.

Dale, P. S. (1974). Hesitations in maternal speech. *Language and Speech, 17*(2), 174–181.

Dawkins, R. (2005). *The ancestor's tale: A pilgrimage to the dawn of evolution*. Boston: Mariner.

Dessureau, B. K., Kurowski, C. O., & Thompson, N. S. (1998). A reassessment of the role of pitch and duration in adult's responses to infant crying. *Infant Behavior and Development, 21*(2), 367–371.

Elowson, A. M., Snowdon, C. T., & Lazaro-Perea, C. (1998). Infant "babbling" in a nonhuman primate: Complex vocal sequences with repeated call types. *Behaviour, 135*(5), 643–664.

Falcon, R., Stevens, D. A., & Thompson, N. S. (2001, April). *Features of infant cries as perceived by adults*. Poster session presented at the Eleventh Annual Academic Spree Day, Clark University, Worcester, MA.

Falk, D. (2009). *Finding our tongues: Mothers, infants, and the origins of language*. New York: Basic Books.

Farrell, W. J., & Alberts, J. R. (2002). Stimulus control of maternal responsiveness to Norway rat (*Rattus norvegicus*) pup ultrasonic vocalizations. *Journal of Comparative Psychology, 116*, 297–307.

Feeney, J. A., & Noller, P. (1990). Attachment style as a predictor of adult romantic relationships. *Journal of Personality and Social Psychology, 58*(2), 281–291.

Fernald, A. (1985). Four-month-old infants prefer to listen to motherese. *Infant Behavior and Development, 8*(2), 181–195.

Fernald, A. (1992a). Meaningful melodies in mother's speech to infants. In U. J. Hanus- Papoušek & M. Papoušek (Eds.), *Nonverbal vocal communications* (pp. 262–282). New York: Cambridge University Press.

Fernald, A. (1992b). Human maternal vocalizations to infants as biologically relevant signals: An evolutionary perspective. In J. H. Barkow, L. Cosmides, & J. Tooby (Eds.), *The adapted mind: Evolutionary psychology and the generation of culture* (pp. 391–428). New York: Oxford University Press.

Fernald, A., & Kuhl, P. (1987). Acoustic determinants of infant preference for motherese speech. *Infant Behavior and Development, 10*(3), 279–293.

Fernald, A., Taeschner, T., Dunn, J., Papoušek, M., de Boysson-Bardies, B., & Fukui, I. (1989). A cross-language study of prosodic modifications in mothers' and fathers' speech to preverbal infants. *Journal of Child Language, 16*, 477–501.

Fleming, A. S., Corter, C., Stallings, J., & Steiner, M. (2002). Testosterone and prolactin are associated with emotional responses to infant cries in new fathers. *Hormones and Behavior, 42*(4), 399–413.

Formby, D. (1967). Maternal recognition of infant's cry. *Developmental Medicine and Child Neurology, 93*(3), 293–298.

Francis, D. D., Champagne, F. A., Liu, D., & Meaney, M. J. (1999). Maternal care, gene expression, and the development of individual differences in stress reactivity. *Annals of the New York Academy of Sciences, 896*, 66–84.

Frodi, A. M. (1981). Contribution of infant characteristics to child abuse. *American Journal of Mental Deficiency, 85*, 341–349.

Frodi, A. M. (1985). When empathy fails: Aversive infant crying and child abuse. In B. M. Lester & C. F. Z. Boukydis (Eds.), *Infant crying: Theoretical and research perspectives* (pp. 263–277). New York: Plenum Press.

Frodi, A. M, Lamb, M. E., Leavitt, L. A., & Donovan, W. L. (1978). Fathers' and mothers' responses to infant smiles and cries. *Infant Behavior and Development, 1*, 187–198.

Gesell, A., & Ilg, F. L. (1943). *Infant and child in the culture of today: The guidance of development in home and nursery school.* New York: HarperCollins.

Gray, P. B., & Anderson, K. G. (2010). *Fatherhood: Evolution and human paternal behavior.* Cambridge, MA: Harvard University Press.

Green, J. A., & Gustafson, G. E. (1983). Individual recognition of human infants on the basis of cries alone. *Developmental Psychobiology, 16*(6), 485–493.

Gustafson, G. E., & Green, J. A. (1989). On the importance of fundamental frequency and other acoustic features in cry perception and infant development. *Child Development, 60*, 772–780.

Harlow, H. F., & McKinney, W. T., Jr. (1971). Nonhuman primates and psychoses. *Journal of Autism and Childhood Schizophrenia, 1*(4), 368–375.

Hausfater, G., & Hrdy, S. B. (1984). *Infanticide: Comparative and evolutionary perspectives.* New York: Aldine.

Hrdy, S. B. (1979). Infanticide among animals: A review, classification, and examination of the implications for the reproductive strategies of females. *Ethology and Sociobiology, 1*(1), 13–40.

Hrdy, S. B. (2009). *Mothers and others: The evolutionary origins of mutual understanding.* Cambridge, MA: Harvard University Press.

Johnston, C. C., & Strada, M. E. (1986). Acute pain response in infants: A multidimensional description. *Pain, 24*, 373–382.

Kaplan, H. S., & Gangestad, S. W. (2005). Life history theory and evolutionary psychology. In D. M. Buss (Ed.), *The handbook of evolutionary psychology* (pp. 68–95). Hoboken, NJ: Wiley.

Karzon, R. G. (1985). Discrimination of polysyllabic sequences by one- to four- month old infants. *Journal of Experimental Child Psychology, 39*(2), 326–342.

Katz, J. (1999). An episode of whining. *How emotions work* (pp. 229–273). Chicago: University of Chicago Press.

Kearsley, R. (1973). The newborn's response to auditory stimulation: A demonstration of orienting and defensive behaviour. *Child Development, 44*, 582–590.

Kuroda, S. (1989). Developmental retardation and behavioral characteristics of pygmy chimpanzees. In P. G. Heltne & L. A. Marquardt (Eds.), *Understanding chimpanzees* (pp. 184–193). Cambridge, MA: Harvard University Press.

Lamb, M. E., Pleck, J. H., Chamov, E. L., & Levine, J. A. (1987). A biosocial perspective on parental behavior and involvement. In J. B. Lancaster, J. Altmann, A. S. Rossi, & L. R. Sherrod (Eds.), *Parenting across the lifespan: Biosocial dimensions* (pp. 111–137). Piscataway, NJ: Transaction.

Lorberbaum, J. P., Newman, J. D., Horwitz, A. R., Dubno, J. R., Lydiard, R. B., Hamner, ... George, M. S. (2002). A potential role for thalamocingulate circuitry in human maternal behavior. *Biological Psychiatry, 51,* 431–445.

Mace, R., & Sear, R. (2004). Are humans communal breeders? In E. Voland, A. Chasiotis, & W. Schiefenhoevel (Eds.), *Grandmotherhood: The evolutionary significance of the second half of female life.* Piscataway, NJ: Rutgers University Press.

Masataka, N., & Symmes, D. (1986). Effect of separation distance on isolation call structure in squirrel monkeys (*Saimiri sciureus*). *American Journal of Primatology, 10*(3), 271–278.

Mead, M., & Newton, N. (1967). Cultural patterning of perinatal behavior. In S. Richardson & A. Guttmacher (Eds.), *Childbearing: Its social and psychological aspects* (pp. 142–244). Baltimore: Williams & Wilkins.

Montagu, M. F. A. (1961). Neonatal and infant immaturity in man. *Journal of the American Medical Association, 178,* 56–57.

Morsbach, G., McCulloch, M., & Clark, A. (1986). Infant crying as a potential stressor concerning mothers' concentration ability. *Psychologia: An International Journal of Psychology in the Orient, 29*(1), 18–20.

Murata, K., & Ohara, T. (1966). The development of verbal behavior: VII. Role of mothers in "dialogues" with their one-year-old children. *Japanese Journal of Psychology, 27*(2), 67–73.

Newman, J. D. (1985). Squirrel monkey communication. In L. A. Rosenbaum & C. L. Coe (Eds.), *Handbook of squirrel monkey research* (pp. 99–126). New York: Plenum Press.

Newman, J. D. (2003). Vocal communication and the triune brain. *Physiology and Behavior, 79,* 495–502.

Newman, J. D. (2007). Neural circuits underlying crying and cry responding in mammals. *Behavioural Brain Research, 182,* 155–165.

Newman, J. D., & Symmes, D. (1982). Inheritance and experience in the acquisition of primate acoustic behavior. In C. T. Snowdon, C. H. Brown, & M. R. Petersen (Eds.), *Primate communication* (pp. 259–278). Cambridge, UK: Cambridge University Press.

Newport, E. (1975). Motherese: The speech of mothers to young children. *Dissertation Abstracts International, 36*(5-B), 2503–2504.

Oller, D. K., & Eilers, R. E. (1988). The role of audition in infant babbling. *Child Development, 59,* 441–449.

Porter, F. L., Miller, R. H., & Marshall, R. E. (1986). Neonatal pain cries: Effect of circumcision on acoustic features and perceived urgency. *Child Development, 57,* 790–802.

Potegal, M., & Davidson, R. J. (2003). Temper tantrums in young children: 1. Behavioral composition. *Developmental and Behavioral Pediatrics, 24*(3), 140–147.

Rondal, J. A. (1980). Fathers' and mothers' speech in early language development. *Journal of Child Language, 7*(2), 353–369.

Rosenberg, K., & Trevathan, W. (2002). Birth, obstetrics, and human evolution. *BJOG: An International Journal of Obstetrics and Gynaecology, 109,* 1199–1206.

Sayer, L. C., Bianchi, S. M., & Robinson, J. P. (2004). Are parents investing less in children? Trends in mothers' and fathers' time with children. *American Journal of Sociology, 110,* 1–43.

Sear, R., & Mace, R. (2008). Who keeps children alive? A review of the effects of kin on child survival. *Evolution and Human Behavior, 29,* 1–18.

Sears, W., & Sears, M. (1995). *The discipline book: How to have a better behaved child from birth to age ten.* New York: Little, Brown, & Co.

Semple, S., Gerald, M. S., & Suggs, D. N. (2009). Bystanders affect the outcome of mother-infant interactions in rhesus macaques. *Proceedings of the Royal Society B, Biological Sciences, 276*(1665), 2257–2262.

Slobin, D. I. (1972). Seven questions about language development. In P. C. Dodwell (Ed.), *New horizons in psychology.* Oxford, UK: Penguin Press.

Snow, C. E. (1977). Mothers' speech research: From input to interaction. In C. E. Snow & C. A. Ferguson (Eds.), *Talking to children: Language input and acquisition* (pp. 31–49). London: Cambridge University Press.

Sokol, R. I., Webster, K. L., Thompson, N. S., & Stevens, D. A. (2005). Whining as mother-directed speech. *Infant and Child Development, 14*(5), 478–490.

Sroufe, L. A. (2005). Attachment and development: A prospective, longitudinal study from birth to adulthood. *Attachment and Human Development, 7*(4), 349–367.

Stefanski, R. A., & Falls, J. B. (1972). A study of distress calls of song, swamp, and white-throated sparrows (*Aves fringillidae*): I. Intraspecific responses and functions. *Canadian Journal of Zoology, 50*(12) 1501–1512.

Sterbing, S. J. (2002). The postnatal development of vocalizations and hearing in the phyllostomid bat, *Carollia perspicillata*. *Journal of Mammology, 83*, 515–525.

Storey, A. E., Walsh, C. J., Quinton, R. L., & Wynne-Edwards, K. E. (2000). Hormonal correlates of paternal responsiveness in new and expectant fathers. *Evolution and Human Behavior, 21*, 79–95.

Symmes, D., & Biben, M. (1985). Maternal recognition of individual infant squirrel monkeys from isolation call playbacks. *American Journal of Primatology, 9*, 39–46.

Symmes, D., Newman, J. D., Riggs, G., & Lieblich, A. K. (1979). Individuality and stability of isolation peeps in squirrel monkeys. *Animal Behaviour, 27*, 1142–1152.

Thompson, N. S., Dessureau, B., & Olson, C. (1998). Infant cries as evolutionary melodrama: Extortion or deception? *Evolution of Communication, 2*(1), 25–43.

Thompson, N. S., Olson, C., & Dessureau, B. (1996). Babies' cries: Who's listening? Who's being fooled? *Social Research, 63*(3), 763–784.

Trainor, L. J., Austin C. M., & Desjardins R. N. (2000). Is infant-directed speech prosody a result of the vocal expression of emotion? *Psychological Science, 11*(3), 188–194.

Trivers, R. L. (1974). Parent-offspring conflict. *American Zoologist, 14*, 249–264.

Van Ijzendoorn, M. H., Sagi, A., & Lambermon, M. W. E. (1992). The multiple caretaker paradox: Data from Holland and Israel. *New Directions for Child and Adolescent Development, 57*, 5–24.

Vigilant, L., Stoneking, M., Harpending, H., Hawkes, K., & Wilson, A. C. (1991). African populations and the evolution of human mitochondrial DNA. *Science, 253*(5027), 1503–1507.

Vuorenkoski, V., Wasz-Höckert, O., Koivisto, E., & Lind, J. (1969). The effect of cry stimulus on the temperature of the lactating breast of primipara: A thermographic study. *Cellular and Molecular Life Sciences, 25*(12), 1286–1287.

Warren-Leubecker, A., & Bohannon, J. N., III. (1984). Intonation patterns in child-directed speech: Mother-father differences. *Child Development, 55*, 1379–1385.

Wasz-Höckert, O., Partanen, T., Vuorenkoski, V., Michelsson, K., & Valanne, E. (1964). The identification of some specific meanings in newborn infant vocalizations. *Experientia, 20*, 154.

Weisenfeld, A. R., Malatesta, C. Z., & Deloach, L. L. (1981). Differential parent response to familiar and unfamiliar infant distress signals. *Infant Behavior and Development, 4*, 281–295.

Werker, J. F., & McLeod, P. J. (1989). Infant preference for both male and female infant-directed talk: A developmental study of attentional and affective responsiveness. *Canadian Journal of Psychology, 43*(2), 230–246.

Whitbourne, S. K., Culgin, S., & Cassidy, E. (1995). Evaluation of infantilizing intonation and content of speech directed at the aged. *The International Journal of Aging and Human Development, 41*(2), 109–116.

Wolff, P. (1969). The natural history of crying and other vocalizations in early infancy. In B. M. Foss (Ed.), *Determinants of infant behavior* (Vol. 4, pp. 81–109). London: Methuen.

Wood, R. M., & Gustafson, G. E. (2001). Infant crying and adults' anticipated caregiving responses: Acoustic and contextual influences. *Child Development, 72*, 1287–1300.

Wrangham, R. (1980). An ecological model of female-bonded primate groups. *Behaviour, 75*(3/4), 262–300.

Zeifman, D. M. (2001). An ethological analysis of human infant crying: Answering Tinbergen's four questions. *Developmental Psychobiology, 39*, 265–285.

Zeskind, P., & Shingler, E. (1991). Child abuser's perceptual responses to newborn infant cries varying in pitch. *Infant Behavior and Development, 14*, 335–347.

# 9

# Fathers Versus Sons

## Why Jocasta Matters

LAURA BETZIG

## Introduction

At the turn of the last century, in his book *The Interpretation of Dreams,* Sigmund Freud laid out his Oedipus Complex. "It may be that we were all destined to direct our first sexual impulses toward our mothers, and our first impulses of hatred and violence toward our fathers; our dreams convince us that we were," he wrote—speaking, as usual, for himself (Freud, 1900, pp. 255–256).

In Sophocles' 5th-century tragedy, 2300 years before Freud, Oedipus, having murdered his father Laius on the road, becomes king of Thebes, and is rewarded with the hand of his mother, Jocasta. "Do you think that the sight of children, born as mine were, was lovely for me to look upon?" Oedipus asks, having blinded himself (Sophocles, *Oedipus Tyrannus, 1,* 1375–1376).

Fathers have been fighting with their sons since the beginning of historical time. And the objects of contention have often been women. In a Freudian world, they compete for the father's wife. Oedpius and Laius, his father, are expected to fight over sexual access to Oedpius' mother, Jocasta.

But in a Darwinian world, the competition is over other women. Fathers should fight with their sons, not over their wives, but over their courtesans and concubines, servants and slaves. And "Jocasta" should determine the winner. The winner of contests over sexual access should be Laius, wherever Jocasta is weak; but Oedipus should win, where Jocasta is strong.

Mothers and fathers share an interest in producing, and raising, sons. But after their sons are grown, their interests diverge. Sometimes, fathers and sons compete over inheritance and succession. Other times they compete over casual affairs, girlfriends, housemaids, or second wives—that is, over sexual access to women.

Again, "Jocasta" should determine the winner. The mother of an adult son may lose a great deal when her husband takes another wife, or has sex with another woman. On the other hand, she may gain many grandchildren by a grown son who has more than one woman. Other things being equal, in genetic terms, a mother should side against her husband, but with her son.

Centuries before Sophocles, Hesiod, who was Homer's contemporary, wrote the oldest of Greek myths, and got the mother's part right. In his *Theogony* the sky god, Ournaos, gets together with the earth goddess, Gaia, who gives birth to a houseful of children. But as soon as Gaia's sons are born, Ouranos hides them away from the light of day. So their mother makes a "saw toothed scimitar," a "great long jagged sickle," and sics her boys on their father. Then her youngest son, Kronos—who goes on to become the father of Zeus—"harvests his father's genitals," and turns himself into a king (Hesiod, *Theogony*, 1.55–1.82).

A Darwinian theory of incest predicts that the sons of strong mothers should succeed their fathers at younger ages, and should have longer reigns, than weak mothers' sons. Queens who are heiresses in their own right—like Eleanor of Aquitaine—should have sons who raise insurrections against their fathers. Queens whose fathers are kings—like Mary Queen of Scots—should raise insurrections, themselves, on behalf of their sons. Overall, the sons of strong queens should succeed their fathers, and reign longer, than the sons of weaker queens. And as a result, they should have access to more women.

This paper tests that hypothesis on English queens (see Table 9.1).

# Theory

Toward the end of the last century, Robert Trivers noted that, in sexually reproducing species, parents and their offspring are genetically related by one-half, but that offspring are fully related to themselves. The result is that offspring should be selected to want twice as much from their parents as parents are selected to give. In most cases, a child should want a bigger share than their brothers and sisters get from their parents. On the other hand, in most cases, a parent should be expected to treat all their children the same. As Trivers put it: "As long as one imagines that the benefit/cost ratio of a parental act changes continuously from some large number to some very small number near zero, then there must occur a period of time during which $1/2 < B/C < 1$. This period is one of expected conflict" (Trivers, 1974, p. 251; compare Hamilton, 1964). Among other things, parents and offspring might conflict about succession, inheritance—and mates.

Trivers was never explicit about the conflict between sons and fathers, but John Hartung was. He suggested that an effect might be the Oedipus Complex. In a polygynous society—the vast majority of human societies are polygnous societies (Betzig, 2012, forthcoming)—the *father* of a grown son may do better, genetically, by continuing to father children by a number of women. The *mother* may do

*Table 9.1* **The successions and reigns of England's kings**

| | Year Reign Began | Age Reign Began | Years Reigned | Rebelled Against Father? | King's Mother | King's Mother's Father | Mother's Inheritance |
|---|---|---|---|---|---|---|---|
| **William I** | 1066 | | | | | | |
| **William II** | 1087 | 31 | 12 | no | Matilda of Flanders | Baldwin V Count of Flanders | |
| **Henry I** | 1100 | 32 | 35 | no | Matilda of Flanders | Baldwin V Count of Flanders | |
| **Stephen** | 1135 | 39 | 5 | no | Adela of Blois | William I of England | |
| **Henry II** | 1154 | 21 | 34 | no | Matilda of England | Henry I of England | England |
| **Richard I** | 1189 | 31 | 9 | yes | Eleanor of Aquitaine | William X Duke of Aquitaine | Aquitaine |
| **John** | 1199 | 31 | 17 | yes | Eleanor of Aquitaine | William X Duke of Aquitaine | Aquitaine |
| **Henry III** | 1216 | 9 | 56 | no | Isabella of Angouleme | Aymer Tailefer Count of Angouleme | Angouleme |
| **Edward I** | 1272 | 33 | 34 | no | Eleanor of Provence | Raymond IV Count of Provence | |
| **Edward II** | 1307 | 23 | 19 | no | Eleanor of Castile | Ferdinand III King of Castile | Ponthieu |
| **Edward III** | 1327 | 14 | 50 | yes | Isabella of France | Philip IV King of France | |
| **Richard II** | 1377 | 10 | 22 | no | Joan of Kent | Edmond Earl of Kent | Kent |
| **Henry IV** | 1399 | 32 | 13 | no | Blanche of Lancaster | Henry Duke of Lancaster | Lancastrian estates |
| **Henry V** | 1413 | 25 | 9 | no | Mary de Bohun | Humphrey Earl of Hereford | Hereford estates |
| **Henry VI** | 1422 | 1 | 38 | no | Catherine of Valois | Charles VI King of France | |
| **Edward IV** | 1461 | 18 | 9 | no | Cecily Neville | Ralph Earl of Westmoreland | |
| **Richard III** | 1483 | 30 | 2 | no | Cecily Neville | Ralph Earl of Westmoreland | |
| **Henry VII** | 1485 | 28 | 23 | no | Margaret Beaufort | John Duke of Somerset | |

(Continued)

Table 9.1 (Continued)

| | Year Reign Began | Age Reign Began | Years Reigned | Rebelled Against Father? | King's Mother | King's Mother's Father | Mother's Inheritance |
|---|---|---|---|---|---|---|---|
| **Henry VIII** | 1509 | 17 | 37 | no | Elizabeth of York | Edward IV of England | |
| **Edward VI** | 1547 | 9 | 6 | no | Jane Seymour | Sir John Seymour | |
| **James I** | 1603 | 36 | 22 | no | Mary Queen of Scots | James V King of Scotland | Scotland |
| **Charles I** | 1625 | 24 | 23 | no | Anne of Denmark | Edward II King of Denmark & Norway | |
| **Charles II** | 1660 | 30 | 24 | no | Henrietta of France | Henry IV King of France | |
| **James II** | 1685 | 51 | 3 | no | Henrietta of France | Henry IV King of France | |
| **George I** | 1714 | 54 | 12 | no | Sophia of Hanover | Frederick V Elector Palatine and King of Bohemia | England |
| **George II** | 1727 | 43 | 33 | no | Sophia of Celle | George Duke of Brunswick-Luneberg | |
| **George III** | 1760 | 22 | 9 | no | Augusta of Saxe-Gotha | Frederick II Duke of Saxe-Gotha | |
| **George IV** | 1820 | 57 | 10 | no | Charlotte of Mecklinburg-Strelitz | Charles Duke of Mecklinburg-Strelitz | |
| **William IV** | 1830 | 64 | 6 | no | Charlotte of Mecklinburg-Strelitz | Charles Duke of Mecklinburg-Strelitz | |
| **Edward VII** | 1901 | 59 | 9 | no | Victoria Queen of England | Edward Duke of Kent | England |
| **George V** | 1910 | 44 | 25 | no | Alexandra of Denmark | Christian IX King of Denmark | |
| **Edward VIII** | 1936 | 41 | 1 | no | Mary of Teck | Francis Duke of Teck | |
| **George VI** | 1936 | 40 | 15 | no | Mary of Teck | Francis Duke of Teck | |

better, however, by helping her son father children. "Put plainly, every successful male has a mother, and every mother with highly successful sons has an extraordinary number of grandchildren," is how Hartung summed up (Hartung, 1982, p. 5; compare Hartung, 1985; Trivers, 1972; Trivers & Willard, 1973). So fathers and sons should be expected to compete with each other—not over the son's mother, but over other women. Against Laius, Oedipus and Jocasta should be on the same side. But incest should be the last thing on their minds.

## Methods

William, the 7th Duke of Normandy, crossed the Channel and conquered England in 1066. The conqueror himself was a bastard: his father Robert, the 6th Duke of Normandy, "smitten" with a poor man's daughter, left William all he had when he died on Crusade (William of Malmesbury, *Chronicle*, 1066). On the other hand, William's 32 successors, England's kings, have been legitimately conceived for almost a thousand years. Every one of them was born to a legitimately married queen.

But some queens were stronger than others. Ten queens were heiresses in their own right: women who inherited Aquitaine, Angouleme, Ponthieu, Kent, Lancaster, Herford, Scotland, or Normandy married England's kings. Eleven queens were the daughters of kings, themselves. Their fathers included Ferdinand III of Castile, James V of Scotland, Edward II of Denmark and Norway, Frederick of Bohemia, kings of England and—in three fatal cases—of France. Queens who lacked royal fathers and inheritances should have been relatively weak. Queens who were heiresses in their own right, or the daughters of kings, or both, should have been in a better to position to help their sons. Those women are scored, here, as strong queens.

## Results

As expected, strong queens promoted their sons. Sons of mothers who were heiresses succeeded younger (see Table 9.2). Sons of mothers who were heiresses had longer reigns. Sons of mothers with royal fathers succeeded younger. And sons of queens whose fathers were kings had longer reigns.

Kings of England whose mothers were heiresses started their reigns almost two years younger, on average, than kings of mothers who were not; and their reigns averaged over 4 years longer. Kings of England whose mothers were the daughters of other kings started their reigns almost three years before kings with nonroyal mothers; and they reigned, on average, for over 10 more years. The trends are consistent for mothers who inherited land. Queens who were heiresses had sons who succeeded at a little over 30, on average, and reigned for more than 23 years; but

*Table 9.2* **Kings whose mothers were the daughters of other kings tended to succeed at younger ages, and reigned longer. P values are associated with one-tailed T-tests**

|  |  | All English Kings | |
|---|---|---|---|
|  |  | Mean | Standard Deviation |
| Age Reign Began | Mother's Father a King | 29.5000 | 15.8372 |
|  | Mother's Father Not a King | 32.2500 | 15.4813 |
|  |  | $p = .3165$ | |
| Years Reigned | Mother's Father a King | 27.2500 | 16.7230 |
|  | Mother's Father Not a King | 16.5000 | 13.7324 |
|  |  | $p = .0287$ | |

queens without an inheritance had sons who succeeded at almost 32, and whose reigns ended after just 19 years. The trends are significant for mothers whose fathers were kings. Queens with royal fathers had sons who succeeded, on average, at 29½, versus 32¼ for queens whose fathers were not kings. And queens whose fathers were royal had sons with reigns of 27¼, versus just 16½ years (see Tables 9.1–9.3; Figures 9.1–9.4). All of which raises the question: What made that happen?

Some kings died suddenly and mysteriously, when their sons were in their minority. King John, who gave his barons *Magna Carta*, was married to Isabella, the heiress of Angouleme. He got dysentery and died in his 48th year, leaving England to Henry III, his 9-year-old son. And Henry V, who routed the French at Agincourt, was rewarded with the hand of Catherine of Valois, the daughter of Charles VI of France. She gave birth to his son the next year, who became Henry VI of England as an infant—his father having succumbed to more dysentery, after the siege of Meaux.

*Table 9.3* **Kings whose mothers were heiresses tended to succeed at younger ages and to reign longer. P values are associated with one-tailed T-tests**

|  |  | All English Kings | |
|---|---|---|---|
|  |  | Mean | Standard Deviation |
| Age Reign Began | Mother an Heiress | 30.0909 | 15.6681 |
|  | Mother Not an Heiress | 31.8095 | 15.6417 |
|  |  | $p = .3850$ | |
| Years Reigned | Mother an Heiress | 23.3636 | 17.9626 |
|  | Mother Not an Heiress | 19.0476 | 14.4308 |
|  |  | $p = .2329$ | |

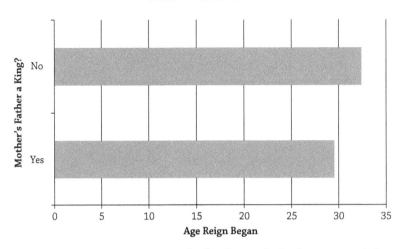

*Figure 9.1* Kings whose mothers were the daughters of other kings succeeded at younger ages.

Other kings passed away as their sons approached their majority. Henry VIII is a case in point. He came to the throne at 17—over the bodies of his brother, Arthur, who died of tuberculosis; and of his father, Henry VII, who died abruptly of respiratory arrest. And Charles II, whose mother Henrietta Maria had taken him back to France, succeeded to the throne of Scotland at just 18—a day after his father, Charles I, was taken to Whitehall and relieved of his head, on the order of Members of Parliament who sat in the High Court of Justice.

Occasionally, heiresses went after their husbands in order to advance their sons. Eleanor of Aquitaine stirred up the "execrable and foul dissension" of her sons against her husband, Henry II—for which she was incarcerated in a series of

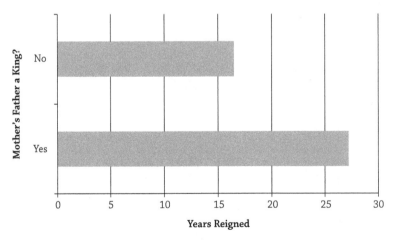

*Figure 9.2* Kings whose mothers were the daughters of other kings had longer reigns.

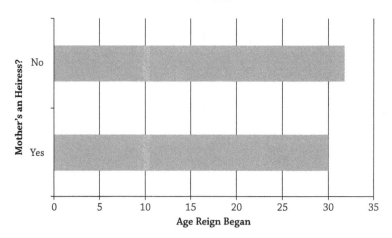

*Figure 9.3* Kings whose mothers were heiresses succeeded at younger ages.

English castles (William of Newburgh, *History*, 2.27). And Mary Queen of Scots had her second husband, Henry Stuart, blown up. She married her third husband, James Hepburn, three months later; then she abdicated in favor of James VI, her 1-year-old son—who went on to become England's James I.

Other kings were defended in battle by mothers who were the daughters of kings. Princess Matilda, the "Empress," for instance—who was a widow of the Holy Roman Emperor, and a daughter of England's Henry I—pitched battles against her cousin, Stephen, so that her son could be crowned Henry II of England at the age of 21. And Isabella the "She Wolf," a daughter of Philip IV of France, invaded England on her son's behalf. She had her husband snuffed out "with a hoote brooch putte thro the secret place posterialle" soon afterward in Berkeley Castle; and Edward III, her long-lived son, became king at the age of 14 (*Life of Edward II*, 1327).

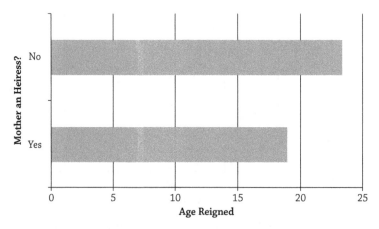

*Figure 9.4* Kings whose mothers were heiresses had longer reigns.

# Discussion

As usual, the numbers only tell part of the story. In the small sample of 32 kings of England descended from William the Conqueror, the sons of strong mothers, on average, had longer reigns. However, the variances were large.

Active maternal intervention is more obvious in some cases than others. At least eight queens of England—four of them heiresses, six of them the daughters of kings—made suspicious or conspicuous efforts on their sons' behalf. Some may have used poison. Others raised armies against their husbands, or hired assassins.

## Isabella of Angouleme and Catherine of Valois

Two kings of England—Henry III, and Henry VI—succeeded their fathers at very young ages. Both of their fathers, John and Henry V, died of dysentery. Their mothers may or may not have been implicated.

On June 15, 1215, in a Runnymede meadow on the banks of the Thames, 25 barons were granted a great charter, or *Magna Carta*, by King John. Just over a year later, making his way south from Lincoln, fighting off rebels in the north, and the future Louis VIII in the south, and having lost the crown jewels in the Wash, "poison'd, ill-fare; dead, forsook, cast off," at the age of 48, King John gave up the ghost. On the other side of England, his 9-year-old son was brought up from Devizes to Gloucester and, with a simple gold circle provided by his mother, Isabella of Angouleme, made King Henry III in St Peter's Abbey on October 28. Isabella might or might not have had anything to do with her husband's death (Shakespeare, *King John*, 5.7; Warren, 1972).

John's wife, "more Jezebel than Isabel," was an heiress. She was the only surviving, legitimate daughter of the only surviving, legitimate son of the count of Angouleme—whose domains stretched from Gascony to Poitou, across a swath of Philip II Augustus' French domains. Isabella was married, in August of 1200, to King John, whose reign had begun in April of 1199. John was 32 years old; and Isabella of Angouleme may have been as young as 8. But the King of England was infatuated, and his wife's inheritance mattered. There were, according to some sources, conjugal arguments as John's territories on the Continent were lost. A source unfriendly to Isabella adds this: "She has often been found guilty of incest, sorcery, and adultery, so that the king, her husband, has ordered those of her lovers who have been apprehended to be strangled with a rope in her own bed." Isabella was at Gloucester when her husband got diarrhea and died at Lynn. A short 9 days later, she was keen to provide her son, Henry III, with a makeshift crown (Paris, 1852, pp. 1211, 1243; Vincent, 1999).

Two centuries later, Henry V died even younger. On May 21, 1420, by the Treaty of Troyes, he was made heir to the King of France; and on June 2, he was married to Catherine of Valois, daughter of the French king Charles VI. She gave birth to their son at Windsor a year later, on December 6; and when Henry V died the next year, that son succeeded him.

"You have witchcraft in your lips, Kate," an admirer wrote. When Catherine delivered, her husband was at the siege of Meaux. But she crossed the Channel after a few months. On May 30, Henry, Catherine, and her parents entered Paris; and at Whitsun, on June 1, Henry hosted a great feast with his wife. An English physician was summoned to treat him by July 14 for "a long standing distemper," diarrhea, or *flux de ventre merveilleux*. On August 13, Henry took to his bed— which he was never to leave. By August 31 he was dead, at the age of 35. And Catherine, who was only 20, returned to England to raise her infant son, who was crowned Henry VI at Westminster in November of 1429 (Walsingham, 2005, p. 1422; Shakespeare, *Henry V*, p. 5.2; Wylie, 1929).

## Elizabeth of York and Henrietta Maria of France

The sons of another two queens—Henry VIII and Charles II—succeeded to the throne in their teens. Henry VII suffocated, suddenly, in his middle age; and during the Civil Wars, Charles I was executed. Again, it isn't clear how responsible their mothers could have been.

When Henry VII passed away as his son came of age, his wife was already dead. On August 22, 1485, Henry Tudor beat King Richard III in a battle on Bosworth Field; and on January 18, 1486, at Westminster, he married the daughter of King Edward IV, Elizabeth of York. Henry Tudor was a bastard grandson of the widowed Catherine of Valois—by Owen Tudor, the keeper of her wardrobe. He won his kingdom by conquest. He consolidated it by marriage.

Elizabeth of York gave her husband four daughters and four sons. On November 14, 1501, at the age of 15, her oldest, Arthur, was married to Catherine, the Princess of Aragon. But tubercular Arthur was dead within a year; and Elizabeth died a year later, giving birth to her last child. But Catherine survived, and was contracted to Arthur's 11-year-old brother. As Catherine's mother wrote to Catherine's father: "God be thanked, the treaty of marriage has been concluded between the Princess of Wales, our daughter, and Henry, the Prince of Wales." But that marriage was put off for years, as the widowed Henry VII thought about taking a second wife. Margaret of Savoy, Margaret of Angouleme, Joan of Naples, and Joanna of Castile were all considered; and there was arguably a "monstrous proposal" to Catherine of Aragon herself. But then on 21 April of 1509, unmarried and unable to breathe, Henry VII unexpectedly died. And on June 11, in a private ceremony at Greenwich, ten days before he was crowned, Catherine got her 21-year-old husband, King Henry VIII (*Calendar of State Papers, Spanish*, p. 308; *Letter and Papers*, 2.27; Chrimes, 1972).

A century and a half after that, Charles II succeeded to the throne of Scotland at the age of 18—a day after his father, Charles I, "a tyrant, traitor, murderer, and public enemy to the good people of this nation," was brought to the block. A dozen years later, royal government in England was restored (Rushworth, 1701, 7.1418).

Henrietta Maria was the daughter of Henry IV of France. There was no doubt that her husband, Charles I, was devoted to her; and there was no doubt that she was devoted to Charles II, her oldest son. "I avow that, without thy company, I can neither have peace nor comfort within myself," Henrietta's husband wrote to his wife. "I do not doubt that God is reserving you for better times," Henrietta wrote to her son. In the summer of 1644, just days after the birth of her last child, and less than two years after the Civil Wars started, Henrietta Maria crossed the Channel to Brest. Seven years later, her oldest son slipped across the Channel to Fécamp; and it was almost a decade before he went back. But on January 30, 1649, a day after his father died, he succeeded as King of Scotland. And more than a decade later, on April 21, 1661, he succeeded as King of England (*The King's Cabinet Opened*, Charles I to Henrietta, 2/1645; *Letters of Henrietta Maria*, Henrietta to Charles II, 6/21/1658; Plowden, 2001).

## Matilda of Flanders and the French "She Wolf"

In other cases, a mother's intervention was obvious. Two queens, both kings' daughters, led armies on their sons' behalf. Both of those boys, Henry II and Edward III, benefited as a result.

On the night of November 25, 1120, Henry I's only legitimate son, William, was drowned when the White Ship went down. So the king made his barons swear that his only legitimate daughter, Matilda, the "Empress," would be his successor. But when Henry I died in 1135, his barons supported a usurper—king Stephen, his sister's son—and a 19-year anarchy began.

Matilda did her best to prevent that. "Always superior to feminine softness and with a mind steeled and unbroken in adversity," she had Stephen captured and put in chains after the battle of Lincoln, in the winter of 1141. She was in Winchester that summer, where she was routed by the townsmen of London; and a year afterward, Stephen's forces besieged her at Oxford—but she was "let down in the night from the tower by ropes," and ran away in a white cape across the snow. In August of 1153, Stephen's legitimate son, Eustace, died of undisclosed causes; and in November of 1153, by the Treaty of Wallingford, Stephen made Henry the heir to his kingdom. Eleven months later, Stephen himself was dead, of other undisclosed causes; and Henry II "FitzEmpress" became king at the age of 21 (*Deeds of Stephen*, 1141; Florence of Worcester, *Continuation*, 1141; *Anglo-Saxon Chronicle*, 1142; Chibnall, 1992).

Roughly two centuries later, Isabella the "She Wolf," a daughter of Philip IV "the Fair" of France, led another army against Edward II of England. In the fall of 1312, she bore her husband a son; but by the winter of 1325, "pleased to visit her native land and her relatives, and delighted to leave the company of some whom she did not like," she'd taken him back home (*Parliamentary Writs*, 1325; Weir, 2005).

So "the Queen reconquered the realm of England" for her son. With a little help from her friends and relatives—from her brother, Charles IV, the King of France; from her son's future father-in-law, William I, the Count of Hainault; and from her lover, Roger Mortimer, the Earl of March—Isabella raised money and recruited troops. They invaded England in September of 1326; and by November, they'd captured her husband. Edward II was presented with half a dozen articles of deposition in January of 1327: he was incompetent to govern; he was given to unseemly works and occupations; wars had been lost; he had disinherited his nobles and destroyed his church; he was not just; and his kingdom was "notoriously" ruined. So, at the age of 14, Edward III inaugurated his 50-year reign (Froissart, 1327; Rhymer, 2.650).

## Eleanor of Aquitaine and Mary Queen of Scots

Another pair of heiresses raised insurrections against their husbands. Richard I waited for years to succeed as king of England after his mother's revolt failed. But James I became king of Scotland as an infant, after his father blew up.

One day in the spring of 1137, the 10th Duke of Aquitaine died. But William of Aquitaine lacked a legitimate son; so his duchy—which stretched from the Pyrenees to Brittany, to the Saone—went to his oldest legitimate daughter, Eleanor. That summer, Eleanor married Louis VII of France. But Louis was a weak king, and his kingdom, at the time, was a fraction of the size of Aquitaine. So in the spring of 1152, Eleanor made Henry II of England her second husband. They raised four adult sons. In the spring of 1170 the oldest, another Henry, was crowned king at the age of 15—while his father looked on; and in the summer of 1172 Young King Henry married Margaret, one of Louis VII's daughters—and was crowned again. And the civil wars began. "The Young King Henry, walking in the counsels of the wicked, left his father, and withdrew to the court of his father-in-law the king of France," Henry II's admirer wrote. On the advice of their mother, Queen Eleanor, his brothers followed; but their father came after them. He worked his way toward the cradle of conspiracy, Eleanor's Aquitaine; but Henry could not find his queen—till his scouts stumbled on a band of Poitevin knights, and found Eleanor herself, in a man's dress, sitting astride her mount. Henry gathered together his renegade sons; and their mother was shuffled about, under guard, to a variety of castles in England, for as long as their father lived (Roger of Wendover, 1173; Kelly, 1950).

That left Henry II free to amuse himself. There were assignations with the wives and daughters of a variety of earls, counts, and knights—and with his daughter-in-law-to-be, Alis, a sister of Philip II Augustus of France. When Philip asked why he had no interest in her, Richard "Lionheart," answered: "On no account would he take his sister to wife, inasmuch as the King of England, his own father, had been intimate with her, and had a son by her." Witnesses were produced to establish the fact (Roger of Hoveden, 1191).

Four centuries later, Mary Stuart became Queen of Scotland. The only surviving, legitimate daughter of Scotland's King James V was married, first, to the future Francis II of France, on April 24, 1558—and widowed after just 19 months; she made her cousin Lord Darnley, a son of the Earl of Lennox, her second husband, on July 29, 1565—and was widowed 18 months later; and she made James Hepburn, the Earl of Bothwell, her third husband on May 15, 1567—then abdicated, two months later, in favor of her 1-year-old son, James.

Mary seems to have been part of a plot to blow her second husband up. And a part of the problem seems to have been that he was more interested in other women, than he was in his infant son. Henry Darnley is supposed to have been a pretty young man—"very lusty," a "polished trifler," a "great cock chick"—and Mary was smitten with him. But becoming King Consort of Scotland turned out not to be enough; he wanted to become King of Scotland, and an heir to throne, in his own right. "She has done him so great honour, contrary to the advice of her subjects, and he, on the other part, has recompensed her with such ingratitude and misuses himself so far toward her that it is a heartbreak for her to think he should be her husband, and how to be free of him she sees no outgait," was the report to the ambassador to Charles IX of France. So, in the wee hours of February 10, 1567, £60 Scots-worth of gunpowder exploded like a volley of 25 or 30 cannon, and Henry Darnley died in the Kirk o' Field. His son became James VI of Scotland that summer—and, 36 years later, King James I of England (Weir 2003).

## Conclusions

The evidence suggests that strong queens of England raised insurrections against their husbands, or subverted them behind the scenes. As a result, their sons started their reigns younger, and ruled longer, than the sons of weaker mothers. No evidence suggests that kings of England wanted to have sex with their mothers. But plenty of evidence suggests that those kings were interested in other women, and willing to fight for them (compare Betzig, 1986, 1997, 2005).

Occasionally, kings of England coveted the wives of their sons. Henry II may or may not have got a bastard on Richard I Lionheart's intended, Alis of France. And Henry VII may or may not have intended to marry his older son Arthur's widow—and keep Catherine of Aragon from his younger son, Henry VIII, along with the English throne.

Plenty of English princes coveted their fathers' households. Eleanor of Aquitaine's oldest son, the Young King, was one of many princes to become "highly indignant, because his father had sparingly supplied him with money to meet the expenses of a royal establishment" (William of Newburgh, *History*, 2.27). And Elizabeth of York's youngest, Henry VIII, was one of many princes to resent being kept under restraint—locked up, in this case, in small quarters next to his father's chambers, with no way out except through a private door that led into a park, and even then, only under strict supervision (Scarisbrick, 1972).

Certainly, kings of England, like other kings, lived with large numbers of women. The *Constitutio Domus Regis*, a record of the household of William the Conqueror's son, Henry I, accounts for the bread, wine, cash, and candle allowances of the hundreds of men and women who worked on their staffs. For centuries, those numbers kept going up. Household Ordinances consistently count hundreds of heads at English courts; and in summer of 1642, the rebels who fought against Charles I were supporting a royal household of well over 1,800—580–620 in the chamber, 305 in the household below stairs, another 195 servants' servants below stairs, 400–800 officers' servants, 210 yeomen of the guard, 263 in the stables, 202 in the chambers of three princes and two princesses, and 172 in the rooms of Henrietta Maria, his French queen (Aylmer, 2002; *Constitutio Domus Regis*; Given-Wilson & Curteis, 1984; Given-Wilson, 1986).

Certainly, some kings of England took advantage of their boarders. After Henry I lost Prince William, his legitimate son, in the wreckage of the White Ship, he spent the last decade and a half of his life trying to promote 20 or more of his bastards (Hollister & Keefe, 1973). And though the first Charles Stuart was notoriously devoted to his wife, the second Charles Stuart was not. Charles II, like Henry I, lacked a legitimate successor; and he promoted a houseful of bastards. "Why art thou poor, O King? Embzzling cunt, that wide mouthed greedy monster, that has done't," is how one of his critics put it (*Essay on Scandal*; compare Fraser, 2002; Poynting 2003; Betzig, 1992, 1995, 2002).

Even before Sophocles' *Oedipus*, and even before Hesiod's *Theogony*, sons coveted their fathers' women. In the Bible, in the book of Genesis, Jacob is the father of 12 sons, eight by Rachel and Leah, his wives, and four by Bilhah and Zilpah, their maids. After they grow up, one of Rachel's boys "lays with" Bilhah, her maid. So Jacob laments: "Reuben, you are my firstborn, my might, and the first fruits of my strength, preeminent in pride and preeminent in power;" but "unstable as water, you shall not have preeminence because you went up to your father's bed; then you defiled it—you went up to my couch!" (Genesis, 35:22–23, 49:3–4; 1 Chronicles 5:1–2).

There were even better stories about Israel's kings. David, who was a 10th-generation descendant of Reuben's younger brother, Judah, would father at least 19 sons of his own. But one of those sons would "go in" to his father's women, and suffer for it. When Absalom—who was the son of Maacah, a daughter of the King of Geshur—raised an insurrection against David, he lay down with his father's women "in the sight of the sun." Absalom pitched a tent on his father's roof, and went in to the 10 women who kept David's house. Twenty thousand men died in the battle they fought in the forests of Ephraim. And Absalom ended up hung in an oak, with three darts in his chest. The concubines in question were put under house arrest, and shut up to the day of their death (Ruth 4:18–22; 2 Samuel 12:11, 16:22, 20:3).

Ever since Genesis, rules against incest between sons and mothers have been conspicuously absent across cultures. But rules against sex with step-mothers, daughters-in-law, and other in-laws have been common. Men almost never have to be reminded to stay away from their mothers. But they almost always have to be reminded to stay away from each other's step-kin and in-laws, servants, and secondary wives (Thornhill, 1991).

In contemporary cultures, sons in Freud's Oedipal (age 2–6) stages are no more likely to be killed by their fathers than daughters are. When toddlers have strong feelings for their mothers, neither parent is threatened. Fathers are much more likely to kill, or to be killed by, their grown up sons (Daly & Wilson, 1990).

Even in bonobos, mothers seems to matter. *Pan paniscus* males at LuiKotale, in the Congo, mate significantly more often if their mothers are members of the party, than if their mothers are not. And that "is at least partly because their mothers help. Mothers actively break up the consortships of unrelated males; and they actively keep unrelated males from breaking their sons" consortships up (Surbeck, Mundry, & Hohmann, 2010). All of which suggests that Freud was wrong about the Oedipus Complex. But that the Darwinians—Trivers and Hartung—were right. Sons fight with their fathers over inheritances, successions, and sexual access to women. And mothers tend to side with their sons.

# References

Aylmer, G. E. (2002). *The crown's servants: Government and service under Charles II*. Oxford: Oxford University Press.

Bergenroth, G. A. (Ed.). (1862). *Calendar of state papers, Spanish, 1485–1509*. London: Longman.

Betzig, L. (1986). *Despotism and differential reproduction: A Darwinian view of history*. New York: Aldine.

Betzig, L. (1992). Roman polygyny. *Ethology and Sociobiology*, 13, 309–349.

Betzig, L. (1995). Medieval monogamy. *Journal of Family History*, 20, 181–215.

Betzig, L. (1997). People are animals. In L. Betzig (Ed.), *Human nature: A critical reader* (pp. 1–13). Oxford: Oxford University Press.

Betzig, L. (2002). British polygyny. In M. Smith (Ed.), *Human biology and history*, pp. 30–97. London: Taylor and Francis.

Betzig, L. (2005). Politics as sex: The Old Testament case. *Evolutionary Psychology*, 3, 326–346.

Betzig, L. (2012). Means, variances and ranges in reproductive success: Comparative evidence. *Human Behavior and Evolution*, 33, 309–317.

Betzig, L. (forthcoming). Eusociality in history. *Human Nature*, 23.

Chibnall, M. (1992). *The empress Matilda*. Oxford: Blackwell.

Chrimes, S. (1972). *Henry VII*. London: Methuen.

*Constitutio Domus Regis*. (1983). (C. Johnson, Trans.). London: Oxford University Press.

Daly, M., & Wilson, M. (1988). *Homicide*. New York: Aldine-de Gruyter.

Daly, M., & Wilson, M. (1990). Is parent-offspring conflict sex-linked? Freudian and Darwinian models. *Journal of Personality*, 58, 163–189.

*Deeds of Stephen*. (1976). (K. R. Potter & R. H. C. Davis, Trans.). London: Oxford University Press.

*Essay on scandal*. (1976). In J. H. Wilson, *Court satires of the restoration*. Columbus: Ohio State University Press.

Fraser, A. (2002). *King Charles II*. London: Orion.

Freud, S. (1932). *The interpretation of dreams* (A. A. Brill, Trans.) (3rd ed.). New York: Macmillan.

Froissart, J. (1978). *Chronicle* (G. Brereton, Trans.). Harmondsworth, UK: Penguin.

Gairdner, J. (Ed.). (1965). *Letters and papers illustrative of the reigns of Richard III and Henry VII*. Weisbaden, Germany: Kraus Reprint.

Given-Wilson, C. (1986). *The royal household and the king's affinity*. New Haven, CT: Yale University Press.

Given-Wilson, C., & Curteis, A. (1984). *The royal bastards of medieval England*. London: Routledge and Kegan Paul.

Guy, J. (2004). *My heart is my own: The life of Mary Queen of Scots*. London: Fourth Estate.

Hall, E. (1965). *Chronicle containing the history of England*. New York: AMS Press.

Hamilton, W. D. (1964). The genetical evolution of social behavior. *Journal of Theoretical Biology*, *7*, 1–52.

Hartung, J. (1982). Polygyny and the inheritance of wealth. *Current Anthropology*, *23*, 1–12.

Hartung, J. (1985). Polygyny, bride-price, inheritance, and Oedipus. In G. Volger & R. Weld (Eds.), *The bride, given away, sold, bartered, stolen* (pp. 794–797). Koln, Germany: Rautenstrauch-Joest Museum.

Hesiod. (1973). *Theogony* (D. Wender, Trans.). Harmondsworth, UK: Penguin.

Hollister, C. W., & Keefe, T. K. (1973). The making of the Angevin Empire. *Journal of British Studies*, *12*, 1–25.

*King's cabinet opened*. (1645). London: Bostock.

*Life of Edward II (Vita Edwardi Secundi)*. (2005). (W. R. Childs, Trans.). London: Oxford University Press.

Milton, J. (1650). *Eikonoklastes*. London: T. N.

Palgrave, F. (Ed.). (1827–1834). *Parliamentary writs and writs of summons*. London: Records Commission.

Paris, M. (1852). *English history* (J. A. Giles, Trans.). London: Henry Bohn.

Plowden, A. (2001). *Henrietta Maria*. London: Sutton.

Poynting, S. (2003). "In the name of all the sisters": Henrietta Maria's notorious whores. In C. McManus (Ed.), *Women and culture at the courts of the Stuart Queens* (pp. 163–185). London: Palgrave.

Rhymer, T. (1971). *Foedera*. In C. A. Zimansky (Ed.). Westport CT: Greenwood Press.

Roger of Hoveden. (1853). *History of England* (H. T. Riley, Trans.). London: Bohn.

Roger of Wendover. (1849). *Flowers of history* (J. A. Giles, Trans.). London: Bohn.

Rushworth, J. (1701). *Historical collections*. London: Boulter.

Scarisbrick, J. J. (1968). *Henry VIII*. Berkeley: University of California Press.

Sophocles. (1994). *Oedipus Tyrannus* (H. Lloyd-Jones, Trans.). Cambridge, MA: Harvard University Press.

Surbeck, M., Mundry, R., & Gottfried, H. (in press). Mothers matter! Maternal support, dominance status, and mating success in male bonobos *(Pan paniscus)*. *Proceedings of the Royal Society B*.

Thornhill, N. W. (1991). Evolutionary theories of rules regulating incest and inbreeding. *Behavioral and Brain Sciences*, *14*, 249–293.

Trivers, R. (1972). Parental investment and sexual selection. In B. Campbell (Ed.), *Sexual selection and the descent of man, 1871–1971* (pp. 136–179). Chicago: Aldine.

Trivers, R. (1974). Parent-offspring conflict. *American Zoologist*, *14*, 249–264.

Trivers, R., & Willard, D. (1973). Natural selection of parental ability to vary the sex ratio of offspring. *Science*, *179*, 90–92.

Vincent, N. (1999). Isabella of Angouleme: John's Jezebel. In D. S. Church (Ed.), *King John: New interpretations* (pp. 165–219). Woodbridge, NY: Boydell.

Walsingham, T. (2005). *English history* (D. Preest, Trans.). Woodbridge, NY: Boydell.

Warren, W. L. (1973). *Henry II*. London: Eyre Methuen.

Weatherhead, P. J., & Robertson, R. J. (1979). Offspring quality and the polygyny threshold: The "sexy son" hypothesis. *American Naturalist*, *113*, 201–208.

Weir, A. (2003). *Mary Queen of Scots and the murder of Lord Darnley.* New York Ballantine.

Weir, A. (2005). *Queen Isabella: Treachery, adultery, and murder in medieval England.* New York: Ballantine.

William of Malmesbury. (1847). *Chronicle of the Kings of England* (J. A. Giles, Trans.). London: Bohn.

William of Newburgh. (1988). *The history of English affairs* (P. G. Walsh & M. J. Kennedy, Trans.). Warminster, UK: Aris.

Worcester, Florence of. (1854). *Continuation* (T. Forester, Trans.). London: Henry Bohn.

Wylie, J. H. (1929). *The reign of Henry the Fifth.* Cambridge, UK: Cambridge University Press.

# HEALTH AND REPRODUCTION

# 10

# Women's Health at the Crossroads of Evolution and Epidemiology

CHRIS REIBER

## Introduction

In recent years, women's reproductive health has become a major focus of medical and epidemiological research, and has become embedded in the public consciousness. Research on women's reproductive cancers has expanded. Educational programs and public service announcements promoting regular Papanicolaou (pap) tests are now commonplace in the media. Massive public events in the streets of major cities use little pink ribbons to marshal support for mammography for all women. The human papillomavirus (HPV) vaccine has been developed and marketed, and public campaigns urge parents to vaccinate their pubescent daughters, who all should want to be "one less." New and updated contraceptive choices are available, and are heralded in television advertisements by women taking control of their own destinies, even if they are still clad in swimsuits. Advances keep coming.

However, despite the fact that female humans have walked the earth for just as long as male humans, many aspects of women's bodies and their functionality are still viewed as either mysterious or problematic, and some of the most basic questions have still not been adequately addressed. For instance, *why* do women menstruate? Much research has been aimed at understanding *how* women menstruate, via an intricate endocrinological symphony orchestrating a web of cascading physiological responses. But few have asked, and no one yet has provided adequate scientific data to answer, *why* women menstruate in the first place. If we fail to understand even this most basic detail about human female reproductive biology, women's health research and treatment can hardly be expected to be maximally productive.

Other aspects of women's reproductive health are wrapped in an almost mysterious shroud. Premenstrual syndrome (PMS) is truly a puzzle. It has been written about at least since the time of the early Greeks (see Adams, 1939), recognized in medical and psychiatric contexts for centuries (see Prichard, 1837; Rubinow & Schmidt, 1995), and documented and studied in rural and urban women the world over (Asia, Africa, Europe, Australia, and the Americas; Ericksen, 1987). Prevalence estimates range from about 7% (Gaulrapp, Backe, & Steck, 1995) to 90% (Riley, 1986) of women affected; and consensus among PMS researchers is that most women experience some symptom fluctuations premenstrually, even if it is subclinical (Halbreich et al., 2007). Yet no etiologic agent or underlying mechanism has been revealed in spite of many decades of (proximate) research (see Connolly, 2001). Over 150 different symptoms can be manifested as part of PMS (Dalton, 1986), so women with nothing in common but their gender can be diagnosed with the same syndrome! In essence, we know that PMS is real, and we recognize it when we see it or experience it, but no one knows what it really is. It drags women down, making them cranky and hostile, and preventing them from going about their daily lives with grace and ease. *Why?*

Another poorly understood aspect of women's health is menopause. There is tremendous variability in the experience, both within populations and between. Women go through menopause at different ages; some women experience many symptoms, while others have few; symptoms are nearly incapacitating for some women, while they are hardly noticeable to other women. Treatment options are many and changing, and run the gamut from physician-prescribed hormones to a wide variety of herbal remedies and lifestyle changes. Like menstruation, however, answers to the most basic questions are lacking. Every single woman who survives past a certain age will experience menopause; not a single man will. *Why?*

These questions are really about organismal design. Over millions of generations of evolution by natural selection, (female) humans have come to be characterized by particular features, including patterns of menstruation (sometimes), PMS (also sometimes), and menopause. Why did evolution design women as menstruators? There are many organisms—some primates included—that do not menstruate (Strassmann, 1996); so why do humans? Why did evolution design women such that they (sometimes) feel suboptimal premenstrually? If men can reproduce throughout their lives, why can't women? Why are we designed the way we are?

The crux of evolutionary medicine lies in pursuing an understanding of design, seeking answers to *ultimate* questions like these about *why* organisms are the way they are. On the other hand, the questions asked by epidemiologists and medical researchers have traditionally been mechanism-focused, or *proximate*; they ask "how." Ultimate and proximate explanations are neither mutually exclusive nor contradictory. In fact, they are complementary, and both types of explanation are needed for a full understanding of any biological process (Nesse, 2001a). Taken together, they can produce a more thorough understanding of human health and disease. Answers to the basic evolutionary questions will shore-up the foundation on which the field of women's health is growing, and point the field in novel and fruitful directions for advancing women's health.

# An Evolutionary Approach to Medicine: The Basics

The process of natural selection underlies all evolutionary medicine. The logic of natural selection is simple and inescapable: heritable traits that augment reproduction (relative to their alternatives) become proportionately more common in subsequent generations. Evolution is nothing more than a "statistical bias in the rate of perpetuation of alternatives" (Williams, 1966, p. 22). Thus, reproduction is what shapes organisms over evolutionary time, and modern organisms are the products of reproductive competition that has gone on, unabated, for millennia. This means that traits such as health, happiness, well-being, strength, vigor, and even survival itself—the very heart of modern medicine—are not *independently* important to the evolutionary process. They are favored by evolution only to the extent that they contribute to an organism's ability to reproduce. It also means that attempts to understand modern human anatomy and physiology, endocrinology, health, disease and disorder, *must* be consistent with the concept that humans are both products of, and participants in, the historical and still ongoing process of natural selection.

Evolutionists thus approach features of organisms by asking questions such as, is this feature adaptive?—that is, was this feature favored through the process of natural selection because it contributed to augmented reproduction in some way? If so, how and why? If not, why does the organism still exhibit the feature? Is it merely a consequence or by-product of some other, adaptive, feature?

Similarly, evolutionary medicine attempts to understand why features are the way they are. But diseases and disorders—the "stuff" of modern medicine—are unlikely to contribute to augmented reproduction! It is unlikely that diseases/disorders are adaptive in and of themselves; after millions of years of evolution, shouldn't organisms be fairly perfectly evolved to survive, thrive, and reproduce in their environment(s)? Why do we still get sick? Diseases and disorders can be understood by reframing the question: given how the process of natural selection works, why are organisms vulnerable in the particular ways that they are?

It turns out that there are a few relatively simple issues that lead to the vulnerabilities that explain most of human suffering (see Nesse & Williams, 1994). First, organisms have to defend themselves; hence we have symptoms that can be unpleasant even though they are in our best interest. Self-defense against micropredators—viruses and bacteria, for example—leads to fevers and other symptoms of infection. (See Ewald, 1994, 1996, 2002, 2004, for detailed discussions of evolution and infectious disease.) Vulnerabilities are also sometimes created by disease-causing genes. Although such genes will be eliminated by natural selection in some cases, they will not be eliminated in all cases (see Allison, 2004, for a classic example); thus, when thinking about genetic diseases, it is important to deduce how the genes have been able to persist in spite of natural selection. A few other issues—compromises and novel environments—also conspire to generate health-related vulnerabilities (Nesse & Williams, 1994). Organisms often exhibit compromises between related features, reflecting a trade-off between overall costs and benefits of the various features. Novel environments also create vulnerabilities, because organisms are evolved to survive and reproduce well *not* in the environment in which they find themselves, but in the environment of their ancestors. This mismatch between genes and environment can produce vulnerabilities to disease and ill health.

Understanding humans as biological products of evolutionary processes *can* enhance our understanding of women's health. The evolutionary perspective inspires questions that have not yet been asked or answered, but that have direct bearing on women's health. It allows us to consider why particular features of women are the way they are, and to think about the underlying vulnerabilities that lead to various states of (ill) health in women, as well as the reason(s) for those vulnerabilities. The answers to these questions have direct implications for our growing understanding of women's health, and the potential to change how we think about the management and treatment of women's health issues.

## Applications to Women's Health: Menstruation

The menstrual cycle is complex. From a proximate perspective, it is understood through the anatomy, physiology, and endocrinology of the cycle. It involves neuroendocrine components via the hypothalamic-pituitary axis, events of the reproductive organs and genital tract, and endocrinological components within the ovaries. (For excellent and comprehensive proximate discussions of the menstrual cycle, see Ferin, Jewelewicz, & Warren, 1993; and/or Jones, 1991.) Menstruation is generally seen as a nonfunctional by-product of normal reproductive cycling; it is what happens when the egg is not fertilized, and the inner lining of the uterus (the uterine endometrium), which had been enriched in preparation for implantation of a fertilized egg, is shed in anticipation of regenerating for the subsequent cycle. Strassmann (1996, 1997) has argued that menstruation is simply a result of the high cost of maintaining the endometrium; cost-benefit considerations suggest that it is simply less costly to allow the endometrium to degenerate and regenerate cyclically, than it is to maintain the endometrium in a fertility-promoting state.

In contrast to the nonfunctional by-product explanations, several functional explanations for menstruation have been proposed. Ravenholt (1966) suggested that menstruation might act as a physiological eraser of sorts, eliminating endometrial neoplasias (tumors in the uterine lining). Similarly, Shaw and Roche (1985) argued that menstruating might cleanse the uterus of cellular debris and necrotic (dead) tissue; and Garey (1990) proposed that menstruation might rid the uterus of dietary phytoestrogens (plant-derived estrogen-like compounds) that could bind to hormone receptors and interfere with reproduction. Haig (1993) suggested that menstruation would expel fetal cells that might manipulate maternal metabolism.

However, none of these proposed functions for menstruation requires bleeding; each of them could be accomplished simply by sloughing cells.

Profet (1993) argues that menstruation is an evolved, functional adaptation that requires bleeding. There are several lines of evidence supporting this hypothesis, including details of reproductive physiology that are otherwise hard to reconcile. Menstruation is not merely nonspecific bleeding. The spiral arteries of the uterus behave differently than those of other organs, constricting and dilating with timing orchestrated to induce rupture and formation of epithelial hematomas (localized pools of blood under the thin lining inside the uterus) which burst and result in menstrual blood flow. Menstrual blood also differs from venous blood; it lacks many normal clotting factors, has fewer and smaller hemostatic plugs, only 1/10th of the platelets, lower iron levels, and higher lactoferrin (an iron-binding protein that helps prevent infection) and leukocyte (white blood cell) levels than venous blood. While nonmenstrual bleeding is staunched by clotting, menstrual bleeding is staunched by constriction of the spiral arteries. These differences are not merely theoretically interesting. They suggest that the menstrual system is both unique and costly, which in turn indicates that it likely has a specific adaptive function.

The function proposed by Profet (1993) is defensive: menstruation serves to rid the female reproductive tract of pathogens transported there by sperm. In this model, sperm are vectors of disease transport, transferring bacteria and viruses from both the male, and from the female's own cervix and vagina, to the higher reaches of the uterus and/or fallopian tubes. Many predictions follow from this model. First, menstruation is predicted to characterize species in which copulation does not reliably lead to pregnancy; menstruation should be absent in species in which copulation reliably leads to pregnancy. Second, the model predicts that a key feature of reproductive-tract infection is bleeding and spotting—a novel response to infection not found elsewhere in the body. The model also predicts that the number of pathogens in the higher reaches of the female reproductive tract should increase after copulation, and the average load of sexually transmitted pathogens, as well as the number of sperm ejaculated into the female reproductive tract, should correlate with the degree of menstrual bleeding. Postmenopausal women may also be at greater risk of sexually transmitted infections (STIs) since they no longer menstruate.

Sorting out the ultimate explanation of menstruation is not merely academically interesting. If menstruation is nonfunctional, a proximate understanding of how it works will suffice. But if menstruation is, indeed, an evolved defense that rids the reproductive tract of sexually transmitted pathogens, curtailing it has the potential to be harmful (see Nesse & Williams, 1994; Reiber, 2009a). Sexually active women who do not menstruate would be expected to suffer higher rates of STIs than those who menstruate regularly. This is important both clinically and epidemiologically. First, maintenance of fertility in women requires early detection of STIs. Second, undetected STIs threaten public health. And third, if menstruation is protective, newly available menstruation-stopping oral contraceptives (MSOCs) could potentially put large numbers of women at increased risk of infection.

Many studies will need to be carried out to investigate these issues. Many of Profet's (1993) original predictions have not yet been subjected to rigorous testing. Moreover, the more recent advent of MSOC's demands additional research (Reiber, 2009a), since the endocrinological state associated with pharmaceutically induced amenorrhea is *not* equivalent to the nonmenstruating state that would be commonly experienced by hunter-gatherer women (Leidy Sievert, 2008). (Interestingly, Profet, 1993, argues that the nonmenstruating states in hunter-gatherer women, and/or our evolutionary ancestors, do not refute her pathogen-reduction model of menstruation; during pregnancy and lactational amenorrhea, other physiological priorities subvert the protective mechanism.) Longitudinal epidemiologic studies could investigate whether the incidence of STIs in a population increases as the new MSOCs are introduced and adopted by larger numbers of women. Within populations, comparisons of the STI rates in women using MSOCs and those using other, nonbarrier contraceptive methods, would test whether women using MSOCs have a higher rate of STIs than those not using MSOCs. Results from such studies would have myriad implications. They would be clinically beneficial to women; they would shed light on whether or not menstruation is evolutionarily adaptive; and they might provide supporting logic that links medical phenomena that are otherwise seemingly unrelated—a woman's choice of a particular type of oral contraceptive and STIs.

# Applications to Women's Health: Premenstrual Syndrome (PMS)

Premenstrual Syndrome (PMS) is an even bigger puzzle than menstruation itself. For menstruation, the proximate mechanisms are well described, even if the ultimate explanations still require extensive research. For PMS, however, neither the proximate nor the ultimate explanations are well understood. The obvious link between PMS and the menstrual cycle has prompted a search for underlying endocrinological anomalies. In spite of decades of endocrinological—and genetic, physiological, and psychological—research, however, no proximate mechanisms have been found; for a thorough review, see Connolly (2001). No treatments based on any such research have been any more effective than a placebo (Tucker & Whalen, 1991). Clare (1985) and Connolly (2001) argue that no single, proximate causal factor will be capable of explaining the complex patterns of PMS, and Tucker and Whalen (1991) have called for more theoretical development in the field. An evolutionary approach might be just what the field needs; fruitful evolutionary (or ultimate) research might logically point us to underlying proximate mechanisms, and suggest productive treatment avenues.

Recently Doyle, Ewald, and Ewald (2007) proposed that PMS may be the result of the evolved pattern of cyclic changes in immunosuppression across the menstrual cycle; these changes may lead to premenstrual exacerbation of underlying infectious conditions in women, and hence, premenstrual symptoms. It is difficult to imagine how this model could reliably and specifically account for the tremendous variation in symptoms and patterns within and between women, since the most common symptoms of PMS (including, among others, general irritability, moodiness, social friction, impulsivity, and decreased concentration; Halbreich et al., 2007) are so general. Much research will be required to pinpoint specific infectious agents, and to find the proximate links between those agents and specific symptoms or symptom clusters, and rule out confounding factors. However, this line of research opens up an entirely new and unexplored arena of potential causality that deserves serious consideration.

This hypothesis also points to an interesting conundrum. Because evolutionary approaches to disease have different theoretical underpinnings than clinical approaches to disease, they sometimes seem to violate the clinical "ground rules." For instance, Doyle et al.'s (2007) infectious causation model of PMS violates the clinical definition of PMS! There are several different clinical diagnostic definitions of PMS (see APA, 1994; Severino & Moline, 1989; WHO, 1992), and most of them explicitly exclude from consideration any symptoms that reflect the exacerbation of other underlying conditions—which would include infection. Thus, the infectious disease hypothesis runs the risk of being dismissed by the establishment before it can even be fully explored.

However, while diagnostic criteria and definitions are generally useful in the clinic, they represent prototypes of disease rather than logical categories (Nesse, 2001b) and thus can limit understanding rather than encourage novel approaches. Diagnostic criteria and definitions reflect consensus achieved by panels of experts, usually based on their experience with the disorder in the clinical setting. Since most clinical experts are not schooled in evolutionary thinking (see Nesse, Stearns, & Omenn, 2006; Nesse & Schiffman, 2003), the perspectives they bring and the consensus they reach are not likely to take into account the possibilities that an evolutionary approach might encompass. Definitional issues should not therefore be allowed to limit our thinking. After all, evolutionary biology is the basic science underlying all of medicine (Nesse & Stearns, 2008; Nesse et al., 2010), and understanding the essence of disease requires us to question why the body works the way it does (Nesse, 2001b).

Reiber (2008, 2009a) also recently proposed an evolutionary explanation for PMS. In this model, PMS is argued to simply be a by-product of other cyclic adaptations. Instead of focusing on what seems to be going wrong during the premenstruum, this model focuses on what is going really well at other points in the menstrual cycle—specifically, during the ovulatory phase—and how these "positives" can conspire to make women feel suboptimal later on. Much research in evolutionary psychology has shown that,

During the fertile phase of the menstrual cycle, women ornament more (Haselton, Mortezaie, Pillsworth, Blecke-Rechek, & Frederick, 2007) and wear sexier/bolder clothing (Grammer, Renninger, & Fischer, 2004), go to clubs more (Haselton & Gangestad, 2006), are more attentive to "maleness" (Macrae, Alnwick, Milne, & Schloerscheidt, 2002), increase ranging activities including locomotion and volunteering for more social activities (Fessler, 2003), and flirt more with men not their mates (Gangestad, Thornhill, & Garver, 2002; Haselton & Gangestad, 2006). Physical and chemical changes also track the menstrual cycle. Women's facial appearance (Roberts et al., 2004) and body odors (Doty, Ford, Preti, & Huggins, 1975; Singh & Bronstad, 2001; Thornhill et al., 2003) are more attractive to men during the fertile phase of the menstrual cycle. Finally, women's sexual desire is reported to be higher during the fertile phase than during non-fertile phases of the menstrual cycle (Bullivant et al., 2004; Gangestad, Thornhill, & Garver, 2002; Haselton & Gangestad, 2006). (Reiber, 2008; formatting of textual references has been changed from the original: original had numbered references, APA style references given here)

These phenomena are cyclic adaptations; the positive side of each is expressed during the ovulatory phase of the cycle, when women can potentially become pregnant. However, after the ovulatory phase, women can no longer become pregnant, and the potential evolutionary benefit of maintaining all of these heightened states is reduced; so the positive states remit during the premenstruum. Relative to the "highs" of the ovulatory phase, the premenstruum is therefore characterized by a lower-energy state: women are less social, less active, feel less sexy and flirtatious, and men find them less attractive. Interestingly, the symptoms of PMS mirror exactly these lower states, and taken together may lead to a sense of suboptimal well-being, and in their extreme form, even clinical distress.

The implications of this model are many. For instance, this model points to a whole new set of potential proximate mechanisms underlying the symptoms of PMS, and thus, a whole new set of potential treatment options. What is it, exactly, that causes women to alter their ranging patterns over the cycle? Similarly, what specific elements of physical appearance are changing across the cycle, and what causes these changes? If we can discover the proximate cause of each of the "positives" of the fertile phase of the cycle, there is tremendous potential to find ways of preventing their remission during the premenstruum. Notice that multiple proximate mechanisms are likely acting in concert to produce the particular suite of symptoms and intensity experienced by different women. The variation is expected; and it allows a shift from thinking in terms of *the* cause, which has thus far been futile, to thinking about complex, multiple causality for a complex, highly variable syndrome.

There is still much to learn about PMS, but these evolutionary approaches to PMS are important in the field of women's health. They make testable predictions and point in novel directions for future research (see Reiber, 2009b). They also highlight critical definitional and diagnostic issues. In addition, they may begin to provide psychological relief for women who have been unable to understand what is happening to their bodies, and who are getting conflicting messages from traditional medical wisdom. One study (Reiber, 2007) found that 93% of women reported a priori that they suffer from PMS, but only 12% qualified for a diagnosis after keeping symptom diaries for 1–2 months. Most interestingly, amongst the 12% meeting the diagnostic criteria, the a priori ratings of symptoms ranged all the way from "none" to "extreme"; and of those who rated their symptoms as "severe" or "extreme," only one-sixth met diagnostic criteria! To the extent that one's assessment of one's own well-being is validated by concurrence of experience and diagnosis, these disjunctions devalue women's assessments of their own health, and may impact attitudes toward PMS and impair appropriate treatment-seeking behavior in general. Broader evolutionary models can potentially correct such problems by changing how we think about definitions and diagnoses.

## Applications to Women's Health: Menopause

Menopause is another feature of the human female reproductive system for which there is much proximate, but little ultimate, understanding. In terms of proximate mechanisms, the cause of menopause is that women literally run out of eggs (Ellison, 2001; Leidy, 1994). There is a huge professional literature on menopause, ranging from physiology and symptomatology, to clinical treatment and/or management, to behavioral, sociocultural, and psychological influences, interpretations, and consequences. The scope of this literature is well beyond that of this chapter; readers are referred to Korenman (1990) for a discussion of the proximate biology and clinical issues related to menopause. What *is* important about this literature, however, is that no one has figured out (and indeed, most researchers have not even asked) *why* women experience menopause in the first place.

From an evolutionary point of view, menopause might seem paradoxical. Evolution optimizes reproduction, yet has produced organisms in which fully one-half of the species undergoes an unavoidable cessation of reproductive ability roughly two-thirds of the way through life! How can this be? There are two common answers to this question. One proposed answer is that humans are currently simply mismatched to their environment; the advent of public health and medicine have led to a rapid and large increase in the human lifespan, and women's reproductive systems just could not "keep up" (Austad, 1994). But this explanation fails to explain why, when all the other systems of the body can continue functioning throughout this extended lifespan, only the reproductive system fails, and why it fails only in women and not in men (Reiber, 2010).

The other common answer to the question is that women give up their own direct reproduction and instead behave in ways that augment the survival and/or reproduction of their children and/or grandchildren (for various incarnations of this general argument, see Hamilton, 1966; Hawkes et al., 1989; Hill & Hurtado, 1991; Lancaster & Lancaster, 1983; Peccei, 1995a, 1995b; Williams, 1957). Theoretically, this could potentially lead to a woman having a greater genetic representation in future generations than she would have if she continued reproducing directly; if this were the case, evolution would favor the switch. The problem with this argument is that it is mathematically very difficult to tip the genetic balance to favor (grand)mothering over direct reproduction (see Rogers, 1993); and after decades of research, there are no real-world data available that show that women actually do *better* through (grand)mothering than they would do by continuing to reproduce directly (Reiber, 2010). Of course, aiding kin can be evolutionarily beneficial in many situations, and once menopausal, such kin-directed behavior would be the only means through which women could continue to alter the evolutionary destiny of their genes; but aiding kin has not been demonstrated to override direct reproduction to an extent capable of *causing* menopause (Cohen, 2004; Reiber, 2010).

Both the extended human lifespan hypothesis and the (grand)mother hypothesis are also plagued by another major problem: they are incapable of explaining the existence of postreproductive lifespans in nonhuman organisms (Reiber, 2010). The reproductive systems of many nonhuman organisms are now known to cease functioning well before the end of life (Cohen, 2004). But unlike humans, none of these organisms are characterized by recent artificial increases in lifespan, and many of them do not provide (grand)maternal aid to (grand)children (Cohen, 2004). Any general evolutionary explanation of menopause must take this into account.

Reiber (2010) takes a novel evolutionary approach and argues that menopause is a result of competition between female gametes. When we think in evolutionary terms, it is often safe to ask questions like, "what is in the best interest of the individual?" However, this is only because the best interest of an individual is often aligned with the best interest of that individual's genes. If the best interest of the individual diverges from the best interest of the genes, the best interest of the genes will prevail at the apparent expense of the individual. From the perspective of whole individuals, any individual who had a longer reproductive lifespan ought to be evolutionarily favored; it would be in an individual's best interest to be able to reproduce throughout the entire adult lifespan, without experiencing menopause. From the perspective of the gamete, however, the best strategy is not to sit and wait in an aging ovary for a diminishing chance of being ovulated. The best strategy for a gamete would be to fight to ensure its ovulation as quickly as possible, since the chances of dying increase as women age, and a gamete that waited might lose its opportunity. Female gametes are competing to achieve ovulation, and the high rate of gamete loss that results is directly responsible for the follicular depletion that marks the onset of menopause.

The female gamete competition hypothesis implies that female reproductive systems are vital and active, in stark juxtaposition to the commonly portrayed passive view. Female gametes—eggs—are, indeed, larger and less mobile than male gametes (sperm). However, the eggs are in direct contact with each other for decades of a woman's life, and anything that an egg could do to increase its chances of being ovulated would be evolutionarily favored. For instance, at different stages of development, follicles differ in their susceptibility to the hormonal milieu of the ovary. Thus, starting to develop earlier versus later, or developing slower versus faster, could differentially situate a gamete for success or failure. Moreover, at particular stages of development, the follicles themselves secrete hormones and can thereby affect the gametes around them. In the final stages of development, just before ovulation, the largest follicle secretes estradiol and inhibin, which reduces follicle-stimulating-hormone levels in the ovarian environment and thereby kills less-developed follicles that were competing for ovulation. The facts of female reproductive biology are not changing; female gamete competition simply requires that we interpret those facts through an active perspective rather than a passive one.

Many predictions can be made on the basis of the female gamete competition hypothesis (see Reiber, 2010). Since competition will result in depletion of gametes only if the supply is limited, the most obvious prediction is that postreproductive lifespans should only characterize females in species in which there is a discrete, limited period of gametogenesis. This is supported by current data. Female fish, amphibians, and reptiles continuously produce new gametes throughout their lives and are not characterized by postreproductive life (Leidy,1994); female mammals, on the other hand, have limited periods during which they produce all the gametes they will ever possess (Leidy,1994), and most are now known to also have substantial periods of postreproductive life (Cohen, 2004).

Again, there is much research yet to be done, but like the evolutionary ideas presented about menstruation and PMS, the female gamete competition hypothesis may also have clinical implications for women's health. If extending the reproductive lifespan in women is deemed desirable, an understanding of the underlying cause of menopause will certainly be germane. Moreover, the specific competitive tactics employed by gametes, or the intensity of particular tactics, might contribute to some types of premenopausal infertility. Once understood, it might be possible to restore fertility by counterbalancing the competitive tactics or preventing them altogether.

# Conclusions

The field of women's health has made great strides in recent years. This is particularly astounding because most of the work has been done in the absence of an evolutionary perspective that could theoretically frame the issues and point to logical avenues for progress. Imagine a mechanic who is trying to diagnose and fix a problem in an automobile without knowing why the car is put together the way it is. Our impaired mechanic would likely poke around for a long time, trying all sorts of approaches, before hitting on a solution that works—if she ever does; and she would have little, if any, confidence that any working solution she finds is actually the best possible solution. Without an evolutionary perspective, women's health researchers and clinicians are at a disadvantage similar to that of our impaired mechanic. They can look at how things fit together, and employ various strategies, one after another, in the attempt to achieve a particular outcome. But the understanding will not be complete until the evolutionary level is also mastered, because evolutionary biology is the primary science underlying all of medicine (Nesse et al., 2006). Preventing, diagnosing, and correcting problems with human health require knowledge of evolutionary function—of the individual as a whole, and of various component parts and systems.

An evolutionary perspective elucidates novel predictions about women's health that are epidemiologically and clinically important, and that have not been obvious thus far from the traditional proximate perspective of medical researchers. The particular examples given here show that evolutionary approaches to some of the most basic features of women's health—menstruation, PMS, and menopause—have a multitude of implications, even in the face of modern technological advances. The synergy of evolutionary theory, epidemiological methods, and women's health will benefit the public, public health practitioners, epidemiologists, clinicians, and evolutionary theorists alike. But most importantly, it will benefit women themselves, by shoring up the foundation on which women's health science is growing and promoting more direct progress.

# References

Allison, A. C. (2004). Two lessons from the interface of genetics and medicine. *Genetics, 166,* 1591–1599.

American Psychiatric Association. (1994). *Diagnostic and statistical manual of mental disorders* (4th ed.; DSM-IV). Washington, DC: Author.

Austad, S. N. (1994). Menopause: An evolutionary perspective. *Experimental Gerontology, 29,* 255–263.

Bullivant, S. B., Sellergren, S. A., Stern, K., Spencer, N. A., Jacob, S., Mannella, J. A. & McClintock, M. K. (2004). Women's sexual experience during the menstrual cycle: Identification of the sexual phase by noninvasive measurement of luteinizing hormone. *Journal of Sex Research, 41*(1), 82–93.

Clare, A. W. (1985). Premenstrual syndrome: Single or multiple causes? *Canadian Journal of Psychiatry, 30*(7), 474–482.

Cohen, A. A. (2004). Female post-reproductive lifespan: A general mammalian trait. *Biological Reviews, 79,* 733–750.

Connolly, M. (2001). Premenstrual syndrome: An update on definitions, diagnosis, and management. *Advances in Psychiatric Treatment, 7,* 469–477.

Dalton, K. (1986). Premenstrual syndrome. *Hamline Law Review, 9,* 143–154.

Doty, R. L., Ford, M., Preti, G., & Huggins, G. R. (1975). Changes in the intensity and pleasantness of human vaginal odors during the menstrual cycle. *Science, 190*(4221), 1316–1317.

Doyle, C., Ewald, H. A., & Ewald, P. W. (2007). Premenstrual syndrome: An evolutionary perspective on its causes and treatment. *Perspectives in Biology and Medicine, 50*(2), 181–202.

Ellison, P. T. (2001). *On fertile ground.* Cambridge, MA: Harvard University Press.

Ericksen, K. P. (1987). Menstrual symptoms and menstrual beliefs: National and cross-national patterns. In B. E. Ginsburg & B. F. Carter (Eds.), *PMS: Ethical and legal implications in a biomedical perspective* (pp. 175–188). New York: Plenum.

Ewald, P. W. (1994). *Evolution of infectious disease.* New York: Oxford University Press.

Ewald, P. W. (1996). Guarding against the most dangerous emerging pathogens: Insights from evolutionary biology. *Emerging Infectious Diseases, 2*(4), 245–258.

Ewald, P. W. (2002). *Plague time: The new germ theory of disease.* New York: Anchor Books.

Ewald, P. W. (2004). Evolution of virulence. *Infectious Disease Clinics of North America, 18*, 1–15.

Ferin, M., Jewelewicz, R., & Warren, M. (1993). *The menstrual cycle: Physiology, reproductive disorders, and infertility.* New York: Oxford University Press.

Fessler, D. M. T. (2003). No time to eat: An adaptationist account of periovulatory behavioral changes. *Quarterly Review of Biology, 78*(1), 3–21.

Gangestad, S. W., Thornhill, R., & Garver, C. (2002). Changes in women's sexual interests and their partners' mate retention tactics across the menstrual cycle: Evidence for shifting conflicts of interest. *Proceedings of the Royal Society of London. Series B, Biological Sciences, 269*(1494), 975–982.

Garey, J. D. (1990). Phytoestrogens and the evolutionary significance of menstruation [Abstract]. *American Journal of Physical Anthropology, 81*, 225–226.

Gaulrapp, K., Backe, J., & Steck Y. (1995). Assessment of the prevalence of pre- and perimenstrual symptoms in female personnel of a university clinic. *Gynakol Geburtshilfliche Rundsch, 35*(4), 199–208.

Grammer, K., Renninger, L. A., & Fischer, B. (2004). Disco clothing, female sexual motivation, and relationship status: Is she dressed to impress? *Journal of Sex Research, 41*(1), 66–74.

Haig, D. (1993). Genetic conflicts in human pregnancy. *Quarterly Review of Biology, 68*, 495–532.

Halbreich, U., Backstrom, T., Eriksson, E., O'Brien, S., Calil, H., Ceskova, E., . . . Yonkers, K. (2007). Clinical diagnostic criteria for premenstrual syndrome and guidelines for their quantification for research studies. *Gynecological Endocrinology, 23*(3), 123–130.

Hamilton, W. D. (1966). The moulding of senescence by natural selection. *Journal of Theoretical Biology, 12*, 12–45.

Haselton, M. G., & Gangestad, S. W. (2006). Conditional expression of women's desires and men's mate guarding across the ovulatory cycle. *Hormones and Behavior, 49*(4), 509–518.

Haselton, M. G., Mortezaie, M., Pillsworth, E. G., Blecke-Rechek, A., & Frederick, D. A. (2007). Ovulatory shifts in human female ornamentation: Near ovulation, women dress to impress. *Hormones and Behavior, 51*(1), 40–45.

Hawkes, K., O'Connell, J. F., & Blurton Jones, N. G. (1989). Hardworking Hadza grandmothers. In V. Standen, & R. A. Foley (Eds.), *Comparative socioecology* (pp. 341–366). Oxford: Blackwell Scientific Press.

Hill, K., & Hurtado, A. M. (1991). The evolution of premature reproductive senescence and menopause in human females: An evaluation of the "grandmother hypothesis." *Human Nature, 2*, 313–350.

Hippocrates. (1939). *The genuine work of Hippocrates* (F. Adams, Trans.). Baltimore: Williams & Wilkins.

Jones, R. E. (1991). The menstrual cycle. In *Human reproductive biology* (pp. 143–165). New York: Academic Press.

Korenman, S. G. (Ed.). (1990). *The menopause: Biological and clinical consequences of ovarian failure; Evolution and management.* Norwell, MA: Serono Symposia, USA.

Lancaster, J. B., & Lancaster, C. S. (1983). Parental investment: The hominid adaptation. In D. Ortner (Ed.), *How humans adapt: A biocultural odyssey* (pp. 33–66). Washington, DC: Smithsonian Institution Press.

Leidy, L. E. (1994). Biological aspects of the menopause: Across the lifespan. *Annual Reviews Anthropology, 23*, 231–253.

Leidy Sievert, L. (2008). Should women menstruate?: An evolutionary perspective on menstrual-suppressing oral contraceptives. In W. R. Trevathan, E. O. Smith, & J. J. McKenna (Eds.), *Evolutionary medicine and health* (pp. 181–195). New York: Oxford University Press.

Macrae, C. N., Alnwick, K. A., Milne, A. B., & Schloerscheidt, A. M. (2002). Person perception across the menstrual cycle: Hormonal influences on social-cognitive functioning. *Psychological Science, 13*(6), 532–536.

Nesse, R. M. (2001a). Medicine's missing basic science. *The New Physician, Dec 2001, 50,* 8–10.

Nesse, R. M. (2001b). On the difficulty of defining disease: A Darwinian perspective. *Medicine, Health Care, and Philosophy, 4,* 37–46.

Nesse, R. M., Bergstrom, C. T., Ellison, P. T., Flier, J. S., Gluckman, P., Govindaraju, D. R.,…Valle, D. (2010). Making evolutionary biology a basic science for medicine. *Proceedings of the National Academy of Sciences of the United States of America, 107,* 1800–1807.

Nesse, R. M., & Schiffman, J. D. (2003). Evolutionary biology in the medical school curriculum. *BioScience, 53,* 585–587.

Nesse, R. M., & Stearns, S. C. (2008). The great opportunity: Evolutionary applications to medicine and public health. *Evolutionary Applications, 1,* 28–48.

Nesse, R. M., Stearns, S. C., & Omenn, G. S. (2006). Medicine needs evolution. *Science, 311,* 1071.

Nesse, R. M., & Williams, G. C. (1994). *Why we get sick: The new science of Darwinian medicine.* New York: Times Books (Random House).

Peccei, J. S. (1995a). A hypothesis for the origin and evolution of menopause. *Maturitas, 21,* 83–89.

Peccei, J. S. (1995b). The origin and evolution of menopause: The altriciality–lifespan hypothesis. *Ethology and Sociobiology, 16,* 425–449.

Prichard, J. C. (1837). *A treatise on insanity and other disorders affecting the mind.* Philadelphia: Haswell, Burlington, & Haswell.

Profet, M. (1993). Menstruation as a defense against pathogens transported by sperm. *Quarterly Review of Biology, 68,* 335–386.

Ravenholt, R. T. (1966). Malignant cellular evolution: An analysis of the causation and prevention of cancer. *Lancet, 1*(436), 523–526.

Reiber, C. (2007). PMS: Diagnostic and definitional issues [Abstract]. *American Journal of Human Biology, 19*(2), 275–276.

Reiber, C. (2008). An evolutionary model of premenstrual syndrome. *Medical Hypotheses, 70,* 1058–1065.

Reiber, C. (2009a). Evolution for epidemiologists. *Annals of Epidemiology, 19*(4), 276–279.

Reiber, C. (2009b). Empirical support for an evolutionary model of premenstrual syndrome. *Journal of Social, Evolutionary, and Cultural Psychology, 3*(1), 9–28.

Reiber, C. (2010). Female gamete competition: A new evolutionary perspective on menopause. *Journal of Social, Evolutionary, and Cultural Psychology 4*(4), 215–240.

Riley, T. L. (1986). Premenstrual syndrome as a legal defense. *Hamline Law Review, 9,* 193–202.

Roberts, S. C., Havlicek, J., Flegr, J., Hruskova, M., Little, A. C., Jones, B. C.,…Petrie, M. (2004). Female facial attractiveness increases during the fertile phase of the menstrual cycle. *Proceedings of the Royal Society of London. Series B, Biological Sciences, 271*(Suppl. 5), S270–S272.

Rogers, A. R. (1993). Why menopause? *Evolutionary Ecology, 7,* 406–420.

Rubinow, D. R., & Schmidt, P. J. (1995). The treatment of premenstrual syndrome: Forward into the past. *New England Journal of Medicine, 332*(23), 1574–1575.

Severino, S. K., & Moline, M. L. (1989). *Premenstrual syndrome: A clinician's guide.* New York: Guilford Press.

Shaw, S. T., & Roche, P. C. (1985). The endometrial cycle: Aspects of hemostasis. In D. T. Baird & E. A. Michie (Eds.), *Mechanisms of menstrual bleeding* (pp. 7–26). New York: Raven Press.

Singh, D., & Bronstad, P. M. (2001). Female body odour is a potential cue to ovulation. *Proceedings of the Royal Society of London. Series B, Biological Sciences, 268*(1469), 797–801.

Strassmann, B. I. (1996). The evolution of endometrial cycles and menstruation. *Quarterly Review of Biology, 71*, 181–220.

Strassmann, B. I. (1997). The biology of menstruation in *Homo sapiens*: Total lifetime menses, fecundity, and nonsynchrony in a natural-fertility population. *Current Anthropology, 38*(1), 123–129.

Thornhill, R., Gangestad, S. W., Miller, R., Scheyd, G., McCullough, J. K., & Franklin, M. (2003). Major histocompatibility genes, symmetry, and body scent attractiveness in men and women. *Behavioral Ecology, 14*(5), 668–678.

Tucker, J. S., & Whalen, R. E. (1991). Premenstrual syndrome. *International Journal of Psychiatry in Medicine, 21*(4), 311–341.

Williams, G. C. (1957). Pleiotropy, natural selection, and the evolution of senescence. *Evolution, 11*, 398–411.

Williams, G. C. (1966). *Adaptation and natural selection: A critique of some current evolutionary thought*. Princeton, NJ: Princeton University Press.

World Health Organization. (1992). *International classification of diseases* (10th ed.; ICD-10). Geneva, Switzerland: WHO.

# 11

# Fertility

## Life History and Ecological Aspects

BOBBI S. LOW

## Introduction

When we think about human fertility, we may think about social and cultural rules, even laws, as governing forces—and, by and large, they are, both to some degree in traditional societies and especially in our modern world. But there are strong, even inescapable, influences of ecological forces such as resource richness, dispersal, accessibility, and defensibility that have underlying impacts on fertility. Exploring these, and their impacts, may help clarify some of the complexity in the human patterns we see. Of course, sociocultural and ecological impacts interact (e.g., Low, Hazel, Parker, & Welch, 2008), so although I will focus on the ecological, the social influences will creep in.

Here I use a life history/behavioral ecology approach to human fertility. Behavioral ecology examines the impacts of environment on life history: the trade-offs that arise from, for example, conceiving now or waiting in specific conditions. Fertility patterns are a major component of life history strategies in all vertebrates: when to begin reproducing, whether to reproduce once or repeatedly; whether to invest more in protoplasm or care (and within protoplasm, many small or few large offspring); when to stop (e.g., see Roff, 1992, 2001; Stearns, 1992). By examining age-specific fertility and mortality patterns, life history theory can inform predictions about optimal patterns. Fertility is an important trait under selection; yet, regardless of the species one is interested in, optimization (in terms of lineage persistence) is a complex process. Simply maximizing fertility (by, e.g., starting early, spacing children closely, stopping late) is seldom a good strategy for complex social mammals like humans (e.g., see Strassmann & Gillespie, 2002). Too-early fertility can harm a woman's health and growth, can result in less-able child care, and in the worst-off nations of the world, can result in high infant and child mortality.

# How Unusual Are Human Reproductive Traits?

Human life histories are unusual in some regards among primates, but typical in others (Figure 11.1). Early work by Harvey, Martin, and Clutton-Brock (1986; see also Low, 2000) examined primate, including human, life history traits. Harvey et al. had data on 139 species, and sometimes a "family" was represented by only one species; today, far more data exist, and primate taxonomy has changed. This is important because, since taxonomy is hierarchical, one needs "family" to understand patterns—and in Harvey et al.'s time, the only hominid was *Homo sapiens*, which we now know skewed comparisons.

Thus we need new analyses. More recently, Low et al. (under review; see also van Schaik and Isler 2012) gathered data from 214 species of primates, using current phylogeny, thus allowing us to compare humans more appropriately than was possible in Harvey et al.'s time (when, e.g., the only species in the Hominidae was *Homo sapiens*). Like the Harvey et al. data, these were orthogonally regressed against maternal size, because size dictates the pace of much life history. Human females mature slightly later than we would predict from our size (Figure 11.1). Gestation length is almost exactly what we would predict, but infants are about 12.5% larger than we would predict (when occasional twinning is counted, weight of newborn(s) is 23% greater than predicted). Infants are relatively heavy at birth (Kusawa, 1998), but are weaned 10% lighter than predicted. Many scholars suggest that these differences from predictions arise because humans are highly social, and women, unlike other primate mothers, are not solely responsible for their infants' nutrition—they have a lot of help (e.g., Kramer, Greaves, & Ellison,2009; Reiches et al., 2009; also Newson & Richerson, this volume).

Women's reproductive lives differ in another very basic way: although their life expectancy at birth is 25% longer than expected from size, their reproductive life is about 22% shorter than expected. Most primate females live about 10% of their lives after the birth of their last infant, but women live roughly 30% of their lives. There are other species in which females stop reproducing relatively early (below), but details of timing and physiology differ (Donaldson, 2004).

# Ecology of Fertility

Across most traditional societies, girls in their early teens are subfecund: they may be able to conceive, but a full-term healthy birth occurs rarely (Lancaster, 1986, 1991). Another indication that nutrition affects fecundability, and thus fertility, becomes clear when comparing the total fertility rate (TFR) across traditional hunter-gatherer societies versus traditional agriculturalists: agriculturalists have higher fertility (Bentley, Goldberg, & Jasienska, 1993) but more health problems than hunter-gatherers.

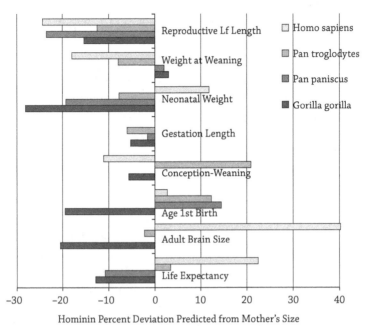

*Figure 11.1* A number of important human life history traits (as they are treated
in the aggregate) differ from values expected from our size (Author's data; Low
et al., under review.) In comparing species, because taxonomy is hierarchical, it is
important to take family into account. Earlier analyses rested on Harvey et al.'s
(1986) work—but at that time only humans were considered to be in the hominidae.
Now, chimpanzees, bonobos, and gorillas are included, so the within-family variation
is shown here. Earlier estimates of human uniqueness (Harvey et al., 1986; Low,
2000) overestimated human deviation from expected patterns.

Female mammals are not fertile at birth; they have some age at maturation,
an age-specific pattern of fertility, and an end to fertility before death. Obviously
nutritional effects on physiology can influence maturation in modern as well as
traditional societies (e.g., Reiber, this volume). For example, there are well-known
data suggesting that the age of menarche has been declining (e.g., Wyshak &
Frisch, 1982), and that fertility can vary nonrandomly within populations (e.g.,
Rosetta & Mascie-Taylor, 1996).

It is widely recognized from life history theory (e.g., Roff, 1992, 2001; Stearns,
1992) that a female's age at first birth (AFB) is strongly tied to her life expectancy
at birth ($e_0$). In turn, AFB strongly predicts total fertility. Because organism size
sets the pace of so many life history events, analyses must control for adult female
size; once that is done (typically by orthogonal regression against adult female size;
cf. Harvey et al., 1986), the consistency of this relationship across species as different as meadow voles and warthogs is strong and consistent (Harvey & Zammuto,
1985; Stearns, 1972, his Figure 5.10). Within the primates, including humans, the
relationship also holds, and humans fit the regression well (Figure 11.2).

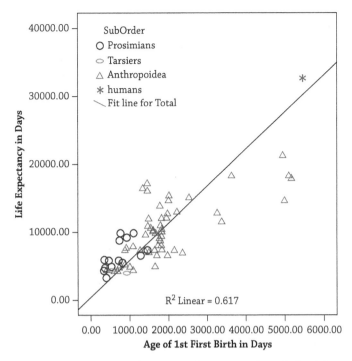

*Figure 11.2* The basic argument of Harvey and Zammuto (1986) that life expectancy at birth is a strong predictor of age at first birth, holds within primates, including humans (Author's data; Low et al., 2008 and under review).

However, such cross-species comparisons, common in the biological litera-ture, make assumptions that we can test with human data. They ignore vari-ation, assuming that a sample from any population can represent the entire species; they also assume that the relationships are not changing—they are at equilibrium. Is this true? Figure 11.3, modified from Low et al. (2008), sug-gests that the general relationship (short life expectancy at birth leads to early reproduction) holds in humans, but that there is considerable variation across populations—and, perhaps surprisingly, this variation is greatest in the shortest-life-expectancy populations (Low et al., 2008). Further, as Figure 11.4 shows, life expectancy at birth has been changing relatively rapidly for a num-ber of countries, so that we cannot assume equilibrium. It will be fascinating to follow these changes over time, particularly in least-developed nations, where we are making efforts to increase life expectancy (but typically with little under-standing of these relationships).

Life expectancy at birth, through influencing age at first birth, is a strong pre-dictor for total fertility rate (TFR; Figure 11.5), a widely used demographic meas-ure: the number of births a woman would have if (1) she lived throughout her entire reproductive period, and (2) at every age, had the average number of births. Note, however, that in terms of actual realized lifetime fertility, this measure will

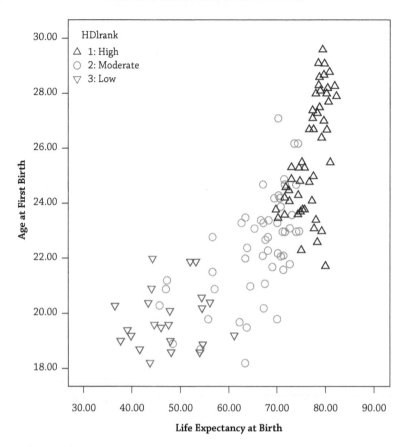

*Figure 11.3* Aggregate comparisons such as Harvey and Zammuto (1986) and Figures 11.1 and 11.2 assume that any population, or some mean or median calculation, can accurately represent a species. It is clear within the human data (even when some aggregation, at the national level, exists) that this is not true (modified from Low et al., 2008).

overestimate fertility for women in countries in which both and/or maternal death rates are relatively high.

Life expectancy appears to affect not only the optimal time to begin having offspring, but also age-specific patterns of fertility for iteroparous mammals. In the transnational data reviewed here, there is a very clear pattern (Figure 11.3): women in wealthier countries (with high life expectancies) begin having children later than women in countries with low life expectancies; they also have fewer children at every age (Figure 11.6, also Daly & Wilson, 1997). Within well-off countries, women in better circumstances begin having children later than other women, and have fewer children in a lifetime (see Low, Simon, & Anderson, 2002, 2003). This later-and-lower-fertility pattern was first seen in Europe and North America in the nineteenth century; scholars associated it with industrialization and called it "the demographic transition" (below).

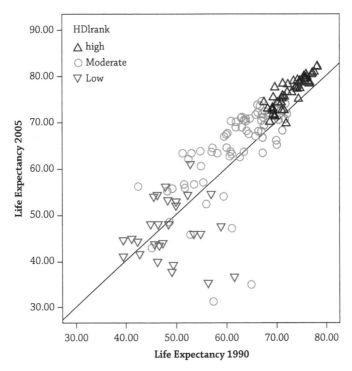

*Figure 11.4* Aggregate comparisons also assume that the relationship between life expectancy and age at first birth is at equilibrium, and not changing. Data from a number of countries show this is seldom true (also see Low et al., 2013).

## When Not to Conceive

Pregnancy is expensive, and lactation is three to five times as expensive as pregnancy. Thus, for iteroparous species (including most mammals), there are better and worse times to begin a pregnancy. For seasonal breeders, there are "better" and "worse" years. In humans, maternal nutrition can matter: in traditional societies, malnourished women or those with heavy workloads (Ellison, 1990), and underweight women or intensely training athletes such as marathon runners (Ellison, Panter-Brick, Lipson, & O'Rourke, 1993) are all more likely to have rare and irregular menstruation and associated failures of ovulation. Social stress, as reflected by cortisol levels in women not using modern birth control, also matters: stressed women are only one-third as likely to conceive as other women (Nepomnaschy et al., 2006).

## Size, Sex, and Number

Not all pregnancies are equally expensive; in many mammals, sons cost more than daughters—they are carried longer in utero, they are larger at birth, and

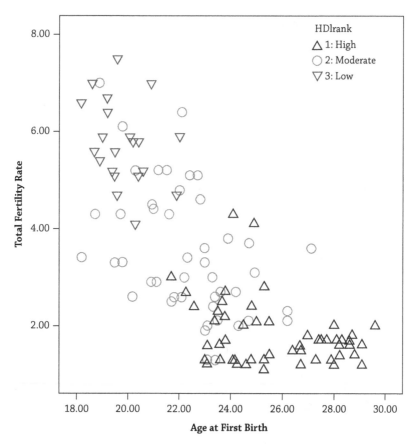

*Figure 11.5* Age at first birth is a strong predictor of TFR, the total fertility rate, which typically is higher for less-developed nations. Note, however, that TFR overestimates actual successful reproduction for these countries, because it does not account for either infant or maternal mortality, both of which are higher in least-developed nations.

they nurse more frequently (and longer in a nursing bout). Most mammals are polygynous, with male reproductive success varying more than female success; one common outcome is that mothers who produce poorly invested sons will not get grandchildren from them. If you are a female in poor condition, it is better reproductively to produce a daughter; even wimpy daughters will be able to have offspring. Consider red deer, well-studied in this regard (Clutton-Brock, 1991; Clutton-Brock, Guinness, & Albon, 1982). Females in excellent condition (those in good territories) and high-status females produce more sons than do females in poor condition or of low status. Another reflection of the high cost of sons in this polygynous system is that after having a son, females are likely to "skip" a year, not producing an offspring in the following year. In humans, for whom offspring are quite costly to rear

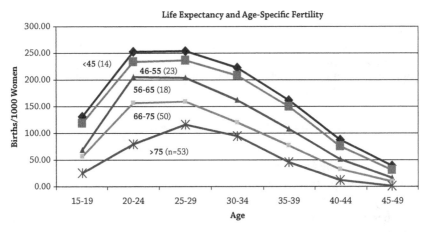

*Figure 11.6* When life expectancy (lines shown here) at birth is short, not only does fertility begin earlier, but age-specific fertility is higher at all ages (modified from Low et al., 2008; see also Daly & Wilson, 1997 for a smaller-scale comparison).

to independence, it is probably no surprise that twins are rare, and son-son twins are exceptionally rare.

The relatively higher expense of producing a son in many species, and the importance of high investment for a son's success, are also reflected by the male-biased sex ratio of (chromosomally normal, corrected for maternal contamination) spontaneous abortions (Hassold, Quillen, & Yamine, 1983) and stillbirths (Machin & Crolla, 1974; Sutherland, Carter, Bauld, Smith, & Bain, 1978). Hassold et al. estimated the sex ratio as 132/100 after correcting for maternal contamination (which in some studies leads to estimation of a less strongly biased sex ratio).

## Spacing Births

The help of others can matter for a mother's ability to space children. As Trivers (1974) first noted, the time of weaning is a moment of potent mother-offspring conflict of interests. Infants clearly would "prefer" a mother to continue investment far beyond the optimal time, while from her outlook, she should shift to production and investment in new offspring. When older children can take care of younger children (and when others are contributing food), this sometimes means a woman can have more children (e.g., Turke, 1988). But there are clear limits; Hrdy (1992) found a dramatic example in 18th-century Paris. Wealthy women could afford wet-nurses, and as a result had very short interbirth intervals. Women who could afford the best wet-nurses had the lowest infant mortality. But these women faced trade-offs: they experienced a range of problems, including chronic anemia and prolapsed uteruses. Wet-nurses fared quite badly:

they had very long interbirth intervals (nursing amenorrhea), resulting low fertility, and high infant mortality.

Birth spacing remains an issue in some least-developed nations, where public health infrastructure, and even simple clean water, may be lacking. In developed nations, low fertility means that interbirth intervals tend to be relatively long.

## Reproductive Value and the Marriage Market

Although we usually focus on how social parameters affect fertility, it is also true that fertility prospects can affect sociocultural rules. *Reproductive value* is a concept devised by R. A. Fisher (1958): the number of daughters a woman will have in the rest of her life, given the prevailing age-specific fertility and mortality schedules. It can thus vary across populations (e.g., Low & Clarke, 1991). Reproductive value peaks at the optimal (population) age at first reproduction, and declines inexorably after that. This has an interesting influence in bridewealth societies, in which men purchase their wives: a younger, higher-reproductive-value woman costs more than an older woman (e.g., Borgerhoff Mulder, 1988, 1989). Reproductive value may also speak to modern confusion about why well-dressed older men are typically seen as "silverbacks" with status, while older women are seen simply as uninteresting.

## Terminations: Resources, Abortion, and Infanticide

Spontaneous abortion appears to be related to chromosomal abnormalities, malnutrition, serious illness, and sometimes structure of reproductive organs; it is more common among women over 35 in Western nations. Much intentional abortion appears similar to spontaneous abortion, and relatively straightforward in an evolutionary perspective: mothers who are unwell and unlikely to be successful in the current pregnancy, mothers who have no support system, mothers who are newly paired with a male not the father, are most likely to abort. But there is a difference: intentional abortion is more likely among mothers with high reproductive value—that is, women who have further chances to carry a successful pregnancy to term when conditions are more favorable (e.g., Hill & Low, 1991). This contrasts with spontaneous abortion patterns; basically, older women, with fewer future chances, may decide to carry a pregnancy to term.

Guttmacher Institute (http://www.alanguttmacher.org/pubs/fb_induced_ abortion.html) figures add additional information for the United States. Almost half of pregnancies are unintended, and 40% of these are terminated by abortion. Of all pregnancies, excluding spontaneous abortions (miscarriages), 22% end in termination. Deliberate abortion tends to be highest among Black women, then Hispanics, lowest among Caucasian women. This should not be surprising, given the conditions prompting women to seek abortion (above). Basically, at least half of American women will experience an unintended pregnancy by age 45, and about one-third will have had an abortion. There are age and status biases: women in their 20s account for more than half of all intentional abortions (as above); and women never married and not cohabiting account for 45%. The reasons women give for seeking abortion reflect their understanding of parental responsibilities. Three-fourths of women cite concern for or responsibility to other individuals; three-fourths say they cannot afford a child; three-fourths say that having a baby would interfere with work, school, or the ability to care for dependents; and half say they do not want to be a single parent or are having problems with their husband or partner. In the United States today, political opinion and health care options affect the Medicaid fund availability (which makes medical aid available to the poor), which in turn can influence the pattern of abortion with socioeconomic status (e.g., Wetstein, 1996).

Patterns of parental infanticide (not the most common type; see Low, 2000) are similar to those of abortion: infanticide is more likely when the current infant is ill, deformed, or otherwise unlikely to thrive; and when the mother has little chance of rearing this child successfully, but has high reproductive value, and thus good future chances. Both abortion and infanticide patterns suggest that resource scarcity may lead to termination of maternal investment when that investment is unlikely to produce a successful, reproductive adult offspring (see review by Low, 2000).

# When to Stop?

Human females are unusual in spending almost a third of their lifetimes after ceasing reproduction; in most other mammals, females might spend perhaps 10% of their lifetimes postreproductive. However, relatively long postreproductive life, something like menopause, exists also in bonobos (de Waal, 1997), odontocyte whales (Marsh & Kasuya, 1984; 1986), elephants (Poole, 1997), baboons (Packer, Tatar, & Collins, 1998), lions (Packer et al., 1998), and rhesus monkeys (Walker, 1995). Because women's reproductive lives are shorter than predicted from our size (Figure 11.1), and grandmothers in many societies care for grandchildren, one possible explanation, the "Grandmother Hypothesis" has arisen (e.g., Hawkes et al., 1999). This argues that because children take so very long to become independent, very late reproducing mothers—and their late-born children—might die, so that switching from reproduction to simply caring for existing children might be optimal (see also Johow, Voland, & Willführ, this volume).

Despite the attractiveness of this hypothesis, there are few data, and results conflict. The first analysis of human lifetime fertility among women who stopped earlier versus later is that of Hill and Hurtado (1991, 1996), who worked with the Ache of Paraguay. They found some positive effects of grandmothers' help:

men and women with a living mother experienced slightly higher fertility than others, and children with a living grandmother survived slightly better than others. But these effects were small, and women who remained fertile longer had higher lifetime reproductive success than other women. Recent simulation models similarly find that, probably because of the weak selection on relatively few women toward the end of life, grandmothering benefits are not likely to be large enough for selective benefit (Kachel, Premo, & Hublin, 2011). Because the value of a grandmother may vary with age-specific fertility and mortality patterns, a grandmother's value to a mother's fertility may vary across societies. Studies in The Gambia have found that maternal grandmothers improve the survivorship of their grandchildren (Sear, Mace, & McGregor, 2000); and that the presence of a woman's in-laws increases her fertility (Sear, Mace, & McGregor, 2002). In contrast, no such effects existed in Malawi (Sear, 2008). Similarly, conflicting results arise from cross-cultural reviews (Hill & Hurtado, 1991, 2009; Sear & Mace, 2008; Shanley, Sear, Mace, & Kirkwood, 2007). In different societies, various relatives may or may not affect women's fertility and children's survival. Here is a problem for future analysis.

Packer et al. (1998) tested the grandmother hypothesis with field data from baboons and lions—in these species two results countered the grandmother hypothesis: first, old-reproducing females had no higher mortality costs of reproduction than younger females; and second, grandmother help did not improve the fitness of either grandchildren or reproductive-age offspring.

## Mating Systems and Parental Care: One Parent, Two, or a Village?

Across birds and mammals, the mating system (polygyny, polyandry, monogamy, and even polygynandry) is strongly correlated with who cares for offspring (e.g., Clutton-Brock, 1991; also reviews in Clutton-Brock, 1988; Low, 2000). Males are unlikely to be paternal in expensive ways unless their paternity is certain. This leads to a dichotomy: when biparental care is much more effective than single motherhood, males develop ways to ensure certainty of paternity: mate-guarding, for example. Or, males simply defect on the paternal care front or (below) do things that are not very expensive.

Cross-culturally, most human societies are polygynous: male reproductive success varies more than does female reproductive success (a common description—that males have multiple mates simultaneously, is incomplete; Bateman, 1948). Note that *marriage rules* are not the same as *mating systems*. Or, to put it differently, *social monogamy* is not the same as true *genetic monogamy* (Reichard & Boesch, 2003); true genetic monogamy, as in some penguins, is very rare. In mating system terms, many nations are currently polygynous: divorce is common; men remarry and have children in second and subsequent marriages more often than do women; but at the same time, more men go without ever having children than do women. The result is that most women have some number of children; among men, a larger proportion fail to have children at all, while some men have many children, usually in repeated marriages. Thus variance in male reproductive success is greater than variance in female reproductive success—the system is biologically polygynous (cf. Bateman, 1948).

In systems that are not genetically monogamous (with equal male and female variance in reproductive success), males will either spend considerable effort guarding access to females, or they will spend very little in true parental investment (Trivers, 1972). They will either do nothing for offspring (as in, e.g., red deer: Clutton Brock et al., 1982), or their parental effort (Low, 1978) will be of a generalizable sort, as in redwing blackbirds: males hold territories encompassing several females' nests, and give warnings of approaching dangers (which works for all nests)—but do not feed offspring (which would increase the cost with each offspring).

Humans have created variations around this general theme. Males are relatively quite parental for a mammal, although the degree of investment in children does vary with certainty of paternity (e.g., Alexander, 1979; Flinn, 1991; Anderson et al. 1999, 2007). From menstrual huts to chastity belts to DNA tests, we humans have invented novel ways to detect particular males' paternity. In traditional societies, marriage residence is often with the man's family (patrilocality)—and marriage residence affects who marries, and who contributes to child care (e.g., Flinn & Low, 1986).

Human sociality comes into play in the care and feeding of children, despite these constraints. Above, I noted that children are weaned earlier than expected; we can wean our children early because women, unlike, say, gorilla females, are not the only source of an infant's food. Others besides the mother bring back food for both the mother and (usually with some processing) the child. Even in polygynous societies, a man's contributions can be vital. Consider the Ache (Hill & Hurtado, 1996). They are polygynandrous; by their mid-thirties, both men and women have had numerous spouses (sleeping together openly in camp for several days is recognized as a marriage). People track and assign paternity. Men hunt, and better hunters get more spouses than poorer hunters; men also trade meat with other men. If a man dies, and his children are younger than ten, other men will not give meat to his widow, and the children are likelier than others to die.

## Fertility Trade-offs and Competition: "The" Demographic Transition

Family sizes fell dramatically in Europe and North America during the 19th century. Although demographers at one time considered industrialization to be a "cause" of demographic transitions (certainly it was a major correlate), at a finer scale, fertility patterns tended (and tend) to be local and reversible, and linked to resource availability (e.g., Lockridge, 1981; Low, 1991; Schofield, 1985, 1989; Wrigley & Schofield, 1981). Rather than a singular, large-scale change, studies continue to find family-size shifts in response to resource conditions and the costs of various investments (e.g., education) necessary for children's success.

A variety of cultural phenomena can influence shifts in fertility, and in fertility decisions (Newson & Richerson, 2009; Newson et al., 2007; Newson, Richerson, & Boyd, 2007). Modern transitions in developing nations may be linked to opportunities for children's success, and such opportunities are frequently linked to expensive parental investment (e.g., Knodel, 1994; Schreffler & Dodoo, 2009). In the case of Thailand, Knodel and colleagues found that as employer preferences shifted, preferring employees with (nonfree) secondary-school education, parents explicitly calculated how many children they could afford to send to secondary school.

Obviously, cultural secular trends are a major driving force in demographic transitions, and, as I explain below, today just such trends may be driving Western women's fertility to levels that are biologically suboptimal in terms of lineage persistence and success. But if we set the empirical data in the context of the competitiveness of children's environments—the investment necessary to mature, settle, marry—and intergenerational transfers (e.g., Bogerhoff Mulder et al., 2009; Kaplan, 1996; Kaplan & Bock, 2001; Shenk et al., 2009), several things are clear: parents everywhere try to give their children advantages, and there are often clear ecological aspects to these life history shifts. Trading off numbers for parental care, when that is sufficiently effective, is a winning strategy: the "quantity-quality" trade-off is real in humans as well as in other species.

Darwin himself described the quantity-quality trade-off, and Lack (1966) documented empirical examples in birds. MacArthur and Wilson (1967) generated a theoretical example, using islands: they noted that the direction of selection changed when very few conspecific competitors existed, versus when the environment was replete with competitors. They used islands as their context: how the direction of selection shifted in terms of competition for first arrivals, versus when the (typically limited) habitat was full of competitors (italics added):

> In an environment with no crowding (r-selection), genotypes which harvest the most food (even if wastefully) will rear the largest families and be most fit. *Evolution here favors productivity.* At the other extreme, in a crowded area *(K-selection)*, genotypes which can at least replace themselves with a small family at the lowest food level will win, the food density being so lowered that large families cannot be fed. *Evolution here favors efficiency* of conversion of food into offspring—there must be no waste.

Thus, in open, relatively low-competition environments, maximizing number of offspring, with little investment for each, is a viable strategy—while in highly competitive environments, more investment per offspring is required for those offspring to succeed competitively. This is true, of course, only when parental investment can be effective in aiding offspring competitiveness. Note the parallels to Goody's (1988) "Mediterranean" versus "European" family patterns: produce many with small per capita investment, or produce fewer, more intensely invested offspring. In the United States today, there is concern about rising educational and income inequality (e.g., Leonhardt, *New York Times*, January 11, 2011; Tavernise, *New York Times*, February 9, 2012). In particular, daughters of families with high socioeconomic status have increasingly high educational attainment, marry late, and have fewer children than other women.

In a way, MacArthur and Wilson's naming of the concept contributed to its being misunderstood; because they named it after the slope, $r$, and the limit (carrying capacity, K), of the logistic growth curve, many ecologists misused the terms. Selection—how the environment affects our lives—is not about "$r$ and K" but "b and d"—births and deaths, and far more than density affects those parameters. When resources become limiting in any population, birth rates drop (mothers are less able to bear and raise healthy offspring), and death rates increase. In fact, life history theorists (Roff, 1992, 2001; Stearns, 1992) typically avoid the use of the term "$r$-K selection" because of ecologists' misuse. But in its original formulation, it is appropriate in this context: the quantity-quality trade-off as it affects offspring competence and competitiveness.

The crucial question is this: In differentially competitive environmental conditions, how well invested must offspring be to succeed, to survive, and to reproduce? Parents in all species are in a "constant-sum game": What they invest in themselves, they cannot invest in offspring; what they invest specifically in *this* offspring, they cannot invest in *that* one (Trivers, 1972). Thus, the more invested in each offspring, the fewer offspring it is possible to raise successfully, unless the parents get (in nonhumans) larger, or higher metabolic rates, or (in humans) wealthier. MacArthur and Wilson's model uses the density of conspecific competitors as the important metric—and that is a reasonable assumption for most nonhuman species. However, many pressures clearly increase competition for humans, yet are only loosely, or not at all, connected to density: market forces, employer preferences, technological advances....and more.

I suggest the theoretical underpinnings of both r- and K-selection and demographic transitions can be stated generally: What level of parental investment best enhances offspring success in different conditions? Figure 11.7a (ceteris paribus: all else equal) is characteristic of many traditional societies (e.g., Hill & Hurtado, 1996) and many nonhuman species. In these conditions, the influence of parental investment on offspring survival and reproductive success levels off rather early, so it thus is optimal for parents to allocate relatively little investment to many offspring, and to terminate investment early. Figure 11.7b represents modern,

(a)    Routes to familial success *ceteris paribus*

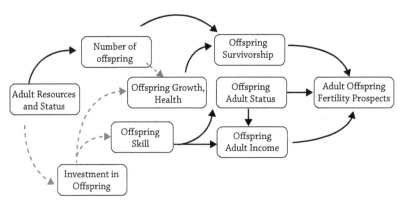

(b)    Routes to familial success in competitive environments

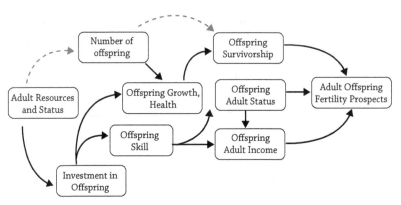

*Figure 11.7* Successful parental investment patterns will differ with environmental conditions. Thicker lines indicate the major routes to familial/lineage success.
[a] Under many conditions, resources contribute to reproductive success by increasing the number of offspring conceived, and do not greatly affect survivorship and future offspring success. For males, this is commonly because those who have achieved costly status can make expensive advertisements (a peacock's tail), or can offer potential mates useful resources; this means they have more mates, and more offspring than other males. For females, this relationship will hold when only females with sufficient resources can raise healthy offspring successfully to independence.
[b] When conditions become highly competitive, and it is difficult for offspring to get established and reproduce, parental resources are more effective when shifted into more intense, higher per capita offspring investment. Better-invested offspring can survive better, develop better skills, be more competitive, gain status, and reproduce successfully. In non-human species, this condition is typically connected to density (MacArthur & Wilson, 1967); in humans, other factors can operate. See text for further explanation

postdemographic transition pathways (and life history paths of species such as elephants, various cetaceans, and some other primates). This path shows great amounts of investment in each child, because investment affects survivorship and adult success. Increasing the per capita investment in each offspring means that, unless the parent develops a faster metabolism or gets larger (or, in humans, becomes wealthier), fewer children can be produced successfully (above). Note that in both pathways, *resource consumption is key to lineage success*; the important difference is the effectiveness of numbers of offspring versus per capita allocation of effort to offspring.

## Modern Novelties

Demographic transitions may well have arisen when shifting from high fertility to lowered fertility and better-invested children, but it seem likely that women in Western developed nations today (upward-pointing triangles in Figure 11.3) may have such delayed first births that they are at a selective disadvantage (e.g., Low et al., 2002, 2003). Delaying fertility to increase resources for parental investment has clearly nonlinear effectiveness: women who delay fertility to the late 20s or more have lineages that decline, compared to other women; the observed fertility of modern women is suboptimal from a biological point of view. Interestingly, the same may be true for men, as well (Kaplan, Lancaster, Johnson, & Bock, 1995). This is, of course, a trade-off: producing many children with low investment, in a highly competitive environment, will not succeed either.

Modern women face additional challenges, more fully explored in other chapters (e.g., Reiber, this volume). A number of pollutants, which lower fertility and/or increase mortality, are widespread in ways that are evolutionarily novel. Arsenic exposure, for example, increases a woman's risk of spontaneous abortion, low birth weight, infant mortality, and (though less clear) possibly stillbirth (Hopenhayn et al., 2000; Hopenhayn et al., 2003; Rahman et al., 2010). A variety of pesticides disrupt women's menstrual cycles, which in turn may affect ovarian function (e.g., Farr, Cooper, Cal, Savitz, & Sandler, 2004; Windham et al., 2005). Modern evolutionary novelties can pose serious risks to women's fertility. In developed nations, delays in first births appear to be primarily culturally influenced, a matter of delaying pregnancy until after advanced education. Ecological stresses that affect fertility may arise from a number of pollutants.

## Conclusion

Underneath our cultural influences, we humans must solve the same problems as all other species, of getting resources and using them to reproduce successfully. Ecological forces still affect human fertility, as they do the fertility of other primates. Human life histories differ in predictable ways from expectations based on adult female size, and these differences, arising from social patterns, are apparent even in traditional hunter-gatherer societies; they stand in sharp outline in developed nations.

Today, in both least-developed and developed countries, perhaps the strongest ecological forces acting on fertility are apparent at the extremes. That is, for least-developed nations, stresses—from civil war, poor nutrition, pollutants, and sometimes STDs, result in low life expectancy at birth and often heightened infant mortality (Low et al., 2008). In developed nations, our environments are so unusual, and reproductive patterns so striking, that Henrich, Heine, and Noranzayan (2010) called us "weird." Marked delays in first births (e.g., New Zealand AFB = 29.5; Low et al., 2008) appear to be primarily culturally influenced, a matter of postponing pregnancy until after advanced education. Ex-Soviet countries are an exception, with earlier childbirth, then a return to work for the mother. Ecological stresses that affect fertility may arise from a number of pollutants, a set of novel evolutionary stresses that can affect both men and women.

In most-developed nations, later fertility and few offspring mean fragile, easily extinguished lineages. If you and I each have two daughters, but you have them at 20 and 22, and I have mine at 38 and 40 (not unusual today in the Western World), and our daughters follow the same path, you have grandchildren when I am having my children: my lineage declines, compared to yours. Interestingly, the *generation time* is far more important that the number of children in generating this pattern (Low et al., 2002). On the other hand, very early fertility tends, in Western nations, to conflict with education, so poor urban women who drop out of school to have children are likely to remain poor and have difficulty obtaining competitive jobs, or good education for their children. So within-species variation in human fertility today is great, and has multiple causes, both ecological and cultural.

# References

Alexander, R. D. (1979). *Darwinism and human affairs*. Seattle: University of Washington Press.

Anderson, K. G., Kaplan, H., Lam, D., & Lancaster, J. B. (1999). Paternal care by genetic and stepfathers: II. Reports by Xhosa High School Students. *Evolution and Human Behavior, 20*, 433–451.

Anderson, K. G., Kaplan, H., & Lancaster, J. B. (2007). Confidence of paternity, divorce, and investment in children by Albuquerque men. *Evolution and Human Behavior, 28*(1), 1–10.

Bateman, A. J. (1948). Intra-sexual selection in *Drosophila melanogaster*. *Heredity, 2*, 349–368.

Bentley, G. R., Goldberg, T., & Jasienska, G. (1993). The fertility of agricultural and nonagricultural traditional societies. *Population Studies, 47*, 269–289.

Borgerhoff Mulder, M. (1988). Kipsigis bridewealth payments. In L. Betzig, M. Borgerhoff Mulder, & P. W. Turke (Eds.), *Human reproductive behavior: A Darwinian perspective* (pp. 65–82). Cambridge, UK: Cambridge University Press.

Borgerhoff Mulder, M. (1989). Earlier-maturing Kipsigis women have higher lifetime reproductive success, and cost more. *Behavioural Ecology and Sociobiology, 124*, 145–153.

Borgerhoff Mulder, M., Bowles, S., Hertz, T., Bell, A., Beise, J., Clark, G., ... Weissner, P. (2009). The intergenerational transmission of wealth and the dynamics of wealth in pre-modern societies. *Science, 326*(5953), 682–688.

Clutton-Brock, T. H. (Ed.). (1988). *Reproductive success: Studies of individual variation in contrasting breeding systems.* Chicago: University of Chicago Press.

Clutton-Brock, T. H. (1991). *The evolution of parental care.* Princeton, NJ: Princeton University Press.

Clutton-Brock, T. H., Guinness, F. E., & Albon, S. D. (1982). *Red deer: The behaviour and ecology of two sexes.* Chicago: University of Chicago Press.

Daly, M., & Wilson, M. (1997). Life expectancy, economic inequality, homicide, and reproductive timing in Chicago neighborhoods. *British Journal of Medicine, 314,* 1271–1274.

de Waal, F. (1997). *The forgotten ape.* Berkeley: University of California Press.

Ellison, P. T. (1990). Human ovarian function and reproductive ecology: New hypotheses. *American Anthropologist, 92,* 933–952.

Ellison, P. T., Panter-Brick, C., Lipson, S., & O'Rourke, M. (1993). The ecological context of human ovarian function. *Human Reproduction, 8,* 2248–2258.

Farr, S. L., Cooper, G. S., Cal, J., Savitz, D. A., & Sandler, D. P. (2004). Pesticide use and menstrual cycle characteristics among premenopausal women in the Agricultural Health Study. *America Journal of Epidemiology, 160,* 1194–1204.

Fisher, R. A. (1958). *The genetical theory of natural selection.* New York: Dover Books.

Flinn, M. V. (1991). Paternal care in a Caribbean village. In B. S. Hewlett (Ed.), *Father-child relations: Cultural and biosocial contexts* (pp. 57–84). New York: Aldine de Gruyter.

Flinn, M. V., & Low, B. S. (1986). Resource distribution, social competition, and mating patterns in human societies. In D. Rubenstein & R. Wrangham (Eds.), *Ecological aspects of social evolution* (pp. 217–243). Princeton, NJ: Princeton University Press.

Goody, J. (1988). *The development of family and marriage in Europe.* Cambridge, UK: Cambridge University Press.

Harvey, P., Martin, R. D., & Clutton-Brock, T. H. (1986). Life histories in comparative perspective. In B. Smuts, D. Cheney, R. Seyfarth, R. Wrangham, & T. Struhsaker (Eds.), *Primate societies* (pp. 181–196). Chicago: University of Chicago Press.

Harvey, P., & Zammuto, R. M. (1985). Patterns of mortality and age at first reproduction in natural populations of mammals. *Nature, 315,* 319–320.

Hassold, T., Quillen, S. D., & Yamine, J. A. Y. (1983). Sex ratio in spontaneous abortions. *Annals of Human Genetics, 47,* 39–47.

Hawkes, K., O'Connell, J. F., Blurton Jones, N. G., Alvarez, H., & Charnov, E. L. (1999). The grandmother hypothesis and human evolution. In L. Cronk, N. A. Chagnon, & W. G. Irons (Eds.), *Adaptation and human behavior: An anthropological perspective* (pp. 237–258). Hawthorne, NY: Aldine de Gruyter.

Henrich, J., Heine, S. J., & Noranzayan, A. (2010). The weirdest people in the world? *Behavioral and Brain Sciences, 33,* 61–135.

Hill, E. M., & Low, B. S. (1991). Contemporary abortion patterns. A life-history approach. *Ethology and Sociobiology, 13,* 35–48.

Hill, K., & Hurtado, A. M. (1991). The evolution of premature reproductive senescence and menopause in human females: An evaluation of the "Grandmother Hypothesis." *Human Nature, 2,* 313–350.

Hill, K., & Hurtado, A. M. (1996). *Ache life history: The ecology and demography of a foraging people.* New York: Aldine de Gruyter.

Hopenhayn, C., Browning, S. R., Hertz-Picciotto, I., Ferreccio, C., Peralta, C., & Gibb, H. (2000). Chronic arsenic exposure and risk of infant mortality in two areas of Chile. *Environmental Health Perspectives, 108,* 667–673.

Hopenhayn, C., Ferreccio, C., Browning, S. R., Huang, B., Peralta, C., Gibb, H., & Hertz-Picciotto, I. (2003). Arsenic exposure from drinking water and birth weight. *Epidemiology, 14,* 593–602.

Hrdy, S. B. (1992). Fitness tradeoffs in the history and evolution of delegated mothering with special reference to wet-nursing, abandonment, and infanticide. *Ethology and Sociobiology, 13,* 409–442.

Kachel, A. F., Premo, L. S., & Hublin, J. J. (2011). Grandmothering and natural selection. *Proceedings of the Royal Society B, 278*, 384–391.

Kaplan, H. (1996). A theory of fertility and parental investment in traditional and modern human societies. *Yearbook of Physical Anthropology, 39*, 91–135.

Kaplan, H., & Bock, J. (2001). Fertility theory: Caldwell's theory of intergenerational wealth flows. In J. M. Hoem (Ed.), *International encyclopedia of social and behavioral sciences* (Vol. 8, pp. 5561–5568). New York: Elsevier.

Kaplan, H., Lancaster, J. B., Johnson, S. E., & Bock, J. A. (1995). Does observed fertility maximize fitness among New Mexican men? A test of an optimality model and a new theory of parental investment in the embodied capital of offspring. *Human Nature, 6*, 325–360.

Knodel, J. (1994). Gender and schooling in Thailand. *Population Council, 60*, 1–60.

Kramer, K. L., Greaves, R. D., & Ellison, P. T. (2009). Early reproductive maturity among Pume foragers: Implications of a pooled energy model to fast life histories. *American Journal of Human Biology, 21*, 430–437.

Kuzawa, C. W. (1998). Adipose tissue in human infancy and childhood: An evolutionary perspective. *Yearbook of Physical Anthropology, 41*, 177–209.

Lack, D. (1966). *Population studies of birds.* Oxford, UK: Oxford University Press.

Lancaster, J. B. (1986). Human adolescence and reproduction: An evolutionary perspective. In J. B. Lancaster & B. A. Hamburg (Eds.), *School-age pregnancy and parenthood* (pp. 17–38). New York: Aldine de Gruyter.

Lancaster, J. B. (1991). A feminist and evolutionary biologist looks at women. *Yearbook of Physical Anthropology, 34*, 1–11.

Lockridge, K. (1981). *The fertility transition in Sweden: A preliminary look at smaller geographic units.* Umea, Sweden: Umea University.

Low, B. S. (1978). Environmental uncertainty and the parental strategies of marsupials and placentals. *American Naturalist, 112*, 197–213.

Low, B. S. (1991). Reproductive life in nineteenth century Sweden: An evolutionary perspective on demographic phenomena. *Ethology and Sociobiology, 12*, 411–448.

Low, B. S. (2000). *Why sex matters: A Darwinian look at human behavior.* Princeton, NJ: Princeton University Press.

Low, B. S., & Clarke, A. L. (1991). Family patterns in 19th-century Sweden: Impact of occupational-status and landownership. *Journal of Family History, 16*, 117–138.

Low, B. S., Hazel, A., Parker, N., & Welch, K. B. (2008). Influences on women's reproductive lives: Unexpected ecological underpinnings. *Cross-Cultural Research, 42*, 201–219.

Low, B. S., Hazel, A., Parker, N., & Welch, K. B. (2012). Life expectancy, fertility, and women's lives: A life-history perspective. *Cross-Cultural Research, 47(2)*.

Low, B. S., Simon, C. P., & Anderson, K. G. (2002). An evolutionary ecological perspective on demographic transitions: Modeling multiple currencies. *American Journal of Human Biology, 14*, 149–167.

Low, B. S., Simon, C. P., & Anderson, K. G. (2003). The biodemography of modern women: Tradeoffs when resources become limiting. In J. L. Rodgers & H. P. Kohler (Eds.), *The biodemography of human reproduction and fertility* (pp. 105–134). Boston: Kluwer Academic.

MacArthur, R., & Wilson, E. (1967). *The theory of island biogeography.* Princeton, NJ: Princeton University Press.

Machin, G. A., & Crolla, J. A. (1974). Chromosome constitution of 500 infants dying during the perinatal period. *Human Genetics, 23*, 182–198.

Marsh, H., & Kasuya, T. (1984). Changes in the ovaries of the short-finned pilot whale, *Globocephala macrorhynchus,* with age and reproductive activity. *Reports of the International Whaling Commission, Special Issue 6*, 259–310.

Marsh, H., & Kasuya, T. (1986). Evidence for reproductive senescence in female cetaceans. *Reports of the International Whaling Commission, Special Issue 8*, 57–74.

Nepomnaschy, P., Welch, K., McConnell, D., Low, B. S., Strassmann, B., & England, B. (2006). Cortisol levels and very early pregnancy loss. *Proceedings National Academy of Sciences, 103*, 3938–2942.

Newson, L., Postmes, T., Lea, S., Webley, P., Richerson, P. J., & McElreath, R. (2007). Influences on communication about reproduction: The cultural evolution of low fertility. *Evolution and Human Behavior, 28*, 199–210.

Newson, L., & Richerson, P. J. (2009). Why do people become modern? A Darwinian explanation. *Population and Development Review, 35*, 117–158.

Newson, L., Richerson, P. J., & Boyd, R. (2007). Cultural evolution and the shaping of cultural diversity. In S. Kitayama & D. Cohen (Eds.), *Handbook of cultural psychology* (pp. 454–476). New York: Guilford Press.

Packer, C., Tatar, M., & Collins, A. (1998). Reproductive cessation in female mammals. *Nature, 392*, 807–811.

Poole, J. (1997). *Elephants*. Stillwater, MN: Voyageur Press.

Rahman, A., Persson, L. A., Nermell, B., El Arifeen, S., Ekstrom, E. C., Smith, A. H., & Vahter, M. (2010). Arsenic exposure and risk of spontaneous abortion, stillbirth, and infant mortality. *Epidemiology, 21*, 797–804.

Reichard, U., & Boesch, C. (2003). *Monogamy: Mating strategies and partnerships in birds, humans, and other mammals*. Cambridge, UK: Cambridge University Press.

Reiches, M. W., Ellison, P. T., Lipson, S., Sharrock, K., Gardiner, E., & Duncan, L. (2009). Pooled energy budget and human life history. *American Journal of Human Biology, 21*, 421–429.

Roff, D. A. (1992). *The evolution of life histories: Theory and analysis*. New York: Chapman and Hall.

Roff, D. A. (2001). *Life history evolution*. Sunderland, MA: Sinauer.

Rosetta, L., & Mascie-Taylor, C. (1996). *Variability in human fertility*. Cambridge, UK: Cambridge University Press.

Schofield, R. (1985). English marriage patterns revisited. *Family History, 10*, 1–20.

Schofield, R. (1989). Family structure, demographic behaviour, and economic growth. In J. Walter & R. Schofield (Eds.), *Famine, disease, and the social order in early modern society* (pp. 279–304). Cambridge, UK: Cambridge University Press.

Schreffler, K., & Dodoo, F. N. A. (2009). The role of intergenerational transfers, land, and education in fertility transition in rural Kenya. *Population and Environment, 30*, 1–13.

Sear, R. (2008). Kin and child survival in rural Malawi. *Human Nature, 19*, 277–293.

Sear, R., & Mace, R. (2008). Who keeps children alive? A review of the effects of kin on child survival. *Evolution and Human Behavior, 29*(1), 1–18.

Sear, R., Mace, R., & McGregor, I. A. (2000). Maternal grandmothers improve nutritional status and survival of children in rural Gambia. *Proceedings of the Royal Society B, 267*, 1641–1647.

Sear, R., Mace, R., & McGregor, I. A. (2002). The effects of kin on female fertility in rural Gambia. *Evolution and Human Behavior, 24*, 25–42.

Shanley, D. P., Sear, R., Mace, R. & Kirkwood, T. B. L. (2007). Testing evolutionary theories of menopause. *Proceedings of the Royal Society B, 274*, 2943–2949.

Shenk, M. K., Borgerhoff Mulder, M., Bowles, S., Beise, J., Clark, G., Irons, W., ... Piraino, P. (2009). Intergenerational wealth transmission among agriculturalists. *Current Anthropology, 51*(1), 65–82.

Stearns, S. C. (1992). The evolution of life histories. Oxford, UK: Oxford University Press.

Strassmann, B. I., & Gillespie, B. (2002). Life-history theory, fertility, and reproductive success in humans. *Proceedings of the Royal Society B, 269*, 553–562.

Sutherland, G., Carter, R. F., Bauld, R., Smith, I. I., & Bain, A. D. (1978). Chromosome studies at the pediatric autopsy. *Annals of Human Genetics, 42*, 73–181.

Trivers, R. L. (1972). Parental investment and sexual selection. In B. Campbell (Ed.), *Sexual selection and the descent of man* (pp. 136–179). Chicago: Aldine de Gruyter.

Trivers, R. L. (1974). Parent-offspring conflict. *American Zoologist, 14*, 249–264.

Turke, P. W. (1988). Helpers at the nest: Childcare networks in Ifaluk. In L. L. Betzig, M. Borgerhoff Mulder, & P. W. Turke (Eds.), *Human reproductive behaviour: A Darwinian perspective* (pp. 173–188). Cambridge, UK: Cambridge University Press.

van Schail, C., & K. Isler. (2012). Life-history evolution in primates. Ch. 10 in J. Mitani, J. Call, P. M. Kappeler, Ryne A. Palombit, and J. Silk (eds.). *The Evolution of Primate Societies.* University of Chicago Press, Chicago.

Walker, M. (1995). Menopause in female rhesus monkeys. *American Journal of Primatology, 35,* 59–71.

Wetstein, M. (1996). *Abortion rates in the United States: The influence of opinion and policy.* Albany: State University of New York Press.

Windham, G. C., Lee, D., Mitchell, P., Anderson, M., Petreas, M., & Lasley, B. (2005). Exposure to organichlorine compounds and effects on ovarian function. *Epidemiology, 16,* 182–190.

Wrigley, E. A., & Schofield, R. (1981). *The population history of England 1541–1871.* Cambridge, MA: Harvard University Press.

Wyshak, G., & Frisch, R. E. (1982). Evidence for a secular trend in age of menarche. *New England Journal of Medicine, 306,* 1033–1035.

# 12

# Reproductive Strategies in Female Postgenerative Life

JOHANNES JOHOW, ECKART VOLAND, AND KAI P. WILLFÜHR

## Introduction

Probably many of us have had the chance of coming to know at least one of our grandmothers during our lifetime. Perhaps some of our readers may even experience being grandmothers while reading this book. In order to answer the nontrivial question of how the phenomenon of postgenerative longevity could have been produced by natural selection, this chapter pursues two main goals. First, it aims to provide a broad overview of the current debate on the evolutionary significance of grandmothers. To do this, we will briefly review the currently available empirical data on fitness-relevant behavioral traits that have been described for postmenopausal mothers. Second, we aim to show that grandmaternal strategies are conditional strategies. One of the most relevant conditions to which grandmothers adaptively react is the question of who made them grandmothers: Their sons or their daughters? Ultimately, we hope to be able to demonstrate that the postmenopausal phase of life is not only characterized by reproductive interests, but that these interests can be manifested in a considerable strategic flexibility and diversity in behavior.

## Evolution of the Postgenerative Lifespan

As is well known, the life history of humans differs in two essential aspects from those of the other apes (Robson, Van Schaik, & Hawkes, 2006). On the one hand, humans are characterized by a comparatively extended juvenile phase, and on the other, by a comparatively extended postgenerative lifespan. The latter brings the social role played by grandparents on the stage of evolution—a role which might be unique in the kingdom of organisms. Although Richardson, Burke, and Komdeur (2007) describe grandparental help in the Seychelles warbler, yet in contrast to human beings, the older helpers (mostly females) in this species are not physiologically constrained by infertility. Instead, they become helpers after they have been socially deposed from dominant positions and therefore have few opportunities for continuing their own reproduction. As they are relatively closely related to the young birds (r = 0.24), the helper role offers them a promising option for increasing their indirect fitness. Thus, older Seychelles warblers are postgenerative, but by no means postreproductive.

Since Williams (1957) placed the issue of reproductive senescence on the agenda of evolutionary research with his classic paper, various hypotheses have been proposed concerning how the evolutionary origin of the postgenerative lifespan could fit into Darwinian theory. At first glance the discontinuation of reproduction possibly some decades prior to the end of life appears to be anything but plausible, because how can one explain that natural selection, which rewards nothing but genetic reproduction, can produce sterility in senescence? Why age, if it does not increase the number of offspring? What must have appeared to be a paradox prior to Williams's contribution can be harmonized with modern views of Darwinian theory because now reproductive fitness is viewed as having three components, only one of which is fertility. The survival of one's offspring and their social and ecological placement, that is, their provisioning with social and ecological opportunities that are as advantageous as possible, are the two other factors. It is now clear that the term "postreproductive lifespan," which dominates the literature, is very misleading, namely because as long as individuals can influence the fate of their offspring and of other kin, they may be considered to be in their postgenerative lifespan, but not of postreproductive age.

While it appears to be possible to explain the postgenerative lifespan in keeping with evolutionary theory, no consensus has been reached with regard to the details. Which selective benefits of the postgenerative lifespan (and thus the latter's psychosocial correlate of the grandparental role) have gained in evolutionary significance (Voland et al., 2005) is unclear and remains controversial in the literature. In our view, the various theories offered in this regard may be classified into three categories, depending on which life history trait the selective benefits are correlated with: menopause, longevity, or premenopausal vitality.

## Selection Favors Menopause

It was originally thought that menopause resulted from an optimal trade-off between continued investments in existing offspring versus the investment necessary to start new offspring. The fundamental observation is that continued parturition becomes riskier, because with increasing age the probability of obstetric complications and thus of maternal death increase. However, due to the longer dependence of children on their mother, her death ultimately jeopardizes not only the lastborn child, but possibly all existing dependent children as well. For this reason, it appears to be more advantageous to cease with the production of additional children at a certain point in time, and instead, to invest one's remaining vitality in raising children that have already been born. From this perspective, menopause is an evolved trait and selection will favor its optimal timing. This is the heart of Williams's (1957) argument, which subsequently was also discussed in the literature as the "good-mother hypothesis" (Sherman, 1998), or as the "stopping-early hypothesis," or the "altriciality-life span hypothesis" (Peccei, 1995).

Recently, a second evolutionary scenario has been proposed, which also sees menopause as the result of a selective process. Starting from the observation that in natural fertility populations, menopause commences at an age once the following generation begins to reproduce, Cant and Johnstone (2008) modeled a reproductive conflict between the generations. The conflict is won by the younger women under the conditions of the patrilocal context due to the relatedness asymmetries within families. The result of this conflict is the reproductive division of the generations and a change in strategy by older women away from their own reproduction and toward kin support. However, it must be noted that there is an ongoing debate in the literature about whether or not menopause is actually subject to selection, or instead is a genetically fixed constraint that is practically unchangeable from an evolutionary viewpoint (Lummaa, 2007; Peccei, 2005). On the one hand, the fact that the age at the onset of menopause shows genetic variance (Peccei, 1999) seems to indicate a selective preservation of menopause. On the other hand, doubts have been expressed concerning the issue of whether the kin-selected fitness benefits of helping would be able to more than compensate for the costs of postmenopausal sterility (Austad, 1994; Rogers, 1993). If the costs of obligate old-age sterility are higher than the benefit(s) of the helper strategy, menopause cannot be interpreted as a functional adaptation of *Homo sapiens*. Instead, one may assume that it has persisted as a constraint from the evolutionary history of the Great Apes (but cf. Pavard, Metcalf, & Heyer, 2008). These considerations lead us to the second of the three cited bundles of theories.

## Selection Favors Longevity

This hypothesis, according to which natural selection does not primarily begin with menopause, but with longevity, also assumes that the postgenerative lifespan evolves because women are able to increase their fitness after menopause. They are essentially able to do so because they release their adult daughters from having to complete their subsistence tasks, and thus they support their daughters' reproduction and indirectly increase their own individual fitness. This is the core of the argument of Hawkes's (2003) version of the "grandmother hypothesis." The key difference to the idea that selection might favor menopause (1) consists of the interpretation of menopause as a barely changing phylogenetic constraint from our ape heritage. Interestingly enough, the reproduction physiology of women does not notably differ from that of female chimpanzees. The supply of follicles determined before birth and the rate of follicle atresia, that is, the regression of the follicles that do not ovulate are practically identical. Consequently, the reproductive senescence in female chimpanzees (and in the other apes as well, apparently), occurs at about the same age as in women. This means, however, that the extended postmenopausal life expectancy of women in comparison to other Homininae is a derived trait (cf. Robson et al., 2006). The fitness gains that can be achieved through kin support within a cooperative breeding system are deemed to be responsible for the extended life expectancy.

## Selection Favors Premenopausal Vitality

Another argument, which is also known as the "fly-by" phenomenon, is also based on the assumption that menopause is a genetically fixed trait of ape life evolution (Wood et al., 2001). Female chimpanzees also have only a limited lifetime supply of follicles and would undergo menopause if only they lived long enough. However, because selection favored those females in our phylogenetic history who actually achieved menopause, that is, who were able to fully exploit their fecund lifespan, phenotypes automatically arose, which were still vital enough at the time of their menopause to continue to live for a while. From this perspective, the postgenerative lifespan is a nonfunctional by-product of the selection for premenopausal vitality and, in this sense, simply a "fly-by" phenomenon. If one ages anyway, one can also help others. The difference to the hypothesis that selection favors longevity (2) consists, therefore, of the assumption that the postgenerative lifespan is primarily not an adaptation, but was secondarily co-opted by nepotistic helping strategies through the mechanism of kin selection.

Models (2) and (3), that is the ideas that selection favors longevity or premenopausal vitality, respectively, are essentially less sophisticated than the idea that selection favors menopause (1) with regard to the necessary fitness effects required to further an adaptation. So that menopause can function in an adaptive way, the considerable costs of childlessness in senescence must be more than compensated for by the effects of kin support, whereas regarding menopause as phylogenetic inertia and postmenopausal survival as the target of natural selection as in (2) and (3) merely require slightly positive kin effects in senescence. Compared to the alternative of doing nothing, helping is already advantageous even with minor effects and can contribute to the evolutionary spread of the genes for postgenerative life.

All three hypotheses interpret the postgenerative lifespan as a biologically functional stage of life. Whether this functionality is the result of a process of adaptation (1, 2) or a co-option (3), is of subordinate importance for this chapter. The still unresolved issue of whether menopause is a biological adaptation of human life history evolution (1) or a phylogenetic constraint from our ape heritage (2, 3) is not going to be explored any further here either. As Coall and Hertwig (2010, p. 4) stated, "Once women started living past their reproductive ceiling, the only way that they could improve their inclusive fitness was by caring for their children and grandchildren. Whether human longevity, and specifically the postreproductive longevity associated with menopause, is adaptive or an epiphenomenon, grandparents are still in the right place, at the right time."

## What Effects Do We Observe?

### Who Benefits From Elderly Women: Children or Grandchildren—or Both?

Human behavioral ecologists describe adaptive behavioral strategies as conditional strategies. That is, depending on the context, including the type of subsistence, division of labor and inheritance rules, and mating and residence patterns, different payoffs for family transactions might occur. As a consequence, evolved behavioral inclinations are able to lead to varying manifestations of behavior. This also applies to the reproductive strategies of postgenerative women, which makes generalizations about their influence on familial reproduction difficult.

This also concerns the issue of who actually benefits from elderly women: their children or their grandchildren? Or to rephrase the question: Is the postgenerative lifespan primarily strategically filled by maternal or grandmaternal investment? Do women continue to live after menopause because their female ancestors increasingly looked after their late-born children or their grandchildren (or helped their adult children with the latter's reproduction, respectively)? Peccei (2005) correctly points out that these two strategic options do not mutually rule each other out because in both scenarios a gain in fitness is achieved by continued investment. Whether this postmenopausal investment is in the improved survival of their own children or the support of their already adult children with the latter's reproduction, that is, ultimately in their grandchildren, is irrelevant, insofar as both can promote fitness. As long as the investment meant a significant gain in the fitness in one's genetic kin, the younger generation will benefit from the extended postgenerative lifespan of their mothers and grandmothers. If, for example, the postgenerative lifespan is solely traceable to maternal investment, grandmotherly welfare motivations would be unknown, and it would tend to be improbable that grandmothers would be able to function as a "secure base" in their grandchildren's emotional bonding (Flinn & Leone, 2006). On the other hand, if the postgenerative lifespan is solely due to grandmaternal investment in their grandchildren, one should expect that grandmothers would prove to be obligate helpers with childcare. What has been observed, however, is that postgenerative women voluntarily assume the role of "helping" grandmothers and that the probability of altruistic behavior toward their grandchildren is determined by constraints (Coall & Hertwig, 2010). This would also explain why in some populations no grandmotherly effect is to be found, whereas it is clearly demonstrable in others (Sear & Mace, 2008, for the impact of grandmothers on child survival; Sear & Matthews, 2010, for impact of grandmothers on a child's fertility).

To give two examples: Hawkes et al. (1997) were able to show that weaned children of nursing mothers among the Hadza of Tanzania are better nourished if they received support from their (mostly maternal) grandmothers. However, contradictory results come from a population of rural Malawi, where Sear (2008) has demonstrated a detrimental effect of maternal grandmothers. Here grandchildren have poorer survival if their grandmother lives nearby. Similar to these mixed results in case of the maternal grandmother, diverse effects have been recognized for the paternal grandmother's effect on child mortality when comparing different populations: While in the case of the demographically saturated population of the historical Krummhörn, a harmful effect of the paternal grandmother can be found (Beise & Voland, 2002), this is not the case where early French settlers in Québec are concerned (Beise, 2005). So, although maternal grandmothers in general are assumed to be more reliable in their support than paternal grandmothers (see next section), available evidence suggests that—depending on ecological conditions—both can function in highly different ways with highly different outcomes for family reproduction.

## Matrilineal Bias

The existence of a matrilineal bias in kin support (Euler & Michalski, 2007, Holden, Sear, & Mace, 2003) is due to the basic tendencies of evolved reproductive strategies in old age. The ultimate reason for this lies in the known asymmetry of kinship relationships. On average, fathers are genetically always a little less related to the children of their wives than mothers to their children (Anderson, 2006). As a result, typically in mammals and especially in primates, matrilineal cooperative societies can occur with a higher probability than patrilineal ones; females tend to stay close to their mothers and other female kin while males disperse. Accordingly, the early social evolution of humans was characterized by an adaptive complex comprising female philopatry and matrilinearity, and the first symbolic kinship systems are likely to have been developed by female kin as well (Opie & Power, 2008). Thus, the helping grandmother was the self-reinforcing germ cell for the origin of complex human family systems, including cognitive and emotional adaptations for family life (see Hrdy, 2009, for an overview). In this perspective, postmenopausal survival functions as a key feature in human life history from which other characteristics like a relatively late but rapid reproduction have been derived (e.g., Robson et al., 2006).

The matrilineal bias in the helping behavior of postgenerative women can also be found in modern times. In general, maternal kin tend to render more reproductive support than paternal kin (Euler & Michalski, 2007; Pollet, Nelissen, & Nettle, 2009; Mace & Sear, 2005, Sear & Mace, 2008). Furthermore, grandchildren regularly report varying emotional closeness to their four grandparents that are congruent with the predictions of *"pater semper incertus,"* that is, the maternal grandmother is the emotionally most significant and the paternal grandfather is the emotionally least significant grandparent (Bishop, Meyer, Schmidt, & Gray, 2009; Euler & Weitzel, 1996). This said, one must remember that humans adjust to local conditions and thus the matrilineal bias may show some variation cross-culturally (Kemkes-Grottenthaler, 2005; Pashos, 2000).

Interestingly, the help provided by postgenerative women in the patriline show significantly more variation than in the matriline, as Sear and Mace (2008) have demonstrated in their meta-analysis on the influence of grandmothers (and other kin) on grandchild survival. Paternal grandmothers can also be helpful, but because they lack a matrilineal bias and thus an increased unconditional basic motivation to support the family, other circumstances gain a higher conditioning influence. This includes the circumstance that paternal grandmothers not only play their role in the supportive transactions between the generations, but over and above that, they also play a prominent role in sexual conflict. Sexual conflict arises when the sexes have different fitness optima and one sex can gain by exploiting the other. Humans solve the sexual conflict in different ways with enduring consequences not only for the configuration of pair bonds but also for family life, in general (Borgerhoff Mulder & Rauch, 2009). On this evolutionary battleground, paternal grandmothers can be expected to act as the extended arm of their sons' interests. In principle, this also applies for maternal grandmothers, of course. So another strategy comes into play in addition to kin support, namely that individuals engage in the manipulation and exploitation of family relationships in the interests of their own descendants. This situation is expressed as the "in-law conflict."

## Grandmothers and In-law Conflicts

A Japanese proverb recommends the following: "Never rely on the glory of the morning or the smiles of your mother-in-law," whereas the American comedian Joan Rivers jeers: "I told my mother-in-law that my house was her house, and she said, 'Get the hell off my property.'" Well, we could easily expand the enumeration of more or less malicious jokes and proverbs that exist around the world at the expense of mothers-in-law. It seems that the topos of "evil mothers-in-law" might represent a kind of transcultural mental concept. Viewed from an evolutionary perspective, in-law conflicts are ultimately rooted in sexual conflicts, which also extend to the helpers within cooperative breeding communities who are always asymmetrically related (Leonetti, Nath, & Hemam, 2007). Differences of opinion within families and extended kinship networks are, therefore, unsurprising to behavioral ecologists and evolutionary psychologists because, after all, the genetic interests of individuals from various lines of parentage automatically conflict with one another (e.g., Euler & Michalski, 2007). Significant sex differences in the scope of parental investment and thus in the reproduction-related opportunity costs between males and females (Penn & Smith, 2007) ensure varying optimums for mothers and fathers with regard to certain trade-offs. Males will tend to assert their reproductive interests at the expense of females (for which sexually selected infanticide serves as a good example: Van Schaik & Janson, 2000), and vice versa, females will tend to assert their reproductive interests at the expense of the males (for which the concealment of paternal relationships serves as a good example: Hrdy, 2000). The result of this conflict-laden situation in the reproductive cooperation of the sexes is a culturally and mentally negotiated, but always remains an individually and evolutionarily fragile compromise in the balance of power between the sexes (e.g., Borgerhoff Mulder, 2009).

According to the logic of kin selection, the evolutionary battle of the sexes extends to the parties' kin, which is why kin tend to work toward the interests of the male or the female, depending on to which of the two they are related. If kin function as allomothers, that is, as persons who care for offspring that are not their own, sexual conflict will even pervade the reproductive strategies in the kinship network. Since humans are facultative cooperative breeders who may organize their reproduction within an extended family context (Hrdy, 2005, 2009; Reiches et al. 2009; Sear & Mace, 2005, 2008, 2009), we can expect the in-law conflict to constitute an intrinsic and inevitable aspect of human social evolution.

Owing to the universal precept of exogamy (Bischof, 1985), kinship is always asymmetric, that is, with the mother *or* the father. Whether and to what extent the parties involved in the sexual conflict are confronted with their "partner's" genetic alliance depends on the predominating mating and family system (Strier, 2008). Accordingly, there is theoretically the expectation of a high degree of plasticity regarding grandmotherly behavior. Depending on whether their (future) grandchildren are the offspring of their son or their daughter, different criteria can influence the socioemotional relationship to their child's partner and the treatment of any grandchildren.

Studies conducted to date provide the first hints that sexual conflict can also have an impact on the adaptive investment decisions on the part of grandmothers (Leonetti et al., 2007; Pollet et al., 2009; overview in Coall & Hertwig, 2010; Sear & Mace, 2008). For example, it was shown for the historical population (18th and 19th century) of the Krummhörn (Ostfriesland, Germany) that postgenerative mothers exerted a different influence on the reproductive behavior of their child, depending on whether the child was a son or a daughter. While the presence of a maternal grandmother increased infant survivorship, the presence of a paternal grandmother did not show the same effect. On the contrary, her presence led to an increase in neonatal mortality (Voland & Beise, 2002). The same contrast can also be seen with regard to stillbirths: whereas the existence of their own mother did not have any influence on the risk of a stillbirth, the existence of a mother-in-law increased the relative risk of a stillbirth by 34.9% (Voland & Beise, 2005).

The fact that the correlation between the existence of a mother-in-law and the risk of a stillbirth is actually an expression of a behavioral conflict is underlined by the observation that the spatial proximity between the mother-in-law and the daughter-in-law models this effect, similar to the findings on neonatal mortality (Voland & Beise, 2002). If the villages in which the mother-in-law and the daughter-in-law reside were identical, a living mother-in-law significantly increased the relative risk of a stillbirth or neonatal mortality. If the villages were different, however, the effect disappeared below the significance threshold.

The background for these correlations comprised the fact that daughters-in-law were constrained to work more than genetic daughters and increased contributions to the family economy were demanded of them. Mothers-in-law and daughters-in-law are not genetically related to one another, and therefore it is to be expected according to sociobiological theory that the motive for sparing a daughter-in-law is not as strongly developed as sparing one's own daughter. Sparing daughters-in-law even during pregnancy or after they give birth may not have been ultimately worthwhile in the unsentimental balance sheets of Darwinian selection. Even if the economic exploitation of a daughter-in-law cost a just-born grandchild or one not yet born now and again, the strategy could have had a positive net effect under certain socioeconomic constraints, because dead grandchildren were possibly easy to replace. Even a dead daughter-in-law was not irreplaceable. We are dealing with a system of exploitation, in which the daughter-in-law's work performance was demanded as naturally as their fertility. From the logic of the sexual conflict, it is clear that this motive for exploitation automatically has a patrilineal origin.

What consequences this can have for the daughter-in-law's physical and mental health is then a question of the respective social and economic living circumstances, such as the status that women and their work performance have in a society. Where women enjoy a high market value by virtue of their rarity, such as among the French settlers of Québec and in founder settlements, which typically show a surplus of men, a mother-in-law cannot at all afford to confront her daughter-in-law with inappropriate demands (Beise, 2005). If, however, demographic stagnation does not allow a shortage of women to emerge, as was the case in the Krummhörn, with its almost zero growth in population and a surplus of births and outmigration, a mother-in-law may increase her demands. Social ties are strategic ties and therefore sensitive to the market and dependent on the situation.

How in-law conflicts are impacted by biographical and sociocultural contexts is also shown, for example by Skinner (2004) for a Japanese population with patrilineal inheritance patterns in the 18th and 19th century. In this case, if the daughter-in-law moves into the household of the paternal natal family, there is frequently an idealized sequence of births, with a first-born daughter followed later by a male heir, which simultaneously coincides with reduced interbirth intervals overall and consequently higher marital fertility. The prevalence of this strategy is often achieved by manipulative measures (infanticide, adoption), and as Skinner (2004) shows, is very much more likely to happen if both the paternal grandmother is present in the family and if the father is much older than the mother. On the one hand, the large age differences mean that grandfathers are much more likely to die earlier than grandmothers, which leads to the fact that in this population, a parental couple frequently only lives together with the paternal grandmother at the time of the first birth. On the other hand, the age difference between the mother and the father can also influence the relative power among the spouses in the reproductive conflict (Beekman, Komdeur, & Ratnieks, 2003). Although the wife's younger age at the beginning of a marriage allows her to make higher demands of the man, possibly due to a higher residual reproductive value, it also offers less opportunity for the accumulation of energetic, material, social and/or informational resources. Therefore, a large age difference could mean a weakening of the younger partner in reproductive conflicts. Skinner (2004, p. 142) concludes:

> A [paternal] grandmother gets her way only when she and her son gang up on the daughter-in-law, but that coalition is likely only when her son dominates the conjugal relationship, which in turn reflects the grandmother's success in binding the son tightly to her emotionally and in delaying his marriage. Otherwise, the grandmother may be shut out from reproductive decision-making by the conjugal coalition that acts in solidarity.

This finding indicates the dynamics of in-law conflicts. Quite obviously in-law conflicts sensitively mirror the participants' age structure, and it can therefore be expected that the compromises found in the in-law conflict will vary over time. This parallels the finding that the conflict between parents over care is also time-dependent (Houston, Székely, & McNamara, 2005).

Investment in existing offspring creates costs because it restricts future possibilities for reproduction. However, the remaining possibilities for reproduction change in different ways over time by virtue of other constraints for both sexes. This "drifting apart" of the opportunity costs for parental investment should, therefore, ensure that the patrilineal interest in existing offspring does not increase over time to the degree that the matrilineal interest does. In addition, it follows from the consequences of uncertain paternity described earlier that patrilineal investment is lower overall by virtue of differences in the probability of kinship but is more selective in particular and therefore should be more variable than matrilineal investment. The patrilineal investment strategy does not always have to be disadvantageous for the offspring: preferred children, who can guarantee a high degree of paternal certainty on the basis of certain criteria, benefit under certain circumstances from the discriminatory patrilineal channeling of parental resources. It is self-evident that this has to have an impact on "sibling rivalry" and ultimately even be a possible source of intrafamilial "spite" (West & Gardner, 2010).

It is theoretically plausible, for the time being at least, that the genetic distance between the matriline and the patriline ensures "closed fronts" in the conflict between the matriline and the patriline. The orientation of the reproductive strategy within sexual conflict influences the direct fitness of the man or the woman in the same direction as the indirect fitness of their kin. In other words, whatever increases the direct fitness of the male also increases the indirect fitness of his kin, and whatever increases the direct fitness of the female also increases the indirect fitness of her kin. As the next section is intended to show, however, special features in the heredity of the sex chromosomes could lead to the fact that even within the patriline there is a lack of agreement concerning the allocation of resources to existing offspring.

## Grandmothering and X Chromosomal Relatedness

Sexual conflict was only able to escalate during the evolution of the sex chromosomes, because the genetic discrepancy between homogametic (the sex with both sex chromosomes being the same, i.e., females) and heterogametic sex (i.e., males) enormously increases the possibility for the occurrence of antagonistic adaptations, that is, traits being beneficial to the one sex but harmful to the other (Rice 1984). In heterogametic sex, sexual recombination is completely suppressed for discrete chunks of the highly dimorphic sex chromosomes (e.g., Lahn & Page, 1999), so that during the course of male meiosis almost all genes of the paternal sex chromosomes cosegregate in a closed manner to future daughters or sons. Because of the asymmetrical inheritance of the sex chromosomes, additional competition over reproductive resources (e.g., oocytes and parental investment) arises between parts of the sex chromosomes (Rice et al., 2008). X-linked alleles are thus engaged in an intragenomic conflict for reproductive resources; the reproduction of the one sex chromosome costs the other sex chromosome potential resources, (e.g., oocytes or parental investment), but do not deliver any comparable reproductive benefit. Similar to the "meiotic drive" of certain alleles, a potential shift in the sex ratio during spermatogenesis, (i.e., the production of sperms carrying either the X chromosome or the Y chromosome disproportionately) would eventually be advantageous for the reproduction of the sex chromosome. The same holds true for the later "adjustment" of the sex ratio (Rice et al., 2008). This circumstance could have consequences for sibling interactions and in-law conflicts. Whereas the genetic correlation, as a rule, decreases evenly with kinship distance, this gradient is extremely asymmetrical for the sex chromosomes. Rice et al. (2008) show that within "sibling rivalry," mutations can establish on the sex chromosomes to a certain degree, which also lead to postzygotic damage to the noncarriers ("sexually antagonistic zygotic drive"), even if this effectively harms the carrier's inclusive fitness. This is a little reminiscent of the phenomena in social hymenoptera, where reproductive skew and "policing" cause costs for the colony that constrain the queen's (or queens') genome in the latter's reproduction (overview in Beekman et al., 2003).

The idea that these genetic models are definitely psychologically relevant could explain part of the variance in the relationships of postgenerative grandmothers with their grandchildren is shown by Fox et al. (2010). On the basis of the data from different populations, they have shown that daughters obviously survive better under the influence of the paternal grandmothers than sons do, which serves as a reminder that daughters always share an X chromosome with their paternal grandmothers while sons do not. Besides a series of relatively minor quantitative differences in the genetic correlation, features coupled with the X chromosome (e.g., face morphology or odor) could allow the estimated parental uncertainty for daughters to be lower than for sons (Fox et al., 2010; Johow, Fox, Knapp, & Voland, 2011). In contrast, the effect predicted by Rice's sexually antagonistic zygotic drive leads to additional discrimination against male descendants, which is associated with fitness costs for all parties, both in the matriline and in the patriline. Precisely the fact that that they constrain the reproductive success of the remaining genome is characteristic for adaptations in intragenomic conflicts, such as the described "harmful adaptations" on the X chromosome (Rice, Gavrilets & Friberg, 2008, 2010).

Among the Krummhörn population, a difference is found in interbirth intervals (IBIs) following the birth of infants surviving their early toddlerhood, which is consistent with the prediction that the investment made by paternal grandmothers is biased toward granddaughters (Johow et al., 2011). Figure 12.1 shows that IBIs generally tend to be shorter by some weeks on average after daughters than after sons. However, it is interesting in connection with Rice's theory of the sexually antagonistic drive that this correlation between IBI and the foreborn child's sex significantly changes in the presence of the paternal grandmother (see Figure 12.1 panel B). Accordingly, the influence of the paternal grandmother over the reproductive rate, even within the in-law conflict, does not unconditionally accelerate but reacts to the sex of the grandchild born. Only after the birth of a girl but not after the birth of a boy, does the presence of a paternal grandmother coincide with the delayed birth of another sibling. This finding from the Krummhörn supplies another indication that the asymmetric transmission of the sex chromosomes can also influence the paternal grandmother's reproductive strategy. She not only appears to have a different impact on the reproductive behavior of a family than the maternal grandmother but also obviously influences the production of granddaughters differently than the production of grandsons, namely as predicted by the genetic theory of social behavior in general and of family relationships in particular.

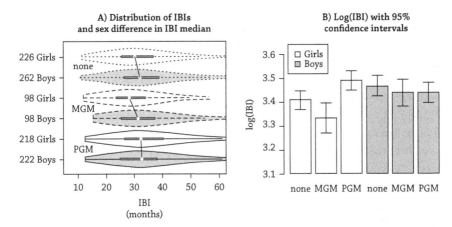

*Figure 12.1* Panel A gives violin plots (a combination of boxplot and kernel density distribution plot) for interbirth intervals (IBIs) following the birth of a girl or a boy separated for families where the PGM is present, where both grandmothers are absent, or where the MGM is present. Panel B presents asymptotic tests with 95% confidence intervals to show differences in logtransformed IBI values. (Figure taken from Johow et al. 2011.)

Consequently, Fox et al. (2011) recently suggested that X-linked alleles could also lead to increased longevity even in complete absence of any fitness advantage to the X chromosome's carrier. In this perspective, postmenopausal survival could instead result from evolutionary constraints imposed by the reproduction of the X chromosome than from functional benefits in regard to the carrier's reproductive success. Genes affecting discriminative behavior and longevity could be clustered on the X chromosome because among the sex chromosomes there is stronger selection for these traits compared to the autosomal genome (Fox et al., 2011; Rice et al., 2008).

## Evolution's Elderly Empress

This rough sketch of intrafamilial behavioral tendencies in the postgenerative age of women underlines the fact that no lifespan phase—not even senescence—is excluded from evolution and its adaptive pressure. Even if the selection pressures decline with age, because the fitness effects of behavioral decisions logically decrease with age, humans will never be released from Darwinian principles. To this extent, the conclusion about senescence as a postreproductive lifespan is theoretically unjustified. Instead, conceptualizing this period of life as postgenerative is more accurate, and is definitely characterized by evolutionarily functional behavioral adaptations.

However, it is also clear, completely in line with the assumptions of behavioral ecology, that these strategies are conditional ones. As also suggested elsewhere (e.g., Sear, 2008) one must highlight the fact that grandmaternal behavior, like any kin relations, can take many forms depending on the context. This plasticity would explain the apparent behavioral diversity found between different populations and even between different social groups within a population. For example, Johow and Voland (2012) demonstrate that the effects of the maternal grandmother on reproductive behavior may also be contingent on socioeconomic stratification. Only for the landless people of the historical Krummhörn population (but not in case of commercial farmers) was it revealed that those women who lived near their mother at the time of marriage and thus at the time of their first birth are about one year younger compared to females living near their husband's mother. Although brides married to commercial farmers were generally several years younger than brides married to landless laborers (which allows for a comparably higher total number of births), fertility differences between landless families and commercial farmers seem to be buffered by the conditional influences of maternal grandmothers (Johow & Voland, 2012).

Basic inclinations, such as the matrilineal bias in kin support, can manifest themselves in various ways as specific behaviors. Depending on which cultural institutions predominate, be it in the utilization of resources, the marriage and philopatry rules, and many others, the last third of a person's life has an adaptive function with different accents. Helping is only one fitness-maximizing strategy in senescence, and it is a behavior that is frequently overlooked. Manipulation and taking sides in sexual conflict are other examples. Thus, sexual conflict expands into an in-law conflict, to a conflict that is ultimately between the matriline and the patriline, and it seems that evolution has shaped the special role played by older women.

Recent studies suggest the script for this role is to be found on the X chromosome. There is undoubtedly an immense need for more research here, because the path from intragenomic conflict to a social grandmotherly role is, without a doubt, long and complex, but one idea seems to be emerging: the image of the unconditionally good and helpful grandma imprecisely reflects the mental and social reality. Like all family members in their respective roles, grandmothers are managers of their own interests that have been shaped by evolution.

# References

Anderson, K. G. (2006). How well does paternity confidence match actual paternity? *Current Anthropology, 47*, 513–520.

Austad, S. N. (1994). Menopause: An evolutionary perspective. *Experimental Gerontology, 29*, 255–263.

Beekman, M., Komdeur, J., & Ratnieks, F. L.W. (2003). Reproductive conflicts in social animals: Who has power? *Trends in Ecology and Evolution, 18*, 277–282.

Beise, J. (2005). The helping and the helpful grandmother: The role of maternal and paternal grandmothers in child mortality in the seventeenth- and eighteenth-century population of

French settlers in Québec, Canada. In E. Voland, A. Chasiotis, & W. Schiefenhövel (Eds.), *Grandmotherhood: The evolutionary significance of the second half of female life* (pp. 215–238). New Brunswick, NJ: Rutgers University Press.

Beise J., & Voland E. (2002). A multilevel event history analysis of the effects of grandmothers on child mortality in a historical German population (Krummhörn, Ostfriesland, 1720–1874). *Demographic Research, 7*, 469–497.

Bischof, N. (1985). *Das Rätsel Ödipus: Die biologischen Wurzeln des Urkonflikts von Intimität und Autonomie*. Munich, Germany: Piper.

Bishop, D. I., Meyer, B. C., Schmidt, T. M., & Gray, B. R. (2009). Differential investment behavior between grandparents and grandchildren: The role of paternity uncertainty. *Evolutionary Psychology, 7*, 66–77.

Borgerhoff Mulder, M. (2009). Tradeoffs and sexual conflict over women's fertility preferences in Mpimbwe. *American Journal of Human Biology, 21*, 476–487.

Borgerhoff Mulder, M., & Rauch, K. L. (2009). Sexual conflict in humans: Variations and solutions. *Evolutionary Anthropology, 18*, 201–214.

Cant, M. A., & Johnstone, R. A. (2008). Reproductive conflict and the separation of reproductive generations in humans. *Proceedings of the National Academy of Sciences, 105*, 5332–5336.

Coall, D. A., & Hertwig, R. (2010). Grandparental investment: Past, present, and future. *Behavioral and Brain Sciences, 33*, 1–59.

Euler, H. A., & Michalski, R. L. (2007). Grandparental and extended kin relationships. In C. A. Salmon & T. K. Shackelford (Eds.), *Family relations: An evolutionary perspective* (pp. 230–256). Oxford, UK: Oxford University Press.

Euler, H. A., & Weitzel, B. (1996). Discriminative grandparental solicitude as reproductive strategy. *Human Nature, 7*, 39–59.

Flinn, M. V., & Leone, D. V. (2006). Early family trauma and the ontogeny of glucocorticoid stress response in the human child: Grandmother as a secure base. *Journal of Developmental Processes, 1*, 31–65.

Fox, M., Johow, J., & Knapp, L. A. (2011). The selfish grandma gene: The roles of the X-chromosome and paternity uncertainty in the evolution of grandmothering behavior and longevity. *International Journal of Evolutionary Biology, 2011*, Article ID 165919. doi:10.4061/2011/165919

Fox, M., Sear, R., Beise, J., Ragsdale, G., Voland, E., & Knapp, L. A. (2010). Grandma plays favourites: X-chromosome relatedness and sex-specific childhood mortality. *Proceedings of the Royal Society B, 277*, 567–573.

Hawkes, K. (2003). Grandmothers and the evolution of human longevity. *American Journal of Human Biology, 15*, 380–400.

Hawkes, K., O'Connell, J. F., & Blurton Jones, N. G. (1997). Hadza women's time allocation, offspring provisioning, and the evolution of post-menopausal lifespans. *Current Anthropology, 38*(4), 551–577.

Holden, C. J., Sear, R., & Mace, R. (2003). Matriliny as daughter-biased investment. *Evolution and Human Behavior, 24*, 99–112.

Houston, A. I., Székely, T., & McNamara, J. M. (2005). Conflict between parents over care. *Trends in Ecology and Evolution, 20*, 33–38.

Hrdy, S. B. (2000). The optimal number of fathers: Evolution, demography, and history in the shaping of female mate preferences. In D. LeCroy & P. Moller (Eds.), *Evolutionary perspectives on human reproductive behavior* (pp. 75–96). New York: New York Academy of Sciences.

Hrdy, S. B. (2005). Cooperative breeders with an ace in the hole. In E. Voland, A. Chasiotis, & W. Schiefenhövel (Eds.), *Grandmotherhood: The evolutionary significance of the second half of female life* (pp. 295–317). New Brunswick, NJ: Rutgers University Press.

Hrdy, S. B. (2009). *Mothers and others: The evolutionary origins of mutual understanding*. Cambridge, MA: Harvard University Press.

Johow, J., Fox, M., Knapp, L., & Voland, E. (2011). The presence of a paternal grandmother lengthens interbirth interval following the birth of a granddaughter in Krummhörn (18th and 19th centuries). *Evolution and Human Behavior, 32*, 315–325.

Johow, J., & Voland, E. (2012). Conditional grandmother effects on age at marriage, age at first birth, and completed fertility of daughters and daughters-in-law in historical Krummhörn. *Human Nature, 23*, 341–359.

Kemkes-Grottenthaler, A. (2005). Of grandmothers, grandfathers, and wicked step-grandparents: Differential impact of paternal grandparents on grandoffspring survival. *Historical Social Research, 30*, 219–239.

Lahn, B. T., & Page, D. C. (1999). Four evolutionary strata on the human X chromosome. *Science, 286*(5441), 964–967.

Leonetti, D. L., Nath, D. C., & Hemam, N. S. (2007). In-law conflict: Women's reproductive lives and the roles of their mothers and husbands among the matrilineal Khasi. *Current Anthropology, 48*, 861–890.

Lummaa, V. (2007). Life-history theory, reproduction, and longevity in humans. In R. I. M. Dunbar & L. Barrett (Eds.), *The Oxford handbook of evolutionary psychology* (pp. 397–414). Oxford, UK: Oxford University Press.

Mace, R., & Sear, R. (2005). Are humans cooperative breeders? In E. Voland, A. Chasiotis, & W. Schiefenhövel, (Eds.), *Grandmotherhood: The evolutionary significance of the second half of female life* (pp. 143–159). New Brunswick, NJ: Rutgers University Press.

Opie, K., & Power, C. (2008). Grandmothering and female coalitions: A basis for matrilineal priority? In N. J. Allen, H. Callan, R. Dunbar, & W. James (Eds.), *Early human kinship: From sex to social reproduction* (pp. 168–186). Oxford, UK: Blackwell.

Pashos, A. (2000). Does paternal uncertainty explain discriminative grandparental solicitude? A cross-cultural study in Greece and Germany. *Evolution and Human Behavior, 21*, 97–109.

Pavard, S., Metcalf, C. J. E., & Heyer, E. (2008). Senescence of reproduction may explain adaptive menopause in humans: A test of the "mother" hypothesis. *American Journal of Physical Anthropology, 136*, 194–203.

Peccei, J. S. (1995). The origin and evolution of menopause: The altriciality-lifespan hypothesis. *Ethology and Sociobiology, 16*, 425–449.

Peccei, J. S. (1999). First estimates of heritability in the age of menopause. *Current Anthropology, 40*, 553–558.

Peccei, J. S. (2005). Menopause: Adaptation and epiphenomenon. In E. Voland, A. Chasiotis, & W. Schiefenhövel (Eds.), *Grandmotherhood: The evolutionary significance of the second half of female life* (pp. 38–58). New Brunswick, NJ: Rutgers University Press.

Penn, D. J., & Smith, K. R. (2007). Differential fitness costs of reproduction between the sexes. *Proceedings of the National Academy of Sciences, 104*, 553–558.

Pollet, T. V., Nelissen, M., & Nettle, D. (2009). Lineage based differences in grandparental investment: Evidence from a large British cohort study. *Journal of Biosocial Science, 41*, 355–379.

Reiches, M. W., Ellison, P. T., Lipson, S. F., Sharrock, K. C., Gardiner, E., & Duncan, L. G. (2009). Pooled energy budget and human life history. *American Journal of Human Biology, 21*, 421–429.

Rice, W. R. (1984). Sex chromosomes and the evolution of sexual dimorphism. *Evolution, 38*(4), 735–742.

Rice W. R., Gavrilets S., & Friberg, U. (2008). Sexually antagonistic "zygotic drive" of the sex chromosomes. *PLoS Genetics, 4*(12), e1000313.

Rice, W. R., Gavrilets, S., & Friberg, U. (2010). The evolution of sex-specific grandparental harm. *Proceedings of the Royal Society B, 277*(1694), 2727–2735.

Richardson, D. S., Burke, T., & Komdeur, J. (2007). Grandparent helpers: The adaptive significance of older, postdominant helpers in the Seychelles warbler. *Evolution, 61*, 2790–2800.

Robson, S. L., Van Schaik, C. P., & Hawkes, K. (2006). The derived features of human life history. In K. Hawkes & R. R. Paine (Eds.), *The evolution of human life history* (pp. 17–44). Santa Fe, NM: School of American Research Press.

Rogers, A. R. (1993). Why menopause? *Evolutionary Ecology, 7*, 406–420.

Sear, R. (2008). Kin and child survival in rural Malawi: Are matrilineal kin always beneficial in a matrilineal society? *Human Nature, 19*, 277–293.

Sear, R., & Mace, R. (2008). Who keeps children alive? A review of the effects of kin on child survival. *Evolution and Human Behavior, 29*, 1–18.

Sear, R., & Mace, R. (2009). Family matters: Kin, demography, and child health in a rural Gambian population. In G. Bentley & R. Mace (Eds.), *Substitute parents: Biological and social perspectives on alloparenting in human societies* (pp. 50–76). New York: Berghahn.

Sear, R., & Matthews, P. (2010, March 25–27). *The impact of kin on female fertility: A systematic review*. Paper presented at the Annual Conference of the European Human Behavior and Evolution Association, Wroclaw, Poland.

Sherman, P. W. (1998). The evolution of menopause. *Nature, 392*, 759–760.

Skinner, G. W. (2004). Grandparental effects on reproductive strategizing: Nobi villagers in early modern Japan. *Demographic Research, 11*, 111–147 (article 5).

Strier, K. B. (2008). The effects of kin on primate life histories. *Annual Review of Anthropology, 37*, 21–36.

Van Schaik, C. P., & Janson, C. H. (Eds.). (2000). *Infanticide by males and its implications*. Cambridge, UK: Cambridge University Press.

Voland, E., & Beise, J. (2002). Opposite effects of maternal and paternal grandmothers on infant survival in historical Krummhörn. *Behavioral Ecology and Sociobiology, 52*, 435–443.

Voland, E., & Beise, J. (2005) "The husband's mother is the devil in house": Data on the impact of the mother-in-law on stillbirth mortality in historical Krummhörn (1750–1874) and some thoughts on the evolution of postgenerative female life. In E. Voland, A. Chasiotis, & W. Schiefenhövel (Eds.), *Grandmotherhood: The evolutionary significance of the second half of female life* (pp. 239–255). New Brunswick, NJ: Rutgers University Press.

Voland, E., Chasiotis, A., & Schiefenhövel, W. (Eds.). (2005). *Grandmotherhood: The evolutionary significance of the second half of female life*. New Brunswick, NJ: Rutgers University Press.

West, S. A., & Gardner, A. (2010). Altruism, spite, and greenbeards. *Science, 327*, 1341–1344.

Williams, G. C. (1957). Pleiotropy, natural selection, and the evolution of senescence. *Evolution, 11*, 398–411.

Wood, J. W., O'Connor, K. A., Holman, D. J., Brindle, E., Barsom, S. H., & Grimes, M. A. (2001). *The evolution of menopause by antagonistic pleiotropy* (Working paper 01-4). Seattle, WA: Center for Demography and Ecology.

# 13

# Now or Later

## *Peripartum Shifts in Female Sociosexuality*

MICHELLE J. ESCASA-DORNE, SHARON M. YOUNG, AND PETER B. GRAY

## Introduction

An egg is a potential store of reproductive wealth. While human females during fetal life have several million follicles, these diminish rapidly in number, with less than half a million remaining by age 5, and attrition continuing through pre-pubertal years (Gluckman, Bittles, & Hanson, 2009). By their late teens, about 200,000 follicles may remain. In the case of human hunter-gatherers, females might experience menarche—their first menstruation—around age 16, form long-term bonds in which they first reproduce around age 18–20, and then spend the bulk of their reproductive years pregnant or subject to postpartum lactational amenorrhea (not cycling, in part due to intensive breastfeeding and energetic constraints) (Kelly, 1995; Marlowe, 2005). It is the rare egg indeed that enjoys the possibility of a reproductive legacy—few are ever released during ovulation. Even fewer are fertilized, and of those fertilized an estimated 30–70% are spontaneously aborted (Ellison, 2001). The culmination of these diminishing odds is the remarkable feat of an actual birth, much less that newborn surviving long enough to perpetuate the reproductive chain.

A successful conception heralds dramatic changes in a female's life. During the peripartum period (the months of gestation through shortly after giving birth), a woman's physiology and behaviors change to focus more on her offspring. Here, we address peripartum shifts in female sociosexuality, or shifts in sexual behaviors, preferences, and views. There are at least three reasons to investigate the effects of pregnancy and lactational amenorrhea on female sociosexuality. As one rationale, an evolutionary perspective reminds us that hunter-gatherer females were subject to shifts across their reproductive years from rare spells in which they cycled, to a majority of time spent pregnant or in a state of postpartum amenorrhea

ily

(Eaton et al., 1994). Another rationale is that considerable scholarly attention has been devoted to shifts in female sociosexuality across the ovulatory cycle—a topic certainly of merit—but one that also misses potentially more dramatic influences during pregnancy and postpartum. As we shall see, the subtle shifts in female coital frequency observed across the ovulatory cycle pale in comparison to the more dramatic fluctuations in coital frequency late in pregnancy and postpartum. Finally, we can employ tools of life history theory to make sense of both the adaptive patterning and complementary alterations in hormonal physiology that structure peripartum shifts in female sociosexuality. Increased maternal investment (taking care of that rare baby) may supplant mating effort, a shift in priorities that may enhance female reproductive success. However, the maintenance of long-term sociosexual bonds with a mate may also foster enhanced female sexual expressiveness, helping favor continued investment by that partner in a woman and her offspring.

In the present chapter, we outline a framework, couched in life history theory, examining why female sociosexuality may fluctuate across the peripartum period. We then discuss sociosexuality in its different forms, followed by empirically based sections on the sociosexuality of nonhuman primate females and human females respectively. Finally, we consider some of the implications for future research on female sociosexuality.

# Sociosexuality

## Sociosexual Trade-offs Across the Reproductive Years

A fundamental premise of life history theory is that organisms have limited time and resources to devote to growth, maintenance, and reproduction (Stearns, 1992). Faced with "budget constraints," organisms may allocate their limited time and resources in ways that maximize reproductive success. Sometimes these allocations entail trade-offs, or mutually exclusive allotments to competing ends of growth, maintenance, and reproduction. The resources devoted to reproduction may come at expense to growth, one reason why still-growing adolescent females who bear children tend to have offspring of lower birth weight (Stearns, 1992). Across the life course, life history theory helps account for why juveniles grow rapidly while maintaining a quiescent reproductive system, and why older individuals tend to senesce in parallel with reproductive investment (though of course, extended human postreproductive life poses a notable challenge to this typical nonhuman pattern) (Hawkes & Paine, 2006).

Across mammals, including humans, females and males tend to invest differently in reproductive effort, or the allocation of resources to produce live offspring to maturation (Low, 2000). Female mammals tend to specialize in parenting effort, allocations such as gestation, breastfeeding, and maternal care. Male mammals tend to specialize in mating effort, behaviors such as same-sex competition and courtship designed to obtain reproductive access to mates.

Apart from the typical sex difference in reproductive effort, females face several life history allocation challenges that entail fluctuations in mating and parenting effort across the reproductive years. Early in their reproductive careers, females may focus on mating effort, competing with other females and attempting to attract the interest of potential mates. Increases in mating effort around the time of ovulation compared to nonreproductive phases of the ovulatory cycle may also occur, a topic on which we will touch below. After forming a bond with a mate, perhaps with that codified as marriage, females may shift their reproductive effort toward parental investment, entailing the utilization of resources during pregnancy and postpartum that benefit a woman's reproductive success by enhancing the prospects of her offspring. The tremendous investment in parenting effort may come at expense to mating effort. Couched in life history theory, this trade-off can be viewed as one between competing agendas of current versus future reproduction. Put another way, females can focus their limited time and resources on the current—the now, the fetus they are gestating, the baby they are nursing—and worry about the next reproductive bout later.

The shifts in peripartum female sociosexuality, situated in this trade-off between current and future reproduction, are underpinned by various physiological mechanisms (see Ellison & Gray, 2009; Masters & Johnson, 1966; Nelson, 2005). Changes in hormonal physiology during gestation promote adaptive maternal investment, as do related mechanisms postpartum. For example, estrogens, which are important in female sexual development and in ovulation prior to conception, rise across pregnancy to increase breast tissue in preparation for breast milk production, and facilitate the deposition of fat during gestation, stores that can serve as metabolic substrates for lactation postpartum (Taylor & Lebovic, 2007). Following parturition, oxytocin, a hormone important in the uterine contractions that initiate and facilitate labor, is released in pulsatile surges that facilitate milk letdown during lactation and maternal attachment to the infant (Bancroft, 2005; Taylor & Lebovic, 2007).

Especially in humans, however, there is plenty of higher cognitive function guiding the details of peripartum allocation decisions. After all, postpartum maternal investment can be highly variable and behaviorally flexible (Hrdy, 1999). While hunter-gatherer females typically breastfeed 2–4 years, many women around the world today elect not to breastfeed (Ellison, 2001). In a 2010 survey, 22.4% of US women were breastfeeding at 6 months, with only 13.3% exclusively breastfeeding (CDC, 2010). The decline in breastfeeding may be due to several factors including scheduled feedings to accommodate dual home and work schedules, and the addition of supplemental foods at an earlier age. Some females may find cause to seek a new mate amid intensive parental effort if another prospect offers better potential, particularly in contrast to inadequate or inconsistent support from a current mate. Such considerations highlight the importance of embedding female peripartum sociosexual shifts with respect to ongoing mating relationships (e.g., with the child's father).

## Female Sociosexuality

An individual's sexual behaviors, preferences, and views about sexuality are referred to as sociosexuality (Penke & Asendorpf, 2008; Schmitt, 2005). Sociosexuality includes attitudes toward sexual intercourse, desired number of sexual partners, fantasies about sexual intercourse, frequency of intercourse, and number of sexual partners (Simpson & Gangestad, 1991). An influential and useful conceptual scheme suggests that female sociosexuality can be distinguished with respect to attractivity, proceptivity, and receptivity (see Dixson, 1998). Attractivity refers to the stimulus value of a female. In humans, attractivity can include traits like facial symmetry, desirable waist-to-hip ratio, youthful appearance, and an overall healthy appearance (see Sugiyama, 2005). A large body of scholarship on human sexuality suggests that young adult females of high reproductive value, or prospects for future reproductive success, are viewed as particularly attractive. An interpretation of this finding is that because humans tend to mate within long-term reproductive relationships often entailing coparenting multiple offspring, males value the long-term reproductive capacity of females when making evaluations of attractiveness. Interestingly, males in our close relatives, chimpanzees, find older mothers most attractive, likely a reflection of their shorter-term, multimale, multifemale mating system (Muller, Emery Thompson, & Wrangham, 2006).

Proceptivity refers to proactive female mating attempts (e.g., a female approaching a male), whereas receptivity entails female acceptance of mating attempts (e.g., a female accepting a date request). These two concepts are worth disentangling for several reasons, including attempting to discern female motivations that may underlie involvement in sexual behavior. As an expression of mating effort, females may exhibit overt mating interest, often reflective of hormonally related and socially contextualized elevations in sexual desire. With respect to late pregnancy and postpartum sexual behavior, much female behavior may also highlight receptivity; despite low sexual desire, females may engage in sexual behavior to maintain reproductive bonds, satisfying male proceptive behaviors and fostering continued investment.

Hormonal physiology appears to adaptively attune female attractivity, proceptivity, and receptivity across the ovulatory cycle. The ovulatory cycle can be divided into two phases, the follicular phase, characterized by follicle development, and the luteal phase, characterized by potential implantation of a fertilized egg in the uterus. During the follicular phase, the hypothalamus, a structure near the base of the brain, sends a hormonal signal (gonadotropin-releasing hormone, or GnRH) to the pituitary gland (which rests below the base of the brain) stimulating it to release luteinizing hormone (LH) and follicle stimulating hormone (FSH).

These hormones slowly increase across the follicular phase, which lasts about 14 days, and they act on the ovaries to release an egg (ovulation) and to stimulate the production of estrogen, a female sex steroid, which primes the uterine lining for the anticipated implantation of a fertilized egg. Following ovulation, during the approximately 14 day luteal phase, there is an increase in progesterone, a hormone necessary for maintaining the uterine lining and supporting pregnancy. In the absence of conception, estrogen and progesterone decline, causing the uterine wall to shed, leading to menstruation (Rosen & Cedars, 2007).

Estrogens, along with androgens such as testosterone, are the main hormonal drivers of female sociosexuality (Bancroft, 2005). Peak levels of estrogens and androgens across the ovulatory cycle occur around the time of ovulation, potentially facilitating female attractivity, proceptivity, and receptivity. While estrogens also rise during part of the luteal phase, progesterone offsets the priming effects of estrogens to some degree. Indeed, it has been argued that elevated progesterone levels of the luteal phase might orient females more toward social support, since the luteal phase serves as a state of "early-stage pregnancy" (Jones et al., 2008).

An explosion of studies in recent years has addressed cycle-related shifts in female sociosexuality. Among the most provocative of these, Miller, Tybur, and Jordan (2007) found that normally cycling female lap dancers received significantly higher tip earnings around the time of ovulation compared with the luteal phase, though it was not clear if the difference was due to noticeable cues emanating from the female lap dancers (e.g., attractivity) or if there was a behavioral difference in the dancers (e.g., receptivity). A study of 88 female undergraduates found that women near ovulation chose outfits that revealed more skin (Durante, Li, & Haselton, 2008). Another study at a singles bar suggested that women tend to dress in more revealing attire around ovulation (Grammer, Renninger, & Fisher, 2004), suggestive of a change in female proceptivity in sexual behavior. In two naturalistic studies, Guéguen (2009a, 2009b) observed higher rates of female receptive behavior around the time of ovulation rather than during the luteal phase or menstruation: among women accepting offers to dance in a nightclub and among women giving their phone numbers to men in an outdoor setting. These ovulatory cycle shifts, however, appear to have only subtle influences on actual fluctuations in female sexual behavior: a massive study reporting on partnered women's recent sexual activity across 13 countries including Haiti and Bolivia revealed no differences in intercourse frequency around the time of ovulation compared to times before and afterward (Brewis & Meyer, 2005a). The most precise of studies, entailing measurement of female cycle stage through hormonal assays, sometimes find subtle increases in partnered women's intercourse frequency around the time of ovulation (Wilcox et al., 2004). The reasons we see stronger shifts in some behaviors (e.g., clothing choice, accepting dates) and not in others could be due to several reasons. One notable reason may be the methods employed for the different studies (e.g., vignettes, self-reported questionnaires, observations, or hormonal assays). Another reason could be that some scenarios incite female-female competition; women may shift behaviors that can appear to gain more attention from male partners, without necessarily having to engage in sexual intercourse. Further studies should more closely examine why we tend to see shifts in some behaviors but not others.

In addition to the studies on female shifts in active and receptive behaviors, preferences for whom women find attractive change across the ovulatory cycle. Several studies indicate that around ovulation women prefer more masculine male faces, deeper voices, higher body symmetry, and more aggressiveness (reviewed in Jones et al., 2008; Thornhill & Gangestad, 2008). Many of these traits are associated with testosterone levels in males. For example, behavioral traits correlating with lower paternal investment (Gray, Kahlenberg, Barrett, Lipson, & Ellison,2002) and dominant personalities (Mazur & Booth, 1998) are associated with higher testosterone levels. During nonfertile phases, females do not desire these "testosterone laden" traits as strongly as during fertile phases. There may be good reason for this. Some of these traits may not be desirable in a long-term partner. For example, high aggressiveness may not be a desirable trait in a father-figure. Masculinity and high physical attractiveness may also be signals that a male may not be as willing to stick around in the long-run. Preferences during times of low pregnancy risk may be reflective of females' preferences for males who can provide higher paternal investment, more desirable personality traits, and less aggressive behaviors.

While the elucidation of female ovulatory-cycle shifts in sociosexuality has attracted much interest recently, the wider contexts in which these shifts play out merit attention. From a female's standpoint, it is best to find a partner who is trustworthy, dependable, and can provide resources (typically in the form of wealth or food). David Buss (1994) found in his classic cross-cultural study of 37 societies that females rank dependability and trustworthiness as highly desirable traits, more so than physical attractiveness. A male who can provide resources to a female and her offspring is more desirable than one who does not have the skill or cannot afford to provide sufficient resources for his mate and family. In addition to tangible resources, females also desire a male who will likely stick around after conception to assist the female in caring for their offspring. To better understand female shifts in sociosexuality, let us first explore the changes in sexuality in the nonhuman primate world.

## From Conception to Weaning in Nonhuman Primates

Suppose all of that mating effort has translated into a long-term and fertile partnership—the typical context for human reproduction, both over evolutionary contexts and in most contemporary ones. An array of cultural and behavioral factors can impact sexuality during pregnancy and postpartum (e.g., postpartum sex taboos). Hormonal fluctuations may also play a role, such as during breastfeeding (e.g., the hormone prolactin, which increases across pregnancy and is maintained postpartum in lactating mothers, both promotes continued milk production and inhibits ovulation). Changes in time allocation may be a factor, since mom now has less time to focus on herself (and her partner) and spends more time looking after her infant. For reasons such as these, patterns of sociosexuality tend to fluctuate during pregnancy and postpartum generally, with marked reductions in sexual behavior late in gestation and early postpartum compared with times when women are cycling. However, the specifics of those fluctuations also exhibit considerable variation cross-culturally.

Before we steep ourselves in the available human data, we situate peripartum shifts in female sociosexuality in a nonhuman primate comparative context. Employing a comparative primate perspective is important because, as Sarah Hrdy put it, "a broader understanding of other primates is going to help us expand the concept of human nature" (Hrdy, 1981, p. 10). Females in many nonhuman primate species engage in sexual behavior at least occasionally during gestation, and sometimes during postpartum amenorrhea. At face value, this illustrates the quite common expression of nonreproductive coitus among our primate kin, reminding us that we are hardly alone in this feature. The socially monogamous gibbon has been observed to mate during pregnancy, but only one female of seven groups was observed mating postpartum (Barelli, Heistermann, Boesch, & Reichard, 2008). Females of other primate species such as baboons, mangabeys, and long-tailed macaques—all of which are nonmonogamous—also continue some sexual relationships during pregnancy (Ziegler, 2007). While pregnant West African gorillas mated sporadically during pregnancy, Doran-Sheehy and colleagues (2009) noted the decline in postpartum sexual behavior, which might include over three years' abstinence. Among white-faced capuchin monkeys in Costa Rica, potentially cycling females exhibited the highest rates of proceptive behavior, with rates among pregnant females fairly similar, but rates considerably lower postpartum; similarly, rates in which females were courted by males were comparable when females were potentially cycling and pregnant, but notably lower postpartum (Manson, Perry, & Parish, 1997).

Sexual behaviors in nonhuman primates during pregnancy and postpartum may occur for several reasons. Hormonal changes may facilitate female sexuality during pregnancy, with rising estrogens and androgens in some primate species perhaps enhancing female proceptivity and attractivity in ways that could be interpreted as by-products; enhanced female midgestational proceptivity in long-tailed macaques could be simply a by-product of the rising steroid hormone levels whose main functions are to coordinate gestation and postpartum investment. For example, nonfertile female rhesus macaques injected with estradiol began seeking coitus more frequently than macaques not injected with estradiol (Maestripieri, 2007).

Apart from a by-product interpretation, other adaptive functions for gestational sex could be advanced. In langur monkeys and chimpanzees, female mating during pregnancy has been interpreted as paternity confusion (Stumpf & Boesch, 2005); if a male is uncertain whether he might have fathered a given offspring, perhaps he will be more inclined to leave the female and her offspring alone and coerce another mother or harass or even kill a different female's offspring. In blue monkeys, females will have sex with more males while pregnant during years when more males are in the group (Pazol, 2003). Female baboons will continue to have sex during pregnancy to maintain "friendships" with male cohorts who may provide resources or protection to her and her offspring (Palombit, 1997, 1999). Similarly, Sarah Carnegie and colleagues observed that white-faced capuchin monkeys who were pregnant mated frequently, but only with subordinate males. One explanation for this is to build social bonds and solicit help from males who do not have the same mating options as alpha males (2006). Capuchin monkeys have been observed having sex during pregnancy and postpartum, perhaps to garner attention for a new infant (Perry & Manson, 2008). In one case, a new capuchin mother named Miffin proactively recruited sex with multiple partners and vocalized 60 times more than normal to gain attention for her new infant, Mowgli. In the case of gorillas, which mate in polygynous groups, female sexual behavior during pregnancy is generally rare, but when it does occur it tends to appear in response to the male mating with another female in the group. An interpretation of this pattern is female-female competition over maintenance of adaptive relationships with a mate (Doran-Sheehy, 2009).

In an interesting discussion of captive data on cotton-top tamarin and common marmoset sexual behaviors, Snowdon and Ziegler (2007) note that these South American monkeys tend to engage in frequent sex across the ovulatory cycle and pregnancy. In these species females and males tend to mate within long-term reproductive bonds that are generally monogamous, and males provide considerable parental investment. They interpret the patterns of sexual behavior among cotton-top tamarins:

> Frequent sexual behavior across the ovulatory cycle and during pregnancy may be one way in which adults maintain the relationship . . . pairs increase sexual behavior following the challenges of separation and following presentation of odors from a novel female, especially when the novel female is fertile . . . . Increased sexual arousal in males coupled with increased proceptivity by females led to increased sexual behavior that appears to maintain and reinforce pair bonds in the face of threats to the relationship. (Snowdon & Ziegler, 2007, pp. 46–47)

These comparative data highlight patterns of female sociosexuality that are both similar and different with respect to humans. One similarity is that rates of sexual behavior are higher during gestation compared to postpartum lactational amenorrhea. Female sexuality may be more readily expressed during gestation than postpartum due to hormonal support for female sexuality and the absence of a newborn demanding care. Rates of sexual behavior among nonhuman primates during lactational amenorrhea are so low that many primatologists (and the nonhuman primates they study) might find the notion of sexual behavior during this period strange. If primate females are focused on a young infant they are nursing, they may be enmeshed in the "now" side of the life history trade-off, focusing their reproductive effort on a needy offspring, foregoing sexual behavior and any possibility of begetting the next offspring (which their noncycling physiology shuns too).

As far as distinguishing human female sociosexuality from other primates, it is important to embed the discussion in long-term pair bonds and paternal care. In part due to paternal care, humans have shorter interbirth intervals and durations breastfeeding than would be expected of an ape of our body size (Gray & Anderson, 2010; Hrdy, 2009). Resources contributed by males enable females to more readily overcome the energetic challenges to resume cycling, meaning that human females spend shorter durations in a state of lactational amenorrhea. Still, human females regularly engage in sexual behavior before they are cycling postpartum, a pattern that, like commonly engaging in sex during pregnancy, may be part of the way human females maintain long-term pair bonds with their mates; this idea converges with the cotton-top tamarin interpretation above. Put another way, human females may benefit by maintaining an existing pair bond during pregnancy and into postpartum as fathers can largely aid in assisting both the mother and the infant. It becomes detrimental if a new mother's attention is steered away too much from her partner and toward her infant, as she then runs the risk of seeing declines in male parental investment.

## Peripartum Patterns in Human Female Sociosexuality

Across pregnancy and postpartum phases, the data indicate demonstrable shifts in human female sociosexuality. A number of studies document these changes in sociosexuality, some drawing on large international samples, others based on cross-cultural attitudinal surveys, and still others more focused on specific societies. The data almost always rely on self-report, unlike the observational studies that can be conducted on small samples of nonhuman primates. But the patterns are consistent with life history allocation shifts between mating and parenting effort and can be situated within the nonhuman primate comparative data above. Of course, there is notable cross-cultural variation too, calling for explanation itself, which we attempt first for patterns in female sociosexuality during pregnancy, then postpartum respectively.

In a classic survey of human sexuality, Ford and Beach (1951) compiled cross-cultural data on sexuality from 60 small-scale societies of hunter-gatherers, horticulturalists, pastoralists, and farmers. Although they lacked quantitative data on sexual behavior, they observed patterns in attitudes toward sexuality across pregnancy. They found that 70% of societies permitted sexual intercourse during early pregnancy, with that percentage remaining relatively high through the middle of pregnancy before dropping steadily. By the 7th month of gestation, 50% of societies allowed intercourse, but only 25% did during the 9th month of pregnancy. There are several reasons why these taboos are in place, with many societies believing that sex during pregnancy can harm the growing fetus. Furthermore, the societies that tended to prohibit female sex during pregnancy the earliest were also most likely to be polygynous societies; the implication is that a husband whose pregnant wife is tabooed from having sex may have other wives with whom he can have sex.

In a large quantitative, international compilation of data specifying effects of pregnancy on female sexuality, Brewis and Meyer (2005b) integrated data on over 90,000 women's recent sexual behavior from 19 countries including Bolivia, Nepal, Peru, Dominican Republic, and Cameroon. They concluded that effects of pregnancy on women's sexual activity the past 4 weeks are robust and patterned: "Pregnancy has a negative effect for the most part on sexual frequencies... generally, coital frequencies are significantly lower in pregnancy compared with the non-pregnant state... overall... sexual frequencies decline in the first trimester, decrease further in the second, and still further in the third" (Brewis & Meyer, 2005, p. 508). These data buttress the cross-cultural conclusions resting on sexual attitudes but also leave room within the overarching patterns for additional contributors to variation in female sociosexuality during pregnancy.

In some societies, sex during pregnancy is thought to serve important functions. For example, among the Aka of central Africa, semen is thought to help promote growth of the infant, and thus pregnant women and their husbands have frequent sex during pregnancy (Hewlett & Hewlett, 2008). Some Aka men report their exhaustion—that sex with a demanding pregnant wife is hard work—based on the need to have repeated sex. Another interpretation of this pattern could be that a pregnant woman solicits frequent sex in order to enhance her marital bond and recruit her husband's sexual fidelity and continued investment. Among many native Amazonian societies, all men having intercourse with a pregnant woman are thought to contribute to a fetus's conception and growth in a process that anthropologists have labeled "partible paternity." As an example, Bari women have sex with multiple males throughout pregnancy, and the men with whom she has sex are considered secondary fathers (Beckerman & Valentine, 2002). It may be no coincidence that most of these Amazonian societies characterized by partible paternity are matrilocal, meaning that a mother tends to live with her maternal kin, and her mating relationships with men tend to be more fluid. In this context, an interpretation of pregnant females mating with multiple men could be that it recruits the potential investment of typically two men, an advantage over a mating context in which a single partner may be unreliable or insufficient to provide resources such as fish, meat and other means of support. In a study of 128 South American societies with partible paternity beliefs, both men and women could gain from this context (Walker et al., 2010). For example, men have the advantage of multiple sexual outlets with little or no repercussions from either female partners or male rivals, while females gain by having multiple sources of social and material resources.

In a narrower cultural scope, with almost all studies conducted in the United States and Western Europe, Von Sydow (1999) reviewed 59 sexuality studies addressing patterns of sexual behavior across the full length of pregnancy. Coital frequency tended to remain high the 1st trimester, was quite variable the 2nd trimester, and dropped considerably the 3rd trimester. These patterns are generally similar, then, to the international findings reported above. Positions during intercourse also changed across gestation, with most 3rd-trimester intercourse entailing positions with males from behind and partners side-by-side, a contrast to more frequent face-to-face positions previously employed.

Another means of understanding female sexuality during pregnancy entails further consideration of the physiological changes women undergo during each trimester. Having briefly touched on relevant hormonal mechanisms earlier, we build on classic lab studies of the physiology of human sexuality by Masters and Johnson (1966) along with additional hormonal mechanisms. These studies provide insight into some features of pregnancy that may heighten female sexuality, but others impacting mood, fatigue, body image, and concern over a fetus's health that may account for diminished sexuality.

During the 1st trimester, the development of the fetus creates vasocongestion in the pelvic region from increases in blood volume (Masters & Johnson, 1966). This vasocongestion persists throughout gestation and can cause feelings of "sexual tension" due to the increased pressure in the pelvic region. The breasts prepare for lactation by increasing blood flow and glandular beds in the breast tissue. Many women report breast tenderness during the 1st trimester due to these changes. After the 1st trimester, some of the breast tenderness may subside; however, women still report continued nipple erections and breast engorgement throughout pregnancy. These changes in the breasts may be discomforting for some women. For other women, the changes in the breasts, including engorgement of the areolar tissue, may cause sexual tension during pregnancy. Hormones released initially from the ovary but later from the placenta orchestrate the changes in blood volume and breast development mentioned above. Some of these hormones are specific to pregnancy and circulate at much higher concentrations than prepregnancy levels (Petraglia, Florio, & Torricelli, 2006), contributing to nausea and alterations in mood and fatigue that may impact a woman's sexual desire.

During the 2nd trimester, many women have less or none of the tiredness or nausea experienced during the first 3 months. Women often note a jump in their sex drives during the 2nd trimester, likely due to the lessened pregnancy symptoms experienced during the 1st trimester and increases in steroid hormones that are associated with libido. Although placental production of estrogens and progesterone become significant by around 10 weeks, the 2nd trimester is marked by rapid increases in these hormones (Speroff, Glass, & Kase, 1994). Although the role of progesterone in sexual desire is debated, estrogen is at least indirectly responsible for increased sexual interest by enhancing vaginal elasticity and lubrication (Regan, 1999), including during pregnancy. Testosterone also increases steadily throughout pregnancy (Taylor & Lebovic, 2007), which could play a role in increased libido during this time.

During the 3rd trimester, many of those pregnancy symptoms that disappeared after the 1st trimester reappear. For example, women report feeling more fatigued during the 3rd trimester than the second (Masters & Johnson, 1966). Once again, during the last few months of pregnancy, a woman's sex drive can be dampened by the physiological changes that affect her mood and energy levels. Changing physiology may cause some women to feel less attractive during these times, impinging on her desire to engage in sexual activities with a partner. In addition, prolactin, a hormone that promotes lactation but is associated with decreased sexual desire, has been climbing steadily throughout pregnancy, peaking at delivery (Taylor & Lebovic, 2007), and oxytocin, a hormone related to uterine contractions and bonding rather than libido (Bancroft, 2005), can be detected in late gestation as well (Petraglia et al., 2006).

As pregnancy and alterations in female sociosexuality wane, a baby is born, demanding intensive parental care with the mother at center stage. The postpartum phase can have large impacts on female sociosexuality. In a dramatic cultural anecdote, the Marquesans of Polynesia specify that on the day of the birth the mother and father should go to a stream to engage in intercourse there (Suggs, 1966). However, this is a one-time event, followed by more typical reductions in postpartum sexuality.

A notable feature of female sociosexuality that varies cross-culturally is the duration of postpartum sex taboos. These are taboos that specify how long a new mother should refrain from intercourse. Cross-culturally, postpartum sexual taboo durations are longest in societies where males have sexual access to other women (e.g., polygynous societies). For example, women in certain Malaysian groups refrain from sexual activity for years after giving birth. Their partners, however, are free to have sex with new mothers' younger sisters during the postpartum abstinence period (Dentan, 1997). Postpartum sex taboos are longest (restraint from sexual activity for 1 or more years after giving birth) in African societies, where polygyny is more frequently practiced. For example, the Nso and Fulani of Cameroon are highly polygynous groups that have a 2-year postpartum sex taboo. These groups believe that semen can poison the breastmilk, afflicting the infant (Yovsi & Keller, 2003). Sex taboos after birth are shortest in Eurasia and the Mediterranean region, lasting around 1–5 months (Frayser, 1985). When men have alternative sexual outlets, there may not be as strong of a push for women to resume sexual intercourse with their partners. Providing international reports on behavior rather than taboo lengths, Brewis and Meyer (2005a) explored a sample drawn from 13 countries to investigate various influences on pair-bonded women's recent sexual behavior.

Among the negative predictors of recent female sexual behavior was being involved in a polygynous union and currently breastfeeding, factors which both highlight the importance of marital context and postpartum maternal care.

In the same review of 59 largely North American and western European societies discussed above, all of which only allow monogamous marriage, reductions in sexual behavior postpartum are typical, but still marked by relatively short durations of postpartum abstinence in cross-cultural perspective or with respect to other primates. As von Sydow (1999, p. 23) notes, across these Western samples "compared with the prepregnancy period, coital frequency is reduced in most couples during the first year after birth." That reduction in female sociosexuality postpartum makes sense in light of life history trade-offs: with literally a helpless baby demanding maternal care, this offsets investment in mating effort devoted to potential new partners. Instead, much of the focus rests with her current partner. By continuing sexual activities with a valued partner, this may reduce the chance of his seeking extra-pair sexual liaisons and foster his ongoing investment in her and their offspring. Indeed, marital quality is associated with earlier resumption of sexual behavior postpartum in Western samples (De Judicibus & McCabe, 2002). Indicating an active role of women in these patterns, one US study found that over 80% of women reported a desire to have sexual intercourse with their partners, as early as 4 weeks postpartum in nonbreastfeeding women (Kenney, 1973). Women are not just "persuaded" by their partners to jump back into a sexual routine; they report *wanting* to have sex with their partners even if, as we shall see, their non-cycling postpartum physiology undercuts features of their sexuality.

A focus on postpartum female physiology provides insights into life history shifts highlighting parenting effort over mating effort. After 9 months of dramatically increasing hormone levels, with the expulsion of the placenta, these levels suddenly plummet. Progesterone rapidly declines within the first 24 hours after birth and reaches follicular phase levels within a few days, while estrogen takes between 1 and 3 days to return to this level (Taylor & Lebovic, 2007). Levels of these hormones can matter: the diminished estrogens reduce vaginal lubrication, often making intercourse more painful. In addition, mothers experience a spike in oxytocin and prolactin during birth (Petraglia et al., 2006; Taylor & Lebovic, 2007). Although hormone levels return to normal after pregnancy, breastfeeding impacts this process. Women who breastfeed experience increases in oxytocin, important in the letdown of milk, and prolactin, important in milk production (Goodman, 2003), which delays the return of these hormones to prepregnancy levels when compared to bottle-feeding moms (Petraglia et al., 2006). Furthermore, prolactin suppresses the release of GnRH from the hypothalamus, which is necessary for ovulation, and therefore delays the return to menstrual cycling in breastfeeding moms (Taylor & Lebovic, 2007).

Lactation is another key factor in the resumption of sexual activity. Women who cease breastfeeding shortly after giving birth or who do not breastfeed begin cycling sooner than women who do breastfeed, and lactating women tend to experience lower sexual desire (Hyde, DeLamater, Plant, & Byrd, 1996; Lamarre,

Paterson, & Gorzalka, 2003). The physiological changes during breastfeeding may also have effects on sexual behaviors, such as the men lactating moms find attractive. For example, Hadza women who were breastfeeding preferred higher pitched, less masculine voices compared to nonbreastfeeding women (Apicella & Feinberg, 2009). Unfortunately, we know relatively little beyond this isolated study of how lactation, or postpartum amenorrhea more generally, influences women's perceptions of desirable traits in a mate.

## Pair Bonds, Divorce, and the Risky Peripartum Period

The peripartum period entails high stakes. If women are lacking necessary social support, including by children's fathers, they may not wish to continue investment in their current offspring. Among rhesus macaques, younger, first-time mothers may abandon newborns; however, older mothers do not abandon infants unless the mother or infant is sick (Maestripieri, 2007). The regular occurrence of abortion and infanticide in the historical and cross-cultural record in the contexts of perceived inadequate partner support and young female ages indicates that women often opt out of current reproduction to wait for a later, perhaps better, time (Hrdy, 1999). Another option may be continuing with a pregnancy or postpartum investment in a child but eventually seeking a new mate. In this latter track, women may find a mate's investment inadequate—indeed, this is one of the most cross-culturally salient reasons females divorce their husbands (Betzig, 1989)—but wait to separate from him until having progressed through the most intensive of postpartum parental investment. Fisher's (1989) recognition that divorce rates in a sample of 58 societies tend to peak approximately four years after the birth of a child would be consistent with this view. More overt female solicitation of new mates in the peripartum period might detract from even inadequate perceived parenting effort provided by a child's father. A poorly investigated area of research is how peripartum women involved in low quality reproductive bonds go about separating from these undesirable mates and seek a better prospect for the next reproductive bout. Indeed, we know little about even the attractivity of women during gestation and with nurslings, an important consideration if such women attempt to find a new mate. The demographics of divorce, both in large countries like the United States and small-scale societies such as the Tsimane of Bolivia (Winking, Kaplan, Gurven, & Rucas, 2007), indicate that divorce is most common among young adult women, the time when juggling considerations of partner quality and investment from the standpoint of current versus future reproduction are especially salient.

In better-quality relationships, as we have suggested, female maintenance of these through relatively high expression of sociosexual behaviors may be adaptive. While fathers may experience alterations in their physiology and some impacts on their libido, these tend to pale in comparison to those experienced by mothers, generating a wider chasm between the sexual desire of men and women in these peripartum periods (Gray & Anderson, 2010). Notably, Masters and Johnson (1966, p.168) cautioned, "Six weeks before and six weeks after delivery usually are proclaimed restricted periods by medical interdiction. Many male partners first break marital vows during this three-month period." Of course, their observations were derived in a US society only allowing monogamy, whereas in other societies, as discussed previously, women may have less concern with a husband straying if she is already in a polygynous union providing him with alternative sexual outlets. However the competing agendas of females and males play out in these peripartum periods, the measurable outcomes of sexual behavior can be viewed as compromises between them, in addition to the life history allocation challenges women have negotiated between the now and later in reproduction.

There are several implications stemming from a deeper recognition of peripartum shifts in female sociosexuality. Importantly, fluctuations in female peripartum proceptivity, receptivity, and attractivity can be situated within the adaptive (trade-offs between current and future reproductive success) and competitive (differing fitness agendas of females and males) viewpoints, a contrast with a nascent medical approach suggesting that low female peripartum libido may be a "pathology" requiring intervention (Abdool, Thakar, & Sultan, 2009; Carter et al., 2007). A greater understanding of how and why women's sociosexuality shifts during the peripartum period may have clinical relevance, allowing medical practitioners and therapists to counsel their patients on these changes. Changes in sociosexuality are also important for new parents to know. For example, shifting sociosexualities during lactation and pregnancy can affect the mother-father relationship, where male and female sexual desires may conflict. During the postpartum period, women's attunement to some of these changes may be relevant to decisions governing when to resume intercourse and what that may entail for successive conceptions. Further, more basic research on peripartum shifts in sexuality is warranted in order to facilitate a more complete understanding of female behaviors and preferences during these critical time frames. For example, the 2010 National Survey of Sexual Health and Behavior represents the most recent nationally representative study of US sexuality, sampling over 5,500 men and women (Herbenick et al., 2010). While this survey indicated patterned sexual behavior according to sex, age, and other variables, it did not include separate analyses based on peripartum states, arguably a major oversight given the work presented here.

## Conclusion

In summary, the peripartum period is an active one during which females face life history allocation challenges between current and future reproduction. Hormones and other features of women's physiology help coordinate the increased investment in maternal behavior at expense to sexuality. Comparative nonhuman primate data indicate that females may maintain sexual behavior during pregnancy at variable rates, but these tend to plummet postpartum when females are focused on caring for a new offspring. In humans, "Evolution's Empress" may negotiate continued partner investment through greater expression of peripartum sexuality than would be expected, but reductions in female proceptivity during this phase could be construed as adaptive and contributing to observed reductions in sexual behavior during gestation and postpartum.

# References

Abdool, Z., Thakar, R., & Sultan, A. H. (2009). Postpartum female sexual function. *European Journal of Obstetrics and Gynecology and Reproductive Biology, 145*, 133–137.

Apicella, C. L., & Feinberg, D. R. (2009). Voice pitch alters mate-choice-relevant perception in hunter-gatherers. *Proceedings of the Royal Society B, 276*, 1077–1082.

Bancroft, J. (2005). The endocrinology of sexual arousal. *Journal of Endocrinology, 186*, 411–427.

Barelli, C., Heistermann, M., Boesch, C., & Reichard, U. H. (2008). Mating patterns and sexual swellings in pair-living and multimale groups of wild white-handed gibbons, Hylobateslar. *Animal Behavior, 75*(3), 991–1001.

Beckerman, S., & Valentine, P. (Eds.). (2002). *Cultures of multiple fathers: The theory and practice of partible paternity in South America*. Gainesville: University of Florida Press.

Brewis, A., & Meyer, M. (2005a). Demographic evidence that human ovulation is undetectable (at least in pair bonds). *Current Anthropology, 46*, 465–471.

Brewis, A., & Meyer, M. (2005b). Marital coitus across the life course. *Journal of Biosocial Science, 37*, 499–518.

Buss, D. M. (1994). *The evolution of desire*. New York: Basic Books.

Carnegie, S. D., Fedigan, L. M., & Ziegler, T. E. (2006). Post-conceptive mating in white-faced capuchins, *Cebus capucinus*: Hormonal and sociosexual patterns of cycling, noncycling, and pregnant females. In A. Estrada, P. A. Garber, M. S. M. Pavelka, & L. Luecke (Eds.), *New perspectives in the study of Mesoamerican primates: Distribution, ecology, behavior, and conservation* (pp. 387–409). New York: Springer Science.

Carter, F. A., Carter, J. D., Luty, S. E., Jordan, J., McIntosh, V. V. W., Bartram, A. F.,...Bulik, C. M. (2007). What is worse for your sex life: Starving, being depressed, or a new baby? *International Journal of Eating Disorders, 40*(7), 664–667.

DeJudicibus, M. A., & McCabe, M. P. (2002). Psychological factors and the sexuality of pregnant and postpartum women. *Journal of Sex Research, 39*, 94–103.

Dentan, R. K. (1997). *Malaysia and the "original people": A case study of the impact of development on indigenous peoples*. Boston: Allyn and Bacon.

Dixson, A. F. (1998). *Primate sexuality*. New York : Oxford University Press.

Doran-Sheehy, D. M., Fernandez, D., & Borries, C. (2009). The strategic use of sex in wild female western gorillas. *American Journal of Primatology, 71*(12), 1011–1020.

Eaton, S. B., Pike, M. C., Short, R.V., Lee, N.C., Trussell, J., Hatcher, R. A.,...Hurtado, A. M. (1994). Women's reproductive cancers in evolutionary context. *Quarterly Review of Biology, 69*, 353–367.

Ellison, P. T. (2001). *On fertile ground*. Cambridge, MA: Harvard University Press.

Ellison, P. T., & Gray, P. B. (Eds.). (2009). *Endocrinology of social relationships*. Cambridge, MA: Harvard University Press.

Fisher, H. (1989). Evolution of human serial pairbonding. *American Journal of Physical Anthropology, 78*, 331–354.

Ford, C. S., & Beach, F. A. (1951). *Patterns of sexual behavior*. New York: Ace Books.

Frayser, S. (1985). *Varieties of sexual experience*. New Haven, CT: HRAF Press.

Gangestad, S. W., & Thornhill, R. (2008). Human oestrus. *Proceedings of the Royal Society B, 275*, 991–1000.

Gluckman, P., Bittles, A., & Hanson, M. (2009). *Principles of evolutionary medicine*. New York: Oxford University Press.

Goodman, M. H. (2003). *Basic medical endocrinology* (3rd ed.). San Diego, CA: Academic Press.

Grammer, K., Renninger, L., & Fischer, B. (2004). Disco clothing, female sexual motivation, and relationship status: Is she dressed to impress? *Journal of Sex Research, 41*(1), 66–74.

Gray, P. B., & Anderson, K. G. (2010). *Fatherhood: Evolution and human paternal behavior*. Cambridge, MA: Harvard University Press.

Gray, P. B., Kahlenberg, S. M., Barrett, E. S., Lipson, S. F., & Ellison, P. T. (2002). Marriage and fatherhood are associated with lower testosterone in males. *Evolution and Human Behavior, 23*, 193–202.

Gueguen, N. (2009a). Menstrual cycle phases and female receptivity to a courtship solicitation: An evaluation in a nightclub. *Evolution and Human Behavior, 30*(5), 351–355.

Gueguen, N. (2009b). The receptivity of women to courtship solicitation across the menstrual cycle: A field experiment. *Biological Psychology, 80*(3), 321–324.

Hawkes, K., & Paine, R. (Eds.). (2006). *The evolution of human life history*. Santa Fe, NM: School of American Research.

Herbenick, D., Reece, M., Schick, V., Sanders, S. A., Dodge, B., & Fortenberry, J. D. (2010). Sexual behavior in the United States: Results from a national probability sample of men and women ages 14–94. *Journal of Sexual Medicine, 7*, 255–265.

Hewlett, B. L., & Hewlett, B. S. (2008). A biocultural approach to sex, love, and intimacy in central African foragers and farmers. In W. Jankowiak (Ed.), *Intimacies: Love and sex across cultures* (pp. 37–64). New York: Columbia University Press.

Hrdy, S. (1981). *The woman that never evolved*. Cambridge, MA: Harvard University Press.

Hrdy, S. (1999). *Mother nature: A history of mothers, infants, and natural selection*. New York: Pantheon.

Hrdy, S. (2009). *Mothers and others: The evolutionary origins of mutual understanding*. Cambridge, MA: Harvard University Press.

Hyde, J. S., DeLamater, J. D., Plant, E. A., & Byrd, J. M. (1996). Sexuality during pregnancy and the year postpartum. *Journal of Sex Research, 33*, 143–151.

Jones, B. C., DeBruine, L. M., Perrett, D. I., Little, A. C., Feinberg, D. R., & Law Smith, M. J. (2008). Effects of menstrual cycle phase on face preferences. *Archives of Sexual Behavior, 37*, 78–84.

Kelly, R. (1995). *The foraging spectrum*. Washington, DC: Smithsonian Press.

Kenny, J. A. (1973). Sexuality of pregnant and breastfeeding women. *Archives of Sexual Behavior, 2*(3), 215–229.

LeMarre, A. K., Paterson, L. Q., & Gorzalka, B. B. (2003). Breastfeeding and postpartum maternal sexual functioning: A review. *Canadian Journal of Human Sexuality, 12*, 151–168.

Low, B. (2000). *Why sex matters*. Princeton, NJ: Princeton University Press.

Maestripieri, D. (2007). *Macachiavellian intelligence*. Chicago: University of Chicago Press.

Manson, J. H., Perry, S., & Parish, A. R. (1997). Nonconceptive sexual behavior in bonobos and capuchins. *International Journal of Primatology, 18*, 767–786.

Marlowe, F. (2001). Male contribution to diet and female reproductive success among foragers. *Current Anthropology, 42*, 755–760.

Marlowe, F. (2005). Hunter-gatherers and human evolution. *Evolutionary Anthropology, 14*, 54–67.

Masters, W. H., & Johnson, V. E. (1966). *Human sexual response*. Boston: Little, Brown, and Company.

Mazur, A., & Booth, A. (1998). Testosterone and dominance in men. *Behavioral and Brain Sciences, 21*, 353–363.

Miller, G., Tybur, J. M., & Jordan, B. D. (2007). Ovulatory cycle effects on tip earnings by lap dancers: Economic evidence for human estrus? *Evolution and Human Behavior, 28*(6), 375–381.

Muller, M. N., Emery Thompson, M. E., & Wrangham, R. W. (2006). Male chimpanzees prefer mating with old females. *Current Biology, 16*(22), 2234–2238.

Nelson, R. J. (2005). *An introduction to behavioral endocrinology.* Sunderland, MA: Sinauer.

Pazol, K. (2003). Mating among the Kakamega Forest blue monkeys (*Cercopithecus mitis*): Does female sexual behavior function to manipulate paternity assessment? *Behavior, 140,* 473–499.

Penke, L., & Asendorpf, J. B. (2008). Beyond global sociosexual orientations: A more differentiated look at sociosexuality and its effects on courtship and romantic relationships. *Journal of Personality and Social Psychology, 95,* 1113–1135.

Perry, S., & Manson, J. (2008). *Manipulative monkeys.* Cambridge, MA: Harvard University Press.

Petraglia, F., Florio, P., & Torricelli, M. (2006). Placental endocrine function. In J. D. Neill (Ed.), *Knobil and Neill's physiology of reproduction* (Vol. 2, 3rd ed., pp. 2847–2898). Amsterdam, The Netherlands: Academic Press.

Regan, P. C. (1999). Hormonal correlates and causes of sexual desire: A review. *Canadian Journal of Human Sexuality, 8*(1), 1–16.

Rosen, M. P., & Cedars, M. I. (2007). Female reproductive endocrinology and infertility. In D. G. Gardner & D. Shoback (Eds.), *Greenspan's basic and clinical endocrinology* (8th ed., pp. 502–561). New York: McGraw-Hill Medical.

Schmitt, D. P. (2005). Sociosexuality from Argentina to Zimbabwe: A 48-nation study of sex, culture, and strategies of human mating. *Behavioral and Brain Sciences, 28,* 247–311.

Simpson, J. A., & Gangestad, S. W. (1991). Individual differences in sociosexuality: Evidence for convergent and discriminant validity. *Personality Processes and Individual Differences, 60*(6), 870–883.

Snowdon, C. T., & Ziegler, T. E. (2007). Growing up cooperatively: Family processes and infant care in marmosets and tamarins. *Journal of Developmental Processes, 2*(1), 40–66.

Speroff, L., Glass, R. H., & Kase, N. G. (1994). *Clinical gynecologic endocrinology and infertility* (5th ed.). Baltimore: Williams & Wilkins.

Stearns, S. C. (1992). *The evolution of life histories.* Oxford, UK: Oxford University Press.

Stumpf, R. M., & Boesch, C. (2005). Does promiscuous mating preclude female choice? Female sexual strategies in chimpanzees (*Pan troglodytes verus*) of the Tai National Park, Cote d'Ivoire. *Behavioral Ecology and Sociobiology, 57*(5), 511–524.

Suggs, R. (1966). *Marquesan sexual behavior.* New York: Harcourt, Brace, & World.

Sugiyama, L. (2005). Physical attractiveness in adaptationist perspective. In D. M. Buss (Ed.), *The handbook of evolutionary psychology* (pp. 292–343). Hoboken, NJ: Wiley.

Taylor, R. N., & Lebovic, D. I. (2007). The endocrinology of pregnancy. In D. G. Gardner & D. Shoback (Eds.), *Greenspan's basic and clinical endocrinology* (8th ed., pp. 641–660). New York: McGraw-Hill Medical.

Von Sydow, K. (1999). Sexuality during pregnancy and after childbirth: A metacontent analysis of 59 studies. *Journal of Psychosomatic Research, 47,* 27–49.

Von Sydow, K., & Palombit, R. A. (1999). Infanticide and the evolution of pair bonds in nonhuman primates. *Evolutionary Anthropology, 7*(4), 117–129.

Walker, R. S., Flinn, M. V., & Hill, K. R. (2010). Evolutionary history of partible paternity in lowland South America. *Proceedings of the National Academy of Sciences, 107*(45), 19195–19200.

Wilcox, A. J., Baird, B. B., Dunson, D. B., McConnaughey, D. R., Kesner, J. S., & Weinberg, C. R. (2004). On the frequency of intercourse around ovulation: Evidence for biological influences. *Human Reproduction, 19,* 1539–1543.

Winking, J., Kaplan, H., Gurven, M., & Rucas, S. (2007). Why do men marry and why do they stray? *Proceedings of the Royal Society B, 274*(1618), 1643–1649.

Yovsi, R. D., & Keller, H. (2003). Breastfeeding: An adaptive process. *Ethos, 31*(2), 147–171.

Ziegler, T. E. (2007). Female sexual motivation during non-fertile periods: A primate phenomenon. *Hormones and Behavior, 51,* 1–2.

MATING AND COMMUNICATION

# 14

# Sexual Conflict in White-Faced Capuchins

## *It's Not Whether You Win or Lose*

### LINDA MARIE FEDIGAN AND KATHARINE M. JACK

## Introduction

This inquiry into the nature (the how and why) of male-female conflict in primates begins with the conundrum of the white-faced capuchin male as a social creature. Is he best characterized as a "new age sensitive male" or an "aggressive, despotic abuser" of females and their offspring? Our several decades of observing these male monkeys have shown us the many facets of their paradoxical social attributes. Within his group, a capuchin male will tolerate playful infants bouncing on his head while he is resting, he will try to retrieve an infant from the grasp of a predator, allow it to suckle from his nonfunctional nipples, carry it through the trees and present his body as a bridge when the gap between branches is too wide for the infant to cross. But when he changes groups, this same capuchin male may snatch a small infant from its mother's body and kill it with canine punctures to its skull or body, despite the efforts of the mother and others to protect it. Capuchin males routinely supplant females from preferred feeding locations, causing the females to avoid and cower away from them. But alpha males also readily form coalitions with coresident females against other group members and outsiders. A capuchin male will sit pressed up against another adult male, grooming him and gently placing the other's fingers in his mouth; he will hurdle around the forest giving lost calls until he locates a "missing" male who has moved far away from his group and then engage in an affiliative reunion display that is very similar to the courtship display for this species. Or conversely, he will gang up with other males to slash a rival male with his large, sharp canines until the victim dies of his wounds. What could be the source of such apparently contradictory behavior on the part of capuchin males, how do females respond to it, and why would females live with such volatile social partners?

These are the questions that underlie this chapter, in which we will describe how evolutionary biologists are increasingly identifying sexual conflict (conflict between the sexes for the control of reproduction: Arnqvist & Rowe, 2005; Chapman, Arnqvist, & Rowe, 2003; Clutton-Brock & Parker, 1995; Eberhard, 1996; Parker, 1979) as the driving force behind many of the variable behavior patterns we observe during social interactions (e.g., Gowaty, 2004; Muller & Wrangham, 2009; Smuts & Smuts, 1993; Stumpf, Martinez-Mota, Milich, Righini, & Shattuck, 2011). To exemplify the general points we make about the probable chain of adaptations and counteradaptations that led to the behaviors we observe in male and female capuchin monkeys today, we will use our findings from nearly 30 years of studying a Costa Rican population of wild, white-faced capuchin monkeys (*Cebus capucinus*) in the Santa Rosa Sector of the Área de Conservación Guanacaste.

## Starting Points: Anisogamy, Sexual Selection, and Parental Investment

Explanations of sex roles and of conflicts between males and females usually begin with anisogamy (sexual reproduction via the union of two dissimilar gametes) and with Bateman's Principle (1948)—the theory that because eggs are larger, less mobile and more resource-rich than sperm, females initially invest more in reproduction than do males and therefore females are the limiting resource over which males compete for access. Bateman's experiments with fruit flies demonstrated that males exhibit greater variance in mating success than do females, which, following Darwin (1871), Bateman attributed to the indiscriminate eagerness of males to mate versus the discriminating choosiness of females regarding their mates. Williams (1966), Parker (1979), and Trivers (1972) all extrapolated from anisogamy and Bateman's work to develop theories of sexual conflict. Parker and Williams focused on sexual selection (male-male competition and female choice) as resulting from the original unequal investment made by females in eggs and males in sperm. Trivers focused on asymmetrical parental care patterns (females typically provide more care of their offspring than do males) as arising from anisogamy and as resulting in choosy females and competitive, promiscuous, males.

These very influential evolutionary models of sexual reproduction and their successors have typically portrayed females, both implicitly and explicitly, as the "losers" when the reproductive interests of males and females diverge. The traditional depiction of females as losers in sexual conflict is based mainly on the assumption that the initial higher investment of females in their gametes forces them to continue to invest more in their offspring than do males. This "constrained-by-prior-investment" argument is carried even further in assumptions about sexual conflict in mammals. Because female mammals gestate and lactate for their young, they are seen by many evolutionary biologists to invest more than males in the rearing of their young; to be more constrained than are males in the quantity of young they can produce in their lifetimes; and, unlike males who have only invested sperm, to be largely constrained by prior investment from the option of abandoning their costly offspring (Trivers, 1972).

There have been many criticisms of Bateman's experiments and conclusions (e.g., Dewsbury, 2005; Snyder & Gowaty, 2007; Tang, Martinez, & Ryder, 2005) and of the assumption that females are constrained in their options by their initial high investment in eggs (e.g., Dawkins & Carlisle, 1976; Kokko & Jennions, 2008a; Trillmich, 2010). A common misapprehension about optimal decisions (the "Concorde Fallacy") is that investment strategies should be based on prior costs (what micro economists call "sunk" or lost costs) rather than future benefits. Named after the construction of the Concorde jet on which the governments of Britain and France lost so much money, the Concorde Fallacy is the mistaken assumption that large prior costs justify continued investments, when it is in fact the likelihood of future benefits that justify investment (see Kokko & Jennions, 2008a for detailed review). Some researchers (e.g., Hrdy, 1986; Kokko & Jennions, 2008b) have also called into question the assertion (originating with Darwin) that females are coy in their choice of mates whereas males are indiscriminate. And there have been counterarguments made to the assertion that females are the losers in sexual conflict (e.g., Arnqvist & Rowe, 2005; Gowaty, 2004; Green & Madjidian, 2011). Over the course of this chapter, we will return to these assumptions and outline some of the criticisms and counterarguments. We now turn to what is arguably for many animal species another important starting point for conflict between males and females over reproduction: internal fertilization.

In most aquatic animals, the sperm unites with the egg external to the body of the reproducing individuals after the male and female release their gametes into their watery surroundings. Internal fertilization, which occurs in land dwelling animals, is thought to be a reproductive adaptation that evolved to protect eggs and sperm (and ultimately the zygote) from desiccation. Most mammals carry this pattern of protecting the zygote even further by gestating the young internally, rather than secreting fertilized eggs as do birds and reptiles. In the same way that anisogamy may have originally evolved for selective reasons (competition among gametes) but then had a side-effect on male-female conflict, it is possible that the process of internal fertilization evolved to protect the gametes from drying out but also set off a chain of reactions from males and then subsequent reactions from females. This is because an important epiphenomenon of internal fertilization is that it created the possibility of cryptic conception and increased the ability of the female to exert female choice.

Thus, we could say that the widespread pattern of internal reproduction has benefits for females as well as the costs identified by Trivers (1972) and others. Indeed, if we return to the traditional winner/loser metaphor of most evolutionary models of sexual reproduction, one could make the argument that females hold the trump card in the game of competing with males for control of reproduction. Females may not be capable of producing as many offspring as the males of their species, although it is important to remember that many male animals are not reproductively successful whereas almost every female that reaches adulthood produces some offspring. And because of gestation and lactation costs, female mammals may invest more energy in rearing their offspring than do males. But for viviparous females, their offspring are guaranteed to be their own and thus the possibility of cuckoldry does not act on females as a powerful selective force as it does on males, driving the latter to engage in costly and dangerous competitive/coercive measures. Evolutionary biologists maintain that the ultimate purpose of life is to reproduce one's own genetic material. Thus, from an evolutionary point of view, paternity uncertainty imposes a serious constraint on a male's life purpose and is believed to set off an entire chain of events (an "arms race" as some have called it, e.g., Dawkins & Krebs 1979; Mulder & Rauch, 2009; Palombit, 2010) in which males behave in a strategic manner and/or evolve morphological and physiological features that not only improve their reproductive success in comparison to other males but also reduce ambiguity about which offspring they have truly sired. And females respond with countermeasures that maintain paternity uncertainty and that protect themselves and their offspring from the features that males have evolved to improve their reproductive success (Hrdy, 1974, 1977, 1979).

Sexual selection theory and its applications (going all the way back to Darwin and up through recent papers) have been criticized for assuming that conventional Western gender roles apply to animals (e.g., see critiques in Clutton-Brock, 2007; Fausto-Sterling, 1997; Gowaty, 1982, 1997; Martin, 2008; Roughgarden & Akçay, 2010). Green and Madjidian (2011) wondered whether researchers of sexual conflict, like those of sexual selection, approach their topic with a preconceived view of how the sexes should act. Thus, they carried out a quantitative analysis of the terminology used in publications on sexual conflict. These authors found that in the literature on sexual conflict, researchers use many terms to describe how males and females respond to one another (28 in total) but that male behaviors are consistently described with terms implying *action* and female behaviors with terms implying *reaction*. When a male responds to a problem presented by the environment or by female patterns, it is called an *adaptation*. When a female responds, it is labeled *resistance* or *counteradaptation*. Green and Madjidian argue that the use of these sex-stereotyped terms implies that the male has the upper hand (the male adapts and the female resists or counteradapts). Furthermore, they found that theoretical models are focused almost solely on costs for females even though costs for both sexes must occur in any coevolutionary process. They conclude by arguing that anthropomorphic stereotyping of sex roles seriously constrains rather than enhances our understanding of sexual conflict, but that nonetheless, it is difficult to avoid the trap of conventional terminology.

In this review of sexual conflict in capuchins, we will try to interpret our findings on male and female interactive patterns more neutrally as a chain of actions and reactions or a sequence of problems set and solutions developed/evolved, without making assumptions about which sex has the upper hand, the first move, or the fewest costs. We choose to enter the chain of actions and reactions with the advent of, and responses to, the process of internal fertilization. Other researchers might start at another point in the sequence.

## White-Faced Capuchins and Sexual Conflict

White-faced capuchins occur across Central America from Honduras in the north down to Panama and into limited areas of northwestern Ecuador and Colombia in South America (Fragaszy, Visalberghi, & Fedigan, 2004). Like other members of the genus Cebus, white-faced monkeys are arboreal omnivores with an eclectic diet consisting of fruit, insects and small invertebrates. They live in social groups made up of kin-related adult females and their offspring ("matrilines") associated with temporarily resident adult males. Group size averages 15 members, ranging from 3 to 40 individuals, with approximately equal numbers of adult females and adult males residing together (Fedigan & Jack, 2011,2012). Males disperse from their natal groups into neighboring groups at around 4.5 years of age, well before being capable of reproducing (6 years; Hakeem, Sandoval, Jones, & Allman, 1996) or attaining full adult body size (10 years; Jack, Sheller, & Fedigan, 2011). After this initial move from the birth group, males continue to change groups repeatedly over the course of their adult lives at approximately 4-year intervals (Jack & Fedigan, 2004b). Females, with a few exceptions, remain in their natal groups and first give birth around 6 years of age and then produce additional infants approximately every 2 years after that. Female white-faced capuchins copulate with the multiple resident males of their groups and then gestate their young for 5.5 months before giving birth and suckling their infants for approximately one year (Carnegie, 2011).

Because capuchin females conceive via internal fertilization and mate with multiple males, it is difficult for the researcher, and presumably for the male capuchin, to be certain who sires the resultant infant. (The researcher's solution to paternity uncertainty is to collect fecal samples from mothers, infants, and potential sires and subject the samples to DNA relatedness analyses.) As described earlier, the replication of one's genetic material (in this case, the production of viable offspring) is believed by evolutionary biologists to be the driving force of living forms. Therefore, an adult male monkey has a good evolutionary reason to invest effort and energy in the survival of his own offspring but not in the offspring of unrelated males. Thus, the lack of assurance that he is the sire sets up a problem for the male monkey to which we believe he has adapted various solutions: competition with other males for access to a female; the offering of benefits to a female that increase the chances she will choose him as a mate; and male coercion of a female to the same ends.

# Male Solutions to the Uncertainty Problem Set by Internal Fertilization

## Male-Male Competition

All male animals compete for opportunities to inseminate eggs, and capuchin males are no exception. Since female capuchins reside in permanent, kin-related social groups, males compete for the opportunity to immigrate into and retain residency within these groups, which is where the mating occurs (we have only rarely observed females to mate with outsider males during brief periods of group instability). To gain entry into groups, small parties of males periodically attempt to take over the positions of resident males, via physical intimidation and fighting with the male members of the group (Fedigan & Jack, 2004; Jack & Fedigan, 2004a, 2004b; Jack et al., 2011). If successful, these invading males become resident and then cooperatively attempt to keep other males out of the group. This pattern of male-male competition for residency within the established groups of related females results in the complete replacement of adult males in our study groups approximately every 4 years. Either before or during the takeover process, or once in the group, immigrating males sort themselves into a dominance hierarchy, after which relationships among group males are generally tolerant and cooperative in nature. Indeed, once in a group, overt male-male competition over mates is rare; we observe all resident males of a group to mate with females, regardless of male rank, and the top-ranking (alpha) male of the group does not overtly harass or interrupt the copulations of subordinate males. Despite these behavioral observations suggesting that overt mating competition does not occur among coresident males, genetic paternity tests (Jack & Fedigan, 2006; Muniz et al., 2010) find that alpha males sire most of the offspring (70–90% in our Santa Rosa study groups). This suggests that even though reproductive competition is high (as evidenced by high reproductive skew), it is not manifested aggressively among coresident males. Although female choice is not as conspicuous in our species as in brown capuchins (e.g., Janson, 1984), it is possible that female white-faced capuchins allocate their receptive and proceptive behaviors in such a way that they mate more often with alpha males when they are ovulating and with subordinate males when they are not conceptive (Izar, Stone, Carnegie, & Nakai, 2009). It is also possible that male mating competition is occurring at an inconspicuous level (e.g., sperm competition or subordinate male avoidance of mates sought by the alpha male).

Knowing that alpha males are more reproductively successful than subordinate males, has helped us understand the frequent movement of males between social groups. Male white-faced capuchins are truly only transient members of any one group, continually dispersing throughout their lives. In some years these changes in male group members occur through aggressive evictions, when outsider males cooperatively take over a group by evicting resident males, while in other years the male changeovers occur voluntarily. In these latter cases, subordinate males are usually the first to go, often leaving the alpha male on his own to defend the group (from predators and would-be immigrants) while they seek out residency in a new group. In such circumstances, it is only a matter of time before a lone alpha male will be challenged by a coalition of extragroup males looking to take over the group in which he resides (and the mating opportunities that go along with it). Sometimes the resident alpha male is actually killed by invaders, other times he joins a neighboring group, and sometimes he simply disappears. This pattern of frequent male dispersal enables subordinate males to increase their dominance rank and, in the process, increase their reproductive chances (Jack & Fedigan, 2004b).

## Male Benefits to Females (Influencing Female Mate Choice)

Alpha male capuchins have exaggerated secondary sexual characteristics (i.e., pronounced jaw line and brow ridge) and are in a permanent state of piloerection, making them look larger and more impressive than the other males of the group (Perry, 1998a). These traits likely result from their heightened testosterone levels compared to those of subordinate males (Schoof & Jack, 2009). Alpha males are conspicuously active in defending their groups against predators, neighboring groups, invading males, and anthropogenic disturbances. And they will do so to the point of being sometimes fatally wounded during aggressive interactions with outsiders (e.g., by nonresident males, large carnivores, angry humans, and passing vehicles). From an ultimate or adaptive perspective, we suspect that the females choose the alpha male to sire their young, because along with his fighting strength, the alpha male offers special benefits to the adult females of the group. Top-ranking males spend more time than other group members monitoring the surrounding environment and are often the first to alert the group to danger and to rush to its defense (Gould, Fedigan, & Rose, 1997; Jack, 2001; Rose & Fedigan, 1995). They are also more likely than subordinate males to perform impressive arboreal displays that involve a swaggering walk, exaggerated leaps through the trees and heavy landings onto tree limbs, causing large branches to sway violently or crash to the ground. All males in the group will court females (and/or respond to female courtship) via whirling "dances" that include distinctive body movements, facial expressions, and vocalizations. And all resident males will respond to the distress call of an infant in their group by hurrying to retrieve it, but alpha males are particularly prone to do so (Fragaszy et al., 2004; MacKinnon, 2002). These behavioral patterns (protection of females, their young, and their resources; male courtship displays; and "ornamental" features) are all believed to entice females to accept these males as residents in their group (Rose, 1994) and to preferentially choose alpha males as their copulation partners when the female is ovulating.

## Male Coercion of Females

As described by Smut and Smuts (1993) and more recently explored in an entire volume (Muller & Wrangham, 2009), male primates may also attempt to coerce females to choose them as copulation partners. This pattern of males endeavoring to forcibly bend females to their own ends is widespread in the animal kingdom and can take a variety of forms (e.g., intimidation, harassment, and attempted sequestering or "guarding" of females as well as physical attacks on them and killing of infants sired by unrelated males). Smuts and Smuts (1993) argued that male coercion of females to mate with them is sufficiently common as to constitute a third mechanism of sexual selection (Darwin had originally outlined only two: male-male competition and female choice). Other researchers of sexual conflict have since agreed with Smuts and Smuts (e.g., Clarke, Pradhan, & van Schaik, 2009; Clutton-Brock & Parker, 1995; Stumpf et al., 2011; Watson-Capps, 2009). In many respects, sexual coercion is the place where male-male competition and female choice converge under the label of "sexual conflict": males compete with one another for mating opportunities and the chance to influence female mate choice and sometimes they use force to override and/or influence this mate choice (often at the expense of not only female reproductive success but that of other males).

As mentioned above, once male white-faced capuchins have established themselves as residents within a group, we see few overt behavioral manifestations of mating competition among them and they rarely direct aggression against females residing in their group. Females mate with most or all group males with no interference or harassment from higher ranking males, even when they mate in full view of the alpha male. This means that forms of sexual coercion frequently observed in other primate species (e.g., sexual harassment and intimidation, reviewed in Palombit, 2010) are not common occurrences in our study species, although alpha males do groom and follow females when the latter are periovulatory, suggesting a mild form of mate guarding (Izar et al., 2009). Extreme forms of mate guarding or attempted sequestering of females would be difficult for any one male, including the alpha male, to achieve due to the dispersed nature in which our capuchins travel and forage, their rapid locomotor patterns and the often dense foliage in which they reside. We simply do not see alpha males in "hot pursuit" of periovulatory females, although the fact that they follow them more than they follow other females (and do so more than subordinate males) suggests that alpha males might have an enhanced ability to detect ovulation and/or the females may be providing them with cues (e.g., olfactory ones) that we have yet to document (Izar et al., 2009).

However, we do observe infanticide in our study groups, a manifestation of sexual coercion that has, by far, the most damaging consequences to female reproductive success. To be sure, infanticide, specifically the killing of infants by adult males, is the number one cause of infant death in white-faced capuchins, and infanticide is only observed in the context of a changeover in male group membership or in the rarer instances of male rank reversals (i.e., when a resident male establishes himself as the group's new alpha male) (Fedigan, 2003; Perry, 1998b; Perry, Godoy, & Lammers, 2012). In our study population, 82% of infants <12 months of age die following group takeovers, whereas during times of group stability, the mortality rate for infants is 12% (Fedigan, 2003). By killing the dependent offspring of group females, newly immigrant males (or new alpha males) can influence female reproduction by shortening her interbirth interval (i.e., causing her to resume cycling earlier than she would have if she raised her current infant to weaning age), thereby increasing that male's mating opportunities and ultimately his reproductive potential. This behavior enables a male to influence the timing of female reproduction while at the same time decreasing the reproductive fitness of other males (by killing their offspring). In this way, infanticide is not only the ultimate manifestation of male sexual coercion of females but also of male-male mating competition.

## Costs of Male-Male Competition and Coercion

The costs to females of male competitive and coercive patterns are large and extensive. Over the years of our long-term study, we have gathered ample evidence that the lives of female capuchins are enormously affected by the ubiquitous and persistent efforts of males to compete with other males for mating access and to gain some control over how, when, and with whom the females copulate/reproduce. First and most obvious is that the killing of infants by adult males is very costly to the female who has gestated and suckled that infant, in both an energetic and reproductive sense. Since infanticide usually occurs in the context of male invasions and takeovers of groups, this is a period during which all members of the group (females, juveniles, and males) are at risk of being wounded and also a time when group members expend a lot of energy either fighting off the invaders (in the case of resident males) or avoiding them (in the case of females and their young) (Fedigan, 2003; Fedigan & Jack, 2004).

It is sometimes the case that the characteristics selected for in male-male competition (large size, aggressive behaviors, and "armaments"; Darwin, 1871) can also be directed at females and their young to improve a male's control over reproductive outcomes. Furthermore, females may suffer collateral damage simply if they are present when males compete with other males for reproductive access (Watson-Capps, 2009). In capuchins, takeovers generally occur over a period of weeks, during which time the group is highly destabilized in its social patterns and disrupted in its ranging and feeding patterns. Cortisol levels of adult females are significantly elevated during and after takeovers, indicating heightened stress levels and energy expenditure (Carnegie, Fedigan, & Ziegler, 2011). Even though female capuchins exhibit strong and stable linear dominance hierarchies (Bergstrom & Fedigan, 2010), we have been unable to demonstrate that higher ranking females are more reproductively successful than subordinate females. We suspect this is because frequent male takeovers and infanticide confound the effects of female-female dominance relations on reproductive success (Fedigan, Carnegie, & Jack, 2008) and particularly affect higher ranking females who are more central to the group and easier for invading males to locate and target for aggression than the more subordinate, peripheral females.

Patterns of male-male competition and male-female coercion (as well as male-female benefits) are also not without costs to the males. First of all, there are considerable energetic investments made by males during these interactions. Alpha males have higher testosterone and, for the most part, higher cortisol levels than do subordinates (Schoof & Jack, 2009). These higher cortisol levels indicate greater amounts of stress experienced by alpha males and the higher testosterone levels are hypothesized to be associated with greater male vulnerability to parasites and other forms of infections (Poulin, 1996; Schalk & Forbes, 1997). Furthermore, the strategy of male dispersal to neighboring groups, thought to be an adaptation to increase their chances of copulating with fertile females (Jack & Fedigan, 2004b), also comes with very high costs. These males must move to new and unfamiliar ranges, which increases their risks of starvation, dehydration, and predation, along with the high probability that they will be wounded while battling their way into new groups. Janson, Baldovino, and Di Bitetti (2011) report 38% mortality for males of dispersing age in the closely related brown capuchin (Cebus*[apella]* *nigritus*). Mortality for dispersing males of our species of capuchin is likely lower because our males disperse in cohorts (Jack & Fedigan, 2004a, 2004b; Perry et al., 2012) rather than alone, as is the case for brown capuchins. However, aggression from unknown conspecifics nonetheless poses a real threat to dispersing males. We have observed many cases of males being seriously injured in the course of take-overs, and this aggression can sometimes be lethal, either immediately or from infections of the wounds they incur (Gros Louis, Perry, & Manson, 2003). Even the behaviors engaged in by males in their attempts to influence female mate choice are not without costs; alpha males expend more time and energy engaged in vigilance behaviors and often put themselves directly into harm's way in their attempts to protect females and infants from predators or aggressive conspecifics.

## Female Solutions to the Problems Set by Male-Male Competition and Male Coercion

The literature on sexual conflict indicates that female animals have evolved many mechanisms that lower the costs imposed on them by male-male competition and male coercion; in other words, patterns that help the females to exert and maintain some control over their reproductive lives (e.g., Gowaty, 2004; Mulder & Rauch, 2009; Stumpf et al., 2011; Watson-Capps, 2009). We will briefly describe some of these patterns here (typically referred to as "female counteradaptations" in the sexual conflict literature) and indicate which ones we have documented in our white-faced capuchin females.

## Polyandrous, Nonconceptive, and Post-Male-Takeover Mating

Females in many primate species mate with multiple males (polyandry, or polygynandry in the case of multiple females residing and mating with multiple males). It has been shown in several studies that male primates are more favorably disposed toward females with whom they have mated (Clarke et al., 2009; Palombit, 2010), so that even if males are unable to make a conceptual association between copulation and siring an infant (which is probably the case), they are predisposed to be protective and nonaggressive toward the infant of a female with whom they have recently consorted. If a female mates with several males, this exacerbates the paternity uncertainty already imposed by internal fertilization and predisposes several males instead of just one to be protective. So we can understand why there would be selection for female primates who live in groups with multiple males to mate polyandrously and this is what we have commonly seen in our capuchins.

Furthermore, we have hormonal evidence that female capuchins mate with males when they are not cycling reproductively and continue to mate with them after they have already conceived (Carnegie, 2011; Carnegie, Fedigan, & Ziegler 2005, 2006; Manson, Perry, & Parish, 1997; and see below on female choice). Additionally, we have observed females to mate with newly resident males who have recently invaded and taken over the group, even when these females are already pregnant. This may represent a form of "situational receptivity" (Clarke et al., 2009; Hrdy, 1979) in which females initiate mating and/or respond positively to male sexual initiations (whether or not the females are conceptive) in order to predispose the new males to be nonaggressive toward future infants.

## Female Mate Choice, Concealed/Unpredictable Ovulation, and Cryptic Female Choice

Female brown capuchins exhibit very obvious proceptive behavioral patterns and actively pursue males sexually over a period of days (Fragaszy et al., 2004; Janson, 1984). Although females of our study species do sometimes initiate sexual behavior with distinctive proceptive behaviors, these are much more subtle, fleeting signals than those exhibited by brown capuchins, and mating in white-faced capuchins is just as likely to be initiated by males as females. As noted by Kappeler and van Schaik (2004), there is surprisingly little direct evidence for female choice in free-living primates. This is in large part because field conditions limit our ability to perform experiments of the type typically performed on invertebrates to sort female choice from male-male competition and coercion. However, there is considerable indirect evidence for female choice in wild primates, such as our capuchins, some examples of which we just described—females choose to mate polyandrously, postconceptively, and after takeovers ("situationally"), all of which increase paternity uncertainty in the males and helps females to counter male attempts to control reproduction.

The fact that females can successfully encourage males to copulate when they are not in fact ovulating, suggests that their ovulatory phases may be concealed and/or unpredictable from the perspective of at least some of the males (Carnegie et al., 2006; Carnegie, 2011). One might argue that male capuchins are just always ready to copulate with any female at any time (i.e., the "indiscriminate eagerness of males to mate" identified by Bateman in fruit flies), but there is evidence that male primates do become sperm deleted and physically exhausted from multiple copulations (Dixson, 1998) and we know that capuchin males do sometimes reject female sexual advances (Fragaszy et al., 2004). Unpredictable/concealed ovulation has been argued to occur in many primate species where females show proceptive and receptive behavior over periods of time that are much longer than their actual conceptive phases and where males readily mate with nonconceptive females (van Schaik et al., 2000). As noted by Strier (2010), there is little that females can do to alter their olfactory or physical cues, but many female primates are adept at modifying their behavior to stimulate sexual interest from males.

The fact that we see females mate with all the males of the group but our paternity tests indicate that alpha males sire 70–90% of the groups' infants (Jack & Fedigan, 2006, see also Muniz et al., 2010), may indicate that alpha males are better at detecting cues to ovulation (see above) or it may also suggest that some form of "cryptic female choice" is operating in our study animals. "Cryptic female choice" is the term coined by Thornhill (1983) and a concept extensively developed by Eberhard (1996) to indicate the many different mechanisms by which a female can mate with a male but reject him as the sire of her offspring—and therefore exert female control over reproduction. Cryptic female choice typically refers to postcopulatory patterns by which females may preferentially use sperm from one male over that of another –via differential sperm storage and transport to the egg. Again, there is no direct evidence for postcopulatory female choice in primates, probably because of the invasive nature of the experiments required to document it (Birkhead & Kappeler, 2004), but there is some indirect evidence, for example the discrepancy between those male capuchins that we observe to copulate and those who actually sire the infants (see Schwensow, Eberle, & Sommer, 2008, for similar findings in grey mouse lemurs, *Microcebus murinus*).

### Reproductive Synchrony

The pattern whereby the multiple females of a group all cycle simultaneously and/ or give birth in the same season, is believed to be primarily an adaptation to the seasonality of resources, but it can also function to decrease the ability of any given male to monopolize mating opportunities. In our capuchins, we have demonstrated that, although births do occur throughout the year, 44% of births occur in the 3-month period (May–July) that immediately precedes the peak of food availability (Carnegie, Fedigan, & Melin, 2011). The fruits eaten by these monkeys are most abundant about 8 weeks after the peak in births (Carnegie, Fedigan, & Melin, et al., 2011). Since we also know that lactation is the most energetically costly part of female reproduction and that lactation costs peak when the infants are 8 weeks of age (McCabe & Fedigan, 2007), we have concluded that reproductive seasonality in this species is geared toward enhancing maternal ability to lactate for their young. Nonetheless, a side-effect of reproductive seasonality may be that if many of the females of a group cycle more or less simultaneously, it is more difficult for any one male to monopolize mating access to these females.

## Female-Female Alliances and Female Avoidance of Nonpreferred Males

Female primates also exhibit a number of social behaviors that may function to help them maintain control over their reproduction. It is possible that these patterns originally evolved for other reasons, but proved adaptive in the context of sexual conflict. In many (but not all) monkey species, females usually remain throughout their lives in the groups and home ranges in which they were born. This pattern is known as female philopatry and results in the stable core of social groups being made up of matrilineally related females and their offspring. If the males of the species commonly disperse between groups, then adult males are only temporarily associated with each kin-related cohort of female monkeys. Kinship is a powerful basis for permanent alliances, because these females spend their entire lives together and because their inclusive fitness is enhanced by protecting not only their own direct offspring, but also those of their relatives.

Females who grow up and remain in their natal groups throughout their lives have an intimate knowledge of their home range (e.g., where to find water and food during low-resource seasons and drought years), which enhances their survival and their ability to "lose" newly immigrant males. Antiphonal calling (when one individual's vocalization elicits answering calls from other members of the group) is very common in capuchins. Group members typically forage in a highly dispersed pattern in the dense canopy, but commonly vocalize back and forth to one another. As well as near-distance antiphonal "contact calling," we have found that group members respond to the long distance "lost calls" of individuals who have become greatly separated from the group and are vocalizing loudly in an apparent attempt to relocate their group (Digweed, Fedigan, & Rendall, 2007). However, we have also observed that group residents may literally run away from a newly immigrant male and then fall silent and fail to answer that male's lost calls. In the long run, this does not appear to be a successful strategy to avoid a group takeover, but it can temporarily protect females and their infants from agitated and aggressive newcomer males.

Invasions of immigrant males, and takeovers that result in the ejection of prior resident males, appear to be inevitable in white-faced capuchins—sometimes occurring despite the best efforts of females to support the resident males (Perry, 1997, 2008). While females do not have much choice as to which males ultimately join their groups, we have found in some cases that the females will disperse with the former alpha male when he is ejected from the group and will travel with him into a new group (Jack & Fedigan, 2009). Although capuchins are characterized by male dispersal and female philopatry, 14% of the adult females that have resided in our main study groups have been immigrants. Immigrating females are not readily accepted into established groups, they often receive aggression from resident females, and they are never very well integrated as group members, likely because they lack the kin network that is so important for females of this species (Perry, Manson, Muniz, Gros-Luis, & Vigilant, 2008). Immigrant females usually remain on the group's periphery, occupy low dominance ranks, have low reproductive success, and often end up dispersing again. In our analysis of these immigrant females and females that emigrated or disappeared from our study groups, we found that female dispersal is much more common in years where takeovers occur than during times of group stability (Jack & Fedigan, 2009). Female dispersal is yet another (albeit costly) way in which females can exert female choice of their mates and it also demonstrates that females sometimes form relationships with males that are as strong as their alliances with their female kin.

## Female-Male Alliances and Encouragement of Multimale Groups

Female primates may also react to attempted male coercion by forming close alliances with certain males, who protect them against others ("hired guns," Cowlishaw, 1998). After newly immigrant capuchin males have settled into a group, they begin to actively protect the group from predators and defend its resources against neighboring groups. Once the aggressive, unsettled period of a takeover has calmed down, the infants sired by prior males are less and less in danger and indeed the males start to protect the young of the group. It is clearly in the interest of the females to form positive relations with these males through grooming and mating with them. Although females direct most of their affiliative behaviors to the new alpha male, they also groom, sit beside, and mate with subordinate males. We believe that female capuchins actively encourage multimale groups because groups with low ratios of adult males are at greater risk of takeovers and resultant infanticide (Fedigan & Jack, 2004). We have recently demonstrated that females in groups with higher proportions of adult males are more reproductively successful than those in groups with smaller proportions of adult males (Fedigan & Jack, 2011a). Interestingly, the same is not true for the males—their reproductive success is negatively associated with the proportion of adult males in the group. The differential effect of adult sex ratios on reproductive success may be another example of sexual conflict in that male capuchins are better served by lower numbers of males in the group whereas females experience reproductive benefits from residing in groups with sex ratios skewed toward adult males.

## Costs of These Female Adaptive Strategies

All of these female adaptive strategies to counter male-male competition and coercion involve some costs to the females. Perhaps the main one is feeding competition—by living with other females and their young as well as with multiple adult males, there is inevitable competition for access to food and water. As already mentioned, adult males commonly supplant adult females from preferred sitting/sleeping/foraging locations and food sources. In some groups, it is only the alpha male who is dominant to all the females but in others, many of the adult males are able to supplant individual females. On the other hand, coalitions of females (or of a female and a male) can evict almost any male from a feeding tree, and triadic forms of aggression are relatively common in our white-faced capuchins (Perry, Barret, & Manson, 2004)

There are also obviously costs of these female capuchin behaviors to the males of our study groups. Almost all of these patterns result in lowered ability of males to control the reproductive lives of females and they increase male levels of paternity uncertainty and their risk of caring for infants that are not their biological kin. Furthermore, along with the fact that alpha males need other males to defend their residency in groups (Fedigan & Jack, 2004), several of these female choice patterns force males to coreside in social groups and to cooperate with other adult males, which reduces their individual reproductive success (Fedigan & Jack, 2011).

## Further Male Solutions to the Problems Set by Female Reproductive and Social Strategies

Some of the patterns we observe in male primates may be interpreted as reactions to the female patterns just outlined, especially to polyandrous mating, cryptic female choice, and female encouragement of multimale groups. For example, male chimpanzees, spider monkeys, and muriquis have large testes size relative to body size (Strier, 2010) and some primate males produce copulatory plugs (parts of their ejaculate harden and block the female vaginal tract, Dixson, 1998). Large relative testes and large ejaculate size (i.e., many sperm per ejaculate) are hypothesized to be forms of sperm competition in response to cryptic female choice.

Ejaculatory plugs help a male's ejaculate to remain in a female's vaginal tract, even if she mates with a subsequent male (Birkhead & Kappeler, 2004).

Male primates may also lower some of their reproductive costs of multimale social living, by residing in groups of related males. That way, even if their individual reproductive success is negatively affected by competing with the other males of their group to sire infants, their inclusive fitness will still be strong. We hypothesize that this is accomplished in white-faced capuchins by parallel dispersal behavior in which brothers or cousins immigrate into a new group together (Jack & Fedigan, 2004a, 2004b; Perry et al., 2012). Given that a single male (the group's alpha male) sires the majority of group infants, and that females residing in groups together are closely related, natal males born during the tenure of a single alpha male will be very closely related. Parallel dispersal of these closely related males may be why subordinate capuchin males are content, for at least a few years, to reside in groups where the alpha male (who is related to them) is experiencing greater individual siring success than their own and who also supplants them regularly out of their preferred feeding and resting spots! For his part, the alpha male does not harass the subordinate males in his group when they copulate, which can be interpreted as him "ceding" reproductive opportunities to them (Clutton-Brock, 1998; Henzi, Clarke, van Schaik, Pradhan, & Barrett, 2010). In capuchins, we have found that alpha males "need" the subordinate males to help ward off takeover attempts (Fedigan & Jack, 2004) and in chacma baboons, Henzi et al. (2010) found that alpha males showed restraint against copulating at every possible opportunity, which resulted in subordinate males having more mating opportunities. They also found that those subordinate males who had mated with group females acted as extra protectors of the infants.

## Why Do Female Capuchins Live Year Round With Males?

Like most other primate species (and unlike most nonprimate mammals), capuchin males and females reside together year round. Given the conflicts that arise between the sexes, it begs the question of why females bother. Why do they put up with these rather volatile males that are capable of imposing enormous reproductive costs on them? Returning to the questions posed in the beginning of this chapter, we have shown that the apparently contradictory ("good cop/bad cop") behavior of male capuchins results in large part from their attempts to improve their reproductive success relative to other nonrelated males and to reduce ambiguity about which offspring they have actually sired—that is, to have as much control as possible over when and with whom females conceive their young. Male capuchins behave positively toward offspring likely to be their own, toward females who are likely or recent copulatory partners, and toward males who are their allies and relatives. These positive behaviors, however, change dramatically when males take up residency in a new group. It is at that time that we see them behave aggressively toward male competitors and the latter's offspring. Female capuchins respond to competitive and coercive male patterns with a variety of behaviors that maintain or increase paternity uncertainty in the males and reduce male abilities to control them. They respond to beneficial male patterns, typically exhibited by alpha males, by concentrating their conceptive mating on those males.

In the long run, female capuchins cannot keep out males who are determined to live in association with their kin-related groups. However, they can and do exact numerous concessions out of them, which are costly to the resident males—vigilance, defense of resources, multimale social groups, and protection from predators, humans, and invading males.

# Metaphors of Sexual Conflict: Winners/Losers, Dialectics and More

Because Parker (1979) used game theory to understand male and female mating strategies, he consistently referred to "winners and losers," as have many of his successors. Dawkins (1976) popularized the phrase: "battle of the sexes." However, as noted by Arnqvist and Rowe (2005), one sex does not win a conflict against the other in the way that some parasites may be said to win or lose a conflict with their hosts. That is, the average fitness of one sex in a population does not increase at the expense of the other, they are not independent. In this respect, sexual conflict is quite unlike antagonistic interactions between species (e.g., predator/prey or parasite/host interactions), where the fitness of one party (in this case, one species) can increase at the expense of the other. As succinctly said by Arnqvist and Rowe (2005, p. 221), what happens to the average fitness of one sex in a population also happens to the other.

If we insist on labeling one party as the winner and the other as the loser, then we should note that the actual "battle" for reproductive success is within each sex. A given male may exhibit a strategy that results in him having greater control over reproduction than does the female in a particular interaction (or vice versa)—but at the population level, males can only be as reproductively successful as the females. On the other hand, some females (as a result of genes, behavior, and a certain amount of serendipity) reproduce more successfully than do other females and some males reproduce more successfully than do others. Or as Gowaty (2004, p. 48) put it, although the contests over control of reproduction are between opposite sexes, the outcomes of these contests work to affect fitness variation *within* each sex.

Rather than perpetuating an anthropomorphic attribution of males as active winners and females as passive losers, researchers such as Gowaty (2004) have argued that sexual conflict is a form of dialectics, an ongoing dialogue between two parties holding different points of view and that the dialogue in this case is about who holds control over reproduction. Mulder and Rauch (2009, p. 201) defined sexually antagonistic coevolution as "a chain of adaptations and counter adaptations during the struggle over sex-specific optimality in a given conflict trait." Gowaty (1997) has argued that sexually antagonistic coevolution occurs when each sex sets up problems that the other must solve in order to survive and reproduce. This vivid metaphor is one that we prefer because it is neither male- nor female-biased. "Problem setting and solving" is reminiscent of Newton's Third Law of Motion, that every action has an equal and opposite reaction, and even resembles the Buddhist view that envisions life forms as a vast net (Indra's Net) made up of jewels at every juncture (Kabat-Zinn, Watson, Batchelow, & Claxton, 2000). Each jewel represents a life form that is connected to the others such that a change in one is reflected in the others. Indra's Net seems an apt metaphor for socially cognitive animals such as primates, who are constantly negotiating and adjusting their lives and their reproductive success through a web of other individuals, similarly engaged.

## Conclusion

Some primatologists (e.g., Snowdon, 1997; Sussman & Garber, 2004, 2007; Sussman, Garber, & Cheverud, 2005) emphasize the strong degree of cooperation found between males and females in many primate species, especially in relation to the rearing of their "joint investment," the infants. It is truly a joint investment since, as pointed out by Arnqvist and Rowe (2005), every individual has one father and one mother. Snowdon (1997) notes that male primates may often assist during the female's lactation period to enhance infant survival and thus may make considerable, sometimes comparable, parental investments to those of females. There are, of course, many benefits of social living as well as the high frequencies of affiliative behavior and low frequencies of aggressive behavior that typify most primate societies. Indeed, resident adult and subadult male capuchins seldom direct physical aggression toward the females in their groups, and capuchins spend the vast majority of their social time in affiliative interactions.

Roughgarden (2009) has argued that evolutionary biologists emphasize intra- and intersexual competition to the exclusion of recognizing the strong and widespread evidence for cooperation within and between the sexes. It is of course not possible to directly compare the importance of affiliation between the sexes to that of sexual conflict. Whether or not Roughgarden's assertion is justified, it is clear that the two main principles of sexual selection (male-male competition and female choice) need to be augmented by better consideration of the many ways in which male and female strategies conflict and coincide and by better understanding of how females and males affect, constrain, and enhance each other's lives and ability to reproduce. It is also clear that both females and males play active roles in these interactions and adaptations.

## Acknowledgments

We thank the Costa Rican National Park Service for permission to work in SRNP from 1983 to 1989 and the administrators of the Área de Conservación Guanacaste (especially Roger Blanco Segura) for allowing us to continue research in the park through the present day. Many researchers (both graduate students and assistants) have contributed to the long-term database on the Santa Rosa monkeys and we are grateful to all of them. We are also thankful to John Addicott, who developed the Santa Rosa database, and Greg Bridgett, who maintains it. LMF's research is supported by NSERC (the Natural Sciences and Engineering Research Council of Canada) and the Canada Research Chairs Program. KMJ's research is supported by grants from Tulane University's Research Enhancement Fund, the Stone Center for Latin American Studies, and the Newcomb Institute. We also thank the Zemurray Foundation for support of our project. Research protocols reported in this paper complied with all institutional and government regulations regarding ethical treatment of our study subjects.

## References

Arnqvist, G., & Rowe, L. (2005). *Sexual conflict*. Princeton, NJ: Princeton University Press.
Bateman, A. J. (1948). Intrasexual selection in *Drosophila*. *Heredity, 2*, 349–368.
Bergstrom, M. L., & Fedigan, L. M. (2010). Dominance among female white-faced capuchin monkeys (*Cebus capucinus*): Hierarchical linearity, nepotism, strength, and stability. *Behaviour, 147*, 899–931.
Birkhead, T. R., & Kappeler, P. M. (2004). Post-copulatory sexual selection in birds and primates. In P. Kappeler & C. P. van Schaik (Eds.), *Sexual selection in primates: New and comparative perspectives* (pp. 151–171). Cambridge, UK: Cambridge University Press.
Carnegie, S. D. (2011). *Reproductive behaviour and endocrinology of female white-faced capuchins (Cebus capucinus)*. Doctoral dissertation, University of Calgary.
Carnegie, S. D., Fedigan, L. M., & Melin, A. D. (2011). Reproductive seasonality in female capuchins (*Cebus capucinus*) in Santa Rosa (Área de Conservación Guanacaste), Costa Rica. *International Journal of Primatology, 32*, 1076–1090.
Carnegie, S. D., Fedigan, L. M., & Ziegler, T. (2005). Behavioral indicators of ovarian phase in white-faced capuchins (*Cebus capucinus*). *American Journal of Primatology, 67*, 51–68.
Carnegie, S. D., Fedigan, L. M., & Ziegler, T. (2006). Post-conceptive mating in white-faced capuchins, *Cebus capucinus*: Hormonal and sociosexual patterns of cycling, noncycling, and pregnant females. In A. Estrada, P. Garber, M. Pavelka, & L. Luecke (Eds.), *New perspectives in the study of Mesoamerican primates: Distribution, ecology, behavior, and conservation* (pp. 387–409). New York: Springer.
Carnegie, S. D., Fedigan, L. M., & Ziegler, T. (2011). Social and environmental factors affecting fecal glucocorticoids in wild, female white-faced capuchins (*Cebus capucinus*). *American Journal of Primatology, 73*, 1–9.

Chapman, T. G., Arnqvist, J. B., & Rowe, L. (2003). Sexual conflict. *Trends in Ecology and Evolution, 18,* 41–47.

Clarke, P., Pradhan, G., & van Schaik, C. (2009). Intersexual conflict in primates: Infanticide, paternity allocation, and the role of coercion. In M. N. Muller & R. W. Wrangham (Eds.), *Sexual coercion in primates and humans: An evolutionary perspective on male aggression against females* (pp. 42–77). Cambridge, MA: Harvard University Press.

Clutton-Brock, T. H. (1998). Reproductive skew, concessions, and limited control. *Trends in Ecology and Evolution, 13,* 288–292.

Clutton-Brock, T. H. (2007). Sexual selection in males and females. *Science, 318,* 1882–1885.

Clutton-Brock, T. H., & Parker, G. A. (1995). Sexual coercion in animal societies. *Animal Behaviour, 49,* 1345–1365.

Cowlishaw, G. (1998). The role of vigilance in the survival and reproductive strategies of desert baboons. *Behaviour, 135,* 431–442.

Darwin, C. (1871). *The descent of man in relation to sex.* London: John Murray.

Dawkins, R. (1976). *The selfish gene.* Oxford, UK: Oxford University Press.

Dawkins, R., & Carlisle, T. R. (1976). Parental investment, mate desertion, and a fallacy. *Nature, 262,* 131–133.

Dawkins, R., & Krebs, J. R. (1979). Arms races between and within species. *Proceedings of the Royal Society London B, 205,* 489–511.

Dewsbury, D. (2005). The Darwin-Bateman paradigm in historical context. *Journal of Integrative and Comparative Biology, 45,* 831–837.

Digweed, S. M., Fedigan, L. M., & Rendall, D. (2007). Who cares who calls: Selective responses to the lost calls of socially dominant group members in the white-faced capuchin. *American Journal of Primatology, 69,* 829–835.

Dixson, A. F. (1998). *Primate sexuality.* New York: Oxford University Press.

Eberhard, W. G. (1996). *Female control: Sexual selection by cryptic female choice.* Princeton, NJ: Princeton University Press.

Fausto-Sterling, A. (1997). Feminism and behavioral evolution: A taxonomy. In P. A. Gowaty (Ed.), *Feminism and evolutionary biology: Boundaries, intersections and frontiers* (pp. 42–60). New York: Chapman & Hall.

Fedigan, L. M. (2003). The impact of male takeovers on infant deaths, births, and conceptions in *Cebus capucinus* at Santa Rosa, Costa Rica. *International Journal of Primatology, 24,* 723–741.

Fedigan, L. M., & Jack, K. M. (2004). The demographic and reproductive context of male replacements in *Cebus capucinus. Behaviour, 141,* 755–775.

Fedigan, L. M., & Jack, K. M. (2011). Two girls for every boy: The effects of group size and composition on the reproductive success of male and female white-faced capuchins. *American Journal of Physical Anthropology, 144,* 317–326.

Fedigan, L. M., & Jack, K. M. (2012). Tracking neotropical monkeys in Santa Rosa: Long-term lessons from a regenerating Costa Rican dry forest. In P. Kappeler & D. Watts (Eds.), *Long-term field studies of primates* (pp. 165–184). Heidelberg, Germany: Springer.

Fedigan, L. M., Carnegie, S. D., & Jack, K. M. (2008). Predictors of reproductive success in female white-faced capuchins (*Cebus capucinus*). *American Journal of Physical Anthropology, 137,* 82–90.

Fragaszy, D. M., Visalberghi, E., & Fedigan, L.M. (2004). *The complete capuchin: The biology of the genus Cebus.* Cambridge, UK: Cambridge University Press.

Gould, L., Fedigan, L. M., & Rose, L. M. (1997). Why be vigilant? The case of the alpha animal. *International Journal of Primatology, 18,* 401–414.

Gowaty, P. A. (1982). Sexual terms in sociobiology: Emotionally evocative and, paradoxically, jargon. *Animal Behaviour, 30,* 630–631.

Gowaty, P. A. (1997). Sexual dialectics, sexual selection, and variation in reproductive behavior. In P.A. Gowaty (Ed.), *Feminism and evolutionary biology: Boundaries, intersections, and frontiers* (pp. 351–384). New York: Chapman & Hall.

Gowaty, P. A. (2004). Sex roles, contests for control of reproduction, and sexual selection. In P. Kappeler & C. van Schaik (Eds.), *Sexual selection in primates: New and comparative perspectives* (pp. 37–54). Cambridge, UK: Cambridge University Press.

Green, K. K., & Madjidian, J. A. (2011). Active males, reactive females: Stereotypic sex roles in sexual conflict research? *Animal Behaviour, 81*, 901–907.

Gros-Louis, J., Perry, S., & Manson, J. (2003). Violent coalitionary attacks and intraspecific killing in wild, white-faced capuchins (*Cebus capucinus*). *Primates, 44*, 341–346.

Hakeem, A., Sandoval, R. G., Jones, M., & Allman, J. (1996). Brain and life span in primates. In J. E. Birren & K. W. Schaie (Eds.), *Handbook of the psychology of aging* (4th ed., pp. 78–104). San Diego, CA: Academic Press.

Henzi, S. P., Clarke, P. M. R., van Schaik, C. P., Pradhan, G. R., & Barrett, L. (2010). Infanticide and reproductive restraint in a polygynous social mammal. *Proceedings of the National Academy of Sciences, 107*, 2130–2135.

Hrdy, S. B. (1974). Male-male competition and infanticide among the Langurs (*Presbytis entellus*) of Abu, Rajasthan. *Folia primatologica, 22*, 19–58.

Hrdy, S. B. (1977). Infanticide as a primate strategy. *American Scientist, 65*, 40–49.

Hrdy, S. B. (1979). Infanticide among animals: A review, classification, and the implications for the reproductive strategies of females. *Ethology and Sociobiology, 1*, 13–40.

Hrdy, S. B. (1986). Empathy, polyandry, and the myth of the "coy" female. In R. Bleier (Ed.), *Feminist approaches to science* (pp. 119–146). New York: Pergamon.

Izar, P., Stone, A., Carnegie, S., & Nakai, E. S. (2009). Sexual selection, female choice, and mating systems. In P. A. Garber, A. Estrada, J. C. Bicca-Marques, E. Heymann, & K. B. Strier (Eds.), *South American primates: Comparative perspectives in the study of behavior, ecology, and conservation* (pp. 157–189). New York: Springer.

Jack, K. M. (2001). Effect of male emigration on the vigilance behavior or coresident males in white-faced capuchins (*Cebus capucinus*). *International Journal of Primatology, 22*, 715–732.

Jack, K. M., & Fedigan, L. M. (2004a). Male dispersal patterns in white-faced capuchins, *Cebus capucinus*: Part 1. Patterns and causes of natal emigration. *Animal Behaviour, 67*, 761–769.

Jack, K. M., & Fedigan, L. M. (2004b). Male dispersal patterns in white-faced capuchins, *Cebus capucinus*: Part 2. Patterns and causes of secondary dispersal. *Animal Behaviour, 67*, 771–782.

Jack, K. M., & Fedigan, L. M. (2006). Why be alpha male? Dominance and reproductive success in wild white-faced capuchins (*Cebus capucinus*). In A. Estrada, P. Garber, M. Pavelka, & L. Luecke (Eds.), *New perspectives in the study of Mesoamerican primates: Distribution, ecology, behavior, and conservation* (pp. 367–386). New York: Springer Verlag.

Jack, K. M., & Fedigan, L. M. (2009). Female dispersal in a female-philopatric species, *Cebus capucinus. Behaviour, 146*, 471–497.

Jack, K. M., Sheller, C., & Fedigan, L. M. (2011). Social factors influencing natal dispersal in male white-faced capuchins (*Cebus capucinus*). *American Journal of Primatology, 73*, 1–7 (Early view).

Janson, C. H. (1984). Female choice and mating system of the brown capuchin monkey, *Cebus apella* (Primates: Cebidae). *Zeitschrift fur Tierpsychologie, 65*, 177–200.

Janson, C. H., Baldovino, M. C., & Di Bitetti, M. (2011). The group life cycle and demography of Brown Capuchin monkeys (*Cebus apella nigritus*) in Iguazu National Park. In P. Kappeler & D. Watts (Eds.), *Long-term field studies of primates*. Heidelberg, Germany: Springer.

Kabat-Zinn, J., Watson, G., Batchelow, S., & Claxton, G. (2000). *Indra's net at work: The mainstreaming of dharma practice in society*. Newburyport, MA: Weiser Press.

Kappeler, P. M., & van Schaik, C. P. (2004). Sexual selection in primates: Review and selective preview. In P. Kappeler & C. van Schaik (Eds.), *Sexual selection in primates: New and comparative perspectives* (pp. 3–23). Cambridge, UK: Cambridge University Press.

Kokko, H., & Jennions, M. D. (2008a). Parental investment, sexual selection, and sex ratios. *Journal of Evolutionary Biology, 21*, 919–948.

Kokko, H., & Jennions, M. D. (2008b). Sexual conflict: The battle of the sexes reversed. *Current Biology, 18*, R121-R123.

McCabe, G. M., & Fedigan, L. M. (2007). Effects of reproductive status on energy intake, ingestion rates, and dietary composition of female white-faced capuchins (*Cebus capucinus*) at Santa Rosa, Costa Rica. *International Journal of Primatology, 28*, 837–851.

MacKinnon, K. C. (2002). *Social development of wild white-faced capuchin monkeys (Cebus capucinus) in Costa Rica: An examination of social interactions between immatures and adult males*. Doctoral dissertation, University of California, Berkeley.

Manson, J. H., Perry, S., & Parish, A. (1997). Non-conceptive sexual behavior in bonobos and capuchins. *International Journal of Primatology, 18*, 767–786.

Martin, E. (2008). The egg and the sperm: How science has constructed a romance based on stereotypical male-female roles. *Signs, 16*, 485–501.

Mulder, M. B., & Rauch, K. L. (2009). Sexual conflict in humans: Variations and solutions. *Evolutionary Anthropology, 18*, 201–214.

Muller, M. N., & Wrangham, R. W. (2009). *Sexual coercion in primates and humans: An evolutionary perspective on male aggression against females*. Cambridge, MA: Harvard University Press.

Muniz, L., Perry, S., Manson, J. H., Gilkenson, H., Gros-Louis, J., & Vigilant, L. (2010). Male dominance and reproductive success in wild white-faced capuchins (*Cebus capucinus*) at Lomas Barbudal, Costa Rica. *American Journal of Primatology, 72*, 1118–1130.

Palombit, R. (2010). Conflict and bonding between the sexes. In P. M. Kappeler & J. B. Silk (Eds.), *Mind the gap* (pp. 53–83). Berlin: Springer Verlag.

Parker, G. A. (1979). Sexual selection and sexual conflict. In M. S. Blum & N. A. Blum (Eds.), *Sexual selection and reproductive competition in insects* (pp. 123–166). New York: Academic Press.

Perry, S. (1997). Male-female social relationships in wild white-faced capuchins (*Cebus capucinus*). *Behaviour, 134*, 477–510.

Perry, S. (1998a). Male-male social relationships in wild white-faced capuchins, *Cebus capucinus*. *Behaviour, 135*, 139–172.

Perry, S. (1998b). A case report of a male rank reversal in a group of wild white-faced capuchins. *Primates, 39*, 51–70.

Perry, S. (2008). *Manipulative monkeys: The capuchins of Lomas Barbudal*. Cambridge, MA: Harvard University Press.

Perry, S., Barret, H. C., & Manson, J. H. (2004). White-faced capuchin monkeys show triadic awareness in their choice of allies. *Animal Behaviour, 67*, 165–170.

Perry, S., Godoy, I., & Lammers, W. (2012). The Lomas Barbudal monkey project: Two decades of research on *Cebus capucinus*. In P. Kappeler & D. Watts (Eds.), *Long-term field studies of primates* (pp. 141–163). Heidelberg, Germany: Springer.

Perry, S., Manson, J. H., Muniz, L., Gros-Luis, J., & Vigilant, L. (2008). Kin-biased social behavior in wild adult female white-faced capuchins, *Cebus capucinus*. *Animal Behaviour, 76*, 187–199.

Poulin, R. (1996). Sexual inequalities in helminth infections: A cost of being a male? *American Naturalist, 147*, 287–295.

Rose, L. M. (1994). Benefits and costs of resident males to females in white-faced capuchins, *Cebus capucinus*. *American Journal of Primatology, 32*, 235–248.

Rose, L. M., & Fedigan, L. M. (1995). Vigilance in white-faced capuchins, *Cebus capucinus*, in Costa Rica. *Animal Behaviour, 49*, 63–70.

Roughgarden, J. (2009). *The genial gene: Deconstructing Darwinian selfishness*. Berkeley: University of California Press.

Roughgarden, J., & Akçay, E. (2010). Do we need a sexual selection 2.0? *Animal Behaviour, 79*, E1–E4.

Schalk, G., & Forbes, M. R. (1997). Male biases in parasitism of mammals: Effects of study type, host age, and parasite taxon. *Oikos, 78*, 67–74.

Schoof, V. A. M., & Jack, K. (2009). Rank-based differences in fecal androgen and cortisol levels in male white-faced capuchins, *Cebus capucinus*, in the Santa Rosa Sector, Área de Conservación Guanacaste, Costa Rica. *American Journal of Primatology, 71*(Suppl. 1), 76.

Schwensow, N., Eberle, M., & Sommer, S. (2008). Compatibility counts: MHC-associated mate choice in a wild promiscuous primate. *Proceedings of the Royal Society B: Biological Sciences, 275*, 555–564.

Smuts, B. B., & Smuts, R. W. (1993). Male aggression and sexual coercion of females in nonhuman primates and other mammals: Evidence and theoretical implications. *Advances in the Study of Behavior, 22,* 1–63.

Snowdon, C. C. (1997). The "nature" of sex differences: Myths of male and female. In P. A. Gowaty (Ed.), *Feminism and evolutionary biology* (pp. 276–293). New York: Chapman and Hall.

Snyder, B. F., & Gowaty, P. A. (2007). A reappraisal of Bateman's classic study of intrasexual selection. *Evolution, 61,* 2457–2468.

Strier, K. B. (2010). *Primate behavioral ecology* (4th ed.). Boston: Pearson.

Stumpf, R. M., Martinez-Mota, R., Milich, K. M., Righini, N., & Shattuck, M. R. (2011). Sexual conflict in primates. *Evolutionary Anthropology, 20,* 62–75.

Sussman, R. W., & Garber, P. A. (2004). Rethinking sociality: Cooperation and aggression among primates. In R. W. Sussman (Ed.), *The origin and nature of sociality* (pp. 161–190). New York: Aldine.

Sussman, R. W., & Garber, P. A. (2007). Cooperation and competition in primate societies. In C. J. Campbell, A. Fuentes, K. C. MacKinnon, M. Panger, & S. K. Bearder (Eds.), *Primates in perspective* (pp. 636–651). New York: Oxford University Press.

Sussman, R. W., Garber, P. A., & Cheverud, J. M. (2005). Importance of cooperation and affiliation in the evolution of primate society. *American Journal of Physical Anthropology, 128,* 84–97.

Tang-Martinez, Z., & Ryder, B. T. (2005). The problem with paradigms: Bateman's world view as a case study. *Journal of Integrative and Comparative Biology, 45,* 821–830.

Thornhill, R. (1983). Cryptic female choice and its implications in the scorpionfly, *Harpobittacus nigriceps. American Naturalist, 122,* 765–788.

Trillmich, F. (2010). Parental care: Adjustments to conflict and cooperation. In P. Kappeler (Ed.), *Animal behavior: Evolution and mechanisms* (pp. 267–298). Heidelberg, Germany: Springer.

Trivers, R. L. (1972). Parental investment and sexual selection. In B. Campbell (Ed.), *Sexual selection and the descent of man* (pp. 136–179). Chicago: Aldine.

Van Schaik, C. P., Hodges, K., & Nunn, C. L. (2000). Paternity confusion and the ovarian cycle of female primates. In C. P. van Schaik & C. Janson (Eds.), *Infanticide by males and its implications* (pp. 361–387) Cambridge, UK: Cambridge University Press.

Watson-Capps, J. J. (2009). Evolution of sexual coercion with respect to sexual selection and sexual conflict theory. In M. N. Muller & R. W. Wrangham (Eds.), *Sexual coercion in primates and humans: An evolutionary perspective on male aggression against females* (pp. 22–41). Cambridge, MA: Harvard University Press.

Williams G. C. (1966). *Adaptation and natural selection.* Princeton, NJ: Princeton University Press.

# 15

# The Importance of Female Choice

*Evolutionary Perspectives on Constraints, Expressions, and Variations in Female Mating Strategies*

DAVID A. FREDERICK, TANIA A. REYNOLDS, AND MARYANNE L. FISHER

## Introduction

All animals face two major challenges. The first challenge is simply to survive to an age at which they can produce offspring. If animals are killed by predators or succumb to failing internal organs before developing the ability to reproduce, their genes are lost forever. Animals that spend all of their energy on maintaining their bodies and avoiding predators, however, face a similar fate: the end of their genetic lines. Thus, the second challenge for individuals is to find ways to successfully pass on their genes. Reproduction is the engine that drives evolution. Genes that produce traits, tactics, and behaviors that promote reproduction, even at the expense of long-term survival, can carry forward to future generations.

The solutions to the challenge of reproduction vary dramatically across species, and these solutions often differ between females and males. Honey bees and bowerbirds serve as useful examples of two extremely different mating systems. Among honey bees, the queen bee launches into a mating flight and is chased by drone males. When the male catches up to her and they copulate, his genitals explode, snapping off inside the queen. The snapped off penis acts as a genital plug to prevent other males from fertilizing the queen (for a review of insect sexual behaviors, see Zuk, 2011). Male bowerbirds, on the other hand, attempt to impress females with their skills at building nests. These nests, called bowers, are complex structures shaped like small huts. The males decorate the bowers with flowers, feathers, stones, and even small bits of plastic and glass if found. They may steal decorations from other male bowers to put the finishing touches on their structures. The females then inspect the bowers carefully and are more likely to mate with males with more impressive bowers (Borgia, 1985).

There can also be considerable variation in mating behaviors *within each sex*. Not all females of a species display the same mating preferences or behaviors. There can also be considerable variation in preferences and choices of a given female over time and across different situations. Rather than being coy and passive, females may display a wide array of preferences and behaviors, from nearly iron-clad monogamy to seeking matings with many males. Although the importance of female choice in shaping sex differences in behavior and morphology was historically underappreciated, female preferences and behaviors can substantially shape male behaviors, male traits, and entire mating systems.

In writing this chapter, we have three overarching goals. The first is to briefly introduce the reader to some of the influential perspectives on sexual selection and female mate choice in evolutionary biology over the past few decades, with a focus on parental investment theory (Trivers, 1972). The second goal is to then present two influential theories in evolutionary psychology that have been applied to understand variations in women's mating preferences and choices: sexual strategies theory (Buss & Schmitt, 1993) and strategic pluralism theory (Gangestad & Simpson, 2000).

Although the importance of female choice has gained widespread acceptance in the biological sciences (see Milam, 2010, for a review), the influence that female choice has on mating systems can be limited by many factors (Andersson, 1994). For example, it has been proposed that active choices by women played a relatively unimportant role in shaping the human mating system across evolutionary history because women's parents often maintained firm control over reproductive decision-making (Apostolou, 2007). Moreover, some scholars argue that male-male competition, rather than female choice, shaped many male traits (e.g., Puts, 2010). Readers might infer that this latter view harkens back to earlier days of evolutionary biology, where "very few scientists framed their research in terms of Darwinian sexual selection, and when they talked about courtship behavior, their attention was focused on male-male competition" (Milam, 2010, p. 167). However, we agree with Puts (2010) that in the recent human literature there has been an overemphasis on contexts where individuals are relatively free to express their mate preferences. As Puts suggests, the shift towards studying mate choice has sometimes come at the expense of studying the influence of intrasexual competition in humans. Theories relating to the development of male traits have sometimes underestimated the role of male-male competition in their explanations for these traits. The advent of patriarchal systems and male control over sexuality likely constrained women's ability to exercise free choice of mates across human evolutionary history (Smuts, 1995). The third goal of this chapter is to examine and critique these claims regarding the factors that limit female choice, and to show how women exercise choice even in societies where parents and men attempt to severely restrict women's mate choice.

# Parental Investment Theory and the Power of Female Choice in the Animal Kingdom

## Eager Males and Coy, Discriminating Females?

According to the theory of *natural selection*, individuals with certain traits are more likely to survive than individuals without these traits. When heritable genetic predispositions are partly or completely responsible for the development of these traits, they can be passed on from parent to offspring. In his text *On the Origin of Species by Means of Natural Selection*, Charles Darwin (1859) puzzled over the existence of sex differences in behavior and morphology. If all individuals are under the same selective pressures to survive and reproduce, why would differences emerge?

He reasoned that in addition to the process of natural selection, the process of *sexual selection* shaped the evolution of traits that function to maximize reproductive success rather than survival. In his view, however, males competed with each other to display these traits whereas females did not. He wrote, "This depends, not on a struggle for existence, but on a struggle between males for possession of females: the result is not death to the unsuccessful competitor, but few or no offspring" (Darwin, 1859; p. 136). Through the process of *intrasexual selection*, males competed with other males for access to mates, developing traits that made them more effective in deterring, defeating, or intimidating other males. *Intrasexual competition* can involve situations in which males fight in order to gain a higher rank in the dominance hierarchy. Dominant males may effectively exclude subordinate males from the mating pool through intimidation and fights. In extreme cases, females can only mate with the most dominant males, because these males are the only ones available to mate with. Female choice becomes nonexistent.

Through the process of *intersexual selection*, males of some species developed traits that are attractive to members of the other sex, even when these traits hamper survival. Whereas males were described as active competitors, females were described as "less eager" to engage in sex than the male; and Darwin notes that, "as the illustrious Hunter long ago observed, she 'requires to be courted'; she is coy, and may often be seen as endeavoring for a long time to escape from the male" (Darwin, 1859; p. 273). In this view, females had to develop a discerning sense to appreciate visual, auditory, and olfactory beauty, and males had to develop the capacity to compete in these arenas. In *The Descent of Man*, Darwin (1871) proposed that these different selection pressures lead men to develop superior physical and mental capacities in order to effectively compete for mates, whereas the rather passive selection of mates by females did not necessitate the evolution of strong female bodies or minds (for a review, see Milam, 2010).

Darwin's observations of sex differences in mating strategies were later supported by Bateman (1948). Bateman proposed that the coyness of females produces greater variance among males than females in terms of reproductive success: Some males have many mates and other males have none, whereas females tend to differ little from each other. For example, in a study of fruit flies, he reported that males had more variance in their number of offspring than did females. Borrowing language from Charles Darwin, he attributed this observed difference to the "undiscriminating eagerness in males and discriminating passivity in females." Although later research showed that his results failed to establish this claim convincingly (Gowaty, Kim, & Anderson, in press; Gowaty, Steinichen, & Anderson, 2003; Tang-Martinez & Ryder, 2005) and more generally it is now recognized that intrasexual competition for mates can be intense among females (Rosvall, 2011), his framework laid the groundwork for scientists to endorse the myth of the passive and coy female.

Noted evolutionary theorist George Williams (1966) later summarized these proposed differences between females and males, which lead to sex differences in mate preferences and mating behaviors. Williams (1966, pp. 183–185) stated:

> It is commonly observed that males have a greater readiness for reproduction than females. This is understandable as a consequence of the greater physiological sacrifice that is made by females for the production of each surviving offspring. A male mammal's essential role may end with copulation, which involves a negligible expenditure of energy and materials on his part, and only a momentary lapse of attention from matters of direct concern to his safety and well-being. The situation is markedly different for the female, for which copulation may mean a commitment to a prolonged burden, in both the mechanical and physiological sense, and its many attendant stresses and dangers. Consequently, the male having little to lose in his primary reproductive role, shows an aggressive and immediate willingness to mate with as many females as may be available. If he undertakes this reproductive role and fails, he has lost very little. If he succeeds, he can be just as successful for a minor effort as a female could be only after a major somatic sacrifice. Failure for a female mammal may mean weeks or months of wasted time. The mechanical and nutritional burden of pregnancy may mean increased vulnerability to predators, decreased disease resistance, and other dangers for a long time. Even if she successfully endures these stresses and hazards she can still fail completely if her litter is lost before weaning. Once she starts on her reproductive role she commits herself to a certain high minimum of reproductive effort. Natural selection should regulate her reproductive behavior in such a way that she will assume the burdens of reproduction only when the probability of success is at some peak value that is not likely to be exceeded.
>
> The traditional coyness of the female is thus easily attributed to adaptive mechanisms by which she can discriminate the ideal moment and circumstances for assuming the burdens of motherhood...

The greater promiscuity of the male and greater caution of the female is found in animals generally.

The emergence of these perspectives was seized upon by Trivers (1972), who coalesced them into the highly influential parental investment theory.

## Parental Investment Theory

*Parental investment* is the time, energy, and resources that parents allocate to offspring, which then reduces their ability to invest in any other offspring. Trivers (1972) proposed that the existence of sex differences in parental investment leads to sex differences in mating behavior. In general, when one sex invests more in an individual offspring, that sex is thought to be more selective when choosing a mate.

One key difference between females and males of many species is the physiologically *obligatory costs of reproduction*. For males, costs of reproduction are highly variable. The minimum cost for a male mammal is potentially as low as a few seconds or minutes of sexual intercourse. In mammals, the possibility of an extremely low cost reproductive act always exists for males and never exists for females. Mammalian reproduction requires pregnancy and lactation for females, setting a high obligatory minimum investment in offspring. For example, a woman's investment begins with 40 weeks of pregnancy in which caloric needs are elevated by 8–10% (Dufour & Sauther, 2002). Pregnancy is followed by a period of lactation, lasting about 2.5 years in hunter-gatherers (Kaplan, Hill, Lancaster, & Hurtado, 2000), in which caloric needs are elevated by 26% (Dufour & Sauther, 2002). According to parental investment theory, males can afford to be less choosy than females because their act may pose minimal cost. The costs are usually more than minimal, however, and can include care by males of offspring. The proposed overall higher costs of reproduction for females than for males may lead females to be more selective in whom they choose as mates.

A second noteworthy difference between females and males is their *reproductive potential*, particularly among mammals. For females, the number of offspring that can be produced is limited by life history factors such as gestational length and length of time between births. For males, the number of offspring that can be produced and live to the age of reproduction is limited by access to females and the extent to which offspring require male care to survive. Thus, according to this logic, there is greater incentive for males to seek out multiple partners in order to maximize the number of offspring produced, particularly for species where male caretaking of offspring is unnecessary or results in fewer surviving offspring than a promiscuous strategy.

A third important distinction between female and male mammals is the *internal gestation of offspring*. Females always have *maternal certainty*, meaning that they can be sure that the offspring they give birth to is genetically related to them. Males, on the other hand, always face *paternal uncertainty*. They can never be entirely confident that the offspring they are raising is genetically related to them because they can never be sure that they were the only male to have intercourse with their female partner.

This theory then allows one to hypothesize that behavioral patterns, psychological predispositions, and physical structures evolved in response to the specific challenges each sex faced. The choosiness of females forces males to engage in intense intrasexual competition. Males compete with each other to develop traits that are attractive to females or that enable them to successfully bully other males. For example, males in some species have evolved physiological traits such as horns or large body sizes that enable them to acquire desirable territories and resources, as well as potentially enabling the use of force to prevent competitor males from mating with a preferred female. Males can often produce offspring at a higher rate than females (number of offspring in a given unit of time), perhaps favoring the evolution of preferences for seeking multiple mates (Clutton-Brock & Parker, 1992). Overall, from Darwin until the 1970s, this vision of males as eager and aggressive and females as passive and coy dominated the early work on sexual selection and female choice.

## Eager Females and Coy, Discriminating Males?

Females across many species, however, are anything but coy. In her cheeky take on animal sexual behavior, Olivia Judson (2003) dons the persona of Dr. Tatiana, a sex advice columnist for the forlorn, curious, and insecure members of the animal kingdom. Many of her readers express concern regarding the seemingly "promiscuous" behavior of females:

> Dear Dr. Tatiana,
> I'd prefer to keep my identity secret, since I am writing to you not about me or my species but about my noisy neighbors—a group of chimpanzees. When those girls come into heat, it's enough to make a harlot blush. Yesterday I saw a girl screw eight different fellows in fifteen minutes. Another time I saw one swing between seven fellows, going at it 84 times in eight days. Why are they such sluts?

Observations of highly *proceptive* behavior by female primates—initiating sexual behavior with multiple males—directly challenged traditional views of female sexual motivations in the field of primatology, and even in popular culture. Hrdy (1977, 1981) provided some of the first challenges to the conclusions drawn from parental investment theory. Her accounts of sexual behavior among Hanuman langur monkeys revealed sexually ardent behavior by females, who would mate with multiple males. Hrdy proposed that this female promiscuity had adaptive benefits for females because it created *paternity confusion*, so that males would not know which infants were genetically related to them. This paternity confusion would be important among langurs because the males in this species routinely engage in infanticide, killing off the infants of rival males when joining a troop of new females. Behaviors that deter infanticide would be highly advantageous, because infanticide represents a loss of considerable energy, time, and resources that was invested by females in their offspring. Thus, if males perceived a possibility of genetic relatedness, they might be less likely to engage in infanticide, and the females would not lose their investment.

The strongly held view that females were passive and coy began to fall to the wayside. Primatologists discovered that the social partner of a female was not necessarily the father of her offspring, which called into question prior work on mate selection and extrapair copulations. The males involved in these extrapair sexual relationships were actively sought out by females (Fedigan, 1992). Thus, the role of female choice, as opposed to male competition or coercion, has been a subject of debate in both the empirical and theoretical literature on extrapair mating (Arnqvist & Kirkpatrick, 2005; Griffith, 2007; Griffith, Owens, & Thuman, 2002; Westneat & Stewart, 2003), but it is clear that females of many species seek out opportunities to mate with some males over others.

It is not the case that females are choosy and males are indiscriminate in their mating, although it is true that the minimum obligatory costs to reproduction are higher for females than males. Less often discussed, however, is the fact that males may face very high costs if they are required to allocate energy, time, and resources prior to conception. These costs can include energy expended while seeking mates, securing the necessary territories to attract mates, competing with other males for limited resources, guarding resources, and producing sperm. Males simply cannot mate indiscriminately because doing so may result in a waste of their energy. Greater choosiness by females induces males to engage in costly displays, which in turn may limit the reproductive potential of males by decreasing the energy they would otherwise dedicate toward finding alternative mates. In this view, females exert substantial influence over the mating system by systematically choosing some males over others.

The implication of parental investment theory is that there are key differences (e.g., obligatory costs, reproductive potential, and internal gestation) between female and male mammals that may influence females to be choosier than males on average. There can be, however, incentives for both sexes to be choosy, just as there are varying reasons why one might engage in short-term mating versus long-term pair bonds, which we review later in the chapter. The exact balance of these incentives depends on a wide variety of factors, such as the costs of bearing offspring, fragility of offspring, the potential reproductive benefits, and the relative reproductive potential of females and males given the local ecological circumstances. Parental investment theory falls short of capturing all of these nuances; the differences in obligatory costs and reproductive potential between the sexes are just two of the many factors that potentially influence the relative sex differences and similarities that lead to distinct sexual preferences and choices.

# What Are Females Choosy About?

Females can seek direct and indirect benefits from their mates. When researchers speak of selection for *direct benefits*, they generally are referring to the idea that females choose a mate because he possesses a trait that directly increases her health, survival, or lifetime reproductive output. This can include selection of males who are more fertile, provide superior resources, offer more parental care, or otherwise reduce females reproductive costs (Kokko, Brooks, Jennions, & Morley, 2003). Kirkpatrick and Ryan (1991) specify some of the forms of direct selection, including choosing a male because he provides resources, because the male has high sperm fertility, and because choosing the male reduces the costs of searching for other potential mates. Further, parental ability may also be one such trait in species where males provide care to offspring (Goodenough, McGuire, & Wallace, 2001). This form of selection simply suggests that a male will be chosen because of the tangible benefits he can immediately provide the female, regardless of what kind of genes the male will pass on to offspring. This form of selection has been rather uncontroversial, because it is easy to see how females directly benefit by mating with males who provide resources such as food and protection to their mates.

In contrast, *indirect benefits* are conferred to the offspring of the females through genetic inheritance. Males with genes that promote robust or attractive bodies will produce offspring who are more likely to inherit these genes and therefore be more likely to develop robust or attractive bodies. Several types of indirect selection have been identified. Historically, two of these forms have been pitted against each other: Runaway selection and good-genes selection. Recent evidence, however, suggests that these two forms of selection are not as different as was once thought.

## Runaway Selection

*Runaway selection* occurs when a female preference and a male trait evolve together (Fisher, 1930). It has typically been claimed that this trait may be "arbitrary"— that these traits don't necessarily signal anything about the general quality or condition of the individuals. For example, a gene might predispose males to develop orange spots and predispose females to prefer orange spots. Males who display brighter and brighter orange markings then become even more prevalent in future generations, producing stronger and stronger attractions by females. These traits, however, can directly reduce the likelihood that a male will survive (e.g., predators will find him easier to spot). This runaway selection process is also referred to as the *sexy sons hypothesis*: females who mate with males with sexy traits (e.g., orange markings) will produce sons with sexy traits. In this way, females who mate with these males are receiving a strong indirect benefit because their sons will go on to attract many females, improving the female's genetic representation in future generations (Fisher, 1930; Goodenough, McGuire, & Wallace, 2001; Hall, Kirkpatrick, & West, 2000; Kirkpatrick, 1989; Kirkpatrick & Barton, 1997; Kokko, Brooks, McNamara, & Houston, 2002).

## Markers of Heritable Fitness

In contrast to runaway selection, females may choose males with certain traits and behaviors that indicate a male is in robust condition. For example, males with larger weapons, more attractive features, or higher energy levels may possess genes that contribute to the creation of these traits. The physical traits and behavioral patterns that are associated with these genetic predispositions are sometimes called "indicators of good genes." We instead recommend calling these traits *"markers or indicators of heritable fitness."* The term "good genes" (and the implied converse, "bad genes") carries with it evaluative connotations that may be misinterpreted. Males who are better able to display these markers of heritable fitness may be preferred as mates, especially if the female is seeking indirect benefit with limited outlook toward any future paternal investment.

Women might improve their reproductive success by mating with men whose offspring may inherit genes predisposing the development of robust bodies. This is not a surefire strategy of course: due to recombination of genetic material during meiosis and the unique combination of genes created when two individuals reproduce, offspring may not develop these traits to the same extent as their parents. Although this form of female choice was historically contrasted with runaway selection, Kokko et al. (2002) point out that both forms of selection can be placed along the same continuum. Kokko et al. reason that as runaway selection for a trait occurs in a population, only males with certain advantageous qualities will be able to produce the most extravagant examples of these traits. Runaway selection will ultimately lead to preferences for males who are signaling good genes through the production of these extravagant traits. Preferences for good genes traits likely start in the same manner that preferences for runaway traits start. In order for females to preferentially select males with traits associated with a good genes trait, females must have some form of sensory bias favoring these traits—otherwise, there is no way for females to selectively choose men with this trait. Thus, to a large degree, similar processes are operating for both forms of selection.

It is reasonable to expect that both sexes seek mates who show indicators of heritable fitness. It is interesting, then, that in the literature on nonhuman animals, there has been much research devoted to male attractiveness and far less on female attractiveness (e.g., Alcock, 2005; Andersson, 1994). Females appear to value male attractiveness because it is a cue of genes that confer fitness benefits to offspring through increased viability or reproductive success (e.g., Kokko et al., 2003; Møller & Thornhill, 1997). A variety of traits have been proposed as markers of heritable fitness, including the degree of fluctuating asymmetry. It has been proposed that more symmetrical individuals possess fewer genetic mutations and have encountered fewer parasites and diseases during development. Thus, females may attend to symmetry, or to traits correlated with symmetry, when selecting a mate (Møller & Thornhill, 1997).

Some traits are markers of heritable fitness because they demonstrate that a male is in *good condition*. The exact definition of "condition" varies, but it can refer to aspects of the organism such as nutritional state or energy reserves, and higher condition confers greater reproductive fitness.

*Life history theory* provides one means for understanding this concept of good condition. Life history theorists think of organisms as entities that capture energy from the environment and then convert it to survival and reproduction enhancing activities. These actions include the development of metabolically expensive physical features that are attractive to the opposite sex (for a review, see Kaplan & Gangestad, 2005). Due to differences in genetic composition, combined with the challenges faced during development, individuals differ in their ability to allocate energy to generating energetically costly traits that are attractive to the other sex. According to the *handicap principle* proposed by Zahavi (1975), males who display traits that are costly to maintain (e.g., the peacock's train) are attractive to females precisely because the traits are difficult to produce. Hence, the traits serve as an *honest signal* that the male is in good enough condition to produce them.

The logic of the markers of heritable fitness argument, however, does not entail that these males are healthier. For example, male peacocks with large trains can have high parasite loads because they are using more of their energy budgets on developing the sexy traits than on immune system maintenance. Depending on ecological circumstances, a male in good condition might be better served by burning through his metabolic resources to vigorously display, even if this erodes his long-term health and leads to death before the male with a smaller energy budget. There can be a negative, positive, or neutral correlation between costly signals and various indicators of health (Kokko et al., 2002).

The idea that females would be attracted to a trait that requires males to waste their energies on developing useless traits like the peacock's train is initially counterintuitive. Why would females prefer a trait that is harmful to the well-being of the male? It is useful to consider an analogy provided by Dawkins (2006), who asked readers to imagine two men running a race. One of the men is carrying a large boulder and the other man is not. The man carrying the boulder reaches the finish line around the same time as the man with no such encumbrances. Which man would be more impressive? Obviously, the man carrying the boulder grabs our attention because he has displayed his strength despite bearing a burdensome handicap. Females who mate with males displaying these metabolically burdensome traits increase the likelihood that their offspring will possess these traits. Their male offspring who display these traits will then have an advantage over other males when seeking mates, increasing their mothers' ultimate reproductive success.

As an extension of Zahavi's hypothesis, Folstad and Karter (1992) introduced the *immunocompetence signaling hypothesis*. This hypothesis suggests that secondary sexual characteristics are reliable indicators of mate quality because the reproductive hormones required for their development, including testosterone, suppress the immune system (e.g., Peters, 2000; Rantala, Vainikka, & Kortet, 2003). The expression of testosterone-linked traits reveals that men are in good enough condition to withstand the deleterious effects of immunosuppression, and women who selected these men as mates would have transmitted features associated with good condition to their offspring. The link between testosterone level and immunosuppression has been challenged as weak to nonexistent (Roberts, Buchanan, & Evans, 2004), however, with some researchers suggesting that testosterone redistributes the number of circulating leukocytes into target tissues rather than suppressing the immune system (Braude, Tang-Martinez, & Taylor, 1999).

An alternative perspective suggests that testosterone-linked traits are costly signals for reasons other than immunocompetence (see Kaplan & Gangestad, 2005; Kokko et al., 2003). In this view, males in good condition benefit more than other males from devoting a greater share of their energy budget toward mating effort (e.g., competing for mates, displaying attributes desired by mates) than parenting or somatic effort. Higher testosterone is associated with more effort allocated to mating (McIntyre et al., 2006) as well as greater size and muscle mass (Bhasin, 2003), which may be used to attract potential mates. It is critical to note that one has limited efforts to devote to tasks. Effort allocated to developing and maintaining these mating-related attributes reduces the budget that is available for maintaining other attributes (e.g., immunocompetence, somatic upkeep) and can increase other energy demands (e.g., increased metabolism; Buchanan et al., 2001). This view suggests that there is a wider array of costs beyond simply immunosuppression that cause these traits to be indicators of heritable fitness.

Regardless of whether the evidence favors the immunocompetence or the more general cost model, the prediction is the same: the traits produced by high levels of testosterone are cues of heritable fitness and/or good condition because they reliably indicate that the male can afford to generate these costly traits. Consequently, there would be advantages for evolved female preference of these traits because, all else equal, males displaying them sire more viable offspring.

In practice, however, it can be difficult to distinguish between female preferences for direct versus indirect benefits. As Wong and Candolin (2005) observe,

Mate choice can present choosy individuals with both direct mate-rial gains that increase their fecundity and/or survival, as well as in-direct benefits that improve offspring viability and/or attractiveness. Competitive ability may correlate with some of these benefits if, for example, males that are adept in competition also monopolise the best resources or territories... Moreover, dominance could correlate with genetic benefits if sons inherit their father's competitive prowess, re-sulting in dominant males siring successful sons. (p. 2)

For example, Frederick and Haselton (2007) suggest that displays of behav-ioral dominance and greater levels of muscularity could be preferred by females because of direct benefits (i.e., greater protection to her and offspring) and indi-rect benefits (i.e., these males may produce offspring with genetic predispositions to rapidly develop muscularity). These two types of benefits—direct and indi-rect—can be obtained by females through short-term sexual liaisons or longer-term partnerships with an investing male.

## Evolutionary Psychology and Female Choice of Short-Term and Long-Term Partners: Sexual Strategies Theory and Strategic Pluralism Theory

The processes and preferences identified by these biological perspectives helped to inspire two highly influential theories of mate choice in evolutionary psychol-ogy: Sexual strategies theory (Buss & Schmitt, 1993) and strategic pluralism the-ory (Gangestad & Simpson, 2000). Both of these theories are consistent with the logic of Trivers (1972), who proposed that females and males do not follow one fixed mating strategy. Rather, they deploy multiple or mixed strategies depending on species-specific characteristics. For example, Trivers proposed that in "species where there has been strong selection for male parental care, it is more likely that a mixed strategy will be the optimal male course—to help a single female raise young, while not passing up opportunities to mate with other females whom he will not aid" (p. 145) and that "Psychology might well benefit from attempting to view human sexual plasticity as an adaptation to permit the individual to choose the mixed strategy best suited to local conditions and his own attributes" (p. 146). Sexual strategies theory and strategic pluralism theory emphasize the variety of mating strategies that women and men follow, and how these strategies may differ for each sex, on average. Both of these perspectives provide logic for understand-ing the importance of female choice, and the motivations that women may have for seeking short-term affairs. According to these theories, humans have evolved the capacity to follow a mix of short-term and long-term strategies depending on fitness-related circumstances.

## Sexual Strategies Theory: The Mating Strategy Menu

Buss and Schmitt (1993) proposed an evolutionary theory of human mating strategies, which they called *sexual strategies theory*. This theory focuses on variations in mating preferences and strategies within each sex and between women and men. They proposed that men and women pursued short-term and long-term reproductive strategies in the ancestral past. Regarding sex differences, they reason that women and men differed on average in the challenges that they faced over the course of human ancestral history. The fact that these challenges may have differed in their intensity or frequency for women and men may have led to the evolution of different physical traits and psychological predispositions to help each sex overcome these challenges. The theory leads to the prediction that men will devote a larger proportion of their total mating effort toward short-term mating than do women because of the higher obligatory costs of sex for women (for a review, see Schmitt, 2010).

They specify, however, that women will also seek short-term mates, and that women and men face different challenges evaluating or attracting a potential short-term mate. They propose that men are more likely to face the problem of finding numerous, willing short-term partners who do not require substantial commitment or investment, as well as the problem of identifying women who are likely to be currently fertile. Men may solve the problem of identifying fertile women by attending to cues of age such as wrinkles in the skin and the presence or absence of secondary sexual characteristics (e.g., breast development). They propose a different set of challenges for women. For example, they propose that access to sexual partners has been less of challenge for women than for men. In contrast, women are faced with the need to identify partners who are willing and able to invest time and resources in the relationship, and who can provide protection from potentially violent males.

Central to the sexual strategies theory is the idea that women can benefit from pursuing both short-term and long-term strategies. For women, short-term affairs can lead to the securing of a new mate, or finding a potential back up mate. It can also enable women to mate with men who have markers of heritable fitness, such as symmetry and masculinized faces: traits that are hypothesized to be associated with genetic predispositions for healthier, sexier, or more robust body types.

## Strategic Pluralism Theory: The Importance of Individual Differences and Mating Context

*Strategic pluralism theory* builds on the logic of parental investment theory and sexual strategies theory (Gangestad & Simpson, 2000). Gangestad and Simpson proposed that one's genetic sex and one's physical traits can influence whether a person pursues a short-term or long-term mating strategy and the traits they prefer in these partners. According to this view, men have evolved predispositions to pursue reproductive strategies that are contingent on their value on the mating market. More attractive men accrue reproductive benefits from spending more time seeking multiple mating partners and relatively less time investing in offspring. In contrast, the reproductive effort of less attractive men, who do not have the same mating opportunities, is better allocated to investing heavily in their mates and offspring, and spending relatively less time seeking additional mates.

From a woman's perspective, the ideal is to attract a partner who confers both direct long-term benefits and indirect genetic benefits. Not all women, however, will be able to attract long-term mates with markers of heritable fitness who are willing and able to make substantial investments in terms of resources, protection, and care of offspring. Males with these attractive traits may be desirable to more women and therefore may have more opportunities to pursue a short-term mating strategy and to provide fewer direct benefits to their partners. Consequently, women face *mating trade-offs* when choosing a partner, between men who display markers of heritable fitness but lack inclination to provide direct benefits and men who are willing to provide benefits but lack these markers.

One solution to these trade-offs is to simply seek short-term mates who will not provide long-term investment, but who will pass on beneficial heritable traits to their offspring. A second partial solution to the problem of trade-offs is that women may pursue a dual-mating strategy by securing investment from a long-term mate and obtaining genetic benefits from extrapair mates (Fisher, 1992, 2011; Haselton & Gangestad, 2006). Consistent with this logic, women are most attracted to men other than their primary mate when fertility is highest within the ovulatory cycle (and thus the benefits of extrapair mating for genetic benefits are highest; Gangestad, Thornhill, & Garver-Apgar, 2005). This is especially true for women whose primary mates lack sexual attractiveness—the women who, in theory, have the most to gain from extrapair mating for good genes (Gangestad, Thornhill, & Garver-Apgar, 2005; Haselton & Gangestad, 2006; Pillsworth & Haselton, 2006). More generally, women find men with traits linked to higher testosterone levels more attractive during the highest fertility phase of their cycle relative to luteal and menstrual phases (DeBruine et al., 2010; Gangestad & Thornhill, 2008)

One prediction that follows from the dual-mating logic is that men who display cues to fitness will be chosen most often as affair partners. One such proposed cue is low fluctuating asymmetry: the extent to which the left half of the body develops differently than the right half. It has been proposed that higher fluctuating asymmetry is associated with genetic mutations and history of disease and parasite infection (see Møller & Thornhill, 1997). Therefore, more symmetrical individuals may be in better condition. Women may attend to symmetry per se or to traits that are correlated with symmetry when evaluating a man as a potential partner. Thornhill and Gangestad (1994) examined the self-reported number of sexual partners of men varying in symmetry. As predicted, more symmetrical men reported having a greater overall number of sex partners, more sexual affairs, and a greater number of sex partners who were themselves mated to other men at the time of the affair. Hughes and Gallup (2003) found a similar pattern in men with higher shoulder-to-hip ratios, as did Frederick and Haselton (2007) with muscularity, both traits that are linked with testosterone. In sum, both theory and existing evidence suggest that women attend to cues of fitness when selecting sex partners, particularly short-term mates and affair partners (for a brief review of research on mate preferences, see Gallup & Frederick, 2010).

These two theories have provided useful guides for generating testable predictions regarding the variation in mating preferences, the distinct choices faced by the sexes, and the choices faced by members within each sex. A key point of contention, however, has been the extent to which female choice is exercised in humans.

# Constraints on Female Choice: Particularly Stark in Humans?

The literature on women's mating preferences in evolutionary psychology has been dominated by the idea that preferences have a strong influence on choice, that these preferences emerged across the course of our evolutionary history, and that women have the ability to exercise choice (Buss, 1996; Miller, 1998). Female choice can be limited by males, however, through tactics such as mate-guarding, where males attempt to monitor and curtail the movements of their partner (Buss, 1988; Kokko & Morrell, 2005). This importance of female mate choice has been recently challenged through two influential articles focusing on the constraints placed on female mate choice by males (Puts, 2010) and by parents (Apostolou, 2007). More generally, Darwinian feminists have argued that several unique factors have contributed to the emergence of particularly patriarchal cultures with extensive control over female behaviors (Smuts, 1995). After reviewing these claims, we discuss evidence that women have found ways to exercise choice, even in the context of severe constraints.

## Constraints on Female Choice by Males

Puts (2010) suggests that research on sexual selection in humans has been overly skewed toward investigations of mate choice and that research on *contest competition*—where force or threats of force have been used to control mating opportunities—have been relatively neglected. More specifically, the claim is that contest competition was the main form of mating competition among men. Frequent contest competitions create strong selection pressures on males to become larger and more powerful, which provides advantages over smaller males and increases the average size difference between males and females across evolutionary time. The increased size of males enables males to more effectively monopolize females.

Traditionally, it has been argued that sexual dimorphism in humans is rather modest, suggesting a lack of contest competitions. For example, sexual dimorphism in height is a modest 8% (Gaulin & Boster, 1985) and sexual dimorphism in overall body mass is also a modest 15–20% (Mayhew & Salm, 1990). Puts (2010) proposes, however, that these measures are misleading. In Western societies, men are 40% heavier than women when examining fat-free mass index (Lassek & Gaulin, 2009; Mayhew & Salm, 1990) and men have 60% more total lean muscle mass than women. Men also have 80% greater arm muscle mass and 50% more lower body muscle mass (Abe, Kearns, & Fukunaga, 2003). Lassek and Gaulin (2009) note that the sex difference in upper-body muscle mass in humans is similar to the sex difference in fat free mass in gorillas (Zihlman & MacFarland, 2000), the most sexually dimorphic species of all living primates. This sexual dimorphism in muscle mass leads men to have approximately 90% greater upper body strength and the average man is stronger than over 99% of women (Abe et al., 2003; Lassek & Gaulin, 2009). The extent to which this is true across a wide variety of cultures would be informative as to the extent to which these sex differences are exacerbated or limited by ecological or cultural factors.

One source of this greater upper body strength may be unrelated to contest competitions. Greater upper body strength, combined with faster running speeds, may have been adaptations that facilitated big-game hunting. They may have also arisen in part from violent confrontations between men. Traits associated with testosterone, such as deep voices, jaw size, brow size, and muscularity enhance perceptions that a male is physically intimidating. Although much research has examined the extent to which women prefer these traits, Puts (2010) notes that women often prefer only moderate or average levels of some these features. Thus, it may be the case that males are not displaying these traits in order to attract women.

Although men lack "weapons" commonly seen in species with frequent contest competitions (e.g., horns, large canines, antlers), men have had the ability to construct weapons such as sharpened stones for millions of years. This ability can allow strong upper body strength to be used as a deadly weapon. Puts (2010) proposes that violent contests aided individual men in their competitions against other men in securing mates. Further, he proposes that males formed alliances with other males that enabled them to take over other groups or threaten members of their own group in order to acquire additional mates.

Taken as a whole, these arguments suggest that male-male competition was a more important factor than female choice in generating male testosterone-linked traits, and perhaps that contest competition had a more significant impact on whom women partnered with than did women's choices and preferences. In this view, women's preferences were not the primary force in shaping men's physical appearance. Not all reviews have come to the conclusion that the evolution of human sexual dimorphism emerged primarily from contest competitions, noting that a variety of processes could have lead to the dimorphism seen in humans (e.g., mate choice, resource competition, intergroup violence, and female choice; Plavcan, 2012). Puts' proposal is intriguing, however, and merits further consideration.

## Constraints on Female Choice by Relatives

In addition to constraints placed on women's mating choices by men, parents can strongly influence or restrict women's choices. Evidence presented by Apostolou (2007) has been particularly influential in emphasizing this point. Parents wield a great deal of power over offspring in many societies. Girls are often dependent on parents for food, protection, and access to influential social networks within the community. Parents have a direct interest in controlling the mating choices of their offspring. The fate of parental genes is at stake when offspring select mates, as is the social reputation and influence of the parents. Although some preferences between parents and offspring may overlap, others may diverge. A family with two sons and one daughter may find it beneficial to arrange a marriage with a family with two daughters and one son so that each child has a partner, even if the arranged marriage is not ideal for the single daughter. These potentially different priorities could generate conflicts between parents and offspring regarding mate choice.

In contrast to the freedom of choice experienced in Western and other industrialized cultures, arranged marriages are more common in most preindustrial societies (Murdock, 1967, 1981). For example, Apostolou (2007) claims that in 190 modern forager societies, only 4% allow individuals to select their mates free of much, or any, influence from their parents. If high levels of *parental control over mate choice* has been a long-standing pattern in human evolutionary history, it may suggest that current evolutionary models of human mating that assume free female choice are highly problematic and misleading (Apostolou, 2007). This work highlights the importance of examining the influence parents have in the mate selection process, and the traits that parents take into account when arranging or influencing their offspring's mating choices.

## Evolutionary Origins of Patriarchy

Several such constraints on women's social influence were highlighted by Darwinian feminist Barbara Smuts (1995), who noted that human societies appear to exhibit greater male control over female sexuality than is typical in most nonhuman primate species. Smuts posits that this desire for control over female sexuality was one of the key factors facilitating the emergence of patriarchy, which has strongly constrained women's reproductive choices.

In particular, she proposes six factors that diminished women's reproductive choices and control over their own lives. First, patrilocal societies in which females moved away from kin led to reduced social support for women from families and allies. Second, men's alliances became increasingly well developed across human evolutionary history, which enabled men to exert greater influence over women. Third, men's alliances allowed them to increase control over resources needed by women to survive and reproduce, making women more dependent on men. Fourth, control over resources by some men's alliances created increased variance in men's wealth and power, which left women increasingly vulnerable to the will and whims of a few powerful men. Fifth, women engaged in behaviors that promote male control over resources, such as preferring and choosing more dominant and wealthier men as partners. This pattern of choice increases pressure on men to control these resources. Last, the evolution of language enabled the creation of ideologies supporting men's dominance and supremacy, and women's subordinance and inferiority. Smuts (1995) was not proposing that female choice was unimportant, but it is clear that this constellation of factors would have reduced women's ability to act on their preferences.

## Resistance to Constraints on Female Choice

Research over the past few decades in evolutionary psychology on mating in Westernized cultures has led to a relative overemphasis on mate choice as a mechanism of sexual selection. In contrast, contest competition and parental influence on mate choice have been relatively underemphasized.

We present evidence, however, that women's preferences and choices can be exercised, even in the face of strict constraints. We examine methods that women use to subvert attempts at mate guarding, that daughters use to influence parental control over mating decisions, and the cultural factors that enable women's choices. The extent to which women are able to break through these constraints has implications for the importance assigned to female choice as a factor in human evolution.

### Subverting Mate Guarding

The fact that men engage in *mate guarding* suggests that women engage in behaviors that require guarding against. If women were uniformly and strictly sexually monogamous, then mate guarding would only need to be exerted in limited circumstances. Men would only need to guard against rival males who were attempting to gain access to their sexual partner. If women did not at some level exert choice in mates, then there would be no other pressure on men to mate guard.

In Western societies, approximately 11–15% of women indicate that they have had extramarital sex in their current marriage. These numbers exclude, however, relationships that have ended in divorce caused by infidelity, and infidelity is frequently cited as one of the leading causes of divorce in the United States and across cultures. Estimates vary, but approximately 20–25% of heterosexual married women will have an extramarital affair during their lifetime, and the incidence of extrapair sex is far higher for dating couples (for reviews, see Allen et al., 2005; Betzig, 1989; Tsapelas, Fisher, & Aron, 2010). In the Standard Cross-Cultural Sample, female extramarital affairs are common among foragers, horticulturalists, and pastoralists (Marlowe, 2000). These data are consistent with numerous ethnographic accounts describing female infidelity among the !Kung (Hill & Hurtado, 1996), Ache (Hill & Hurtado, 1996; Kaplan & Hill, 1985), Bari (Beckerman et al., 1998), Tsimane (Winking, Kaplan, Gurven, & Rucas, 2007), and Tiwi (Goodale, 1971).

Extramarital affairs can lead to extrapair paternity, which occurs when the purported biological father is not the actual biological father of a child. In general population samples taken primarily from European and North American cultures, the estimated human extrapair paternity rates range from 2 to 4%. This extrapair paternity rate jumps to 30% among men who specifically seek out paternity tests (for reviews, see Anderson, 2006; Voracek, Fisher, & Shackelford, 2009). It remains unknown how comparable these rates are among other populations because systematic data on nonpaternity rates are not available for nonindustrialized societies. The only known study of genetic paternity from a small-scale natural fertility (noncontraceptive using) population is from research with the Yanomamo in the 1960s, showing a nonpaternity rate of 9.1% (Neel & Weiss, 1975). The figure for the Yanomamo is at the high end of global reported prevalence rates.

Other types of data on nonindustrialized cultures are available, however, and these data shed light on the potential frequency and impact of women's extrapair mating on men's paternal certainty. Gaulin and Schlegel (1980) attempted to assess degree of paternal certainty using three variables from the Standard Cross-Cultural Sample of nonindustrialized societies. They classified societies as having low paternal confidence if the society had some form of culturally sanctioned sharing of wives, at least a moderate frequency of extramarital sex, or a lack of a double standard regarding attitudes toward extramarital sex by women versus men. Relevant data was available in 145 of the 190 societies. Based on this criteria, they estimated that 61 (45%) of the societies had low paternal confidence and 74 had high paternal confidence (55%). The actual number of societies with low paternal confidence may be higher, however, because the authors frequently treated missing data as evidence of high paternity (for example, a society with a sexual double standard, wife sharing, and no information on frequency of extramarital sex was coded as high paternal certainty; Wolfe & Gray, 1981).

Huber, Linhartova, and Cope (2004) used four measures of extramarital sexual activity from 57 nonindustrialized cultures to create a 16-level measure of paternity confidence. The measures included frequency of premarital and extramarital sex, and strength of the social deterrents to premarital and extramarital sex. In their sample, 36 of the cultures were classified as having moderate to very high frequencies of extramarital affairs and 44 were classified as having moderate to very high frequencies of premarital sex.

The aforementioned studies relied on broad ethnographic data available from many cultures. To examine the paternal uncertainty in a given society in more specific detail, Scelza (2011) collected reproductive histories from Himba women. The Himba are a seminomadic pastoral population living the northwest corner of Namibia. They are largely isolated from the market economy and rely primarily on livestock for subsistence and trade. Marriages can be arranged or can result from love matches. In this study, reproductive histories were collected from 110 women, and showed 421 births, of which 329 occurred within marriage. The women were asked to identify whether the child resulted from liaisons with an extramarital affair partner or from their husband. Nearly one-third of women indicated having at least one extrapair birth in their lifetimes (32%), which accounted for 18% of all marital births. None of the women in love marriages reported extrapair births (0 of 79), whereas for the arranged marriages, 23% of the births were described as extramarital births. The results may be somewhat skewed due to the self-report nature of the data, but these findings demonstrate the potentially high rates of extrapair paternity in some natural fertility populations.

In contrast to the view that female choice is highly constrained by parents and males, these findings collectively suggest that in many nonindustrial societies, mate choice is occurring outside the purview of parental influence and possibly outside the context of contest competitions. The results of Scelza (2011) indicate that arranged marriages may be a risk factor for extrapair paternity. It is likely that the rates of extramarital affairs and births will vary considerably according to one's culture, depending on social and ecological factors. The existing evidence, however, provides support for the claim that women are able to exercise choice, even in the face of constraints. Through extramarital affairs, women exercise a tremendous influence over the mating system and the evolutionary process by controlling reproduction (Tsapelas, Fisher, & Aron, 2010).

## Subverting Parental Choice and Mate Guarding

Arranged marriages and parental influence on mate choice are common across cultures. In most of these cultures, however, women are still able to exercise substantial influence over mating choices. As Pillsworth and Barrett (2011) have shown in a broad sample of nonindustrialized cultures, women have some degree of sway on parental choices in many societies where there are arranged marriages. This influence can range from having veto power, having some input, or having substantial input on parental choice, as well as the option of entering love or arranged marriages.

Pillsworth and Barrett (2011) documented the various ways in which women among the Shuar of Ecuador, a hunter-horticuluralist society, are able to exercise choice in the face of strict constraints. Through ethnographic interviews, they identified strategies that women use to escape marriages, despite the fact that among the Shuar it is said that "marriage is forever." Corporal punishment is regularly meted out against both women and children as way to control and constrain their options. One mechanism of escape from abusive or undesirable marriages is simply to run away. Women most frequently return to their father's home or run away with another man, although they may occasionally seek employment in one of the cities. A second method of escape is to attempt suicide. By attempting suicide, a woman gains the attention of her family. It is also a clear signal to the husband that she is unhappy, which may motivate the husband to change (either from genuine concern or from fear that her family will kill him or his kin if he is viewed to be the cause of the suicide). Women will also engage in adultery or seek a new partner. If a girl disagrees with the marriage her parents are arranging, she may elope with a different boy.

Men in this society expend a great deal of energy to attract women and woo them, even if the parents are officially the ones to approve or arrange the marriage. Failing to woo the daughter can lead to a conflict between daughter and parents, which may cause the parents to withdraw from the marriage negotiation. There is pressure on men to display traits that the daughters, not just the parents, will find attractive.

The extent to which women choose relatively more or less dominant men as partners may depend in part on the local ecological and cultural settings. Frederick and Haselton (2007) found that women perceived muscular men as more attractive and dominant, but also as more volatile. Snyder et al. (2011) proposed that women face a trade-off when choosing a man with domineering personalities and powerful body types as a mate (e.g., men described as dominant, domineering, tough-guy, strong, could win a fight if necessary). These men may provide better protection from other males, for example, but they may also be more controlling of their mates. Snyder et al. reasoned that women who perceived the world as relatively more dangerous would more strongly prefer domineering men because the benefits of a potential protector in a dangerous world outweigh the costs, whereas the costs may outweigh the benefits in a relatively safe world. Women may facultatively adjust their preferences based on actual or perceived environmental conditions.

## Concluding Comments: The Future of Mating Research

Western cultures and other industrialized cultures have provided women with the opportunities to exercise a great deal of choice over their mates, perhaps more so than at any other time in recent or ancestral history. It is particularly interesting to explore how women's preferences are expressed in this context and how these preferences differ from the preferences exhibited in cultures where choices are more constrained. In general, our examination indicates that there is tremendous variability in female choice that can be exercised across different societies, which leaves some reason to suspect that this may have been true across different isolated groups in human ancestral history.

The theories of parental investment, sexual strategies, and strategic pluralism have generated a wealth of hypotheses regarding men's and women's long-term and short-term mating strategies. Much work has been done documenting the presence of sex differences, and more recent work examines the individual differences within each sex. The current focus on understanding how ecological factors, cultural ideologies, life history factors, parental influences, female choice, and contest competitions interact will provide greater insight into how evolution shaped individual and sex differences in mating preferences and choices.

The field of evolutionary psychology has generated a wealth of novel and interesting predictions using the perspectives in evolutionary biology related to sexual selection. As cultural attitudes toward female sexuality have changed, these theories have evolved by more fully incorporating notions of active female choice and reproductive decision. The current debates in evolutionary biology and animal behavior regarding the role of sex, ecological factors, developmental factors, and social factors provide evolutionary psychologists with new perspectives to draw from when generating predictions regarding human sexual behavior (e.g., Gowaty & Hubbell, 2005). One conclusion from the changing understanding of female sexuality in evolutionary biology and psychology is clear: Women have been, and will likely continue to be, active agents in shaping the course of human evolution.

# References

Abe, T., Kearns, C. F., & Fukunaga, T. (2003). Sex differences in whole body skeletal muscle mass measured by magnetic resonance imaging and its distribution in young Japanese adults. *British Journal of Sports Medicine, 37*, 436–440.

Alcock, J. (2005). *Animal behavior: An evolutionary approach.* Sunderland, MA: Sinauer.

Allen, E. S., Atkins, D. C., Baucom, D. H., Snyder, D. K., Gordon, K. C., & Glass, S. P. (2005). Intrapersonal, interpersonal, and contextual factors in engaging in and responding to extramarital involvement. *Clinical Psychology: Science and Practice, 12*, 101–130.

Anderson, K. G. (2006). How well does paternity confidence match actual paternity? Evidence from worldwide nonpaternity rates. *Current Anthropology, 47*, 435–461.

Andersson, M. (1994). *Sexual selection.* Princeton, NJ: Princeton University Press.

Apostolou, M. (2007). Sexual selection under parental choice: The role of parents in the evolution of human mating. *Evolution and Human Behavior, 28*, 403–409.

Arnqvist, G., & Kirkpatrick, M. (2005) The evolution of infidelity in socially monogamous passerines: The strength of direct and indirect selection on extrapair copulation behavior in females. *American Naturalist, 165*, S26–S37.

Bateman, A. J. (1948). Intra-sexual selection in Drosophila. *Heredity, 2*, 349–368.

Beckerman, S., Lizarralde, R., Ballew, C., Schroeder, S., Fingelton, C., Garrison, A., & Smith, H. (1998). The Bari partible paternity project: Preliminary results. *Current Anthropology, 39*, 164–167.

Betzig, L. L. (1989). Causes of conjugal dissolution: A cross-cultural study. *Current Anthropology, 30*, 654–676.

Bhasin, S. (2003). Regulation of body composition by androgens. *Journal of Endocrinological Investigation, 26*, 814–822.

Borgia, G. (1985). Bower quality, number of decorations, and mating success of male satin bowerbirds (*Ptilonorhynchu violaceuous*): An experimental analysis. *Animal Behaviour, 33*, 266–271.

Braude, S., Tang-Martinez, Z., & Taylor, G. T. (1999). Stress, testosterone, and the immunoredistribution hypothesis. *Behavioral Ecology, 8*, 345–350.

Buchanan, K. L, Evans, M. R., Goldsmith, A. R., Bryant, D. M., & Rowe, L. V. (2001). Testosterone influences basal metabolic rate in male house sparrows: A new cost of dominance signaling. *Proceedings of the Royal Society of London B, 268*, 1337–1344.

Buss, D. M. (1988). From vigilance to violence: Tactics of mate retention in American undergraduates. *Ethology and Sociobiology, 9*, 291–317.

Buss, D. M. (1996). Sexual conflict: Evolutionary insight into feminism and the "battle of the sexes." In D. Buss & N. Malamuth (Eds.), *Sex, power, and conflict: Evolutionary and feminist perspectives* (pp. 296–318). New York: Oxford University Press.

Buss, D. M., & Schmitt, D. P. (1993). Sexual Strategies Theory: An evolutionary perspective on human mating. *Psychological Review, 100*, 204–232.

Clutton-Brock, T. H., & Parker, G. A. (1992). Potential reproductive rates and the operation of sexual selection. *Quarterly Review of Biology, 67*, 437–456.

Darwin, C. (1859). *On the origin of species by means of natural selection*. London: Murray.

Dawkins, R. (2006). *The selfish gene (30th Anniversary edition)*. New York: Oxford University Press.

Debruine, L. M., Jones, B. C., Frederick, D. A., Haselton, M. G., Penton-Voak, I. S., & Perrett, D. I. (2010). Evidence for menstrual cycle shifts in women's preferences for masculinity. *Evolutionary Psychology, 8*, 768–775.

Dufour, D. L., & Sauther, M. L. (2002). Comparative and evolutionary dimensions of the energetics of human pregnancy and lactation. *American Journal of Human Biology, 14*, 584–602.

Fedigan, L. M. (1992). *Primate paradigms* (2nd ed.). Chicago: University of Chicago Press.

Fisher, H. E. (1992). *Anatomy of love: The natural history of monogamy, adultery, and divorce*. New York: Norton.

Fisher, H. E. (2011). Serial monogamy and clandestine adultery: Evolution and consequences of the dual human reproductive strategy. In S. C. Roberts (Ed.), *Applied evolutionary psychology*. New York: Oxford University Press.

Fisher, R. A. (1930). *The genetical theory of natural selection*. Oxford, UK: Clarendon Press.

Folstad, I., & Karter, A. (1992). Parasites, bright males, and the immunocompetence handicap. *American Naturalist, 139*, 603–622.

Frederick, D. A., & Haselton, M. G. (2007). Why is muscularity sexy? Tests of the fitness indicator hypothesis. *Personality and Social Psychology Bulletin, 33*, 1167–1183.

Gallup, G. G., Jr., & Frederick, D. A. (2010). The science of sex appeal: An evolutionary perspective. *Review of General Psychology, 14*, 240–250.

Gangestad, S. W., & Simpson, J. A. (2000). The evolution of human mating: Trade-offs and strategic pluralism. *Behavioral and Brain Sciences, 23*, 573–644.

Gangestad, S. W., & Thornhill, R. (2008). Human oestrus. *Proceedings of the Royal Society of London B, 275*, 991–1000.

Gangestad, S. W., Thornhill, R., & Garver-Apgar, C. E. (2005). Women's sexual interests across the ovulatory cycle depend on primary partner developmental instability. *Proceedings of the Royal Society of London B, 272*, 2023–2027.

Gaulin, S. J. C., & Boster, J. S. (1985). Cross cultural differences in sexual dimorphism: Is there any variance to be explained. *Ethology and Sociobiology, 6*, 193–199.

Gaulin, S. J. C., & Schlegel, A. (1980). Paternal confidence and paternal investment: A cross cultural test of a sociobiological hypothesis. *Ethology and Sociobiology, 1*, 301–309.

Goodale, J. C. (1971). *Tiwi wives: A study of the women of Melville Island, North Australia*. Seattle: University of Washington Press.

Goodenough, J., McGuire, B., Wallace, R.A. (2001). *Perspectives on animal behavior*. New York: Wiley.

Gowaty, P. A., & Hubbell, S. P. (2005). Chance, time allocation, and the evolution of adaptively flexible sex role behavior. *Integrative and Comparative Biology, 45*, 931–944.

Gowaty, P. A., Kim, Y. K., Anderson, W. W. (in press). No evidence of sexual selection in a repetition of Bateman's classic study of Drosophila melanogaster. *Proceedings of the National Academy of Science.*

Gowaty, P. A., Steinichen, B., & Anderson, W. W. (2003). Indiscriminate females and choosy males: Within and between species variation in Drosophila. *Evolution, 57*, 2037–2045.

Griffith, S. C. (2007). The evolution of infidelity in socially monogamous passerines: Neglected components of direct and indirect selection. *The American Naturalist, 169*, 274–281.

Griffith, S. C., Owens, I. P. F., & Thuman, K. A. (2002). Extra pair paternity in birds: A review of interspecific variation and adaptive function. *Molecular Ecology, 11*, 2195–2212.

Hall, D. W., Kirkpatrick, M., & West, B. (2000). Runaway sexual selection when female preferences are directly selected. *Evolution, 54*, 1862–1869.

Haselton, M. G., & Gangestad, S. W. (2006). Conditional expression of women's desires and men's mate guarding across the ovulatory cycle. *Hormones and Behavior, 49*, 509–518.

Hill, K., & Hurtado, A. M. (1996). *Ache life history: The ecology and demography of a foraging people.* New York: Aldine de Gruyter.

Huber, B. R., Linhartova, V., & Cope, D. (2004). Measuring paternal certainty using cross cultural data. *World Cultures, 15*, 48–59.

Hrdy, S. B. (1977). Infanticide as a primate reproductive strategy. *American Scientist, 65*, 40–49.

Hrdy, S. B. (1981). *The woman that never evolved.* Cambridge, MA: Harvard University Press.

Hughes, S. M., & Gallup, G. G., Jr., (2003). Sex differences in morphological predictors of sexual behaviors: Shoulder to hip and waist to hip ratios. *Evolution and Human Behavior, 24*, 173–178.

Judson, O. (2003). *Dr. Tatiana's sex advice to all creation: The definitive guide to the evolutionary biology of sex.* London: Vintage.

Kaplan, H. S., & Gangestad, S. W. (2005). Life history theory and evolutionary psychology. In D. Buss (Ed.), *The handbook of evolutionary psychology* (pp. 68–95). New York: Wiley.

Kaplan, H., & Hill, K. (1985). Hunting ability and reproductive success among male Ache foragers. *Current Anthropology, 26*, 131–133.

Kaplan, H., Hill, K., Lancaster, J., & Hurtado, A. M. (2000). A theory of human life history evolution: Diet, intelligence, and longevity. *Evolutionary Anthropology, 9*, 156–185.

Kirkpatrick, M. (1989). Is bigger always better? *Nature, 377*, 116–117.

Kirkpatrick, M., & Barton, N. (1997). The strength of indirect selection on female mating preferences. *Evolution, 94*, 1282–1286.

Kirkpatrick, M., & Ryan, M. J. (1991). The evolution of mating preferences and the paradox of the lek. *Nature, 350*, 33–38.

Kokko, H., Brooks, R., Jennions, M. D., & Morley, J. (2003). The evolution of mate choice and mating biases. *Proceedings of the Royal Society of London B, 270*, 653–664.

Kokko, H., Brooks, R., McNamara, J. M., & Houston, A. I. (2002). The sexual selection continuum. *Proceedings of the Royal Society of London B, 269*, 1331–1340.

Kokko, H., & Morrell, L. J. (2005). Mate guarding, male attractiveness, and paternity under social monogamy. *Behavioral Ecology, 16*, 724–731.

Lassek, W. D., & Gaulin, S. J. C. (2009). Costs and benefits of fat-free muscle mass in men: Relationship to mating success, dietary requirements, and natural immunity. *Evolution and Human Behavior, 30*, 322–328.

Marlowe, F. (2000). Paternal investment and the human mating system. *Behavioural Processes, 51*, 45–61.

Mayhew, J. L., & Salm, P. C. (1990). Gender differences in anaerobic power tests. *European Journal of Applied Physiology and Occupational Physiology, 60*, 133–138.

McIntyre, M., Gangestad, S. W., Gray, P. B., Chapman, J. F., Burnham, T. C., O'Rourke, M. T., & Thornhill, R. (2006). Romantic involvement often reduces men's testosterone levels—but not always: The moderating role of extrapair sexual interest. *Journal of Personality and Social Psychology, 91*, 642–651.

Milam, E. L. (2010). Looking for a few good males: Female choice in evolutionary biology. Baltimore: Johns Hopkins University Press.

Miller, G. F. (1998). How mate choice shaped human nature: A review of sexual selection and human evolution. In C. B. Crawford & D. Krebs (Eds.), *Handbook of evolutionary psychology: Ideas, issues, and applications* (pp. 87–130). Mahwah, NJ: Erlbaum.

Møller, A. P., & Thornhill, R. (1997). A meta-analysis of the heritability of developmental stability. *Journal of Evolutionary Biology, 10*, 1–16.

Murdock, G. P. (1967). Ethnographic atlas: A summary. *Ethnology, 6*, 109–236.

Murdock, G. P. (1981). *Atlas of world cultures.* Pittsburgh, PA: University of Pittsburgh Press.

Neel, J. V., & Weiss, K. M. (1975). The genetic structure of a tribal population, the Yanomama Indians: 12. Biodemographic studies. *American Journal of Physical Anthropology, 42*, 25–52.

Peters, A. (2000). Testosterone treatment is immunosuppressive in superb fairy-wrens, yet free-living males with high testosterone are more immunocompetent. *Proceedings of the Royal Society of London B, 267*, 883–889.

Pillsworth, E., & Barrett, H. C. (2011, June). *Female choice and parent-offspring conflict in human mating: Evidence from the Shuar of Ecuador.* Paper presented at the annual meeting of the Human Behavior and Evolution Society, Montpellier, France.

Pillsworth, E. G., & Haselton, M. G. (2006). Male sexual attractiveness predicts differential ovulatory shifts in female extra-pair attraction and male mate retention. *Evolution and Human Behavior, 27*, 247–258.

Plavcan, J. M. (2012). Sexual size dimorphism, canine dimorphism, and male-male competition in primates: Where do humans fit in? *Human Nature, 23*, 45–67.

Puts, D. A. (2010). Beauty and the beast: Mechanisms of sexual selection in humans. *Evolution and Human Behavior, 31*, 157–175.

Rantala, M. J., Vainikka, A., & Kortet, R. (2003). The role of juvenile hormone in immune function and pheromone production trade-offs: A test of the immunocompetence handicap principle. *Proceedings of the Royal Society of London B, 270*, 2257–2261.

Roberts, M. L., Buchanan, K. L., & Evans, M. R. (2004). Testing the immunocompetence handicap hypothesis: A review of the evidence. *Animal Behaviour, 68*, 227–239.

Rosvall, K. A. (2011). Intrasexual competition among females: Evidence for sexual selection. *Behavioral Ecology, 22*, 1131–1140.

Scelza, B. A. (2011). Female choice and extra-pair paternity in a traditional human population. *Biology Letters, 7*, 889–891.

Schmitt, D. P. (2010). General mate choice. In M. P. Muehlenbein (Ed.), *Human evolutionary biology* (pp. 295–308). Cambridge, UK: Cambridge University Press.

Smuts, B. B. (1995). The evolutionary origins of patriarchy. *Human Nature, 6*, 1–32.

Snyder, J. K., Fessler, D. M. T., Tiokhin, L., Frederick, D. A., Lee, S. W., & Navarette, C. D. (2011). Trade-offs in a dangerous world: Women's fear of crime predicts preferences for aggressive and formidable mates. *Evolution and Human Behavior, 32*, 127–137.

Tang-Martinez, Z., & Brandt Ryder, T. (2005). The problem with paradigms: Bateman's worldview as a case study. *Integrative and Comparative Biology, 45*, 821–830.

Thornhill, R., & Gangestad, S. W. (1994). Human fluctuating asymmetry and sexual behavior. *Psychological Science, 5*, 297–302.

Trivers, R. R. (1972). Parental investment and sexual selection. In B. Campbell (Ed.), *Sexual selection and the descent of man, 1871–1971* (pp. 136–179). London: Heinemann.

Tsapelas, I., Fisher, H. E., & Aron, A. (2010). Infidelity: When, where, why. In W. R. Cupach & B. H. Spitzberg (Eds.), *The dark side of close relationships II* (pp. 175–196). New York: Routledge.

Voracek, M., Fisher, M., & Shackelford, T. K. (2009). Sex differences in subjective estimates of non-paternity rates in Austria. *Archives of Sexual Behavior, 38*, 652–656.

Westneat, D. F., & Stewart, I. R. K. (2003). Extra-pair paternity in birds: Causes, correlates, and conflict. *Annual Review of Ecology, Evolution, and Systematics, 34*, 365–396.

Williams, G. C. (1966). *Adaptation and natural selection.* Princeton, NJ: Princeton University Press.

Winking, J., Kaplan, H., Gurven, M., & Rucas, S. (2007). Why do men marry, and why do they stray? *Proceedings of the Royal Society B, 274*, 1643–1649.

Wolfe, L. D., & Gray, J. P. (1981). Comment on Gaulin and Schlegel (1980). *Ethology and sociobiology, 2*, 95–98.

Wong, B. B. M., & Candolin, U. (2005). How is female mate choice affected by male competition. *Biological Reviews of the Cambridge Philosophical Society, 80*, 559–571.

Zahavi, A. (1975). Mate selection: A selection for a handicap. *Journal of Theoretical Biology, 53*, 205–214.

Zihlman, A. L., & MacFarland, R. K. (2000). Body mass in lowland gorillas: A quantitative analysis. *American Journal of Physical Anthropology, 113*, 61–78.

Zuk, M. (2011). *Sex on six legs: Lessons on life, love, and language from the insect world.* New York: Houghton Mifflin Harcourt.

# 16

# Swept off Their Feet?

*Females' Strategic Mating Behavior as a Means of Supplying the Broom*

CHRISTOPHER J. WILBUR AND LORNE CAMPBELL

## Introduction

A common thread to several classic fairy tales (e.g., Sleeping Beauty, Cinderella), reinforced by their modern cinematic instantiations, is that women are timid, delicate souls requiring rescue from their humble existence by dashing, daring, princely saviors. The fairy tale's contemporary counterpart, the romantic comedy, frequently perpetuates this theme. Most people, perhaps biased by their exposure to those stereotypical depictions, believe that real-world dating scripts involve men actively pursuing prospective romantic partners and women patiently and passively waiting for the man of their dreams to sweep them off their feet. As another stereotype of women's passivity, though decidedly less romantic, the lay conception of prehistoric relationships involves brawny cavemen clubbing one another over the head and staggering away with female conquests in tow.

Evolutionary psychological approaches to human mating are often accused of reinforcing stereotyped representations of mating processes (see Smith & Konik, 2011, for a review of such critiques). Indeed, a general conclusion of several lines of research is that men opportunistically seek multiple mating prospects with young, attractive, fertile women who are portrayed as the spoils in male-male competition (e.g., Buss, 1989; Schmitt et al., 2003; Schmitt & Buss, 1996). Although men are generally inclined toward short-term mating opportunities and women are generally inclined toward long-term mating opportunities, a more refined analysis of the evolutionary psychological literature reveals that individuals' mating strategies are flexible in response to contextual factors, individual differences, and life history stages (Buss & Schmitt, 1993; Gangestad & Simpson, 2000; Schmitt, 2005). Indeed, psychological and anthropological evidence has been used to argue for humans being monogamous, polygynous, and/or promiscuous (see Schmitt, 2005, for a review). Humans are highly altricial, requiring significant parental investment, a quality typically observed in monogamous species (Lovejoy, 1981). But opportunistic promiscuity has likely pervaded human evolutionary history as well, given the several adaptations to sperm competition possessed by modern humans (Shackelford, Pound, Goetz, & Lamunyon, 2005). We adopt a pluralistic perspective, suggesting that women (and men, for that matter) often seek long-term committed mates, but that short-term trysts occur when such liaisons offer certain advantages (e.g., copulating with a partner of high genetic quality). Important for the present purpose, whether they are seeking a long-term companion or a short-term sexual partner, women actively and judiciously select their suitors—there may be some truth to the claim that men sweep women off their feet, but we argue that women clearly provide the broom.

The remainder of the chapter will paint a richer portrait of female mating behavior by reviewing sexual selection theory which argues that females ought to be very selective about with whom they mate. We will illustrate this argument with analogues from the animal behavior literature and by describing research that highlights females' active control over the mating process. The core of our chapter will focus on the role of humor in human mating. Research in this domain is an illustrative microcosm of the contrast between passive and active accounts of women's role in the mating process, with findings from our own research program supporting the active account (Wilbur & Campbell, 2011).

## Sexual Selection and Female Choice

Women do not sit idly by and accept the advances of any male suitor. Traditional evolutionary theory argues that women's greater parental investment impels them to be very selective about with whom they mate (Trivers, 1972). According to Trivers's (1972) parental investment theory, because women incur the costs of internal fertilization, placentation, gestation, and lactation, they seek to maximize returns on their significant investment, selecting high-quality partners who can ensure offspring survival and reproductive success. Partner quality is ascertained through the process of sexual selection. Darwin (1981[1871]) advanced sexual selection theory to explain how some traits, seemingly superfluous or even detrimental to survival, could persist in species by virtue of their appeal to prospective mates. Elaborate traits, such as the peacock's ostentatious train, initially puzzled Darwin because, at first glance, they appear to impose survival costs on the bearer. The peacock's ornate plumage requires a significant degree of physiological resources to maintain and renders the peacock conspicuous to predators. But Darwin reasoned that if the peacock's train is attractive to peahens, then the heritable constituents of the trait would be propagated to successive generations due to increased mating opportunities.

Only relatively recently did Darwin's hypothesis first receive empirical support—many traits are transmitted through generations via sexual selection (e.g., Andersson, 1982; Petrie, Halliday, & Sanders, 1991; Rosenqvist, 1990). Furthermore, in several cases, sexually selected traits are not superfluous—they are reliable indicators of the bearer's underlying quality. In the case of *intrasexual competition*, sexually selected traits result in greater mating opportunities because they fashion the bearer with an edge in same-sex competition for access to mates. For example, extreme body size in male elephant seals is sexually selected because larger males usually win physical confrontations, allowing them to maintain access to harems of females while their smaller, vanquished adversaries bound away across the beach to wait for another shot (McCann, 1981). The image of enormous elephant seals engaging in quasi sumo matches in front of an awaiting female audience, dramatized by nature programs, serves to reaffirm people's representations of passive females.

But several contemporary accounts of sexual selection argue that, in some cases, females too engage in intrasexual competition (see Drea, 2005; Rosvall, in press, for a review). For example, female callitrichid primates physically aggress against rival females during periods of heightened fertility. As a more subtle variant of intrasexual competition, dominant females can suppress ovulation in subordinate females via behavioral and olfactory cues. Such tactics contribute to female reproductive success, as dominant females exhibit superior outcomes on several measures of reproductive success compared to their subordinate counterparts (Wasser, Norton, Kleindorfer, & Rhine, 2004). Females of several primate species not only exhibit characteristics of female-female competition, they also engage in promiscuous sexual behavior, counter to the notion that they are merely the spoils of male-male competition (e.g., Soltis, 2002). Benefits to female promiscuity might entail, among other things, paternity confusion. If males cannot be certain which offspring they have sired, females might recruit more males to assist in offspring care.

Another means by which females exert a more active role in the mating process is through *intersexual competition*—one sex (typically females) controlling with whom fertilization occurs based on partner quality. Again, given that females of most species commonly allocate greater effort to reproduction, at least in terms of initial biological investments (Trivers, 1972), it sensibly follows that females will prefer to procreate with males of high quality. In this way, then, females are far from passive pawns in the mating chess game—they are powerful queens that exert significant control on the reproductive process. As one compelling example, male bowerbirds spend an inordinate amount of time constructing elaborate twig structures (bowers) that are adorned with shells, leaves, flowers, and other decorative pieces. When females come to visit the bowers, the male birds are inspired to perform an elaborate mating ritual, replete with frenetic movements and production of song. Female bowerbirds choose which males they mate with based on an inspection of the male bowers and rituals, with the result being the rejection of most males and multiple matings being afforded to only a lucky few (Borgia, 1995). The ability to construct and defend bowers is predictive of males' immunocompetence, and females rely on bower-holding as a marker of males' underlying quality, showing discernment in their mating choices (Borgia, Egeth, Uy, & Patricelli, 2004). The great variance in male reproductive success in a given breeding season is powerful evidence against the notion that males simply have their way in the mating process.

Several examples in the animal literature illustrate female mate choice. For example, female scorpionflies prefer males with more symmetrical wings (Thornhill, 1992), female wild turkeys prefer males with larger beak ornaments (Buchholz, 1995), female Tungara frogs prefer males who emit lower-pitched mating calls (Ryan, 1985), and female katydids prefer males who offer a more nutritious gift (i.e., a spermatophore) made from the male's own bodily resources (Gwynne & Brown, 1994). Nicely demonstrating female control over reproduction is evidence that female katydids strategically invest the spermatophore's resources, diverting most of it to their eggs when they are in good health and instead to body tissues when deprived of food (Gwynne & Brown, 1994).

Although our later discussion of humor use in mating contexts largely reflects traditional female choice (i.e., choosing partners with whom to have committed or sexual relationships), female choice is not simply limited to *precopulatory* decisions. Intriguing evidence indicates that when females copulate with multiple partners, they can exert *postcopulatory* choice, a phenomenon referred to as *cryptic female choice* (Eberhard, 1996; see Reeder, 2003, for a review of evidence among primates). For instance, females can control whose sperm ultimately contributes to fertilization by retaining sperm of high quality mates and/or by ejecting sperm from lower quality mates following copulation. Cryptic female choice contributes to viability of offspring by ensuring that offspring are sired by high quality mates and contributes to paternity confusion by disguising the identity of the true biological father.

Several mechanisms are purported to underlie female choice of male partners (Andersson & Simmons, 2006). Among these are the hypothesis that male traits are indicative of being better providers of tangible benefits for offspring and the hypothesis that male traits are indicative of underlying genetic quality, which can be transmitted to offspring. Gangestad and Simpson (2000) suggest that good provider benefits and good genes benefits are not mutually exclusive. Research shows, however, that women tend to be particularly attracted to men possessing good genes (e.g., having greater bodily symmetry, more masculine facial appearance) as sexual partners primarily when they are ovulating (e.g., Alvergne & Lummaa, 2009; Gangestad & Thornhill, 2008), and men with good genes are more likely to pursue a short-term mating strategy, including having more extrapair partners when involved in long-term relationships (Gangestad & Thornhill, 1997). Although men's preferred strategy may be to pursue multiple matings (Buss & Schmitt, 1993), the ability of men to successfully pursue a short-term mating strategy is likely driven by female choice. Given that women's short-term preferences are for men possessing traits indicating good genes, men lacking these traits will be relatively less successful in pursuing a short-term mating strategy and will likely adopt a long-term mating strategy that involves a greater commitment of resources to one partner.

## Women's Strategic Mating Behavior

Provocative data have emerged in recent years to suggest that women strategically and surreptitiously seek romantic partners in a manner that jointly maximizes good provider *and* good genes benefits. When women consider long-term romantic partners, they report a preference for traits that imply an ability and willingness to invest in family, such as kindness, earning potential, and ambition (e.g., Buss, 1989; Li, Bailey, Kenrick, & Linsenmeier, 2002; Wilbur & Campbell, 2010). When considering short-term sexual partners, however, ovulating women and women approaching ovulation place greater emphasis on traits indicative of genetic quality, such as symmetry (Thornhill & Gangestad, 1999), facial masculinity (Penton-Voak et al., 1999), and intrasexual competitiveness (Gangestad, Simpson, Cousins, Garver-Apgar, & Christensen, 2004).

Women, then, adjust their preferences depending on the nature of the relationship they are seeking, even imposing different standards for the same trait in different relationship contexts. For example, women report relatively exacting standards for most traits (e.g., intelligence) when considering a potential long-term committed partner or a casual sex partner, but relax those standards when considering a partner for a first date (Kenrick, Groth, Trost, & Sadalla, 1993; Kenrick, Sadalla, Groth, & Trost, 1990). Even though both a casual sexual relationship and a simple first date imply no long-term commitment, the former carries a greater risk of conception, and thus women strive to limit such relationships to men of high quality, particularly genetic quality, because good genes can be transmitted to any resultant children of a causal affair. Women also seek long-term partners of high quality, seeking evidence of both high genetic quality and high parenting quality (Wilbur & Campbell, 2010), because such relationships are typically characterized by conceiving children and subsequent biparental care of those children.

Women not only modify their preferences when considering long-term relationship partners versus short-term sexual partners, they also behave in ways that allow them to have the best of both worlds. Women in long-term committed relationships report heightened attraction to men other than their primary partners during ovulation, particularly when their primary partners lack the traits most preferred in short-term sexual mates (Gangestad, Thornhill, & Garver-Apgar, 2005; Haselton & Gangestad, 2006; Pillsworth & Haselton, 2006). Thus, women value the security of a long-term committed relationship while remaining watchful of opportunities to seek sexual involvement with genetically superior men when conception risk is highest. Indeed, estimates of the incidence of cuckoldry—deceiving men into raising genetically unrelated children—range between 10 and 15% (Cerda-Flores, Barton, Marty-Gonzalez, Rivas, & Chakraborty, 1999; Macintyre & Sooman, 1991).

In accordance with shifts in women's partner preferences across the menstrual cycle are shifts in women's overt behavior that improve their chances of attracting desired short-term mates. Women express greater interest in going out to dance clubs and parties in order to meet men around the time of ovulation than during other times of the menstrual cycle (Haselton & Gangestad, 2006). Moreover, women make more concerted efforts to appear attractive and dress more provocatively around the time of ovulation than during other times of the menstrual cycle (Durante, Li, & Haselton, 2008; Haselton, Mortezaie, Pillsworth, Bleske-Rechek, & Frederick, 2007). In short, women actively engage in strategies designed to solicit desired men's attention when conception probability is high. Intriguingly, evidence is accruing that men are influenced by women's psychological and behavioral changes across the menstrual cycle: Men are more vigilant of their female partners around the time of ovulation, possibly in response to their partners' increased interest in other men (Gangestad, Thornhill, & Garver, 2002; Haselton & Gangestad, 2006; Pillsworth & Haselton 2006). In addition, unmated men exhibit an increase in testosterone, a response linked to sexual interest, when confronted with ovulating women (S. L. Miller & Maner, 2010). In short, the data on menstrual cycle shifts strongly suggest that women judiciously allocate their mating efforts in ways best suited for their needs, and in doing so, exert influence on men's own mating behavior.

One might argue that even if women control the process of mating in the broad sense of adjusting their preferences and strategies, with cascading influence on men's subsequent responses, men still take a more active role in specifically initiating courtship. Consistent with this logic, men do apply more overt relationship initiation strategies than do women, including physical approach of prospective partners and initiation of physical contact (Clark, Shaver, & Abrahams, 1999). Even in the specific domain of initial courtship, however, women appear to subtly select their suitors. Moore (1985) documented a wide range of nonverbal behaviors women employ in a classic mating context—the singles bar. These behaviors included lip licks, smiles, neck presentations, and parades (exaggerated swaying of the hips while walking). She observed that women selectively direct such behaviors toward men in whom they have interest as a means of soliciting advance only from desired suitors. A validation of these nonverbal displays revealed that women do indeed perform the displays more frequently in mating contexts (e.g., singles bars) than in nonmating contexts (e.g., a library) and that regardless of context, higher rates of nonverbal displays are associated with a greater number of male approaches. In this subtle, nonverbal manner, then, women "choose" their potential partners, contrary to assumed wisdom that men commonly make advances on passively naïve female targets.

# Interim Summary

To sum thus far, sexual selection theory articulates how members of the sex which invests more in offspring (typically females) should confine their reproductive engagements principally to partners who demonstrate evidence of high quality (either in the form of parental investments, good genes, or both). Sometimes, evidence of quality is demonstrated by the outcomes of male-male competition. But often these selective engagements proceed after females have exerted active partner choice based on their appraisal of male traits—females control the means of reproduction (Waage, 1997).

Numerous examples abound from the animal literature to illustrate the mechanisms of female choice (e.g., Borgia et al., 2004; Eberhard, 1996). Human females, too, are strategic and discerning, typically favoring long-term romantic relationships, but in some instances, seeking short-term sexual trysts, even if involved in a principal long-term relationship (Gangestad et al., 2002; Haselton & Gangestad, 2006; Pillsworth & Haselton, 2006). Whether they are evaluating prospective short-term or long-term partners, women carefully evaluate potential mates, placing differential emphasis on various traits, depending on which sort of relationship is desired (Fletcher, Tither, O'Loughlin, Friesen, & Overall, 2004; Kenrick et al., 1990; Kenrick et al., 1993; Li & Kenrick, 2006; Wilbur & Campbell, 2010). Furthermore, women subtly, yet actively, behave in ways to elicit approach from preferred mates (Moore, 1985). And women's behavioral repertoire to attract desired mates is highly nuanced, changing as a function of the menstrual cycle to maximize good genes benefits even when they are involved in committed long-term romantic relationships (Gangestad et al., 2005; Haselton & Gangestad, 2006; Pillsworth & Haselton, 2006).

# Humor Evaluation as an Illustration of Women's Strategic Mating

Evidence from the animal literature and from research on women's strategic mating behavior converge to illuminate females' active, consequential role in controlling reproduction—the centerpiece of the evolutionary process. Traditional sexual selection models of female choice have also been applied to the study of humor use in romantic contexts (Bressler & Balshine, 2006; Bressler, Martin, & Balshine, 2006). As we will review, our own research has contributed to this investigation (Wilbur & Campbell, 2011), with our central argument being that women actively evaluate the humor of prospective suitors in service of making prudent mate selections. We believe that the study of humor use in romantic contexts provides a convenient illustration of the contrast between passive and active accounts of women's mating behavior. We thus review findings from that literature and describe how our own findings buttress the account of women's active role in driving reproduction.

The adornments and display rituals of several animal species are thought to have evolved via sexual selection as indicators of underlying quality (Andersson & Simmons, 2006). G. F. Miller (2000a, 2000b, 2007) conjectured that humor, too, evolved as a fitness indicator, advertising evidence of genetic quality or of being a good partner or parent. Because successful attempts at humor require specific skills such as cognitive flexibility, theory of mind, and social adroitness, G. F. Miller (2007) contends that proficient displays of humor convey reliable information about underlying mate quality. Indeed, most people consider showcasing a sense of humor to be the single most effective mate attraction tactic (Buss, 1988).

Initial tests of G. F. Miller's sexual selection account of humor displays observed that women prefer humorous men to nonhumorous men for various sorts of relationships, but that humorous women are not preferred by men (Bressler & Balshine, 2006; Bressler et al., 2006). Instead, men value a prospective mate's receptivity to their own humorous offerings (Bressler et al., 2006); that is, men prefer women who appreciate their humor. Bressler et al.'s (2006) research was consistent with sexual selection theory in showing that men's humor displays are more consequential in determining their appeal as both long-term and short-term partners. Concerning women, Bressler et al.'s (2006) research focused on humor *appreciation*, which entails displays of enjoying another's humorous attempts, such as laughing and compliments. Humor appreciation can be feigned, however, and might be displayed for various reasons even when an individual does not find the humorist to be particularly amusing. In contrast, humor *evaluation* entails deliberative judgment, which may or may not be explicitly articulated, as to whether a target is indeed amusing.

The logic of sexual selection, and female choice in particular, reasons that women should not report indiscriminate tendencies to appreciate the humor of any possible suitor; rather, women should be attuned to the quality of prospective partners' humorous offerings in order to select the best possible mate and should thus carefully evaluate such offerings. Intriguing neuroimaging data support this distinction: when observing humorous stimuli, left prefrontal cortex and right nucleus accumbens activation is stronger in women than in men (Azim, Mobbs, Jo, Menon, & Reiss, 2005). The left prefrontal cortex is implicated in language comprehension and decoding the semantic meaning of stimuli; the right nucleus accumbens mediates the experience of reward, such as the experience of amusement in response to a joke's punchline. Those neuroimaging data imply, then, that women recruit resources for making sense of jokes and experience reward from viewing particularly amusing stimuli, processes consistent with evaluative responses.

Whereas past research on humor use within romantic contexts (Bressler & Balshine, 2006; Bressler et al., 2006) has (unintentionally) reaffirmed the stereotype that women assume a predominantly passive role in the mating process, our own research on this topic (Wilbur & Campbell, 2011) suggests a more active role for women. Our research was largely inspired and informed by the work of Bressler and his colleagues, but our efforts were directed toward offering the first direct empirical evidence that women evaluate the humorous offerings of potential suitors.

Another aspect of the sexual selection account of humor displays that had previously remained unaddressed was whether men's humor displays do indeed reveal information about underlying quality that women use to make informed mating choices. Intelligence and warmth are two highly valued traits in romantic partners (e.g., Evans & Brase, 2007; Li et al., 2002) and producing humor as a way to convey these attributes might be particularly effective for tacitly advertising mate quality. Simply stating one's purported qualities in more direct ways offers little information to prospective partners because without any substantiating evidence, such boasts are nondiagnostic. In short, our research on the use of humor in romantic contexts (Wilbur & Campbell, 2011) extends prior work by examining whether women evaluate the humorous offerings of male suitors and if these evaluations carry implications for their relationship decisions. A second contribution of our research is the demonstration of systematic associations between humor and traits desired in romantic partners, such as intelligence and warmth. Our research substantiates the sexual selection account of humor use in relationship initiation and exemplifies the active role that women play in the mating process.

Our examination of men's and women's use of humor in romantic settings included three studies. With Study 1, we aimed to document sex differences in the use of humor to initiate relationships, predicting that men, relative to women would report employing humor production strategies, and that women, relative to men, would report engaging in humor evaluation. With Study 2, we intended to show that these sex differences emerge in an ecologically valid context: online dating websites. In Study 3, we assessed whether women's (but not men's) evaluation of a prospective partner's humor bears a relation to their expressed long-term romantic interest. In the latter two studies, we also explored associations of humor with underlying attributes, namely intelligence and warmth.

In Study 1, a large sample of introductory psychology students were asked to imagine being in a social context, being attracted to a prospective romantic partner, and then to think of how they would go about trying to get to know this person better. Specifically, they were asked to rate their likelihood of using several humor strategies, including forms of humor production (e.g., I would make a lot of jokes) and humor evaluation (e.g., I would attempt to evaluate how naturally amusing he/she is), in service of getting to know a potential partner. As expected, men reported a greater likelihood to produce humor than did women; women, on the other hand, reported a greater likelihood to evaluate partners' humorous offerings than did men. The results of this study imply that women do not simply sit back and passively absorb men's attempts to impress them; on the contrary, women are actively and prudently evaluating men's humorous displays, as such displays might reveal important information about men's underlying qualities.

In a second study, we aimed to adduce evidence that sex differences in humor production and humor evaluation are apparent in an online dating environment. Recent surveys indicate that more than 800 dating websites exist, and that in the United States alone, three million users have developed long-term relationships with partners met through dating websites (Sritharan, Heilpern, Wilbur, & Gawronski, 2010)—mating behavior in the online realm clearly carries important relationship implications. We coded online dating profiles posted by men and women in major cities all across Canada for instances in which users advertised their own tendency to produce humor (humor production offers) and for instances in which users sought partners with a penchant for humor production (humor production requests). Phrases coded as representing humor production included "can make me/you laugh," "funny," "witty," and "likes to make jokes," among others. When individuals indicated that they possessed these qualities, the phrase was coded as an offer of humor production. When individuals indicated that they were seeking a partner possessing these qualities, the phrase was coded as a *request* for humor production. Consistent with predictions, men, compared to women, were nearly twice as likely to *offer* humor production. Women, compared to men, were nearly twice as likely to *request* humor production. Within both sexes, humor production offers were not systematically associated with humor production requests, suggesting that producing humor and seeking humor production are distinct, sex-differentiated strategies.

G. F. Miller (2000a) surmised that humor might have evolved as an indicator of underlying traits, such as intelligence, but prior research supporting his claim (Bressler & Balshine, 2006; Bressler et al., 2006) has generally taken this link as a given, rather than providing evidence for its existence. Study 2 provided evidence for this link: humor production offers were systematically associated with intelligence offers among both men and women. Likewise, humor production requests were associated with intelligence requests among both men and women. These findings imply that both men's and women's humor production might advertise underlying quality. We argue that men's inclination toward humor production and women's inclination toward humor evaluation are components of *strategies* that men and women enact in the service of particular goals, and are not the result of differential *abilities*. Though humor production used by either sex might convey similar information, the logic of female choice contends that it is more advantageous for men to advertise their humor to attract mates and for women to evaluate these humorous displays when choosing potential suitors.

Study 3 was designed to test explicitly that women's (but not men's) evaluation of potential partners' humor predicts their romantic interest. Participants first examined an opposite-sex online dating profile ostensibly submitted to a developing campus dating service. Profiles opened with one of five "one-liner" jokes (e.g.,

"Sign in restaurant window: Eat now, pay waiter"). The profile did not include a photograph and, other than the joke, the content of the profile was identical for all participants. After taking time to scrutinize the profile carefully, participants provided their impression of the target on several traits, including humor, intelligence and warmth, and rated their long-term romantic interest in the target.

Consistent with our hypotheses, we observed a significant interaction between participant sex and humor ratings, whereby ratings of target humor positively predicted romantic interest for women, but not for men. Men's romantic interest was unrelated to their ratings of the target's humor. Thus, women's evaluations of prospective partners' humor do indeed carry implications for their romantic desire. And women evaluate men's humor because they perceive humor to indicate important underlying qualities. Women's ratings of target humor were significantly correlated with both their ratings of target intelligence and their ratings of target warmth. On the other hand, men's ratings of target humor did not correlate with either their ratings of target intelligence or their ratings of target warmth. The results of Study 3 underscore that demonstrating a flair for good humor might be one test men must pass to pique women's romantic interest.

Our research offers the general conclusion that in initial courtship, women evaluate men's humorous productions to make prudent mating decisions, inferring important attributes about prospective partners from their evaluations. Whereas past research has focused on women's *appreciation* of prospective partners' humor (Bressler and Balshine, 2006; Bressler et al., 2006), we provide evidence that accords more strongly with the tenets of sexual selection theory: Women, as the more-investing sex, judiciously *evaluate* the humorous offerings of prospective mates to make sensible mating decisions.

To date, most research on the role of humor in mating does not distinguish among various forms of humor (e.g., Bressler et al., 2006; Bressler & Balshine, 2006; Li et al., 2009; Wilbur & Campbell, 2011). However, specific forms of humor likely convey specific pieces of information about the humorist's qualities. One classification scheme delineates four types of humor: (1) self-enhancing humor, often used to cope with adverse life events; (2) affiliative humor, often used to bond with others; (3) aggressive humor, often used to belittle others; and (4) self-defeating humor, often used to belittle the self (Martin, Puhlik-Doris, Larsen, Gray, & Weir, 2003). In our research, women inferred warmth and intelligence from humorous productions and expressed greater long-term interest in men they perceived as funny (Wilbur & Campbell, 2011, Study 3), implying that they perceived the humor as affiliative in nature. Using affiliative humor is likely most effective for men seeking to establish long-term committed relationships and women seeking the same might be especially attuned to this variety of humor.

Martin et al.'s (2003) scheme reveals that not all forms of humor are adaptive; in fact, some might be maladaptive in the context of mating. The use of self-defeating humor, for example, might imply low self-esteem, low social dominance, or other negative traits and women might be disinclined to seek long-term or short-term relationships with self-defeating men. Future research needs to be sensitive to specific forms of humor and establish which forms in particular are evaluated by women as indicative of good partner quality. Intriguingly, the same form of humor could indicate evidence of good or bad partner quality, depending on the romantic context. For example, because women are drawn to socially dominant men as short-term sexual partners, but prefer warmer, gentler partners as long-term mates (Gangestad, Garver-Apgar, Simpson, & Cousins, 2007), they might be especially attracted to men using aggressive humor when seeking a short-term tryst, yet find the same form of humor unappealing when seeking a committed long-term relationship. Future research examining the role of humor in mating should begin to establish links between specific types of humor and the specific underlying forms of quality each conveys.

# Conclusion

Numerous pieces of evidence exist to support the idea that females are very active players in the mating game, contrary to assumed wisdom. The females of several species choose their reproductive mates, based on assessing reliable cues of mate quality (e.g., Borgia et al., 2004; Gwynne & Brown, 1994; Reeder, 2003; Thornhill, 1992; see Andersson & Simmons, 2006, for a review). Human females appear to be no different, typically seeking evidence of long-term commitment (Buss & Schmitt, 1993; Trivers, 1972), but strategically adjusting their preferences and their behavior when obtaining mates of high genetic quality becomes paramount (Gangestad et al., 2007; Haselton & Gangestad, 2006; Pillsworth & Haselton, 2006). In contrast to how they are commonly depicted in classic fairy tales and contemporary media, women clearly exert a powerful influence in the realm of reproduction, a realm at the core of the evolutionary process.

The review of our own recent research focused specifically on humor production and evaluation in a mating context. Consistent with prior research, we found that men place more effort than women on using humor to attract potential mates. At first blush the active use of humor by men to woo women implies that women play a more passive role in the mating game. On the contrary, we found that women actively evaluate the quality of men's humorous offerings, seek partners that can make them laugh, and are more smitten with men they deem to have a good sense of humor. When a woman laughs at a man's jokes, she therefore may be providing him the broom with which to sweep her off her feet.

# References

Alvergne, A., & Lummaa, V. (2009). Does the contraceptive pill alter mate choice in humans? *Trends in Ecology and Evolution, 25,* 171–179.

Andersson, M. (1982). Female choice selects for extreme tail length in a widowbird. *Nature, 299,* 818–820.

Andersson, M., & Simmons, L. W. (2006). Sexual selection and mate choice. *Trends in Ecology and Evolution, 21,* 296–302.

Azim, E., Mobbs, D., Jo, B., Menon, V., & Reiss, A. L. (2005). Sex differences in brain activation elicited by humor. *Proceedings of the National Academy of Sciences, 102,* 16496–16501.

Borgia, G. (1995). Why do bowerbirds build bowers? *American Scientist, 83,* 542–547.

Borgia, G., Egeth, M., Uy, A., & Patricelli, G. L. (2004). Juvenile infection and male display: Testing the bright male hypothesis across individual life histories. *Behavioral Ecology, 15,* 722–728.

Bressler, E. R., & Balshine, S. (2006). The influence of humor on desirability. *Evolution and Human Behavior, 27,* 29–39.

Bressler, E. R., Martin, R. A., & Balshine, S. (2006). Production and appreciation of humor as sexually selected traits. *Evolution and Human Behavior, 27,* 121–130.

Buchholz, R. (1995). Female choice, parasite load, and male ornamentation in wild turkeys. *Animal Behaviour, 38,* 298–308.

Buss, D. M. (1988). The evolution of human intrasexual competition: Tactics of mate attraction. *Journal of Personality and Social Psychology, 54,* 616–628.

Buss, D. M. (1989). Sex differences in human mate preferences: Evolutionary hypotheses tested in 37 cultures. *Behavioral and Brain Sciences, 12,* 1–49.

Buss, D. M., & Schmitt, D. P. (1993). Sexual strategies theory: An evolutionary perspective on human mating. *Psychological Review, 100,* 204–232.

Cerda-Flores, R. M., Barton, S. A., Marty-Gonzalez, L. F., Rivas, F., & Chakraborty, R. (1999). Estimation of nonpaternity in the Mexican population of Nuevo Leon: A validation study of blood group markers. *American Journal of Physical Anthropology, 109,* 281–293.

Clark, C. L., Shaver, P. R., & Abrahams, M. F. (1999). Strategic behaviors in romantic relationship initiation. *Personality and Social Psychology Bulletin, 25,* 709–722.

Darwin, C. (1981). *The descent of man, and sexual selection in relation to sex* (Vols. 1 & 2). Princeton, NJ: Princeton University Press. (Original work published 1871).

Drea. C. M. (2005). Bateman revisited: The reproductive tactics of female primates. *Integrative and Comparative Biology, 45,* 915–923.

Durante, K. M., Li, N. P., & Haselton, M. G. (2008). Changes in women's choice of dress across the ovulatory cycle: Naturalistic and laboratory task–based evidence. *Personality and Social Psychology Bulletin, 34,* 1451–1460.

Eberhard, W. G. (1996). *Female control: Sexual selection by cryptic female choice.* Princeton, NJ: Princeton University Press.

Evans, K., & Brase, G. L. (2007). Assessing sex differences and similarities in mate preferences: Above and beyond demand characteristics. *Journal of Social and Personal Relationships, 24,* 781–791.

Fletcher, G. J. O., Tither, J. M., O'Loughlin, C., Friesen, M., & Overall, N. (2004). Warm and homely or cold and beautiful? Sex differences in trading off traits in mate selection. *Personality and Social Psychology Bulletin, 30,* 659–672.

Gangestad, S. W., Garver-Apgar, C. E., Simpson, J. A., & Cousins, A. J. (2007). Changes in women's mate preferences across the ovulatory cycle. *Journal of Personality and Social Psychology, 2007,* 151–163.

Gangestad, S. W., & Simpson, J. A. (2000). The evolution of human mating: Trade-offs and strategic pluralism. *Behavioral and Brain Sciences, 23,* 573–644.

Gangestad, S. W., Simpson, J. A., Cousins, A. J., Garver-Apgar, C. E., & Christensen, P. N. (2004). Women's preferences for male behavioral displays change across the menstrual cycle. *Psychological Science, 15,* 203–207.

Gangestad, S. W., & Thornhill, R. (1997). The evolutionary psychology of extrapair sex: The role of fluctuating asymmetry. *Evolution and Human Behavior, 18,* 69–88.

Gangestad, S. W., & Thornhill, R. (2008). Human oestrus. *Proceedings of the Royal Society B, 275,* 991–1000.

Gangestad, S. W., Thornhill, R., & Garver, C. (2002). Changes in women's sexual interests and their partners' mate retention tactics across the menstrual cycle: Evidence for shifting conflicts of interest. *Proceedings of the Royal Society B, 269*, 975–982.

Gangestad, S. W., Thornhill, R., & Garver-Apgar, C. E. (2005). Women's sexual interests across the ovulatory cycle depend on primary partner developmental instability. *Proceedings of the Royal Society of London B, 272*, 2023–2027.

Gwynne, D. T., & Brown, W. D. (1994). Mate feeding, offspring investment, and sexual differences in katydids (Orthoptera: Tettigoniidae). *Behavioral Ecology, 5*, 267–272.

Haselton, M. G., & Gangestad, S. W. (2006). Conditional expression of women's desires and men's mate guarding across the ovulatory cycle. *Hormones and Behavior, 49*, 509–518.

Haselton, M. G., Mortezaie, M., Pillsworth, E. G., Bleske-Rechek, A., & Frederick, D. A. (2007). Ovulatory shifts in human female ornamentation: Near ovulation, women dress to impress. *Hormones and Behavior, 51*, 40–45.

Kenrick, D. T., Groth, G. E., Trost, M. R., & Sadalla, E. K. (1993). Integrating evolutionary and social exchange perspectives on relationships: Effects of gender, self-appraisal, and involvement level on mate selection criteria. *Journal of Personality and Social Psychology, 64*, 951–969.

Kenrick, D. T., Sadalla, E. K., Groth, G., & Trost, M. R. (1990). Evolution, traits, and the stages of human courtship: Qualifying the parental investment model. *Journal of Personality, 58*, 97–116.

Li, N. P., Bailey, J. M., Kenrick, D. T., & Linsenmeier, J. A. W. (2002). The necessities and luxuries of mate preferences: Testing the tradeoffs. *Journal of Personality and Social Psychology, 82*, 947–955.

Li, N. P., Griskevicius, V., Durante, K. M., Jonason, P. K., Pasisz, D. J., & Aumer, K. (2009). An evolutionary perspective on humor: Sexual selection or interest indication? *Personality and Social Psychology Bulletin, 35*, 923–936.

Li, N. P., & Kenrick, D. T. (2006). Sex similarities and differences in preferences for short-term mates: What, whether, and why. *Journal of Personality and Social Psychology, 90*, 468–489.

Lovejoy, O. (1981). The origin of man. *Science, 211*, 341–350.

Macintyre, S., & Sooman, A. (1991). Non-paternity and prenatal genetic testing. *Lancet, 338*, 869–871.

Martin, R. A., Puhlik-Doris, P., Larsen, G., Gray, J., & Weir, K. (2003). Individual differences in uses of humor and their relation to psychological well-being: Development of the Humor Styles Questionnaire. *Journal of Research in Personality, 37*, 48–75.

McCann, T. S. (1981). Aggression and sexual activity of male southern elephant seals, *Mirounga leonina*. *Journal of Zoology, 195*, 295–310.

Miller, G. F. (2000a). The mating mind: How sexual choice shaped the evolution of human nature. New York: Anchor Books.

Miller, G. F. (2000b). Sexual selection for indicators of intelligence. In G. Bock, J. Goode, & K. Webb (Eds.), *The nature of intelligence* (pp. 260–275). Chichester, England: John Wiley.

Miller, G. F. (2007). Sexual selection for moral virtues. *Quarterly Review of Biology, 82*, 97–125.

Miller, S. L., & Maner, J. K. (2010). Scent of a woman: Men's testosterone responses to olfactory ovulation cues. *Psychological Science, 21*, 276–283.

Moore, M. M. (1985). Nonverbal courtship patterns in women: Context and consequences. *Ethology and Sociobiology, 6*, 237–247.

Penton-Voak, I. S., Perrett, D. I., Castles, D., Burt, M., Koyabashi, T., & Murray, L. K. (1999). Female preference for male faces changes cyclically. *Nature, 399*, 741–742.

Petrie, M., Halliday, T., & Sanders, C. (1991). Peahens prefer peacocks with elaborate trains. *Animal Behaviour, 41*, 323–332.

Pillsworth, E. G., & Haselton, M. G. (2006). Male sexual attractiveness predicts differential ovulatory shifts in female extra–pair attraction and male mate retention. *Evolution and Human Behavior, 27*, 247–324.

Reeder, D. M. (2003). The potential for cryptic female choice in primates: Behavioral, anatomical, and physiological considerations. In C. B. Jones (Ed.), *Sexual selection and reproductive* competition in primates: New perspectives and directions (pp. 255–303). Norman, OK: American Society of Primatologists.

Rosenqvist, G. (1990). Male mate choice and female-female competition for mates in the pipefish Nerophis ophidian. Animal Behaviour, 39, 1110–1116.

Rosvall, K. A. (in press). Intrasexual competition in females: Evidence for sexual selection? Behavioral Ecology.

Ryan, M. J. (1985). The Tungara frog. Chicago: University of Chicago Press.

Schmitt, D. P. (2005). Fundamentals of human mating strategies. In D. M. Buss (Ed.), The handbook of evolutionary psychology (pp. 258–291). New York: Wiley.

Schmitt, D. P., Alcalay, L., Allik, J., Ault, L., Austers, I., Bennett, K. L., et al. (2003). Universal sex differences in the desire for sexual variety: Tests from 52 nations, 6 continents, and 13 islands. Journal of Personality and Social Psychology, 85, 85–104.

Schmitt, D. P., & Buss, D. M. (1996). Strategic self-enhancement and competitor derogation: Sex and context effects on the perceived effectiveness of mate attraction tactics. Journal of Personality and Social Psychology, 70, 1185–1204.

Shackelford, T. K., Pound, N., Goetz, A. T., & Lamunyon, C. W. (2005). Female infidelity and sperm competition. In D. M. Buss (Ed.), The handbook of evolutionary psychology (pp. 372–393). New York: Wiley.

Smith, C., & Konik, J. (2011). Feminism and evolutionary psychology: Allies, adversaries, or both? An introduction to a special issue. Sex Roles, 64, 595–602.

Soltis, J. (2002). Do primate females gain nonprocreative benefits by mating with multiple males? Theoretical and empirical considerations. Evolutionary Anthropology, 11, 187–197.

Sritharan, R., Heilpern, K., Wilbur, C. J., & Gawronski, B. (2010). I think I like you: Spontaneous and deliberate evaluations of potential romantic partners in an online dating context. European Journal of Social Psychology, 40, 1062–1077.

Thornhill, R. (1992). Female preference for the pheromone of males with low fluctuating asymmetry in the Japanese scorpionfly (Panorpa japonica: Mecoptera). Behavioral Ecology, 3, 277–283.

Thornhill, R., & Gangestad, S. W. (1999). The scent of symmetry: A human pheromone that signals fitness? Evolution and Human Behavior, 20, 175–201.

Trivers, R. L. (1972). Parental investment and sexual selection. In B. Campbell (Ed.), Sexual selection and the descent of man 1871–1971 (pp. 136–179). Chicago: Aldine.

Wasser, S. K., Norton, G. W., Kleindorfer, S., & Rhine, R. J. (2004). Population trend alters the effects of maternal dominance rank on lifetime reproductive success in yellow baboons (Papio cynocephalus). Behavioral Ecology and Sociobiology, 56, 338–345.

Waage, J. K. (1997). Parental investment – minding the kids or keeping control? In P. Gowaty (Ed.), Feminism and evolutionary biology: Boundaries, interactions, and frontiers (pp. 527–553). New York: Chapman and Hall.

Wilbur, C. J., & Campbell, L. (2010). What do women want? An interactionist account of women's mate preferences. Personality and Individual Differences, 49, 749–754.

Wilbur, C. J., & Campbell, L. (2011). Humor in romantic contexts: Do men participate and women evaluate? Personality and Social Psychology Bulletin, 37, 918–929.

# 17

# Sex and Gender Differences in Communication Strategies

ELISABETH OBERZAUCHER

## Introduction

For decades a goal of the feminist movement has been equal living conditions for men and women. Still, gender inequality is part of our lives. This chapter focuses on one possible source of inequality: communication strategies. The selection of a specific communication strategy in a given situation results from the assessment of the situation and the interaction partner, individual traits such as personality, and individual goals. Communication success is thus strongly linked to social intelligence. Based on the predictions of evolutionary theory and empirical findings, the social skills of women should be more elaborate than those of men regarding sex differences found in cognition, perception, and behavior. Thus, women should be more likely to choose successful strategies for establishing and maintaining long-lasting, reliable social relationships (see Moscovice, this volume). On the other hand, men should be more successful in securing immediate profit. Rather than giving answers, this chapter aims to provide a theoretical and methodological framework for the investigation of sex differences in communication.

## Gender Inequality: A General Framework

Gender inequality is a persisting issue, despite efforts that have been made to equalize the living conditions of men and women. The Global Gender Gap Report 2008 (Hausmann, Tyson, & Zahidi, 2007) reveals the vast ground that has to be covered before equality of the genders is reached. In the global gender gap index the United States ranks 27th, behind several third-world countries. The United States only ranks first for educational attainment of women (sharing this position with several other countries); regarding economic participation and opportunity it ranks 12th; for health and survival, 37th. The political empowerment index (rank 56) gives little hope that politics alone can change the situation. Although the legal basis is in place for equality, reality looks very different. Women still earn lower wages for similar work than men, such that women's incomes are only 63% of men's. Norway ranks first in this report in overall scores (Hausmann et al., 2007).

What are the differences between nations ranking high and those ranking low in these reports? Can the lack of gender equality in low-ranking states be explained by differences in communication styles and behavior?

We are currently witnessing a new trend in the feminist movement, rooted in "sustainable feminism." This trend is characterized by a demand for a deeper understanding of the way men and women think and act, with the goal to employ those insights to improve cross-sex interactions. Knowledge about the sexes (from perception and cognition to preferences and behavior) can also help to better adjust gender mainstreaming to women's needs and thus help to close the gender gap in a satisfying and sustainable way.

Deborah Tannen (1990) argues that "communication between men and women can be like cross-cultural communication, prey to a clash of conversational styles" (p. 42). Her argument follows the line that women look at the world in a different way than men do, and communicate for different reasons: Female communication is centered on establishing and maintaining relationships, whereas male communication serves specific goals (Wood, 1994).

Thus, cross-sex communication should be studied like cross-cultural communication with an awareness of the stumbling blocks of cross-cultural communication. This perspective involves five considerations. First, there is an assumed similarity, which might blind us to differences and thus lead to misconceptions. Second, language must be considered, which is differently acculturated in men and women. Third, there are nonverbal misinterpretations, which can thoroughly alter the verbal information. Fourth, preconceptions and stereotypes, can, like assumed similarity, mislead our interpretations; and fifth, there is a tendency to evaluate, considering our own way of thinking and acting as superior to that of others (Barna, 1985). These misconceptions lead to decreased communication success, as well as to a negative perception of the communication partner.

By dropping the assumption that men and women are the same, and accepting the possibility that men's and women's values and goals may differ, and their verbal and nonverbal language might vary as well, science might begin to pursue research paths leading to new insights. Conversely, awareness of societal preconceptions and stereotypes, which portray the other sex as "different" or "opposite" is the pretext for avoiding such stereotypes (Mulvaney, 1994). Gender stereotypes seem to persist despite decades of activity by the feminist movement (Lueptow, Garovich, & Lueptow, 1995). A better understanding of sex and gender differences on an empirical basis can contribute to a more refined picture of the sexes.

This chapter will focus on cultural and sex differences in conversational styles—because these variables determine the way men and women treat each other and affect the outcome of social interactions.

Communicative styles shape everyday life, yet they have gained attention mainly in economic research and in clinical psychology (Roter, Hall, & Aoki, 2002). Insights gained from behavior observation could shed light on sex differences in communication and might provide some explanation of the origins and maintenance of the socioeconomic inequality of men and women.

## What Is Communication?

The most basic definition of communication is that a sender A produces a signal that is perceived by a receiver B (Figure 17.1).

John Locke (2004, p. 272) called this mechanism "semeiotics":

All that can fall within the compass of human understanding, being either, FIRST, The knowledge of things, as they are in their own proper beings, then constitution, properties, and operations; {…} or, SECONDLY, [word in Greek: praktika], The skill of right applying our own powers and actions, for the attainment of things good and useful.{…} THIRDLY, the third branch may be called [word in Greek: Semeiotika], or

THE DOCTRINE OF SIGNS; the most usual whereof being words, it is aptly enough termed also [word in Greek: Logika], LOGIC: the business whereof is to consider the nature of signs, the mind makes use of for the understanding of things, or conveying its knowledge to others. For, since the things the mind contemplates are none of them, besides itself, present to the understanding, it is necessary that something else, as a sign or representation of the thing it considers, should be present to it: and these are IDEAS. And because the scene of ideas that makes one man's thoughts cannot be laid open to the immediate view of another, nor laid up anywhere but in the memory, a no very sure repository: therefore to communicate our thoughts to one another, as well as record them for our own use, signs of our ideas are also necessary: those which men have found most convenient, and therefore generally make use of, are ARTICULATE SOUNDS. The consideration, then, of IDEAS and WORDS as the great instruments of knowledge, makes no despicable part of their contemplation who would take a view of human knowledge in the whole extent of it. And perhaps if they were distinctly weighed,

*Figure 17.1* Basic definition of communication. The sender encodes the information in a signal, which is sent to the receiver, who decodes it.

and duly considered, they would afford us another sort of logic and critic, than what we have been hitherto acquainted with.

Note that here no intentionality of the sender is necessary. This means that we communicate all the time, whether we are aware of it or not.

There has been a long discussion whether actual information is transferred through the signal, which seems to be resolved by now (Stiles, 2011). Thus I will not discuss it further at this point. The general agreement is that the signal per se does not carry information, but that the receiver interprets the signal based on her or his knowledge and thus information is created. The pretext of successful communication, then, is that the interpretation of the signal by the receiver corresponds to what the sender—intentionally or unintentionally—encoded in the signal. Therefore, a certain amount of common ground is necessary for two individuals to be able to communicate at all. But how is this common ground created?

The main foundation for sharing a basis of knowledge is a common evolutionary history. This commonality can refer to shared evolutionary roots, as applicable for within-species communication, as well as shared evolutionary history, meaning interspecific communication. Within a species, the shared manifold is made up of knowledge about the environment, of the species-specific needs and constraints. In other words, belonging to the same species contributes greatly to successful communication. The recent identification of the so-called mirror system casts light on how these commonalities could be processed in the brain (Gallese et al., 2001; Rizzolatti, Fadiga, Gallese, & Fogassi, 1996). The mirror system seems to be well suited to be employed as a sort of interpreter: By simulating the behaviors another individual shows, like pretending one would behave oneself, a very immediate access to the intraorganismic context of such behaviors is opened. This also casts a completely new light on communication research: Whereas explaining the whole process of communication previously required a rather complicated encoding and decoding procedure of a message transferred through a signal, communication can now be boiled down to simply putting oneself in the other's shoes. Building on this evolutionary foundation, social and cultural exchange further increase the common ground. The more background information that is shared among two individuals, the more smoothly communication proceeds.

Communication always involves sharing information and self-disclosure. This might not always be the intention of the sender, nevertheless communication seems to be omnipresent. Even though leaking information that one would rather keep private can occur when communicating, we find some sort of communication in all animal species. Moreover, communication skills might be the most important tool for ensuring social success. The basic setup for the evolutionary stage of communication are: (1) the need for successful cooperation, (2) the establishment of trust, (3) the control of communication success, (4) mutual manipulation attempts, and (5) the possibility of deception (Allwood et al., 2008).

Consequently, specific mechanisms should exist that are able to cope with the basic constraints on communication. Communication is employed not only to share information but also to establish social relations and to motivate others to do what we want them to do. Thus, the usual approach to the analysis of communication seems unfeasible, given the complexity of the task. Most communication models focus on the notion of information transfer, which results in a structural model like a ping-pong game, where communicative tokens of any kind move sequentially between two interactants. The analysis of communication is then limited to the analysis of behavior markers on either the verbal or nonverbal level. The problem with this approach is that it provides a rather stunted view on communicative processes insofar as it fails to take the dynamic nature of communication into account. Furthermore, it looks at specific signals in a rather isolated way, thus neglecting the multimodal interaction of communicative tokens.

In contrast to the sequential ping-pong model of communication we (Oberzaucher & Grammer, 2008) have introduced a dynamic communication model that involves signaling on three different levels, in which all communicative channels interact permanently (see Figure 17.2). These levels have to fulfill two main functions: The first function is information sharing, and the second is communication management (e.g., turn-taking, feedback, or back-channel behavior). The levels we propose are signals, displays, an analog index level, and appearance. On the symbolic level, verbal content is shared. On the display level, behaviors,

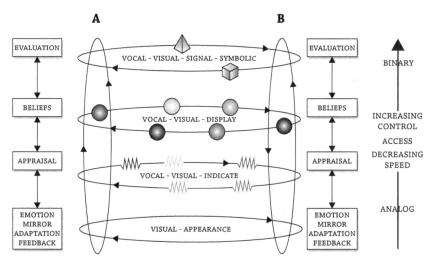

*Figure 17.2* Overview of the communication model. This figure illustrates the levels of our dynamic communication model as communication takes place between two communicators, A and B. Three different levels are differentiated according to the aforementioned types of communicative tokens (index, display, symbol) and the time scales on which they operate. At each level, vocal as well as visual expressions can be exchanged, concurrently and in both directions. (Oberzaucher & Grammer, 2008)

which can be identified as entities, that is, gestures and postures, are located. The index level can modify the information conveyed by the other levels, for instance by using verbal pauses, prosody, or movement quality. Finally, physical appearance of the communicator conveys biologically relevant information about the communicator, and modulates the meaning of communicative tokens on the above levels. All four levels are continuously and simultaneously active, and thus cannot be strictly separated from each other. Multimodality and dynamic interaction of representation in communication are basic features of communication, which demand simultaneous analysis of the different levels. At the same time, the interactants, depending on the evaluation of the situation and their motivation, continuously adjust to the ongoing communication process. The model also indicates that only the upper levels are accessible to conscious processes—both in production and decoding—while the lower level cannot be controlled so easily.

The model has been tested in the analysis of feedback and it was successfully used to understand communicative strategies involving feedback in embodied agents (Kopp, Allwood, Grammer, Ahlsen, & Stocksmeier, 2008). Communication success itself can be monitored by a feedback system. Mutual manipulation can be achieved by displaying signals, which promote the action tendencies of the signaler. The communication process also gives rise to deception, which is an important element in generating and maintaining one's adaptive communicative advantage over potential competitors. As Dawkins and Krebs (1984) propose, communicating one's intentions openly may be a costly mistake, since the goals of communication partners might be in conflict. This is one reason for the existence of unobtrusive levels in communication.

The assumption that the different communication channels interact requires the analysis of all levels, since the signals sent via one channel modify the meaning of other signals. In direct interactions verbal and nonverbal behavior as well as appearance play a role. That is, the number and types of social cues like voice hesitance, tone, immediacy of response, eye contact, body language, facial expression, and physical appearance combined determine the communicative meaning (Elfenbein, Foo, White, Tan, & Aik, 2007). They are an intrinsic part of interactions and are the basis on which we understand each other.

Communication plays a crucial role in mediating social interactions. When living in groups, individuals need a means to agree on common goals and strategies for how to reach them. However, individual goals might not always correspond to those of the group, and thus, communicative signals are also used by individuals to manipulate others. This leads to two phenomena: Withholding information and using social signals to trigger desired responses in others.

Social signals can trigger desired responses in others. I will name but a few examples to illustrate this function. First, there is appearance, such that features of the so-called Kindchenschema (i.e., large forehead, large eyes, small nose, small lower face, large head) elicit care-taking behavior in conspecifics, and even across species (Lorenz, 1943). There are analogue signals, such that fear changes the scent of sweat and others react to this scent with emotional responses (Prehn-Kristensen et al., 2009). Then, display behavior: Courtship behavior triggers sexual response from the other sex (Grammer, Kruck, Juette, & Fink, 2000). There is also symbolic communication, which is the most direct way: help of others can be recruited through simply asking for it.

Whereas the symbolic level allows us to name our needs directly and appears to be the most efficient way to recruit others' help, it also poses a high risk of being rejected. Someone who is asked a direct question can refuse right away. Having been rejected, there is no easy way for the one asking a favor to reenter the negotiation. This is why indirect communication is widespread: Even in verbal communication, one can observe that people escalate slowly toward their actual goal, avoiding naming it directly as long as possible (Holdcroft, 1976). One well-cited example is the following: Person A enters person B's office where all windows are wide open. Person A considers the room temperature to be too low and wants the windows closed. Instead of asking Person B to close the windows, Person A starts mentioning the low temperature or the noise outside. If this does not have the desired effect, Person A will mention being cold, getting gradually more insistent in the complaints the longer Person B does not react. Only when all other means have been exploited, Person A will ask Person B directly to close the windows. In this example, a steep dominance relation exists between Person A and Person B. First, the interaction happens in Person B's territory, and second, Person A seems to be in a subordinate position to Person B. The larger the status difference between two interlocutors, the more indirect the strategies of the subordinate will become. On the other hand, the dominant role can be very direct, since subordinates do not have the power to refuse their demands. Cross-cultural studies have shown that cultural norms can modify this simple dominance-directness relation (Brown & Lewinson, 1987).

Indirect communication and subtle manipulation of interaction partners involves mainly the lower levels of the communication model from Figure 17.2. Limited access to cognitive control makes the receiver of such signals much more unaware of what is happening and thus unable to take steps against this manipulative effort.

On the analogue level, chemical, acoustic, and visual signals play a role. The tonic modulation model by Schleidt (1973) proposes that the sender sends a uniform signal in time intervals. As the receiver decodes the signal over time, she or he uses a signal-time filter to extract the contextual meaning of the signal. Contextual meaning of a signal emerges through accumulation of discrete content meanings over time. In other words, Person A may be sending several signals simultaneously or sequentially, and depending on the greater context, Person B may respond or not. Thus, Person A manipulates the contextual meaning through signal modulation (Markl, 1985). In general, Schleidt's idea has not received much attention in the area of communication research. What he proposes is communication based on small fractions of signals; the single signal fraction itself will not be decoded as a single entity but will add up over time, building a reaction tendency in the receiver. Schleidt proposes a general dynamical approach to communication, and this view was extended by Michael Argyle's dance metaphor (Argyle, 1988), which denotes communication as a dance-like structure created by the communicators. This form of communication is most likely to take place on the analogue level, and such signals are perfectly suited for tonic signaling.

Etienne Jules Marey (1876) noted that "from the invisible atom to the celestial body in space everything is subject to motion" (p. 9). Indeed, motion is probably the most apparent characteristic of life, manifesting itself in all its functions and being central to some of them. On a most basic level, any behavior can be described as motion. In general, the way we move is at least as informative in communication as what we do. Motion quality has been of interest to scientists for a long time. The first attempts to investigate motion patterns were done with photographs taken at high speed. Through this methodology, Eadweard Muybridge (1887) attempted to decompose movements in their parts to gain knowledge about the mechanics of motion.

Fritz Heider and Mary-Ann Simmel (1944) showed in an experiment that we tend to interpret motions as emotions, intentions, and motivations. They showed a cartoon to people and asked them to describe what was happening in those cartoons. The actors are merely two triangles and a circle. Interestingly, people have no qualms to attribute aggression to the circle, whereas the triangles might show some mischief but in general are perceived as rather nice persons. Obviously, this information has not been taken from the physical appearance of these geometric figures, but from the way they behave and, primarily, how they move. This very impressive finding was later also supported by perception studies on human motion.

Phenomenological studies tried to disentangle physical appearance and motion quality through the implementation of the so-called point-light-display methodology. The results of those studies were impressive and could show not only that human motion can be recognized from such point light displays but also that it is possible for the human observer to attribute sex, personality, and emotional states to the moving points (Johannson, 1973; Sumby & Pollack, 1954). Motion quality, as well as voice properties, is closely linked to the physical properties of the body. The length of body parts in combination with weight distribution defines which movements are possible, and which are most energy efficient (Pfeifer & Bongard, 2007). The same holds true for voice parameters, for example fundamental frequency corresponds to the length of the vocal cords, and so on (Isshinki, 2000). Our visual system is strongly biased toward moving stimuli; moving objects seem to be more accessible to perception and interpretation than still objects (Finlay, 1982). Therefore, it seems to make sense to include some redundancy in the signaling system, communicating some content through both appearance and motion quality or voice, respectively. Motion quality can convey information itself, that is, personality is linked to motion, and the attitude toward the interaction partner affects time patterns in movements (Oberzaucher & Grammer, 2008).

The display level is more accessible to cognitive processes, both in production and perception, though it is not completely controllable. At the same time, the speed at which communicative tokens are exchanged is reduced at this level. Displays can to a certain extent be associated with specific meanings, but recent research indicates that the link between meaning and signal is far less unambiguous than expected. Obviously, a large extent of the variation in meaning can be explained by qualitative differences in the tokens themselves, for example the timing of the behaviors (Krumhuber & Kappas, 2005). On the iconic level of communication we find behaviors that can be classified into different behavior categories, but that are at the same time not directly linked to a distinct meaning. Facial expressions, body postures, and gesturing are accessible to classical behavior observation methods. Here a decomposition of the behaviors into their parts allows for a more detailed insight into the quality of the communicative tokens.

For the analysis of the communicative meaning of iconic communicative tokens, a combination of behavior observation and behavior simulation has proven useful. Behavior observation in natural or experimental settings is usually carried out by means of annotation of defined behavior categories. The behavior is then linked to questionnaire data, for example, emotional state or interpersonal attitude. Once the link between behavior and the information communicated has been established, these findings can be validated through reverse engineering (Grammer et al., 2004; Grammer & Oberzaucher, 2006).

Behavior is deconstructed into its parts using standardized methods. For example, the Facial Action Coding System (Ekman & Friesen, 1978) describes facial expressions as changes on the surface of the face that are caused by contractions of single muscles or muscle groups, the so-called action units. To analyze body postures, the Bernese System (Frey, Hirsbrunner, Florin, Daw, & Crawford, 1983) is used, describing single body angles. Questionnaire data are then linked to the behavior components (i.e., action units or body angles) employing multiple regression analyses, resulting in mathematical descriptions of the relation of each behavior component to the dependent variables. The communicative function of these behavior units is then validated by third-party ratings based on reconstructed facial expressions and body postures (Oberzaucher, Grammer & Schmehl, 2011). The great advantage of this approach is that it allows us to isolate specific behavior units and investigate their communicative value, while keeping all potentially intervening variables constant.

The symbolic level of the communication model consists mainly of verbal communication, and is complemented by symbolic gestures with distinct meaning, such as the gesture "thumbs up." Communication on this level is direct and easily accessible to cognitive control. While information transfer is facilitated by these characteristics, there is a great drawback: Signals on this level can be easily falsified and therefore can be used for deception and manipulation of others. One core aspect of verbal communication is that it needs to be regulated. In successful conversations, only one person speaks most of the time, even though there is a substantial amount of overlap of speech. Turn-taking signals regulate who has the floor, that is, who is allowed to speak when. Feedback regulates the communicative act in a broader sense: In a conversation, the listener has to provide the speaker constantly with information such as "I am listening" (Contact), "I can hear you" (Perceive), "I understand what you say" (Understand), and "I want you to continue/discontinue" (Evoke). Allwood and colleagues (1992) describe these four functions as the main capacities of feedback behavior. Feedback can occur on the verbal level in form of short utterances like "yes," "no," "really," and the like, but it is by far not limited to verbal communication. Head movements and postures play an important role in conversation regulation, as well as gestures and posture shifts.

Feedback is crucial for communication processes to function smoothly and efficiently. It allows us to inform the speaker right away if something in the communication process goes wrong, so he or she can take measures to express the information more clearly. In simulation of communicative behavior, for example for human-machine interactions, the incorporation of feedback seems to be essential (Allwood et al., 2008; Grammer et al., 2007).

# Why and How Sexes Differ

Sex differences in behavior are a popular research topic in both the biological and social sciences. Whereas both approaches yield the same information on sex differences, the explanation for their existence is not the same. Biologists argue that sex differences developed due to specific selection pressures in the course of human evolution. Asymmetric investment in offspring is very pronounced in all mammals: The relatively large female gametes translate into higher parental investment, with conception followed by an energetically expensive gestation and lactation. Collectively, this requires mothers to provide a high energy input toward offspring. Paternal investment, on the other hand, can be as little as providing gametes during one single intercourse. Since female biological minimal investment is much higher, males compete for them and females choose with whom to mate (Trivers, 1972).

Various examples of sex differences demonstrate how morphological, behavioral, and cultural factors complement each other. Many sex differences in human reproductive behavior can be explained with reference to male parental behavior patterns (Trivers, 1972). These include the male's greater aggressiveness, the preponderance of polygyny over polyandry, and differences in the antecedents of jealousy (Weisfeld & Woodward, 2004). The effects of this asymmetry reflect on mate choice criteria (female choice and male competition) and are assumed to be ubiquitous in all cultures (Buss, 1985). Females try to compensate for their higher biological investment by securing male investment in them and their offspring through the provisioning of resources. To ensure paternal investment requires establishing a long-term relationship with males who are well equipped with resources that they are willing to invest. The establishment of long-lasting reliable relationships with their partners and others is therefore even more crucial for females than for males, thus presenting a strong selection pressure toward the development of social skills in females (Hrdy, 1981).

Apart from asymmetric investment, another phenomenon led to different selection pressures on our female and male ancestors—different social environments due to patrilocality. In patrilocal systems, males remain in the group they were born into, while females leave their birth group when entering their reproductive period. The pattern of one sex leaving the birth group and the other remaining is an incest avoidance mechanism observable in many species.

In humans, patrilocality is more frequent both in traditional hunter-gatherers and in so-called modern societies compared to matrilocality and bilocal systems (i.e., choice between matri- or patrilocal residence) (Murdoch, 1981). Recent findings indicate that Neanderthals had a patrilocal mating pattern (Lalueza-Fox et al., 2010). Therefore, it can be assumed that patrilocality was predominant in the hominid lineage and led to the evolution of corresponding adaptations that still can be found nowadays (Wrangham, 1987).

In patrilocal systems, males receive material or emotional support, as well as protection from the members of the group, which improves chances of survival and successful reproduction. Support is provided on the basis of the inclusive fitness principle; male individuals are surrounded by relatives who genetically benefit by providing assistance (Hamilton, 1964; Van den Berghe, 1979).

Due to exogamy and the resulting greater geographic distance, females can rely on support from relatives to a lesser extent. This fact poses a problem for females, because long-term support to ensure their reproductive success is even more crucial for them. While support by the partner is important, additional help from others massively increases both the health status of a mother and the survival rate of her offspring (Clark, 2001). In both humans and other primates the phenomenon of alloparenting occurs, that is, group members who are not the parents of infants engage in childrearing processes (Hrdy, 2005). To ensure such investment, social skills are needed. Therefore, a pronounced selection pressure for female protohominids to evolve elaborate social skills can be assumed, while it was less strong for our male ancestors.

From a biological point of view, these two phenomena are the basis for many sex differences in social behavior. Biology provides a basic framework, which is adapted by sociocultural influences. There is no such thing as a purely genetic behavior, but also no behavior without an environmental basis. Thus, biology should serve as a contributor to a better understanding of sex differences, but is never to be engaged for justification.

# Sex and Gender Differences

This section contains a short overview of empirical studies about sex differences in several aspects of cognition and behavior. Literature in this field is extensive, and research has been carried out in various disciplines. I will focus on sex differences that might be involved in social interactions, from cognitive processes to behavior and communicative differences.

## Cognition

A number of anatomical differences between male and female brains have been described, such as women having smaller brains with a more pronounced connection between the hemispheres. Modern techniques like fMRI (functional magnetic resonance imaging) and EEG (electroencephalogram) allow us to watch the brain while it is preoccupied with specific tasks. This research shows that female brains seem to be more emotional—that is, emotional activations are more intense and involve larger areas (Wildgruber, Pihan, Ackermann, Erb, & Grodd, 2002). Mapping such activation patterns onto task performance (for example, attributing the correct emotional state to a facial expression) allows us to understand the physiological aspects of sex differences in cognition (Baxter, Jackson, & Bain, 2003; Baxter, Saykin, et al., 2003). The development of the brain seems to be affected by testosterone (Knickmeyer et al., 2006), which modulates the differential growth of brain areas toward a masculinization of the brain. The human brain shows plasticity throughout one's lifespan, and hormonal environments continue to affect its functioning. A dramatic change in testosterone and estradiol levels in adult life can modify the physiology and cognitive processing, such that testosterone shifts the processes toward a masculinized brain and estradiol toward a feminized brain, in terms of the distribution of activations (Schoning et al., 2007; Sommer et al., 2007).

There is empirical evidence that men employ different cognitive strategies in problem solving. Error management theory (EMT) describes a general principle in cognitive functioning (Haselton & Buss, 2000). No decision process is perfect, and mistakes are always possible, but some mistakes imply higher costs than others. If a fire alarm goes off without there actually being a fire, this will mainly cause inconvenience. On the other hand, if there is a fire, and the alarm does not go off, the costs are substantially higher. Thus, when constructing an alarm system, one will choose a threshold that ensures that every outbreak of fire will be detected, at the cost of some false alarms. This principle can be applied to cognitive processes, too. For example, we see faces not only in other people and animals, but also in objects (Guthrie, 1993; Windhager et al., 2008). The reason for this overperception error is found in EMT, in that not recognizing an agent might lead to severe consequences. There are also sex differences in error management, rooted in asymmetric investment. It would be a costly mistake for females to choose a partner who is not willing to invest, thus women tend to underestimate the mating interest of men. Men, on the other hand, overestimate the interest of women, thus avoiding the possibility of missing a mating opportunity (Hill, 2007). Interestingly, this form of error management affects the assessment of situations with unknown outcomes, even if they have nothing to do with mate choice. Men tend to overestimate themselves, while women underestimate themselves (Oberzaucher et al., 2012). Consequently, this might lead women to set lower aims in negotiations.

Cognitive functioning is strongly intertwined with emotionality. Antonio Damasio (1998) proposes that there is no cognition without emotion. Thus, emotions have to be taken into account when talking about communication.

## Nonverbal Behavior and Emotions

Women experience emotions more intensely than men (Grossman & Wood, 1993), and they outperform men in reading nonverbal behavior (Baron-Cohen, 2003; Carter & Hall, 2007; Hall, 1990). As compared to men, women are more expressive and send more social and communicative signals (Hall, 1990). This is an advantage for creating trust in an interaction, but makes it more difficult to hide one's intentions from a social partner.

Women are not only better at decoding nonverbal signals, they also outperform men in the production of social signals. For example, they show higher expression accuracy than men, meaning female facial expressions are more accurately recognized than male expressions (Hall, 1990). Women show greater facial expressiveness, and tend to be externalizers (high degree of expressions, lower physiological response). They generally use social smiles more often, which could be explained by their social preoccupation (Weisfeld, 1993). Women look at their social partners more often (i.e., mutual gaze or looking each other into the eyes), which allows for a more permanent monitoring of the facial signals of the partner. They also have a smaller personal distance and a more direct (face to face) orientation, allowing more immediate contact with others, which is enhanced by higher proportions of touching (Hall, 1984).

A pretext to act socially intelligent is the ability to correctly assess a social partner's behavioral tendencies. This ability is called theory of mind (ToM), such that the representation of the other's mind helps us to understand how others see the world (Whiten, 1997). It is necessary to know what the other may and may not know. Knowledge about the communication partner's perception, knowledge, and motivations is a necessary pretext for any social interaction, especially if one is attempting to motivate the other to take specific actions. Women score higher in ToM-tasks (Baron-Cohen, 2003) and should thus be better at assessing the other's intentions (Gordon, 1996).

In order to assess emotional states, motivations, and behavior tendencies of our counterparts, we use simple techniques. We assume that all people function in a comparable way and make predictions about the other through introspection and projection. The neural correlates of mind reading have been found in the so-called mirror neurons. These are neurons in the motor cortex that are active not only when acting out a specific action but also when this action is seen or heard being carried out by another agent (Gallese, Fadiga, Fogassi, & Rizzolatti, 1996). The so-called F5-neurons have been identified in nonhuman animals, and while human's activations in the Area 24 have been shown, individual neurons are not accessible for investigation in humans. These mirror systems serve to create a shared manifold, indicating that they are the means by which we can simulate intentions and behavioral tendencies of others, which is a prerequisite for ToM and social competence (Gallese, 2001).

The signaling behavior of others affects the degree and the accurateness of our predictions. The more expressive a person is (i.e., the stronger and more explicit the nonverbal signaling is), the easier it is to read this person. Consequently, more expressive people are perceived as more likable and attractive (Renninger, 2004). In addition to the immediate assessment of the social partner, we rely on information we have gathered in the past about this person. The acquisition of social knowledge is the prominent topic in everyday conversations, creating a basis for predictions about the others' behavior (Dunbar, 1996).

Since verbal communication is a prerequisite for successful social involvement and facilitates social strategies, elaborate linguistic skills have evolved (Searle, 1969). Women show higher verbal ability, and comprehend more words on average (Miller, 1967). In addition, girls feel usually more efficient and less anxious than boys in the verbal domain (Rouxel, 2000).

## Social Networks and Social Strategies

As I review in this section, communicative behavior serves, among other goals, the establishment and maintenance of relationships. Sex differences found in the context of social relationships fit well in the model of patrilocality, which brought about a stronger selection pressure on women to develop social skills and a social preoccupation. Consequently, the intimate social networks of women are more complex (Bernhard & Oberzaucher, 2004) and involve more relationships than those of men (Vierzigmann, 1995), and they more often name a family member as the closest person in their social network (Rohde et al., 2003). Girls are more successful in reconciliation after conflicts than boys (Butovskaya, Timentschik, & Burkova, 2007). Women's values and goals in social relationships focus on the development of altruistic, reciprocal relationships, while men are "interested primarily in power, competition, and struggle" (Willingham & Cole, 1997, p. 144). Men tend to show higher degrees of both verbal and physical aggression (Knight, Fabes, & Higgins, 1996), whereas women show a higher degree of relationship aggression, such as using blackmail (Butovskaya et al., 2007; Crick & Gropeter, 1995). The social behavior of men seems to be directed toward a gain of power, whereas female behavior pursues social stability (Rubin & Brown, 1975; Weisfeld, Bloch, & Ivers, 1984).

Social competence is defined as a concept that combines the ability to be assertive and keep one's own interests with the ability to start and maintain positive relationships with others. A socially competent person finds a balanced ratio between one's own interest and the interests of others (Asendorpf, 1999). Differences between the sexes in social abilities and activities arise early in ontogeny: It has been demonstrated that girls in kindergarten show more social competence than boys of comparable age (LaFreniere et al., 2002). Schreiner and colleagues (2001) report that female teenagers develop higher social competence during a stay in a holiday camp in comparison to male teenagers. Girls generally play in smaller groups, and their play shows more sharing, more imitation of relationships and more intimacy than boys' play (Grammer, Schreiner, Atzmüller, & Dittami, 2002). This pattern is still observable in adulthood. Women self-report that they have larger social networks of close friends than men (Oberzaucher & Bernhard, in prep.). Women spend more time caring for preschoolers and aging parents and are also far more likely to describe themselves as being empathetic (Asendorpf, 1999). But how does this affect success in social interactions?

When confronted with a negotiation task, men are generally found to be more successful than women. This effect, though, seems to be easily manipulated by providing specific information: If males are told about typically female gender stereotypes and that feminine traits are linked to poor negotiation performance, men outperform women; whereas women, when told that stereotypically male strategies perform worse, outperform men (Kray, Galinsky, & Thompson, 2002). This is another indicator for the plasticity of these phenomena; the specific qualities of the observed interaction have a pronounced effect on the choice of strategies and communicative tokens. Therefore, single findings should not be overestimated.

Women seem to be more relationship-oriented and men more profit-oriented (Rubin & Brown, 1975). Above that, women are less hostile in face-to-face interactions than in virtual negotiations, while there is no comparable difference in men, indicating that the assessment of the interaction partner is more important for choice of strategy in women than in men (Stuhlmacher, Citera, & Willis, 2007). As a consequence, a social incentive should affect female performance by making them even more cooperative. Male cooperation only increases if high immediate profit is involved (Katz, Amichai-Hamburger, Manisterski, & Kraus, 2007). Cooperation is an advantageous behavior if negotiation is part of an ongoing relationship (Putnam & Kolb, 2000). The reason why men score better in negotiation studies might lie in the rather short-lived nature of the experimental interactions. Most of the studies involve one specific situation and do not have long-lasting implications. Thus, the profit-orientation is advantageous, because it allows concentrating on the task at hand, while the sustainable strategy focuses on the establishment of reliable relations, which includes a willingness to forego the maximum profit in the first move. As stated in game theory, altruism can be established as a stable strategy only if future interactions are conceivable (Axelrod & Hamilton, 1981).

Another question pertains to whether women employ less successful negotiation strategies. Do women give the wrong cues in negotiations by taking on a wrong social role? Stereotypically masculine traits (e.g., strong, dominant, assertive, rational) are connected with success, but not female stereotypes (e.g., weak submissive, intuitive, emotional) (Pulkkinen, Ohranen, & Tolvanen, 1999). Or, can these differences be explained by general differences in social strategies?

Based on our assessment of the situation, monitoring of individual goals, and interpreting the social partner's behavior, we have to decide whether and how our goals can most likely be achieved. The selection of the social strategy will strongly influence the outcome of an interaction.

One should refrain from escalating the communicative situation too quickly, especially in situations where stakes are high. Both verbal and nonverbal behavior should follow an indirect path, which allows one to avoid losing everything in the first move. In interactions with a steep dominance relation the high-ranking person is more likely to act direct, and the subordinate will use indirect strategies (Brown & Levinson, 1978; Grammer et al., 2002). Women are more likely to communicate indirectly than men (Brown & Levinson, 1978; Nelson, Batal, & Bakary, 2002).

When entering a social interaction with a new social partner, the impression one evokes in this partner is crucial for the potential benefit one can gain through this interaction. Different strategies and tactics are employed depending on the person him/herself, on the social partner, and on the social setting. Social interactions are framed by factors such as social distance and relative power of the interactants, as well as the absolute ranking of impositions within the respective culture (Brown & Levinson, 1978). Impression management serves the accumulation of social power, which can then be employed to pursue individual goals with the help of others. Several authors (Bolino & Turnley, 1999; Lee, Quigley, Nesler, Corbett, & Tedeschi, 1999) propose a framework of strategies and tactics employed in impression management, as follows.

Assertive impression management strategies serve the acquisition of a lasting positive reputation, which holds true for different situations. Defensive impression management strategies translate into behaviors such as frequent use of excuses, diverse self-handicapping strategies, and the presentation of symptoms of mental illnesses. Assertive impression management tactics aim at immediate situation-specific effects. Defensive impression management tactics serve the defense or reestablishment of reputation in a specific situation. Women are more likely to employ defensive strategies and tactics (Lee et al., 1999).

This is complemented by findings on politeness in speech, where women are found to use more positive politeness strategies, such as endearment, irony, rhetorical questions, negative assertions meaning positives, empathic expression of opinions, exaggerated empathic intonation and prosodics, and hedging expressions of strong feelings than men. In contrast, men tend to employ sexy joking and lecturing styles in same-sex interactions. In cross-sex-interactions, women use more negative politeness, whereas men are brusquer, unless a large social distance demands negative politeness. The negative politeness in women might be the consequence of differences in relative power, and consequently, it could be less pronounced in cultures with smaller differences in power between the sexes (Brown & Levinson, 1978).

These findings are mainly based on differences in verbal behavior. As cognitive accessibility decreases from the symbolic to the analogue level, so does the directness of verbal expression. Therefore, it would be likely to find a shift of the signaling intensity from the upper toward the lower levels when an indirect strategy is chosen.

Impression management defines the roles in an interaction. Selecting a strategy is the next step. Preferences for specific strategies seem to be a personality trait but depend also on the given situation. Machiavellianism, named after Niccolo Machiavelli (Machiavelli, 1513/2009), describes a person's tendency to deceive and manipulate others for personal gain. In general, men score higher in Machiavellianism, as measured by MACH-scales (Wilson, Near, & Miller, 1998). Machiavellianism is not related to success in project managers (Graham, 1996), and therefore Machiavellianism is a short-term strategy, which is bound to be unsuccessful in the long run. It neglects the treatment of others as social partners, and is reckless and goal-oriented. In long-term relationships, this strategy is likely to fail. The success of this strategy depends largely on the control one has in a specific situation and the dominance relations among the involved parties.

Social intelligence is thus a far more complex phenomenon than the mere ability to manipulate others. In this context, Whiten and Byrne (1997) propose that Machiavellian intelligence is an interaction of social knowledge with social perception, strategic abilities, and the ability to produce the necessary behavioral output in socially complex situations. For empirical research, this means that one has to investigate social abilities both in immediate success in a given situation, as well as the ability to maintain sustainable, reliable relationships. The behavior we employ to reach social success is communicative. Thus, we have to try to integrate knowledge about cognition, motivation, and behavior if we want to gain a deeper understanding of communicative processes.

# Discussion

Sex differences in cognition arise due to different hormonal environments during early development. Differential growth of brain areas is associated with sex differences in cognitive performance later on in life, but this association is not hardwired, and instead can be counterbalanced through dramatic changes in hormonal environments in adults. Cognitive processes that are sexually dimorphic, such as error management, play an important role for the assessment of social interactions. The choice of communicative strategies depends largely on social factors, such as dominance relations and escalation potential.

Emotions are central to cognitive and social processes. The stronger responsiveness of women to emotional stimuli might hint at a cognitive strategy: Emotions are a powerful tool in reducing the number of choices. As humans have a very large behavioral repertoire, emotions are very important for narrowing down the options from which to choose in a given situation. By enabling this emotional filter, decisions can be made more quickly and efficiently. Emotional expressions are central to any communicative act. Women are both more expressive and more accurate at decoding emotional expressions. This might be linked to some kind of honesty factor in communication: Emotional expressions are hard to falsify and they are hints about action tendencies. Thus, a person showing emotional expressions enables the interactant to make predictions about the interactions, whereas someone showing a "pokerface" remains unpredictable. Emotional expressiveness combined with accuracy in reading expressions provides the basis for a predictable, long-term interaction.

The higher social competence in women is not associated with higher success in negotiations. Empirical findings indicate that sexually dimorphic abilities connected to communication favor the sexes in different situations: Men tend to be more successful in short-term negotiations, while women seem to be more apt at establishing long-term relationships.

If we could link cognitive and emotional processes via communicative behavior to success in social interactions, we might provide a weak link between sex differences and gender inequality. To aim for anything more than a weak link would be unrealistic and not helpful. As mentioned before, humans are complex organisms whose behavior is shaped by a continuous interaction between biological, environmental, cultural, and social constraints. Thus, it is impossible to explain any aspect of human behavior solely on one level. A more thorough understanding can only be achieved through integration of all of these factors. This is why a holistic view has to be taken when trying to understand sex and gender differences in communication. Interactive effects between the above outlined levels of communication might cast a completely different light on the emergence of meaning in communicative encounters.

# References

Allwood, J., Kopp, S., Grammer, K., Ahlsén, E., Oberzaucher, E., & Koppensteiner, M. (2008). The analysis of embodied communicative feedback in multimodal corpora: A prerequisite for behavior simulation. *Journal of Language Resources and Evaluation, 41*(3–4), 255–272.

Allwood, J., Nivre, J., & Ahlsén, E. (1992). On the semantics and pragmatics of linguistic feedback. *Journal of Semantics, 9*(1), 1–26.

Argyle M (1988). *Bodily Communication.* London, Methuen.

Asendorpf, J. B. (1999). *Psychologie der Psychologie der Psychologie der* (2nd ed.). New York: Springer Verlag.

Axelrod, R., & Hamilton, W. D. (1981). The evolution of cooperation. *Science, 211,* 1390–1396.

Barna, L. M. (1985). Stumbling blocks in intercultural communication. In L. A. Samovar & R. E. Porter (Eds.), *Intercultural communication: A reader* (4th ed., pp. 330–338). Belmont, CA: Wadsworth.

Baron-Cohen, S. (2003). *The essential difference: Men, womenThe essential difference: Men, women-The essential difference: Men, women.* London: Penguin.

Baxter, J. S., Jackson, M., & Bain, S. A. (2003). Interrogative suggestibility: Interactions between interviewees' self-esteem and interviewer style. *Personality and Individual Differences, 35*(6), 1285–1292.

Baxter, L. C., Saykin, A. J., Flashman, L. A., Johnson, S. C., Guerin, S. J., Babcock, D. R., et al. (2003). Sex differences in semantic language processing: A functional MRI study. *Brain and Language, 84*(2), 264–272.

Bernhard, M., & Oberzaucher, E. (2004, 22–25 July). The impact of patrilocality on human social behavior. Paper presented at the HBES conference, Berlin, Germany.

Bolino, M. C., & Turnley, W. H. (1999). Measuring impression management in organizations: A sale development based on the Jones and Pittman taxonomy. *Organizational Research Methods, 2,* 187–206.

Brown, P., & Levinson, S.C. (1978). Universals in language use: Politeness phenomena. In E. N. Goody (Ed.), *Questions and politeness* (pp. 56–289). Cambridge, UK: Cambridge University Press.

Brown, P. & Levinson S.C. (1987). *Politeness. Some Universals in Language Usage.* Cambridge: Cambridge University Press.

Buss, D. (1985). *Human mate selection. American Scientist, 73,* 47–51.

Butovskaya, M. L., Timentschik, V. M., & Burkova, V. N. (2007). Aggression, conflict resolution, popularity, and attitude to school in Russian adolescents. *Aggressive Behavior, 33*(2), 170–183.

Carter, J. D., & Hall, J. A. (2007). Individual differences in the accuracy of detecting social covariations: Ecological sensitivity. *Journal of Research in Personality,42*(2), 439–455.

Clark, L. (2001). La Familia: Methodological issues in the assessment of perinatal social support for Mexicanas living in the United States. *Social Science and Medicine, 53*(10), 1303–1320.

Crick, N. R., & Gropeter, J. K. (1995). Relational aggression, gender, and social psychological adjustment. *Child Development, 66,* 710–722.

Damasio, A. R. (1998). Descartes' Descartes' Descartes' Descartes' Descartes' (3rd ed.). MünchenMünchenDeutscher Taschenbuch Verlag.

Dawkins, R., & Krebs, J. R. (1984). Animal signals: Mind-reading and manipulation. In J. R. Krebs & N. B. Davies (Eds.), *Behavioral ecology: An evolutionary approach* (pp. 380–402). Oxford: Blackwell.

Dunbar, R. I. M. (1996). Groups, gossip, and the evolution of language. In A. Schmitt, K. Atzwanger, K. Grammer, & K. Schaefer (Eds.), *New aspects of human ethology* (pp. 77–86). New York: Plenum Press.

Ekman, P., & Friesen, W.Friesen, W.Friesen, W. (1978). *Investigator's guide: Facial action coding system.* Paolo Alto, CA: Consulting Psychologis.

Elfenbein, H. A., Foo, M. D., White, J., Tan, H. H., & Aik, V. C. (2007). Reading your counterpart: The benefit of emotion recognition accuracy for effectiveness in negotiation. *Journal of Nonverbal Behavior, 31,* 205–223.

Finlay, D. (1982). Motion perception in the peripheral visual field. *PerceptionPerceptionPerceptio n11*(4) 457–462.

Frey, S., Hirsbrunner, H.Hirsbrunner, H.Hirsbrunner, H., Florin, A., DawDawDaw, & Crawford, R. (1983). A unified approach to the investigation of nonverbal and verbal behavior in communication research. In W. Doise & S. Moscovici (Eds.), *Current issues in European social psychology* (pp. 143–199). Cambridge, UK: Cambridge University Press.

Gallese, V. (2001). The The The The The . *Journal of Consciousness Studies, 8*(5–7), 33–50.

Gallese, V., Fadiga, L., Fogassi, L., & Rizzolatti, G. (1996). Action recognition in the premotor cortex. *Brain, 119*(2), 593–609.

Gordon, R. M. (1996). "Radical" simulationism. In P. Carruthers & P. K. Smith (Eds.), *Theories of theories of mind* (pp. 11–21). Cambridge, UK: Cambridge University Press.

Graham, J. H. (1996). Machiavellian project managers: Do they perform better? *International Journal of Project Management, 14*(2), 67–74.

Grammer, K., Fink B., Oberzaucher E., Atzmüller M., Blantar I., & Mitteröcker, P. (2004). The analysis of self reported affect in body posture and body posture simulation. *Collegium Anthropologicum, 28*(Suppl. 2), 159–173.

Grammer, K., Kopp, S., Allwood, J., Stocksmeyer, T., Ahlsen, E., & Oberzaucher, E. (2007). Human machine interfaces and embodied communication. In G. Kempter & M. Dontschewa (Eds.), *uDayV Informieren mit Computeranimation* (pp. 24–37). Berlin: Pabst Science Publishers.

Grammer, K., Kruck, K., Juette, A., & Fink, B. (2000). Non-verbal behavior as courtship signals: The role of control and choice in selecting partners. *Evolution and Human Behavior, 21,* 371–390.

Grammer, K., & Oberzaucher, E. (2006). The reconstruction of facial expressions in embodied systems: New approaches to an old problem. *ZIF Mitteilungen, 2,* 14–31.

Grammer, K., Schreiner, S., Atzmüller, M., & Dittami, J. (2002). Die evolutionäre Psychologie des Kindes: Soziale Intelligenz und Überleben. In K. W. Alt & A. Kemkes-Grottenthaler (Eds.), Kinderwelten. *Anthropologie—Geschichte Kulturvergleich* (pp. 6–24). Cologne, Germany: Böhlau Verlag.

Grossman, M., & Wood, W. (1993). Sex differences in intensity of emotional experience: A social role interpretation. *Journal of Personality and Social Psychology, 65*(5), 1010–1022.

Guthrie, S. E. (1993). *Faces in the clouds: A new theory of religion.* New York: Oxford University Press.

Hall, J. (1984). *Non-verbal sex differences.* Baltimore: John Hopkin.

Hall, J. A. (1990). *Nonverbal sex differences: Accuracy of communication and expressive style.* Baltimore: Johns Hopkins University Press.

Hamilton, W. D. (1964). The genetical evolution of social behaviour. *Journal of Theoretical Biology, 7,* 1–52.

Haselton, M. G., & Buss, D. M. (2000). Error management theory: A new perspective on biases in cross-sex mind reading. *Journal of Personality and Social Psychology, 78*(1), 81–91.

Hausmann, Tyson, L. D., & Zahidi, S. (2007). *The global gender gap report.* Geneva, Switzerland: World Economic Forum.

Heider, F., & Simmel, M. (1944). An experimental study of apparent behaviour. *American Journal of Psychology, 57,* 243–259.

Hill, S. E. (2007). Overestimation bias in mate competition. *Evolution and Human Behavior, 28*(2), 118–123.

Holdcroft, D. (1976). Forms of indirect communication: An outline. *Philosophy and Rhetoric, 9*(3), 147–161.

Hrdy, S. B. (1981). *The woman that never evolved.* Cambridge, MA: Harvard University Press.

Hrdy, S. B. (2005). Evolutionary context of human development: The cooperative breeding model. In C. S. Carter, L. Ahnert, K. E. Grossmann, S. B. Hrdy, M. E. Lamb, S. W. Porges, & N. Sachser (Eds.), Attachment and bonding: A new synthesis. (pp. 9–32). .

Isshinki, N. (2000). Mechanical and dynamic aspects of voice production as related to voice therapy and phonosurgery. *Otolaryngology: Head and Neck Surgery, 122*(6), 782–793.

Johannson, G. (1973). Visual perception of biological motion and a model for its analysis. *Perception and Psychophysics, 14,* 201–211.

Katz, R., Amichai-Hamburger, Y., Manisterski, E., & Kraus, S. (2007). Different orientations of males and females in computer-mediated negotiations. *Computers in Human Behavior, 24*(2), 516–534.

Knickmeyer, R., Baron-Cohen, S., Fane, B. A., Wheelwright, S., Mathews, G. A., Conway, G. S., et al. (2006). Androgens and autistic traits: A study of individuals with congenital adrenal hyperplasia. *Hormones and Behavior, 50*(1), 148–153.

Knight, G. P., Fabes, R. A., & Higgins, D. A. (1996). Concerns about drawing causal inferences from meta-analyses: An example in the study of gender differences in aggression. *Psychological Bulletin, 119*(3), 410–421.

Kopp, S., Allwood, J., Grammer, K., Ahlsen, E., & Stocksmeier, T. (2008). Modelling feedback with virtual humans. In I. Wachsmuth & G. Knoblich (Eds.), *Modeling communication with robots and virtual humans* (pp. 18–37). Berlin, Germany: Springer Verlag.

Kray, L. J., Galinsky, A. D., & Thompson, L. (2002). Reversing the gender gap in negotiations: An exploration of stereotype regeneration. *Organizational Behavior and Human Decision Processes, 87*(2), 386–410.

Krumhuber, E., & Kappas, A. (2005). Moving smiles: The role of dynamic components for the perception of the genuineness of smiles. *Journal of Nonverbal Behavior, 29*(1), 3–24.

LaFreniere, P., Butovskaya, M., Chen, Q., Dessen, M., Atzwanger, K., Schreiner, S., et al. (2002). Cross-cultural analysis of social competence and behavior problems in preschoolers. *Early Education and Development, 13*, 201–219.

Laluleza-Fox, C., Rosas, R., Estalrrich, A., Gigli, E., Campos, P.F., Garcia-Tabanero, A., et al. (2010). Genetic evidence for patrilocal mating behavior among Neandertal groups. PNAS, 20. December 2010, 1–4.

Lee, S.-J., Quigley, B. M., Nesler, M. S., Corbett, A. B., & Tedeschi, J. T. (1999). Development of a self-presentation tactics scale. *Personality and Individual Differences, 26*(4), 701–722.

Locke, J. (2004). *An* Essay Concerning Human Understanding, Volume II, MDCXC,. http://www.gutenberg.org/ebooks/10616, Based on the 2nd Edition, Books III. and IV, An essay concerning humane understanding. In four books. Written by John Locke, Gent. The second edition, with large additions. . . . London, printed for Thomas Dring and Samuel Manship M DC XCIV [1694] [40], 407, [13] p. port. 2°.

Lorenz, K. (1943). Die angeborenen. *Zeitschrift für Tierpsychologie, 5*, 233–409.

Lueptow, L. B., Garovich, L., & Lueptow, M. B. (1995). The persistence of gender stereotypes in the face of changing sex roles: Evidence contrary to the sociocultural model. *Ethology and Sociobiology, 16*(6), 509–530.

Machiavelli, N. (2009). *Il principe* (Ed.). Available from http://www.ibiblio.org/ml/libri/m/MachiavelliNB_IlPrincipe_s.pdf

Marey, E. J. (1876). La méthode graphique dans les sciences expérimentales. Physiologie Expérimentale. Travaux du laboratoire de M. Marey, 2, 133–219.

Markl, H. (1985). Manipulation, modulation, information, cognition: Some of the riddlers of communication. *Fortschritte der Zoologie, 31*, 163–194.

Miller, G. A. (1967). *The psychology of communication: Seven essays.* Baltimore: Penguin.

Mulvaney, B. M. (1994). Gender differences in communication: An intercultural experience. Retrieved July 12, 2007, from http://feminism.eserver.org/gender/cyberspace/gender-differences.txt

Murdoch, G. P. (1981). *Atlas of world cultures.* Pittsburgh, PA: University of Pittsburgh Press.

Muybridge, E. (1887). *Animal locomotion: An electro-photographic investigation of consecutive phases of animal movements.* Philadelphia: Lippincott.

Nelson, G. L., Batal, M. A., & Bakary, W. E. (2002). Directness vs. indirectness: Egyptian Arabic and US English communication style. *International Journal of Intercultural Relations, 26*(1), 39–57.

Oberzaucher, E., & Bernhard, M. (October 2012). *Gender differences in friendships.* Ludwig-Boltzmann-Institute for Urban Ethology, University of Vienna. Manuscript in preparation.

Oberzaucher, E., Filiadis, C., Stockinger, E., & Grammer, K. (submitted, 2012). Sexual dimorphism in error management beyond the mating context. submitted to *Journal of Evolutionary Psychology.*

Oberzaucher, E., & Grammer, K. (2008). Everything is movement: On the nature of embodied communication. In I. Wachsmuth & G. Knoblich (Eds.), *Embodied communication in humans and machines* (pp. 151–178). Oxford, UK: Oxford University Press.

Oberzaucher, E., Grammer, K., & Schmehl, S. (2011). Embodiment and expressive communication on the Internet. In A. Kappas & N. C. Krämer (Eds.), *Face-to-face communication over the Internet* (pp. 237–279). Cambridge, UK: Cambridge University Press.

Pfeifer, R., & Bongard, J. (2007). *How the body shapes the way we think: A new view of intelligence.* Cambridge, MA: A Bradford Book, MIT Press.

Prehn-Kristensen, A., Wiesner, C., Bergmann, T. O., Wolff, S., Jansen, O., et al. (2009). Induction of empathy by the smell of anxiety. *PLoS ONE, 4*(6), e5987. doi:10.1371/journal. pone.0005987

Pulkkinen, L., Ohranen, M., & Tolvanen, A. (1999). Personality antecedents of career orientation and stability among women compared to men. *Journal of Vocational Behavior, 54*(1), 37–58.

Putnam, L. L., & Kolb, D. M. (2000). Rethinking negotiation: Feminist views of communication and exchange. In P. M. Buzzanell (Ed.), *Rethinking organizational and managerial communication from feminist perspectives* (pp. 1–52). Thousand Oaks, CA: Sage.

Renninger, L. A. (2004). *Faces in motion: A Darwinian analysis of the roles of facial attractiveness and facial expressiveness in creating a first impression.* PhD Thesis, Faculty of Life Sciences, University of Vienna.

Rizzolatti, G., Fadiga, L., Gallese, V., & Fogassi, L. (1996). Premotor cortex and the recognition of motor actions. *Cognitive Brain Research, 3*, 131–141.

Rohde, P. A., Atzwanger, K., Butovskaya, M., Lampert, A., Mysterud, I., Sanchez-Andres, A., et al. (2003). Perceived parental favoritism, closeness to kin, and the rebel of the family: The effects of birth order and sex. *Evolution and Human Behavior, 24*(4), 261–276.

Roter, D. L., Hall, J. A., & Aoki, Y. (2002). Physician gender effects in medical communication. A meta-analytical review. *Journal of the American Medical Association, 288*(6), 756–764.

Rouxel, G. (2000). Cognitive-affective determinants of performance in mathematics and verbal domains: Gender differences. *Learning and Individual Differences, 12*(3), 287–310.

Rubin, J., & Brown, B. (1975). *The social psychology of bargaining and negotiation.* New York: Academic Press.

Schleidt, W. M. (1973). Tonic communication: Continuous effects of discrete signs in animal communication systems. *Journal of Theoretical Biology, 42*, 369–386.

Schoning, S., Engelien, A., Kugel, H., Schafer, S., Schiffbauer, H., Zwitserlood, P., et al. (2007). Functional anatomy of visuo-spatial working memory during mental rotation is influenced by sex, menstrual cycle, and sex steroid hormones. *Neuropsychologia, 45*(14), 3203–3214.

Schreiner, S., Atzwanger, K., & Grammer, K. (2001). Soziale Kompetenz von Jugendlichen. Homo—Unsere Herkunft und Zukunft (Proceedings 4. Kongress der GfA), 533–536.

Searle, J. R. (1969). *Speech acts: An essay in the philosophy of language.* London: Cambridge University Press.

Sommer, I. E. C., Cohen-Kettenis, P. T., van Raalten, T., vd Veer, A. J., Ramsey, L. E., Gooren, L. J. G., et al. (2007). Effects of cross-sex hormones on cerebral activation during language and mental rotation: An fMRI study in transsexuals. *European Neuropsychopharmacology, 18*(3), 215–221.

Stiles, J. (2011). Brain development and the nature versus nurture debate. *Progress in Brain Research, 189*, 3–22.

Stuhlmacher, A. F., Citera, M., & Willis, T. (2007). Gender differences in virtual negotiation: Theory and research. *Sex Roles, 57*, 329–339.

Sumby, W. H., & Pollack, I. (1954). Visual contributions to speech intelligibility in noise. *Journal of the Acoustical Society of America, 26*, 212–215.

Tannen, D. (1990). *You just don't understand: Women and men in conversation.* New York: William Morrow.

Trivers, R. (1972). Parental investment and sexual selection. In B. Campbell (Ed.), *Sexual selection and the descent of man 1871–1971* (pp. 136–179). ChicagoChicagoAldine.

Van den Berghe, P. L. (1979). *Human family systems: An evolutionary view.* New York: Elsevier.

Vierzigmann, G. (1995). Entwicklung von. *Zeitschrift für Differentielle und Diagnostische Psychologie, 16.*

Weisfeld, G., Bloch, S. A., & Ivers, J. W. (1984). Possible determinants of social dominance among adolescent girls. *The 144*, 115–129.

Weisfeld, G. E. (1993). The adaptive value of humor and laughter. *Ethology and Sociobiology, 14*(2), 141–169. doi:10.1016/0162-3095(93)90012-7

Weisfeld, G. E., & Woodward, L. (2004). Current evolutionary perspectives on adolescent romantic relations and sexuality. *Journal of the American Academy of Child and Adolescent Psychiatry, 43*(1), 11–19. doi:10.1097/00004583-200401000-00010

Whiten, A. (1997). The Machiavellian mindreader. In A. Whiten & R. W. Byrne (Eds.), *Machiavellian intelligence* (p. 173). Cambridge, UK: Cambridge University Press.

Whiten, A., & Byrne, R.W. (1997). Machiavellian intelligence. In A. Whiten & Byrne, R.W. *Machiavellian intelligence II: Extensions and evaluations* (pp. 1–24). Cambridge, UK: Cambridge University Press.

Wildgruber, D., Pihan, H., Ackermann, H., Erb, M., & Grodd, W. (2002). Dynamic brain activation during processing of emotional intonation: Influence of acoustic parameters, emotional valence, and sex. *NeuroImage, 15*(4), 856–869.

Willingham, W. W., & Cole, N. S. (1997). *Gender and fair assessment.* Mahwah, NJ, US: Lawrence Erlbaum Associates Publishers.

Wilson, D. S., Near, D. C., & Miller, R. R. (1998). Individual differences in Machiavellianism as a mix of cooperative and exploitative strategies. *Evolution and Human Behavior, 19*(3), 203–212.

Windhager, S., Slice, D. E., Schaefer, K., Oberzaucher, E., Thorstensen, T., & Grammer, K. (2008). Face to face: The perception of automotive designs. *Human Nature, 19*(4), 331–346.

Wood, J. T. (1994). *Gendered lives: Communication, genderGendered lives: Communication, gender-Gendered lives: Communication, gender.* Belmont, CA: Wadsworth.

Wrangham, R. W. (1987). The significance of African apes for reconstructing human social evolution. In W. G. Kinzey (Ed.), *The evolution of human behavior: Primate models* (p. 71).

# NEW DISCIPLINARY FRONTIERS

# 18

# A New View of Evolutionary Psychology Using Women's Priorities and Motivations

TAMI MEREDITH

## Introduction

There are many sex differences that have been documented in evolutionary psychology, and while these studies have been informative, they do not necessarily tell the whole story. We propose that at least some, or elements, of these differences are a product of unexplored phenomena pertaining to motivation. In this chapter, we look at the specific examples of combat, competition and goal attainment, and risk aversion in order to explore the possibility that when sex differences in motivation and priorities are considered, documented behavioral sex differences become more readily understandable and satisfying. That is, we suggest that women will perform these behaviors, but that because they do so for different reasons and, consequently, less frequently or in a less explicit and obvious manner.

## Establishing the Bias in Evolutionary Psychology

Evolutionary psychology, as is the case with most subfields of psychology, has been primarily developed by male scholars who have used their experiences and perspectives as men to develop theory and design programs of research. Scholars' own experiences indubitably influence their research, although perhaps only at an unconscious level, such as when interpreting "objective" data (Kaptchuk, 2003). Indeed, one needs only to consider the preponderance of male authors of journal articles and books within evolutionary psychology to clearly see that men initially dominated the evolutionary psychology scene, and to a lesser extent, still maintain this dominance. For example, in a recent article on feminism and evolutionary psychology (Buss & Schmitt, 2011), where one expects stronger than average female participation, of the total 188 papers referenced, 62 were first authored by women (32.9%) and 126 by men (67.1%). Of the total number of names cited, 158 (32.7%) were women, 261 (62.3%) were men.

We propose that the majority of topics and perspectives in evolutionary psychology have been oriented toward men and male-centric views. Due to the fact that many of the scholars in the area are men, their focus on male perspectives is understandable and unavoidable. Their research has advanced our understanding of male human nature considerably and in a very positive manner. However, our concern is that the field is missing many components that directly impact on women, and that it encourages an interpretation of the existing literature and findings that is limited in scope. We believe that it is necessary for female scholars (and gender aware male scholars) to begin uncovering new research topics that are critical for understanding evolved female psychology, and to reexamine or reinterpret old theories and findings with a new, female-oriented lens. The goal, then, is not merely to use such a lens, but to fully incorporate this viewpoint and either find new directions for work or begin to revise and redirect past work. Rather than subtract from the existing literature, this new focus would ideally add a complementary view, make existing theories more comprehensive, and consequently, create a more accurate and inclusive reflection of all human nature.

Discourse on sex-specific behavior has been informative, but even in these instances the explanations that are offered are not always sound or unbiased. For some topics, sex differences have been exaggerated or misrepresented, potentially due to the priorities or interests of the researchers involved. Perhaps more importantly, though, is that these sex differences became the foundation for later theory building. For example, according to the hunter-gatherer hypothesis of ancestral human behavior, men hunt while women care for children or gather local vegetation (e.g., Eagly & Wood, 1999). This view may be somewhat accurate, but as we will review, subsequent models built on this difference tend to be male-focused, with men as the active agents and women relegated to the activity of childcare. These models may neglect the plethora of other roles women perform. The issue is that the arguments that rely on the traditional hunter-gatherer hypothesis overlook the active and necessary roles that women play in supplying nutrients to the group, maintaining kin alliances, and so on. Our observation concerning the disproportionate level of attention in relation to activity is not new (Slocum, 1975), and yet these arguments have persisted and remained prevalent in the field. In fact, the men's hunting activities may be less important than previously theorized, as some researchers (e.g., Hawkes, 1996) suggest that these activities are more about prestige and social networking than feeding their children and community. If such a view is accurate, perhaps "hunter-gatherer" societies should be referred to as "socialite-worker" societies to more accurately reflect the contributions of men and women.

When a male-biased perspective is applied, it may then lead to further theory that subscribes to the same bias. Using hunting again as an example, it has been suggested that men are superior warriors to women, as the weapons used for hunting in the "environment of evolutionary adaptedness" (EEA; Bowlby, 1969) were likely related to those used in warfare (Harris, 1993; for a review of the critiques concerning the EEA, refer to Bolhuis, Brown, Richardson, & Laland, 2011). As warriors, men are reported to be less risk averse (van Vugt, De Cremer, & Janssen, 2007) due to their natural inclination for highly risky activities such as hunting or combat and their focus on intergroup as opposed to intragroup relationships. As Stanford (1990) reports, the canonical work of Washburn and Lancaster (1968) placed men in the prestigious position of obtaining high caloric meat, and the process of hunting meant that there were opportunities to develop intelligence and communication skills. Women were not afforded these opportunities. Stanford continues,

> Washburn and Lancaster linked the deep human love of hunting to the equally deep human love of going to war and to acts of aggression in general. The fact that it is almost always males who carry out these acts served to reinforce the idea that men had a natural right to occupy the glamour role of clever minded forager, meat provider, and conqueror in human societies. Ever since, theories of human evolution have focused on male activities rather than female as the core human adaptations. (p. 38–39)

As an aside, we note that there are alternative hypotheses to this hunter-gatherer hypothesis. Hart and Sussman (2005 p. 12) suggest that for early humans it is more likely that "hunted man took advantage of predator kills" and were commonly preyed upon by large predators, banding together and learning to use weapons for defensive purposes. It has also been proposed that warfare is not a by-product of male hunting skills but is instead a necessary population control mechanism (Divale, 1972). Kuhn and Stiner (2006) provide evidence that the hunter-gatherer division of labor did not occur until the Upper Paleolithic and is therefore less evolutionarily important than many scholars believe. Thus, the male-biased tenets on which later theories have been built are still subject to dispute and cannot be considered as unquestionable facts. Interestingly, though, the traditional view of man the hunter, and similarly woman the gatherer, remain in modern, introduction to evolutionary psychology textbooks (e.g., Workman & Reader, 2008).

## Sex Differences in Behavior

It is well known that sex-based differences in behaviors exist, such as those previously mentioned, and we generally agree with these findings. What we are questioning is the accuracy and depth of the perspective used to create and motivate the studies that lead to the findings themselves. The view of "Man the Hunter" (as Lee & DeVore named their 1968 Symposium) and how it led to men's advanced mental rotation and spatial perception (Voyer, Voyer, & Bryden, 1995), proclivities toward risk-taking (Byrnes, Miller, & Schafer, 1999), and greater receptivity toward sexual behavior (Joseph, 2000) is only part of the picture. We propose that one must step further back and that the root issue is one of priorities and motivations; men and women have different priorities and motivations due to evolution, and that these are what lead to the observed sex differences in behavior.

In this chapter, we propose that some of the sex differences documented in evolutionary psychology are a product of unexplored phenomena that concern motivation. Rather than focus on differences due to hunting, for example, a more satisfying explanation is that there are differences between women's and men's motivations, and the priorities assigned to these motivations. That is, perhaps men are not better warriors per se, but merely more apt to engage in this behavior because it has a higher, evolved priority for them. We will provide evidence that when given the necessary motivation, women are also effective warriors, albeit using different, often complementary (but not inferior), tactics or strategies than men. Similarly, it may be the case that women are only more risk averse with respect to combat, as it does not have a high priority, but for other activities which are of high priority, such as reproduction, women will not exhibit the same levels of risk aversion. In other words, women have been considered as risk averse because the situations explored by academics are ones to which men give a high priority. We also suggest that risk aversion can be alternatively framed with respect to goal attainment; women can be viewed as setting more achievable goals for which risk is not as necessary to ensure success.

To whet the reader's appetite, consider for a moment one of the most sexually differentiated behaviors: combat performance. When most of us think about soldiers or tribal warriors, we think about men. Why? Typically, one will suggest that men are usually larger and stronger than women, on average, although this relative difference seems to be decreasing over the course of evolution (see Flinn, 2011, for a review). Thus, we pause here to note that we recognize sexual dimorphism obviously favors men's use of physical aggression and strength, but point out that there is no reason to believe that direct physical combat is the only way to address conflict. We will argue that, just as the sexes have evolved to be physically different and consequently possess distinct cognitions, there are evolutionary-based sex-specific solutions to problems. For example, rather than be involved in direct physical combat, women were extensively used as snipers by the Soviet Union in defense of its homeland during World War II. This example demonstrates that women can fully, voluntarily, and meaningfully engage in combat, albeit of an indirect form, when motivated by the necessity to defend their homes. Thus, we are not questioning the existence of sex differences whatsoever. Instead, we contend the sexes have been presented with similar problems, but due to their evolved psychology and sex-specific priorities and motivations, solve them in a sex-specific manner.

There are additional examples of where sex differences have been documented, but for which alternative and deeper interpretations are possible. In this chapter, we will explore the ways that motivations and priorities clearly impact on behavior, and lead us to distinct and incongruous conclusions that differ to those in the current literature. In particular, we will explore the research on sex differences in combat performance, competition and risk-taking. Our overarching goal is to show that the truly ultimate explanation for these differences lies in priorities and motivations, and that the existing explanations do not achieve this depth of explanation.

## Combat Performance

As mentioned, researchers have proposed that, for a variety of reasons, warfare will almost always be primarily a male activity (e.g., Goldstein, 2001; Malagón-Fajar, 1999; van der Dennen, 1995; van Vugt et al., 2007). A review of the literature by van der Dennen (2003; previously published in van der Dennen, 1990), suggested that compared to women, men are more biologically expendable, preadapted as hunters to be warriors, and more aggressive, which makes them predisposed to waging war. Thus, by virtue of their aggression, lack of risk aversion, greater physical strength, and lesser involvement in child rearing, among other factors, men are better warriors than women. What is wrong with this seemingly "logical" perspective is that historical evidence shows that women are equally capable of performing a combat role when motivated to do so. This evidence is apparent across time and among various cultural groups.

During the Great Patriotic War, otherwise known as World War II, over 800,000 women served in the Soviet armed forces, comprising 8% of the mobilized troops (O'Brien & Jefferies, 1982). Nearly 200,000 women were decorated (Sakaida, 2003), and 89 of them received the Soviet Union's highest award, the Hero of the Soviet Union (Sakaida, 2003). They served as pilots, snipers, machine gunners, tank crew-members and partisans, which are all roles that can be classed as "warriors." Additionally, similar to other nations involved in the conflict, women served in administrative, nursing, and other noncombative auxiliary roles, thereby showing their support for the military's efforts in defending their country.

The Soviet Union extensively used women for sniping duties (O'Brien & Jefferies, 1982). Women performed this role very effectively, as can be seen by the achievements of Nina Alexeyevna Lobkovska (who achieved the rank of lieutenant and commanded a company of female snipers) and Ukrainian Lyudmila Pavlichenko (who killed over 300 enemy soldiers). The Soviets found that sniper duties fit women well, since good snipers are patient, careful, deliberate, avoid hand-to-hand combat, and need higher levels of aerobic fitness than other troops.

This role therefore permitted women to actively engage in combat with their enemies in a manner unhindered by their comparatively smaller body size and lower physical strength.

Very few of these women were ever promoted to officers (O'Brien & Jefferies, 1982), so we can conclude that it was not the lure of promotion and leadership that drew Soviet women into battle. Why would the Soviet Union use women more than other countries, and why would women so readily engage in combat? The answer, we believe, is in the location of the conflict. The forces of the United States, Canada, England, Japan, and Germany were predominantly fighting in foreign countries whereas in the Soviet Union, the conflict was taking place on Soviet soil. Soviet women were fighting in defense of their homes and families, and consequently were motivated differently in comparison, for example, to a 21-year-old American soldier heading off to fight in Europe. We propose that women tend to shun military service when they are asked to leave their homes and families to fight for political and abstract nationalistic purposes.

History has shown us that women, when fighting to defend what they value, such as their homes or their families, will readily engage in combat activities. McLaughlin (1990) has documented that in medieval Europe, women were frequently forced, in emergencies, to perform as "wives of nobles who defended castles..., women who snatched up weapons in defense of their homes when invaders threatened, nuns who... used force to defend their convent's property" (pp. 197–198). In the words of Saunders (2011), "The most common occasion on which women would take part in battles was when their home, castle or town was attacked."

Similarly, during the Cuban revolution, when the Cuban people fought to free their homeland from the US-backed Batista regime, the revolutionary leader, Fidel Castro, was asked by some of his men why women were armed when they were not. His reply was simple and concise, "Because they're better soldiers than you are. They're more disciplined" (Waters, 2011). As the Mariana Grajales Women's Platoon showed, women were able to effectively participate in the freeing of their country from oppression. The effectiveness of the platoon caused Castro to use them as his personal security detail due to their courage, discipline, and calmness under fire (Waters, 2011). On January 2, 1959, Castro stated that "a people whose women fight alongside men—that people is invincible," indicating the successful leader's belief in the effectiveness and ability of women to engage in combat.

There are many restrictions that men have put into place to limit women's military service. It has been incorrectly argued that women lack the physical strength, endurance, and emotional strength to become effective soldiers, when in reality they can fight as well as men and should be permitted to do so (Segal, 1982). What differs between the sexes is the type of combat that they might be best suited toward, and how motivation depends on the context of the combat. Sexual dimorphism, and the greater strength of men, is often and erroneously used to state that women cannot effectively engage in combat activities. Rather, it is more accurate to state that an untrained and unarmed woman, when pitted against a larger and stronger man, is at a disadvantage in direct hand-to-hand combat. However, as Carrie Rentschler (1999) states, "it takes only 12 pounds of pressure to break a knee," which is a force that a child could generate and successfully apply if trained in the appropriate techniques. Rentschler provides many additional examples of how women can subdue, harm, and defeat more powerful assailants when they have been trained to do so. Furthermore, she states that women possess an advantage in leverage because of their relatively stronger hips and legs. Although many different variations in the tale exist, it is generally agreed that the Wing Chun martial arts discipline made famous by Bruce Lee was developed by the nun Wumei and her female disciple Yongchun specifically to allow women to subdue stronger opponents (ColorQ World, 2011). Women, therefore, do not lack the strength necessary for successful physical combat.

Another factor that limits females' military participation is men's attitudes toward women. As described by Wilson and Daly (1992), men take a proprietary view of women's sexuality and reproductive capacity, to the extent that women are viewed as chattel, or, more succinctly, as a resource to be protected, sold, exchanged, and for which redress can be demanded in the event of theft or damage. Using this view, one can readily see why men would go to war to protect their homes, and hence their resources, and similarly, why men would deny women the opportunity to engage in combat unless threatened to the extent that it was necessary for their survival.

In a similar vein, while men can readily leave a wounded comrade in order to complete a mission, they are considerably less likely to do so if the comrade is a woman rather than a man (Kemp, 1999). For example, Grossman (1996) suggested that women had been prevented from performing combat roles prior to 2001 in the Israeli Defense Forces because male soldiers were believed to display uncontrollable, instinctual protective aggression for female comrades. That is, men's protective "instincts" for women apparently override their desire to capture a foreign nation for political purposes. Interestingly, this policy provides an example of a behavior with clear evolutionary roots being used to set military policy. Meanwhile, it seems that the examples of women being effective defenders of their homeland are ignored, both by policy makers and by scholars. Alternative military policies based on peace-oriented feminist strategies have been proposed by women (Reardon, 1993), but have not been explored within evolutionary psychology nearly to the extent that male-oriented warfare has been.

The evidence shows that women can be successful in combat, and without aversion, if sufficiently motivated. Women defend their homes and families, but seem far less interested in acquiring new land or resources. Indeed, one reason that women are sometimes not allowed to engage in combat is because they are thought to have divided loyalties; women who have moved from their natal families to marry into a new community may have loyalties to both groups (Jones, 2011). Furthermore, although we readily acknowledge that women generally prefer to avoid directly aggressive situations (Björkqvist, 1994) and prefer more peaceful alternatives (Smith, 1984), we contend that they will actively participate in combat when they see no alternative. Past work that has focused on men as warriors has advanced our understanding of male evolved psychology, but what of the women? The exclusion of the view of women as warriors is significant; our view of "war" must be expanded to include various forms of combat, and to better understand human nature, we must also better comprehend the motivations underlying behavior. It is simply incorrect to state that there is a sex difference in the ability to effectively engage in combat. Instead, there are sex differences in the motivations for engaging in combat, the type of combat each sex is potentially best suited for, and the desire to avoid high-risk intergroup confrontational situations.

# Competition

One could argue that war is a competition for a limited resource such as land, influence, or mates, all of which have repercussions on one's reproductive fitness. Thus, because war is a contest, it is hardly surprising that men have remained the focus of research on competition. Numerous researchers have shown that men are more physically aggressive than women (e.g., Cashdan, 1998; Fry, 1998; Maccoby & Jacklin, 1974), and this difference has often been equated with the belief that men are competitive and women are not (e.g., Symons, 1979). Indeed, it is commonplace to talk about men's competitive behavior in evolutionary psychology, but much less common to discuss women's competitive behavior, especially when it enters into the mating arena.

The idea that women are not physically aggressive, and by extension, not competitive, is simply wrong. For example, in a cross-cultural examination, Burbank (1987) found that in 61% of the 137 cultures she analyzed, women engaged in physical aggression, typically fighting other women over men. Although acknowledging that men's involvement in violent crimes is higher, Campbell (1995) has described how women's age-violence curve for assault is similar, and centers around competition for, or retention of, mates. Other researchers have even argued that the sexes do not differ significantly with respect to the frequency of aggressive behavior in general (e.g., Bettencourt & Miller, 1996; Ramirez, Andreu, & Fujihara, 2001).

Researchers have demonstrated that women also compete in ways other than by physical aggression, such as by using verbal attacks or indirect social aggression (e.g., Campbell, 1999; Mealey, 2000). It may be the case that, because women possess less physical strength than men, women develop alternative methods of competing, and thus rely on different strategies to men (Björkqvist, 1994). Campbell (1999) suggests that this lack of physical competitiveness reflects a successful female adaptation that results in reproductive benefit (but see also Liesen, this volume, who presents three limitations of Campbell's arguments). She argued that mothers are the primary caregivers and protectors of their children, and hence, their survival is more critical for children's well-being, than that of the father. Children's reliance on their mothers leads to less risk-taking by women and the use of indirect, low-risk strategies to resolve disputes. Furthermore, mothers may be more likely to invest in their children since they are assured of their genetic relatedness through the act of birthing, whereas fathers may be uncertain of their paternity and may invest less. In summary, "female choice... and... reproductive strategies are selected not by virtue of being the female half of a reproductive pair, but by being an individual woman reproducing in competition with other women to raise her offspring successfully" (Lancaster, 1991, p. 2).

It is clear that women are competitive (see Fisher, this volume), but they are less likely to overtly demonstrate this behavior in contests of physical strength. Again, we suggest that the sex difference is a product of women's motivations, and not of any inability to compete effectively. One confounding issue may be the way competition is itself defined; if one considers only physical contests as competition, then men are more competitive than women. However, it seems more reasonable to state that competition occurs when there is a scarcity of a needed resource (including mates), thus causing competition between the resource's users. Using this definition, one can view competition as any act that helps one obtain the desired resource, possibly by preventing another from obtaining it first.

For example, if high-quality men are considered a scarce resource, then behaviors related to mate acquisition represent competition between women. Likewise, when a woman suggests to her mate that they have a quiet dinner at home, with the possible intention of keeping other women away from her desired mate, she is "mate guarding." In this context, mate guarding can be considered as a competitive act (Fisher & Cox, 2011). The act is very passive in nature and avoids confrontation with rivals while assisting her in securing her desired mate. Similarly, using gossip to devalue her competition in the eyes of the target male can also be considered as a competitive act, and seems particularly effective if the male considers her attractive (Fisher, Shaw, Worth, Smith, & Reeve, 2010). Using this perspective, we can readily see that women are highly competitive in mate acquisition and retention. Finally, if the use of fashion and beauty products to self-promote and appear more attractive relative to potential rivals is considered a competitive act, then the sales figures for cosmetics, perfume, fashion, and cosmetic surgery are strong indicators of the amount of time and resources that women will expend in order to compete for a high quality mate. Currently, Americans spend approximately $10 billion annually, with the majority of the consumption performed by women (Hoovers.com, 2012).

Competitive athleticism is another way to examine sex differences in "competition." Men are widely considered as more competitive with respect to sports and athletic activities. However, women's participation in athletic events such as the Olympic Games is an undeniable indicator that women can and will compete, albeit at a different level of performance for some activities due to sexual dimorphism. There are noticeable differences in the number of professional athletes who are female versus male, possibly due to the necessity of dismissing other areas of one's life to make time for training, or because there is less economic and social support for women's teams. In addition, the demands of an athletic lifestyle can hinder the performance of other, potentially higher-priority activities such as reproduction. It has been documented that female athletes are more likely than nonathletic women to display menstrual irregularities such as primary and secondary amenorrhoea, oligomenorrhoea, short luteal phases, and anovulation (Warren, 2000). Furthermore, pregnancy can directly affect performance as well, by making it difficult to run long distances quickly, for example. The decision to forgo reproduction in favor of professional sports is not one men typically encounter, whereas it is a decision some women must face. In the end, the lack of women involved in professional athletics may reflect their differing priorities and motivations, and highlight how these are distinct from the issues faced by male athletes. This may be true of women pursuing any career; the trade-offs for women are larger than those faced by men, which may be then linked to differential priorities and motivations.

Other examples of women competing are numerous. Women will readily compete for position within their social hierarchies (Cashdan, 1995), for access to educational resources for their children (e.g., De Sena, 2006), or simply to obtain a bargain when shopping. In situations where bargaining is required, women have been shown to use different strategies and to bargain with a different propensity than men (Schneider, Rodgers, & Bristow, 1999), but they do not avoid bargaining altogether. While we do not fully explore bargaining behavior, it has been shown that differences in bargaining can be linked to sex differences in altruism (Andreoni & Vesterlund, 2001) and thus provide further evidence that women will compete, but do so using different motivations than men.

The belief that women are not competitive is accurate only if one exclusively views competition in terms of direct physical aggression, which is a highly male-biased perspective. When one takes a more comprehensive view, it is readily seen that women are highly competitive. Thus, the focus on forms of competition for which men are more likely to engage has led to an incomplete and inaccurate understanding of how humans compete.

## Goal Achievement and Risk-Taking

In this section, we argue that sex differences in motivations lead to differences in goal-setting and risk-taking behavior. Overall, our examples, which include mate selection, financial investing, and computer programming, indicate that women set more realistic, readily achievable goals with a focus on reliably obtaining the outcome, while men employ more risky strategies that lead to a greater variability in the quality of a result, if one is even obtained. It may be that bias has framed these differences in terms of what women avoid (i.e., taking risk) and not on what women may excel at doing (i.e., setting effective goals).

Numerous studies from within evolutionary psychology have shown the dichotomy that men seek attractive mates, while women seek mates with plentiful resources, particularly if desiring a long-term partner. When looking for a long-term mate, it seems that women place a premium on a potential mate's resources (and indicators of securing more resources in the future) because historically, women and their children have extensively relied on men's provisioning of resources. This reliance stems from sex differences in biology, in that women are the ones who become pregnant, gestate, and lactate, and in parenting behavior, as women provide the majority of childcare. In order to find a mate with material resources as well as intangible resources (e.g., time, energy, parenting skills), women presumably have lower standards for other characteristics, such as attractiveness. We note, though, that women seeking short-term, sexual interactions increase their standards for men's attractiveness (Kenrick, Groth, Trost, & Sadalla, 1993).

This willingness to trade off certain characteristics against each other is congruent with the social psychological literature that indicates women are more practical in their romantic relationships (e.g., Sprecher & Metts, 1989). Women appear to believe that trade-offs are necessary to obtain their goals. We propose that women are setting achievable standards with respect to mate selection, in light of a variety of factors, including the reliance of children on them. Although women may fantasize about having a wealthy husband who is also extremely handsome and has a winning personality, such as seen in romance novels (Cox & Fisher, 2009), in reality, women seem to generally accept that men vary in their characteristics and they have to acquire one that satisfactorily matches their multiple and diverse needs.

Indeed, when it comes to mate selection, women are likely to examine more factors than men for a wide array of socially desirable personality traits (Botwin, Buss, & Shackelford, 1997). It is possible that, as a result of being more practical, women consider a greater number of characteristics and place less emphasis on any individual characteristic. That is, women are more likely to settle for a mate of average attractiveness, with a good personality and a moderate income, rather than waiting for Prince Charming to come along. We do not wish to confuse practicality with compromise, as it has been shown that once women establish a set of mate selection criteria, they are unlikely to compromise on satisfying those criteria (Hatfield & Sprecher, 1995). In other words, it seems that women establish achievable standards for reasons of practicality when creating their mate selection criteria.

It has been found that women are more "choosy" than men when it comes to mate selection (e.g., Hatfield & Sprecher, 1995). This selectivity may be a consequence of women's higher mating investment, and results in a need to examine all the factors and to finally select a realistically obtainable mate. In contrast, the literature suggests that men focus on fewer factors, and in particular attractiveness, but establish higher and potentially unreachable standards that they are more willing to compromise. Perhaps, then, men are less able, or find it less important, to establish attainable standards with respect to mate selection.

We realize that mate selection is a complex issue, since women's fecundity is intimately tied to age, and age is linked to female attractiveness; thus, there is a connection between attractiveness and the likelihood of viable offspring. However, using the same argument, women should also be careful to select mates with characteristics displaying high gene quality, as indicated by male attractiveness and age, and be even more careful than men due to the higher parental investment. We believe that women tend to focus on obtaining a satisfactory result for an activity such as mate selection, and that as women evaluate potential long-term mates, they keep the end goal of reproduction in focus, albeit perhaps tangentially, as tied to the desire to have a family, for example. In contrast, men pursue highly attractive mates, and while attractiveness may indicate higher genetic fitness, it does not equate with a willingness to mate, or an ability to raise children. Thus, by extension, one could say that men are seeking the best possible mate by focusing on her genetic fitness and tolerating the variability in her desire to mate and her ability to raise children. It may be that men, because they can have more mates, place less importance on any single mating attempt, in the belief that they can always "try again tomorrow."

Interestingly, when actual behavior is examined, people's reactions and behaviors suggest that the sexes equally value attractiveness in potential mates (Feingold, 1990; Sprecher & Metts, 1989). One of the best demonstrations of this phenomenon randomly matched 376 first-year university students (Hatfield, Aronson, Abrahams, & Rottman, 1966). After an arranged dance, participants evaluated their dates in terms of how much they liked them and stated whether or not they wanted to see them again. The only significant factor that predicted liking behavior and desire to continue was physical attractiveness, regardless of the participant's sex. Together with the literature reviewed above, this example illustrates that sex differences in mate preferences may not necessarily be due to what one likes but are potentially the result of differences in motivations and the goals we set.

As previously mentioned in our discussion on combat, women are more likely to seek peaceful solutions to conflict. When it comes to warfare, women tend to seek a compromise that achieves a mutually agreeable solution rather than the high cost alternative of conflict. Men are more willing to endure the cost in terms of life and resources that is associated with war. History has shown that men idealize warfare and can consider it glorious, heroic, and an act of valor, often ignoring the misery, grief, and losses it causes. Thus, when it comes to engaging in war, men use high-cost and potentially high-risk strategies while women engage in more practical, lower cost approaches. Negotiating a peaceful solution may not win one the rewards that a successful military victory would obtain, but neither does it risk the losses that a defeat would inflict.

This difference can be seen in even an activity like computer programming. When programming, it has been suggested that women are more likely to use a bottom-up approach (Turkle & Papert, 1990) while men are more likely to use a top-down approach. Bottom-up programming builds an application by assembling smaller, previously constructed components. As a constructive process that builds on previous results, bottom-up programming is highly likely to achieve programming goals. Top-down approaches, which begin with a design that is slowly developed on an abstract level, are more likely to lead to better quality computer source code but are also more likely to fail because the design is too complex or may be impossible to implement. The male-biased top-down approach is therefore a riskier strategy with highly variable outcomes, while the female-biased bottom-up approach ensures gradual and consistent success.

This pattern can be seen elsewhere, and interpreted similarly with respect to a sex difference in goal setting and achievement. For example, researchers (e.g., Eckel & Grossman, 2008) have consistently found that women, when investing, tend to take less financial risk than men, though this result tends to be more pronounced in abstract experiments than actual investment contexts. While this difference is often attributed to women's risk aversion, it can also be viewed in terms of practicality. Women take sufficient risk to ensure growth of their investments such that they can have a satisfactory retirement income, and thus achieve their investment goals. Moreover, women's investment strategies will, on average, yield better results than men's higher-risk strategies (Barclays Wealth, 2011). When a situation such as this is viewed with regard to goal achievement rather than risk, women can be seen as being more realistic in that they focus on reliably reaching an achievable goal.

When gambling is considered, it has been documented that women have a narrower scope of gambling behavior, but the sexes are not significantly different on frequency, wagering, and time spent at gambling (Hraba & Lee, 1996). Although conflicting reports exist (e.g., Blanco, Hasin, Petry, Stinson, & Grant, 2006), they only tend to dispute the amount that women will gamble or the likelihood of pathological gambling and not the fact that women participate in gambling activities. Since gambling by its very nature involves risk-taking, it provides further evidence that women will take risks if they are motivated to do so.

This said, we do not dispute that in some areas, men take more risks than women, and as a result, have greater variability in success. The problem, though, is that the idea that men are always more risk-taking than women is simply incorrect. We suggest that women take risks, but do so in less obvious ways. For example, women engage in many highly risky sexual behaviors where the outcome could be disease, pregnancy, or physical harm caused by their male partner. Mortality due to childbirth has diminished due to modern medical technology, but historically, and for women in many developing nations, it remains a significant cause of death (Mayor, 2004). Sexually transmitted diseases have a greater rate of morbidity and mortality for women (see Smith, 2007, pp. 338–340, for a review). For example, gonorrhea is more likely to be contracted and less likely to be detected by women than by men. Sexual activity, and any resulting pregnancy, is consequently much more risky for women than for men. We propose that rather than being risk-averse, women do take substantial risks but in the pursuit of activities, such as reproduction, where the goal has sufficient priority to require the taking of the risk.

Taking this argument one step further, we propose that the ways in which risk-taking has been studied are primarily applicable to men. The risks that are considered by researchers are often for activities that have little or minimal meaning to many women. Engaging in mountaineering and other adventure sports (e.g., parachuting, cliff jumping) are activities that men perceive as less risky than women (Demirhan, 2005) but that one does not need to take in order to survive, have a family, eat well, and live in a protective shelter. They are behaviors that can demonstrate fearlessness and bravado, which presumably more directly impact on men's social dominance and status. However, if there is a situation when it is necessary for quality of life, women will invest and will accept the risks associated with investment. Where men and women differ in this arena is the amount of risk that they are willing to incur. Women tend to minimize the risk such that they can accomplish achievable goals with a high likelihood of success, while men are more likely to take greater risks in search of greater rewards, and as a consequence, tolerate greater failures. We note that there has been much written, from within the field of evolutionary psychology, about sex differences in risk (e.g., Wilson & Daly, 1985; or see Byrnes et al., 1999, for a meta-analysis of 150 studies on sex differences in risk-taking). However, our reading of this literature indicates the area has primarily reduced women to being risk-averse without examining areas that women do take risks, and by overlooking women's motivations and priorities (but see also Fessler, Pillsworth, & Flamson, 2004; and Harris, Jenkins, & Glaser, 2006). Sex differences in risk-taking may be a secondary difference that results from sex differences in goal setting, which is an area that needs more attention from researchers.

## Sex Differences in Motivation

We have reviewed three different themes: combat, competition, and goal setting as it relates to risk-taking. In retrospect, although these subjects seemed distinct to us, they do converge and allow us to arrive at a comprehensive description of women's behavior, as suggested by their priorities and motivations. Women can be combative, but do so for the sake of defense of what they own or deeply care about, such as their home and families.

They can also be competitive when it matters to them, albeit often in an indirect manner. They will engage in physical aggression for the purposes of acquiring or retaining a mate, but do so less often than men. Instead, they seek ways that are more circuitous, and free of the dangers involved in physical aggression and competition. As well, women, compared to men, tend to establish more achievable goals that can be considered as more practical. They also will take risks that are personally relevant, and that allow them to achieve their goals. Together, these topics point to the fact that women seek "sure things" with a steady payoff, rather than gambling for a variable chance of a big reward. Moreover, these sections clearly indicate that women have distinct motivations and priorities. Going one step further, we propose that women's role as active agents in human evolution has often been dismissed due to the focus on men's motivations and priorities.

A difference in motivation can perhaps be explained using the concept of time perspective. Zimbardo and Boyd (1999) found that women scored significantly higher than men with respect to striving toward future goals and rewards, and thus have a greater "future orientation." This sex difference in future time perspective is consistent within the context of mortality; cross-culturally, men have reduced longevity to women (Kruger, 2007). Women may thus be forming longer-term goals and establishing motivations with respect to a longer time perspective. Zimbardo and Boyd (1999) also found that future orientation positively corre-lates with conscientiousness and desire for consistency, and negatively correlates with novelty and sensation seeking. As many risks are associated with sensation seeking one can readily see the relationships between sex, time perspective, goal setting, and risk-taking.

Alternatively, one could argue that since women are the primary caregivers for children, women's priorities are more focused on external factors, while men's are more internally based. Swap and Rubin (1983) indirectly support this view, as they found that women had a higher interpersonal orientation (IO) than men. A higher IO is associated with greater interest in and reaction to other people and lower interest in the economic issues of relationships. We argue that many of women's priorities and motivations rest on long-term think-ing that is needed to maintain and support interpersonal relations and provide childcare, whereas men's priorities and motivations rest on short-term success. Women are also faced with determining and managing the trade-off between their fertility and offspring survival (e.g., Strassmann & Gillespie, 2002), while this issue is not faced by men. Therefore, women's parental investment requires a considerably longer time span than men's, and can be performed a limited number of times, so it makes sense that women use a longer frame of reference and consider the future more than men. It also seems reasonable that, when using a long-term perspective, women tend to view the average result of activi-ties, such as investing, and attribute less value to any singular short-term loss or gain.

We suggest that much of the literature on sex differences is incomplete. Although many of the researched sex differences have been framed with respect to evolved differences that rest on physiology, the existing explanations and theoretical foundations do not dig conceptually deep enough. Motivations and priorities also have evolutionary roots, and by understanding how these impact on one's cognitions and behavior, we will attain a much more comprehensive understanding of human nature. Furthermore, knowing about motivations and priorities might enable us to review research that has already been performed and acknowledge there are gaps, particularly when it comes to issues that are pertinent to women. As evolutionary psychologists expand their outlook to encompass women's priorities and motivations, a more comprehensive and accurate view of human behavior will be achieved.

# References

Andreoni, J., & Vesterlund, L. (2001). Which is the fair sex? Gender differences in altruism. *Quarterly Journal of Economics, 116*(1), 293–312.

Barclays Wealth. (2011). Barclays wealth insights, volume 13: Risk and rules. Retrieved from http://www.barclayswealth.com/Images/BWA-Barclays-Wealth-Insights.pdf

Bettencourt, B., & Miller, N. (1996). Gender differences in aggression as a function of provocation: A meta-analysis. *Psychological Bulletin, 119*, 422–447.

Björkqvist, K. (1994). Sex differences in physical, verbal, and indirect aggression: A review of recent research. *Sex Roles, 30*(3–4), 177–188.

Blanco, C., Hasin, D., Petry, N., Stinson, F., & Grant, F. (2006). Sex differences in subclinical and DSM-IV pathological gambling: Results from the National Epidemiologic Survey on Alcohol and Related Conditions. *Psychological Medicine, 36*, 943–953.

Bolhuis, J., Brown, G., Richardson, R., & Laland, K. (2011). Darwin in mind: New opportunities for evolutionary psychology. *PLoS Biology, 9*, e1001109. doi:10.1371/journal.pbio.1001109

Botwin, M. D., Buss, D. M., & Shackelford, T. K. (1997). Personality and mate preferences: Five factors in mate selection and marital satisfaction. *Journal of Personality, 65*, 107–136.

Bowlby, J. (1969). *Attachment and loss: Vol. 1. Attachment.* New York: Basic Books.

Burbank, V. (1987). Female aggression in cross-cultural perspective. *Behavior Science Research, 21*, 70–100.

Buss, D., & Schmitt, D. (2011). Evolutionary psychology and feminism. *Sex Roles, 64*, 768–787.

Byrnes, J., Miller, D., & Schafer, W. (1999). Gender differences in risk-taking: A meta-analysis. *Psychological Bulletin, 125*(3), 367–383.

Campbell, A. (1995). A few good men: Evolutionary psychology and female adolescent aggression. *Ethology and Sociobiology, 16*, 99–123.

Campbell, A. (1999). Staying alive: Evolution, culture, and women's intra-sexual aggression. *Behavioral and Brain Sciences, 22*, 203–252.

Cashdan, E. (1995). Hormones, sex, and status in women. *Hormones and Behavior, 29*, 354–366.

Cashdan, E. (1998). Are men more competitive than women? *British Journal of Social Psychology, 37*, 213–229.

ColorQ World. (2011). Yan Yongchun and the Venerable Wumei. Retrieved August 20, 2011, from http://www.colorq.org/articles/article.aspx?d=asianwomen&x=yongchun

Cox, A., & Fisher, M. (2009). The Texas billionaire's pregnant bride: An evolutionary interpretation of romance fiction titles. *Journal of Social, Evolutionary, and Cultural Psychology, 3*, 386–401.

Demirhan, G. (2005). Mountaineers' risk perception in outdoor-adventure sports: A study of sex and sports experience. *Perceptual and Motor Skills, 100*, 1155–1160.

De Sena, J. (2006). "What's a mother to do?" Gentrification, school selection, and the consequences for community cohesion. *American Behavioral Scientist, 50*(2), 241–257.

Divale, W. (1972). Systemic population control in the middle and upper Palaeolithic: Inferences based on contemporary hunter-gatherers. *World Archaeology, 4*(1), 222–243.

Eagly, A., & Wood, W. (1999). The origins of sex differences in human behavior: Evolved dispositions versus social roles. *American Psychologist, 54*(6), 408–423.

Eckel, C., & Grossman, J. (2008). Men, women, and risk aversion: Experimental evidence. In C. R. Plott & V. L. Smith (Eds.), *Handbook of experimental economics results* (Vol. 1, pp. 1061–1073). Amsterdam, The Netherlands: Elsevier B.V.

Feingold, A. (1990). Gender differences in the effects of physical attractiveness on romantic attraction: A comparison across five research paradigms. *Journal of Personality and Social Psychology, 59*, 981–993.

Fessler, D. M. T., Pillsworth, E. G., & Flamson, T. J. (2004). Angry men and disgusted women: An evolutionary approach to the influence of emotions on risk taking. *Organizational Behavior and Human Decision Processes, 95*, 107–123.

Fisher, M., & Cox, A. (2011). Four strategies used during intrasexual competition for mates. *Personal Relationships, 18*, 20–38.

Fisher, M., Shaw, S., Worth, K., Smith, L., & Reeve, C. (2010). How we view those who derogate: Perceptions of female competitor derogators. *Journal of Social, Evolutionary, and Cultural Psychology, 4*(4), 265–276.

Flinn, M. V. (2011). Evolutionary anthropology and the human family. In C. A. Salmon & T. K. Shackelford (Eds.), *The Oxford handbook of evolutionary family psychology* (pp. 12–32). New York: Oxford University Press.

Fry, D. (1998). Anthropological perspectives on aggression: Sex differences and cultural variation. *Aggressive Behavior, 24*, 81–95.

Goldstein, J. (2001). *War and gender: How gender shapes the war system and vice versa.* Cambridge, UK: Cambridge University Press.

Grossman, D. (1996). *On killing: The psychological cost of learning to kill in war and society.* New York: Little, Brown.

Harris, M. (1993). The evolution of human gender hierarchies: A trial formation. In B. Miller (Ed.), *Sex and gender hierarchies* (pp. 57–80). Cambridge, UK: Cambridge University Press.

Harris, C. R., Jenkins, M., & Glaser, D. (2006). Gender differences in risk assessment: Why do women take fewer risks than men? *Judgment and Decision Making, 1*, 48–63.

Hart, D., & Sussman, R. (2005). *Man the hunted: Primates, predators, and human evolution.* Cambridge, MA: Westview Press.

Hatfield, E., Aronson, V., Abrahams, D., & Rottman, L. (1966). The importance of physical attractiveness in dating behavior. *Journal of Personality and Social Psychology, 4*, 508–516.

Hatfield, E., & Sprecher, S. (1995). Men's and women's preferences in marital partners in the United States, Russia, and Japan. *Journal of Cross-Cultural Psychology, 26*(6), 728–750.

Hawkes, K. (1996). Foraging differences between men and women: Behavioral ecology of the sexual division of labor. In J. Steele & S. Shennan (Eds.), *The archeology of human ancestry: Power, sex, and tradition* (pp. 283–305). London: Routledge.

Hoovers.com. Cosmetics, beauty supply and perfume stores industry overview. Retrieved April 11, 2012, from http://www.hoovers.com/cosmetics,-beauty-supply,-and-perfume-stores/ – ID__294 – /free-ind-fr-profile-basic.xhtml

Hraba, J., & Lee, G. (1996). Gender, gambling, and problem gambling. *Journal of Gambling Studies, 12*(1), 83–101.

Jones, D. (2011). The matrilocal tribe: An organization of demic expansion. *Human Nature, 22*(1–2), 177–200.

Joseph, R. (2000). The evolution of sex differences in language, sexuality, and visual-spatial skills. *Archives of Sexual Behavior, 29*(1), 35–66.

Kaptchuk, T. (2003). Effect of interpretive bias on research evidence. *British Medical Journal, 326*(7404), 1453–1455.

Kemp, M. (1999) Femme fatale: Women in the military service. *Women in Action, 3*. Online publication of Isis International. Retrieved from http://www.isismanila.org/index.php?option=com_content&task=view&id=594&Itemid=200

Kenrick, D., Groth, G., Trost, M., & Sadalla, E. (1993). Integrating evolutionary and social ex-change perspectives on relationships: Effects of gender, self appraisal, and involvement level on mate selection criteria. *Journal of Personality and Social Psychology, 64*, 951–969.

Kruger, D. (2007). Human life history variation and sex differences in mortality rates. *Journal of Social, Evolutionary, and Cultural Psychology, 2*, 281–288.

Kuhn, S., & Stiner, M. (2006). What's a mother to do? The division of labor among Neandertals and modern Humans in Eurasia. *Current Anthropology, 47*(6), 953–980.

Lancaster, J. B. (1991). A feminist and evolutionary biologist looks at women. *Yearbook of Physical Anthropology, 34*, 1–11.

Lee, R., & DeVore, I. (Eds.). (1968). *Man the hunter*. Chicago: Aldine.

Maccoby, E., & Jacklin, C. (1974). *The psychology of sex differences*. Stanford, CA: Stanford University Press.

Malagón-Fajar, M. (1999). *Hubris, warriors, and evolution* (US Army War College Strategy Research Report). Carlisle Barracks, PA: US Army War College.

Mayor, S. (2004). Pregnancy and childbirth are leading causes of death in teenage girls in devel-oping countries. *British Medical Journal, 328*(7749). Retrieved from http://www.bmj.com/content/328/7449/1152.2.extract

McLaughlin, M. (1990). The woman warrior: Gender, warfare, and society in medieval Europe. *Women's Studies, 17*, 193–209.

Mealey, L. (2000). Anorexia: A "losing" strategy? *Human Nature, 11*, 105–116.

O'Brien, M., & Jefferies, C. (1982). Women and the Soviet military. *USAF Air and Space Power Journal: Air University Review, 33*(2), 76–85. Retrieved from http://www.airpower.maxwell.af.mil/airchronicles/aureview/1982/jan-feb/obrien.html

Ramirez, J., Andreu, J. M., & Fujihara, T. (2001). Cultural and sex differences in aggression: A comparison between Japanese and Spanish students using two different inventories. *Aggressive Behavior, 27*, 313–322.

Reardon, B. (1993). *Women and peace: Feminist visions of global security*. Albany: State University of New York Press.

Rentschler, C. (1999). Women's self-defense: Physical education for everyday life. *Women's Studies Quarterly, 27*(1/2), 152–161.

Sakaida, H. (2003). *Heroines of the Soviet Union, 1941–45*. Botley, UK: Osprey.

Saunders, N. (2011). *Women warriors from 3500BC to the 20th Century*. Retrieved August 20, 2011, from http://www.lothene.org/others/women.html

Schneider, K., Rodgers, W., & Bristow, D. (1999). Bargaining over the price of a product: Delightful anticipation or abject dread? *Journal of Product and Brand Management, 8*(3), 232–244.

Segal, M. (1982). The argument for female combatants. In N. Goldman (Ed.), *Female soldiers: Combatants or non-combatants?* (pp. 267–268). Westport, CN: Greenwood Press.

Slocum, S. (1975). Woman the gatherer: Male bias in anthropology. In R. Reiter (Ed.), *Toward an anthropology of women* (pp. 36–50). New York: Monthly Review Press.

Smith, B. (2007). *The psychology of sex and gender*. Boston: Allyn and Bacon.

Smith, T. (1984). The polls: Gender and attitudes towards violence. *Public Opinion Quarterly, 48*(1), 384–396.

Sprecher, S., & Metts, S. (1989). Development of the "Romantic Beliefs Scale" and examina-tion of the effects of gender and gender-role orientation. *Journal of Social and Personal Relationships, 6*, 387–411.

Stanford, C. (1990). *The hunting apes: Meat eating and the origins of human behavior*. Princeton, NJ: Princeton University Press.

Strassmann, B., & Gillespie, B. (2002). Life-history theory, fertility, and reproductive success in humans. *Proceedings of the Royal Society of London Series B, 269*, 553–562.

Swap, W., & Rubin, J. (1983). Measurement of interpersonal orientation. *Journal of Personality and Social Psychology, 44*(1), 208–219.

Symons, D. (1979). *The evolution of human sexuality*. New York: Oxford University Press.

Turkle, S., & Papert, S. (1990). Epistemological pluralism: Styles and voices within computer culture. *Signs, 16*(1), 128–157.

van der Dennen, J. (1990). *Why is the human primitive warrior virtually always the male of the species?* Paper prepared for the conference on Kriegsbegeisterung, Groningen, The Netherlands.

van der Dennen, J. (1995). *The origin of war: The evolution of a male-coalitional reproductive strategy* (2 vols.). Groningen, The Netherlands: Origin Press.

van der Dennen, J. (2003). [Review of Goldstein, 2001—in this reference list]. *Human Ethology Bulletin, 18*(2), 4–7.

van Vugt, M., De Cremer, D., & Janssen, D. (2007). Cooperation and competition: The male-warrior hypothesis. *Psychological Science, 18*(1), 19–23.

Voyer, D., Voyer, S., & Bryden, M. (1995). Magnitude of sex differences in spatial abilities: A meta-analysis in consideration of critical variables. *Psychological Bulletin, 117*(2), 250–270.

Warren, M. (2000). The female athlete. *Best Practice and Research Clinical Endocrinology and Metabolism, 14*(1), 37–53.

Washburn, S. L., & Lancaster, J. B. (1968). The evolution of hunting. In R. B. Lee & I. DeVore (Eds.), *Man the hunter* (pp. 293–303). Chicago: Aldine.

Waters, M.-A. (2011). Women's role in Cuba's 1956–58 revolutionary war. *The Militant, 74*(6). Retrieved August 20, 2011, from http://www.themilitant.com/2010/7406/740649.html

Wilson, M., & Daly, M. (1985). Competitive, risk taking, and violence: The young male syndrome. *Ethology and Sociobiology, 6*, 59–73.

Wilson, M., & Daly, M. (1992). The man who mistook his wife for a chattel. In J. Barkow, L. Cosmides, & J. Tooby (Eds), *The adapted mind: Evolutionary psychology and the generation of culture* (pp. 289–322). New York: Oxford University Press.

Workman, L., & Reader, W. (2008). *Evolutionary psychology: An introduction* (2nd ed.). Cambridge, UK: Cambridge University Press.

Zimbardo P., & Boyd J. (1999). Putting time in perspective: A valid, reliable individual-difference metric. *Journal of Personality and Social Psychology, 77*, 1271–1288.

# 19

# From Reproductive Resource to Autonomous Individuality? Charlotte Brontë's *Jane Eyre*

NANCY EASTERLIN

## Introduction

Feminism's animus to evolutionary psychology has been particularly pronounced in the academic humanities, where a prevailing constructionist viewpoint has dominated since the advent of poststructuralism, generally dated to Jacques Derrida's 1968 landmark lecture "Structure, Sign, and Play in the Discourse of the Human Sciences" (Derrida, 1968). The dogmatic insistence on constructionism, the perspective that differences are socially produced rather than the result of innate predispositions, assumes a misguided correlation between *difference* and *inequality*. Generally speaking, of course, difference does not presuppose inequality; red, blue, and green are all different but value-neutral. Objectively, the same is true of women and men. But the equation of difference with inequality results from the superimposition of postmodern social analysis onto realms outside of patriarchal society, casting reality in terms of hierarchically organized pairs, including active/passive and male/female (Cixous, 1975). While all of us should be concerned that research on the differences among kinds of people will be manipulated to the disadvantage of some groups, only the misapplication of theory and research, not *difference itself*, puts certain groups in a subordinate positions.

In this chapter, I claim, first, that feminism—a movement that eschews social and other forms of bias against women, seeking to bring its causes to consciousness and thus lead to the elimination of sexual discrimination—ignores research on evolved sex differences to its peril. Second, I claim that combining the resources of evolutionary psychology along with traditional literary criticism and other forms of cultural analysis provides the basis for specifically Darwinian feminist forms of literary interpretation. The ensuing literary analysis of the novel *Jane Eyre* will demonstrate to feminists in all fields that an understanding of evolved psychological predispositions does not determine social outcomes but may help explain motivations and behaviors. In my analysis of *Jane Eyre*, I suggest that the research on sex-differential mating strategies presents feminists with a finding that should be of paramount concern: men typically seek to control women as part of a psychological profile derived from their normative reproductive strategy, a strategy that is in conflict with the basic human desire for autonomous individuality. This unconscious conflict between the prototypical male desire to control women as a sexual resource and every person's desire for autonomous individuality has repercussions for both the life satisfaction and inclusive fitness of *women and men*, neither of whom is motivated solely by normative mating strategies. Because mimetic (realistic) literature attempts to represent the complexity of experience, it is particularly useful for considering how evolved dispositions are, or are not, realized in specific sociocultural and psychological conditions.

For several reasons, Charlotte Brontë's *Jane Eyre* is an ideal text to consider from a perspective that focuses on the conflict between male control of women as a sexual resource and the desire for autonomous individuality. This novel is a widely read work of nineteenth-century English literature, telling the story of a young girl who must make a life for herself in difficult circumstances. More importantly, male-female power dynamics are a prominent feature of the plot. Finally, since the rise of academic feminism in the 1970s, the novel has undergone numerous constructionist feminist literary analyses of these male-female power dynamics, which suggests that the novel may be due for an evolutionary analysis of these same dynamics.

## Overview of Sex-Differential Mating Strategies

According to standard evolutionary psychological accounts of mate selection, men and women, on average, pursue somewhat different strategies in keeping with their roles in the reproductive process. Contemporary evolutionary psychology recognizes that strategies will vary depending on social, political, ecological, and other environmental conditions (Buss, 1994/2003; Geary, 1998). My overall perspective is particularly influenced by David Geary's *Male, Female*, because that text places Darwinian accounts of mating strategies within discussions of culture, environment, and other aspects of psychology that elucidate the functionally dynamic nature of mate selection.

Robert L. Trivers's 1972 paper "Parental Investment and Sexual Selection" established a theoretical paradigm for sex-differential mating strategies. Citing an overlooked 1948 paper by A. J. Bateman, Trivers noted a relationship between relative parental investment and reproductive success among males of a variety of species, for whom reproductive success varies more widely than it does for females. In his reformulation of Bateman's argument, Trivers states, "Since the total number of offspring produced by one sex of a sexually reproducing species must equal the total number produced by the other...then the sex whose typical parental investment is greater than that of the opposite sex will become a limiting resource for that sex. Individuals of the sex investing less will compete among themselves to breed with members of the sex investing more, since an individual of the former can increase its reproductive success by investing successively in the offspring of several members of the limiting sex" (Trivers, 1972/2002, p. 68).

Although parental investment is more equal between the sexes among pair-bonding or relatively monogamous species, investment between human partners hardly appears equivalent, and this has bearing on mating strategies and mate preferences (Buss, 1994/2003; Geary, 1998). Women typically exhibit a preference for dominant males who provide resources and monogamy in the interest of inclusive fitness (Geary, 1998, p. 123–128). These priorities are governed by the costs of fertilization, childbearing, and child rearing for women, all *expensive* in fitness terms. A devoted mate who helps protect and provide for offspring best serves the woman's genetic interests by increasing the likelihood that her children will survive and reproduce—that is, her *inclusive fitness*.

However, a number of recent theorists have taken issue with the basic assumption of the Bateman-Trivers hypothesis that *parental investment* is the crucial factor governing sexual selection. Barbara Smuts (1996) points to the significance of weak female coalitions among humans and suggests that the human pairbond may have evolved to protect against rape rather than to ensure parental investment. In other primate species, strong female coalitions provide protection against male sexual aggression, but human females notably lack such coalitionary support. In her study of the Tanzanian Pimbwe, Mulder (2009) finds that women do not pursue long-term pair-bonds under certain ecological conditions, employing a strategy of serial monogamy prototypically defined as male. Studies like these raise important questions about whether the Bateman-Trivers hypothesis legitimately characterizes human sexual selection. Notably for the present analysis, however, these challenges to the long-prevailing explanation of mating strategies do not generally dispute that women seek resources, protection, and support through short- or long-term bonds with men.

Men typically pursue a mixed reproductive strategy, seeking both long-term mates requiring high investment and short-term mates demanding little investment (Trivers, 1972/2002). Whereas reproduction is relatively expensive for women, it is much less so for men, who produce millions of sperm in contrast to a woman's fixed supply of eggs, and who do not bear the physical costs of pregnancy and reproduction. For this reason, their inclusive fitness may be better served, on average, by this mixed strategy, which allows for the possibility that a greater number of offspring will reach adulthood and reproduce. Crucially, for men, the control of resources is linked to reproductive success, even in cultural conditions where women have power and control resources, because even powerful women prefer powerful, resource-rich men (Buss, 1994/2003, pp. 46–47). In general, then, the research supports the scenario in which men seek to acquire status and resources as a means of access to and control over women, thus pursuing their fitness interests.

Because of this mixed strategy, evolutionary psychologists characterize men as less selective or "choosy" than women, but it is worth noting that a man may be every bit as choosy about his long-term mate (wife or wives) as is a woman. Most especially, monogamous marriage systems, whether state or ecologically imposed, affect selection strategies as well as male-male and female-female competition. At present, analyses explain the anomalous fact of state-imposed monogamy's evolution within patriarchy as a social agreement *between males* that equalizes reproductive opportunity (relatively speaking) *among men* by providing low-status males with an opportunity to mate (Alexander, in Wright, 1994; Scheidel, 2009). The reduction in male-male aggression diminishes social violence overall but, notably, increases female-female competition, which tends to take less direct forms than male-male competition, and female choice (Geary, 1998). As it restricts the power of elite males by limiting the number of wives they may have, monogamy increases the choosiness of these resource-rich men and, correspondingly, catalyzes competition between the women who desire them as mates.

Complicating the picture of mate selection are the personal characteristics frequently sought in a long-term partner, and women and men exhibit continuity in their preference for kindness, intelligence, and a sense of humor (Geary, 1998, pp. 128–131, 147–148). Putting this in the context of the generalized mate selection strategies, women and men may often prioritize these personal characteristics in a partner over those ranked high by their mate selection strategies, such as dominance and resource provision or beauty. Indeed, Geary (1998) suggests that these priorities have been reordered in line with the demands of the nucleated modern family, which places emotional and social needs largely within the family unit and the pair bond, rather than allowing for the fulfillment of some of these needs in an extended kinship network, as is the case in traditional societies. Thus, for example, a woman may choose a kinder, less dominant male, and a man may choose a less beautiful but wittier wife than would have been the case in a traditional society. In this way, because the pair bond now serves an increasing portion of human social and emotional needs, a major sociocultural change—the breakdown of large kinship networks—has transformed the modern environment of mate selection. Thus the "culture" so often hypostatized as a discrete and separate force from "nature" is a central aspect of the environment of mate selection.

## Female Choice Versus Autonomous Individuality

Evolutionary studies have undergone a sea change in their understanding of the female role in the reproductive process in the past five decades, and female choice and female-female competition are now identified as two of the four central factors of sexual selection (the other two being male choice and male-male competition) (Geary, 1998, pp. 136–146). Understanding sexual selection, however, must be separated from feminism, and feminists across the disciplines should be clear that the term *female choice* refers to the mating and reproductive decisions of a range of species and not to human progress toward social equality. If this point is obvious to a biological anthropologist, it is less so to a sociologist or literary scholar, both of whom conduct cultural analysis and assume the denotative meaning of "choice" (decision by conscious intention). For a human being, the choice of a mate is conscious in varying degrees, and the evolved motivation that evolutionary psychology addresses is inclusive fitness, not individual self-determination or equal rights. Although a number of seminal evolutionary literary analyses have pointed to the operation of female choice within the marriage plots of the eighteenth-century novelist Jane Austen, I argue here that emphasis on this feature of sexual selection alone is typically insufficient to constitute a *Darwinian feminist* perspective in the analysis of a cultural artifact, particularly when male dominance receives thorough legal and cultural sanction in the historical era portrayed therein (Boyd, 1998; Carroll, 2005; Stasio & Duncan, 2007). When the only life opportunity available to women in the historical era depicted in the literary work was to make discerning choices about the men they would marry, it should be recognized that adult life was a matter of complete material dependence on one's partner and little or no personal autonomy. Because women have been granted suffrage and rights since the publication of Austen's and Brontë's novels in the period spanning the late eighteenth to mid-nineteenth century, there is good reason to think that the enculturation of dependent, homebound women was an unsatisfactory cultural and economic formulation for many women and men, particularly when the nuclear family was beginning to serve more fully the social and emotional needs of its members.

As Geary (1998) points out, "the desire for control is the fundamental motivation underlying the behavioral and psychological development *of human beings*" (Geary, 1998, p. 161; italics mine). Like much simpler organisms, through control over ourselves as physical entities we seek to negotiate our survival and reproduction, but as human beings, we do so through a complex sense of autobiographical selfhood and evolved culture (Damasio, 1999; Donald, 1991). If simple organisms require only a sense of organismic integrity as a fundamental point of reference, then humans need a far more elaborate sense of self to facilitate prospective planning and retrospective memory through the agency of narrative thought. All of these integral functions evolved within men and women and promoted bonding mechanisms within the kinship group in the ancestral past; over the long term, they contributed to the development of a profound sense of autonomous individuality, out of which all human beings, women and men, provide order, control, and meaning over their lives.

Geary's (1998) discussion of mate selection is particularly helpful for highlighting several areas of possibly conflicting motivations within the psyches of and between potential mates. (1) All individuals desire autonomy, but (2) men often try to control women, whom they view as sexual resources, through the control of resources. Such control (3) compromises the autonomous individuality of the women. At the same time, (4) the tendency to control may also conflict internally (psychologically) with the desire of the man to find a mate who has the sought-after personal attributes of kindness, intelligence, and humor. By the same token, (5) women often seek out dominant, resource-rich men who may be somewhat controlling, or whose personal characteristics do not lend themselves to intimacy within the pair bond. (6) The culturally sanctioned submissiveness of women who mate (or consider mating) with dominant men comes into conflict with the motivation of these women for autonomous individuality. (7) The relative isolation of the modern family, which places so much need for emotional and social fulfillment within the pair bond, brings these conflicts to the fore.

## Plot Summary of *Jane Eyre*

Published in 1847, Charlotte Brontë's *Jane Eyre* is a bildungsroman, an example of the novelistic subgenre that traces the growth and development of a single character. Jane, an orphan, leaves the home of her uncongenial aunt Sarah Reed to attend the charity school Lowood early in the novel. Jane acquires a sound education under somewhat harsh conditions, completing her schooling and serving for several years as a teacher. Desiring broader experience, she places an advertisement and obtains a position as governess for Adèle Varens, the ward of Edward Rochester, at Thornfield, an estate about fifty miles from Lowood. When Jane first arrives, Rochester is not in residence at Thornfield, and she at first thinks the housekeeper is her new employer. In her first months at Thornfield, Jane and her employer develop a mutual regard based on intellectual affinity. During this time, several disruptions during the evening (loud laughter, running in the halls) are explained as the eccentric behavior of Grace Poole, a woman who comes to sew in the attic in the evening. In the midst of an extended house party, an unexpected visitor from the West Indies, Richard Mason, is injured in the attic, and Jane discretely helps Rochester and the doctor tend him and precipitate his departure from Thornfield. All this time, Rochester is courting a beautiful and eligible woman named Blanche Ingram, but, finding out through devious means that Jane is in love with him, he proposes to her. As the wedding service is in progress, Richard Mason and a lawyer step forward to announce that Rochester is already married to Mason's sister, a madwoman confined to Thornfield's attic. The wedding is called off, and Jane learns of Rochester's arranged marriage to Bertha Mason, an unstable Creole planter's daughter.

Early the following morning, Jane flees Thornfield, taking a coach as far as she can afford to a desolate crossing, Whitcross. Inadvertently, she leaves her parcel of belongings under the seat and is rendered destitute. After several desperate days inquiring about work and begging, she seeks refuge at a house in the village of Morton, giving her name as Jane Elliot. The clergyman St. John Rivers and his two sisters, temporarily staying in their recently deceased father's house, take Jane in and nurse her back to health. Jane asks for assistance in finding employment and is firm that she has no living family or friends to whom St. John might write. St. John asks Jane to become the schoolmistress for the village school for girls he is opening at Morton. Jane learns that St. John is in love with Rosamond Oliver, the daughter of a wealthy gentleman, but also that he willfully resists his love for Rosamond out of his ambition to become a missionary. During a visit to Jane's cottage, St. John sees Jane's real name on one of her drawings. The next day, he reveals to her that they are cousins, and that she has recently inherited a fortune from their uncle in Madeira. Jane insists on dividing the fortune with her three cousins. The four cousins now living together and studying languages, St. John begins pressuring Jane to marry him, calculating that she will make a good missionary's wife. Jane is almost persuaded by St. John's missionary zeal, but the supernatural intervention of Rochester's voice calling her name prevents her from accepting the proposal. She returns to Thornfield, finds the estate a burned ruin, and learns that Bertha Mason died after setting it afire and that Rochester was blinded and maimed trying to save her. Jane seeks out Rochester at Ferndean, his home in the woods. The novel's conclusion provides an account of their happy marriage and Rochester's partially restored sight.

## *Jane Eyre* in Critical and Evolutionary Context

Since the emergence of feminist literary criticism in the seventies, critics have offered a range of feminist interpretations of Brontë's novel, adopting various socially contextualizing and generic paradigms. In a chapter from the classic work of feminist scholarship *The Madwoman in the Attic*, Sandra M. Gilbert asserts that Bertha, Rochester's mad Creole wife, symbolizes Jane's irrationality and repressed anger, embodying impulses that she must learn to control in her progress toward selfhood (Gilbert & Gubar, 1979). Gilbert and Gubar's inclusion of analysis of *Jane Eyre* in *Madwoman* has established the canonical stature of the novel as a work of rebellious feminism. Along somewhat different lines, in "Jane Eyre: The Development of Female Consciousness," Margaret Fulton focuses not on the journey from childhood dependence to maturity but on the reconciliation of opposites, particularly the bringing into balance of male and female elements (Fulton, 1979). Placing the novel within generic conventions and analyzing it specifically from the perspective of gothic fiction, Cynthia Griffin Wolff maintains that Brontë treats feminine sexuality within realistic limitations and asserts that Rochester embodies projected passion rather than a realistically embodied character (Wolff, 1979). Also using genre as her paradigm for analysis, though deviating from Wolff somewhat, Robin Warhol claims that *Jane Eyre* is neither fully realistic nor gothic, masculine or feminine, as when Jane is submissive to Rochester, calling him "Master," but fraternal toward St. John (Warhol, 1996). In somewhat stark contrast to the persistent feminist strain of these analyses, Bette London argues that *Jane Eyre* provides a psychobiography of submission to the sociocultural construct of woman (London, 1991). Regarding the novel in the context of class shifts during the Victorian era, Esther Godfrey analyzes Jane's androgyny within her working-class background and her ultimate power within her marriage to Rochester (Godfrey, 2005).

These analyses offer varying—in some cases, conflicting—judgments about whether Jane achieves feminist selfhood in her marriage at the novel's conclusion, and they provide no means of mediating between their assessments and contradictory analyses. The Darwinian feminist perspective employed here establishes a grounding theory of the root cause of sexual inequality. It does not render a single one of the foregoing interpretations irrelevant, and it by no means seeks to cancel healthy debate among interpretations. Rather, it expands the framework of explanation for the themes of Brontë's novel, therein providing a starting point for sociocultural explanation. In *Jane Eyre*, two different men with different proximate motives wish to marry Jane, and both exhibit prototypically controlling behavior. This proprietary behavior is not only apt to serve as a constraint on Jane, undercutting her individuality, but to limit the growth of Edward Rochester in the long-term relationship he desires with Jane as well. St. John Rivers, furthermore, seeks to control Jane and use her in his pursuit of religious and spiritual status. Faced with a patriarchal culture that endorses male control of women as well as Christian self-renunciation, Jane must struggle for her autonomy and fight the impulse to submit to male aggression.

Brontë clearly dramatizes the internal conflict between sexual control and the desire for a strong pairbond founded on autonomous individuality in the character of Edward Rochester. Both Jane and Rochester exhibit a desire for autonomous individual expression in the development of a heterosexual relationship, because Brontë establishes unambiguously that intellectual affinity is the ground of attraction between Rochester and Jane. For example, about halfway through the novel, when Rochester finally proposes to Jane, she does not think his proposal is genuine, because she believes that he is going to marry Blanche Ingram. Rochester says to Jane, "'My bride is here'...'because my equal is here, and my likeness'" (Brontë, p. 217). The words confirm what is dramatically developed from the time these two people come together at Thornfield: that their love is based on authentic intellectual regard and mutual understanding.

Brontë develops the theme of likeness or intellectual affinity between Jane and Rochester from the time of their first meetings. Rochester expresses an interest in seeing Jane's drawings soon after she has arrived at Thornfield, and they become absorbed in a discussion of these as well as possible future projects (Brontë, pp. 106–108). This curiosity on the part of the governess's new employer is not only highly unusual but points to their mutual intellectual deprivation, which evolves into the ground of regard and love. Likewise, on another evening when Rochester somewhat imperiously requests Jane's company but she refuses to make small talk, Rochester clarifies the situation by saying he only claims such superiority (that is, by demanding conversation) that his greater age confers. Jane responds: "'I don't think, sir, you have a right to command me merely because you are older than I, or because you have seen more of the world than I have; your claim to superiority depends on the use you have made of your time and experience'" (Brontë, p. 114). Then, amused by the fact that Rochester forgets he *does* have the right to command her because he pays her a salary, she nonetheless distinguishes between the simple enumeration of years and true experience. On these and other points, she shows herself unwilling to acquiesce to some of his softer conversational points, and it is on the basis of this individuality that their mutual regard is established. Ready as she is to *serve* because brought up to a life of servitude, Jane is never intellectually *submissive*, and Rochester recognizes her as his intellectual partner and likeness from these first conversations. In sum, he comes to love her for the strength of an autonomous individuality characterized by intellectual curiosity and independence, the very characteristics he prizes in himself.

Simultaneously, however, Rochester exhibits the prototypical tendency to treat women as sexual resources, a tendency supported by several features of Victorian culture and of Brontë's narrative as well. As the second son in a family still abiding by the practice of primogeniture, Rochester inherited no family wealth, instead marrying his aristocratic title to the fortune of the Creole heiress Bertha. Upon his older brother's untimely death, and with his wife's increasing insanity, he was able to pursue a new partner on the continent. Speaking to Jane about his past after Richard Mason has revealed that Rochester has a living wife, he tells her how he sought a true companion after the failure of his marriage and how he consorted with many beautiful, but incompatible, women (including Adèle's mother). When Jane questions the morality of this behavior, he says, '"Hiring a mistress is the next worst thing to buying a slave: both are by nature, and always by position, inferior: and to live familiarly with inferiors is degrading"' (Brontë, p. 266). Yet to feel degraded by one's choices and behavior, as Rochester acknowledges he does here, is not the same as either recognizing the need for penitence—the point that Jane addresses, and one that feeds into the Christian ideology of the novel—or foregoing an approach to women which sees them as objects of barter. This attitude, which Rochester acknowledges creates relationships of inequality, nevertheless motivates some of his behavior toward Jane in preparation for their marriage. In short, Brontë invests Rochester with a complex sexual psychology, one further complicated by the circumstances of his marriage to Bertha Mason but not entirely explained by that fact. That is, Rochester makes explicit that he feels tricked by his father and brother and therefore has difficulty trusting others, but his controlling and manipulative behavior toward Jane cannot be explained by this fact alone, because he never specifically distrusts *her*.

Thus, although Rochester loves Jane for her intelligence and her forthright nature—for the strength of her autonomous individuality—as soon as he has proposed to her and they have begun preparations for their marriage, he attempts to secure the relationship through forms of material possession. In other words, his behavior becomes overtly proprietary, as he acquires material resources in an effort to secure the sexual resource he desires, Jane. Rochester tells Jane he has written, for instance, to his banker for "'heir-looms for the ladies of Thornfield. In a day or two I hope to pour them into your lap: for every privilege, every attention shall be yours, that I would accord a peer's daughter, if about to marry her'" (Brontë, p. 220). Jane replies that such things seem unnatural and strange for herself. A moment later Rochester expresses a desire to dress her in satin and lace, and Jane responds that she would then no longer be the same person, "'but an ape in a harlequin's jacket,—a jay in borrowed plumes'" (Brontë, p. 221). Still, as they continue to prepare and shop for the wedding trousseau, Jane has to remain adamant that she will not accept the elegant dresses that do not suit her temperament, habits, and looks. At the close of this conversation, they have a joking exchange about harems, and Jane finally says: "'I only want an easy mind, sir; not crushed by crowded obligations. Do you remember what you said of Céline Varens?—of the diamonds, the cashmeres you gave her? I will not be your English Céline Varens. I shall continue as Adèle's governess'" (Brontë, p. 230). In sum, Jane recognizes that the acceptance of these unwelcome resources (things she truly does not want) subjects her to Rochester in a way that neither of them desires and that is additionally, within the simultaneously Christian and feminist value system of the novel, inappropriate. In spite of his intelligence, Rochester himself is less able to see the conflict between desiring Jane as an equal and treating her as a sexual resource. This is psychologically comprehensible, given that (1) the evolved desire to treat women as sexual resources is unconscious; (2) patriarchal reinforcement of such control of women, especially by elite men, was pervasive in Victorian culture; and (3) class differences between the two characters in the novel also encourage Rochester's dominance and control.

Like his general distrustfulness and sexually controlling behavior, Rochester's emotional manipulation is not adequately explained by his past experiences alone. During the house party, for instance, he disguises himself as a gypsy and sneaks back into his house to tell fortunes for the ladies, meeting with each privately. He tells Jane, "'Chance has meted you a measure of happiness: that I know. I knew it before I came here this evening. She has laid it carefully on one side for you. I saw her do it. It depends on yourself to stretch out your hand, and take it up; but whether you will do so, is the problem I study. Kneel again on the rug'" (Brontë, p. 171). Although Jane is not particularly susceptible to fortune-tellers, this does not alter the fact that Rochester has taken on the mantle of yet another form of authority, one that can glean the future. In this guise, he casts his wishes in terms of Jane's desires. When Rochester reveals himself to Jane halfway through their interview, Jane says, "'I shall try to forgive you; but it was not right'" (Brontë, p.173). Rochester concedes that Jane is "sensible" and "correct" in her disapproval, but he does not acknowledge that his behavior toward Jane or the other young ladies—including Blanche Ingram, whom he has misled about the size of his fortune—has been unethical. Slightly later in the novel, after Jane has helped Rochester nurse the injured Mason, Rochester asks Jane, "'You are my little friend, are you not?'" Having become alert to mysteries at Thornfield that she does not understand and in which Mason is somehow implicated, Jane replies, "'I like to serve you, sir, *and to obey you in all that is right*'" (Brontë, p. 185; italics mine). Rochester's subsequent remarks show that he recognizes the ethical conditions Jane puts on obedience in her reply, but he also repeats the word "friend," the intimacy of which Jane implicitly rejects in the formality of her answer. Violating the traditional boundary between master and governess through disguise and emotional manipulation, Rochester's behavior underscores a propensity to treat Jane as a sexual resource, a propensity that contradicts his wish to acquire her as a mate on equal terms. For her part, Jane must work to maintain the proper boundary between governess and master.

All in all, given cultural conditions that reinforce the tendency to treat women as sexual resources and inferiors and to remind Rochester and Jane that theirs will be a marriage of unequal class, it seems unlikely that these conflicts would have been reasonably resolved in the novel without the dramatic plot events that precipitated the separation of the two characters and ultimately led to Jane's inheritance and Rochester's maiming, the reduction of his material estate, and his seclusion at Ferndean. A standard cultural interpretation of Rochester's maiming and property loss is that these acts serve, within the novel's Christian ideology, as retribution for his promiscuity and his intended bigamy. Such a lesson logically coheres with the novel's austere piety, and it doubtless pleased contemporaneous audiences; nonetheless, the necessity of Rochester's chastening on religious grounds does not obviate its capacity to highlight sexual conflicts or its implications for the novel's feminist themes. From a Darwinian feminist perspective, the conclusion suggests that Rochester must be largely disempowered to forego the proprietary behaviors that inhibit the pair bond based on autonomous individuality that he desires with Jane.

Comparatively little critical attention is given to Jane's relationship with her cousin St. John Rivers, who is not only a serious suitor but whose marriage proposal Jane nearly accepts. This is because the *romantic plot* is clearly focused on the Jane-Rochester story. However, any full treatment of the novel must address the Jane–St. John relationship, which Brontë develops at length, and which is of particular interest to feminists. St. John, whose conscious intentions differ from Rochester's in his relationship with Jane, also poses a threat to her autonomy and to the equality of the pair bond. Whereas the tendency to treat women as sexual resources by buying sexual favors with material possessions is an acknowledged part of Rochester's life history and a part of his behavioral profile that, through habit, carries over into and conflicts with the new pair bond he wishes to form with Jane, St. John Rivers never directly displays these mating behaviors. To the contrary, his great effort is channeled through the force of his religious zeal, and he controls his own sexual desire and love, ultimately attempting to control Jane, in the service of his religious ambitions. In St. John, then, the proximate cause of controlling behavior differs substantively from the ultimate cause of such behavior (sexual access). Whereas evolutionary psychologists typically argue that, for men, there is a strong correlation between high status and reproductive success, for St. John Rivers not only has status become an end itself, but its ultimate rewards are deferred to the afterlife.

Conscious control and denial of emotion is a program that St. John enacts in the service of his religious ambition, in effect transferring his reproductive motives toward religious goals. At the same time, however, prototypical patterns of control, both over women and himself, are perhaps especially apparent because they have become divorced from their evolved sexual motivations. The novel's first examples of St. John's pitilessly controlling nature display him in the act of quashing his own love and sexual desire. Before he turns his attentions toward Jane, Jane notices that he loves Rosamond Oliver, and she suggests to him that he need not become a missionary and leave England for the harsh climate and conditions of India. Rosamond, who reciprocates St. John's love, is beautiful and wealthy, and her family would approve his suit, since he is of old, local family. But St. John wonders how Jane could ask that he relinquish his "'foundation laid on earth for a mansion in heaven? [His] hopes of being numbered in the band who have merged all ambition in the glorious one of bettering their race—of carrying knowledge into the realms of ignorance....Must I relinquish that? It is dearer than the blood in my veins'" (Brontë, p. 319). Jane speaks to him forthrightly of his attraction to Rosamund; although taken aback that a woman would speak to him so directly, St. John denies the significance of his feelings, and says, "'Know me to be what I am—a cold, hard man'" (Brontë, p. 319). St. John is not yet as hard-hearted as he claims, but Jane has seen him in the process of aspiring to such control in the presence of Rosamond Oliver. As Rosamond bends to pat the dog's head, Jane observes, "I saw his solemn eye melt with sudden fire, and flicker with resistless emotion. Flushed and kindled thus, he looked nearly as beautiful for a man as she for a woman. His chest heaved once, as if his large heart, weary of despotic constriction, had expanded, despite the will, and made a vigorous bound for the attainment of liberty. But he curbed it, I think, as a resolute rider would curb a rearing steed" (Brontë, pp. 310–311). In the character St. John Rivers, the replacement of individual autonomy with self-renunciation is consistent with Victorian Evangelical religious piety and, in itself, not subject to criticism in the novel. However, while Brontë, through Jane's narration, exhibits respect for Christian self-renunciation in general, her depiction of St. John's repudiation of human feeling—including his repression of his feelings for Rosamond, his insistence that Jane join him in a loveless marriage, and his disapproval of the domestic pleasure Jane enjoys with her cousins (her first true family)—cast his character in a negative light.

Just as St. John's self-control appears especially merciless because displaced from sexual motives onto the supernatural authority of God, his attempts to control Jane are calculating, manipulative, and insensitive, because all such procedures are rationalized in terms of a divine authority. And just as his willed subjugation of his sexual desire ("despotic constriction") has an element of brutality missing from Rochester's conflicting motives, St. John's proprietary behavior toward Jane evinces an element of cruelty that appears unsettlingly intentional. Having realized that the devout and hard-working Jane will make an excellent "help-meet and fellow-labourer" in India, St. John waits until his sisters are away at Morton one day, approaches Jane as she is studying German, and says, "'I want you to give up German, and learn Hindostanee'" (Brontë, p. 342, p. 338). Although he says he wants help only until his departure for India in three months, it is clear that he has already formulated a plan to propose marriage to Jane. Hardly by nature a shrinking violet, Jane nevertheless reports that

> By degrees, he acquired a certain influence over me that took away my liberty of mind: his praise and notice were more restraining than his indifference. I could no longer talk or laugh freely when he was by, because a tiresomely importunate instinct reminded me that vivacity (at least in me) was distasteful to him. I was so fully aware that only serious moods and occupations were acceptable, that in his presence every effort to sustain or follow any other became vain: I fell under a freezing spell. When he said "go," I went, "come," I came; "do this," I did it. But I did not love my servitude: I wished, many a time, he had continued to neglect me. (Brontë, p. 339).

At this same juncture in the narrative, St. John offers Jane, one evening at bedtime, what she designates "an experimental kiss," and she says, "he viewed me to learn the result....I might have turned a little pale, for I felt as if this kiss were a seal affixed to my fetters" (Brontë, p. 339). Some time (about a month) later, thinking that Jane looks ill, Diana proposes a trip to the seaside, which St. John opposes, pressing her to continue her "lessons in Hindostanee"; Jane defers because, as she reports, "I, like a fool, never thought of resisting him—I could not resist him" (Brontë, p. 340). Shortly thereafter, St. John proposes marriage and the missionary's life to Jane. Jane agrees to accompany him as his curate only on the condition that they will not marry, a condition that St. John considers indecent.

In sum, Brontë's narrative makes it clear that Jane sees St. John's behavior as constraining and confining not only *retrospectively* but also *initially*, at the time she first experienced the request to learn Hindi, the kiss, and the offer of marriage (Beaty, 1996). The question that arises with respect to Jane, then, who has fought so hard for her selfhood and survival from the time she was effectively disowned by her Aunt Reed, is why she would be so susceptible to a man so controlling that she recognizes he robs her of her autonomous individuality. There are several answers to this question. First, Jane is still in love with Rochester, and at the time of St. John's first proposal, she has tried to acquire news of Rochester through Mrs. Fairfax, but has received no reply. For this reason, she assumes erroneously (not knowing of the fire at Thornfield) that he has left England, which is thus rendered empty for her. Second, Jane is deeply religious, and it is this, in addition to family ties, which subjects her to St. John's power. As the literary critic Jerome Beaty points out, modern readers have difficulty accepting that Brontë endorses self-renunciation in the service of Christian mission for both St. John and Jane, because these values—religious, colonial, and psychological—diverge rather far from our own. But what Brontë does not endorse is the conjunction of such religious self-renunciation with sexually consummated, loveless marriage. Having twice turned down St. John's proposals, Jane, deeply moved by his evening scriptural readings and prayers, reports that she "felt veneration for St. John—veneration so strong that its impetus thrust me to the point I had so long shunned. I was tempted to cease struggling with him—to rush down the torrent of his will into the gulf of his existence, and there lose my own" (Brontë, p. 356). As, at Jane's request, they pray together so she may know God's will regarding St. John's proposal, she hears the voice of Edward Rochester call her name three times. By conferring supernatural insight upon Jane at this crucial moment, Brontë disrupts the ideological support, tied exclusively to male power systems, underwriting St. John's status. Jane insists that she must go to her room alone and pray, and the devout, ordained man of God is left without privileged access to the divine. The next day, Jane leaves to find Rochester.

# Conclusion: From Reproductive Resource to Autonomous Individuality?

Cultural critics often object to evolutionary analyses because they assume that such analyses are deterministic. By contrast, this reading attempts to demonstrate how an understanding of the gendered power dynamics in Brontë's *Jane Eyre* is augmented by considering it in light of differential reproductive strategies as well as historical and ideological factors. Importantly, because the work considered is fictional, it can (and does) subvert male power in unlikely ways and at crucial moments: Richard Mason stops the wedding at the altar; Bertha burns Thornfield, killing herself and maiming her husband in the process; God intervenes to call Jane back to Rochester and away from a self-denying marriage to St. John. Unlikely to occur in real life, within the novel these events check religious and marital systems that militate against Jane's individual autonomy and satisfying marriage. From the Darwinian feminist perspective adopted here, Brontë exposes the evolved male proprietary attitude toward women, reveals some of the specific cultural forms it takes in the nineteenth century, and illustrates its potential harmfulness to individual autonomy and pair bonding for both men and women. Although the novel itself provides readers with a classic fairytale ending—Jane and Rochester reunited, their love nothing diminished by their hardships, Rochester's sight restored and their family growing after two years—Brontë's penetrating portrayal of power dynamics, cast within a Darwinian perspective, is a rather sobering reminder of how difficult it was for actual women of this historical period to achieve such autonomy or to find loving, respectful partners.

# References

Beaty, J. (2001). St. John's way and the wayward reader. In C. Brontë, 491–503.

Boyd, B. (1998). Jane, meet Charles: Literature, evolution, and human nature. *Philosophy and Literature, 22*(1), 1–30.

Brontë, C. (1847/2001). *Jane Eyre* (R. J. Dunn, Ed., 3rd ed.). New York: Norton.

Buss, D. M. (1994/2003). *The evolution of desire: Strategies of human mating* (Rev. ed.). New York: Basic Books.

Carroll, J. (2005). Human nature and literary meaning: A theoretical model illustrated with a critique of *Pride and Prejudice*. In J. Gottschall & D. S. Wilson (Eds.), *The literary animal: Evolution and the nature of narrative* (pp. 76–106). Evanston, IL: Northwestern University Press.

Cixous, H. (1975/1986). Sorties. In H. Cixous & C. Clément, *The newly born woman* (B. Wing, Trans., pp. 63–131). Minneapolis: University of Minnesota Press.

Damasio, A. (1999). *The feeling of what happens: Body and emotion in the making of consciousness.* New York: Harcourt.

Derrida, J. (1968/1989). Structure, sign, and play in the discourse of the human sciences. In R. C. David & R. Schleifer (Eds.), *Contemporary literary criticism: Literary and cultural studies* (pp. 229–248). New York: Longman.

Donald, M. (1991). *The origins of the modern mind: Three stages in the evolution of culture and cognition.* Cambridge, MA: Harvard University Press.

Fulton, M. (1979). *Jane Eyre:* The development of female consciousness. *English Studies in Canada, 5,* 432–447.

Geary, D. C. (1998). *Male, female: The evolution of sex differences.* Washington, DC: American Psychological Association.

Gilbert, S. M., & Gubar, S. (1979). A dialogue of self and soul: Plain Jane's progress. In S. M. Gilbert & S. Gubar (Eds.), *The madwoman in the attic: The woman writer and the nineteenth-century literary imagination* (pp. 336–371). New Haven, CT: Yale University Press.

Godfrey, E. (2005). *Jane Eyre,* from governess to girl bride. *Studies in English Literature, 45*(4), 853–871.

London, B. (1991). *Jane Eyre* and the production of the text. *English Literary History, 58,* 195–213.

Mulder, M. B. (2009). Serial monogamy as polygyny or polyandry? Marriage in the Tanzanian Pimbwe. *Human Nature, 20,* 130–150.

Scheidel, W. (2009). A peculiar institution? Greco-Roman monogamy in global context. *History of the Family, 20,* 1–12.

Smuts, B. (1996). Male aggression against women: An evolutionary perspective. In D. Buss & N. Malamuth (Eds.), *Sex, power, and conflict: Evolutionary and feminist perspectives* (pp. 231–268). Oxford, UK: Oxford University Press.

Stasio, M. J., & Stasio, K. (2007). An evolutionary approach to Jane Austen: Prehistoric preferences in *Pride and Prejudice*. *Studies in the Novel*, *39*(2), 133–146.

Trivers, R. L. (2002). Parental investment and reproductive success. In *Natural selection and social theory: Selected papers of Robert Trivers* (pp. 56–110). Oxford, UK: Oxford University Press.

Warhol, R. R. (1996). Double gender, double genre in *Jane Eyre* and *Villette*. *Studies in English Literature, 1500–1900*, *36*(4), 857–875.

Wolff, C. G. (1979). The Radcliffean model: A form for feminine sexuality. *Modern Language Studies*, *9*(3), 98–113.

Wright, R. (1994). *The moral animal: Evolutionary psychology and everyday life*. New York: Random House/Vintage Books.

# 20

# The Empress's Clothes

JULIE SEAMAN

## Introduction: Interrogating the Dressmaker

Nature has given women so much power that the law has very
wisely given them little (Johnson, S., Letter to Doctor Taylor).

[W]hen the males and females of any animal have the same general
habits of life, but differ in structure, colour, or ornament, such
differences have been mainly caused by sexual selection....
—Darwin, 1859/2009, pp. 137–138

Women and men, girls and boys in contemporary Western society are subject
to myriad social norms regarding dress. Indeed, it appears that gendered dress
norms exist in all human cultures, and that "their principal messages are about
the ways in which women and men perceive their gender roles or are expected
to perceive them" (Crane, 2000, p. 16). According to sociological and anthropological accounts of human dress and adornment, fashion and clothing both reflect
existing gender roles and work to shape social understandings of gender identity
(Barnard, 1996). Thus, one could say that humans are a relatively sexually mono-
morphic species (Mealey, 2000) that has amplified its slight sexual dimorphism
through dress, broadly defined.[1] In this chapter, I seek to apply insights from an
evolutionary explanation of sexual dimorphisms in animal "dress" in order to critically examine the manner in which courts treat employment rules that require
women and men employees to conform to dimorphic dress and makeup norms
while at work.

Given the pervasiveness in human culture of social norms that differentiate
appropriate female from male dress, it is not surprising that the workplace is also
an arena of gendered dress expectations. Whether written or unwritten, explicitly
stated or merely understood, sex-specific norms governing what employees should
wear exist in many—probably most—workplaces (Bartlett, 1994). These policies

often go unremarked and unchallenged. Occasionally, however, an employee objects and a lawsuit ensues. In these cases, courts must grapple with the difficult question whether, and if so when, an employer may condition employment on adherence to different sets of rules for male and female employees.

The outcomes of these cases, along with their reasoning and analysis, are increasingly difficult to reconcile with one another and with the equality values that underlie federal and state antidiscrimination laws. Rather than engaging in principled analysis, courts in this area seem instead to fall back on intuitive notions of appropriate gendered expectations regarding dress. This has resulted in vague and malleable legal doctrines as well as legal opinions in which the reasoning is entirely circular: courts declare that particular dress rules are instantiations of benign social norms and therefore find them nondiscriminatory. As for what makes them benign in the first place, there is little or no explanation.

One of the great contributions of feminist theory in general, and legal feminism in particular, has been to uncover the power dynamics that may be hidden behind seemingly neutral and benign laws and social practices—their soiled undergarments, so to speak. In the context of dress, however, these underlying power dynamics are complex and obscure; indeed, sometimes they are counterintuitive. In this chapter, I hope to begin to remove the veil from common dress rules and practices by drawing on insights from evolutionary theory and experimentation. In particular, I look to the literature on sexual selection to inquire whether an understanding of the adaptive pressures that can result in sexual dimorphisms might provide some guidance to courts and legal scholars as they navigate the tangled bank of dress rules and norms.

In nonhuman animals, it is widely accepted that the primary cause of sex differences is sexual selection (Darwin, 1871). Most notably for the purposes of this chapter, sexual selection has resulted in rather spectacular ornamental features in the males of many species, which we might think of as sexually dimorphic "dress." Thus it seems sensible to wonder whether insights gleaned from the sexual selection literature (both theoretical and empirical) might offer something useful to the analysis of workplace sex discrimination, and in particular to the treatment of sex-differentiated dress and grooming codes. As is well known, sexual dimorphisms are common among many species of nonhuman animals. Such differences have been studied extensively by evolutionary scholars and are widely understood as adaptations caused primarily by sexual selection (Darwin, 1871; Hamilton & Zuk, 1982). According to (a highly simplified version of) the most common explanation, eager males "dress up" in order to be chosen as mates by picky females. There are, of course, several serious alternative hypotheses about why "males dress up." But the important point for present purposes is that each of the proposed evolutionary explanations for differences in male and female animal "dress" involves communication, status, or mating behavior (or some combination of these three elements).

Sexual selection theory is currently in something of a state of flux, and many of the classic paradigms have been challenged (Snyder & Gowaty, 2007; Roughgarden

& Akcay, 2010). On the other hand, gendered dress norms in human societies are not inherent but rather are behavioral. Indeed, even in unclothed societies, humans decorate their bodies and do so in gender-normative ways. Thus sociologists of dress have argued that the original, primary function of dress is not protection from the elements but is communicative. It therefore makes sense to ask what function these communicative, decorative behaviors may have evolved to serve and to question whether existing law and policy relating to sex and dress are in line with the values that federal antidiscrimination law is designed to serve.

## Legal Feminism and Evolution: A Mismatched Set?

Over the past several years, legal scholars have begun to look to evolutionary theory to enrich their understanding of a wide variety of legal doctrines and law-relevant behaviors. As legal scholar Owen Jones (1999) has emphasized, given that the legal system is largely concerned with regulating human behavior, it follows that a more robust theory of behavior can only help the law more effectively influence and regulate these law-relevant human actions in whatever direction is desired by policy makers. Thus, recent "law and evolution" scholarship has looked to evolutionary theory to inform legal analysis in such diverse areas as child abuse, rape, economic irrationalities, wage and gender gaps in employment, the "glass ceiling," workplace sexual harassment, women in combat, free speech, criminal responsibility, property and inheritance, and contract law, among others (Seaman, 2005).

Perhaps nowhere is evolutionary theory more potentially illuminating—or more fraught—than in the arena of workplace sex discrimination law, with its potent mix of sex and gender dynamics, resource acquisition, competition, changing roles and stereotypes, and status jockeying and signaling. Furthermore, the substantial tension in antidiscrimination theory between sameness and difference equality makes the extent, cause, and relevance of sex differences especially salient to feminist legal theorists. And yet it often seems that legal feminists and evolutionary theorists talk past, rather than to, one another. Reference to evolutionary biology in the context of sex differences has sometimes been offered to explain or justify gender disparities in the workplace (Browne, 2002; Epstein, 1990), male-only public educational institutions (United States v. Virginia, 1991), and policies that restrict women from military combat roles (Browne, 2001). With respect to workplace imbalances, if women on average have different cognitive skills, preferences, and behavioral tendencies than do men as a result of divergent adaptive pressures, it might be that the smaller number of women in certain fields—say, science or engineering—might be caused not by societal discrimination but by merit and self-selection (Browne, 2002; Epstein, 1990). Because such arguments have been advanced in the past by some "law and evolution" scholars, many feminist legal scholars tend to be extraordinarily suspicious of any argument that raises the possibility of sex differences grounded in biology or genetics.

In addition, discussions of biology in the context of law invariably raise the specter of the naturalistic fallacy: the notion that what is corresponds to what ought to be. Legal scholars are usually careful to include the obligatory disclaimer that simply because a particular behavior might be grounded in genes, this does not require that it be validated or even tolerated either legally or normatively. To cite perhaps the most controversial example, Thornhill and Palmer (2000) have argued that sexual coercion by males can be adaptive under certain circumstances and that behaviors defined by law as rape might usefully be understood with reference to the findings of behavioral biology. Jones, citing Thornhill and Palmer, argued that advances in behavioral biology might usefully inform legal policy approaches to rape law (Jones, 1999). Despite Jones's careful analysis and clear explanation of why his argument did not sound in genetic determinism, many feminists were outraged by the suggestion that rape was not a wholly "socially constructed" behavior and that biology might be invoked to justify male sexual aggression.

But a refusal to engage with—or even to acknowledge as legitimate—the vibrant and diverse fields that make up contemporary evolutionary studies risks throwing out the genuine insights with the invidious stereotypes. Particularly in the realms of sexual selection and male-female difference, today's scholarly work is not your grandfather's sociobiology. Recent theoretical and empirical work in evolutionary biology, evolutionary anthropology, evolutionary psychology, and related fields has much to offer legal scholars who are concerned with questions of difference and discrimination, if only we are willing to listen with open—though still skeptical—minds. It is in this spirit that I consider the analogy to nonhuman animal "dress" in an attempt to illuminate the underlying dynamics of gendered dress dimorphism and to suggest a possible framework within which to analyze employer appearance rules.

## Sex Based Dress Codes: The Naked Emperor

Title VII is the federal statute that prohibits employment discrimination on the basis of race, color, religion, national origin, and sex. Among other things, the statute makes it unlawful for an employer to subject a person to discriminatory working conditions because of that person's sex or gender. Workplace rules that delineate permissible (or required) dress, makeup, jewelry, or other body decorations are understood to be a "term or condition of employment" under the statute. Normally, a "term or condition" that makes a distinction based on one of the protected characteristics—imagine a dress code that explicitly allowed white employees to wear business attire but required black employees to wear uniforms—would be considered per se discriminatory and would be exceedingly difficult, if not impossible, for an employer to justify.

However, there is one exception to this general framework, one type of explicit distinction based on a prohibited trait that, under current case law, does not automatically raise an inference of discrimination. When an employer maintains an employee dress or grooming code, different treatment of employees based on their sex—what would otherwise be considered "facial discrimination"—is typically permitted so long as the dress and grooming requirements conform to widespread "social norms" rather than improper "sex stereotypes." Yet when it comes to explaining the distinction between benign social dress norms on the one hand, and invidious stereotype on the other, courts are largely at a loss. Despite the strong negative reaction of most feminist legal theorists to arguments implicating biology and evolution, a consideration of sexual selection research and theory might offer fresh insights into this very muddled area of sex discrimination law. Indeed, the lessons of evolutionary biology tend to suggest that many—or most—workplace dress and grooming codes of this kind should be invalidated under Title VII and similar state and local antidiscrimination laws.

Social norms regarding body modification, ornamentation, and covering exist in every known human society (Entwistle, 2001). And in every known human society, such norms are gendered: individuals are expected to adhere to certain sex-differentiated dress and grooming practices. According to scholars of dress, these gendered dress norms do not simply reflect the gender expectations of a particular culture, they are also "part of the process by which attitudes to and images of both men and women are created and reproduced" (Rouse, 1989, as quoted in Barnard, 1996, p. 111). It is hardly surprising, then, that the workplace is no exception to gendered dress rules, whether embodied in formal written policies or informal understandings and practices (Bartlett, 1994; Seaman, 2007). Courts have addressed sex-differentiated dress policies in a growing body of case law in which plaintiffs—both male and female, but more often male—have challenged these rules as unlawful sex discrimination (Case, 1995; Seaman, 2007). For example, male plaintiffs have challenged rules that prohibited them from wearing long hairstyles or jewelry, and female plaintiffs have challenged rules that required them to wear uniforms, skirts, or makeup. Though some early cases viewed such appearance codes as sex discrimination, this formal equality framework, under which different treatment based on sex was equated to discrimination, soon gave way to the view that it was perfectly appropriate—and perfectly legal—for an employer to instantiate social dress and appearance norms even where these differed according to sex.

In the widely discussed case of *Jespersen v. Harrah's Operating Company*, a federal appeals court addressed a challenge to an employer-mandated appearance code that required female bartenders to wear foundation, blush, and lipstick to work, and to tease or style their hair every day, while prohibiting male bartenders from doing so (*Jespersen v. Harrah's Operating Co.*, 2006). Darlene Jespersen, a long-standing and highly regarded employee, was fired after she refused to wear makeup to work. In addressing her claim, the *en banc* Court of Appeals for the Ninth Circuit applied an "unequal burdens" standard to hold that the Harrah's grooming code "impose[d] different but essentially equal burdens on men and women" and therefore did not amount to sex discrimination under Title VII of the Civil Rights Act of 1964. The court stated that "[g]rooming standards that *appropriately differentiate* between the genders are not facially discriminatory" (*Jespersen v. Harrah's Operating Co.*, 2006, p. 4127; emphasis mine).

According to the *Jespersen* court, there are two distinct ways that a plaintiff claiming discrimination based on a sex-differentiated dress or grooming code might prevail. Under an "unequal burdens" analysis, a workplace policy discriminates unlawfully if it differentially impacts one sex, such as by requiring added expense or time to conform to the dress or grooming rules. Alternatively, a plaintiff may prevail under a "sex stereotyping" theory by showing that the policy imposes on members of one or the other sex a requirement that they conform to a stereotypical gender norm (*Jespersen v. Harrah's Operating Co.*, 2006; *Price Waterhouse v. Hopkins*, 1989). The thorny issue in these cases is how a court is to distinguish a sex-differentiated dress code that merely requires employees to adhere to "benign" social gender norms—which is permissible—from one that embodies sex stereotypes—which is not.

The difference between a gender norm on the one hand, and an impermissible stereotype on the other, was only imprecisely defined in *Jespersen*. However the court did offer some clues as to what sorts of sex-differentiated appearance codes could raise a question of sex stereotyping. These clues are significant because they are representative of the threads of analysis that run through the appearance code case law in general. And these themes, it turns out, raise some intriguing analogies to the lessons of animal "dress" in the literature of sexual selection and the evolution of communication.

First, the *Jespersen* majority reasoned that the Harrah's dress code did not amount to "impermissible stereotyping" because it was not "intended to be sexually provocative" or to "stereotype women as sex objects." Were a policy to do so, the court suggested, it could amount to an impermissible sex stereotype that would violate Title VII (*Jespersen v. Harrah's Operating Co.*, 2006, p. 1112). This focus on the gender stereotype of sexual attractiveness and availability—on employer rules or practices that cause female employees to appear "sexy" and available at work—is a prominent underlying theme in the grooming cases. In those relatively rare instances in which female plaintiffs have prevailed in challenges to workplace grooming codes, several have involved what a court perceives as a sexually suggestive requirement that is unrelated to the main purpose of the defendant's business. In one of the first cases to hold that an employer dress code violated Title VII, for example, a court found in favor of a female "lobby hostess" in a New York City office building who was constructively discharged because she refused to wear what the court viewed as a revealing and sexually provocative costume (*EEOC v. Sage Realty Corporation*, 1981).

Similarly, in a series of cases in which courts struck down various airline rules governing the appearance, age, and lifestyle of female flight attendants, courts closely scrutinized the employers' reasons for the policies and determined that they were "part of an overall program to create a sexual image for the airline" by catering to the flying public's desire to be served by thin, attractive, young, single women (*Gerdom v. Continental Airlines, Inc.*, 1982). Thus, courts have invalidated airline rules that restricted flight attendant positions to young, single, childless women, holding that policies that prevented flight attendants from being married, having children, or working beyond their early- to mid-thirties all constituted sex discrimination in violation of Title VII. Notably, in their attempts to control these particular traits of female flight attendants, the airlines tracked very closely those characteristics that the traditional evolutionary psychology literature posits as the desirable mating characteristics of human females: youth, fertility, health, and availability (Buss, 2003).

The difficulty inherent in distinguishing between so-called benign gender norms and invidious sex stereotypes is illuminated by considering Gowaty's (1992) discussion of femininity and the evolution of human communication systems. Gowaty defines femininity as "what women do to ourselves to make ourselves attractive to men" (p. 239). She describes the two primary features of then-current fashions of femininity—in 1992, but I would argue that, at least in recent fashion trends, *plus ca change, plus c'est la meme chose*—as "hobbling" and "juvenilization." Hobbling femininity, most literally such fashions as high heels and foot-binding but also other features that restrict women's ability to move freely and drain their physical, mental, and financial resources, is not obviously tied to what courts view as the invidious gender stereotype of blatant sexual availability. Likewise, the connection between female juvenilization and sexual attractiveness to males is not necessarily apparent. Standard evolutionary psychology would tend to explain shaved legs and underarms, made-up faces, and exaggerated thinness as youth and fertility signals, whereas Gowaty views them as "neotenic characteristics that signal juvenalization and its attendant dependence and subordination" (p. 240). However, insofar as ideals of femininity in a society conform to norms—or at least suppositions—of sexual attractiveness, such features will implicitly communicate sexual signals even if they do not do so explicitly. The point here is that both standard evolutionary psychology and feminist contributions suggest that it is no easy task to draw a line that could reasonably distinguish improper gender stereotypes from "benign" norms of femininity. Though we in the contemporary West might see a vast gulf between foot-binding and high heels, any such difference is likely to be one of degree rather than kind.

Apart from the sexualized appearance and flight attendant cases, female plaintiffs have also prevailed in challenging policies that required women, but not men, to wear uniforms at work. In the leading case of *Carroll v. Talman Federal Savings & Loan Association of Chicago*, the Seventh Circuit Court of Appeals struck down such a policy because the court perceived that the requirement acted as a signal of lesser professional status on the part of the uniformed women employees. The employer's stated justifications for the policy revealed to the court that the uniform requirement was grounded in "offensive stereotypes prohibited by Title VII" (p. 1033). In another case, a court found it "demeaning" to require uniforms for women where men in similar positions were permitted to wear professional business attire (*O'Donnell v. Burlington Coat Factory Warehouse, Inc.*, 1987; *EEOC v. Clayton Federal Savings and Loan Association*, 1981). These cases show that where a dress code imposes a demeaning image on one sex only—here, an unfounded implication of inferior rank or status—it may rise to the level of discrimination under Title VII.

In sum, it appears that the gender norms that courts view as invidious are those that relate either to enforced female sexual attractiveness or to signaling lower female competence and status. Reading between the lines of these cases, one can deduce that these factors are what distinguish an "appropriate" or "reasonable" sex-differentiated dress code from one that is unduly burdensome, a benign cultural gender norm from an inappropriate stereotype. The categories of cases in which female plaintiffs have prevailed are those in which employers are viewed as attempting to enhance the sexual attractiveness of female employees in a position for which sexual attractiveness should not be relevant, or where female employees are compelled to wear uniforms though male employees of similar rank are not. In the latter context, courts reason that such policies imply to customers that the uniformed female employees are of lesser status than the nonuniformed male employees. In addition, there is a patronizing implication that women are not capable of good judgment as to appropriate business attire because they are competitive and subject to fashion's whim (*Carroll v. Talman Federal Savings and Loan Association of Chicago*, 1979).

These judgments on the part of the courts stem more from intuition than from any principled analysis; therefore, the parameters of permissible dress rules are vague and the results unpredictable. The *Jespersen* opinion, for example, created shock waves among legal scholars not for its recitation of the rule (which, it should be noted, was nothing new), but rather for its seeming blindness both to the social stereotypes evoked by a policy that required women to be adorned with makeup and teased hair in order to achieve their "personal best," and to the cost and effort behind such a daily routine. For the *Jespersen* majority, a female face painted with lipstick, rouge, and eyeliner was a social convention no different in kind from that of a male face unadorned and cleanly shaven; a female head sporting a teased, styled mane was no different from a closely cropped male head. Thus, the court held that the policy did not violate Title VII's prohibition against discrimination on the basis of sex.

## Animal Dress: The Emperor's Fancy Clothes

As discussed in *On the Origin of Species*, and elaborated in *The Descent of Man, and Selection in Relation to Sex*, Charles Darwin recognized sexual dimorphism within species and coined the term "sexual selection" to describe the process by which many such sex differences could evolve (Darwin, 1859/2009; 1871). As Jones and Ratterman (2009) recently noted, "Darwin correctly realized that sexual selection could be mediated by male-male combat or by a female's choice of attractive males" (p. 10002). Darwin argued that sexually dimorphic male secondary traits arise where "individual males have had, in successive generations, some slight advantage over other males whether in their weapons, defence, or charms; and have transmitted these advantages to their male offspring" (Darwin, 1859/2009, p. 222). Included in those "charms" would be traits (often along with their accompanying displays), such as brightly colored crests or elaborate tail feathers in birds, which females for some reason might prefer in a mate.

Sexual selection as a process thus creates a dynamic through which males may come to possess weaponry, status badges, bright coloration, lovely song, dramatic tail feathers, combs, and wattles (among other traits). All of these may have evolved via competition among males for access to females. Though it is something of an oversimplification, as a general matter it is fair to say that where such competition tends toward a male-male struggle in which the victor "gets the girl," intrasexual competition predominates and favors development of such "masculine" characteristics as extreme size and aggression, status badges, and weaponry such as tusks, horns, or fangs. Alternatively, the competition may emphasize intersexual mechanisms: female choice rather than male power. In the most extreme example, males in lekking species gather in a large group—a "lek"—to display their charms, and females freely choose the males with which to mate. As Ridley (1994) colorfully described the lek of the sage grouse:

> Each knows his place; each runs through his routine of inflating the air sacs in his breast and strutting forward, bouncing the fleshy sacs through his feathers for all the world like a dancer at the Folies Bergere. The females wander through this market, and after several days of contemplating the goods on offer, they mate with one of the males. That they are choosing, not being forced to choose, seems obvious: The male does not mount the female until she squats in front of him. (p. 141)

Under the common understanding of sexual selection, where competition for mates takes the form of mate choice by females, which emphasizes female agency rather than male power, males are most likely to possess the fanciest dress (Wilson, 2000). Though evolutionary biologists long professed to be baffled by the seemingly irrational preferences of females that could lead to a male trait such as the peacock's tale, in recent years there has been an upsurge of interest and research in the area of female choice. As Paul (2002) notes, "since the 1970's, the theory of sexual selection and mate choice has experienced a fulminant revival, with major new theoretical insights and empirical findings" (p. 878). Among these new insights are the important evolutionary role played by female mate choice, the consequences of constraints on free female (and male) choice (Gowaty, 1996, 1997, Gowaty et al., 2002, 2003; Bluhm & Gowaty, 2004) and the role of social learning and experience in mate selection.

With respect to the important role of female choice in the model of sexual selection, once again the extreme exemplified by lekking species is noteworthy. In their recent review, Jones and Ratterman (2009) point out that in species in which the males provide no resources to the female beyond genetic material, "the benefits of choice are not at all obvious" and therefore a "tremendous amount of effort has been devoted to creating explanatory models of female-choice evolution in such systems" (p. 10003). Ironically, where female choice is most apparent— recall Ridley's description of the female grouse window shopping the shimmying, dancing males—its function is the most obscure. Darwin fell back in explanation on an aesthetic sense on the part of the females, but even he did not seem entirely convinced (Darwin, 1871).

Recent empirical research has begun to suggest answers to this puzzle; several studies offer some support for the proposition that female trait preferences (in the examined species, at the very least) play more than just a Fisherian "sexy sons" role in reproductive success, whereby success would flow simply from choosing males that other females would also find attractive (for any reason, not necessarily to do with substantive fitness), which attractive trait would then be passed on to that female's sons. Rather, female preferences for various traits, some showy and some not, may reflect an astute assessment of genetic quality: the traits may represent honest signals of the males' "good genes." In the most straightforward version of the good genes model, for which there is growing empirical support, the appearance of the ornament or other characteristic directly correlates with the good health of the fancy male because, for example, bright colors indicate low parasite load. In an early study, for example, Hamilton and Zuk (1982) offered some evidence that the showiest species of North American birds were those that were most susceptible to parasite infection. More recently, Petrie (1994) and Manning and Hartley (1991) have found that the degree of symmetry and ornamentation of peacock trains are correlated with one another and with offspring survival.

In another example in which the trait is behavioral rather than physiological, Byers and Waits (2006) showed that "the free mate choices that pronghorn (*Antilocapra americana*) females make by means of an energetically expensive mate sampling process have a strong effect on offspring survival" (p. 16343). In the latter study, involving a species in which males cannot force or coerce mating and females therefore exercise a high degree of autonomous choice, paternity in any season was highly skewed toward a small set of males. Offspring survival to weaning as well as to subsequent ages was significantly correlated with sire attractiveness despite the fact that female mates of less attractive males appeared to compensate (Bluhm & Gowaty, 2004; Gowaty, 2008) by increased rates of nursing.

Other recent studies further reveal that constraints on mate choice can have detrimental consequences to reproductive success. As summarized by Gowaty and Hubbell (2009), "female and male choice studies in flies, cockroaches, ducks, and mice have demonstrated that offspring viability was significantly higher when choosers were mated with discriminates they preferred, as was productivity (the number of offspring surviving to reproductive age)" (p. 10018). Interestingly, some of these studies also showed that the preferred mate was different for different females, suggesting that "fitness" is not an absolute but a relative quality (Anderson et al. 2007; Bluhm & Gowaty, 2004; Drickamer et al., 2000, 2003). In other words, the fittest mate for one individual is not necessarily the fittest mate for another. While the data suggest that these variable fitness findings are related to underlying variation in immunity genes, which are probably chosen based on such information as chemical signs, the findings highlight the potential relevance of subtle variations in the "dress" of individuals and the dangers of uniformity, both genetic and apparent. Other research has demonstrated assortative mating patterns whereby lower-quality females preferred lower-quality males (Holveck & Riebel, 2010). Gowaty and Hubbell (2009) have recently proposed a new theory of sex differences in mating behavior and preferences, which takes into account the ecological constraints within which individuals make reproductive decisions. This "switch point" theory provides a theoretical framework showing that selection favors mate assessment by both sexes in all species, and that the behavior of "choosy" versus "indiscriminate" is expressed adaptively and flexibly by all individuals, regardless of their sex, depending on various ecological factors. Others have also argued that "[e]nvironmental factors—for example, ambient color, temperature and lighting, predation, food availability, seasonal timing, or climatic events—can…influence mate selection and reproductive behavior" (White, 2004). Collectively, much of this recent research suggests that "artificial" manipulation of, or constraints on, male and female dress, resources, mobility, and status can have a significant effect on what is communicated, and the environments that affect an individual's well-being, survival, and reproductive success.

Finally, several intriguing studies have begun to flesh out an empirical case for the somewhat obvious proposition that social learning and experience, like other environmental factors, can affect mate choice. As White (2004) notes, "[b]ecause mating is a social activity in sexually reproducing species, social information surrounding mating is ubiquitous" (p. 111). Perhaps less obvious, social learning has been shown to influence mating preferences in nonvertebrates such as field crickets (Bailey & Zuk, 2009) and wolf spiders (Hebets, 2003). Some of this social learning takes the form of female copycat mating, whereby females show increased preference to mate specifically with males whom they have observed mating with other females, as well as generally with males who share a trait of the observed male (Swaddle, Cathey, Correll, & Hodkinson, 2005). In other species, familiarity gained through experience increases female preference for males of the known phenotype (Hebets, 2003). Bailey and Zuk (2009) emphasize that "flexibility in mate choice can fundamentally alter sexual selection pressure, and the consequences for selection on male ornaments can be profound if social experience causes predictable changes in mating preferences" (p. 449). Gowaty and Hubbell (2005, 2009) tie these findings back to some of the prior research on relative fitness and ecological variability by suggesting that what is learned during social experience is who an individual is relative to others in the population.

## The Moral of the Story: Dress, Power, and Status

Two strong themes emerge quite vividly from a review of the sexual selection literature, and are echoed by the sociological scholarship on human dress. First, it is likely that many sex differences in animal dress are, in the broadest sense, a result of sexual selection. This means that they are ultimately driven by sexual attraction and mating behaviors. Second, status and power are intimately entwined with many expressions of ornamentation and other forms of dress. The most highly ornamented *males* are typically found in species in which *females* have the greatest degree of unconstrained choice and power in the mating dance; that is, the degree of sexual dimorphism—including dimorphisms in behaviors relating to communication and the morphology of display—is likely to be intimately related to relative degrees of status and power. Similarly, interdisciplinary scholarship demonstrates that among the primary functions of human dress are gender expression, modesty, and seduction on the one hand, and creating, reflecting and enforcing power and status hierarchies on the other (Entwistle & Wilson, 2001).

Likewise, the two most prominent strands of concern in the appearance code cases revolve around sexuality and status. Courts have invalidated appearance codes when they appeared either to be based on stereotypes about female sexual attractiveness or to signal power and status differences not justified by the relative positions of the employees in question. An examination of, and analogy to, the evolutionary literature reveals that these judicial intuitions are valid. Indeed, they are likely two sides of the same coin because mate preference, status, and power are intimately intertwined. Insights about the relationship of dress dimorphisms and female autonomy, choice, and status from the evolutionary and sociological literature have important implications when considering employer policies that mandate female ornamentation. While sexual attractiveness and status signals are not the only relevant considerations, at the very least those employer grooming codes that reflect such stereotypes should be considered sex discrimination under Title VII. What the analogy adds to the existing judicial intuitions is that it suggests that the categories of dress codes that implicate these two concerns of sexuality and status are far broader than courts have usually found. Thus, for example, it seems clear that the makeup requirement in *Jespersen* should be invalidated because it requires women to be more colorful and elaborately ornamented than the males.

Dickemann (1982) proposed three decades ago that certain social practices, including some that involve female dress, might fruitfully be understood by reference to sexual selection theory. In particular, Dickemann hypothesized that intense claustration and veiling of females in highly socially and economically stratified polygynous societies could be attributed to female competition for resources controlled by high-status males. Claustration, of which veiling was a physical and symbolic element, served to guard against paternity uncertainty by these males who, in return, offered the potential of a high return in terms of resources to the woman's (male) offspring. In return for such reproductive bounty, lower-status females' kin paid with dowry and with transfer of control over her autonomy in movement, dress, and physical integrity.

I certainly do not mean to suggest that workplace dress codes that exist in the United States today are akin to the practices of foot-binding, head-to-toe veiling, female genital mutilation, or claustration. They may, however, be distant relations of these practices in the sense that they reflect an impulse to control women's sexuality and access to resources by prescribing permissible dress. Dress rules may appear benign because they simply reflect cultural gender conventions. However, as is apparent from the sexual selection literature, features of dress serve as a mode of social communication and carry hidden dangers of unconscious discrimination and retrenchment of invidious gender stereotypes. In nonhuman animals, a primary cause of sexual dimorphisms in coloration, decoration, and ornamentation is often said to be sexual selection and, notably, intersexual selection. That is, the primary way that male animals acquire their fancy dress is through some advantage they gain in mating. The very best dressed, fanciest males are those that are members of lekking species. In these species, the female exercises a rare degree of reproductive choice. The correlation between fancy dress and female choice is that the males must entice the females to choose them or else risk losing out in the contest for reproductive success. The females, therefore, are possessed of a good deal of reproductive choice and a certain degree of power and autonomy. The males, conversely, are looking to be chosen.

In humans, in contrast, the contemporary Western norm positions females as the showier sex. Women are expected to wear more colorful clothing, to decorate their faces with makeup, and to display certain body parts. Just as this is a reversal of the more typical dress dimorphism pattern among nonhuman animal species, so might we hypothesize that it is a reversal of the power/autonomy dimorphism as well: the most constrained sex is the most decorated. In other words, the prevalent gender norm that requires women to be the fancier sex is likely to reveal a power differential that is both reflected in, and perpetuated by, this gender dress norm. Indeed, it may be that more recent trends toward male body enhancement reflect a changing gender dynamic whereby women are gaining both economic and reproductive power. Thus, any dress policy that requires female employees to be more colorful, more decorated, or to reveal more of their bodies than their male counterparts should raise a strong inference that the policy is discriminatory. Like uniform policies that imply status differences between men and women, these policies reinforce unconscious gender norms regarding power, autonomy, and status. Viewed through the prism of sexual selection, power and decoration are closely related and forcing women to wear makeup or reveal their legs, as much as forcing them to wear uniforms, implies that they are primarily viewed as objects of selection rather than competent agents of choice and authority.

In 1898 feminist Charlotte Perkins Gilman published *Women and Economics*. In it, "she argued that women's economic independence from men would allow women the freedom to exercise their intuitive choice in partners, thereby unfettering the natural processes of social evolution and restoring the normal balance of the sexes" (Milam, 2010, p. 25). This sentiment was in line with some other early reactions to Darwin's books: feminist contemporaries focused on Darwin's descriptions of female choice and sexual selection to argue that "the place of women in Victorian culture was 'unnatural'" and that "to exercise free choice in husbands, women needed to be freed from the social and economic chains that bound them" (Milam, 2010, p. 24).

Some one hundred years later, animal experiments have demonstrated that constraints on female choice—the "social and economic chains" of behavioral ecology—do indeed have detrimental consequences in terms of fitness and reproduction. When such constraints take place in an arena of resource acquisition—for example, in the form of workplace rules that enforce social gender norms—these consequences may be especially pernicious. Moreover, female within-sex competition often takes the form of competition over resources rather than competition for males (Clutton-Brock, 2009), which suggests that women in the workplace are particularly susceptible to negative gender stereotypes surrounding dress and other features that mimic or emphasize sexually dimorphic traits. And competition in the workplace may also take the form of between-sex competition, whereby constraints on female dress are likely to put women at a disadvantage relative to men where the dress code exacts financial, time, or energy costs.

In the animal world, as revealed in the sexual selection literature, sexual behavior and power dynamics are two sides of the same coin and cannot logically be disentangled: males may be fancier precisely *because* females have more power to exercise unconstrained mating choice. Courts in the workplace dress cases have already exhibited some sensitivity to the factors of sexuality and power status where women have challenged sex-differentiated dress requirements, though they have not explicitly related these two concerns nor applied them systematically. But all dress dimorphisms are essentially intertwined with the elements of sexuality and power. The fancier the dress, the more power and autonomy typically exercised by the unadorned sex. Viewed through this lens, it seems quite clear that enforcing cultural dress norms, particularly those that involve color, decoration, status, and skin, on men and women in the workplace reifies gender stereotypes, decreases female agency and autonomy, and amounts to unlawful sex discrimination.

# Note

1. I use here the broad definition of dress suggested by interdisciplinary scholars of dress Joanne Eicher and Mary Roach-Higgins. Combining the related categories of "body modifications" and "body supplements," Eicher and Roach-Higgins recognize that "the dressed person is a *gestalt* that includes body, all direct modifications of the body itself, and all three-dimensional supplements added to it." Dress, as thus defined, includes clothing as well as all manner of body modifications and supplements such as deliberately made scars, tattoos, perfumes, hairstyles, foot coverings, jewelry, and hand-held accessories (Eicher & Roach-Higgins, 1993, p. 13).

# References

Anderson, W. W., Kim, Y.-K., & Gowaty, P. A. (2007). Experimental constraints on female and male mate preferences in *Drosophila pseudoobscura* decrease offspring viability and reproductive success of breeding pairs. *Proceedings of the National Academy of Sciences of the United States of America, 104*, 4484–4488.

Bailey, N. W., & Zuk, M. (2009). Field crickets change mating preferences using remembered social information. *Biology Letters, 5*, 449–451.

Barnard, M. (1996). *Fashion as communication*. New York: Routledge.

Bartlett, K. (1994). Only girls wear barrettes: Dress and appearance standards, community norms, and workplace equality. *Michigan Law Review, 92*, 2541–2582.

Bluhm, C. K., & Gowaty, P. A. (2004). Social constraints on female mate preferences in mallards, *Anas platyrhynchos*, decrease offspring viability and mother productivity. *Animal Behavior, 68*, 977–983.

Browne, K. R. (2001). Women at war: An evolutionary perspective. *Buffalo Law Review, 49*, 51–248.

Browne, K. R. (2002). *Biology at work: Rethinking sexual equality*. New Brunswick, NJ: Rutgers University Press.

Buss, D. M. (2003). *The evolution of desire: Strategies of human mating*. New York: Basic Books.

Byers, J. A., & Waits, L. (2006). Good genes sexual selection in nature. *Proceedings of the National Academy of Sciences of the United States of America, 103*(44), 16343–16345.

Carroll v. Talman Federal Savings and Loan Association of Chicago, 604 F.2d 1028 (7th Cir. 1979).

Case, M. A. C. (1995). Disaggregating gender from sex and sexual orientation: The effeminate man in the law and feminist jurisprudence. *Yale Law Journal, 105*, 1–106.

Clutton-Brock, T. (2009). Sexual selection in females. *Animal Behavior, 77*, 3–11.

Crane, D. (2000). *Fashion and its social agendas: Class, gender, and identity in clothing*. Chicago: University of Chicago Press.

Darwin, C. (1859/2009). *The origin of species by means of natural selection*. New York: Penguin Classics.

Darwin, C. (1871). *The descent of man, and selection in relation to sex*. London: Murray.

Dickemann, M. (1982). Paternal confidence and dowry competition: A biocultural analysis of purdah. In R. A. Alexander & D. W. Tinkle (Eds.), *Natural selection and social behavior: Recent research and new theory* (pp. 417–438). New York: Chiron Press.

Drickamer, L. C., Gowaty, P. A., & Holmes, C. M. (2000). Free female mate choice in house mice affects reproductive success and offspring viability and performance. *Animal Behaviour, 59*, 371–378.

Drickamer, L. C., Gowaty, P. A., & Wagner, D. M. (2003). Free mutual mate preferences in house mice affect reproductive success and offspring performance. *Animal Behavior, 65*, 105–114.

EEOC v. Clayton Federal Savings and Loan Association, 1981 WL 152 (E.D. Mo. 1981).

EEOC v. Sage Realty Corporation, 507 F. Supp. 599 (S.D.N.Y. 1981).

Eicher, J. B., & Roach-Higgins, M. (1993). Definition and classification of dress: Implications for analysis of gender roles. In R. Barnes & J.B. Eicher (Eds.), *Dress and gender: Making and meaning* (pp. 8–28). Oxford, UK: Berg.

Entwistle, J. (2001). The dressed body. In J. Entwistle & E. Wilson (Eds.), *Body dressing (dress, body, culture)* (pp. 33–58). Oxford, UK: Berg.

Entwistle, J., & Wilson, E. (2001). Introduction: Body dressing. In J. Entwistle & E. Wilson (Eds.), *Body dressing (dress, body, culture)* (pp. 1–9). Oxford, UK: Berg.

Epstein, R. A. (1990). The varieties of self-interest. *Social Philosophy and Policy, 8*, 102–120.

Gerdom v. Continental Airlines, Inc., 692 F.2d 602 (9th Cir. 1982) (en banc).

Gilman, C. P. (1898). *Women and economics: A study of the economic relation between men and women as a factor in social evolution*. Boston: Small, Maynard.

Gowaty, P. A. (1992). Evolutionary biology and feminism. *Human Nature, 3*(3), 217–249.

Gowaty, P. A. (1996). Battles of the sexes and origins of monogamy. In J. L. Black (Ed.), *Partnerships in birds* (pp. 21–52). Oxford, UK: Oxford University Press.

Gowaty, P. A. (1997). Sexual dialectics, sexual selection, and variation in mating behavior. In P. A. Gowaty (Ed.), *Feminism and evolutionary biology: Boundaries, intersections, and frontiers* (pp. 351–384). New York: Chapman & Hall.

Gowaty, P. A. (2008). Reproductive compensation. *Journal of Evolutionary Biology, 21*, 1189–1200.

Gowaty, P. A., Drickamer, L. C., & Schmid-Holmes, S. (2003). Male house mice produce fewer offspring with lower viability and poorer performance when mated with females they do not prefer. *Animal Behavior, 65*, 95–103.

Gowaty, P. A., & Hubbell, S. P. (2005). Chance, time allocation, and the evolution of adaptively flexible sex role behavior. *Journal of Integrative and Comparative Biology, 45*, 931–944.

Gowaty, P. A., & Hubbell, S. P. (2009). Reproductive decisions under ecological constraints: It's about time. *Proceedings of the National Academy of Science, 106*(Suppl. 1), 10017–10024.

Gowaty, P. A., Steinichen, R., & Anderson, W. W. (2002). Mutual interest between the sexes and reproductive success in drosophila pseudoobscura. *Evolution, 56*, 2537–2540.

Hamilton, W. D., & Zuk, M. (1982). Heritable true fitness and bright birds: A role for parasites? *Science, 218*, 384–387.

Hebets, E. A. (2003). Subadult experience influences adult mate choice in an arthropod: Exposed female wolf spiders prefer males of a familiar phenotype. *Proceedings of the National Academy of Science, 100*(23), 13390–13395.

Holveck, M.-J., & Riebel, K. (2010). Low-quality females prefer low-quality males when choosing a mate. *Proceedings of the Royal Society B, 277*, 153–160.

Jespersen v. Harrah's Operating Co., 444 F.3d 1104 (9th Cir. 2006) (en banc).

Jones, A. G., & Ratterman, N. L. (2009). Mate choice and sexual selection: What have we learned since Darwin? *Proceedings of the National Academy of Science, 106*(Suppl. 1), 10001–10008.

Jones, O. (1999). Sex, culture, and the biology of rape: Toward explanation and prevention. *California Law Review, 87*, 827–942.

Manning, J. T., & Hartley, M. A. (1991). Symmetry and ornamentation are correlated in the peacock's train. *Animal Behavior, 42*, 1020–1021.

Mealey, L. (2000). *Sex differences: Developmental and evolutionary strategies*. San Diego, CA: Academic Press.

Milam, E. L. (2010). *Looking for a few good males: Female choice in evolutionary biology*. Baltimore: Johns Hopkins University Press.

O'Donnell v. Burlington Coat Factory Warehouse, Inc., 656 F. Supp. 263 (S.D. Ohio 1987).

Paul, A. (2002). Sexual selection and mate choice. *International journal of primatology, 23*, 877–904.

Petrie, M. (1994). Improved growth and survival of offspring of peacocks with more elaborate trains. *Nature, 317*, 598–599.

Price Waterhouse v. Hopkins, 490 U.S. 228 (1989).

Roughgarden, J., & Akcay, E. (2010). Do we need a sexual selection 2.0? *Animal Behavior, 79*, e1–e4.

Ridley, M. (1994). *The red queen*. New York, NY: HarperCollins.

Rouse, E. (1989). *Understanding fashion*. Oxford, UK: Blackwell Science.

Seaman, J. (2005). Form and (dys)function in sexual harassment law: Biology, culture, and the spandrels of Title VII. *Arizona State Law Journal, 37*, 322–433.

Seaman, J. (2007). The peahen's tale, or dressing our parts at work. *Duke Journal of Gender Law and Policy, 14*, 423–466.

Snyder, B. F., & Gowaty, P. A. (2007). A reappraisal of Bateman's classic study of intrasexual selection. *Evolution, 61*(11), 2457–2468.

Swaddle, J. P., Cathey, M. G., Correll, M., & Hodkinson, B. P. (2005). Socially transmitted mate preferences in a monogamous bird: A non-genetic mechanism of sexual selection. *Proceedings of the Royal Society B, 272*, 1053–1058.

Thornhill, R., & Palmer, C. T. (2000). *A natural history of rape: Biological bases of sexual coercion*. Cambridge, MA: MIT Press.

United States v. Virginia, 766 F. Supp. 1407 (1991).

White, D. J. (2004). Influences of social learning on mate-choice decisions. *Learning and Behavior, 32*(1), 105–113.

Wilson, E. O. (2000). *Sociobiology: The new synthesis*. Cambridge, MA: Belknap Press of Harvard University Press.

# 21

# Consuming Midlife Motherhood

## Cooperative Breeding and the "Disestablishment" of the Biological Clock

MICHELE PRIDMORE-BROWN

## Introduction

*Homo sapiens* are the only extant Great Ape species whose females have a sig-nificant postmenopausal lifespan. In the case of other species of Great Apes, all physiological systems more or less fail in tandem, including fertility (Hawkes et al., 1998). Unique to *Homo sapiens* then is the gendered reproductive clock. This clock applies only to females and regulates their fertility from menarche to menopause at 50 or so, when fertility categorically ends, often decades before other physiological systems wear out.[1] In addition to having an extended post-menopausal postfertile lifespan, *Homo sapiens* are, reproductively speaking and in contradistinction to other apes, characterized by three interrelated traits. They are cooperative breeders—not just mothers but a retinue of "others" provision the young. They are behaviorally flexible—the dynamics of cooperative breeding are immensely variable across individuals and cultures. And, in addition, moth-ers invest strategically rather than unconditionally in their offspring—how much they invest, if at all, depends on timing (where they are in their reproductive lifespan) and the availability of resources and of helpers. Mothers in other species of Great Apes invest in a more unconditional non-context-dependent fashion in their infants (Hrdy, 1999, 2009).

In this chapter I will splice together the recent work of the biological anthro-pologist Sarah Hrdy on cooperative breeding with the insights of gender theory to address the feedback loop between biology and culture—and more specifically the radically altered role of the reproductive clock in the postindustrial era. Hrdy argues that the intricate social dynamics implicit in cooperative breeding (flex-ibility, strategic investment, "helpers at the nest") were the evolutionary lever of "big brains" in *Homo sapiens* (Hrdy, 2009). I will focus on the relevant correlates of that evolutionary narrative—postmenopausal (PM) life spans and the hormonally mediated glue that draws myriad adults other than the mother (including surviving grandmothers) to the care of the young.

In the first part, I argue that the gendered reproductive clock—which most likely evolved in the Pleistocene along with an inordinately long childhood (Konner, 2010)—has tacitly served to stabilize patriarchal norms and institutions. In the last half-century, however, maternal delay—amplified by biomedicalization and postindustrialization—has been correlated with what I call the "disestablishment of the biological clock." In the second part, I will argue that the clock is being disestablished as a barometer of values, with implications for the stages of life, the relationship of female to male bodies, and the use-value of offspring. As a result of this disestablishment, professional Western women now strategically "consume" maternity decades past their prime fertile years, when their forebears might have had a last child, or been grandmothers several times over. This biological backstory—and the ongoing feedback loop between biology and culture—has been neglected in more ideologically motivated feminist narratives.

## The Biological Clock: Patriarchy, Early Births, and the Grandmother Lifespan

Until the later 20th century, the reproductive biological clock was never named as such—although plenty of pundits and medics have, naturally, assumed this gendered clock as the nature of nature; some have used it to naturalize social and political agendas as well. For instance, Plato, citing Aristotle, wrote in *The Republic* that young women should marry at 20–22 and men could wait until 37 in order to create the most robust future citizens and soldiers, and so that their reproductive declines could felicitously coincide (Plato, 2007). According to modern estimates of fertility, the clock does in fact dictate that women are most fertile on average at about 20–22, which is also when they are most likely to produce a healthy full-term infant. Fertility declines significantly at 27 and precipitously at 37, with the average female being mostly although not entirely infertile about 10 years before menopause. At older ages women are indeed marginally more likely to produce a child with chromosomal or other abnormalities—but, as we now know, so are men (Reichenberg, 2006; Yang et al., 2007). Aristotle, however, blithely asserted that children born to women of 40 should not see the light of day regardless of their health-status; they should be culled outright lest they dilute the quality of the race. At 40, men by contrast were still deemed to be in their reproductive prime—and if old men produced a disproportionate number of compromised children, this was most likely not attributed to them but to the mothers. The 2nd-century Greek physician practicing in Rome, Soranus of Ephesus, whose textbook on gynecology prevailed in the ensuing centuries, thought women 15 to 40 would do for the production of offspring so long as they were not mannish, too compact, or too flabby (Soranus of Ephesus,1956/1991). Second-century Roman patriarchal law states that the patriarch's responsibility is to fecundate only youthful healthy wombs. In short, in these pundits' texts, women's wombs were troped as resources—for nation, men, and later for God or species.

My point is that, while patriarchy may well be socially constructed, its condition of possibility is the gendered reproductive clock, which has been instrumental in stabilizing patriarchal institutions—precisely because it created an amplified valuation of youth in women and not men, and in turn early childbearing typically rendered women dependent on men and kin for resources. The gendered clock also implied accelerated social aging for women as compared to men insofar as social roles were tied to reproduction. Interestingly, in other apes, including our closest relatives, chimpanzees, who practice exclusive maternal-infant care, the situation is quite different. Aging female chimpanzees are prime reproductive players and do not undergo the same sort of age-related devaluation (Hrdy, 1996)—even though available data do in fact indicate marginally lower survival probabilities for late-borns (Hawkes et al., 1998). It may then be that the gendered clock in *Homo sapiens*, coupled with the cooperative breeding backdrop (which enables experienced "helpers at the nest" to make up for the inexperienced young mother), accounts for what anthropologists see as the "universal" gut-level valuation among humans of nubile young females—and the discounted valuation of slightly older ones. Youth is, as sociobiologists readily remind us, the most obvious marker of fertility in females (Buss, 1994).

This said, the clock has been reified by cultural dictates in ancient and more modern times. Aristotle's teleological ethics, or "natural law" as he, and many centuries later the medieval theologian Thomas Aquinas, called it, famously states that the natural purpose of sex is procreation—and hence inhibiting the operation of natural law is to inhibit "God's Law" (Murphy, 2008). Christian ethics thus advocated passive deference to nature—which in theory meant no culling or contraception; this led to early births as well as ongoing births until the end of female fertility. Such a view of nature, which consigned women to childbearing throughout their reproductive lifespan, aggressively tightened the feedback loop among "nature," biblical or Christian views of virtue, and women's subservience as encoded in patriarchy—and of course, at the same time, ensured the multiplication of the faithful. In other words, if women were tied down by repeated childbearing, they were necessarily dependent on others, especially men. Christian ethics made a virtue out of female subservience and promised recompense in the afterlife. The pertinent point here is that such interpretations of nature—or natural law—are inherently political, by which I mean that "natural" and so-called moral/civic/religious obligations were conflated in a kind of politicized biological determinism.

Delaying a first birth is correlated historically with destabilizing patriarchy. It is no accident that the first wave of mass maternal delay occurred exactly when women had access to alternatives and when women's "rights" were being articulated. In the years around 1900 in the United States, middle-class women took on jobs as typists and telegraph workers—which enabled them deliberately to delay reproduction by delaying marriage. As a result, President Teddy Roosevelt vituperatively attacked maternal delay in his 1903 presidential address to the nation. While his response seems inordinately shrill, it could also be said he was presciently aware of the threat posed by maternal delay and rising rates of childlessness to patriarchal norms and institutions. Bent on expansion, he famously argued that women delaying maternity were "criminals" against the race and acting *contra naturae*; they were, he expounded in this speech and others, implicated in "national degeneration"; "race suicide"; and the unmanning, devirilization, and denaturalization of men (Roosevelt, 1910). Such themes would reverberate throughout the 20th century. Significantly for my purposes, female age of first birth did not just steadily rise thereafter. On the contrary: age of first birth rose and fell in the ensuing decades of the 20th century in tandem with the status of women. In fact, a few decades later, in the 1950s, the average age of first marriage for women was about 20 and the mean age of first birth as low as 21.4, with little variance among classes (NCHS/CDC). This mean age of first birth was the lowest of the century. Not coincidentally, it was also the era of patriarchal retrenchment marked by a return to rigid gender roles. My point then is that early age of first birth facilitates patriarchal norms—and, as I will argue, and as Roosevelt divined with so much alarm, maternal delay is correlated with the destabilization of those norms.

If, historically, nature and culture have conspired, as it were, to privilege female youth and early births, then what about the other end of the clock? I have pointed out that the biological clock is implicated in gendered aging—or more rapid age devaluation for women than for men—as Jane Austen–like discourses of spinsterhood at 26 or 27 make evident. As for the actual end of fertility and postmenopause, Hrdy (2009) draws on fieldwork among hunter-gatherers to argue that post/menopausal women are the hardest workers (the first to leave camp to gather roots or tubers and the last to return) and the most reliable sharers or "helpers at the nest." They provision the young far more reliably on average than fathers; as she points out, this is not necessarily out of altruism but because of their precarious position in scarce contexts. If a grandmother becomes a burden—requiring resources rather than providing them—she may well be excised (Hrdy, 2009). In other words, the back-story of our longer life spans is not necessarily rosy or ennobling. Here's an illustrative anecdote cited by Hrdy: an old Ache man (from a hunter-gatherer tribe in South America) happily described to a fieldworker how he would sneak up with an axe on the old women who had become a burden to the group: "I would step on them, then they all died, there by the big river" (Hill & Hurtado, 1996).

The gendered biological clock must perforce be the result of a postmeno-pausal evolutionary advantage. According to Hawkes's grandmothering hypothesis, it is due to grandmothers' contribution to the survivability of the young and to their daughters' annual fecundity (Hawkes, 2004). This said, it is correlated with the marked devaluation of aging postfecund females in patriarchal contexts—especially since men also enjoy longer life spans but, by contrast, retain their fertility, at least in theory. This devaluation is especially marked in the industrial era when grandmothers, however able-bodied, are often nonessential to the survival of the young and to resource acquisition. The cultural anthropologist Margaret Lock, writing in the 1990s, notably pointed out the ways in which postmenopausal women have been pathologized in the United States in particular: she argued that PM women have been relegated to social obscurity, biological superfluity, and even medical qua hormonal pathol-ogy insofar as menopause became an "estrogen deficiency disease," even while the culture at large admires old but still fecund Lotharios à la Picasso or Saul Bellow (Lock, 1995).

We can thus understand tweaking the gendered clock, and its correlated social and cultural norms, as inherently about politics or, to use Michel Foucault's term: about the biopolitics of bodies (Foucault, 1984). In a nutshell, it is about increas-ingly entitled aging women (whose raison d'être is no longer gathering tubers to provision their young kin) tweaking the patriarchal variant of the Darwinian script, as it were. It could be argued that notions of "equal rights" were articulated in the Constitution, applied to women during the feminist revolutions, and then refined during the postindustrial era. Ultimately, as I will show in the next pages, they are now being applied to reproduction and the reproductive lifespan itself. Disestablishing the clock is then not just about destabilizing patriarchal norms by delaying reproduction, but just as much about the co-optation of the PM lifespan for feminist and postfeminist ends.

## Biopolitics: Disestablishing the Clock via Maternal Delay

During Roosevelt's era, women delayed maternity by delaying marriage. Now, of course, for the most part, maternal delay is predicated on the separation of sex and reproduction; the mantra of second-wave feminism and of the allied sexual revolution of the '60s and '70s was that young women ought to realize a self before realizing another—which assumes that separation (Rich, 1976/1995). In this section I want to argue that the disestablishment of patriarchy in the 20th century went hand in hand with the cultural as well as biological dises-tablishment of the clock as a barometer of values tied to "natural law." I use the word "disestablishment" precisely because the clock was in some sense the tacit invisible omnipresent axis of practice, normative behavior, morals, and beliefs about nature, sex, and gender. An apt analogy is provided by the Church's disestablishment in Western Europe, or by the possible disestablishment of marriage in the future. To disestablish the biological clock is then to replace one dominant indeed rigid script for the female stages of life (i.e., adolescence, fleeting youth, motherhood, aging, grandmothering) with multiple permutations based in the variability of lives, of life spans and lifestyles, of ambition and beliefs, of bodies and contexts.

As women gained rights—especially after the 1970s and '80s, college-educated women in the United States and much of the West delayed maternity well past their prime fertile years. Delaying motherhood then enabled them to level the playing field with men—in other words, to accrue resources of their own, to gain social capital not linked to fertility, and eventually from the vantage of well-established resourced selves, to have a first child in their 30s or even later (Livingston & Cohn, 2010). First births for female college grads averaged about 30 in 2009, and was higher for those with postgraduate degrees. A first birth after 30 is thus fairly normative for college-educated women (Hamilton et al., 2010). First births after 40 are increasingly common as well, if still not routine. For example, there were 1 in 100 first births to women over 40 in 1970 and 1 in 12 in 2006, when data are available; the proportion is likely to rise further. Indeed, between 2007 and 2009, the birth rate decreased in all age groups except the over 40s, where it rose 6% (Sutton et al., 2011). This represents a massive unprecedented demographic shift, which has taken place in a remarkably short amount of time. In short, many women are having a first child when their forebears would have had a last or become grandmothers helping a daughter or niece. In an ongoing autocatalytic process: maternal delay has led to penetration of the professions, which in turn led to more delay by ever greater numbers of women and the articulation of further rights or rather new notions of what "equal rights" entails, and so on to the further colonization of the professions and of positions of power, and then ever greater numbers of women delaying reproduction, and so forth.

Maternal delay destabilizes patriarchy in many ways that are all variations on a theme. As already mentioned, it severs the link between sex and reproduction and so undermines the tenets of "natural law" and of the social order stabilized by the clock. It undermines the centrality of males and of the bread-winner resource-securing father. If motherhood is the anvil of sexual inequality, then it loosens that anvil by enabling women to have the same career objectives as men and the same economic and social capital objectives. In addition, it reveals the self-sacrificing early mother (a resource for others) to be a cultural construct rather than women's a priori or essential nature. It rewrites women as *strategic owners of their wombs* who delay for their own ends. In other words, the old feminist mantra "a baby if I want when I want" implies not just choice and control but the ability consciously to choreograph life (in theory if not always in practice) rather than to inhabit a patriarchal narrative revolving around procreation. Delay then derigidifies the female life-course, fracturing the reified clock into individual clocks or chronotopes that involve the (strategic) timing of maternity, or what may well become default timing, or indeed permanent postponement.

Of course, this said, no amount of rights or politics can entirely override the limits of the biological clock—or indeed of aging in general, or the fact that "choice" (i.e., having options) can be fraught. The fact is that women in the West may reliably postpone reproduction thanks to the routinization of contraception, but all women cannot as reliably extend fertility into the second half of adulthood. In other words, while the cost of motherhood to careers and resource acquisition declines with age in the postindustrial context, thus rendering it more desirable as women age, fertility declines as well—it seems, only about half or so of women can get pregnant unaided at age 40 or 41. If gender convergence operates in the professional world (at least up to a point, and certainly in relation to the past), then this serves to highlight the fact that, for women, the career clock does indeed collide head-on with the age-old biological clock—which means some women who want progeny will not be able to have them unaided, or at least will not be able to have progeny who share their genes. This situation, if it endures, will most likely introduce new selective pressures. But, in an immediate sense, this is precisely where technology—and what I referred to earlier as the biomedical paradigm—enters the equation, extending choice and possibilities for procreation in ways adaptive to postindustrialism, without of course entirely overriding the limits imposed by aging, nor entirely overriding the unequal costs of procreation (by way of pregnancy and lactation) to women.

First the pill and then in vitro fertilization, IVF, can be understood as instantiating a biotech self. It is these technologies that have biomedicalized infertility precisely in order to override the clock (Friese, 2006). The biomedical era, which according to medical sociologist Adele Clarke can be deemed to start roughly around 1990, marked the rise of a biomedical self—that is, a self coconstituted by technology (Clarke, Mamo, Fosket, Fishman, & Shim, 2010). To be sure, the female self altered by the pill prefigured that biotech self—and then medical screening and in vitro fertilization enhanced it. As Clarke et al. argue, this coconstituted or technologically mediated self is, almost by definition, "scientized" (in contradistinction to being, for instance, an unconscious channel for Darwinian imperatives). Theoretically, if not always in practice, this self is aware of risks, of age-related infertility, of changing scientific and technological possibilities. In theory, it is educable—hence the copious literature and ad campaigns run by the medical establishment and alternative bodies to educate the public—and young women in particular—about the clock and age-related infertility. If we think in terms of Clarke et al.'s historical paradigm, then in 1990 the scientized self applies to a prominent and growing subset of the female population in the United States: basically those with college degrees who are expected to delay as a matter of course for cultural and socioeconomic reasons (to accrue educational capital in order to become productive workers in a knowledge economy).

# Gender Convergence and Queering Mother Nature via Biomedicalization

In vitro fertilization (IVF)—whereby an egg and a sperm are combined in a petri dish before being transferred to a womb—has destabilized the clock's regime, as it were, in all sorts of other ways, most obviously because it allows a young egg to be transferred to an old womb. While the aging egg is an impediment to fertility, the aging womb is generally not (Paulson, 2002; Sauer, Paulson, & Lobo, 1993). In the last section, I listed some of the ways in which maternal delay destabilizes patriarchy. It could be said that biomedicalization and especially IVF post-1990 has sounded its death knell, as I will describe in this section.

Before 1990 or so, IVF was used to mimic nature rather than overturn it. In other words, as was the case for the first so-called test-tube-baby, Louise Brown in 1978, IVF was typically deployed, for instance, to circumvent blocked fallopian tubes in a standard-aged prospective mother using her own egg and her husband's sperm. It thus did not significantly alter cultural or social realities. Since 1990, when the first donor eggs were transferred to postmenopausal wombs, this has irrevocably changed (Angell, 1990; Sauer, Paulson, & Lobo, 1990). The circulation of gametes irrevocably alters the heterosexual monopoly on reproduction and the making of families (Franklin 1995, 2006; Franklin & Ragone, 1998). Single women and lesbian women can purchase sperm. And, in theory, well-resourced older women can use surrogates and donor eggs, strategically tweaking the definition of "infertility" to include postfecund and even postmenopausal women who "want" a child (Mamo, 2007). The word queering, which I borrow from gender studies, is rather apt—in that reproductive delay coupled with biotechnologies has, it could be said, queered nature and gender roles: denaturalized the most fundamental of biological processes, first by separating sex from reproduction and then, via biotechnologies, by extending fertility to normally nonreproductive bodies, enabling them to make babies in artefactual (technologically mediated) ways. If "queer" describes "a horizon of possibility" enabled by tweaking a dominant paradigm "whose precise extent and heterogeneous scope" cannot, as one theorist puts it, "be delimited in advance" (Halperin, 1995), then IVF fits that definition. We do not know what procreative realities the technologies will enable in the future. At present, men themselves can now consume "mother nature" by commissioning a surrogate to carry their child, and Hung-Ching Liu at Cornell is working on a tissue-culture womb that could be transplanted into men, as well as women who lack a functional uterus (Ball, 2011), thus further expanding options in unexpected directions.

Because babies nonetheless remain the most "natural" of products, regardless of how they are made, their existence goes on in fact to socially "naturalize" their unnatural or "queer" coming into being, in effect normalizing new kinds of cooperative breeding bonds—including so-called queer ones. PM motherhood—when an egg is transformed from a young donor to an older womb; or when an embryo is created, then frozen for later implantation; or indeed, as is now becoming increasingly possible, when eggs themselves are frozen for future use—necessarily positions the older woman as consumer (Fletcher, 2006), and implies a scientized consumer. If she has economic resources in the manner of the patriarchs of old, she can even purchase gametes or a womb from another continent, and, then, through her midlife motherhood, remake the social world: revamp the life-course rather than fading into the twilight as her forebears were expected to do, or playing the supportive "tuber-gathering" role to younger fertile kin. While most aging women have no intention of becoming PM mothers—quite the contrary—still, my point then is that, symbolically, they are a visible and potent cultural force. In the past decades, they have risen to positions of prominence, and they grace our magazine covers. It is no accident that the single, lesbian, postmenopausal, new mother Annie Leibovitz—a famous photographer whose family graced the cover of *Newsweek* in 2006, was positioned in that portrait as having her hand on the control button of the camera (October 2, 2006). Several aging, 39+-year-old women (Sandra Tsing Loh, Lori Gotlieb, Kate Bollick) have been featured in the *Atlantic Monthly* in the years 2009 to 2011 writing about men and babies in terms of trade-offs that they may or may not opt for. Hanna Rosin has, in those pages, famously theorized the "end of men" as prime players in the new socioeconomic and reproductive/family mix (Rosin, 2010).

Indeed, perimenopausal, menopausal, and postmenopausal mothers and their childless counterparts are tweaking the cooperative context of premodern *Homo sapiens* in postmodern directions. Multiple players do not just raise the young but, via the circulation of gametes and wombs, take part in bringing them into being. In the future, it may well be that freezing eggs in youth will become routine, and amount routinely to freezing the reproductive clock. Queering then happens on an individual material level, but also in the culture at large. It comes with a new set of values—tied no longer to natural law (and its patriarchal instantiation). Rather, I am suggesting here, this new set of values is increasingly tied to a vision of politics embedded in disembodied notions of equal rights. In short, culture—an articulation of culture—is actively remaking nature.

## "Equal Rights," the ASRM, and the Transformation of (Reproductive) Bodies

In this section and the remainder of this chapter, I will more specifically explore how culture by way of politics transforms so-called natural bodies. As a specific case in point, consider the example of the American Society of Reproductive Medicine, or ASRM, which is the umbrella organization of the fertility profession in the United States. Because reproductive technologies are largely unregulated in the United States, it is this body that issues bioethics statements regarding their "ethical" uses and set protocols. Arguably, it explicitly expresses the power of medicine to adjudicate morals. Indeed, it could be thought of as having the power of the Church in previous eras, although in a more underground, less explicit fashion. It expresses the prevailing generally forward-looking views of the fertility profession while at the same time, in a sense, institutionalizing those views. In 1997 it issued a three-page bioethical document, which it reviewed in 2004, on postmenopausal motherhood (ASRM, 1997, 2004); I would argue this document presciently articulated a new postmodern, postpatriarchal, post-reified-clock ethics. The document is then symbolically important for cultural reasons, for material practice, and for the creation of bodies. Three features of that statement are relevant. One, it assumes that evidence-based medicine is the adjudicator of morals: in other words, what Niklas Rose and others have subsequently called "health" and "life" are the new moral imperatives (Rose, 2006), which are supposed to drive decision-making. What-can-be-via-technology then replaces Nature as a barometer of values. If age-related risks and screening options are taken into account, then the verdict is that, while PM motherhood may not be advisable in most cases, it is not unethical. The fact is that there is no age at which risk skyrockets; rather, it steadily but slowly increases over the course of the lifespan, and markedly more slowly for some than for others.

The second point articulated by the ASRM document is an explicit extrapolation of *equal rights* to the reproductive lifespan. Given that men are allowed *by fiat of nature* to have babies later in life, healthy women ought to be enabled to have them later as well—again, conditional on appropriate risk assessments and screening. Here is the exact wording: "because old men may father children, denying women a successful alternative for reproduction at ages equivalent to men is sexist and prejudicial, especially as women generally live longer than men." This statement explicitly casts biology in terms of politics (i.e., women should not be penalized for the inequities of the gendered clock).

And, finally, the article highlights that the body always occurs in context—of others, of resources, and of age understood as time from birth or as the more nebulous time until expected death—and, indeed, what it implicitly but does not explicitly say is that the body occurs in the context of cooperative breeding. *Homo sapiens*, unlike other Great Apes, do not practice exclusive maternal-infant care except under duress (Hrdy, 2009). As a matter of course, IVF obviously ought not to be used to create orphans, but, given that young women with cancer are allowed to use IVF, the tenets of equal rights suggest there is no legitimate reason for denying older women the right to have a child if they are healthy—especially since, as the statement notes, in human societies, "it is not unusual for children to be raised by grandparents." In short, this document makes a case for what we might term "equal opportunity motherhood across the able-bodied lifespan" and, if we extrapolate further, across sexualities. It assumes a biotech self, and, not only that, it assumes the presence of others. It thus completely abandons the old tenets of "natural law." Interestingly enough, if we look at age cutoffs for acceptance into donor egg programs at fertility clinics: while some do still use a hard cutoff (such as 45, 50, or 55), others use a combined parental age cut off of 100 or 110, thus emphasizing social realities—that is, the social or cooperative context—over the singular "natural" or average body.

## Consuming Mother Nature: PM Motherhood and the Temporal Dynamics of Bonding

The most obvious fallout of severing the link between sex and reproduction is of course the fact that it overturns the unconscious Darwinian script, which depends on that link. It turns women into quasi-scientized consumers who in theory are expected to strategically time motherhood for their own ends: weighing ambition against the vagaries of their (aging) bodies and their desire for (biogenetic) children. As aforementioned, freezing eggs literally freezes the clock. Buying services and gametes literally transfers reproduction to the realm of consumption and conscious calculation. A scientized biotech female self obviously affects men as well, who, in the cooperative breeding context, are expected to adapt to a new reproductive economy. Not only are they expected proactively to parent their young, but to evolve a new toolkit of soft or relational skills, and indeed to reproduce responsibly (Coontz, 2005). The fact that they are nonessential—in biological terms (since sperm can easily be purchased) and in social terms (because women no longer need men for resources or social status)—also alters the sexual, reproductive, and social dynamic.

But here I want to merely highlight two aspects of the cooperative breeding backdrop that are most relevant in the new reproductive economy. First, babies have evolved to draw not just mothers but myriad others to their care. As Hrdy puts it, those infants and children especially adept at reading faces and at being charismatic were, in the Pleistocene and after, more likely to enlist helpers and so to survive to reproductive age. Over generations this would have resulted in directional Darwinian selection favoring infants marginally better at "mind-reading" and charismatic enough to draw others to their aid (Hrdy, 2009). Adults in turn are rigged to be susceptible to the charms of the young—holding a baby raises a cocktail of nurturing and so-called "feel-good" hormones (like oxytocin and prolactin) in kin and non-kin (Hrdy, 2009). It could be said that babies are a bit like hormonal "fly-traps," which is why adoptive parents can bond with adoptees, and why older women can felicitously and knowingly consume the donor eggs of younger women—and experience similar levels of emotional investment as they might with a biogenetic child. In other words, the dynamics of the postmodern emotional economy is predicated on the inherent flexibility of the premodern cooperative breeding backdrop.

Second, Hrdy makes another relevant point: whereas historically, and in patriarchal narratives, females were often troped as passive resources, with the competitive game occurring among males, Hrdy emphasized in her early work on lemurs that females have always been strategic reproductive players—not just in terms of mating but also in terms of whether, and when, they invest in their off-spring (Hrdy, 1999). For instance, across the primate world, an old female invests more heavily in her late-born offspring than she would if she were young and could always have more. Young *Homo sapien* mothers are more likely to practice infanti-cide; old mothers never do, Hrdy writes, drawing on her own and others' fieldwork (Hrdy, 1999). If a young human mother has insufficient resources and helpers, or if her child is sickly or of the wrong sex, then she is more likely to abandon it, whereas when she is older she is more likely to invest unconditionally. My point is that the increased valuation of children with advancing maternal age is amplified in the postindustrial context—for the same reasons but also because a late-born, and especially a late-born who is also a firstborn, may amplify self-expression or social capital in midlife whereas it might diminish or truncate them in youth.

Indeed, we can infer that the "use value" of children has radically altered in an era of predictably longer lives, of sex separated from procreation, of the viabil-ity of alternative ways of arranging life that do not involve procreation, and of an ethics of individualism and self-realization, or of what economists call "utility functions." There is little evidence that having children brings happiness (Eibach & Mock, 2011), but it would seem that they have existential value in the con-text of lengthening life spans. Recent cross-national research suggests that only people over 40 are happier with kids than without; and only parents over 50 are happier with each additional child (Margolis & Myrskyla, 2011). This research is still admittedly sketchy, but one could posit that for some individuals, consciously or calculatedly having a child in midlife is about the creation of meaning when other sources are declining. In a sense, those parenting behaviors, and coopera-tive bonding mechanisms that have evolved for one use are being co-opted or *operationalized* for another existential, postindustrial use that does not necessar-ily depend on transmitting genes—in much the same way that the grandmother lifespan has been *operationalized* for the purposes of delayed reproduction.

The term "co-optation" is apposite precisely because aging women are active agents rather than unconscious channels for Darwinian imperatives. Take the case of the photographer and late-in-life mother Annie Leibovitz again. We know that, in general, for professional women, the "opportunity cost" of motherhood declines with age (i.e., women have to give up less in terms of lifetime earnings if they postpone maternity; Miller, 2009). Arguably, in midlife, women like Leibovitz or any number of prominent professionals and celebrities consume motherhood for strategic ends (Pridmore-Brown, 2009). Joan Lunden, a rapidly aging early baby boomer celebrity, graced the July 2005 cover of *Good Housekeeping* with two sets of twins, one newborn and the other set of toddler age. A young husband com-pletes the picture. She was in her mid-50s at the time. Midlife motherhood sig-nals youth—these women's slow-aging status. Leibovitz and Lunden, like a host of other baby boomer and Gen X celebrities, sell their motherhood to the public via photos and references to their young children to suggest that, even though they are 50 or 60+, they are still in the game, as it were—active players in social life and indeed in professional life (Leibovitz, 2006; Johnson, 2005). Scientific research in turn underlines the adaptive value of motherhood in midlife—again, in the postindustrial context. Neurological evidence suggests that, as is the case in rodents for instance (Kingsley, 2011), pregnancy and new motherhood in midlife can increase brain volume and behavioral plasticity, and of course this happens in human mothers right when these traits would otherwise be declining (during perimenopause or menopause; Kim et al., 2010); research on social cuing suggests that through feedback mechanisms new motherhood also cues the body to inhabit a younger self, as it were, in ways that have biological implications (Clarke et al., 2010). Again, in line with the consumption nexus: Leibovitz's photos of her children highlight their apparent health, thus ostensibly serving to morally ratify her single, lesbian, postmenopausal motherhood as an act of responsible reproductive consumption (Pridmore-Brown, 2009). In photos that are part of her public portfolio, she also foregrounds her extended kin, as if to say that, should she die, the cooperative nature of her parenting ensures her progeny's well-being.

## Conclusion: Reproductive Stratification as a Form of Speciation

I have shown that the flexibility inherent in the cooperative context, the strategic nature of maternal investment, and new reproductive technologies have together enabled the radical reconfiguration of the human lifespan and of reproduction for feminist or postindustrial ends. A new ethics of conscious consumption based in notions of equal rights has replaced Darwinian or patriarchal scripts. Tweaking or overriding the clock via technologically mediated reproductive postponement is inherently adaptive—it increases fitness in the postindustrial context; it serves postindustrial ends because delay enables women to succeed in a postindustrial economy, to contribute to that economy, to accrue status and then to invest their capital in their offspring, who in turn require intense outlays to prepare them for the workforce of tomorrow. In Rosin's rather dramatic words, it marks the "end of men" as the dominant sex (Rosin, 2010).

In a sense we could speak of a kind of Lamarckian adaptation or even speciation because postponement along with biomedicalization transforms humans at the most fundamental of levels: it transforms their reproductive behavior and the way they make new bodies. It transforms the balance of power between the sexes. It enables gender mobility. If technology coconstitutes new selves, then it changes not just culture but nature itself—and in reconstituting women reconstitutes men as well. It also creates new competitive playing fields among women: maternal delay helps level the terrain with men, but, this said, in somatic terms, it could be argued that slower-aging women have a new reproductive advantage over faster-aging ones—those on slow reproductive and lifespan clocks can more easily wrest a biogenetic child from the jaws of menopause or advancing age. In short, the variability of bodies comes into play in new ways.

Class, or education as a marker for class, has an even more obvious influence with respect to the changing politics of reproduction. If maternal delay and associated technologies help level the playing field with men, thus undermining patriarchy, then they also magnify and indeed polarize class inequality. Indeed, it could be argued that, loosely speaking, *speciation* is taking place at the class level as a form of reproductive stratification. Reproductive delay among the privileged accentuates class differences between them and the "have nots." We become two subspecies. The disadvantaged have nothing to lose from early childbearing and so still have them early—according to the dictates of the old unreconstituted clock. As behavioral scientist Daniel Nettle points out, this makes a kind of Darwinian sense: a fast life history is a response to an ecological context of poverty and the expectation of less healthy and so less long lives (Nettle, 2010). The privileged have them later and later, they bank on long lives as well as screening technologies, plus they have plenty of alternatives if the old way of making babies fails. In short, reproductive timing impacts nature and culture at once in a tight feedback loop—and poignantly reifies class and educational differences.

# Note

1. Hawkes notes that postmenopausal longevity, not early termination of fertility, appears to be the derived characteristic of our species. There are other theories besides Hawkes', which I do not discuss here, that supplement her grandmother hypothesis. Males seem to have been the beneficiaries of the PM advantage: their life-spans increased but they retained their fertility—hence the existence of a gendered reproductive clock that applies only to women. It is notable, as Johnstone and Cant (2010) point out, that, while humans are the only primates with a PM lifespan, two other species also have postmenopausal life-spans: killer whales and pilot whales. Notably all three are cooperative breeders and, it turns out, become increasingly genetically related to those they live with as they get older—setting the stage, evolutionarily-speaking, for a grandmother role.

# References

Angell, M. (1990). Editoiral: New ways to get pregnant. *New England Journal of Medicine, 323*(17), 1200–1202.

ASRM. The ethics committee of the American Society of Reproduction Medicine (1997, 2004). Oocyte donation to postmenopausal women. *Fertility and Sterility, 82,* Suppl. 1 (September), S253–255.

Buss, D. M. (1994). The strategies of human mating. *American Scientist, 82,* 238–249.

Ball, P. (2011). *Unnatural: The heretical idea of making people.* London: Bodley Head.

Clarke, A., Mamo, L., Fosket, J. R., Fishman, J., & Shim, J. (Eds.). (2010). *Biomedicalization: Technoscience, health, and illness in the U.S.* Durham, NC: Duke University Press.

Coontz, S. (2005). *Marriage: A history.* New York: Penguin.

Eibach, R., & Mock, S. (2011). Idealizing parenthood to rationalize parental investments. *Psychological Science, 22*(2), 203–208.

Franklin, S. (1995). Postmodern procreation. In F. Ginsburg & R. Rapp (Eds.), *Conceiving the new world order* (pp. 323–345). Berkeley: University of California Press.

Franklin, S. (2006). Origin stories revisited: IVF as an anthropological project. *Culture, Medicine, and Psychiatry, 30*(4), 547–555.

Franklin, S., & Ragone, H. (Eds.). (1998). *Reproducing reproduction: Kinship, power, and technological innovation*. Philadelphia: University of Pennsylvania Press.

Fletcher, R. (2006). Reproductive consumption. *Feminist Theory, 7*(1), 24–47.

Foucault, M. (1984). Biopower. In P. Rabinow (Ed.), *The Foucault reader* (pp. 258–289). New York: Pantheon.

Friese, C. (2006). Rethinking the biological clock: Eleventh hour moms, miracle moms, and meanings of age-related infertility. *Social Science and Medicine, 63*(6), 150–160.

Halperin, D. (1995). *Saint Foucault: Towards a gay hagiography*. New York: Oxford University Press.

Hamilton, B. E., Martin, J. A., & Ventura S. J. (2010). Births: Preliminary Data for 2009 [online]. National Vital Statistics Reports, 59(3). National Center for Health Statistics.

Hawkes, K. (2004). Human longevity: The grandmother effect. *Nature, 428,* 128–129.

Hawkes, K., Connell J. K., Blurton Jones, N. G., Alvarez, H., & Charnov, E. L. (1998). Grandmothering, menopause, and the evolution of human life histories. *Proceedings of the National Academy of Science, 95,* 1336–1339.

Hill, K, & Hurtado, A. M. (1996). *Ache Live History: The ecology and demography of a foraging people.* Hawthorne, New York: Aldine de Gruyter.

Hrdy, S. (1996). Raising Darwin's consciousness: Female sexuality and the prehominid origins of patriarchy. *Human Nature, 8*(1), 1–49.

Hrdy, S. (1999). *Mother nature: Maternal instincts and how they shape the human species.* New York: Ballantine Books.

Hrdy, S. (2009). *Mothers and others: The evolutionary origins of mutual understanding.* Cambridge, MA: Harvard University Press.

Johnson, B. (2005). Joan Lunden: Twins again at 54. *Good Housekeeping, 241*(1), 138.

Johnstone, R. A., & Cant, M. A. (2010). The evolution of menopause in cetaceans and humans: The role of demography. *Proceedings of the Royal Society B, Biological Sciences, 277*(1701), 3765–3771.

Kinsley, C. H., Bardi, M., Karelina, K., Rima, B., Christon, L., Friedenberg, J., & Griffin, G. (2011). Motherhood induces and maintains behavioral and neural plasticity across the lifespan in the rat. *Archives of Sexual Behavior, 37*(1), 43–56.

Kim, P., Leckman, J. F., Mayes, L. C., Feldman, R., Wang, X., & Swain, J. E. (2010). The plasticity of human maternal brain: Longitudinal changes in brain anatomy during the early postpartum period. *Behavioral Neuroscience, 124,* 695–700.

Konner, M. (2010). *The evolution of childhood: Relationships, emotion, mind.* Cambridge, MA: Harvard University Press.

Leibovitz, A. (2006). *Anne Leibovitz: A photographer's life, 1990–2005.* New York: Random House.

Livingston, G., & Cohn, D. (2010, May). *The new demography of American motherhood.* Washington, DC: Pew Research Center.

Lock, M. (1995). *Encounters with aging: Mythologies of menopause in Japan and North America.* Berkeley: University of California Press.

Mamo, L. (2007). *Queering reproduction: Achieving pregnancy in the age of technoscience.* Durham, NC: Duke University Press.

Margolis, R., & Myrskyla, M. (2011). A global perspective on happiness and fertility. *Population and Development Review, 37*(1), 29–56.

Miller, A. (2009). Motherhood delay and the human capital of the next generation. *American Economic Review Papers and Proceedings, 99*(2), 154–158.

Murphy, M. (2008). The natural law tradition in ethics. In E. N. Zulta (Ed.), *The Stanford encyclopedia of philosophy*. Retrieved from http://plato.stanford.edu/archives/fall2008/entries/natural-law-ethics/

Nettle, D. (2010). Dying young and living fast: Variations in life history across English neighbor-hoods. *Behavioral Ecology, 21*, 387–395.

Paulson, R. (2002). Pregnancy in the sixth decade of life. *Journal of the American Medical Association, 288*(18), 2320–2232.

Plato. (2007). *The republic* (D. Lee, Ed.; M. Lane, Trans.). New York: Penguin Classics.

Pridmore-Brown, M. (2009). Annie Leibovitz's queer consumption of motherhood. *Women's Studies Quarterly, 37*(3/4), 81–95.

Reichenberg, A., Gross, R., Weiser, M., Bresnahan, M., Silverman, J., Harlap, S., et al. (2006). Advancing Paternal Age and Autism. *Archives of General Psychiatry, 63*(9), 1026–1032.

Rich, A. (1976/1995). *Of woman born*. New York: Norton.

Roosevelt, T. (1910). *Presidential addresses and state papers and European addresses* (8 vols., Homeward Bound Edition). New York: Review of Reviews.

Rosin, H. (2010, July/August). The end of men. *Atlantic Monthly, 306*(1), 56–70.

Rose, N. (2006). *The politics of life itself, biomedicine, power, and subjectivity in the 21st century*. Princeton, NJ: Princeton University Press.

Sauer, M. V., Paulson, R. H., & Lobo, R. A. (1990). A preliminary report on oocyte donation extending reproductive potential to women over 40. *New England Journal of Medicine, 323*,1157–1160.

Sauer, M. V., Paulson, R. H., & Lobo, R. A. (1993). Pregnancy after 50: Application of oocycte donation to women after natural menopause. *Lancet, 341*, 321–345.

Soranus of Ephesus. (1956/1991). *Gynaecology* (O. Temkin, Trans.). Baltimore: Johns Hopkins University Press.

Sutton, P. D., Hamilton, B. E., & Mathews, T. J. (2011). Recent declines in births in the United States, 2007-2009. NCHS data brief. no. 60. National Center for Health Statistics.

Yang, Q., Wen, S. W., Leader, A., Chen, X. K., Lipson, J., & Walker, M. (2007). Paternal age and birth defects: how strong is the association? *Human Reproduction, 22*(3), 696-701.

# 22

# The Quick and the Dead

### Gendered Agency in the History of Western Science and Evolutionary Theory

LESLIE L. HEYWOOD

## Introduction

In the summer of 2009, in his EvoS blog report "The Launching of the Feminist Evolutionary Psychology Society," then North Eastern Evolutionary Psychology Society (NEEPS) president Glenn Geher brought together two seemingly irreconcilable ideas when he began his entry with Cheris Kramarae's and Paula Treichler's famous quotation, endemic on tee-shirts and bumper stickers, that "feminism is the radical notion that women are people." Kramarae and Treichler's statement came about in reaction to the wide range of, to anyone with any knowledge of the field, off-target ideas about feminism, such as this, from Pat Robertson: "Feminism is a socialist, anti-family, political movement that encourages women to leave their husbands, kill their children, practice witchcraft, destroy capitalism and become lesbians" (http://www.brainyquote.com/quotes/authors/p/pat_robertson.html). "Feminism is the radical notion that women are people" encapsulates what feminism in its various waves has always been about: "the advocacy of women's rights on the grounds of equality to men" (*New Oxford American Dictionary*). Geher had this slogan in mind, and the way it captures the disjunction between what feminism actually is and what various detractors accuse it of being, when he came up with the slogan: "Evolutionary Psychology is the radical notion that human behavior is part of the natural world." By providing this echo to the feminist slogan (incidentally, the word "slogan" is from Scottish Gaelic in the early sixteenth century, and referred to a Scottish Highland war cry), Geher invokes a host of associations that highlight similarities between the public reception of feminism and the reception, albeit in different contexts, of evolutionary psychology.

# Evolutionary Theory and Feminism: Compatible Types?

Both words, "feminism" and "evolutionary psychology," seem to be polarizing, emotionally freighted with a number of associations that often have little or nothing to do with the ideas those identified with them would endorse. The equivalent quotation to Robertson's quotation about feminism might run something like "Evolutionary psychology is a socially conservative, anti-woman, pseudo-science that encourages people to think that everything is genetically determined, that rape is natural, and that men should drag women off by their hair."

To anyone who has read recent work in evolutionary psychology, this idea of the discipline is ridiculous, an inaccurate caricature that willfully misrepresents the valuable work that has been done. Yet to some who identify with evolutionary psychology, the word "feminism" raises an equivalent specter: science-hating cultural relativist women grimly wielding signs at political rallies and demanding special privileges for themselves. For most feminists, however, academic and otherwise, this view of feminism is just as frustrating as is the aforementioned view of evolutionary psychology. In both cases, the distortions and misunderstandings are legion, and reflect a mutual lack of knowledge by each side about the research of the other. As one of the academic founders of the "third wave" of feminism—that is, feminist theory initially conceptualized in the 1990s that puts the contradiction between an interest in gender equality and beauty culture, for instance, or, to put it in evolutionary terms, interaction effects between nature and culture, human lives and the environment—on center stage, I wholeheartedly endorse Geher's contention that the content of the two ideas embodied in the slogans "feminism is the radical notion that women are people," and "evolutionary psychology is the radical notion that human behavior is part of the natural world" gives us "no reason on earth to believe that these two 'radical' notions are irreconcilable" (http://evostudies.org/blog/?p=215). As the subtitle to the book I edited with Jennifer Drake, *Third Wave Agenda: Being Feminist, Doing Feminism*, asserts, feminism can be as much a way of *being*, of trying to develop an understanding of what is, and strategizing accordingly, as it is of *doing*, acting to facilitate what is seen as desirable change and making prescriptions about what *should be* (Heywood & Drake, 1997). We were criticized in some quarters for making this distinction, and therefore not being political or having enough of an agenda, but were appreciated by others. Indeed, many forms of feminism follow this line of inquiry—describing what *is*—and this kind of description, of course, is also a stated aim of scientific inquiry. In fact, I would argue an unbiased understanding of what *is* should precede the development of prescriptions for what *ought to be*, and this is an idea, believe it or not, that many types of feminism and evolutionary psychology share.

However, perhaps based on the history of stereotypes and misunderstandings, not all in the evolutionary psychology community or in the feminist community would agree that feminism and evolutionary psychology *are* reconcilable. For instance, an exchange on an evolutionary psychology forum showed one contributor in a considerable state of distress about the founding of the Feminist Evolutionary Psychology Society (FEPS) and its announcement as part of the 2010 NEEPS conference. He saw evolutionary psychology and feminism as precisely an "irreconcilable" contradiction in terms, because, he wrote, "many members of my forums have argued passionately that evolutionary psychology is a-political," whereas (he quotes from Wikipedia), "the term feminism can be used to describe a political, cultural, or economic movement.'" This led him to believe that "somebody is trying to destroy the non-political status of EP and stuff it into the same biased trash bin we stuffed behaviorism, social science, eugenics, and other 'sciences' corrupted by political movements." Science is apolitical, feminism is political, and never the twain shall meet.

Psychologist Cordelia Fine comments on this characteristic maneuver in an entry on a PLoS (Public Library of Science) blog, "Let's Say Goodbye to the Straw Feminist," and in her book *Delusions of Gender* (2011). She argues that "straw feminist" and "value free scientist" are untenable stereotypes used to obscure the fact that some "science" about gender differences is bad science. Science is itself political, from its assumptions, questions, and hypotheses, to its presentation of results. The stereotypes of the "political feminist" and "value-free scientist" are actually impeding scientific progress:

> In the interminable sex differences debate it always seems to be those who are critical of scientific claims of essential differences who are accused of allowing political desires to blinker them to the facts of the case...The straw-feminist is getting in the way. When criticisms are dismissed as "political"—to be contrasted with one's own, value-free scientific judgment—we learn nothing about the quality of the scientific evidence, the hidden work of political values in the scientific debate, or where difference of opinion truly lies. Throwing out that prickly, imaginary lady will give us a clearer picture of the landscape of barriers to disagreement. Then we can make better moves to navigate them. (http://blogs.plos.org/blog/2011/02/11/let%E2%80%99s-say-good-bye-to-the-straw-feminist/)

In the spirit of exactly that "clearer picture," let's return to the "radical" notions that women are people and that human behavior is part of the natural world. I think it safe to assume that most evolutionary psychologists would agree that women are people, and furthermore that most feminists would agree that human behavior is part of the natural world—especially if we understand that "natural world" to be shaped by humans as well as shaping them—a key insight in the biological concept of niche construction, which I will return to later. In fact, this is an exciting time for both evolutionary and feminist theory, because new research and insights from all quarters are complicating old paradigms in ways that set the stage for real consilience.

## Sources of Discord: Sameness and Difference in Gender

That said, there are real reasons why feminism and evolutionary psychology (EP) continue to be perceived as antithetical or even hostile. In what follows, I give an account, summarized in Table 22.1, of some of the core tenets of feminism and evolutionary psychology and how they conflict, as well as how an evolutionary psychology conceived in terms of the extended synthesis (ES) of evolutionary biology would help resolve the conflicts and facilitate a conversation that would be mutually beneficial to research paradigms and projects in both disciplines.

As the table shows, some forms of and conceptualizations from evolutionary psychology do seem irreconcilable with feminism on multiple levels. Yet as the first box articulates, feminism has itself been characterized by what has sometimes seemed to be irreconcilable tensions between feminists who embrace gender difference, and those who think those differences are not constitutive of an overall identity for all women. In other words, different strains of feminism define and value biological difference differently. More than twenty years ago, Ann Snitow summed up the conflict in feminism between "equality" (or sameness) and "difference" feminism, a conflict that continues to this day:

> Difference theory tends to emphasize the body; equality theory tends to deemphasize the body and to place faith in each individual's capacity to develop a self not ultimately circumscribed by a collective law of gender. For difference theorists the body can be either the site of pain and oppression or the site of orgasmic ecstasy and maternal joy. For equality theorists neither extreme is compelling as the overriding idea that the difference between male and female bodies is a problem in need of solution. In this view, therefore, sexual hierarchy and sexual oppression are bound to continue unless the body is transcended or displaced as the center of female identity. (Snitow, 1990, p. 24–25)

This split has gone under a number of names in different historical periods: essentialist feminism versus constructivist feminism, radical feminism versus liberal feminism, radical feminism versus cultural feminism, cultural feminism versus poststructuralist feminism. While current feminist thinking is engaged in theorizing the relationship between these positions, and neither side would argue that there are no biological differences, there still exist thinkers who are more interested in revaluing what has traditionally been seen as "feminine" or "women's voice/morality," and those who are more interested in looking at sexual

*Table 22.1*  **Consilience?: Feminism, Evolutionary Psychology, and the Extended Synthesis of Evolutionary Biology**

| Central Feminist Tenets | Central EP Tenets | How ES Mediates Between Each |
|---|---|---|
| Because of their material bodies and reproductive function, women have been symbolically affiliated with nature, men with culture. Tension in feminism between therefore making other roles than motherhood important for women and disassociating women from an exclusive association with that role, revaluing the devalued cultural role of motherhood, and switching the focus from mothering to parenting so men are included. | "Fitness" = reproductive success; men and women confront different "adaptive problems" in mating—therefore fixation on reproductive behavior in EP research; EP's almost exclusive focus on reproductive function when it comes to gender questions reinscribes the exclusive association with that role that feminism has worked so hard to destabilize. | Multiple sites of selection, not just natural selection; questions other than reproductive behavior are also important to the evolutionary puzzle, and their interaction questions the EP model of reproductive behavior |
| Culture has been given higher valuation; nature seen as threatening, in need of transformation/ containment, with negative consequences for women and how they are perceived and treated | EP accurately describes ultimate mechanisms— adaptations that have ensured human species survival—these mechanisms determine how women act, and are perceived and treated | Proximate/ultimate distinction more interactive, relational than previously assumed |
| Sex/gender distinction: sex is the biological, gender the cultural, and the two are related but sex is not the "ultimate" explanation for the "proximate" manifestation of gender— each level affects the other | EEA/gradualism; adaptive "lag"— underlying psychological mechanisms developed in the Pleistocene interact with current inputs to produce manifest behavior | "Fast" evolution: even genetics can change in a few generations; cultural evolution interacts with biological evolution |

*(Continued)*

*Table 22.1* **(Continued)**

| Central Feminist Tenets | Central EP Tenets | How ES Mediates Between Each |
|---|---|---|
| Reproductive function could be interpreted/valued differently, and that valuation and interpretation is a cultural function | Parental investment theory/Sexual strategies theory: differences in reproductive roles based on anatomy determine social organization | Niche construction—humans have reshaped the natural world to the degree that this reshaping has profound evolutionary consequences that effect sex and reproduction and make these forms more variable |
| Woman/women: no one category can accommodate all the differences between women: differences between women as important as similarities | There are universal principles all women share because they have all had to face adaptive problems like pregnancy and breastfeeding | Evo-Devo: "recent trends in developmental biology and cognitive neuroscience recognize that the human brain and behavior are shaped to an important extent by individual and social learning" (Bolhuis, Brown, et al., 2011, p. 6 |
| Language is a constitutive category, creating as well as describing, even in science; it is part of the human "environment" that creates how we think and perceive | Language is neutral and describes rather than inscribes (this is an assumption—language and its role in producing what we think as well as describing what "is" is never an issue EP examines) | Epigenetics: genes express themselves in particular environmental conditions on both the cellular and macro levels, so "innovation, social learning and other aspects of development are capable of introducing novelty into phenotypic design space, thereby establishing new selective scenarios" (Bolhuis, Brown, et al., 2011, p.6). Language is a big part of social learning. |
| The assumed link between women and the primary caretaking of children is not biologically necessary—multiple caregivers are possible | Women solve "adaptive problems" of childcare by showing a "mate preference" for/selecting one man with resources to provide for them and their children | Evolutionary success of groups has been facilitated by "cooperative breeding" and alloparenting; plasticity is a feature of both human biology and culture and the two are indissociable. |

difference on a continuum, with some women falling on the "masculine" side of the continuum more than some men, and some falling more on the "feminine" side than some women. A continuum-based model is more concerned with variability than would be compatible with most classic EP propositions that make universal claims regarding "women" and "men," while a difference-based model is more compatible with classic EP.

David Buss, whose work has been authoritative in EP in terms of establishing a difference perspective, points out in an article coauthored with David Schmitt that the difference model in EP is only partial:

> Evolutionary psychology provides a meta-theory for predicting when and where to expect gender differences and when and where to expect gender similarities. Women and men are expected to *differ* in domains in which they have faced recurrently different adaptive problems over human evolutionary history. They are expected to be *similar* in all domains in which they have faced similar adaptive problems over human evolutionary history. (2011, p. 2)

While this sounds eminently reasonable, because evolutionary psychology discusses the differences *rather than* the similarities, and does so in provocative ways that reinforce crude gender stereotypes, it is often taken to naturalize and thus attempt to legitimize the very stereotypes it has been feminism's aim to change—a prescription for irreconcilability of positions if there ever was one. However, as I will argue later in the paper, the extended synthesis (ES) of evolutionary biology offers a way to incorporate and enhance both strains of feminism, and a "difference" and "similarities" perspective within evolutionary theory overall, especially as these manifest themselves in contemporary human behavior. As evolutionary psychology and feminism develop their research programs in conjunction with the new research that characterizes the extended synthesis, this historical incompatibility will be mitigated.

However, in previous evolutionary psychology work where there is an emphasis on universals that undervalues variation, the 1980s feminist distinction between "Woman"(seen by feminists post-1980 as bias-laden and fundamentally mythic), and "women," (observable individuals whose experiences, situations, and even biologies vary), becomes important to understanding the conflict. Even more importantly, if work proceeding from evolutionary psychology is written in such a way that it appears to reduce women to their reproductive function, that reduction violates a core tenet of women's rights struggles from the eighteenth century onward—the struggle for the vote, access to education and the professions, and access to the public sphere. While it seems clear that such work does *not* claim that women are reducible to reproduction, the nearly exclusive focus on that aspect of a woman's existence may *seem* to be making such a claim, especially to feminists who come from the "equality/sameness" rather than "difference" perspective. Research that makes women's bodies and their functions the central level of inquiry may be interpreted as then reducing women to those functions, creating a great deal of unease for those whose research program has centered around challenging the historical reduction of women to their bodies and their resulting exclusion from the public sphere.

## The Actual Feminist Position on Biology and Culture

In a classic article from second-wave feminism, anthropologist Michelle Zimbalist Rosaldo delineates a "structural model that relates recurrent aspects of psychology and social and cultural organizations to an opposition between the 'domestic' ["private"] orientation of women and the extra-domestic or 'public' ties that, in most societies, were primarily available to men" (1974, p. 18). What Rosaldo emphasizes—and this is one of the key tenets of feminist theory generally—is that women's symbolic and material conflation with the private, domestic sphere, is a function of women's association with childbearing, and therefore, symbolically, the body and nature. These activities or functions are valued in particular ways: "prestige values always attach to the activities of men" (Rosaldo, 1974, p. 19). However, although this is a *biological* difference (only women can bear children), the meanings assigned to that difference are cultural: "biological research may illuminate the range in human inclinations and possibilities, but it cannot account for the interpretation of these facts in a cultural order. It can tell us about the average endowments of groups or of particular individuals, but it cannot explain the fact that cultures everywhere have given Man, as a category opposed to Woman, social value and moral worth" (p. 22). Looking back at Rosaldo's historic formulation helps redress the misconception within EP which says that feminism claims there is no biological difference between the sexes and that everything is cultural. Instead, the point was that cultural systems of meaning and signification determine how that biology is conceptualized. This was the origin of the later feminist distinction between sex and gender, where "sex" is seen as referring to the biological body, and "gender" as referring to the meanings conferred upon or assigned to that body—"meanings" that often took a historical form which said that women are/have to be primary caretakers of infants and therefore are limited to activities associated with the private home instead of public life. It was this constellation of dominant cultural meanings feminism most worked to change, and it has done so quite successfully.

## Irreconcilable Claims

Another antagonism between feminism and evolutionary psychology arises from a specific constellation of claims: that the environment of evolutionary adaptedness (EEA), "Stone Age Brain," "slow evolution" (gradualism), and massive modularity all result in adaptations that influence human behavior today. These include evolutionary psychology formulations that contemporary behaviors are adaptations that evolved to solve the different reproductive problems of human males and females, and therefore led to behavior like forms of mate selection that just happen to reproduce particular economic arrangements such as those where men have greater resources. Claims like parental investment theory and sexual strategies theory (SST) deemphasize variability and flexibility in modern parenting arrangements, and seem to naturalize a woman's function as a caretaker/mother rather than many other possible roles. These claims tend to resemble old sex role stereotypes that feminism categorically devoted itself to denaturalizing and demystifying. While the general claim is that "evolutionary psychology contends that human behavior is enormously flexible—a flexibility afforded by a large number of context-dependent evolved psychological adaptations that can be activated, combined, and sequenced to produce variable adaptive human behavior" (Buss & Schmitt, 2011, p. 2), the actual *conclusions* of the model—that women will choose mates with more resources, and that women will always be the primary caretakers of children—dictate otherwise.

We can see the distinction between general claim and application when, in the above quotation, Buss and Schmitt seem to claim the same kind of plasticity for human behavior that is found in theories of epigenetics, where gene expression is environmentally triggered. But if one looks more closely at what their work actually *does*, it might be seen to utilize a rhetorical device called *occupatio*—where a speaker says they are not going to do/say something, in order to forestall objections to one's point before anyone can object, but then go ahead and do/say the very thing they said they were not going to do. Buss and Schmitt *say* that the evolutionary psychology paradigm predicts behavioral flexibility, but then their entire analysis postulates specific behaviors as inevitable, rather than context-dependent:

> Buss (1998) advanced a hypothesis about the origins of one component of patriarchy. Specifically, he [Buss refers to himself in the third person here] suggested that the *co-evolution* of women's evolved mate preferences for men with resources and men's co-evolved mate competition strategies [i.e., to get resources] to embody what women want created gender differences in the motivational priority attached to resource acquisition. (2011, p. 4)

In other words, women want men with resources to provide for them while they are "incapacitated" by the metabolic costs of pregnancy and lactation ("incapacitation" is itself a debatable construction of pregnancy), and the fact that women want men with resources therefore makes men want to compete with each other to obtain the resources women want. If these particular mate preferences are "evolved," there is the implicit claim that these preferences are therefore robust, not "flexible." This is a rhetorical use of the word "co-evolution," a usage that takes the word out of its usual signifying context associated with behavioral plasticity and puts it into a context that claims behavioral robustness.

Through the use of the term "co-evolution," which is usually used to designate how biological and cultural forces interact to influence evolution, Buss and Schmitt make it sound like SST is more flexible and attentive to cultural forces than it actually is. What "co-evolution" usually means and the way they are using it here are very different. Buss and Schmitt are using the implications of the larger meaning of the term—evolutionary theory that emphasizes culture as an important part of the evolutionary process—in the context of a concept that *deemphasizes* culture or does not examine it at all—in SST women have domain-specific modules in their brains that are adaptations in response to the "adaptive problems" of pregnancy and lactation—occurrences that are "problems" because they leave women vulnerable and in need of resources/support. In this theory, the modules are adaptations that dictate, for instance, that women will choose men with resources for mates. Buss and Schmitt conclude that "there is abundant evidence for this evolutionary psychological hypothesis about the origins of the resource-control component of patriarchy...women are not 'passive pawns in men's game'" (2011, p. 4). Here, Buss and Schmitt seem to attribute agency to women—men with resources are the men women choose—and women "choose" this because they have specialized brain modules that have evolved to solve the "adaptive problems" associated with reproduction. If, according to this theory, there is a mismatch between the contemporary context and these modules, that mismatch is an instance of "adaptive lag," and women will choose men with resources anyway because that is what their brains have evolved to do. This is a facetious notion of female agency and choice because it evokes agency on the one hand while it takes it away with the other. Despite rhetorical claims to the contrary, the bias here is that evolved adaptations are the "ultimate" cause of behavior.

More abstractly but in a related sense, the insistence in these formulations on natural selection as the only mechanism of heritability ignored much of the contextual information and importance of environmental influence and triggers that feminism has always emphasized as a key factor in how our biologies are culturally represented and valued. While insisting on context, Buss and Schmitt nonetheless claim that "evolution by selection is the only known causal process capable of creating such complex organic mechanisms (adaptations)" (2011, p. 2). Naming selection as the *only* causal inheritance mechanism was a key component of the modern synthesis, but the extended synthesis, through epigenetics and other principles such as "fast evolution," posits multiple inheritance mechanisms that actually do allow for behavioral flexibility and environmental inputs in a specific context—there is not necessarily an "adaptive lag" that determines contemporary behavior. The extended synthesis can better account for environmental and cultural inputs, and gives feminists who take it seriously a complicated and scientifically accurate way to describe cultural influence and its integration with biology.

## The Problem of Language

As I hope to have shown above, the role of language is important to scientific formulations and how they are communicated. While many scientists view language as a neutral medium that is used to describe reality, much of the humanities and social sciences view language as having a constitutive role in people's perceptions of reality. An important part of the feminist unease with evolutionary psychology has to do with the way evolutionary psychology (and most science) ignores role of language in constituting meaning. Given the multiplicity of the way words signify, a scientist willing to grant the importance of rhetoric to communication would be attentive to how vocabulary such as the "proximate/ultimate" distinction, for instance, far from being "neutral," carries the burden of its multiple meanings from the start: a reader will not always *understand* the concept in purely scientific terms even if they know the scientific definition, since the word itself carries with it the associations that belong to its other meanings. This is a problem taken up by cyberneticist sociologists Leydesdorff and Hellsten (year, 2006, p. 234), who investigate disciplinary translations in the process of text coding:

> Co-words have been considered as carriers of meaning across different domains in studies of science, technology, and society. Words and co-words, however, obtain meaning in sentences, and sentences obtain meaning in their contexts of use. At the science/society interface, words can be expected to have different meanings...Words and the relations among words ("co-words") mean different things in other contexts, and the meaning of words can be expected to change, particularly in science where novelty production is part of the mission of the enterprise.

Language, even scientific language, is never a purely neutral force for description, but varies contextually, often changes, and is furthermore associated with cultural valuations. We can see this operating in the "proximate/ultimate" distinction, for instance, a key concept in evolutionary theory. Outside of the scientific context, "ultimate" has multiple meanings: "being or happening at the end of a process"; "being the best or most extreme example of its kind"; "basic or fundamental" (*New American Heritage Dictionary*). In the context of evolutionary theory, however, "ultimate explanations are concerned with why a behavior exists, and proximate explanations are concerned with how it works" (Scott-Phillips et al, 2011, p. 38). A possible end effect of this constellation of different meanings for the reader would be that "ultimate" signifies as *the* truth, the "ultimate" level of meaning that determines all others. To the extent that evolutionary psychology claims that ultimate mechanisms explain human behavior, if we take the overall linguistic context into consideration, the implication might be that this behavior then cannot change. Similarly, feminist theory that discusses gender as a "performance" based in the performative nature of language is likewise open to misinterpretation.

## The Importance of Cultural Symbolism and Meaning

In addition to language, some attention to systems of cultural symbols and meaning are crucial to investigate along with other variables. These systems are part of the "context" science needs to consider. Much of feminism has been devoted to this project, because the meanings given to the biological body, rather than just describing biology, have historically contained evaluative judgments. For instance, the Western symbolic tradition Susan Bordo so clearly articulates in her landmark feminist work *Unbearable Weight*: the assumption of "the duality of male as active, striving, conscious subject and female as passive, vegetative, primitive matter," stands behind many cultural traditions, including scientific ones (1993, p. 12). Bordo documents the classic Western philosophical tradition of dualism in its gendered form, demonstrating how thinkers since Plato have conceptualized human existence in terms of a mind/body split, how that split is conceptually problematic, how that split is gendered, and how the residues of these ideas linger in contemporary media representations of medical discourses surrounding the female body. Anthropologist Sherry B. Ortner's classic essay "Is Female to Male as Nature Is to Culture?" (1974) similarly documented the way nature was threatening to human survival for most of human history, the historical association of the female body with nature, the nearly universal devaluation assigned to nature with respect to culture, and therefore the nearly universal devaluation of women. Giving contemporary credence to Ortner's argument is recent work in neuroscience, which has scientifically established the fact that humans and other mammals respond to what is threatening by trying to contain or neutralize it, and recent research into our sympathetic and parasympathetic response systems document this biophysiological/psychological process. Evolutionarily speaking, nature was threatening to human survival for most of the species' life span—humans were prey as well as predators for a good part of species history. When symbolic, cognitive processes evolved, symbolism became a mechanism by which to control that threat. Ortner's work developed an enormously influential interpretive frame that established how our ancestors may have responded symbolically to the survival threat nature posed especially in earlier forms of human development, and how that symbolism became gendered:

Every culture, or, generically, "culture," is engaged in the process of generating and sustaining systems of meaningful forms (symbols, artifacts, etc) by which humanity transcends the givens of natural existence, bends them to its purposes, controls them in its interest. We may thus broadly equate culture with the notion of human consciousness, or with the products of human consciousness (i.e., systems of thought and technology) by means of which humanity attempts to assert control over nature....women are seen as being *closer* to nature than men... It all begins with the body and the natural procreative functions specific to women alone... [there are cultural] levels at which this absolute physiological fact has significance: 1) woman's *body and its functions*, more involved more of the time with "species life," seem to place her closer to nature, in contrast to men's physiology, which frees him more completely to take up the projects of culture; 2) woman's body and its functions place her in *social roles* that in turn are considered to be at a lower order of the cultural process than man's... in other words, woman's body seems to doom her to the mere reproduction of life; the male, in contrast, lacking natural creative functions, must (or has the opportunity to) assert his creativity externally, "artificially," through the medium of technology and symbols. In so doing, he creates relatively lasting eternal, transcendent objects, while the woman creates only perishables—human beings. (1974, pp. 72, 75)

Here Ortner neatly captures the human preoccupation with the transcendence of nature and mortality, a preoccupation that, arguably, serves as a motivation for cultural production, and the way that transcendence is given a particular gendered meaning and set of symbols. By documenting this tradition, which had so many implications for women's social positions and experiences, Ortner's piece also delineates the source of "equality" feminism's unease with the female body and why some forms of feminism might therefore see evolutionary psychology as antithetical to a feminist project. To the extent that *the focus* of some forms of evolutionary psychology is often directly on the female body and its functions, it would seem to participate in the historical tradition Ortner documents here: the cultural association with and correspondent devaluation of women because of their bodies. Ironically, although scientific materialism and functionalism argue that *we all* are "brute matter" subject to physical laws, as those laws are articulated culturally they become gendered in particular ways that have historically effected women very negatively. One of feminism's main achievements has been to call attention to cultural interpretations of biology in order to denaturalize them and question their assumptions—and to look at what assumptions might be more scientifically accurate.

# Reconcilable Models

Those assumptions, however, have changed and are continuing to change, perhaps most excitingly in the arena of evolutionary theory. So what are some developments in evolutionary theory that might be of interest to feminists, and that can begin to reconcile some of the feminisms' fundamental splits? Correspondingly, how can developments in evolutionary theory reconcile tensions that have been the source of much academic and public dismissal of evolutionary psychology? There is much work being developed now, some of it in this volume, that might give feminists and evolutionary psychologists complementary new ways of conceptualizing gender and its role in human behavior.

A number of new analyses of sexual behavior whose theoretical models can be said to function as examples of the extended synthesis question the presuppositions and predictions of SST. For instance, a study on contemporary sexual "hook-up" behaviors concludes that models like SST that are focused on sex-specific adaptations are inadequate, citing the need for a more comprehensive biopsychosocial view that includes consideration of mechanisms, social processes, and the context of contemporary popular culture—an unprecedented medium of social transmission that has tremendous behavioral influence. "All things considered," Garcia et al. conclude,

> the simplest expectation is that evolutionary processes will result in both men and women desiring both sex and pair-bonding. Extra-relational sex is part of the human mating repertoire, as is pair-bonding. Individuals have competing sexual/relational motivations at any given time, which should be expected to go in one direction or the other depending on an individual's environmental context. (Garcia, Reiber, Massey, & Merriwether, 2012, p. 18)

For evolutionary biologist Patricia Adair Gowaty, in this volume, "it is critical that we understand and test alternative hypotheses for the origins of sex roles." (p. 3). Performing an important interrogation of the way scientific research is sometimes practiced and disseminated, she calls attention to the way in which data that questioned the Bateman-Trivers paradigm (which SST is derived from) was conveniently ignored, sometimes even by researchers themselves: "many still posit and conclude Bateman's "principles," even when their data remain inconsistent with COR's [Cost of Reproduction's] assumptions" (p. 5). Gowaty proposes an alternative model to SST, what she calls the "switch point theorem" (SPT). Gowaty stresses the importance of variability when speaking about sexual difference: "we've needed for a long time a theory of individuals that could refocus our gaze on *individuals, not sexes*, and to release the vice-grip on our imaginations" (p. 6). The SPT performs this refocusing by articulating how "the SPT predicts the fraction of potential mates acceptable to a given individual given a specified set of circumstances. Experimentalists can compete the SPT's predictions *about flexible individuals* against the predictions of parental investment and anisogamy theory *about fixed sexes*" (p. 8). Gowaty's work is an indispensable, more scientifically accurate revision of earlier, unconsciously politicized work on evolution and sexual difference.

Another major step in the articulation of new models for gender and human behavior was achieved with the 2009 publication of anthropologist Sarah Blaffer Hrdy's book *Mothers and Others*, which is an application of feminist conceptualizations regarding agency—work that focuses on the active role of women in human history. Hrdy's work is a crucial extension of this kind of feminist analysis to how dualisms about women's social roles based on their biologies are *scientifically* inaccurate, embedding an implicit consideration of *representation* within an explicit consideration of an alternative evolutionary model of parenting that has vast implications for the previously accepted evolutionary models such as the parental investment theory. Her work is also part of the crucial shift within evolutionary theory from an analytic paradigm based around the individual (and the individual, "selfish" gene) as the target of selection to a paradigm that also explores the group as a target of selection, and that investigates multiple levels of selection, and that shows how cooperation rather than competition has been previously undervalued and underexplored as a fundamental contributor to the evolutionary process—in other words, the shift from the modern synthesis of evolutionary biology to the extended synthesis of evolutionary biology. This shift is not without implications for gender and feminism, given the way the group has historically been gendered female, the individual male. The extended synthesis, I argue, gives earlier feminist intuitions about human behavior a scientific basis.

For simplicity's sake, I will briefly spell out the assumptions of and differences between the modern synthesis and the extended synthesis in the summaries below:

### Modern Synthesis

- (Julian Huxley, J. B. S. Haldane, Ronald Fisher, mid-20th century) Emphasizes natural selection to the exclusion of other evolutionary forms
- Emphasizes populations genetics—"gene's eye view"
- Genes not affected by developmental history of individual. Focuses on genetic mutation in individuals as they manifest in populations
- Populations with genetic variation evolve via changes in gene frequency induced by natural selection
- Phenotypic changes are gradual, speciation and diversification only come about over long periods of change (evolution is only a slow process)

### Extended Synthesis (the "Altenberg 16")

The extended synthesis adds to and explores questions that the modern synthesis did not fully account for:

1. The role of development (taken up by Evo-Devo)
2. Whether evolutionary change must be gradual
3. That natural selection is but one of the organizing principles of biological complexity, and that there are additional inheritance mechanisms beyond the standard genetic one
4. That multilevel selectionism is a way that natural selection produces evolution at other hierarchical levels (group level) in addition to the organism (Darwin), and the gene (modern synthesis).
5. The relationship between micro- and macroevolution.
6. Contingent and deterministic processes in evolution.
7. How ecological and evolutionary theories are related.

An extension (not a refutation) of the modern synthesis primarily focused on the gene, all aspects of extended synthesis outlined here have implications for feminist theories of gender.

Hrdy's work, which continues in the biological, scientific context what earlier feminist work did in evaluating more explicitly cultural forms, participates in the work of the extended synthesis and gives feminists (and others) a way to talk about evolutionary conceptions of agency in very different terms from the usual stereotypes such as the "hunting hypothesis," which, in Hrdy's words, postulated "a pact between a hunter and a mate who repaid him with sexual fidelity so the provider could be certain that children he invested in carried at least half his genes. This 'sex contract' assumed pride of place as the 'prodigious adaptation central to the success of early hominids'" (Hrdy, 2009, p. 147). The "hunting hypothesis," which contributed to gender stereotypes such as male agency and female passivity, is shown by Hrdy and others to ignore crucial data such as the contribution women made to the provision of daily calories and the fact that meat was communally shared rather than given to an individual man's family.

In a move that is subtle but has tremendous implications for theoretical bases and specifically gender in evolutionary psychology, Hrdy further revises the hypothesis with her own novel contribution to evolutionary theory—the idea that the supposedly "feminine" traits of empathy and identification with others are actually human traits that had a central role in human evolution:

> I propose that...sometime before the evolution of 1,350 cc sapient brains (the hallmark of anatomically modern humans) and before such distinctively human traits as language (the hallmark of behaviorally

modern humans), there emerged in Africa a line of apes that began to be interested in the mental and subjective lives—the thoughts and feelings—of others, interested in understanding them. (p. 30)

Hrdy holds this interest to be the legacy of human cooperative breeding, which came about since the production of large-brained children was so costly that a mother could not handle child-rearing on her own: "both before birth and especially afterward, the mother needed help from others; and even more importantly, her infant would need to be able to monitor and assess the intentions of both his mother and these others and to attract their attentions and elicit their assistance in ways no ape had ever needed to do before. For only by eliciting nurture from others as well as his mother could one of these little humans hope to stay safe and fed and to survive" (p. 31). This need to elicit nurture led to the evolution of an advanced human theory of mind—the ability to put oneself in another's place and adopt their perspective. Hrdy's "cooperative breeding hypothesis" (32), which she explicitly contrasts with earlier ideas such as the "hunting hypothesis," provides a novel way of reconceptualizing theories of human emotion that previously were articulated in less complicated, and gender-stereotyped ways. She further highlights the ways caregiving is a form of work that, since the division of labor that came about with the rise of industrialism in the late eighteenth and early nineteenth centuries, tended to be seen as "women's work" and therefore less important than "men's work" in the public sphere, was in fact a communal effort absolutely crucial to human survival. This both denaturalizes the idea of one woman as a child's exclusive caregiver, and highlights the importance of female agency, both central feminist concerns. Hrdy provides an evolutionary reading of human history that extends those concerns.

If Hrdy's cooperative breeding hypothesis is right, it challenges SST at its most fundamental levels. Males with resources don't seem so crucial from this point of view, and we can see the origins of the emphasis on males with resources not in deep evolutionary history but rather, in some contexts, in the economic shifts associated with industrialization and the development of the public/private split. Instead of an individual woman cowering back home in the cave, waiting for an individual male to show up with meat to feed her and her baby, in Hrdy's work we have dynamic group interaction in which women are free to pursue multiple roles rather than being confined to the position of the primary caretaker. Breaking the cultural assumption of an absolute link between women and caretaking because of the constraints of the female body was a major goal of feminism, and Hrdy's work shows that throughout evolutionary history, multiple forms of parenting existed and were even responsible for our species' success.

Hrdy's hypothesis further addresses a problem that extends beyond evolutionary psychology to affective neuroscience, which, in its discussion of the development of affect regulation, still assumes that the primary caretaker will be the mother: "the essential task of the first year of human life is the creation of a secure attachment bond between the infant and his or her primary caretaker. Secure attachment depends on *the mother's* sensitive biopsychological attunement to the infant's dynamically shifting internal states of arousal" (Schore, 2009, 116). But if throughout human evolutionary history there have been multiple "primary caretakers," "alloparents," in Hrdy's words, this is a game-changer that is in accordance with the larger shift in evolutionary biology to a multidimensional paradigm that looks at the evolution of groups (it is key that in Hrdy's work, caretaking is performed by the group, not a single individual), considers the role of development, and looks at selection on multiple levels.

## The Extended Synthesis: A Better Model for Feminism and Evolutionary Psychology

As with Hrdy's work, other developments in evolutionary theory now going under the appellation of "the extended synthesis" further provide differential conceptions of "agency" in the context of evolutionary theory. These developments are of interest to and can perhaps more readily include a feminist perspective not because they move away from biology but because they show more than ever how biology and culture are inextricable, and how human behavior, which is irrefutably material, incorporates cultural developments, and the way that humans actively shape their environmental niche and hence their own evolutionary process, as a central part of that materiality. The extended synthesis provides a way of conceptualizing human agency in the context of evolution rather than making it sound like humans are everywhere and at all times subject to the constraints of their genes with no active role in the evolutionary process. In the words of geneticist Eva Jablonka and evolutionary biologist Marion Lamb, for instance, "various inheritance systems (genetic, epigenetic, behavioral, symbolic) are instrumental in construction of the niche in which selection takes place...organisms can engineer the environment in ways that affect the development and selection of their descendants" (Jablonka & Lamb, 2005, p. 237). This "environmental engineering" has implications for the development of patterns related to sex, gender, and reproduction, for technological advancement has so altered the human environment that resource acquisition and provisioning have changed profoundly, and "fast" evolution shows that there has in fact been time to alter patterns such as those claimed by the SST. As Jablonka and Lamb put it,

> a main point of the evolutionary psychologists' arguments is that our uniquely human behavior is *not* the product of our greater general intelligence; rather, it is the result of highly specific neural networks that were constructed by Darwinian selection of genetic variations...an alternative is to see human behavior and culture as consequences of

hominids' extraordinary behavioral plasticity coupled with and enhanced by their powerful system of symbolic communication. According to this view, an important aspect of cultural evolution is the extremely variable ecological and social environments humans construct for themselves....

...

All organisms do a bit of niche construction, but its effects on evolution are particularly significant for animals that inherit a niche in the form of artifacts, behaviors, and cultures of their elders. Changes in habits can result in these animals creating a very different social and physical environment for themselves and their descendants. It is therefore wrong to think of them as passive objects of environmental selection. This is especially true for humans, whose elaborate cultural constructions form such a large part of their environment. What we transmit through our behavioral and symbolic systems obviously has profound effect on the selection of the information that we transmit through our genes. (pp. 213, 286).

The extended synthesis as it is articulated here gives feminist inquiry and research—research that necessarily explores the impact of female biology and behavior on human behavior—an expanded ground on which to enter the conversation than did the mostly genetic focus of the modern synthesis. It stresses the need for examining behavioral and symbolic systems as they interact with genetics, since humans' "elaborate cultural constructions form such a large part of their environment." These developments promise greater consilience not only between feminist and evolutionary approaches but also between the humanities, which have historically been concerned with "behavioral and symbolic systems," and sciences more generally since the former has previously been mostly concerned with so-called culture and the latter with so-called nature. Both feminism and evolutionary psychology will be better descriptors of human behavior in this model, and crucial interaction effects that were ignored in both disciplines will be taken into account. We all benefit here.

Looked at closely, a good deal of the conflict between evolutionary psychology and feminism has been semantic, while only some of it has been conceptual. It is my argument, then, that evolutionary psychology and feminism, especially if developed along the lines of the extended synthesis, are by no means mutually exclusive as the poster to the list-serv whom I mentioned at the beginning of the chapter would have it: the writer who insisted that "science should not come with political baggage" and that a Feminist Evolutionary Psychology Society would "destroy the non-political status of Evolutionary Psychology." They are not mutually exclusive, since, I think he means, a feminist perspective would predetermine results rather than, as I would argue, function as a mode of developing particular research questions and foci, just as feminism has done in many other disciplines.

His comments show that there are as many misunderstandings of feminism as there are of evolutionary psychology. Feminism is marginalized and attacked in the same emotional ways, often by evolutionary psychologists, as evolutionary psychology is often attacked by feminists. This irrationality creates an impasse through which no discussion can take place. For us or against us, if you're one of them you can't be one of us, the in-group/outgroup mechanics sometimes beneficial in our evolutionary history are maladaptive here.

In fact, based on current neuroscientific research, I point to an ultimate-level explanation for why feminists and evolutionary psychologists have had such a difficult time communicating productively: as I have shown, the premises of each group have often been articulated in a way that is fundamentally threatening to the other, and each group needs the lens of the extended synthesis to develop their ideas in affiliative ways. A threatening context prevents cooperation. As the work of Stephen Porges has established, humans have evolved to respond to stimuli according to their "neuroception" of safety in the environment—a detection system that precedes perception. Responses are phylogenetically coordinated, with the most recent evolutionary development as the first line of response. For Porges, that first line of response is what he terms the social engagement system (SES), which is engaged through the myelinated vagus in a way that applies a "vagal brake" to the heart rate. If cues of safety are detected in neuroception, these cues then provoke a "rest and digest," calming response linked to oxytocin release that allows for social engagement. If cues of threat are detected, then the flight/fight system is engaged through the parasympathetic nervous system, triggering cortisol release and elevated heart and respiration rates, all of which cause the SES to disengage and therefore makes communication and affiliation behaviors impossible. If we apply the polyvagal theory to the historical hostilities between evolutionary psychology and feminism, we can trace that hostility to the likely biophysiological responses the theoretical tenets provoke in each group. On both sides, the presuppositions of the one discipline trigger the other's neuroception of threat/lack of a sense of safety, thereby disengaging the SES system and triggering the fight/flight mechanism—at which point no meaningful social exchange can take place. Feminism threatens claims about gender difference as they influence the human behaviors postulated by evolutionary psychology, and evolutionary psychology threatens feminism's careful readings of the cultural meanings assigned to biology that have influenced women's devalued status. In this sense, each discourse can *biologically* trigger each group so that there is no vagal brake, no engagement of the SES, and hence no conversation. As characteristically happens in response to stress, both groups are notable for the error of global thinking, taking one aspect or practitioner of either feminism or evolutionary psychology and making that aspect stand for the whole of the field. In a spectacular error of what I call the "synechdochic logic," based on the rhetorical figure of synechdoche, where the part is taken for the whole, the excesses of each field become representatives of the field.

With the advent of the extended synthesis, there is at this point no conceptual necessity for this kind of hostility and sense of threat. Until now, *both* feminism and evolutionary psychology were constrained by the lack of a theoretical framework through which to adequately formulate the interaction effects between nature and culture, organism and environment, body and mind that are so instrumental in the production of human behavior. An adequate account of these interaction effects, I have argued, necessitates the inputs of *both* disciplines, and is facilitated by the development of the extended synthesis of evolutionary biology. In that feminism *is* committed to "the radical notion that women are human," and humans are unquestionably "part of the natural world" even as we have transformed that world with our technologies by such an enormously successful form of niche construction that the distinction between the natural world and us is a very difficult line to draw, feminism and evolutionary psychology are both engaged in very similar concerns: the study of what it means to be human. Since, because of their earlier lack of an interactionist framework, *both* feminism and evolutionary psychology were often considered by those outside the in-groups to be biased in fundamental ways, each side should stop worrying about contagion by the other. Where their interests converge is in a research program that would explicitly test interaction effects between biological sex difference as it has developed evolutionarily and the particular social, cultural, and economic contexts in which those universals exist, individual variability in terms of difference, and human strategizing—reproductive and otherwise—in the context of biological and environmental constraint. But in order for this to happen, evolutionary psychology postulates need to be brought into alignment with the scientific developments and paradigm shift described under the heading of the extended synthesis in *deed as well as word*. Similarly, the extreme constructivist ends of feminism (such as Judith Butler's claim that all gender difference is performance) need to be attentive to recent work in neuroscience that shows a biological basis for human behavior that has implications for gender, although that gender must be considered on a spectrum of variability with some robust features and some plastic features rather than in terms of fixed polar opposites. The recent developments in the field of evolutionary biology that are collected under the name of the "extended synthesis" give feminists and evolutionary psychologists the ability to create a genuinely "co-evolved" discourse that charts the interactions between and indissociability of "nature" and "culture" and how these impact gender and human behavior in a way that has previously been impossible.

Placed in a historical framework, it can be seen that a main source of discord between feminism and evolutionary psychology lies in philosophical debates about human agency—determinism versus free will—that go back as far as written human history. Are humans the active producers of their own destinies, or are they the passive beings whose behaviors are determined by larger forces such as nature or the gods? Much in these debates hinged on the question of the human relationship to nature and the relative degree of human control. Since, as feminist theory documented, men were symbolically affiliated with active culture that shapes nature and women with the raw matter, women's social status was lower. This had an ironic inversion in scientific discourse, where materialist claims tended to deemphasize agency. Casting these debates in evolutionary terms, it is clear that the presuppositions associated with the modern synthesis of evolutionary biology—natural selection is the single inheritance mechanism and it determines the evolutionary rate and form of populations—took a deterministic bent popularly understood along the lines of "genes determine human behavior," and the role of human agency in the evolutionary process was left relatively unexplored. In that context, women as the residual symbol of a nature to which humans are subject still posed a threat to the human agency that actively shapes the natural world. But new developments in neuroscience, genetics, developmental psychology, and paleoecology have crystallized under the heading of the extended synthesis of evolutionary biology, and provide ways of accounting for human agency that may make "nature" seem less deterministic and threatening, thereby doing away with the threat that nature—and by symbolic extension women—have always seemed to pose to "culture"—human actions on and intervention into the natural world. This account provides a way of reconciling both semantic and conceptual tensions between the disciplines of evolutionary psychology and feminism, giving us new ways to formulate the difference/sameness question in gender and of precisely studying the interactionist elements that have, when they were segregated, been the source of much disciplinary discord.

# References

Bolhuis, J., Brown, G. R., Richardson, R. C., & Laland, K. N. (2011). Darwin in mind: New opportunities for evolutionary psychology. *PLOS Biology, 9*(7), 1–8.

Bordo, S. (1993). *Unbearable weight: Feminism, Western culture, and the body*. Berkeley: University of California Press.

Buss, D. M. (1998). Sexual strategies theory: Historical origins and current status. *Journal of Sex Research, 35,* 19–31.

Buss, D. M., & Schmitt, D. P. (2011). Evolutionary psychology and feminism. *Sex Roles, 64,* 768–787.

Fine, C. (2011). *Delusions of gender: The real science behind sex difference*. New York: Norton.

Garcia, J. R., Reiber, C., Massey, S. G., & Merriwether, A. M. (2012). Sexual hook-up culture: A review. *Review of General Psychology, 16,* 161–176.

Geher, G. (2010). The launching of the Feminist Evolutionary Psychology Society (FEPS). Retrieved from http://evostudies.org/blog/?p=215.

Heywood, L., & Drake, J. (Eds.). (1997). *Third wave agenda: Being feminist, doing feminism*. Minneapolis: University of Minnesota Press.

Hrdy, S. (1999). Mother Nature. A History of Mothers, Infants, and Natural. Selection. Pantheon Books. New York.

Hrdy, S. (2009). *Mothers and Others: The Evolutionary Origins of Mutual Understanding*. Cambridge: Harvard UP.

Jablonka, E., & Lamb, M. J. (2005). *Evolution in four dimensions: Genetic, epigenetic, behavioral, and symbolic variation in the history of life*. Cambridge, MA: MIT Press.

Leydesdorff and Hellsten. (2006). Measuring the meaning of words in contexts: An automated analysis of controversies about 'Monarch butterflies,' 'Frankenfoods,' and 'stem cells'. *Scientometrics*, 67(2), 231–258.

Low, B. S. (2000). *Why sex matters*. Princeton, NJ: Princeton University Press.

Oliver, M. B., & Hyde, J. S. (1993). Gender differences in sexuality: A meta-analysis. *Psychological Bulletin*, 114, 29–51.

Panksepp, J., & Panksepp, J. (2000). The seven sins of evolutionary psychology. *Evolution and Cognition*, 6(2), 108–131.

Petersen, J. L., & Hyde, J. S. (2010). A meta-analytic review of research on gender differences in sexuality, 1993–2007. *Psychological Bulletin*, 136, 21–38.

Porges, S. W. (2011). *The Polyvagal Theory*. New York: Norton.

Rosaldo, M., & Lamphere, L. (1974). *Woman, Culture, and Society*. Stanford, CA: Stanford University Press.

Schore, A. N. (2009). Right-brain affect regulation. In D. Fosha, D. Siegel, & M. Solomon (Eds.), *The Healing Power of Emotion: Affective Neuroscience, Development & Clinical Practice*. New York: Norton.

Scott-Phillips, T. C., Dickins, T. E., & West, S. A. (2011). Evolutionary Theory and the Ultimate–Proximate Distinction in the Human Behavioral Sciences, *Perspectives on Psychological Science*, 6, 38–47.

Snitow, A. (1990). A gender diary. In M. Hirsch & E. Fox Keller (Eds.), *Conflicts in feminism* (pp. 9–43). New York: Routledge.

Trivers, R. (1972). Parental investment and sexual selection. In B. Campbell (Ed.), *Sexual selection and the descent of man: 1871–1971* (pp. 136–179). Chicago: Aldine Press.

# INDEX